THE CANADIAN ANNUAL REVIEW

OF PUBLIC AFFAIRS

THE RT. HON. SIR WILFRID LAURIER, G.C.M.G., P.C., M.P.,
Prime Minister of Canada, and the Dominion's Representative at the Coronation Conference.

*(From the painting by J. Colin Forbes, R.C.A.
By special permission.)*

THE
CANADIAN
ANNUAL REVIEW

OF

PUBLIC AFFAIRS

1902

BY

J. CASTELL HOPKINS, F.S.S.

Editor of " Canada: An Encyclopaedia of the Country," in Six Volumes;
Author of "the Story of the Dominion"; " Queen Victoria: Her
Life and Reign"; "The Progress of Canada," Etc., Etc.

ILLUSTRATED

TORONTO
THE ANNUAL REVIEW PUBLISHING COMPANY
LIMITED

THIS VOLUME

IS

Dedicated

WITH KIND PERMISSION

TO

The Right Honourable Sir Wilfrid Laurier, P.C., G.C.M.G.

PRIME MINISTER OF CANADA

WHO HAS GRACED THE PUBLIC LIFE

OF THE

DOMINION AND THE EMPIRE

WITH SO MARKED A MEASURE OF DIGNITY AND

DISTINCTION

BY

THE AUTHOR.

PREFACE

In this work it is hoped, from year to year, to provide an adequate view of Canadian resources, progress, institutions and history. The record of important events in politics and Parliament is combined with many statements, or tabulated statistics, of trade and commerce and industry and finance. Canadian relations with the Empire, with the United States and other countries, are treated at length as well as the Provincial politics and interests which are usually so slightly known outside of Provincial boundaries.

The progress of Agriculture and the great grain production of Ontario and the West; the development of Mining and of Iron and Steel and other industries; the ever-increasing Transportation requirements and interests of Canada; the expanding and much-discussed Educational facilities of the Provinces; the Militia and defensive interests of the Dominion; are dealt with in a varied detail which, it is believed, will prove of value.

Many other important branches of history or progress, as they develop, will be treated from year to year and, together with a few selected illustrations typical of men, events, or places which have been specially prominent during the period under review, will, it is hoped, convey to the people of Canada, the Empire and other countries a clear and continuous picture of the position of the Dominion amongst the nations of the world.

Toronto, 20th May, 1903.

CONTENTS

I.—GOVERNMENT AND POLITICS

II.—RELATIONS WITH THE EMPIRE

CONTENTS   ix

VII.—TRANSPORTATION INTERESTS

VIII.—AGRICULTURE IN CANADA

IX.—TRADE AND COMMERCE

X.—MINERAL RESOURCES AND PRODUCTION

XI.—FORESTS AND FISHERIES

XII.—MANUFACTURING INDUSTRIES

XIII.—FINANCIAL INTERESTS AND AFFAIRS

XIV.—POPULATION AND IMMIGRATION

XV.—RELIGIOUS AND MORAL INTERESTS

XVI.—EDUCATIONAL AFFAIRS IN CANADA

XVII.—MUNICIPAL INTERESTS

XVIII.—LABOUR QUESTIONS AND CONDITIONS

XIX.—LITERATURE AND JOURNALISM

XX.—CANADIAN OBITUARY FOR 1902

ILLUSTRATIONS OF THE YEAR

GOVERNMENT AND POLITICS

THE CORONATION

THE CLOSE OF THE WAR

EDUCATIONAL AFFAIRS

BUSINESS INTERESTS

SCENES AND MAPS

CHIEF BRITISH GOVERNMENTS—1902

THE SOVEREIGN

His Majesty, Edward VII., of the United Kingdom of Great Britain and Ireland and of the British Dominions beyond the Seas, King, Defender of the Faith, Emperor of India.

THE IMPERIAL ADMINISTRATION

LORD SALISBURY'S GOVERNMENT.

Prime Minister and Lord Privy Seal............Marquess of Salisbury.
Lord High Chancellor...........................Lord Halsbury.
Lord President of the Council...................Duke of Devonshire.
First Lord of the Treasury......................Rt. Hon. A. J. Balfour.
Chancellor of the Exchequer.....................Sir M. E. Hicks-Beach.
Chancellor of the Duchy of Lancaster............Lord James of Hereford.
Secretary of State, Colonial Department.........Rt. Hon. J. Chamberlain.
Secretary of State, Home Department.............Rt. Hon. C. T. Ritchie.
Secretary of State, Foreign Department..........Marquess of Lansdowne.
Secretary of State, War Department..............Rt. Hon. W. St. John Brodrick.
Secretary of State, Indian Department...........Lord George Hamilton.
First Lord of the Admiralty.....................Earl of Selborne.
President of the Board of Trade.................Rt. Hon. Gerald W. Balfour.
President, Local Government Board...............Rt. Hon. W. Hume Long.
Lord-Lieutenant of Ireland......................Earl Cadogan.
Lord-Chancellor of Ireland......................Lord Ashbourne.
Secretary for Scotland..........................Lord Balfour of Burleigh.
First Commissioner of Works.....................Rt. Hon. A. Akers-Douglas.
President of the Board of Agriculture............Rt. Hon. R. W. Hanbury.
Postmaster-General..............................Marquess of Londonderry.

NOT IN CABINET.

Chief Secretary for Ireland ....Rt. Hon. George Wyndham.
Financial Secretary to the Treasury.............Austen Chamberlain.
Patronage Secretary to the Treasury.............Sir W. H. Walrond, Bart.
Paymaster-General..............................Duke of Marlborough.
Secretary to the Admiralty......................H. O. Arnold-Forster.
Parliamentary Under-Secretary, Home Office......Rt. Hon. Jesse Collings.
  " " " Foreign Office....Viscount Cranborne.
  " " " War Office.......Lord Raglan.
  " " " Colonial Office....Earl of Onslow.
  " " " Indian Office.....Earl of Hardwicke.
Financial Secretary of the War Office...........Lord Stanley.
Attorney-General of England.....................Sir R. B. Finley, K.C.
Solicitor-General of England....................Sir E. H. Carson, K.C.
Attorney-General for Scotland...................Andrew Graham Murray, K.C.
Solicitor-General for Scotland..................Charles Scott Dickson, K.C.
Attorney-General of Ireland.....................John Atkinson, K.C.
Solicitor-General of Ireland....................J. H. M. Campbell, K.C.

MR. BALFOUR'S GOVERNMENT.

Prime Minister, Lord Privy Seal and First Lord
 of the Treasury............................Rt. Hon. A. J. Balfour.
Lord High Chancellor............................Earl of Halsbury.
Lord President of the Council...................Duke of Devonshire.
Chancellor of the Exchequer.....................Rt. Hon. C. T. Ritchie.
Secretary of State, Colonial Department.........Rt. Hon. J. Chamberlain.
Secretary of State, Home Department.............Rt. Hon. A. Akers-Douglas.

xiv

Secretary of State, Foreign Department .... Marquess of Lansdowne.
Secretary of State, War Department............Rt. Hon. W. St. John Brodrick.
Secretary of State, Indian Department...........Lord George Hamilton.
First Lord of the Admiralty.. ....Earl of Selborne.
President of the Board of Trade.................Rt. Hon. Gerald W. Balfour.
President of the Local Government Board ....Rt. Hon. W. Hume Long.
Lord Chancellor of Ireland ....Lord Ashbourne.
Secretary for Scotland.........................Lord Balfour of Burleigh.
President of the Board of Agriculture............Rt. Hon. R. W. Hanbury.
Chief Secretary for Ireland.....................Rt. Hon. George Wyndham.
President of the Board of Education.............Marquess of Londonderry.
Postmaster-General. ....Rt. Hon. Austen Chamberlain.

NOT IN CABINET.

Chancellor of the Duchy of Lancaster.............Sir W. H. Walrond.
Lord-Lieutenant of Ireland.................... ..Earl of Dudley.
First Commissioner of Works...................Lord Windsor.
Financial Secretary to the Treasury..............William Hayes Fisher.
Patronage Secretary to the Treasury.............Sir A. Acland Hood, Bart.
Paymaster-General.............................Duke of Marlborough.
Secretary to the Admiralty..................... H. O. Arnold-Forster.
Parliamentary Under-Secretary, Home Office..... Hon. Thomas Cochrane.
"   "   "   Foreign Office.... Viscount Cranborne.
"   "   "   War Office.......Earl of Hardwicke.
"   ."   "   Colonial Office....Earl of Onslow.
"   "   "   Indian Office.....Earl Percy.
Financial Secretary of the War Office............Lord Stanley.
Attorney-General of England................. ..Sir R. B. Finlay, K.C.
Solicitor-General of England,....................Sir E. H. Carson, K.C.
Attorney-General for Scotland..................Andrew Graham Murray, K.C,
Solicitor-General for Scotland...................Charles Scott Dickson, K.C.
Attorney-General of Ireland....,..............John Atkinson, K.C.
Solicitor-General of Ireland.....................J. H. M. Campbell, K.C.

CANADIAN ADMINISTRATION *

Governor-General, His Excellency, The Earl of Minto, P.C., G.C.M.G.

Prime Minister and President of the Privy Council..Rt. Hon. Sir Wilfrid Laurier.
Minister of Trade and Commerce.................Hon. Sir. R. J. Cartwright.
Secretary of State.............................Hon. R. W. Scott.
Minister of Justice............................Hon. David Mills.
Minister of Marine and Fisheries.................
Minister of Militia and Defence..................Hon. Dr. F. W. Borden.
Postmaster-General............................Hon. William Mulock.
Minister of Agriculture.........................Hon. S. A. Fisher.
Minister of Public Works.......................Hon. J. Israel Tarte.
Minister of Finance............................Hon. W. S. Fielding.
Minister of Railways and Canals.................Hon. A. G. Blair.
Minister of the Interior.........................Hon. Clifford Sifton.
Minister of Customs...........................Hon. W. Paterson.
Minister of Inland Revenue.....................Hon. M. E. Bernier.
Minister without Portfolio ....Hon. James Sutherland.
Minister without Portfolio ....Hon. R. R. Dobell.
Solicitor-General (not in Cabinet)...............Hon. Chas. Fitzpatrick, K.C.

Province.	Lieut.-Governor.	Premier.
Ontario	Hon. Sir Oliver Mowat......	Hon. George W. Ross.
Quebec................	Sir L. A. Jetté..............	Hon. S. N. Parent.
New Brunswick.	Hon. J. B. Snowball........	Hon. L. J. Tweedie.
Nova Scotia...........	Hon. A. G. Jones...........	Hon. G. H. Murray.
Prince Edward Island ...	His Honour P. A. McIntyre..	Hon. Arthur Peters.
Manitoba	Sir D. H. McMillan........	Hon. R. P. Roblin.
North-West Territories..	His Honour A. E. Forget....	F. W. G. Haultain, K.C.
British Columbia........	Sir H. G. Joly de Lotbinière..	Hon. Edward G. Prior.

* As on 1st January, 1902. Changes during the year will be found in text.

COMMONWEALTH OF AUSTRALIA

Governor-General, His Excellency, The Lord Tennyson, K.C.M.G.

Prime Minister...............................Rt. Hon. Sir Edmund Barton.
Attorney-General..............................Hon. Alfred Deakin.
Minister for Home Affairs......................Sir William J. Lyne.
Treasurer......................................Rt. Hon. Sir George Turner.
Minister of Trade and Commerce.................Rt. Hon. C. C. Kingston.
Minister of Defence............................Rt. Hon. Sir John Forrest.
Postmaster-General.............................Hon. J. G. Drake.

State.	Governor.	Premier.
New South Wales	Vice-Admiral Sir H. H. Rawdon	Hon. Sir John See.
Victoria	Colonel Sir G. S. Clarke	Hon. W. H. Irvine.
South Australia		Hon. J. G. Jenkins.
Queensland	Maj.-General Sir H. C. Chermside	Hon. Robert Philp.
Tasmania	Sir Arthur E. Havelock	Hon. Sir N. E. Lewis.
Western Australia		Hon. W. H. James, K.C.

BRITISH SOUTH AFRICA

High Commissioner, Lord Milner of Capetown, G.C.B., G.C.M.G.

	Governor.	Premier.
Cape Colony	Sir W. F. Hely-Hutchinson	Rt. Hon. Sir J. Gordon Sprigg.
Natal	Sir H. E. McCallum	Rt. Hon. Sir A. H. Hime.
Basutoland	Sir G. Y. Lagden.	Commissioner.
Transvaal	Hon. Sir Arthur Lawley	Lieutenant-Governor.
Orange River	Major Sir H. J. Goold	" "
Rhodesia	Sir Marshall J. Clarke	Commissioner.

THE EMPIRE OF INDIA

Viceroy and Governor-General, H. E. Lord Curzon of Kedleston.
Commander-in-Chief, General Lord Kitchener of Khartoum.

Madras	Lord Ampthill	Governor.
Bombay	Lord Northcote	"
Bengal	Sir John Woodburn	Lieutenant-Governor.
Punjaub	Sir C. M. Rivaz	" "
North-West	Sir J. J. D. La Touche	" "
Burmah	Sir F. W. R. Fryer	Chief Commissioner.
Assam	H. J. S. Cotton, C.S.I.	" "
Central	A. H. L. Fraser, C.S.I.	" "

NEW ZEALAND

Governor, His Excellency The Earl of Ranfurly, G.C.M.G.
Prime Minister, Rt. Hon. R. J. Seddon.

NEWFOUNDLAND

Governor, His Excellency Sir Cavendish Boyle.
Prime Minister, Rt. Hon. Sir Robert Bond.

THE CANADIAN
ANNUAL REVIEW

I.—GOVERNMENT AND POLITICS

Early in the year several changes occurred in Sir Wilfrid Laurier's Government. On February 8th, it was announced that **Changes in the Dominion Cabinet** the Hon. David Mills, K.C., had been appointed to the Supreme Court of Canada; that the Hon. Charles Fitzpatrick, K.C., was to succeed him as Minister of Justice; that Mr. Henry George Carroll, K.C., M.P., was to replace the last-mentioned as Solicitor-General, without a seat in the Cabinet; and that the Hon. William Templeman was to become a member of the Government without portfolio. Mr. Fitzpatrick was sworn in on February 11th, Mr. Carroll's appointment dated from February 10th, and Senator Templeman was sworn a Privy Councillor of Canada on February 22nd. The Hon. James Sutherland, M.P., who had been a member of the Government since 1899, without portfolio, had already been sworn in as Minister of Marine and Fisheries on January 16th, in place of Sir Louis Davies, who had gone upon the Supreme Court in the preceding December. The appointments were well received as a whole by the press. Of Mr. Justice Mills, the London *Advertiser*, as representing his old home and nearby constituency, declared on February 8th "that he had long been recognized as the ablest constitutional lawyer in Canada. When Sir Oliver Mowat was engaged in contesting the several great questions that arose between the Dominion and the Province of Ontario, it was only natural that he should look to him for help. In these questions Mr. Mills found work that exactly suited him— opportunity for the expenditure of industrious energy, for painstaking research, for sound reasoning, for the application of those principles of law which had been his life study." The Toronto *Globe* paid him high tribute as one of Canada's historic figures and as a staunch Liberal fighter in the Parliaments of 1878-96.

Senator Templeman's appointment was regarded as the recognition of British Columbia's right to representation in the Government. It was not altogether congenial, however, to the friends of Mr. Joseph Martin, M.P.P., who had on February 7th passed a Resolution at a Liberal meeting in Vancouver, asking for the selection of

Mr. George R. Maxwell, M.P., as the representative of the Province in the Dominion Cabinet. The local press was as a whole, however, congratulatory in its expression of opinion, and the Victoria *Colonist*, though belonging to the Opposition camp, declared on February 8th that Mr. Templeman richly deserved this party recognition. "He was an active Liberal here at a time when to be so was not so popular as it is now. He has been consistent in his adherence to his party and taken his share of hard work and defeat on its behalf." The hope was also expressed that he would soon be given a portfolio so as to better combine personal responsibility and Ministerial influence for his Province. Mr. Fitzpatrick's appointment was said by *Le Soleil* of Quebec, on February 18th, to be a tribute to the most distinguished representative of Irish Catholicism in Canada. "Talent, labour, services rendered to nationality, the reward due to merit, are all involved in his elevation." In the House of Commons on February 26th, the Prime Minister paid high tribute to the Hon. Mr. Mills and Sir Louis Davies, and briefly referred to the new appointments which had been made. Mr. R. L. Borden's comments were of a kindly rather than a critical nature.

The next change in the Government took place on October 20th, when the Hon. J. Israel Tarte resigned his position of Minister of Public Works, after precipitating a wide discussion upon questions of tariff, transportation and Ministerial responsibility. After considerable delay, and rumours which connected the names of the Hon. L. P. Brodeur, Speaker of the House of Commons, the Hon. S. N. Parent, Premier of Quebec, and Mr. Raymond Prefontaine, K.C., M.P., ex-Mayor of Montreal, with the appointment, it was announced on November 10th that the Hon. Mr. Sutherland was to be Minister of Public Works and Mr. Prefontaine to succeed him as Minister of Marine and Fisheries. It was stated that the latter Department would have the charge of all works and improvements in the St. Lawrence River and of the building and maintaining of wharves throughout the Dominion added to its responsibilities. The new Ministers were sworn in on November 11th. The Hon. Mr. Prefontaine's appointment was strongly opposed by certain antagonistic interests in Montreal headed by the *Witness* and the *Herald* of that city, and caused by differences arising out of his Mayoralty administration of its affairs. Elsewhere, however, the appointment was highly eulogized in the party press. The Toronto *Globe* described him as "a strong, aggressive man with many of the qualities of leadership," and as being "the incarnation of energy." The Winnipeg *Free Press* described him as a good speaker equally familiar with both languages, as having all the abilities to become a national figure, and as the fighter of more contests in the Montreal district —local, municipal and Dominion—than any other living man. "He has never known defeat." Mr. Sutherland's promotion was approved by the entire Liberal press with the exception of the Winnipeg

Tribune, under the dissatisfied political control of Mr. R. L. Richardson, ex-M.P.

The Dominion Parliament met on February 13th and was opened in due form by H. E. the Earl of Minto, whose Speech from
Dominion Parliament and Public Affairs the Throne declared the new Census returns to be a highly satisfactory evidence of prosperous progress if not of the increase of population; referred to the pending application of the C. P. R. for an increase of its capital and the Government's submission of the regulation of its tolls to the Courts; mentioned the successes of Mr. Marconi and the aid given him by the Government; offered congratulations on the continued expansion of business and trade; promised an increase in the number of Commercial agencies; referred to the coming Coronation Conference in London; stated the Government's intention to establish a steamship service with South Africa; and expressed hope that the Conference in London would promote trade and commerce. The House was prorogued on May 15th by the Governor-General with congratulations upon the unusual number of Acts passed incorporating industrial and railway companies, upon the increased trade and revenue of the country, and upon the expansion of immigration and the development of the Yukon.

During the Session two important measures were introduced for purposes of public consideration and withdrawn under promise from the Government to present them again in 1903. They were Mr. Blair's Bill for the establishment of a Railway Commission and Mr. Mulock's measure for the compulsory arbitration of labour disputes. Another measure in this category was one assuming control of telegraph and telephone rates. An increase in the permanent force of the Militia was promised, and there was much talk of tariff revision, without, however, any Government pledge in the matter. Of the actual legislation passed there were measures giving representation to the Yukon, municipal institutions to Dawson and a Court of Appeal to the same Territory.

An Act was passed revising the position of Post Office employees, prescribing a Departmental instead of Civil Service examination, and amending the terms of remuneration. The Minister of Justice was responsible for amendments to the Bills of Exchange Act and to the law regarding Evidence, as well as for the measure allowing the C. P. R. to increase its capital under condition of spending the $20,000,000 on improvements and $9,000,000 of that amount on rolling stock. County Court Judges were also given improved provisions for retiring allowances. The Government, through Mr. Fielding, obtained power to borrow $15,000,000 to meet maturing obligations, and a measure was passed increasing the Provincial share in the Chinese capitation tax to one-half. The amendments presented by Sir R. J. Cartwright to the Manitoba Grain Act required a railway company upon application of ten farmers, within twenty miles of their nearest shipping point, to erect and maintain a loading platform for grain. Another enactment abolished compulsory pilotage for vessels in inland waters drawing less than sixteen feet, and the coasting laws were amended so as to exclude foreign-built ships of British register without a license and payment of 25 per cent. duty on the average market value of the ship.

The Government took power to exclude and deport immigrants suffering from certain forms of disease and established a system of pensions for the North-West Mounted Police somewhat similar to those now granted the Permanent Force in the Militia. The area of the Rocky Mountain Park was extended to 3,668,480 acres and the law regarding joint stock companies was amended so as to allow the incorporation of certain institutions by letters patent. The law regarding Naturalization was changed so as to compel half-yearly returns to Ottawa as to those taking the oath of allegiance. Certain mining towns in British Columbia were permitted to establish Boards of Trade, and Dr. Roddick's measure for the creation of a Dominion Medical Council—subject to the approval of each Province before coming into operation—was approved and became law. The principal debates, or subjects discussed in the House of Commons, as compiled from the voluminous pages of *Hansard*, were as follows during this Session:

Alaskan Boundary, February 19, March 5, 7.
Agriculture, Encouragement of, April 11, 16.
Binder Twine, April 25.
Bernier's North Pole Expedition, May 1.
Budget, The, March 17, 18, 19, 20, 21, 24, 25, 26, April 1, 2, 3, 4, 7, 8.
Cattle Guards on Railways, February 27, April 21.
Clayton-Bulwer Treaty, February 19, March 5, 7.
Canadian Table of Precedence, February 26.
Coronation Conference, March 26, May 12.
Coronation Contingent, April 9, 30.
Canadian Northern Railway, April 11, 14.
Canadian Pacific Railway, April 17, 21.
Coal Oil, Duties and Prices, March 13.
Census, The, March 18, 24, April 4, 23, May 2.
Colonial Appeals to Privy Council, April 28.
Cattle Embargo, British, May 1.
Defence of the Empire, March 25, 26, April 3, 7, 8, 15, 23, May 12.
Financial Situation, The, May 13.
Georgian Bay Canal, May 7.
Immigration, Encouragement of, April 17, 29.
Immigration, Oriental, March 20, 21.
Intercolonial Railway, April 24, 25.
Imperial Army Commissions to Canadians, February 26.
Judicial Salaries, February 21, May 1.
Labour Disputes, Settlement of, April 29.
Market Produce and the Tariff, April 28.
Militia Affairs, March 7, April 10, 14, 21.
Montreal Turnpike Commission, February 27.
Medical Convention in Canada, March 13, April 9, May 7.
Manitoba Grain Act, May 9.
Nickel, Export of, April 18.
Niagara Electric Power, April 28.

North-West Town Sites, May 7.
Property and Civil Rights—Provincial Uniformity of Laws—March 12.
Public Works and Mr. Tarte, March 4, 11.
Prince Edward Island Communications, February 20.
Preferential Trade, Imperial, April 15, 17, May 12.
Preferential Tariff, March 21, 24, 25, April 1, 2, 3, 8, 15, May 12.
Pensions to Mounted Police, April 23.
Postal Service, April 30, May 2.
Relations with Germany, March 6, April 2.
Reciprocity with United States, February 24, March 20, 21.
Railway Commission, April 9.
South African War, April 14, 23.
Transportation, February 14, 17, 28, March 10, 20, 21, April 7, 11, 14, 22, 28,
    May 7, 14.
The *Labour Gazette*, February 20.
Telegraphic Communication with Prince Edward Island, April 15.
Territories, Condition of, April 18.
Treadgold Yukon Concession, May 14.
Tariff, The, February 14, March 14, 17, 18, 19, 20, 21, 24, 25, 26, April 1, 2,
    3, 4, 7, 8, 28.
Trade and Commerce, March 17, 18, 25, April 2, 3, 8.
Wheat Transportation and Manitoba, March 10.
Yukon Railway Project, May 13.

The incidents leading up to the retirement of Mr. Tarte from the Government were the most discussed political events of the
Mr. Tarte's Tariff Campaign year. Originally a Conservative and then a strong and serviceable supporter of Sir Wilfrid Laurier in the general elections of 1896, he had received the natural reward of his exertions in being appointed to a prominent place in the new Government. His sympathies were always understood to have leaned towards a protective tariff but were not found in any apparent antagonism to the Liberal fiscal re-arrangements of ensuing years. In November, 1901, however, he made a strong protectionist declaration at a banquet in Montreal, and on February 8th of the year under review, at a dinner tendered him by the Reform Club of that city, he commenced what became practically a personal campaign for higher duties. "There is a crisis at hand," he declared. "Our American friends are endeavouring to make a slaughter market of this country. In consequence of this attempt let us have a tariff that will protect our national industries and waterways that will protect our national trade."

During the ensuing summer the Minister made a tour of the lake-ports, visited many of the inland towns of Ontario and also Halifax and St. John on the Atlantic coast. At Peterboro', on June 19th, he declared that he would like to arrange a tariff as high as the interests of the country required and fitted to meet the Americans who were trying to slaughter the Canadian market, while maintaining a 60 per cent. tariff of their own. From Montreal to Fort William he travelled, speaking everywhere of transportation and the tariff, and on his return told the Toronto *Globe* correspondent at Ottawa on August 8th that "unless we intend to close up

shop in the trade business we will have to get to work and develop
our waterways. The Americans are slaughtering us now and they
will continue to do so unless we get to work for ourselves and
build up our harbours, our waterways and our industries. Then
we can afford to put up just as high a tariff wall against them as
they have against us."

Meanwhile, these and similar utterances had provoked a good
deal of discussion in the press, and the Toronto *Globe* of August
11th referred to the Minister's speeches as giving his opponents
plenty of "intellectual exercise." It described him as being a
"retaliationist" rather than a high protectionist. During the
course of the annual banquet of the Canadian Manufacturers'
Association at Halifax on August 14th, Mr. Tarte made a further
contribution to the discussion. He protested against the American
or even British manufacturer being allowed to injure the implement and woollen industries of this country. He urged the
inauguration of a "strong" tariff. "It is my opinion that we can
sell to the Canadian consumer just as cheaply as the American
manufacturer can, provided we have the proper tariff." Following
this occasion some of the French-Canadian papers discussed Mr.
Tarte in a rather frank way, and *Le Courrier de St. Hyacinthe*
on August 17th described him as likely to impose himself upon
his party as Sir Wilfrid Laurier's successor. "He has successfully
defied Beausoleil, Prefontaine and Bernier and all the Clubs and
is stronger than ever in the French-Canadian Liberal party."
Speaking at Bowmanville on August 27th, Mr. Tarte said that if
he were really "Master of the Administration," as the Conservatives called him, he "would take the tariff item by item and
adjust it so as to save to Canada the profit of the exportation of
her resources, and build up a nation here." At the Toronto Exhibition on September 7th Mr. Tarte made a strongly protectionist
speech, referring to the cities as being the farmers' best market,
declaring a "proper tariff" not to be a party question, eulogizing
the American idea of guarding national interests at any expense of
taxation or tariff, and urging an imitation of that example.

By this time the free trade, or low tariff wing, of the Liberal
party had taken alarm at these utterances. Western papers such
as the Winnipeg *Free Press* and eastern ones like the Montreal
Herald protested against Mr. Tarte's views as being opposed to the
policy of his party. The Hon. Mr. Sifton, Minister of the Interior,
was interviewed by the Ottawa *Journal* on September 4th and
declared that "any attempt to increase the protective features of
the tariff will meet with the strenuous opposition of every Liberal
elected west of Lake Superior." There would be no revival of the
"discredited Tory policy" of the past. "My position is that the
tariff as it stands is a compromise; well and carefully worked out.
Its adaptability to the requirements of the trade of Canada is shown
by results. Manufacturers and consumers are alike getting fair
treatment. We would like the tariff lower, but we recognize that

there must be mutual concession and for the present we recognize the present tariff as a reasonable one." The Toronto *Globe* of September 6th declared that the existing tariff was fair, moderate and sufficient and must be retained. In reply Mr. Tarte told *La Patrie* of Montreal on September 11th that he represented the bulk of Canadian sentiment. "My belief and the belief of the Manufacturers' Association, is purely and simply that the tariff of this country should be re-adjusted on certain points for the greater development of our national industries, so as to create a profitable and permanent market for the farming community, to give more and more work to the working classes, to create more and more an interprovincial·and an Imperial trade."

Not satisfied with speeches, however, Mr. Tarte early in September commenced a personal investigation into industrial conditions by visiting a number of important manufacturing establishments, including the Dominion Cotton Company's mills at Hochelaga, the woollen and boot and shoe and other industries of Montreal, the manufacturing interests of Gananoque and other places. Meanwhile, the controversy within his own party increased. The Montreal *Witness* described his action as a "noisy advocacy of protectionism" and other papers took equally strong ground. On September 16th the Toronto *Globe* came out in direct antagonism to the Minister, declared that "only unsympathetic and unromantic people would seek to bind Mr. Tarte by the traditions and usages which govern Ministers of the Crown in British communities," described him as assuming all the functions and work of the entire Government and, finally, told him that the collective wisdom of the Cabinet would still determine Canadian policy. In reply Mr. Tarte told interviewers on the same day that the situation reminded him of the time just after Confederation when a number of French-Canadian Conservatives started a protectionist movement which eventually swept that Province. He declared that the *Globe* displayed "wild malice" in its attack.

At Orillia, on September 19th, in a vigorous speech, he quoted the Hon. Mr. Fielding as supporting his view of the necessity of tariff changes and declared the whole question to be: "Were Canadians to become a nation or were they to depend on Americans for their destiny." There was no reason why we should not manufacture everything for which we have the raw material. Meanwhile, the Conservative press was rejoicing over the apparent differences in the Liberal ranks and *La Patrie*, owned by Mr. Tarte's sons, was vigorously attacking the *Globe*, the *Witness* and the *Herald*. The last-named paper, on September 23rd, it described as the organ of the Hon. Mr. Fisher, Minister of Agriculture and Mr. Fisher himself as a free-trade theorist. At Gananoque, on the following day, Mr. Tarte was presented with an address by the Mayor and citizens declaring that "our tariff should be framed with such ample duties as will not only adequately protect our existing industries but prevent our country from being flooded with the surplus productions of other lands." In his following speech the Minister presented various arguments for tariff revision and higher duties. At the banquet in the evening he referred to the British Preference. "It makes me sick to say, hands off, don't touch it. I would like to try a good strong healthy Canadian tariff for a few years; it would help British connection." He spoke again of the American attitude. "Our friends on the other side of the line have raised a wall against us: they show no disposition to lower it, and if I am not mistaken, they take us by the throat every time they can. Now I want to know why our Canadiam customs laws are not to be just as self-protecting as theirs."

On September 25th the Minister spoke at Strathroy and reiterated his views. The occasion was important for a speech delivered by the Hon. G. W. Ross, Premier of Ontario, in which he expressed strong agreement with Mr. Tarte's tariff opinions. According to the *Globe's* report he spoke as follows: "What we want is a tariff to suit ourselves first, last and always. It mattered not to him how that was adjusted, so long as we get the higher degree of prosperity under it, nor did he care whether it suited anybody else or not so long as it suited ourselves. It mattered not whether the Americans liked it or not. He subscribed thoroughly to Mr. Tarte's doctrine of manufacturing our own raw material, and keeping our industries here and building them up." On the same day the Montreal *Witness* published the following telegram from the Minister: "May I ask you to state in your paper that I will be in the Liberal party long after you are dead and buried? If your views on the fiscal policy of the country were known to be those of the party, we would be defeated at the next general elections by the same overwhelming majority that the same views received in 1878." Meanwhile the Halifax *Chronicle* and Quebec *Le Soleil* had joined the Liberal papers which were rupudiating Mr. Tarte; and the *Globe* of September 26th declared that any revision of the tariff would come in the ordinary way through the Minister of Finance and not be announced in advance by any other person.

Mr. Tarte spoke at Goderich on October 1st—mainly on transportation matters—and on the following day visited the industrial centre of Oshawa and was banqueted after an inspection of various manufacturing concerns. At Chatham, on October 8th, he maintained the right of free speech and declared that no one but the Prime Minister had the power to limit his public utterances while a member of the Government. In any case he would not change. "To-day I stand advocating a tariff for Canadians of every Province as I did in the past. I shall not change my views in this matter. The people of Canada and the country are with me." At Berlin, on October 10th, he declared that he had not gone beyond his right or duty as a Minister in these expressions of opinion. But, "I do not believe that official life has enough charms for me that I will renounce principles that I think of national importance for the sake of office." On October 14th Mr. Tarte addressed the Montreal

THE HON. J. ISRAEL TARTE, M.P.

Resigned the position of Minister of Public Works, Oct. 20th, 1902.

THE HON. JOSEPH RAYMOND FOURNIER PREFONTAINE, K.C., M.P.

Appointed Dominion Minister of Marine and Fisheries, Nov. 11th, 1902.

Board of Trade. He spoke at length upon transportation and tariff matters. A tariff that was good fifteen years before might be no good to-day. "The tariff was not the Gospel." The farmers required protection as well as the manufacturers and the time had arrived when "a strong, vigorous Canadian policy must be adopted and carried out." He might have to go into private life but he would none the less urge a proper adjustment of the tariff. Speaking in Montreal on October 20th, Mr. Hugh Guthrie, Liberal M.P. for South Wellington, endorsed these general views. "There is no concealing and there is no use denying that the Province of Ontario is protectionist. There would be no sense in hurting ourselves by mere blind retaliation against the United States. What we must do is to frame our tariff for our interests, keeping in view the fact that from hard experience we are driven to conclude that our American cousins will hit us without hesitation whenever they think such a course to be for their advantage."

In his later speeches the Minister of Public Works had hinted at the possibility of his retirement when the Premier returned from
England. On October 18th, Sir Wilfrid Laurier
Mr. Tarte arrived in Ottawa and had a couple of interviews
Leaves the with Mr. Tarte. The latter then wrote a letter of
Government formal withdrawal from the Cabinet and went to
Toronto where he spoke on October 20th at a banquet to Colonel Denison, dealing with non-partisan matters and refusing to say whether he was still a member of the Government or not. Two days later the correspondence between himself and the Premier was published. He had written on October 20th in response to a personal demand for the resignation of his portfolio, tendering the same and adding the following remarks: "My views on the tariff are well known to you. I have, on several occasions, stated them publicly in your presence and discussed them often privately with you. Entertaining the opinion that the interests of the Canadian people make it our duty to revise without delay the tariff of 1897 with the view of giving a more adequate protection to our industries, to our farming community, to commerce and to our working men, I cannot possibly remain silent. I prefer my freedom of action and of speech, under the circumstances, even to the great honour of being your colleague." In reply Sir Wilfrid Laurier emphasized the points of difference as follows: "During my absence in Europe, without any communication with me and without any previous understanding with your colleagues, you began an active campaign in favour of an immediate revision of the tariff in the direction of high protection. I regret having been obliged to observe to you that this attitude on your part constitutes a self-evident violation of your duty towards the Government of which you were a member." He proceeded to point out that Mr. Tarte should have first laid his views before the Government "with the object of obtaining that unanimous action of the Cabinet which is the very foundation of responsible government." It would then

have been his duty to win the co-operation of his colleagues or failing that to sever his connection with them. Any other course was an open disregard of constitutional practice and of essential loyalty to his fellow-Ministers.

The event created wide comment from papers and public men. The Conservative press was friendly to the ex-Minister; the Liberal press as a whole the reverse. The Ottawa *Citizen* declared that Mr. Tarte's views were practically those of the Conservative party and that this occurrence was the beginning of the end so far as the Government was concerned. In various forms this view was expressed by the Opposition press, with additional reflections upon Mr. Tarte's popularity in Quebec and his possible leadership once more in the Conservative ranks, subject to the co-operation of Mr. F. D. Monk, the present leader in that Province. The Liberal press praised the Premier's action and his presentation of the constitutional position, described Mr. Tarte as too energetic and too volatile, expressed appreciation in many cases of his administration of a difficult Department, hinted in other cases at his extravagance in promise and expenditure, expressed admiration of his ability but dislike of his impetuosity. This general point of view was summed up in the *Globe* of October 22nd: "The tariff is not the only question in which the Minister's utterances have embarrassed his colleagues. He has been in the habit of making promises and expounding policies not sanctioned by the Ministry and involving heavy expenditures. If these had referred to his own Department he might have claimed a large liberty of speech in regard to them. But he has trespassed on the fields of other Ministers in a manner which he would certainly have resented if others had interfered with the Department of Public Works."

Of the personal comments the most interesting was that of the ex-Minister's old-time rival in the party, Mr. Prefontaine. In the Montreal *Witness*, of October 22nd, he said that the alleged motive for Mr. Tarte's line of action was to force the hand of the party so that he might succeed Sir Wilfrid Laurier as leader instead of Mr. Fielding, whom it was generally understood was to take his place when the time came. He believed the removal of Mr. Tarte would strengthen the Liberal party in Quebec, did not think he had any following in the Province and deprecated the idea of any party difference regarding protection. "I do not believe in the present tariff as a finality; no man who thinks could do that, for the circumstances of the country must be taken into account; but Mr. Tarte knew very well—I may say this much without betraying the secrets of the party caucus—that it was not the intention of the Government to proceed with a revision at present." Some time after this incident, on December 7th, Sir Charles Tupper was interviewed at Montreal and declared that "without a single exception Mr. Tarte is the ablest man in the Liberal party and when the Cabinet lost his services it lost those of the best man in it."

From England came various expressions of approval of the

Premier's action from a constitutional standpoint—the fiscal issue was not judged. The *Standard*, for instance, declared Sir Wilfrid Laurier to be clearly justified in the former connection and Mr. Tarte's conduct to be "contrary to all the traditions of party government." On October 23rd Mr. Tarte assumed editorial charge of *La Patrie* and wrote a valedictory or " word to the country " which described improved transportation arrangements on the St. Lawrence and the great lakes as having been his great ambition in immediately preceding years. Sir Wilfrid Laurier's arguments he termed " shallow " and his reproaches as unjust and due to ill-health. As to the rest he was brief and concise : " My views on the fiscal situation which confronts this country are, I have the profound conviction, those of the very great majority of the Canadian people and of the Liberal party. A tariff of defence for our national interests, of firm protection, without ambiguity, for our industries, our agriculture, our working classes. That is the policy of to-morrow. That is the policy which I will continue to defend with my pen, with my speech, and from my seat in Parliament."

A pronounced agitation developed during the year, in other quarters, for tariff revision in the direction of increased protection to Canadian products. On January 13th the Brant-

Revision of
the Tariff
Discussed

ford Board of Trade passed the following Resolution : " That in view of the present conditions of trade and the expansion of Canadian industries, it is highly desirable that the Government revise the present tariff with a view to the preservation of our markets against unfair competition ; thus assisting to maintain and increase our present industries and to establish new ones." At the annual banquet of the Board on January 28th various approving references were made to this Resolution, while copies of it were sent to all the Boards of Trade in Canada. At a meeting in Toronto of the Executive Committee of the Canadian Manufacturers' Association on January 16th, Mr. James P. Murray read a paper in which he stated the belief that " we cannot hope to have made much of a standing in foreign markets until we are able to supply in a greater way our own requirements. To do this properly we must manufacture much more largely, and we are not warranted in doing so unless we have a larger home market." There were many articles of which the detailed parts should all be manufactured in Canada. " If our importations of last year had been made in Canada we would have employed in round numbers 150,000 more factory hands, who would have earned about $65,000,000 in wages. They and their families and necessary traders, professions, etc., such as doctors, clergymen, teachers, carters and storekeepers, would make up about three cities as large as Toronto. Estimating on these figures, a reasonable increase in the value of our exports would be $40,000,000 worth of manufactures."

Speaking on February 27th at the monthly banquet of the Canadian Manufacturers' Association at Montreal, Mr. Archibald Campbell, a Liberal M.P., was pronounced in his view. He referred to the importance of prosperous industries to a nation, and urged revision of the tariff so as to exclude some portion at least of the $25,000,000 of manufactured goods now brought in from the States as raw material. " It is the duty of the Government to foster and encourage the industries of the Dominion. We are importing altogether too great a proportion of our necessities. The time is at hand when we should look at things from a Canadian standpoint and from that standpoint alone. . . . We should meet the issues as they arise and treat them with the ideas of the present, and not as we thought ten or fifteen years ago."

Mr. Campbell addressed the North Toronto Liberal Club on October 2nd, following, and urged that no tariff was a finality in a progressive country. " He believed that the time had come to revise the tariff, which revision did not mean an increase unless it was necessary not only in the best interests of Canada but of the Empire." On May 13th a meeting of the Montreal Board of Trade discussed the question of German tariff discrimination against Canada and in a formal Resolution pointed out the character of this discrimination, the fact that Canadian exports to Germany and some other countries were not increasing whilst imports from them were steadily growing, and described the desire of the people for a thoroughly Canadian tariff. The motion concluded as follows :

Resolved,—That the Dominion Government is hereby respectfully urged to make such alterations in the tariff upon importations from Foreign countries not having reciprocal relations with this country as will serve to protect the natural products and manufactures of Canada against the present discrimination under which they suffer, and thereby bring about in the near future fairer trade relations between Canada and said Foreign countries.

On October 14th, following, the same Board, after listening to a speech from Mr. Tarte, passed the following Resolution : " That in the opinion of this meeting, in view of the changing conditions in the commercial world, the Dominion Government should examine carefully into the working of our present customs tariff on imports, and should so re-adjust same as to secure Canadian industrial products against the competition of foreign labour." Meanwhile, the Halifax *Chronicle*, a leading Liberal organ of the Maritime Provinces, had been urging a lower tariff rather than increased duties, and criticising, more or less sternly, Mr. Tarte's protectionist views. On August 23rd, the Hon. J. W. Longley, Attorney-General of Nova Scotia, took up the subject in a long letter, which appeared in its columns, and which practically endorsed the attitude assumed by the Minister of Public Works. He deprecated the large import of products from the United States in comparison with the small import from Great Britain, and declared the tariff to be simply a matter of national need and not one of principle. " Under existing conditions it is a question of business and of national interest, and if the Government of Canada, after due investigation, become satisfied that the existing tariff can be improved, even if in such a way as to diminish largely the huge import from the United States and equalize the trade relations between these two countries, then this is a step which it would be fitting and proper to take."

Meantime, at the other end of the Dominion, an agitation was being promoted to increase the duties on lead. At a meeting of the Nelson Board of Trade, in British Columbia, on April 29th, the subject was discussed, and the Secretary instructed to send a telegram asking Mr. W. A. Galliher, M.P., what action the Government was taking in response to a previous request for increased duties, and proceeding as follows: "The situation in this country at present is critical, and the matter is of paramount importance. Board urges you to inform Premier immediately of intense feeling existing regarding this matter and to ask for definite promise of this protection." Public meetings followed at Kamloops, Trout Lake, New Denver, Silverton and other places with similarly vigorous Resolutions. At Ymir, on April 30th, the Citizens' Association urged upon the Dominion Government "the great necessity of imposing a protective tariff on pig-lead in order to make it possible to refine and manufacture lead in this country and thus establish the industries." At a meeting of the Rossland Liberal Association on May 8th, a long Resolution was passed pointing out that the present low price of lead was due partly to hostile American tariff legislation and partly to the influence of American trusts and begging for higher duties and a bounty of double the existing amount in order to encourage the various industries of lead mining, smelting, refining, corroding and manufacturing, independently of a foreign country.

In the British Columbia Legislature, on April 8th, a Resolution was passed without opposition in favour of establishing a lead smelter aided by the Dominion and Provincial Governments. Its cost was estimated by the Minister of Mines at $500,000. On June 11th, the following motion was also unanimously adopted: "That it is desirable, in the interests of the silver-lead mining and smelting industries of British Columbia, that the duties on pig-lead and the products thereof imposed by the Dominion of Canada should be so increased as to protect the capital invested in these industries, and encourage the investment of capital in the establishment of the various manufactures of lead products within the Dominion."

Returning to Ontario we find Mr. Henry Miles, of the Montreal Board of Trade, speaking at Gananoque on September 24th, and declaring the tariff to be the great issue of the day, He deprecated the alleged admission of German goods through and under the Preferential clause, and urged a revision of the system in the direction of greater protection for specific objects. In the *Globe*, of September 27th, appeared a long letter from Senator James McMullen discussing the question as an old-time Liberal politician. He did not believe in a higher tariff to aid the manufacturers, but he did believe the time had come for a revision. He asked why we should continue year after year taking many lines of manufactured goods from the United States when we might just as well make them ourselves. The free list should be enlarged and the tariff adjusted so as to favour British goods at the expense of American wherever possible. He instanced metals and minerals, drugs and dyes, vehicles of various kinds, silks, confectionery, hats, caps, etc. As to the protests of the North-West he claimed that the older Provinces had for long dealt most generously with the newer countries in the West. "If a re-adjustment is made and the Manitoba farmer is asked to have the tariff now collected from him on tea, coffee, spices, crockery, stoneware, and many other lines coming to us from within the Empire removed and put upon agricultural supplies and other manufactured products coming to us from outside countries, what has he to complain of when the gross per capita tax has not been exceeded?"

At a banquet in Gananoque on September 24th, Mr. R. Wilson-Smith, ex-Mayor of Montreal, advocated the establishment of two tariffs—a maximum and a minimum. He declared that "protection is not a party question; it is a fiscal version of Canada for Canadians; it is patriotism not partizanship." Mr. R. L. Borden, M.P., was banqueted at Montreal on his return from the West, and the watchword of the evening of October 25th was "adequate protection to Canadian industries." He declared that this was the doctrine they had preached from the Great Lakes to the Pacific, and expressed strong faith in its approval by the people. Mr. F. D. Monk, M.P., in his speech, stated that "when the Conservative party comes to power every Canadian industry will receive full and adequate protection." Following this occasion, and his own retirement from the Government, Mr. Tarte continued to advocate his policy of revision. Speaking at a banquet at Sault Ste. Marie on October 25th he addressed himself specially to the Americans present; told them that Canada had not been fairly treated by the Republic; and declared that national pride was now running high in Canada and that "we are going to protect ourselves and in doing so we will bring you to time."

At the annual banquet of the Laval law students in Montreal on November 6th, Sir Wilfrid Laurier spoke eloquently upon non-contentious subjects, and Mr. Tarte followed in a vigorous trade and transportation speech. We should cease, he said, to be vassals of the United States. "This is a decisive moment in the history of Canada. This country needs an affirmation of its industrial policy." In his first address as a Minister of the Crown, Mr. Prefontaine on November 12th, told a Liberal Association in Montreal that he was a protectionist as he had declared himself to be in 1896. All legitimate industries should be protected. "The Government would render justice to the legitimate industries of the country and the manufacturers whenever the occasion presented itself." During the contest in Maissonneuve which followed, and resulted in the

Minister's re-election, Mr. F. D. Monk on November 26th attacked
Mr. Prefontaine's claim to be a protectionist. Steel rails should be
manufactured, he declared, and nickel smelted in Canada. Addressing the Canadian Club at Hamilton on December 4th Mr. Tarte
again urged revision of the tariff. American competition and
Canada's geographical position were the reasons advanced. Amongst
other things shipbuilding should be encouraged; United States
bacon and other farm products should be kept out by tariff
regulation; iron-ore and pulp-wood should be kept at home for
Canadian industrial development. The Hon. Mr. Fielding was
banqueted at Halifax on December 11th with the Provincial
Premier, Mr. G. H. Murray, in the chair, and the Hon. L. J. Tweedie,
Premier of New Brunswick, Hon. W. Paterson and Sir Frederick
Borden also present. In the course of his speech the Finance
Minister made the following reference to the tariff and the current
discussion :

We have always attempted to adjust the tariff to meet all classes. There
always has been a measure of incidental protection. If you put on a duty of
15 per cent. on something made in Canada and something made abroad ;
incidentally you confer a protection to that extent. It will be always so for a
considerable time to come. It is a question between a moderate and reasonable
tariff or the high and excessive duties which prevailed under the national policy.
I do not say, and I repeat it again, that the tariff is perfect. It is five years
since that tariff was prepared and but slight changes have been made. We
have held that it is a great improvement to the country to avoid frequent tariff
changes. Every business man appreciates the matter of tariff stability. It is a
matter that sometimes we had better bear the ills we have than fly to others
that we know not of. It is better to bear with some little inequality than to
open up the tariff question and to disturb the equilibrium of trade. But
changed conditions at home and abroad may necessitate looking over these
items from time to time.

The year's discussion of the revision question closed with a
speech by Sir William Mulock, Postmaster-General, before the
Canadian Club at Hamilton on December 26th. He eulogized the
Preferential clause and the Fielding tariff as a whole, and quoted
various figures indicating Canadian prosperity under present fiscal
conditions. He accused the Conservatives of a desire to repeal the
Preference and then proceeded: "Our political opponents in their
intense desire to obtain office at whatever cost, forgetting how dis-
turbing it is to trade that the tariff should be a political issue, constantly seek to make of it a political football by representing the
Liberal party as a free-trade party, hoping thereby to create alarm
in financial and business circles. There is no issue of free trade
against protection in Canada. The only question is between a
high prohibitory tariff and a moderate, just tariff."

In his Budget speech, on April 17th, the Hon. W. S. Fielding
defended the Preferential clause in the tariff, explained his reasons
for not approving the grant of a bounty on beet-root
Parliament and the Tariff sugar and then outlined the position of the Government on the question of fiscal changes in the follow-
ing terms: "We do not propose to make any changes
in the tariff this session. I do not for a moment claim that the

tariff is perfect. I think, that, on the whole, it has proved a very good tariff. Indeed, when we recall the circumstances under which our tariff revision took place, when we remember the very complicated and difficult problem with which we had to deal, we may well congratulate ourselves upon our success in devising a tariff so well adapted to the requirements of the country—a tariff under which Canada has prospered in a greater degree than in any previous period in her history. I have occasionally pointed out the desirability of a reasonable measure of tariff stability. Nothing would be more likely to unsettle business than a practice of introducing frequent tariff changes. Hence, we have resisted applications for many small changes and we think it well to do so to-day. But I would not have it understood that this view can always be held. As time passes, conditions change in our own country and it will be well for us to take note of this, so that we may adjust the tariff accordingly. Nor is that the only reason that might require some change. Conditions arise in other countries of which we are obliged to take account. We do not propose that we shall stand still and that this tariff shall remain unchanged, but we think the time is not opportune for making changes at present."

The principal reasons, in detail, for making no immediate readjustment were the pending appearance of industrial statistics in connection with the Census, the possible settlement of existing fiscal differences with Germany and the coming discussions with Australia and other parts of the Empire at the Coronation Conference. Mr. R. L. Borden, in his reply, presented on the following day an elaborate array of statistics to prove that the present tariff was not protecting Canadian interests and industries. He pointed out that in 1901 Canada took $65,000,000 of manufactured goods from the United States, or nearly one-sixth of that country's total industrial export, and claimed that this was not carrying out the wishes of the Canadian people, but was tending to keep this an agricultural and pastoral country. The people did not want this. "I believe they will look to the Government to so re-adjust the tariff as to prevent Canada being made the slaughter market of the United States, whether of manufactured products or of agricultural products." The Opposition leader went on to attack the Preference as injuring Canadian industries and doing Great Britain no substantial good, and especially as admitting German and Belgian goods in an indirect manner to compete with Canadian manufactures. He concluded by declaring the fiscal statements and views of Mr. Sifton and Mr. Tarte to be antagonistic, the promised future adjustment of the tariff vague and unsatisfactory, and the existing conditions injurious to industrial investment and development. He moved the following Resolution:

That this House, regarding the operation of the present tariff as unsatisfactory, is of opinion that this country requires a declared policy of such adequate protection to its labour, agricultural products, manufactures and industries as will at all times secure the Canadian market for Canadians. While always firmly maintaining the necessity of such protection to Canadian interests this House affirms its belief in a policy of reciprocal trade preference within the Empire.

Sir Richard Cartwright, in following, dealt with the increasing prosperity of the country, the evils of the old-time protective policy and the advantages of Liberal rule under Mackenzie in 1874-78 and under Laurier. As to higher protection being established now he declared that he had no quarrel with the manufacturers of Canada, though many of them looked upon him as their particular enemy. To his mind the Government had treated them with the greatest consideration and care in the preparation of the present tariff. "And in any alterations that may be made in the tariff, I for one shall never advise that injustice be done to the manufacturers or done to anybody. But, I have got to say to them that they have had most uncommonly good fortune and most uncommonly good times. If they have used these well they ought to be most admirably prepared to-day to meet any reverses which may happen to overtake them, as reverses may overtake all classes of the community. I hope they have used their opportunities well. But I do not believe that the way to really advance their interests is to impose higher taxes for their benefit on the rest of the community."

The debate on the Budget was prolonged until April 8th, when Mr. Borden's Resolution was defeated by a party vote of 117 to 67, and during this period every phase of the tariff and every detail of the fiscal condition of the country was gone into by the various speakers from their respective political standpoints.

The tariff is always the chief underlying subject of political difference in Canada, but during 1902 the newspapers were unusually full of comments and criticisms upon the subject. **The Press and the Tariff** On February 28th the Liberal Montreal *Witness* declared that "there is not the slightest doubt that protection is in the air in this community," and thought retaliation against the United States' high duties particularly popular. The Toronto *Globe*, as the leading Liberal organ of Ontario, had a good many important references to the subject during the year. On August 15th it stated that there was no friendship to the manufacturing interests of Canada in any attempt to stir up a tariff discussion. "Stability has advantages that are not fully appreciated. The Government would not be justified in refusing to make an increase or reduction if it were shown that any interest would be thereby benefited without corresponding injuries elsewhere, but the experience of the past decade goes to show that the advantages to be derived from any general revision would be more than offset by the loss of stability and the period of uncertainty that would ensue before the attendant discussions would cease and the trade and industry adjust itself to the new conditions."

Nine days later the same paper defined the tariff as " a moderate

3

one, representing neither free trade nor high protection. "Its moderation is a guarantee of stability." On the following day it defined the old condition of affairs as one of "tariff tinkering," and then added : "The tariff rests upon the consent of the community. The greater the burden the more the community will murmur. Agitation cannot be choked off in a free country. The Western farmers think the tariff is too high already, and if it is increased they will carry on an agitation which may eventually result in sweeping reductions all along the line. The natural result of an agitation for excessive protection will be an agitation for free trade."

On August 23rd the *Globe* described the Preferential clause as devised in the interest of the consumer. The main purpose of a tariff was revenue, but in Canada it had always been incidentally protective. "Stability is perhaps the most important matter in regard to tariffs." On October 4th and again on the 27th tariff stability was described as the most desirable present quality in the fiscal system.

Meanwhile, Conservative papers like the Toronto *Mail and Empire*, the Halifax *Herald* and the Montreal *Gazette* complained that the tariff was not adequately protecting legitimate interests which had developed under recent conditions of prosperity. The Winnipeg *Telegram* thought the Conservatives had kept the tariff down as low as was consistent with efficient protection, and that the Liberals had gone below that point. The Liberal *Telegraph*, of St. John, took a very different view. Though free trade expressions were not much heard just now, it declared, on September 5th, that the sentiment was none the less still widely prevalent. Sir Wilfrid Laurier's hint in an English speech that inter-Imperial trade might be encouraged by a gradual lowering of Colonial tariffs was said to be a very gratifying evidence that the Government had "by no means abandoned their free-trade principles," and the article concluded with the statement that, under present conditions, "no higher tariff propositions could be seriously entertained by the Government." The Manitoba *Free Press*, on September 13th, in an elaborate editorial repudiated the idea that the Liberal party could possibly be protectionist, and indicated its views very clearly in the following words :

The Government formulated its findings on the tariff in a statute which is now the law of the land. This provides for duties at a moderately high rate, sufficient to supply ample revenue for the needs of the country and yet permitting trade, internal and external, to develop along natural lines. This tariff expresses, with some degree of accuracy, the wishes of the Liberal rank and file ; probably a large majority of them would prefer to see it lower, yet they have been reconciled to it in great measure by the success which has attended its administration.

Following Mr. Tarte's retirement on October 22nd a host of tariff comments appeared. The Hamilton *Times* (Liberal) declared that " a moderate, stable tariff has been found advantageous to the

country, fair to industry and productive of revenue. Nothing has
so far occurred to suggest the necessity of a violent change, up or
down." The St. John *Gazette,* of the same party, proclaimed
another revision imminent. " We are being unfairly treated by our
neighbours to the south, and to preserve our own self-respect a higher
tariff must be put in operation against them." Amongst the Conservative papers the principal difference of opinion seemed to be
upon the Preferential clause in the tariff and as to how far it might
be modified or neutralized in its competitive influence. Its abrogation was not directly urged.

The tariff discussions of the year found one of its pivotal points
in the annual meeting of the Canadian Manufacturers' Association
at Halifax on August 13th and 14th. During recent
years this organization had been growing steadily in
scope, in numbers and in influence, and now boasted
strong branches at Montreal, Toronto, and in the
Provinces of Quebec, Nova Scotia, Manitoba and
British Columbia, with headquarters at Toronto and over a thous-
and members. Its objects, according to the constitution, were " to
promote Canadian industries and to further the interests of Canadian manufacturers and exporters." Any political leaning was
strongly disclaimed.

The
Manufacturers'
Meeting at
Halifax.

The Association was welcomed in the Legislative Buildings by
Lieutenant-Governor, the Hon. A. G. Jones, who dealt with the
increasing prosperity of Canada and referred to the aggregate trade
of the Dominion in 1900 as $78.00 per head in comparison with
that of the United States which was $39.00 per head. He urged
attention to South African trade and spoke of the industrial development going on in Nova Scotia. The Hon. J. W. Longley, on
behalf of the Government, and Mayor A. B. Crosby, on behalf of the
City, followed. The latter took a different line from that of the
Lieutenant-Governor. " I would say to you capture the trade of
Canada and you will have all you can do for some time to come." His
policy was Canada for the Canadians. " We should teach the people
to wear goods of Canadian manufacture and to buy goods of Canadian manufacture." When that was done it would be time to seek
foreign markets. After a word of welcome from Mr. George S.
Campbell, President of the Halifax Board of Trade, a formal reply
was made by Mr. Robert Munro, President of the Association. He
referred to the great local developments in steel and iron, and to the
pulp industry and the rolling construction works at Amherst. He
thought that Canada was bound to be a great industrial country
and stated that already one-third of its entire population was
directly or indirectly dependent upon various industries.

In his annual address, which followed, the President described
the year as one of large and substantial growth in every direction.
After dealing with the questions of export trade and expressing
approval of the principle of the Preferential clause in the tariff he

referred to certain textile interests, as suffering from its incidence. Upon the whole the duties should be considerably raised. "The manufacturing classes are not the only sufferers under the present low tariff. Our agricultural classes are similarly affected." He stated that the United States delivered $20,000,000 more of agricultural products to us than they took in exchange and that there was a total balance of trade of $70,000,000 against us. A proper adjustment of the tariff to meet these conditions "would result in a great increase of trade with the Empire." He concluded by deprecating the continued importations of $100,000,000 worth of manufactured goods every year and by urging the patriotism and non-partisan character of his Association.

Various Committees then reported, including that upon the Tariff. This latter was presented by Mr. W. K. McNaught, its Chairman, and dealt with the submission to the Government of a number of suggestions from the Association looking to a general revision of the tariff. A large deputation had waited on the Government on January 21st and 22nd, and had been given the opportunity of going thoroughly into the matters dealt with. They had been accompanied by deputations from the woollen industries and agricultural implement interests. The result had not been satisfactory, although the Government seemed to be strongly in sympathy with the idea of protecting Canadian industry. They had been given to understand that the Government " would make changes just as soon as the electorate of Canada demanded them, and were willing to go just as far as the voice of the people warranted." But Parliament had done nothing at its last Session. "If your Committee can gauge aright the signs of the times public interests now demand a thorough revision of the entire tariff." Education of the people in favour of " a real Canadian tariff" was urged and support asked for the Association's Financial Fund which had been started for that purpose. In moving the adoption of the Report Mr. McNaught declared that the $60,000,000 received for exports to Great Britain over and above the payment for imports from that country was, in the main, practically handed over to the United States in payment for a surplus of imports from the Republic. The following Resolution was then presented by him, seconded by Mr. George E. Drummond, of Montreal, and carried unanimously:

Resolved, That in the opinion of this Association the changed conditions which now obtain in Canada demand the immediate and thorough revision of the tariff upon lines which will more effectually transfer to the workshops of the Dominion the manufacture of many of the goods which we now import from other countries ; that in such revision the interests of all sections of the community, whether of mining, fishing or manufacturing, should be fully considered with a view not only to the preservation, but to the further development of all these great national industries ; that while such tariff should be primarily framed for Canadian interests, it should nevertheless give a substantial preference to the Mother Country, and also to any other part of the British Empire with which reciprocal preferential trade can be arranged to our mutual advantage, recognizing always that under any conditions the minimum tariff must afford adequate protection to all Canadian producers.

THE MANUFACTURERS' MEETING AT HALIFAX

The speakers to the motion dealt largely with the unfair conditions which they claimed to exist in connection with American trade. At the close of the discussion Mr. E. B. Eddy spoke at length on the condition of the pulp-wood industry and Mr. H. E. Croasdaile on the lead industry of British Columbia. Others dealt with ship-building projects and various transportation interests. A number of Resolutions were passed and the following officers elected:—President, Cyrus A. Birge of Hamilton; 1st Vice-President, George E. Drummond of Montreal; Treasurer, George Booth of Toronto; Secretary, R. J. Younge, B.A., of Toronto. The Vice-Presidents for the various Provinces included W. K. George for Ontario; J. J. McGill for Quebec; D. W. Robb for Nova Scotia; John Hendry for British Columbia; E. L. Drewry for Manitoba; and C. J. Osman for New Brunswick.

The annual banquet took place on the evening of August 14th with President Birge in the Chair and the Hon. J. Israel Tarte, M.P., Mr. R. L. Borden, K.C., M.P., Major-General Sir Charles Parsons, Commanding the Imperial forces, the Hon. J. W. Longley, M.P.P., and others, as guests of the Association. Mr. Tarte in his speech dealt with shipping, the Fast Line, and other non-contentious projects and then came to the tariff. He presented his well-known views in favour of "a strong British-Canadian tariff," of meeting American industrial competition with fiscal weapons, of building up Canadian industries. "It is a false notion that if we have a Canadian tariff to suit our own purposes, the Canadian consumer must pay dearer for what he buys." After the Minister came the Leader of the Opposition Mr. Borden urged fair play for every legitimate industry under the tariff. He wanted an honest preference for the Mother-Country but at the same time believed "a factory in Canada was worth as much to the Empire as a factory in Yorkshire." The Hon. Mr. Longley declared that there was no moral issue in the tariff. "It is solely and entirely a question of giving relief and of promoting the best interests of Canada."

Preceding this meeting the Association had asked its members for $50,000 as an educational fund for the purpose of impressing upon Canadians "the advantages of conserving and developing Canadian industries and maintaining as far as practicable the home market for Canadian manufacturers." On October 14th a further circular was issued, signed by the President and Secretary, giving the Resolution which was passed at Halifax and asking the members to indicate any specific changes they would desire in a general re-adjustment of the tariff. Following this action rumours grew apace as to the Association being about to take an active part in politics. This was strongly denied in another circular issued to its members and given to the press. To the Toronto *Globe*, on October 31st, Mr. Younge reiterated this statement and added that the amount asked for was now practically guaranteed and that they were ready to proceed with their educational campaign.

The Leader of the Conservative party in Canada made a six weeks' visit to the Western Provinces during the autumn accompanied by his chief lieutenants. It was Mr. R. L. Borden's first meeting with the people of the West as a political leader, and the arrangements seem to have been well calculated for bringing him into touch with his party. Amongst those who accompanied him and shared the burden of the speaking were Major G. W. Fowler, M.P., Mr. A. C. Bell, M.P., Mr. H. A. Powell, ex-M.P., Mr. A. A. Lefurgey, M.P., and Mr. George V. McInerney, ex-M.P., of the Maritime Provinces, with Messrs. E. F. Clarke, M.P., James Clancy, M.P., W. H. Bennett, M.P., Richard Blain, M.P., W. B. Northrup, M.P., and Dr. T. S. Sproule, M.P., of Ontario. Mr. R. H. Pope, M.P. of Quebec was also in the delegation, and in Manitoba Hon. R. P. Roblin and his colleagues participated in some of the meetings together with Messrs. N. Boyd, M.P., Dr. Roche, M.P., W. Sanford Evans and Mr. A. A. C. La Riviére, M.P. The Leader of the party in Quebec, Mr. F. D. Monk, K.C., M.P., was busy with bye-elections and was only able to attend a meeting in Winnipeg.

Mr. Borden's Political Tour of the West

Leaving Montreal on September 3rd the party went through to Victoria where Mr. Borden addressed a mass-meeting on September 8th. He spoke strongly on tariff matters, declared that Canadian workmen must be protected from American trusts, and took ground against the Dominion Government in their disallowance of anti-Asiatic immigration legislation. "There is no Imperial consideration which should prevail against your views or your wishes as there is no such consideration allowed to prevail against the wishes of Australia." On the following night he spoke at Vancouver to a large audience and on the succeeding day visited Steveston and Ladner, speaking at New Westminster in the evening and supporting a policy of higher duties for the lead industry. Rossland was reached on Sunday the 14th of September, and a meeting addressed on Monday evening. Mr. Borden declared here that the mining industry should be assisted as it had been in the East and that in the matter of Oriental immigration the wishes of the people should prevail. Trail and Nelson were visited on the following day and a meeting addressed at the latter place in the evening. Meanwhile the Conservative Convention at Revelstoke had been attended on the 12th and the representatives of the party in British Columbia addressed by the Leader.

Returning to the Territories Macleod was reached on September 18th and an afternoon meeting addressed. Upon the burning question of Territorial autonomy Mr. Borden declared himself in favour of entrusting the fullest control of local affairs to the people. Lethbridge was visited in the evening and a meeting addressed at Medicine Hat in the afternoon of the next day. Here, as elsewhere throughout the Territories, he reiterated his favourable opinion as to Provincial autonomy and presented the Conservative tariff policy. "It was one of reasonable protection to

ROBERT LAIRD BORDEN, K.C., M.P.,
Leader of the Conservative Party in Canada.

all Canadian industries, and he was prepared to say this before any Canadian audience. Competition amongst Canadian industries had resulted in a marvellous reduction of prices, and he did not think the people of Canada would suffer by a moderate protective tariff." Calgary was reached on September 20th and it was while driving in from the Indian Reserve near this city that a runaway team crashed into the vehicle containing Mr. Borden and other members of his party and seriously endangered their safety for a brief space. Banff was next visited and on the way to the Strathcona meeting of September 23rd gatherings were addressed from the train at Didsbury, Olds, Innisfall, Red Deer and Metaski-win. A mass-meeting was addressed at Calgary on the 24th. Moosejaw was visited on the following afternoon and Regina the same evening. At Qu'Appelle Mr. Borden spoke on the evening of September 27th after addressing the people of Indian Head in the afternoon. Wolseley and Grenfell were visited on the 29th, White-wood and Wapella on the 30th and Moosomin on October 1st.

The tour of Manitoba was commenced at Virden on the following day. Here he repeated the story of protection. "His party had a policy for the whole of Canada, a policy of adequate protection to all Canadian industries." A mass-meeting was addressed at Brandon on October 3rd, and a gathering at Minnedosa on the following day. Sunday was spent in Winnipeg where Mr. Borden expressed to the papers great satisfaction at the political success of his tour and great admiration of the country from the City to the Coast. Then followed meetings at Dauphin on October 6th, Portage la Prairie on the 7th, Morden on the 8th, Boissevain on the 9th, Selkirk on the 10th, Emerson on the 11th, Winnipeg on the 13th, Holland on the 14th, Yorkton on the 16th, Neepawa on the 17th, and Winnipeg again on the 20th. At Morden in reply to a question of great local importance regarding the implement duties Mr. Borden spoke as follows: "We will make the duty adequate, and if it is now high enough, as I believe it is, to enable manufacturers to make implements in Canada, we will not increase it. I am informed that implements are as cheap in Canada as in the United States, so the duty seems to be high enough."

As the two meetings in Winnipeg summarized the events of the tour and the Western policy of the party special reference must be made to them. On October 13th Mr. Borden **Mr. Borden** addressed a mass-meeting in the Winnipeg Theatre. **at Winnipeg** Premier Roblin occupied the chair and the other speakers were Mr. James Clancy, M.P., and Mr. E. F. Clarke, M.P. A great gathering of prominent Conservatives was upon the platform, or in the crowded audience. In his elaborate speech Mr. Borden claimed the prosperity and progress of the West as due to the foundations laid by Conservative policy, dealt with many Liberal promises which he stated had not been kept, denounced that party as having different policies for every section or sectarian interest, and accused them of demoralizing the political standards of the community. He then turned to the practical issues of the moment. He had become satisfied as to the injury done the people of British Columbia by Oriental immigration, he believed the disallowed Acts to be similar to the Natal Act which the Imperial Government had not vetoed, and he was prepared to carry out the wishes of the people of that Province "who seem to be united in sentiment upon a question which affects them more closely than it does the people of other parts of Canada."

Upon the question of Territorial autonomy he believed the people to be locally fitted for the exercise of full self-government and the conditions to be such as to make desirable "the grant of responsible government as given to the people of the Eastern Provinces." As to the exemption of C.P.R. lands from taxation he believed that Parliament should at once pronounce upon the matter and not leave it entirely to the slow action of the Courts. Some decision should be reached even if compensation were deemed just and necessary. After dealing with the Liberal fiscal record and tariff policy and describing the different views of Mr. Sifton and Mr. Tarte, the speaker once more described Conservative policy as the same in all parts of Canada—"adequate protection to all legitimate industries." Every industry should be protected whether it was that of the farmer, the lead miner or the manufacturer. "I do not believe in sending raw materials to the United States, sending Canadians after them to work in United States factories, and then sending good Canadian money to buy the goods made by Canadians from Canadian material in the United States." As to the Preferential clause he declared it to be practically a German preference. His party would never regard any arrangement as satisfactory which did not obtain for Canada a preference in the British market.

An incident of the visit to Winnipeg—as it had been of the visit to other important centres—was a reception held on October 16th by Mrs. Borden, who had accompanied her husband throughout the greater part of the tour. The closing incident of the event was an important banquet given the Conservative Leader in Winnipeg on October 20th. The members of the Provincial Government, the most of the speakers who had accompanied Mr. Borden, the leading Conservatives of the Province, Mr. F. D. Monk, K.C., M.P., the Quebec Leader, Sir Charles Tupper, and the Hon. George É. Foster were present. The Hon. Robert Rogers, Provincial Minister of Public Works, presided. In his speech Mr. Borden paid high tribute to Sir Charles Tupper as a constructive statesman and Conservative leader, hoped soon to welcome the Hon. Mr. Foster back to Parliament, and declared that they had been preaching adequate industrial protection throughout the West with apparent popular favour, and concisely expressed his views of Canadian policy in a general sense as follows: "We stand for the idea that Canada should be an integral part of the British Empire, but it is also the policy of the Conservative party that within the Empire we must stand for Canada first and see that Canadian rights and Canadian interests are protected at all hazards. In this we contend that Canada for the Canadians means not the less Canada for the Empire as well."

Speeches followed from Sir Charles Tupper, Mr. F. D. Monk, and the Hon. George E. Foster. Mr. Monk read a telegram of congratulation upon his success as leader in Quebec from the Presidents of thirteen Montreal Conservative clubs. Other toasts brought brief addresses from the Hon. R. P. Roblin, Mr. E. F. Clarke, M.P., and Mr. W. B. Northrup, M.P. There were some six hundred guests at the banquet and the Winnipeg *Telegram* of the following day declared it the "greatest demonstration" in the history of Western Conservatism. Mr. Borden left for home on the same day, after sending out a message from himself and his associates to the Conservatives of Canada. At Montreal, on October 25th, he was tendered a congratulatory luncheon by the Junior Conservative Club, and at Halifax, two days later, a large crowd welcomed him at the station. The message from Winnipeg to his party was as follows :

In returning East, we wish to leave as a message to the West, first our determination to maintain the policy of progress which we have advocated here, as well as in the East; a policy which includes not only adequate protection to our industries, but also the question of transportion from a national standpoint. Whether our views as to the fiscal policy are sound or unsound, we believe in them, and we are determined to advocate them.

Secondly, we leave the assurance that the party which brought Western Canada into the Confederation values as highly as did our leaders of days gone by the heritage which Canada possesses in the West, and will see to it that the West shall receive at all times the generous consideration to which its importance entitles it.

In the third place, we feel inspired by the spirit of the Conservatives of the West, and we desire to return the assurance that the example and the enthusiasm displayed during our tour, which has now reached its conclusion, will prove an inspiration to our party in the East. To the people of the East we would carry back the assurance, if it were needed, that the people of the West are Canadians to the core, that they are animated by no narrow or sectional spirit, and that they look to the up-building of the great northern half of the continent.

Under the terms of the decision of the Judicial Committee of the Imperial Privy Council in 1901, the Provinces of Canada were recognized as owning the Fisheries within three miles of their coasts. Two of those on the Atlantic thereupon laid claim, or renewed claims, to a division amongst them of the Halifax Award of 1877, amounting to $4,500,000, with interest. There was no reasonable doubt as to the judgment vesting the ownership of the Fisheries in the Provinces, but the right to fix the close seasons, to make regulations and to control the method of fishing was reserved to the Dominion. In the House of Commons on February 28th, 1902, the Minister of Marine and Fisheries declared the decision difficult to understand. The present condition of affairs in connection with revenue and other matters was very unsatisfactory. The points in dispute must, he declared, be settled by some sort of arbitration or else by a Conference. Mr. R. L. Borden urged the special importance of a settlement in view of the claims upon the Halifax Award. Other speakers pointed out that the Provinces got the revenue and the advantages from the Fisheries while the Dominion had to pay for the expense of protecting them by special service.

In his Budget Speech on April 10th, Premier Peters of Prince Edward Island, spoke of this matter as ensuring to his Province $1,000,000 of a lump sum, and $30,000 annually in the future. The claim had been strongly pressed and the indications were that it would soon be submitted to the Supreme Court of Canada for decision. Quebec, he intimated, was also pressing for its share. New Brunswick, it may be added, joined in this pressure, but a little later it was announced that Nova Scotia would refuse to act with the others. The attention of the House of Commons was drawn to the matter on April 30th by Mr. S. Barker, and the Premier replied that it was being considered. As, however, the interest of the Award had been paid for many years to the Provinces in the shape of bounties to the fishermen he did not know that the result would be of much importance.

On May 20th a Conference met at Ottawa composed of the Hon. James Sutherland, the Hon. A. G. Blair, and Hon. Charles Fitzpatrick, representing the Dominion Government; Mr. S. T. Bastedo and Mr. Æmilius Irving, K.C., that of Ontario; Hon. S. N. Parent, Hon. H. T. Duffy and Mr. A. J. Cannon, that of Quebec; Hon. G. H. Murray and Hon. J. W. Longley, that of Nova Scotia ; Hon. L. J. Tweedie and Hon. William Pugsley, that of New Brunswick; Hon. Arthur Peters, Hon. J. F. Whear and Hon. Peter McNutt, that of Prince Edward Island. British Columbia was unable to be represented, and Manitoba was not specially interested. The position of the Provinces in the matter was not identical. Ontario had assumed the ownership of its inland fisheries and was now issuing licences and collecting revenue. Its point of controversy with the Dominion was as to certain regulations which had been embodied in a Provincial law.

The Conference adjourned on the following day to await the return of Sir Wilfrid Laurier in the autumn and with the very general announcement that, in the meantime, the various suggestions made would be considered by the respective Governments and that the Provincial delegates were of the opinion that the Dominion should have control of the Fisheries in tidal and international waters.

During the summer following this somewhat tentative Conference conditions developed a more important meeting, one which ranks with the Provincial Conference at Quebec in 1887. At first it was simply intended to continue the discussions of May 20th, and to also protest against a reduction in Provincial representation at Ottawa under the figures of the new Census and the terms of Confederation.

The Inter-Provincial Conference

This was the view expressed by Premier Peters in an interview on July 30th, and by Premier Tweedie on August 21st. Finally, the question of increased Dominion subsidies to the Provinces came to the front, and in December it was announced that a Conference would be held in Quebec of representatives from all the Provincial Governments and at the call of Premier Parent.

The opening meeting of the Conference was held on December 18th, with the Premier of Quebec, the Hon. Arthur Peters, Premier of Prince Edward Island, the Hon. R. P. Roblin, Premier of Manitoba, Hon. W. Pugsley, Attorney-General of New Brunswick present, together with Hon. H. T. Duffy, Hon. H. Archambeault, Hon. Lomer Gouin, Hon. J. J. Guerin, Hon. A. Robitaille and Hon. A. Turgeon of the Quebec Government. The gathering was a preliminary one, and by the evening Hon. L. J. Tweedie, Premier of New Brunswick, Hon. G. H. Murray, Premier of Nova Scotia, and Hon. J. W. Longley, Attorney-General of Nova Scotia, together with Hon. J. F. Whear, of the Prince Edward Island Government, had arrived and were also present. Premier Parent was chosen Chairman, and Mr. Gustave Grenier, Clerk of the Quebec Executive Council, was appointed Secretary.

During the next two days the deliberations of the Conference proceeded steadily, broken only by a Dinner at Government House, a Luncheon by the Premier, and a Banquet by the Board of Trade. The Ontario Government was represented by an elaborate memorandum submitted by Premier Ross, and British Columbia by a long letter from Premier Prior. The Conference adjourned on December 20th without making any public pronouncement, but it was understood that a delegation of all the Provincial Premiers would wait upon the Dominion Government in the course of a couple of months and present its Resolutions. One or two matters became known, however. At the Board of Trade banquet it was stated that the Conference felt that the proposed Grand Trunk Pacific road should give guarantees as to Canadian ports for the shipment of its produce, and on December 23rd Mr. Pugsley told an interviewer that the Minister of Justice had agreed to the submission of a case re the Fisheries question to the Supreme Court of Canada. As eventually made public the main Resolution of the Conference—endorsed by the presence of all the Provincial Premiers at its presentation to the Federal Government—dealt in detail with the question of larger Dominion subsidies to the Provinces. Summarized, its lengthy preamble may be condensed as follows:

1. That at Confederation in 1867 it was practically impossible to fix a subsidy which should at once be unalterable and adequate to the growing requirements of the future.

2. That it was the undoubted desire of the framers of the Constitution to make this financial provision a fitting one for the management of Provincial affairs.

3. That there is no doubt of the present resources of several of the Provinces, under existing limitations of control, being insuffi-

cient to meet their respective requirements of government and development.

4. That the present specific subsidies are as follows:—Ontario $80,000, Quebec $70,000, Nova Scotia $60,000, New Brunswick $50,000, Manitoba $50,000, British Columbia $35,000, and Prince Edward Island $30,000. That these and the additional 80 cents per head of their population—as established for Ontario and Quebec by the Census of 1861 and for the other Provinces by the last decennial Census—are quite insufficient.

5. That these subsidies and the grants referred to were given in consideration of the transfer to the Dominion Government of Customs and Excise duties which had increased from $11,580,968 in 1868 to $38,245,223 in 1900.

6. That the increase of population in Ontario between 1861 and 1901 had been 786,856, and in Quebec 537,332, while their per capita subsidy on the population of 1861 remained stationary.

7. That this increase of population had involved heavy increases of expenditure and requirements, with no proportionate increase of Dominion grant.

8. That the subsidies should be granted upon the basis of population in each Province at the preceding decennial Census.

In accordance with these varied reasons it was therefore:

Resolved, That this Conference is of opinion that an equitable basis for the settlement of the amounts to be yearly paid by the Dominion to the several Provinces for the support of their Governments and Legislatures be as follows:

(*A*) Instead of the amounts now paid the sums hereafter payable yearly by Canada to the several Provinces for the support of their Governments and Legislatures to be as follows:

    (*a*) Where the population is under 150,000......... $100,000.00
    (*b*) Where the population is 150,000 but does not
        exceed 200,000 .... 150,000.00
    (*c*) Where the population is 200,000 but does not
        exceed 400,000 .... 180,000.00
    (*d*) Where the population is 400,000 but does not
        exceed 800,000 .... 190,000.00
    (*e*) Where the population is 800,000 but does not
        exceed 1,500,000......................... 220,000.00
    (*f*) Where the population exceeds 1,500,000........ 240,000.00

(*B*) Instead of an annual grant per head of the population now allowed, the annual payment hereafter to be at the same rate of 80 cents per head, but on the population of each Province as ascertained from time to time by the last decennial Census, until such papulation exceed 2,500,000 ; and at the rate of 60 cents per head for so much of said population as may exceed 2,500,000.

(*C*) The population as ascertained by the last decennial Census to govern, except as to British Columbia and Manitoba ; and, as to these two Provinces, the population to be taken to be that upon which, under the respective statutes in that behalf, the annual payments now made to them respectively by the Dominion are fixed until the annual population is by the Census ascertained to be greater ; and thereafter the actual population so ascertained to govern.

(*D*) The amounts so to be paid and granted by the Dominion to the Provinces half-yearly and in advance.

It was further declared that the expense of administering the criminal law of Canada should be borne by the Dominion Government. The statement of Ontario's case by the Hon. G. W. Ross, which was submitted to the Conference, compared the position of the various Provinces in 1867 and in 1902, showed the erroneous expectations of the earlier period as to future revenues and expenditures, and declared that the financial provision in the Union Act was made " without adequately anticipating the growth of population and the urgent demands which modern conditions impose upon the Provinces." He claimed that the Provinces taxed themselves very considerably and that if the revenue of the Dominion were the basis of the subsidies the Provinces would receive double the amount now paid. This document formed, in part, the basis of the succeeding Resolutions. The Hon. E. G. Prior, in presenting the position of British Columbia, pointed out that they had a Province of 265,000,000 acres in extent, of which only 6,000,000 acres was a habitable area, with an adult white population of 45,000, and an average contribution by Customs and Inland Revenue taxes to the Dominion of three times that of the other populations of Canada.

Apart from the general election and the Prohibition campaign there were not many political issues of importance in Ontario. On **Political Affairs in Ontario** February 21st, however, a large and representative banquet was given Mr. J. P. Whitney, K.C., M.P.P., the Opposition Leader, in Toronto. It was tendered by the Conservative members of the Legislature and many of the leading men of the party in the Province were present. Messrs. R. L. Borden and F. D. Monk, the Dominion Leaders, addressed the gathering as well as Mr. Whitney and Messrs H. Carscallen and I. B. Lucas of the Provincial Legislature. Meanwhile, Mr. E. J. B. Pense of the Kingston *Whig* had been elected as a Liberal in place of the Hon. W. Harty, who had resigned on January 2nd in order to be a candidate for the Dominion Parliament. The latter also retired from the Government of which for some time he had been a Member without Portfolio. It may be added here that on March 19th the Hon. James T. Garrow, K.C., also a Member without Portfolio, was appointed to the Ontario Court of Appeal and, therefore, resigned his position and his place in the Legislature.

The Assembly was opened on January 8th by Lieut.-Governor, Sir Oliver Mowat with a Speech from the Throne in which he referred to the prosperity of the lumbering industry, the protection of the forest resources from fire, the steady progress of the mining industry, the continued settlement of new areas, the Government's attention to the care of the insane and the promotion of technical education, the compilation of Imperial statutes still in force in Ontario, the continued agricultural prosperity and the improvements made at the Guelph Agricultural College, the good results from the Government's encouragement to the beet sugar industry, the value of recent amendments to the Factories' Act, the inauguration of a system of restocking the inland waters of the Province with fish and the Report of the Royal Commission on Assessment Laws. The Government promised legislation regarding the Liquor traffic, the Temiscamingue Railway and other matters. Various public issues were discussed during the ensuing Session. On February 5th Messrs. A. Miscampbell and H. Carscallen moved that—

In all future agreements made between the Commissioners of the Queen Victoria Niagara Falls Park and any other person, or persons, power shall be reserved to the Provincial Government to, at any time, put a stop to the transmission of electricity and pneumatic power beyond the Canadian boundary ; and that in the opinion of this House, the waters of the Niagara River and its tributaries, as well as the waters of other streams, where necessary, should, at the earliest moment and subject to existing agreement, be utilized directly by the Provincial Government, in order that the latter may generate and develop electricity and pneumatic power for the purposes of light, heat and power, and furnish the same to municipalities in this Province at cost.

After the debate had been adjourned to February 11th this proposal was defeated by a party vote of 30 Conservatives to 41 Liberals. On February 25th, Messrs. T. Crawford and H. Carscallen moved that: " In the opinion of this House it is the duty of the Provincial Government to, without delay, urge upon the Government of Canada the necessity of taking steps to obtain for the people of this Province, cheaper rates for the transportation of agricultural products." The vote was the same as above.

The much-discussed " Act respecting the Sale of Intoxicating Liquors " was presented by the Premier and read a first time on February 12th. It passed the second reading after many speeches had been made, on March 6th, by a vote of 48 to 35. On March 14th, Messrs. T. Crawford and I. B. Lucas moved an amendment eliminating the Referendum clauses from the Bill and this was voted down on a party division of 45 to 34—Mr. G. F. Marter, a former Conservative leader but now independent voting with the Opposition. Another amendment submitted by Mr. Marter and Mr. James Tucker (C) and fixing the date of the voting for the next municipal election day received only four supporters against 75. Mr. Marter then moved to strike out the clause defining the vote which was to make the Act effective but only received four votes to 76. Another amendment increasing the margin of opportunity for the Act to become law was lost by 2 to 81—only Mr. Marter and Mr. Crawford supporting it. The Bill was then read a third time and passed by 47 to 34. Meanwhile, Messrs. Powell and Carnegie had moved a Resolution on March 11th expressing regret that the Government had taken " no sufficient steps " to secure from the Dominion a subsidy for the Temiscamingue Railway and that no complete plans, reports or surveys in the matter had been laid before the House. The vote was a party one of 44 to 33. The following Conservative motion was lost by a similar party vote of 46 to 35, two days later—Mr. Marter voting with the Opposition :

This House denounces the acts of the persons who defaced, switched, tampered with and stole ballots which had been duly and lawfully cast by

electors in the recent elections in West Elgin and North Waterloo, and also
denounces the destruction in the vaults of the Parliament Buildings in Toronto,
of the ballot papers and other documents relating to the West Elgin election,
by which the prosecution and conviction of the guilty parties was rendered
more difficult ; and this House expresses its dissatisfaction and regret that not
one of the malefactors connected with the above-mentioned violations of the
law has been brought to justice or punished for his offense, while one person
connected with the West Elgin frauds has been appointed to a position of trust
and emolument by the Government of the Province.

On March 15th the Government's proposal to ratify their agreement with the Montreal Pulp and Paper Company was approved
by 38 to 36. The Redistribution Bill, increasing the representation
of what is termed " New Ontario," was presented to the House on
February 26th by the Hon. Mr. Gibson and passed on March 15th.
It created four new constituencies. The House was prorogued on
March 17th by Chief-Justice, the Hon. J. D. Armour, acting as
Administrator. His Honour referred to the passage of the Temiscamingue Railway Bill and the proposed construction of this line
under the direct auspices and control of the Government; to the
Liquor Bill and its expected far-reaching influence upon the social
life of the people; to the newly-developed regions of the Province
and the representation given them by the Government's policy ;
and to the numerous charters granted for the construction of
electric railways. One of the closing incidents in the life of this
Legislature was the paying of high tribute by the Attorney-
General and Mr. Whitney to the impartiality and dignity with
which the Hon. F. E. A. Evanturel had acted as Speaker since
1898.

After months of preliminary conflict and preparation upon both
sides, the elections for the Ontario Legislature took place on May
29th, 1902. The central figures in the contest were
the Premier, Hon. George W. Ross, and the Opposition Leader, Mr. J. P. Whitney, K.C. The Hon. J. R.
Stratton, Provincial Secretary, was, probably, the
most active of the Premier's colleagues, while Mr. J. J. Foy, K.C.,
was Mr. Whitney's chief lieutenant. The campaign was opened at
Newmarket by Mr. Ross, on April 4th, in a most elaborate speech.
" How many of the 2,000,000 people in Ontario " he asked, " had
any substantial grievance against the Government ? They had
settled 150,000 people in New Ontario. Had any of them a grievance ? They had spent $10,000,000 for the development of our
railway system and were doing in New Ontario what had been done
in older Ontario many years before, where they had assisted 38
different railways, 2,219 miles in length. They had kept pace with
the wants of the country in regard to public buildings, on which
they had spent $23,563,000 in the last 30 years. They had cared
for the insane, the deaf and dumb and blind, and the expenditure in
Ontario for charitable purposes was greater per head than in Great
Britain or in any State of the Union. They had kept step with the
progressive tendencies of the age in education . . . and with

the agricultural wants of the people." He elaborated the details of useful legislation during the past three decades and declared that the Conservative Opposition had opposed them all.

During the next two months the Premier was at the head and front of the contest in every part of the Province, and his speeches certainly infused fresh vigour into the veins of his party. His principal speeches were at Ottawa on April 24; at Havelock on April 25; at Brampton on April 28; at Lindsay on May 1; at St. Catharines on May 6; at Sarnia on May 5; at Cornwall on May 8; at Ailsa Craig on May 13; at Midland on May 15; at Chatham on May 19; at London on May 21; at Windsor on May 23; at Glencoe on May 26; and in Toronto on May 27. Meanwhile Mr. Whitney had been equally active. His policy was announced as including m·asure; of law reform in the interest of the poorer litigant and in favour of one final and conclusive Provincial appeal; the development of New Ontario and a railway into the Temiscamingue country; grants to railways only for development or colonization purposes and subject to Government control of freight and passenger rates; encouragement to the refining of minerals within the Province; disposition of timber areas in pulp-wood lands under competitive tender; increased grants for agricultural purposes and especially agricultural schools; co-operation with the Dominion Government in promoting facilities for food transportation; educational reform in the direction of improving the curriculum and character of Public Schools; condensation and revision of municipal laws; elimination of alleged corruption and fraud from election procedure. The Opposition Leader's principal speeches were as follows: April 4, Port Hope; April 8, Hamilton; April 9, Aurora; April 10, Lindsay; April 16, Stoney Creek; April 18, Brampton; April 23, Picton; April 24, Stratford; April 25, Creemore; April 28, Sarnia; April 29, Chatham; April 30, Forest; May 1st, London; May 3, Huntsville; May 5, North Bay; May 6, Sudbury; May 7, Thessalon; May 8, Sault Ste. Marie; May 12, Uxbridge; May 13, Burlington; May 14, Galt; May 15, Owen Sound; May 16, Walkerton; May 23, Napanee; May 27, Massey Hall, Toronto; and on May 28 at Kingston. The Premier also made a tour of what was termed New Ontario, commencing at Sudbury on April 9, and some further meetings of his not already mentioned might be included in this list: Alexandria on May 9; Stratford on May 12; Owen Sound on May 16; Simcoe on May 20; and Ottawa on May 28.

Reasons for supporting the Ross Government were given in varied forms and at great length and included almost the entire record of Legislative action during the previous thirty years together with the establishment of the many institutions and reforms which had made Ontario a power in the constitutional framework of Canada. It was claimed that the Liberal party had acquired and developed New Ontario, including the Sault Ste. Marie interests of Mr. Clergue; had given the people vote by ballot and trial of election petitions by Judges; had established

THE HON. GEORGE WILLIAM ROSS, LL.D., M.P.P.

Prime Minister of Ontario

JAMES PLINY WHITNEY, K.C., LL.D., D.C.L., M.P.P.

the School of Practical Science; separated the liquor traffic from Municipal control; made the Agricultural College more efficient; re-organized the Educational Department; established Normal Schools at Ottawa and London; given the franchise to farmers' sons and built colonization roads in many new districts. It was stated that they had encouraged immigration, extended the surveys of Crown Lands, established a female reformatory, erected the Parliament Buildings, asserted successfully the right of the Province to property in rivers and streams, reformed the County Council system, appointed a Good Roads Commissioner and a Provincial Municipal Auditor, taxed Corporations, established a dairy school, dairy farm and Normal College, voted $1,000,000 to encourage good roads and established Provincial timber and mineral rights in a large territory against the Dominion authorities. It was asserted further that the Government or Liberal party had increased the representation of Algoma in 1885 and of New Ontario in 1902, improved the Separate School Act, created a Department of Agriculture, allowed the teaching of French or German in the schools, passed the Succession Duties Act, appointed a Superintendent of Neglected Children and encouraged forestry.

The Opposition view was very different. The Toronto *Mail and Empire* of May 9th declared that Ontario wanted to get rid of its Government of thirty years tenure because the people desired complete reform in their school system and some mitigation of the harshness of an "educational autocracy;" because they wanted relief from monopolies, centralized administration and a political license system; because they disapproved an indebtedness growing at the rate of $2,000 per day and wanted to be free from the burdens of direct taxation; because of the continued menace of corporate interests and the dangerous combination of Dominion and Provincial Governments; because they wished relief from long continued political corruption, the dominance of the "machine" and the power of the "ballot-box stuffer." On May 15th the same paper accused the Government of giving 6,560,000 acres of land, with all their minerals, to railway companies and of granting 15,660 square miles of pulp-wood land, secretly and without competition, to syndicates; with depriving the municipalities of the income from licenses and corporations; with having seized authority to levy direct taxes upon every citizen; with having driven 4,600 settlers out of New Ontario in ten years, squandered colonization roads' money upon politicians, handicapped miners with "rotten" laws, prostituted the license system for political ends and established a school-book monopoly; with having deceived the Prohibitionists, impaired public morals through corrupt electoral methods and used the machinery of justice to save political criminals.

The important incidents of the campaign included the wide use by the Conservatives of an old-time utterance of the Liberal Attorney-General of Nova Scotia—Hon. J. W. Longley—declaring

4

that "it is impossible for any body of men to be in power for a continuous period without getting lax in their ideas of public duty;" the candidature of Mr. G. F. Marter, a former Conservative leader, as an Independent in North Toronto and the issue of his election manifesto on March 22nd; the deliverance of an important speech by Mr. T. H. Preston, Liberal candidate at Brantford, on April 12th, and by Mr. Andrew Pattullo, Liberal candidate in North Oxford, on April 16th. Two addresses by Mr. N. W. Rowell, K.C. of Toronto—one at Aurora on April 25th and the other at Watford on May 9th—were perhaps the most important on the Liberal side apart from the speeches of some of the party leaders. He dealt very largely with the pulp-wood question and the policy of the Government in giving land grants and concessions to various syndicates for the purpose of developing industry. The chief address on the Conservative side, apart from those of the party leaders in the late Legislature, was that of Mr. W. D. McPherson of Toronto, at Niagara Falls, on May 9th. His speech was an elaborate arraignment of the Government for corruption in political organization and in the electoral contests of past years.

Dr. Beattie Nesbitt, the Conservative candidate for North Toronto, made a lengthy speech on May 14th in which he advocated public ownership of utilities and summed up his policy as "the Government at the switch; not corporations." Mr. J. P. Downey, the Conservative candidate in South Wellington, spoke eloquently at Guelph on May 15th, and the Rev. Dr. S. D. Chown of Toronto declared in the same city on May 17th that the Liberal Prohibition policy was "steeped in duplicity." This latter question held a prominent place in the campaign. The *Christian Guardian*, on behalf of Methodism, refrained from direct interference, but the *Canadian Baptist*, on May 1st, declared the Liberal party to be pledged to enforcement of Prohibition, despite the unfortunate conditions of its Referendum, and therefore worthy of support. On the same date the Conservatives issued a printed letter to agents and workers urging care against corrupt influences and the "spoiling, switching and substitution" of ballots. On May 23rd the *Mail and Empire* published a fac-simile of an insurance policy signed by Duncan Bole—who had long been charged with being a corrupt but missing agent of the alleged Liberal machine —in a Company of which the Premier was President.

During a speech at Toronto on May 26th the Hon. J. W. Longley of Nova Scotia paid a high tribute to the leader of the Government. "He believed that in intellectual endowments, in capacity of imagination, in the ability to look abroad, and through the intricacies of the life of a great Empire, there was no man in public life whom he would place ahead of the Hon. G. W. Ross." On the following day Mr. Whitney addressed a mass-meeting in Toronto. "Whitney will win" was the key-note of the speeches. The Opposition Leader vigorously denounced the Government for corruption and for a do-nothing policy in New Ontario as well as in administration generally and demanded clean elections and honest government. The Premier addressed a similar gathering in Toronto on the following night and claimed for his party progressive government, immense industrial development and a patriotic policy. On this occasion as well as throughout the contest there could be no doubt of the personal ability and eloquence of Mr. Ross. The party press laid strong stress upon this fact. The Toronto *Globe* in an editorial on May 1st described what it termed the "personal enthusiasm" roused by his leadership, and by his "virile, hopeful Canadian spirit." The Chatham *Banner-News* of May 20th analyzed his oratory as follows: "Somewhat mellowed by time, it is true, there are the same sparkling wit, the direct and incisive logic, the finished period, the apt metaphor, the sunny optimism and the limpidity of style that enables his audience to keep in sympathetic touch with him from beginning to end of his addresses." Mr. Whitney's influence in the campaign rested upon his clear-cut honesty of sentiment and a forceful, aggressive style of speech.

The nominations took place on May 22nd and only one member was elected by acclamation—Mr. I. B. Lucas, Conservative, in Centre Grey. The elections occurred on May 29th and the returns showed a very close contest. The *Globe* of the following day announced the result as 51 Liberal seats and 46 Conservative, with one to hear from; the *Mail and Empire* gave the same figures and the Toronto *World* placed the Liberal majority at seven. On the next day distant Manitoulin recorded itself Conservative and left the majority as four, for the time being, against straight Liberal majorities of eight in the two preceding elections. The Ministers were all re-elected by large majorities, and the Torontos went Conservative as usual. The most important new men elected to the House were Conservatives—Mayor Adam Beck in London, Mayor John S. Hendrie in Hamilton, Dr. Beattie Nesbitt in Toronto and Mr. J. P. Downey in South Wellington.

With the result, the Premier told the *Globe*, he was well satisfied. "Although the majority is not very large, still, after thirty years tenure of office, it is unprecedented in the history of Governments under our constitution that the Government should have a majority at all." Mr. Whitney expressed the opinion that the victory was only temporary and that inevitable bye-elections would change the result. The *Globe* declared that the "time for a change" cry had had its effect as well as the charges of frauds in the West Elgin election case. The *Mail and Empire* quoted the figures of eighteen constituencies where the Conservative majorities had increased from 7,286 in 1898 to 13,338 in 1902, and on June 9th published figures showing the total Conservative majorities, in all except one undecided seat, as being 21,145 and the Liberal majorities as 13,768—or a popular majority of 7,333 for Mr. Whitney.

The small Government majority kept politics during the next six months at boiling point in Ontario. Through recounts, Judicial decisions, the death of one member and the unseating of others it fluctuated from four to one, and only as a result of bye-elections early in 1903 came back to the figures of the first result. North Norfolk, North Grey, and North Perth were the three constituencies in which the new trial of strength took place and the contest was a very vigorous one on both sides. Leading up to it were several incidents of importance. Soon after election day Mr. Whitney had stated that the Hon. S. H. Blake, K.C., and other prominent Liberals had supported his candidates. Mr. Blake told the *Mail* of June 11th that his reason for doing so was "because of the manner in which the Government dealt with the University question and because one of the principal Departments was so conducted as to destroy confidence in a Government responsible for its administration." On June 25th 300 members of the Ontario Conservative Association met in Toronto with Mr. J. J. Foy, K.C., M.P.P., in the chair and tendered their Leader a rousing reception and a Resolution of gratitude and approval for his "untiring and self-sacrificing efforts to advance the interests of the Province." They promised hearty and unswerving support in his struggle to realize "the desire of the people for reform" and also passed the following motion :

Whereas, In the recent Provincial Elections, by a large majority of the popular vote, the Ross Government was emphatically condemned ; and *whereas*, by an unfair arrangement, or gerrymander, of the constituencies and by disgraceful tampering with ballots, a temporary advantage has resulted (under cover of which the Administration cling to office) ; and *whereas*, this Association recognizes with satisfaction the fact that many independent Liberals joined in the condemnation of the methods of the Administration ; be it therefore

Resolved, That having regard to the grave perils which menace the future of this Province by reason of the fraud and crime through which the Administration retain office, this Association pledges itself and calls with confidence upon all men having the fair fame and honour of the Province at heart to join forces in the determination to preserve the sanctity of the ballot-box, and the rights and franchises of the people, and to give the Province a pure and honest Administration.

A public demonstration and picnic was accorded Mr. Herbert Lennox, the defeated Conservative candidate in North York, at Holland, on July 17th. Mr. Whitney and other leaders of the party were present. On September 10th, the annual meeting of the Ontario Conservative Association was held in Toronto, with Mr. Foy in the chair. Sir Mackenzie Bowell, Mr. R. L. Borden, Mr. J. P. Whitney and Mr. R. Shaw Wood were selected as Honourary Presidents ; Mr. J. J. Foy as President, and Dr. Beattie Nesbitt, R. Blain, M.P., Mr. Edmund Bristol of Toronto, Major Beattie of London, and three other gentlemen as Vice-Presidents ; Mr. A. C. Macdonnell as Secretary, and Mr. E. B. Ryckman as Treasurer. Mr. E. B. Osler, M.P., was appointed Chairman of the Executive Committee. In his speech Mr. Whitney made the following hopeful remark : "I am convinced that the trend of movements and events is so strong in our favour that, I was going to say, we can hardly stop it ourselves. Of course I would not go to that extreme, but I mean to say that as far as human wisdom and judgment can go to form a reasonable opinion I believe that our position to-day is practically certain. In other words, the Government cannot possibly be in power at the expiration of six months from now."

Meanwhile, the Toronto *Globe* had created a political sensation by hinting at the chances or advantages of a coalition. On September 1st it denounced in vigorous language the dangers arising from corruption in politics, the necessity of action to resist the influence of powerful corporate interests upon political parties, the arousing of a public spirit which should regard corruption as a crime. Why, it asked, should there be so much talk about winning members over to one side or the other or seeking to dishonestly control the electorate? " It would be far better to see a combination against all self-seekers, dishonest trimmers and corruptionists, by men who refused to have anything to do with public affairs except upon conditions which would preserve their self-respect. There is not a single issue between the two parties which is worth an hour of intrigue or the expenditure of one dollar in a manner that will not bear the light of day." On September 11th the same paper published an interview with Mr. Goldwin Smith, in which that gentleman declared that the Government could not go on with its majority of one and a popular majority against it, and suggested a coalition— while doubting its possibility. In its editorial comment the *Globe* concluded as follows :

We may find ourselves confronted with a question which has not been much discussed. It is not whether party government or non-party government is the more desirable, but which is feasible. If the country gives a decisive majority to Liberals or to Conservatives there will be party government. If it refuses to do that, some other plan must be devised. There is no use in saying ' England does not love coalitions ' if the people by their votes render any other kind of government impossible. When the Legislature meets, this question ought to be frankly discussed.

Mr. Whitney in discussing the matter in the *Mail and Empire*, two days later, accepted this suggestion as coming from the Government, declared it was a recognition of helplessness, and thought the logical outcome was resignation. " It would be simply absurd to expect that the Opposition should, in defiance of public decency, allow themselves to be absorbed by a Government, the acts of members of which they have denounced in the strongest terms." At a demonstration in honour of the Hon. E. J. Davis, held at Newmarket on October 5th, the Premier dealt with these incidents and the general condition of affairs. He declared that the good of the Province had always been his paramount idea ; stated that there was no necessity and certainly no intention of resigning because of a small majority ; and repudiated the *Globe's* opinions or tentative arguments in favour of a coalition as not being his own or those of the Liberal party. " We are just going to fight ; that is all we are going to do. We believe that we still hold and shall continue to hold a majority of the seats in the Legislature." They would seek the election Courts and then the people and would win out with a working majority.

On September 25th, Mr. Ross had spoken at Strathroy and incidentally endorsed the principle of a strong protective tariff. On the following day the Montreal *Witness* denounced this action from the Dominion Liberal point of view, and declared Mr. Ross to be "politically in extremities." Mr. Whitney was banqueted at London on November 14th, and expressed the hopeful belief that at last "everything is coming our way." Meanwhile the bye-elections were imminent and were finally announced to occur in three seats on January 7th, 1903. As the fate of the Government depended upon the result, the Premier issued a Manifesto on December 16th, which reviewed the charges of corruption, denounced the Conservatives along the same line, indicated various progressive developments in policy and administration, and appealed for public support. The *Globe*, meanwhile, had not pressed its coalition ideas further, and now warmly supported the Premier in his struggle for confirmation in power, on the ground that strong government was greatly required. Mr. Whitney, on December 22nd, described the Manifesto as a "reckless and despairing utterance," and went vigorously into the fight or, as the *Mail* called it, "the campaign against evil."

The chief incident of the bye-elections was a letter published on December 30th, addressed to Mr. J. J. Foy, and dated three days previously, from the Hon. S. H. Blake, which deplored the existing low level of political morality, accused the rulers of the Province of having sought "to obtain the advantage of purchased and perjured evidence" in the Courts, described present political conditions as a "carnival of corruption," and expressed the earnest hope that those who had thus helped to debauch the electorate would be driven from office. Wide discussion and great interest was taken in this epistle, and the Conservatives believed that such criticism, from a life-long Liberal would win them the day. Mr. Blake was strongly denounced in the press of the other party and his action was said to be due to disappointment at not getting certain concessions which he had asked, through his law firm, for a client from one of the Government Departments. The struggle was eventually settled by the election of the three Liberals.

Late in June the Hon. F. G. Miville Déchène, Minister of Agriculture, died, and on July 2nd Mr. Amedée Robitaille, M.P.P.

Political Affairs in Quebec for Quebec Centre, was sworn in as Provincial Secretary, the Hon. Adelard Turgeon being transferred to the Department of Agriculture. On February 1st, Mr. J. A. Godbout, Liberal, was elected to the Legislature by over 800 majority. His opponent was also a Liberal. On October 3rd Mr. G. H. St. Pierre, Conservative, was elected in Stanstead by 397 over Mr. T. B. Rider, Liberal. The Liberal majority for the late member had been 288. In Soulanges, Mr. A. Bissonnette (C.), was elected by 11 majority over Mr. J. A.

Mousseau (L.). The preceding Liberal majority had been 577. In L'Islet Mr. J. E. Caron (Ind.) had been elected by acclamation shortly before.

The Legislature was opened on February 13th by Lieut.-Governor the Hon. Sir L. A. Jetté. In his Speech from the Throne reference was made to the differences of opinion as to the best means of promoting colonization and to the Government's intended appointment of a Commission to study existing conditions and report upon new projects and systems ; to the Government's action in claiming from the Dominion authorities reimbursement of amounts collected since 1867 for fishing licenses and permits and asking a share in the Nova Scotia indemnity paid for Fishery privileges under the Halifax Award ; to the Government's free distribution of school books and maps throughout the Province ; to the aid granted Municipal Councils for the improvement of roads ; and to the encouragement of agriculture by the Government through the improvement of stock-breeding, through premiums granted to cheese factories and by the official diffusion of technical knowledge. The most talked-of legislation of the Session was a measure passed at the instance of property owners on a part of Notre Dame Street East, Montreal, relieving them of certain obligations in connection with local improvements. Protests from the City as a whole were strong and persistent. A delegation waited upon Premier Parent composed of Aldermen Laporte, Lebœuf and Martineau, Mr. L. O. David and others, and claimed that the measure was a serious infringement of vested rights and civic control. Finally, the Bill was defeated in the Legislative Council and the Premier told the *Star* of April 1st that it was done at his instigation. On March 12th Mr. M. Perrault proposed the following motion :

That in the opinion of this House the revenues allotted to the various Provinces by the British North America Act are insufficient to allow of their meeting the requirements of the public service and at the same time of giving the necessary aid to colonization, to agriculture, to the development of our industries and the improvement of our educational system ; that the interpretation given to various clauses of the Constitution has endangered the existence of our local institutions ; and that the Government of Canada and those of the other Provinces should be invited to join the Government of the Province of Quebec in asking the Parliament of the United Kingdom to make such changes in the Confederation Act as may alter the basis on which the Federal subsidy is calculated, secure to the Provinces an exclusive control over their public properties and over the railways within their limits, allow of their imposing export duties on the products of their forests and mines, and confer upon the Government of Great Britain the right of disallowing Provincial laws now exercised by that of Canada.

The Premier stated that the Federal authorities were being approached with a view to the revision of existing financial relations and an amendment was carried by 41 to 6 declaring the confidence of the House in "the patriotism and wisdom of the Government" in this connection and expressing the hope that the Government of Canada would take into favourable consideration the modifications suggested by that of Quebec. On March 17th, Mr. A. Robitaille moved a series of Resolutions declaring that colonization and the forest industries were most important factors in the progress of the Province and empowering the Government to appoint three Commissioners and a Secretary to take evidence under oath and, if need be, to traverse the Province and report to the Lieutenant-Governor-in-Council. The objects of the Commission were to be as follows :

1. To make a critical study of the law and regulations respecting public lands, woods and forests, colonization societies, works and roads, and the protection of settlers, as well as the carrying out of such laws and regulations ;

2. To inquire into the number and causes of the difficulties between settlers and holders of timber licenses and to advise upon methods of their prevention and removal ;

3. To find out what are the sections of the country most suitable for colonization ;

4. To ascertain whether the present colonization roads are sufficient to give access to the good farming lands, and if the extent of surveyed lands is large enough and the work performed by colonization societies deserves encouragement ;

5. To inquire whether, in the interests of the colonization of the Province, it is expedient to contribute towards the building of certain bridges and to grant subsidies in land to certain railway companies ;

6. To study the new proposals or systems which may be submitted to it and, whilst taking into account the financial resources of the Province, to recommend those which tend to amend the laws and regulations so as to foster colonization and the development of forest industries.

The Resolutions were passed without opposition as was also a Bill based upon them. On March 21st, Mr. J. A. Lane moved the following : "That this House deems it its duty to protest against what is called New Imperialism and its dangerous tendencies." This policy he defined as one intended to create new ties between the Mother Country and the Colonies with a view to the final absorption of the latter by Great Britain. It was, he declared, a movement directed against Colonial autonomy. He finally withdrew his motion, after a speech by the Hon. Mr. Turgeon, on the ground of Sir Wilfrid Laurier's recent pronouncements having removed any present danger. Mr. Turgeon stated in his speech that the situation had been serious ten years ago in the days of the Imperial Federation League but was not so now. He defended the Contingents sent to South Africa because they were the result of voluntary enthusiasm and believed that Ontario Imperialistic tendencies would disappear with the war. He concluded with a reference to "the Tory press of Ontario which is so hostile to our race and institutions and, let us say it plainly, to our existence."

The following motion was proposed on March 25th by Mr. J. M. Tellier, Conservative, and lost by a party vote of 55 to 6: "This House regrets that the present Government in distributing the moneys voted for Colonization roads, allows itself to be influenced by party considerations rather than by public interest and the settler's needs and this House hopes that in future these moneys will be distributed equitably in accordance with the true requirements of colonization and the best interests of the Province." Another motion on the following day, moved by Hon. P. E. Le Blanc and seconded by Hon. E. J. Flynn, the Opposition Leader, read as follows and was defeated by 41 to 5 : "This House regrets that the Government has not deemed it advisable to arrange its tariff in connection with the pulp and paper industry in this Province so as to protect our national interests." The House was prorogued on the same day. Meantime, a measure proposing to restrict appeals to the Imperial Privy Council was strongly opposed by the Premier and withdrawn.

Events of a political nature were very quiet during the year in Nova Scotia. The Murray Government, after their sweeping victory in the general elections of 1901, remained

Political Affairs in Nova Scotia

unchanged in composition with the exception of the retirement of the Hon. Angus McGillivary, M.P.P., a Member without Portfolio, who accepted on the last day of 1902, the position of County Judge in Antigonish. On December 3, Mr. J. D. Sperry was elected by acclamation to the Legislature from Lunenburg, and Mr. W. H. Nickerson by 109 majority for Shelburne—both Government supporters. The new Legislature met in its first Session on February 13th and the Speech from the Throne was read by Lieut.-Governor, the Hon. A. G. Jones, after the election of Mr. Thomas Robertson as Speaker of the Assembly in succession to the Hon. F. A. Lawrence. Reference was made by His Honour to the general prosperity which had prevailed in all branches of Provincial industry during the year; to the unprecedented output of coal and promise of a still greater increase; to the Government's policy in constructing and completing the Midland and Inverness and Richmond Railways and thus "enlarging the public conveniences while developing the resources" of the country; to the work commenced on the subsidized line between St. Peter's and the Strait of Canso and the contract accepted by the Government for the construction of a railway from Halifax to Yarmouth; to the steps taken for the establishment of a Sanitarium for the treatment of tubercular diseases; and to the delay in carrying out the plans for constructing a Maritime Agricultural College.

The Premier was absent from the opening through illness and the bill of fare indicated was criticized as being very meagre. The debate on the Address was marked by an eloquent speech from Mr. George Patterson and by varied references to the Government majority of 36 to 2. Mr. C. E. Tanner, for the Opposition, disclaimed the idea of the Government having been factors in the industrial progress of the Province and declared that the coal output was due to the protective policy of the Conservative party at Ottawa. The defeat in the recent elections was said to be due to the Government having assumed the Opposition's policy and to a general use of corrupt methods. The chief subjects of discussion during the ensuing Session were the South Shore, or Halifax and Yarmouth Railway matter and the Agricultural College proposals.

On March 13th the Hon. Mr. Longley moved the second reading of the Government measure regarding the Halifax and South Western Railway Company. This was the last of various attempts to bring the Counties of Queen's and Shelburne into the railway system of the Province and to run a line along the south shore from Halifax to Yarmouth. The speaker explained the conditions which had been unanimously accepted by the preceding Legislature. "The power that the Government asked was power to contract with a company on the basis of giving, instead of the usual subsidy of $3,200 a mile, a sum equal to $10,000 a mile on receiving security by way of mortgage on the road." The distance was 208 miles. Various negotiations had followed and the Government had found it impossible to effect an arrangement upon these terms. Finally, however, they had entered into the contract with Messrs. Mackenzie and Mann, of Toronto, which was now submitted to the House as it had already been presented to the people at the polls The principal change was the increase in the amount advanced to $13,500 a mile. He believed the cost of construction could not be less than $20,000 a mile.

Mr. C. E. Tanner followed and discussed the contract at length, declaring it improvident, hurried, and a matter of electoral exigency. The Company in question was not Messrs. Mackenzie and Mann; they were only shareholders and not directly liable. He stated that 75 per cent. of the money could be advanced before a rail was laid, and objected to this as being dangerous and claimed that there was no word in the contract compelling the Company to put a dollar of their own money into the project. The policy was in fact a change from granting subsidies of $3,200 a mile to that of giving away $13,500 a mile. The Hon. Mr. Drysdale followed at great length and in clear defence of the contract and policy. The proposals passed on March 19th with 31 for and 2 against. Delegations waited on the Government on March 11th and on March 25th asking aid for a railway from Halifax along the Atlantic Coast and the Musquodoboit Valley to the Strait of Canso. On October 28th it was announced that a cash subsidy of $5,000 a mile would be given.

In the House on March 18th Mr. F. A. Lawrence moved the following Resolution regarding the much-discussed arrangement with the other Provinces for the establishment of a Maritime College of Agriculture: "Whereas, by an Act of the Legislature passed at the last session, the Government was authorized to expend $50,000 in the establishment of a College of Agriculture : Resolved, that in the judgment of this House the Government should delay action in the manner indicated in the said Act and, during recess, consider the desirability of establishing a Technical School in connection with some existing University for the purpose of qualifying young men as mining engineers, electrical engineers and like professions." He believed the joint project would be a failure, quoted many illustrations of financial disaster in similar American institutions and deprecated the organization of any more Colleges. Mr. H. H. Wickwire strongly opposed the motion and declared that by legislation and promise to the people the Government were pledged to the project. The Resolution was finally withdrawn by request of acting-Premier Longley. The House was prorogued on March 27th.

There were no changes in the Government of New Brunswick during the year excepting the appointment of Senator Jabez

Political Affairs in New Brunswick Bunting Snowball to succeed the Hon. A. R. McClellan as Lieutenant-Governor. He was sworn in on February 5th by Chief Justice Tuck. During the absence of Hon. L. J. Tweedie at the Coronation, Attorney-General Pugsley was acting Premier. Dr. Robert Carter Ruddick in St. John's County, and Mr. Ora P. King in King's County were elected to the Legislature as Government supporters—the former on February 1st, the latter on March 5th. This contest in King's was one of the chief political events of the year and an aftermath of the much-discussed Rothesay List controversy. The Opposition candidate was Mr. Fred. M. Sproul.

Under date of February 10th the Hon. William Pugsley issued a lengthy Manifesto to the electors in the constituency defending himself from the charges made in the previous year as to his non prosecution of the men who were believed or proven to have manipulated and forged the electoral lists at Rothesay in this county. He pointed to his instant action in countermanding the writ for the election as soon as it was found that something was wrong and in presenting legislation to the House voiding the bogus lists and providing against a repetition of the offence by heavy penalties. He referred to the recent discovery of oil fields in the Province; to the general prosperity of the people; to the Government's policy of building small connecting railways so as to develop the vast deposits of coal existing in Queen's and Lunenburg Counties; to their investigation of the Province's coal resources and arrangements with the Intercolonial and Canadian Pacific Railway Companies for the purchase of a certain yearly quantity. He continued in the following words:

These coal deposits are the property of the Crown, much of the coal being upon ungranted lands. We have been careful to thoroughly safeguard the interests of the Province and have provided by legislation that on all coal hauled by the railways a royalty of ten cents per ton upon that mined on granted lands and of fifteen cents on that mined upon ungranted lands shall be paid into the Provincial exchequer. The present Mining Act has been criticized in some quarters, but its enactment became absolutely necessary if we were going to secure any marked progress in mining, and I am happy to be able to inform you that under its provisions a great development is taking place in the mining of copper at Dorchester where upwards of a quarter of a million dollars of foreign capital has already been invested, and a large amount of labour is being employed. This enterprise will also yield a considerable revenue to the Province. I confidently look forward to the Government receiving a revenue of at least $50,000 a year from the development of its mineral resources in the immediate future.

Mr. Pugsley then stated that he was urging upon the Provincial and Dominion Governments the great desirability of building a railway from St. John up through the fertile St. John River Valley to Edmundstone. He pointed out how the Government had won the Eastern Extension Railway Award of $275,000 from the Dominion and were now expending it upon the construction of bridges and repairs of public works; and how their policy of protest concerning the control of Provincial Fisheries by the Dominion authorities had been practically recognized. But, he added, there was a very important further point in this connection. "If, as we contend, the result of the judgment of the Judicial Committee is that the Fisheries within three miles of the coast belong to the Provinces, the amount of the Halifax Award should have been paid over to the Provincial Governments. New Brunswick's share would be about one million and a-half dollars, and it is the intention of the Government to press earnestly for its payment. We have already brought the matter to the notice of the Dominion Government and have asked that steps may be taken by a reference to the Courts or otherwise to have the right of the Province to this amonnt determined."

Mr. J. Douglas Hazen, K.C., Leader of the Opposition, replied to this document in a speech of great length delivered at Kingston on February 15th. He first handled the Rothesay list charges, declared the Attorney-General responsible for the non-prosecution of the criminals who had created the fraudulent list and accused him of having disfranchised the people of King's County for nearly fifteen months. He spoke of the Opposition efforts to have the "one man, one vote" principle recognized and declared that in 1895 Messrs. A. G. Blair, H. R. Emmerson, James Mitchell and other members of the Government of that day had opposed Dr. Stockton's Resolution along that line. He deprecated the claim that the Government had anything to do with sprouting oil-wells or the development of mines. It was simply a part of the general progress of the country.

The coal industry had, he claimed, been long neglected by the Government while the Fisheries matter would be just as well looked after by a new Administration as by the present one. Mr. Hazen then proceeded to charge the Government with awarding various contracts for the superstructure of its steel bridges at prices two or three times higher than the current market rates and without tender or competition. In financial matters he estimated the increased revenue of the Government at an average of $158,024 per annum since they took office with an imposition, in 1900, of $94,221 in extra taxes. Yet despite this fact the Public Debt had increased from $757,697 on December 31st, 1884, to $2,815,086 on October 31st, 1900. He concluded by attacking Attorney-General Pugsley for receiving, indirectly, a large income from the Province though nominally only entitled to a small salary and with the expression of opinion that 18 years was too long for any Government to be in power and that the people wanted a change. On March 2nd Mr. King was elected for the constituency by 135 majority as against a Government majority in 1900 of 829.

The Legislature was opened on March 6th by the new Lieutenant-Governor. In the Speech from the Throne reference was made to the continued and rapid development in the dairying industries of the Province ; to the good effect which the Government claimed had resulted from financial aid given to roller flour mills in promoting the growth of wheat; to the continued construction of the railway into the coal areas of Queen's and Lunenburg; to the rapid increase of Canadian winter business through the Port of St. John —aided by Government grants towards the building of wharves, etc.; to the expectation of satisfactory results from the pressure upon the Dominion Government in connection with the outstanding Fisheries' question; to the desirability of re-adjusting the Dominion subsidies to the Provinces ; to the necessity of improvement in the management of the branch lines of the Intercolonial Railway system and to the desirability of asking Dominion co-operation in this connection upon some fair and equitable basis.

An address by the Premier in the House on March 10th was notable for the statement that the amount coming to New Brunswick under the claims advanced by the Government for a share of the moneys paid to Canada in the Halifax Award would be $1,750,-000 at ordinary interest and $700,000 more at compound interest. On April 2nd, Mr. Douglas Hazen introduced a Resolution which was important not because it had any chance of passing against the Government's overwhelming majority of 45 to 8 but because it was to constitute the policy of the Opposition in the preliminary election campaign of the following autumn and the general elections of 1903. After a lengthy preamble this motion in favour of " changes and reforms which are desirable in the public interests " made the following demands and proposals :

1. Such amendments in the Election Act as will secure a secret ballot so that electors may vote according to the dictates of their conscience and judgment without fear of intimidation or coercion from employers or creditors.
2. Such changes in the law as to render it easy and less expensive for the prosecution of election trials, as it is important to discourage bribery and corrupt influences at elections, and as the machinery of the Courts for prosecuting violations of the election laws is now expensive, cumbersome and ineffective.
3. That no contract for the construction of any public work be entered into unless tenders for the same be first publicly advertised in the *Royal Gazette*, and in such other ways as may be deemed desirable to give publicity to the same, for a length of time sufficient to enable persons so desiring to tender for the same, and that all public works be performed by means of tender and competition.
4. A change in the system of auditing the public accounts and the appointment of the Auditor-General, so that this office shall, as near as may be, be invested with powers similar to those of the Auditor-General of Canada and the

holder shall not be removed from office except by vote of not less than three-fourths of the members of the House of Assembly, and for cause only.

5. The immediate abolition of the office of Solicitor-General, having in view the reduction of salaried members of the Executive and the amalgamation of offices at present existing.

6. The reduction of the number of members in the House of Assembly to 38 and the division of the Province into 38 electoral divisions, each returning one member ; the different divisions to be as nearly as possible equal in population, having regard to other interests : existing lines to be preserved as far as may be and the divisions into ridings to be made by an independent Commission consisting of three Judges of the Supreme Court.

7. An equitable expenditure in the different counties of the Province of the moneys spent on the great roads' service of the country and of the moneys borrowed for permanent bridges.

8. A progressive agricultural policy to include assistance to dairying, to pork-packing factories and to facilities for exporting the agricultural products of the Province to the markets of Europe.

9. The appointment of an independent Commission to thoroughly investigate the business and medical management of the Provincial Lunatic Asylum, with a view to rendering the institution more efficient.

10. The restitution to the municipal councils of the right to appoint the third revisor and the providing of an appeal to the County Court Judge by any elector whose name has been improperly omitted from the revisors' list.

11. The reduction by at least one-half of the amount allowed the Attorney-General for settling succession duties, a substantial reduction in the cost of public printing, a reduction in the travelling expenses of members of the Executive, a reduction in the controllable expenditure of the Province and such changes in the Legislative and Departmental machinery of the Province as will lead to a substantial reduction in the cost thereof.

12. The passage of such legislation as will ensure the independence of the Legislature and make it unlawful for members' of the House of Assembly other than members of the Executive to receive payment for services rendered the Province.

13. An increase in the salaries of the school teachers in the Province as soon as the finances of the Province will admit of such action, the printing and publication within the Province of the books used in the public schools and a reduction in the cost thereof.

14. The bye-road appropriations for the several counties in the Province to be paid each year to the county councils thereof, to be expended by such councils through the Commissioners appointed by them.

After the introduction of these Resolutions by the Opposition Leader, the Hon. Mr. Tweedie spoke briefly and declared the motion out of order as including matters which were prerogatives of the Crown or of the Governor-in-Council. "The Government has not abdicated all its functions and is not prepared to let the Opposition take charge of affairs at the present juncture." After some discussion the Speaker—Hon. Clifford W. Robinson—quoted Bourinot and May and ruled according to the Premier's contention. The Legislature was prorogued on April 10th, after passing some important railway legislation and a measure prolonging the term of future Legislatures from three to five years. During the rest of the year there was much active political discussion. The St. John Globe, an important Liberal paper and the organ of Senator J. V. Ellis, came out in strong opposition to the Government of Mr. Tweedie and the Moncton Times, edited by Mr. J. T. Hawke, a prominent Liberal, took a similar position. The St. John Gazette and the *Telegraph* were vigorous Liberal supporters, as the St. John *Sun* was an equally strong Conservative critic, of the Administration. Party lines were very fluctuating and hard to define. The *Sun* of October 21st classified 26 Liberals as supporting the Government and one as opposing them in the House while 6 Conservatives supported them with 7 in the Opposition. It claimed that Messrs. Tweedie and Pugsley had once been Conservatives.

On August 22nd the Premier returned from his Coronation visit to England and was warmly welcomed by the people to his home at Chatham. The political situation thereafter increased in public interest. Mr. Douglas Hazen had already commenced a campaign through the Province, organizing his supporters, holding meetings and nominating candidates. He was accompanied at different times by Messrs. F. M. Anderson, G. V. McInerney, ex-M.P., F. M. Sproul, J. B. M. Baxter, Michael McDade, W. A. Mott, M.P.P., S. D. Scott and other speakers. An incident of the time was the defection of Mr. W. A. Mott from the Government. It was announced on September 18th and followed four days later by a formal Address to the electors of his constituency. The chief reason given was dissatisfaction with the Government's local action regarding certain timber limits granted to a Company, but never operated, and finally sold at an alleged profit of $200,000. The political events of the year in New Brunswick terminated in a meeting of Liberals at St. John on December 27th, attended by the Hon. A. G. Blair, Dominion Minister of Railways and formerly Premier of the Province. It was stated that he had urged the policy of nominating only Liberals in support of the Government at the pending elections and on the succeeding day the *Telegraph*—considered to be his special organ—made a strong appeal for a Liberal Convention and for the running of the contest on strict party lines.

The newly-formed Administration in the Island entered upon the year with practically only a change in the Premiership—Mr. Arthur Peters, K.C., succeeding the Hon. Mr. Farquharson. In April Mr. J. F. Whear, M.P.P., became a Member without portfolio in place of the late Hon. Malcolm McDonald. The Legislature was opened on March 11th by Lieut.-Governor P. A. McIntyre and prorogued on April 11th. The most important incident of the Session was the action taken regarding Judge Hodgson's decision *re* corrupt practices, while another interesting development was noted on April 19th by the Charlottetown *Guardian* as follows : " The caucus system was much in evidence, and seems to have obtained a greater prominence here than in any other Province of Canada. In fact, the public business is so fully shaped in caucus as to leave but little for the House to do as a deliberative body. Many matters appear in a clearer and different light after being examined from the Opposition standpoint and the country should have the benefit of this criticism before being committed to important new departures."

During the Session of 1901 and for the first portion of that of 1902 legal complications had kept Mr. Murdoch McKinnon out of a seat in the House to which it afterwards appeared he had been elected by a majority of votes over Mr. A. F. Bruce, the Liberal candidate. At first the returning officers had reported Mr. Bruce elected and Mr. McKinnon then appealed to the Supreme Court of the Province. The case came before Mr. Justice Hodgson, who decided that A. F. Bruce had not been duly elected, but that Murdoch McKinnon had been. The judgment also declared that a number of persons, where names were given, had been guilty of corrupt practices at the election and that they were severally subject to disqualification. When the Judge's Report was presented at the opening of the Legislature, it was at once, on motion of the Government, referred back to him for amendment. Two days later the Speaker announced that a reply had been received. In his reply, Judge Hodgson said that the Legislative Assembly had misapprehended the law in this matter and that his certificate and report were entirely in accordance with the Controverted Elections Act. The reply went on to say:

The Legislative Assembly seem not to apprehend that owing to the form of the election petition in this matter it became my duty to certify and report to you :

1. Which of the two candidates had been duly elected.
2. Whether they or either of them had been guilty of corrupt practices.
3. The names of such persons as had been proved at the trial to have been guilty of corrupt practices.
4. Whether corrupt practices extensively prevailed during the election.

I certified and reported upon these matters essentially in the same form and manner, not only as every Judge in this Province has heretofore done, but as every Judge in England and in the Dominion of Canada, under similar legislation, whose report I have been able to examine. To have divided these matters, and to have made a separate report upon each would have been unusual and unnecessary.

The Judge went on to say that he would never in any circumstances receive suggestions regarding a matter pending before him unless in the presence of the parties concerned, and if possible, of their counsel—not even when they came from so august a body as the Legislative Assembly of Prince Edward Island; that when that Legislature, going beyond its functions, claimed the right to direct and command him when and how to amend his judgments and reform his decrees his reply was that he would never be a party to such a humiliation of the Judiciary. He emphatically declined to do the bidding of the House, and returned his Report just as he had received it.

The Hon. Mr. Gordon, for the Opposition, then moved, seconded by Mr. Mathieson, as follows: " *Resolved,*—That the Report of the Judge selected for the trial of the election petition relating to the fourth electoral district of King's County, be entered in the Journals of the House, pursuant to statute." Mr. Peters, the Premier, opposed this action. He expressed sorrow that such a state of affairs had arisen. In his view the proposal admitted a very simple reply. Mr. Justice Hodgson had to remember that though he was high, the Legislature of the Province stood higher—paramount and higher. The Judge had power, under the statute, to unseat a member of the Legislature, but not the power to disqualify electors. The House had that right and would keep it. The Report could not and would not be adopted. The Premier then announced that a bill would be introduced to give Mr. McKinnon his seat.

On March 20th, 1902, this measure passed the House after speeches by the Premier and others. Mr. Peters declared that the Judge had disqualified and degraded representative citizens who had been guilty of nothing more than treating a friend to liquor; that the nine men in question were not guilty of corrupt practices, and that he would not record them so on the rolls of the House; that he was upheld as to the technicalities of the case by the Attorneys-General of New Brunswick and Nova Scotia. Mr. J. A. Mathieson, for the Opposition, declared that this was the last of a series of disgraceful white-washing Acts passed by the Legislature, and was simply a bold attempt to shield political friends of the Government from the consequences of their corrupt practices.

Meantime Mr. Donald Farquharson, after retiring from the Premiership to contest West Queen's for the House of Commons as the Liberal successor to Sir Louis Davies, had been going through a warm contest. His Address to the electors was published in the first days of the year. It recapitulated and approved the leading articles of Government policy at Ottawa, proclaimed his adherence to Prohibition principles and the Preferential tariff, and promised every effort to keep the Island representation intact under a threatened Census reduction. Mr. A. A. McLean, K.C., was his Conservative opponent, and the election took place on January 15th. Mr. Farquharson received a majority of 493. Late in the year two bye-elections occurred for the Legislature. In Queen's, Messrs. McLean and Wheatley divided the Liberal or Government vote, and Mr. Dougald Currie, Conservative, won the seat held previously by Mr. Farquharson for 25 years. His majority was 27. In King's, Mr. W. A. O. Morson, Conservative, defeated Mr. McLean by 24 majority and succeeded the late Hon. M. McDonald, a member of the Government. These elections left the Assembly with 20 Liberals to 10 Conservatives.

A subject of pronounced political controversy during the year was the establishment of the Dominion Packing Comany, Limited, at Charlottetown, with a capital of $1,000,000, and the announced intention of carrying on a large business in the purchase of living and dressed hogs, cattle, sheep and poultry. They had first approached the Provincial Government and obtained from them an agreement which involved a Provincial guarantee of the Company's bonds to the extent of $150,000 and exemption from taxation, subject to approval by the Legislature. In return the Company was to establish an important business in preserving and canning fruit

5

and in pork-packing and meat-packing and in cold storage arrangements at Charlottetown, and operate the business for 30 years. The project aroused considerable opposition and much discussion, and an important meeting of the Charlottetown Board of Trade was held on October 8th to go into the whole subject. The Premier spoke first and explained the Government's policy at length. Many others spoke, including F. A. McLean, F. L. Hassard, W. S. Stewart, K.C., Horace Hassard, J. J. Hughes, M.P., John McLean, M.P.P., G. E. Hughes, M.P.P., and Hon. D. A. McKinnon, M.P. After discussion, and with a few dissenting voices, the following Resolution was passed :

That *whereas*, the information so far given to the public is too meagre to admit of any possible advantage to be derived by the Government's guarantee, whilst on the other hand it is claimed by those fully competent to judge that the coming here of the Dominion Packing Company under Government patronage would be disastrous to the best interests of this Province ; therefore *Resolved*, in the opinion of this meeting that, whilst capitalists should be encouraged to come to Prince Edward Island to engage in business and that every opportunity should be afforded them of doing business upon equal terms with our own people, we strongly protest against the Government guaranteeing the interest on the bonds of this or any other outside Company without first submitting the question to the people at the polls.

Several other public meetings were held, and on November 13th, at Marshfield, Premier Peters explained that he had been somewhat misled as to the *personnel* of the Company and that it was not now the Government's intention to proceed with the guarantee.

The Government of the Hon. R. P. Roblin—the only Conservative Provincial Administration in Canada—remained unchanged during the year with a Legislative support of 26 Conservatives to 13 Liberals and 1 Independent. The 3rd Session of

Political
Affairs In
Manitoba

the 10th Legislature was opened on January 9th by Lieut.-Governor Sir D. H. McMillan. A brief Speech from the Throne referred to the abundant harvest, the completion of the Canadian Northern Railway to Port Arthur, the failure of the Dominion authorities to pay to the Province the accumulated interest on school moneys and the interest on the sale of school lands which it claimed, and expressed regret at the Federal disallowance of the Real Property Act of the preceding Session. The Legislature was prorogued on March 1. In the House on January 15th the Hon. C. H. Campbell dealt at length with the school lands question.

The territory in dispute, he stated, had been acquired originally by the Imperial Government from the Hudson's Bay Company and handed over to the Dominion authorities in trust for school purposes in the future Province. Afterwards, two sections of each township in the new Province were set aside by Federal enactment as a school endowment. The Province had long claimed the right to administer these lands and opposed the Federal policy of adding the interest on purchase moneys to the endowment. These sums were needed for current educational expenses, though the Province was pledged not to impair the original capital or trust. About $3,000,000 worth of these lands had been sold, and $500,000 placed to capital account. The investment, less certain payments, would, the Attorney-General declared, yield the Province for educational purposes, at 6 per cent., $130,000 a year.

On February 24th Mr. Campbell moved a long Resolution protesting against the Dominion Government's announced policy of reducing the interest on these lands from six to five per cent. He believed it was an error or accident in legislation. The motion passed unanimously. The subject was discussed in the House of Commons on May 6th and Sir Wilfrid Laurier stated that the reduction would have to stand and would be in the interests of the settler. A little later it was announced that the long claimed interest in question would be handed over to the Manitoban Government. In the Winnipeg *Telegram* of May 31, June 2, and June 18, Mr. James Fisher, M.P.P., published elaborate letters dealing with the question historically and endeavouring to prove that the Dominion Government had long admitted the right of the Province to consultation in connection with these lands—a right infringed by the reduction of interest in 1901.

A political factor of the year was the work of the Political Reform Union originally organized by Mr. R. L. Richardson—a one-time Liberal member of Parliament—and strongly supported by his paper, the Winnipeg *Tribune*. Various meetings were held under its auspices throughout the Province and on July 24th a Convention of the party was held at Winnipeg with Mr. John Compton of Manitou in the chair. Resolutions were passed along the following lines:

1. Denunciation of both the Liberal and Conservative parties for betrayal of the temperance people by their support of the Referendum and a declaration in favour of the total abolition of the liquor traffic with immediate legislation toward that end.

2. Declarations against protection as demoralizing and injurious to material interests and in favour of tariff reform and the removal of all restrictions upon trade.

3. In favour of municipal power to erect grain elevators and against the present methods of supplying cars and rolling stock on the railways.

4. Denunciation of the Liberal Government at Ottawa for not carrying out pledges as to reduction of the tariff on agricultural implements and a demand that the duties be greatly reduced or abolished altogether.

5. Condemnation of the Provincial Government in connection with the Referendum and a demand that the whole system of voting in such cases be reformed in the future.

6. Condemnation of the Dominion Government for not accepting the expressed willingness of the Imperial Government to remove duties on Canadian grain in return for the removal of protective duties imposed by Canada on British goods.

It was also announced that the Provincial Executive of the party had expressed its intention of co-operating with the Dominion Alliance in opposing the Roblin Government at the next general election.   The Maple Leaf Conservative Club in Winnipeg had, meanwhile, been addressed on January 10th by the Hon. H. J. Macdonald, Hon. C. H. Campbell and Hon. R. Rogers as to general Conservative policy and on January 31st by the Premier.   Late in the year the 2nd annual Convention of the Young Men's Provincial Conservative Association was held at Brandon on December 11th and 12th.   Mr. Adam Reid was President and Resolutions were passed endorsing the Administration in its railway and school lands policy and in its proposals for an Agricultural College and free text-books for the schools.   Mr. Reid was re-elected President by acclamation and the last meeting of the Association was addressed by the Premier, Dr. Roche, M.P., and Hon. Mr. Campbell.

Mr. Roblin's address was an exhaustive one.   As a result of their protests and pressure he stated that the Dominion Government had paid over $225,000 as interest on school land sales and that his Government were now demanding the right to administer the unsold lands.   They were also resisting a policy under which he claimed that 1,608,551 acres of swamp lands had been selected as transferable to the Province though only 1,178,854 acres had been actually transferred; while four Commissioners had been appointed by the Federal authorities in this connection and paid by the Province although two of them should have been appointed, under the Act, by the latter.   He described the agricultural development of the Province; declared the Government's intention to establish an Agricultural College; reviewed their railway policy and stated that 412 miles were now under construction in the Province; stated that the rates on the Canadian Northern Railway were absolutely controlled by the Government; and gave elaborate tables to prove that their promise of reductions had been amply carried out.

The Hon. Mr. Greenway, Leader of the Opposition, spoke in Winnipeg on December 16th; declared that if it was in his power to remove every vestige of protection from the tariff he would do it in the interest of the Province of Manitoba; denied that the Government's policy had solved the transportation problem and pointed as proof to the crowded elevators everywhere; stated that there were 30,000,000 bushels of wheat still in the farmers' hands involving a loss of nearly $1,000,000; demanded the building of a line to Hudson's Bay and the carrying out of his old plan of a railway to Duluth; and charged the Government with reckless extravagance in financial matters.   At Carberry on December 23rd another preliminary to the pending elections occurred in addresses by Mr. D. W. Bole, President of the Provincial Liberal Association and Senator Robert Watson.   Mr. Bole declared that the Government had kept none of their pledges, that the great need of the country was more railways, denounced Mr. Roblin's Referendum policy and eulogized Mr. Greenway.

The question of boundaries was much discussed during the year

in connection with the claims of the North-West Territories for
Provincial status. In the Manitoba Legislature an important Resolution was presented by the Premier on February 28th

Provincial
Boundaries
of Manitoba

and unanimously passed.   In his speech Mr. Roblin
declared that his motion "substantially embodied the
views of the people." He referred to the objections
raised by various citizens of the Territories against any extension
of Manitoban boundaries and claimed that the charges, as to unfair-
ness in assuming a share of Manitoba's debt and the increased
taxation incurred in any adoption of its municipal system, made
by Premier Haultain, were not well founded.   Messrs. Theodore
Burrows and T. C. Norris followed in speeches of an historical
nature and the Resolution then passed as follows :

Whereas, in the year 1870, the Province of Manitoba was created, comprising what now may be described as Townships one to seventeen, in Ranges one
to eleven, east and west of the first principal Meridian, according to Dominion
survey ;

And *whereas*, the said boundaries of the Province in the year 1881 were
extended or enlarged so as to comprise, as a whole, Townships one to forty-four
in Ranges one to twenty-nine west and east to the westerly boundary of Ontario, which westerly boundary was understood to be a line due north from the
international boundary and passing some distance east of Port Arthur and thus
giving the Province of Manitoba a port on Lake Superior and so increasing our
area from 13,464 square miles to 154,411 square miles ; though unfortunately
as a result of the litigation respecting the boundary between this Province and
the Province of Ontario, our area was reduced by upwards of 100,000 square
miles from what this Province had looked for ;

And *whereas*, the Province of Manitoba possesses legislative powers and
advantages of an educational, commercial, benevolent and charitable character
not at present possessed or enjoyed by the North-West Territories ;

And *whereas*, the large area within the North-West Territories, scattered
settlement, diversity of interests, inadequate revenue for substantial development, and limited railway facilities, cannot but seriously impair and retard the
growth and welfare thereof, making it desirable, therefore, that a portion of the
said area should be attached to and become part of the Province of Manitoba,
where, as aforesaid, more favourable conditions exist for material advancement ;

And *whereas*, similarity of interests, agricultural and otherwise, between
the Province of Manitoba and the proposed extended territory renders the
accomplishment of such extension as aforesaid of paramount importance to
both ;

And *whereas*, the addition of a portion of the area of the North-West Territories to the Province of Manitoba, as aforesaid, does not present financial or
other difficulties incapable of amicable, satisfactory and equitable adjustment ;

Therefore, be it *Resolved*, (1) That this House is of the opinion that it is
desirable, both in the interests and for the welfare of the Province of Manitoba
and the North-West Territories, that the area of the former should be increased
by an extension of boundaries so as to embrace and include a portion of the
Districts of Assiniboia and Saskatchewan and northward to Hudson's Bay.

(2) That a Committee consisting of such members of this House as comprise the Executive and Messrs. Greenway, Mickle and Burrows be appointed
to make all due inquiries into all, singular and the best means of bringing
about the said object and to ascertain the most favourable terms and conditions
upon which the boundaries of the Province may be so extended.

The Legislature of the North-West Territories replied to this
Resolution on April 9th.   A motion was then presented by Messrs.

A. B. Gillis and J. W. Connell, quoting from a Resolution passed on May 20th, 1901, and adding: "That this House reiterates its convictions that any extension of the western boundary of Manitoba will be in direct opposition to the desires and the welfare of the people of these Territories." Mr. D. H. McDonald, the Opposition Leader, proposed an amendment substituting the words "annexation of any part of the Territories to Manitoba," but it was lost by 8 to 22, and the original Resolution carried by 22 to 7. Meanwhile, in March, the *Canadian Magazine* contained several articles upon this question of which the most notable was one by Mr. W. Sanford Evans of Winnipeg.

The last session of the fourth Legislative Assembly of the North-West Territories was opened on March 20th by Lieut-Governor A. E. Forget, and prorogued on April 19th.

Territorial Politics and General Elections The Speech from the Throne dealt chiefly with financial needs, the desirability of autonomy, the prosperity of the people, the immense grain production, and the insufficient transport facilities. The chief subject of discussion was the question of autonomy, but there were other matters dealt with in view of the pending elections. On March 31st, Mr. D. H. McDonald, the Opposition Leader, declared that the Government did not deserve praise for any efforts made to relieve the grain blockade. It was the Grain Growers' Association which deserved the credit, and he quoted a statement at Ottawa that Manitoba and the North-West Territories had lost $7,000,000 during the season because of lack of transportation facilities. He doubted the sincerity and earnestness of the Government in connection with autonomy, criticized the financial statement, deplored dilatoriness in road-work and deprecated any settlement with the Hudson's Bay Company regarding taxes which did not give allowances to other ratepayers. Mr. F. W. G. Haultain's reply may be summed up in his concluding words:

We have a clear and definite policy, and we are united on it. We believe in one Province with all the rights of the other Provinces. We believe we should have control of the lands, minerals and royalties of the country. We believe in adequate compensation for all public lands which have been used for Federal purposes. We believe in getting a fair adjustment of any public debt which may be charged against the country. We believe that the subsidy should not be based on a population of 400,000, but should be as large as any other Province gets.

Mr. G. H. V. Bulyea, for the Government, presented a motion asking the Federal authorities to amend the Elevator Act so as to help the farmers under certain crowded conditions at stations and elevators. It was carried unanimously. Mr. R. B. Bennett, for the Opposition, moved that the action of the Government in accepting less than 100 cents on the dollar in settlement of local improvement taxes from the Hudson's Bay Company was unwarrantable, unjust and unfair discrimination against the people. The principle of compromising taxes was, he declared, bad. The Premier stated that there was no such question involved. They had settled 30

law suits upon technical points, saved indefinite court costs up to the
Privy Council and, instead of taking serious chances on $115,000,
had obtained $54,000 and made satisfactory arrangements for the
future.   On the preceding day Mr. R. S. Lake had moved, seconded
by Mr. A. S. Smith, the following Resolution which carried unanimously: "That in the opinion of this House, as the Canadian
Pacific Railway has signally failed to meet the pressing necessities
of the North-West in the matter of the transportation of grain,
and as the Dominion Government has postponed conferring upon
the North-West powers that would enable the Territories to take
steps to improve this present condition of affairs; therefore, it becomes the imperative duty of the Dominion Government to take
immediately steps looking to the procuring of increased transportation facilities for the Territories, whether by additional trunk
lines or otherwise."

A Convention of the Eastern Assinaboia Liberals was held at
Indian Head on April 2nd, when a series of Resolutions were passed
urging action in connection with the elevator companies and wheat
storage; the grant of increased powers of self-government and control to the Territorial Legislature; the reduction of Dominion fees
under the Land Titles' Act; certain amendments to the homestead
regulations in the Dominion Lands Act; more attention on the part
of the Dominion Government to the transportation question—
especially in districts where farmers had to haul their produce from
15 to 35 miles.   A vigorous protest was also lodged against any
increase in the Federal tariff, and a demand was made for reduced
duties on agricultural implements and other manufactured products.

The Territorial Assembly was dissolved on April 25th; the
nominations took place on May 10th, and the elections on May
21st.   Messrs. A. E. de Rosenroll, A. B. Gillis, R. S. Lake, G. H. V.
Bulyea and A. D. McIntyre, all Government supporters, were
elected without opposition, as were also Mr. D. H. McDonald and
Mr. J. W. Connell.   Fifteen Independents ran and 10 straight
Opposition candidates.   Mr. Haultain's Manifesto to the electors
referred to his long record of useful public service; dealt with the
financial and constitutional position of the Territories; mentioned
the importance of pending negotiations with the Federal authorities
regarding autonomy; and referred as follows to the things for
which his Government were contending and for which he asked
support: "(1) Equal rights with all the other Provinces of the
Dominion and the same financial consideration that has been given
to those Provinces; (2) control of the public domain in the West,
by the West, for the West; (3) compensation for the alienation of
any part of the public domain for purely Federal purposes; and
(4) the removal of the unjust and onerous Canadian Pacific Railway
exemption from taxation."

So far as Dominion politics were concerned the issue was very
mixed.   The Premier was generally considered to be a Conservative

but was a strong opponent of party politics in this connection ; while Mr. Sifton and Mr. Bulyea were Liberals. Messrs. Mc- Donald and Bennett, the Opposition leaders, were Conservatives. The result of the contest was the election of twenty-four Govern- ment supporters, six members of the Opposition and five Independents. Mr. Haultain received a good personal majority, and the other most important individual elections were those of Mr. Sifton, Dr. Patrick, Mr. R. B. Bennett. Mr. J. J. Young and Mr. G. W. Brown. Writing of the Premier, shortly before the election, on May 3rd, the Calgary *Herald* paid him a substantial tribute : " Mr. Haultain is one of the cleanest men in Canadian politics to-day and there has never been a suggestion made even by the most rabid opponent against his personal honour. He is a man of academic training and large, clear perception; straight- forward and manly even towards his enemies. In some respects, he is the most finished debater ever heard on a Western platform, arraying his facts in crisp, clear-cut sentences, and then pressing home his argument with logic and force."

A few days after the result was known Mr. Haultain left to attend the Coronation and did not return until near the end of the year. On December 9th, he was entertained at a banquet in Regina attended by many of the prominent men of the Territories. In his speech Mr. Haultain expressed an academic liking for. Government control of railways and urged, meantime, a greater degree of control over their operations. He favoured a railway to Hudson's Bay and hoped the autonomy question would be kept out of party politics. Meanwhile, a Liberal Convention had been held at Calgary on September 3rd, and Resolutions passed demand- ing a better Post-Office service and the avoidance of higher tariff duties or any increase in customs, asking for additional Dominion expenditure on roads and bridges, increased railway and trans- portation facilities, and more representation for Alberta. Appre- ciation was also expressed of the Laurier Government and especially of the Interior Department's administration of Western affairs.

The question of obtaining full powers of self-government as a Province of the Dominion, and with these powers larger and more adequate revenues, was the chief issue of the year **Provincial** in the North-West Territories. Resolutions upon the **Autonomy** subject had been passed by the Assembly in 1900; **and the** **Territories** Premier Haultain and Mr. J. H. Ross had visited Ottawa in 1900 and in 1901 upon the matter : an elaborate statement of the whole case had been submitted by the Territorial Premier to Sir Wilfrid Laurier under date of December 7th, 1901 ; and a Bill had been prepared and presented to the Ottawa Government embodying the Territorial demands and requirements. The proposal was to join the four Districts of Assiniboia, Saskatchewan, Alberta and Athabasca into a Province of the Dominion under the terms of the British North America

Act, with four members in the Senate and ten in the Commons ; with the same local constitutional powers and rights as the other Provinces ; with the full control of its Crown Lands and with subsidies of $50,000 for legislative purposes, and of $200,000 at the rate of 80 cents per head of its population ; with an increase at the same rate until the population reached 1,396,091 ; with interest at 5 per cent. on all lands previously granted for settlement by the Dominion Government within the bounds of the new Province.

Under date of March 27th, 1902, the Hon. Clifford Sifton, Minister of the Interior at Ottawa, wrote Mr. Haultain as follows : "It is the view of the Government that it will not be wise at the present time to pass legislation forming the North-West Territories into a Province or Provinces. Some of the reasons leading to this view may be found in the fact that the population of the Territories is yet sparse ; that the rapid increase in population now taking place will, in a short time, alter the conditions to be dealt with very materially ; and that there is a considerable divergence of opinion respecting the question whether there should be one Province only or more than one Province. Holding this view, therefore, it will not be necessary for me to discuss the details of the draft bill which you presented as embodying your views." In his reply, dated April 2nd, the Territorial Premier concluded a vigorous protest in the following terms :

We cannot but regret that the Government has not been able to recognize the urgent necessity for the change that has been asked, and can only trust that as you have denied us the opportunity of helping ourselves you will be at least impressed with the necessity and the duty, which is now yours, of meeting the pressing necessities of these rapidly developing Territories. While we may, in your opinion, without inconvenience, mark time constitutionally, we cannot do without the transportation facilities, the roads, the bridges, the schools, and the other improvements which our rapidly growing population imperatively requires—and at once. Whether we are made into a Province or not, our financial necessities are just as real, and in conclusion I can only trust that when the question of an increase to our subsidy is receiving consideration, more weight will be given to our representations in that respect than has been given to our requests for constitutional changes.

A few days later, on April 8th, Mr. Haultain moved the following Resolution in the Territorial Assembly : " Whereas, the larger powers and income incidental to the Provincial status are urgently and imperatively required to aid the development of the Territories and to meet the pressing necessities of a large and rapidly increasing population, be it resolved that this House regrets that the Federal Government has decided not to introduce legislation at the present Session of Parliament with a view to granting Provincial institutions to the Territories." Dr. Patrick, for the Opposition, proposed a 2,000 word amendment supporting the division of the Territories into two Provinces each with about 275,000 square miles of territory and with a view to cheapening administration and making transportation arrangements easier. It was lost by a large majority and Mr. Haultain's motion carried in the same way.

The subject was shortly afterwards debated in the House of Commons at Ottawa—April 18th—in connection with a vote of $357,979 for the North-West schools. All the Western members spoke and Mr. R. L. Borden declared existing grants to be inadequate and supported Territorial autonomy. Mr. Sifton, in reply, stated that the Government were considering the financial question of the future carefully. As to autonomy, he thought a settlement in three or four years would be quite reasonable. Autonomy would not abolish existing difficulties and many of the people in the Territories did not desire it and were not agreed as to the point of one or two Provinces. The Government would not be hurried in so important a matter. On April 16th, Mr. R. B. Bennett, of the Opposition in the Legislature, moved a long Resolution urging autonomy as an imperative necessity. The Premier, however, declared it unnecessary and the mover alone voted for it.

Mr. James Dunsmuir, a wealthy mine owner and respected citizen, had become Premier of British Columbia in June, 1900, and retired in November, 1902. On January 7th of the **Premier Dunsmuir and British Columbia** latter year he wrote to Sir Wilfrid Laurier a lengthy letter presenting his views as to the relations borne by the Province to the Dominion and urging once more upon the Federal authorities a re-adjustment of existing financial arrangements. He renewed previous representations upon this point and felt encouraged, he declared, by the augmented Federal revenues from British Columbia sources. His Government desired only reasonable co-operation. "This has been our position, particularly, in regard to railways, the building of which in this Province involves a great deal that is common to the interests of both Governments."

The railway policy of his Government in the Session of 1901 had been based, he added, largely upon reasonable hopes in this connection. They were anxious to open up the country from the Coast to the Kootenays by means of railways and had already undertaken complete surveys of the proposed route of the Victoria, Vancouver and Eastern line, *via* Hope Mountain. They would be glad of Dominion co-operation in this enterprise and would be willing to negotiate with a view to constructing such a road as a "joint Government undertaking" open to all other railways for "full and equal running rights." The Premier then went on to enlarge upon the willingness of his Government to accept a yearly sum in addition to existing claims. He pointed out the vast difference in conditions between the Eastern Provinces and British Columbia on entering Confederation—the former with public works largely completed and their consequent debts assumed by the Dominion and the latter with roads and bridges, wharves, schools and railways yet to construct, vast resources to develop, distances and physical difficulties to conquer and increasing responsibilities to meet. Yet their sources of revenue were the same as in the East and the disproportion between revenue and neces-

sary expenditure was large and unreasonable. He asked for a
serious conference between the Dominion and the Province and
summed up the situation as follows :

The potential sources of revenue belong to the Dominion. We have proved
to you that we pay three times the average contribution of Canada to the
Dominion and get less than half back. If the people of British Columbia
were able to retain all they contribute in taxes to the Provincial and Dominion
Governments, they could support every public utility of the Province, both
Provincial and Dominion, build their own railways and still have a surplus
each year to their credit.

On January 12th Mr. Dunsmuir published an Address to the
people of British Columbia, reviewing with elaboration and frank-
ness the policy of his Government and the existing political
conditions. He first of all stated that he had never sought the
Premiership, had only accepted it in the hope of helping to restore
political stability, and was anxious to resign it as soon as some one
appeared willing and better able to handle a difficult situation.
Mr. Joseph Martin had not controlled his policy, as was charged.
His railway plans of the past had been guided by the hope of
obtaining Dominion co-operation and when failure had occurred it
was due to the cost of construction and the impossibility of giving
enough to meet this obstacle without raising powerful popular
opposition.

The fact was that three times the amount of revenue was going
to Ottawa from British Columbia than was coming in to the Provincial Treasury. It was, therefore, impossible to properly encourage railways, bonus ship-building and open up the immense inland
country with existing financial resources. In thirty years the
Province had paid the Dominion $15,000,000 more than it received
and his policy was to urge on the Dominion Government " to take
up the burden of railway and ship-building and fishery development or to hand us back such a share of our contributions as will
enable the people of the Province to do it for themselves." As to
local policy he believed that his action in calling Mr. J. C. Brown
to the Cabinet may have been politically a mistake, but in every
other way it was right and a reward for honest support in the
railway crisis of 1901 against the unfair and unjust action initiated
by some of his own supporters.

His future policy he described as including the railway plans
already outlined in his letter to the Dominion Premier; encourage
ment to immigration by placing tracts of land from 1,000 acres
upwards on the market at very easy terms; a careful and just
redistribution of seats; a re-adjustment of mining taxation and
a conference upon joint railway interests with the Dominion
Government; encouragement of ship-building through partial aid
from the Province and part from the Dominion; appointment of a
practical man to investigate conditions of fish life on the Coast;
encouragement to the establishment of cold storage facilities and
abattoirs; an already completed arrangement with the C. P. R. for

material reduction in the rates on agricultural products. A denunciatory criticism of this Manifesto was published on the following day by Mr. R. G. Tatlow, M.P.P., and on January 26th there was made public in the Victoria *Colonist* a second and briefer letter from the Premier. He reiterated at some length his desire to keep the claims and wishes of British Columbia regarding its relations with the Dominion out of party politics. He declared himself opposed to the Government attempting to build railways for three reasons: (1) The Province is not in a position financially to do so. (2) It is the duty of the Dominion Government. (3) Success would depend on the whole Canadian railway system being made uniform.

On September 3rd, 1901, the Hon. Richard McBride had resigned his position as Minister of Mines in the Dunsmuir Government. On February 27th, 1902, it was announced that Lieut.-Col. the Hon. E. G. Prior, ex-M.P., and one-time Minister of Inland Revenue in the Conservative Government at Ottawa, had accepted the post and would contest the vacant seat at Victoria for the Legislature. He announced his policy as a strong endorsation of the railway plans of the Government and of the Canadian-Northern contract. His appointment was of course variously criticized and one quotation may be given here. The British Columbia *Mining Record* of April, after declaring politics to be the curse of Canada, said that mining men could afford to overlook those of Col. Prior "because he is a man of wide experience; well-known in centres from which the money necessary for our development is most likely to come; well liked by those in power at Ottawa; a man with large interests in this Province, not centred at Victoria; and above all because he is a professional and practical mining man."

Political Affairs in British Columbia

The new Minister's opponent in Victoria was Mr. E. V. Bodwell, K.C., a prominent Liberal and able speaker and the contest was close and keen—the Government fighting for its life with a majority variously estimated at one, or two, or nothing, and Mr. Bodwell for a success which might have made him Premier. As to policy Col. Prior's was one of railway construction; while Mr. Bodwell declared at a meeting on February 27th that "the way to secure the railway without trouble was to defeat Col. Prior and thus ensure the defeat of the Government." The discussion turned largely upon the exact meaning and terms of the contract with the Canadian-Northern and the likelihood of Victoria really being its terminus. On March 10th the returns showed 1,539 votes for Col. Prior and 1,484 for his opponent.

Meanwhile the Legislature had been opened on February 20th by Lieut.-Governor Sir Henri Joly de Lotbiniére with a Speech from the Throne which referred to the increased output of the mines; to negotiations with Ottawa regarding the position of the Province; to the Provincial Commission on freight rates and the consequent reductions; to promised measures for cold storage, redistribution of seats, and the settlement of unoccupied lands; to proposed railway construction and the establishment of pulp and paper industries.   The Hon. C. E. Pooley was elected Speaker, and at a caucus of the Opposition, attended by 18 members, the Hon. Mr. McBride was elected Leader, with Messrs. R. F. Green, R. G. Tatlow, Denis Murphy, K.C., Dallas Helmcken, K.C., A. W. Neill and C. W. Munro as an Advisory Committee.   The first division in the House, on February 22nd, gave the Government a majority of two. A couple of days later occurred a remarkable scene during which Mr. Joseph Martin tried to seize the seat always reserved for the Opposition Leader, and precipitated what promised to be a free fight (during prayers) with Mr. McBride.

The succeeding Session was a very stormy one and was marked by the use of much strong language and invective and by many personal charges.   Some of this acrimony was freely reflected in the press.   Motions of censure or non-confidence followed one another in frequent and varied forms.   Mr. McBride moved two of them on April 15th, which were lost by four majority.   Another on April 23rd dealt with the Foreshore or Fisheries matter and was notable for the reading of a letter from Mr. Æmilius Jarvis, of Toronto, in which he described certain negotiations with the Government as involving investments of $1,250,000 and concluded with the statement that British Columbia was, under the circumstances, " a good place to keep our money out of."   The Premier strenuously denied the statements in the letter.   On May 5th a motion to adjourn, made by a Government supporter, was defeated by one majority, and this was claimed as an Opposition victory.   Outside of railway legislation, alien vote and immigration discussions, the chief matter of the Session was the Redistribution Bill, providing for 42 instead of 00 members, altering certain boundaries, giving Vancouver five members and Nelson and Rossland one each.   Mr. McBride criticised the measure as a gerrymander, and Mr. Tatlow would have preferred fewer members rather than an increase.   The second reading, however, only had three opposing votes, and it was finally passed unanimously.

A somewhat discussed incident was the appointment of a Select Committee to inquire into certain charges made against the Gold Commissioner for Atlin, and the Report, submitted on May 30th, declared that Mr. Graham " was not as diligent in the public interests as he might have been."   The Legislature was prorogued on June 21st.   On November 8th, Mr. John Oliver, M.P.P., met his constituents at Ladner and described the reasons of himself and Mr. Kidd for deserting the Government toward the end of the Session; denounced Messrs. Helmcken and Hayward for changing ground and saving the Government with their votes; and bitterly criticized the railway legislation and policy of Mr. Dunsmuir. Meanwhile, Government re-organization was being freely discussed, pending the Premier's return from England and the Coronation, and the question as to whether Col. Prior or the Hon. D. M. Eberts was to succeed to the Premiership was widely debated. It was generally understood that Mr. Dunsmuir intended to resign at the first convenient moment, and it was believed, with every probability as to its truth, that he had long since promised to recommend Col. Prior as his successor.

Transportation was the great public issue of the year in British Columbia. On February 14th Mr. Dunsmuir's organ, the *Colonist*, stated that the construction of the Canadian Northern **Railway** Railway through the Province would be a subject of **Controversies** early consideration for the Legislature. Negotiations **in British** **Columbia** were then continued between the Government and the C. N. R., the representative of the latter being Mr. J. N. Greenshields, K.C., of Montreal. During the Prior-Bodwell contest in Victoria a sort of preliminary contract was made public, and upon the general terms of this Col. Prior took his stand, and promised to resign if they were not realized. About the same time he stated that the Government were negotiating with Mackenzie & Mann to purchase the Esquimault and Nanaimo Railway, in which the Premier was largely interested financially, so as to complete the connection at Victoria with the Canadian Northern. The contract in question was made with the gentlemen above-mentioned under the name of the Edmonton, Yukon and Pacific Railway Company, and in its completed form laid before the Legislature on March 25th, signed by the Premier and the Hon. W. C. Wells, Commissioner of Crown Lands and Works, and by Mr. William Mackenzie, President, and Mr. W. H. Moore, Secretary of the Company. Everything was conditional upon obtaining Dominion aid and co-operation.

The Railway was to run from Victoria, on Vancouver Island, to a point opposite Bute Inlet, thence by ferry and from Bute Inlet to the eastern boundary of the Province in the Yellowhead Pass. It constituted the Pacific connection of the Canadian Northern and was to receive a bonus of $4,800 per mile for the Island section, $4,800 for the first 50 miles from Bute Inlet, $4,000 from there to Quesnel, and $4,500 per mile from there to the boundary line. There was also to be a grant of 20,000 acres of Crown Lands for each mile of standard guage railway, free right of way and all necessary land for terminal facilities, etc. The arrangement was fiercely attacked in the Legislature and especially the bonus clause. Mr. Denis Murphy, on March 5th, described it as involving impossible conditions, outrageous subsidies and non-binding terms. On March 23rd the *Colonist* announced that the Government's negotiations with the E. & N. Railway, instigated by Messrs. Mackenzie & Mann, had been compromised by allowing the new Railway to come into Victoria independently of the Esquimault and Nanaimo line.

The strongest press opposition to this contract and project came from the Vancouver *News-Advertiser*, while the defence by the Victoria *Colonist* was equally vigorous. The objections raised were those of opposition to any cash subsidy whatever, the magnitude of the land grant, the omission of a provision making the subsidy dependent upon completion of the line and the claim that in such an important matter the people should be consulted. Meanwhile the old question of the Victoria, Vancouver and Eastern line—or as it was now largely termed, the Coast-Kootenay Railway project—was being discussed and dealt with. The publication of the Report on the proposed route, which had been submitted to the Government on December 23rd, 1901, by the Hon. Edgar Dewdney, C.E., showed that the Hope Mountains could not be crossed without encountering "serious engineering difficulties which would necessitate a very large expenditure of money."

On April 1st it was stated that the Government were negotiating with Messrs. McLean Bros., the first contractors on the projected V. V. & E., for the construction of the Coast-Kootenay line, and on May 5th a draft contract was submitted to the Legislature together with that of the C. N. R. or Edmonton and Yukon line. By these terms the former Railway was to extend from or near Vancouver to Midway in the Boundary country. For the first 80 miles there was to be a cash subsidy of $4,000 per mile, for the next 100 miles $4,800, and for the balance of line, not to exceed 150 miles, $4,000 per mile. The Company was to receive a land grant of 20,000 acres per mile under similar conditions to those of the Edmonton and Yukon, while the payment of subsidies in each case might be made in fifty-year three per cent. debentures or inscribed stock of the Province. Both contracts were subject to the receipt of satisfactory financial assistance from the Dominion and work was to be commenced before September 1st, 1903.

The contracts were discussed with varying degrees of political intensity and especially the subsidy clause giving heavy land grants and also involving the Province in alleged liabilities of a large amount. Two of their supporters deserted the Government in the Legislature but they gained two others—Mr. W. H. Hayward of Esquimault declaring that this railway policy involved the employment of from 8,000 to 12,000 men for several years and the expenditure of $30,000,000 in the Province. Measures were introduced to ratify the two contracts and were finally amended on May 20th by the Government eliminating the land grants, and fixing the cash subsidy at $5,000 per mile for the C. N. R. (not exceeding 480 miles) and $4,500 for the Coast-Kootenay line for 330 miles. The roads were to be exempt from taxation for ten years and then to pay the Government two per cent. of the receipts. Power was reserved to fix maximum freight and passenger rates. Presumably because of this concession Mr. Martin supported the Government and on May 28th their railway policy was approved in a direct vote by four majority. The second reading of the Coast-Kootenay bill carried by 24 to 11 and after its final passage the contract was signed late in July by McLean Bros.

and the Government.   Meanwhile, the Edmonton and Yukon or
C. N. R. measure had also become law and legislation had been
enacted aiding construction under largely similar conditions of
railways from Midway to Vernon and from Kitimaat Inlet to
Hazelton.   An important matter in this connection was the acquisition in the autumn of 1902 by Mr. Dunsmuir of the entire
holdings in the E. and N. Railway and the consequent removal of
the only bar to an arrangement with the C. N. R. people for entry
into Victoria along satisfactory lines.

Oriental immigration was an incessant subject of discussion at
Pacific Coast during 1902.   Early in the year the Report of the
the Royal Commission, appointed by the Dominion
Oriental Government to inquire into the whole question of
Immigration
and Chinese and Japanese immigration, was presented to
Legislation Parliament.   It defined the men of the latter race as
being "more independent, energetic, apt, and ready
and anxious to adopt, at least in appearance, the manners and mode
of life of the white man," than were the Chinese.   Like the Chinese
the Japanese had a different standard of morals from the white
man and the absence of criminal convictions indicated that he was
law abiding.   He often worked for less wages and in many
industries was driving out the Chinaman.   He came only for a
short time to the country, contributed nothing to public purposes
or interests, had no domestic ties in this country, competed successfully with the labour of family men, lived in over-crowded and
often insanitary quarters, and carried his earnings out of the
country.   There were of course exceptions, but, upon the whole,
the Report said: "Their presence in large numbers delays the
settlement of the country and keeps out intending settlers; and all
that has been said in this regard with reference to the Chinese
applies with equal if not greater force to the Japanese."

The document, signed by Messrs. R. C. Clute, K.C., D. G. Munn,
and Christopher Foley, went on to express satisfaction at the action
of the Japanese Government in stopping the issuance of passports
to British Columbia.   "Nothing further is needed to settle this
most difficult question upon a firm basis than some assurance that
the action already taken by the Government of Japan will not be
revoked."   The Commission strongly approved of Mr. Chamberlain's
advice as to applying the Natal Act to the Chinese and urged
similar legislation by the Dominion Government as being sufficiently stringent and effective.   The Commission favoured the
raising of the Capitation Tax upon Chinese from $100 to $500.

On March 19th Mr. H. B. Gilmour moved in the Provincial
Legislature that the Dominion authorities be petitioned to pass
legislation at the coming Session giving "immediate and full effect"
to these recommendations.   The motion passed without opposition.
Another Resolution was presented by Mr. Dallas Helmcken asking
the Government to communicate with the Premier of Canada and

have the matter brought to the attention and consideration of the Colonial Premiers at the coming Coronation Conference. To this Mr. W. W. B. McInnes moved an amendment pointing out in vigorous language the evils of Oriental immigration; declaring that the legislation of 1900 had been passed in accordance with and along the lines of Mr. Chamberlain's suggestions and yet had been disallowed at Ottawa for "Imperial reasons"; stating that similar legislation was in force elsewhere in the Empire; protesting against this apparent discrimination; and winding up with the same request as that made by Mr. Helmcken. On April 23rd the terms of the amendment were unanimously adopted by the House as being "stronger" and the Resolution then passed.

In connection with Mr. R. F. Green's local Mines' Regulation Act an amendment offered by Mr. McInnes was passed on May 1st indirectly restricting the employment of Chinese or Japanese in coal mines—despite the generally expressed opinion that is would be disallowed. A measure presented by the Minister of Mines dealing with mining and establishing a test of being able to write in the characters of some European language was passed without opposition. It was somewhat similar in terms to Mr. Tatlow's bill of the preceding Session which had been approved by the Provincial Government and operated for a time until disallowed at Ottawa. Another Act passed on the initiative of Mr. Helmcken, provided that workmen employed on works carried out under Legislative charter must be able to read the Act in a European language. Meanwhile strong expressions regarding the whole matter of Oriental immigration were frequent and the following utterance of Mr. C. Foley to a meeting of workmen on Sept. 12th indicates their tone: "He preferred to see all the industries of British Columbia sink to nothing rather than have it the home of Mongolians with an indolent aristocracy made rich by their labour."

On December 13th, it was announced at Ottawa that the three Acts referred to above as having passed the British Columbia Legislature and restricting immigration, or the employment of Oriental immigrants, had been disallowed because of its Japanese application. It had been claimed that the making of the test an educational one, in accordance with the terms of Mr. Chamberlain's despatch of April 19th, 1899, would avert the Federal disallowance. On December 17th, the decision of the Judicial Committee of the Imperial Privy Council in the Tomey Homma case was made public through Mr. Charles Wilson, K.C., of Vancouver, who had represented the Province in the action along with Mr. Christopher Robinson, K.C., of Toronto. It declared, in brief, that Japanese residents, whether naturalized or not, could not exercise the franchise in British Columbia. In other words the Legislature had the right to exclude Asiatics from the franchise, as well as other classes in the community, even though they were British subjects.

6

One of the stormiest scenes in the British Columbia Session of 1902 was that surrounding the presentation of certain charges of corruption by Mr. Smith Curtis on March 19th. He

Opposition Charges and a Royal Commission
accused Premier Dunsmuir of trying to sell the Esquimault and Nanaimo Railway, in which he held large interests, through a deal by which the Government granted excessive subsidies and rights to the Canadian Northern (or Edmonton and Yukon) Railway. He charged the Premier and his colleagues, Messrs. Eberts, Wells and Prentice, with grave misconduct and gross and wilful neglect of their official duty in employing Mr. J. N. Greenshields, K.C., as an accredited agent of the Province in negotiations with the Canadian Northern Railway, at a time when he was acting in a similar capacity for the Railway and Mackenzie & Mann. He accused Col. Prior, Minister of Mines, of similar misconduct and neglect in this connection and demanded an investigation into the whole matter by a Select Committee of the House whom he proceeded to name. Amidst considerable excitement the Premier denied the charges and said he would have a Royal Commission to inquire into and report upon them. On motion of Mr. C. W. D. Clifford, the Lieutenant-Governor was asked to act in accordance with this suggestion by a vote of 33 to 2.

On September 25th Mr. Justice George A. Walkem of the Provincial Supreme Court was appointed a Commissioner to inquire into the matter. The first regular sitting was held on the following day and thereafter, irregularly but frequently, until the middle of April. Mr. R. Cassidy, K.C., acted for the Government and Mr. L. Bond for Mr. Smith Curtis. Several witnesses were examined on March 27th. Mr. Greenshields denied under oath that he had acted in any dual capacity but always for the Canadian Northern Railway. In the interests of Messrs. Mackenzie & Mann he had tried to buy out the Esquimault & Nanaimo Railway and only with difficulty had induced Mr. Dunsmuir to express himself as willing to accept, subject to others who were interested, $2,000,000 for the whole affair. The Premier then followed, denied all the charges, stated that no sale of the Esquimault & Nanaimo had yet taken place and put in evidence certain telegrams which passed between himself and Thomas H. Hubbard, who represented in New York the other parties interested in the line. In these he advised acceptance of the Mackenzie & Mann offer, conditionally on the then Railway Bill passing the House—thus enabling the Canadian Northern Railway to construct across the Province and into Victoria. Finally, the offer of bonds in payment of the $2,000,000 was considered as unsatisfactory by his associates. He would have accepted the offer in order to bring a Trans-continental line into Victoria and risked the chances of personal loss. Mr. Greenshields had only been employed by the Government on another matter—the presentation of Provincial claims at Ottawa.

The Hon. Mr. Wells was examined and denied that Mr. Green-

The Hon. Jabez Bunting Snowball

Lieut.-Colonel, The Hon. Edward Gawler Prior, M.P.P.

shields acted for the Government in this affair while repudiating also certain newspaper interviews with himself, Col. Prior, and Mr. Prentice, which had indicated that he did. The Hon. Mr. Eberts, on March 29th, took the same line and declared that Mr. Greenshields and himself had been at dagger's drawn during the negotiations. During the next few days a number of witnesses were called, including several newspaper men who testified as to the correctness of the reports of interviews and meetings, and a number of members of the Legislature, hostile or otherwise to the Government. The Commission witnessed a number of stormy scenes and discussions of a personal character. On April 7th, during further testimony given by the Premier, a private letter from him to General Hubbard was read admitting that the Canadian Northern Railway offer was not a very good one but pointing out that he was anxious to get that line into Victoria *via* the Esquimault and Nanaimo Railway for public reasons. He was sorry that his colleague had not agreed to the proposition although it might involve some personal loss.

After a prolonged cross-examination of the Premier, a brief one of the Opposition Leader, and the production of certain telegrams, a sudden end came to the Commission by the withdrawal of Mr. Smith Curtis on the ground of the Commissioner refusing to allow a certain unpublished despatch from going in as evidence. The telegrams already produced simply showed a strong desire on the part of the Government during February and March to have Mr. Greenshields given full authority to act for Mackenzie & Mann and to have the contract defined and completed so as to carry Col. Prior's bye-election. With the disappearance of the maker of the charges the investigation closed so far as the Commission was concerned.

On November 21st, the Hon. Mr. Dunsmuir resigned the Premiership of the Province and recommended Lieut.-Col. the Hon. Edward Gawlor Prior, Minister of Mines, as his successor. On November 24th the new Cabinet was completed after various personal negotiations and rumours including the statement that Hon. D. M. Eberts would retire from the Attorney-Generalship, the understanding that Mr. H. Dallas Helmcken, K.C., was offered a Portfolio, and the statement of Mr. R. G. Tatlow, M.P.P., that he and Mr. Richard McBride had declined to become identified with the Ministry. The Cabinet, as finally announced, was as follows:

The New Provincial Government

Premier and Minister of Mines............. Hon. E. G. Prior
Attorney-General......................... Hon. D. M. Eberts
Minister of Finance...................... Hon. J. D. Prentice
Commissioner of Lands and Works......... Hon. W. C. Wells
Provincial Secretary and Minister of Education Hon. Denis Murphy
President of the Council.................. Hon. W. W. B. McInnes.

The last two names were those of the new members and as they were generally counted as being Oppositionists the Government made a substantial gain. The Victoria *Times* "suspended criticism" of the Government and described its new members as "coming men, bright and keen in debate and capable of lifting a debate above the ordinary levels." The Vancouver *Province* expressed the belief that Colonel Prior would disregard partisan politics and conduct affairs on "a thoroughly business basis." The Vancouver *World* took strong position against the new Government. Other papers warmly criticized Mr. Murphy for joining his old opponents and the Nelson *News* described the matter as the result of a system which made politics an affair of persons rather than principles. Mr. Martin declared again that party politics should prevail and indicated antagonism to the new arrangements. Meanwhile Mr. Murphy left for his constituency of West Yale where the bye-election had been fixed for December 20th. Two days later, November 28th, he was back in Victoria and his resignation had been accepted by the Premier. It was retirement not only from the Government but from public life and the reasons given were stated as "personal and private."

On December 1st Mr. Joseph Martin wrote a letter to the press, not taking absolute ground against the new Government, but expressing somewhat severe criticism and demanding to know what their railway policy was. The *Colonist* of December 16th described the issue as one of stable government against the forces of disorder and Col. Prior's policy as one of railway development. Meanwhile the election of Mr. McInnes was proceeding in North Nanaimo where he was opposed by Mr. Parker Williams, a Socialist. North Victoria, long since vacant through the death of the Speaker, Mr. J. P. Booth, was contested by Mr. Robertson for the Government and Mr. W. T. Patterson for the Opposition. In West Yale, the writ was withheld pending action upon Mr. Murphy's sudden retirement. On December 15th the Hon. Mr. McInnes was re-elected by 108 majority and on December 23rd the Government candidate was defeated in North Victoria by 43 majority.

On February 6th a Provincial Convention of Liberals opened in Vancouver, with Senator Templeman, Chairman of the Provincial Executive of the party, in the chair. The object of **Liberal Convention in British Columbia** the gathering was to discuss the question of introducing party lines into Provincial politics and to select a leader, or discuss the advisability of doing so. Amongst those whose names had been suggested for this latter position were Senator Templeman, of Victoria; Dr. Sinclair, of Rossland; Mr. E. P. Davis, K.C.; Mr. E. V. Bodwell, K.C.; Mr. Ralph Smith, M.P.; Mr. Smith Curtis, M.P.P.; Mr. W. W. B. McInnes and Mr. Joseph Martin, K.C., M.P.P. The whole matter, however, soon settled into a struggle as to whether Mr. Martin should be chosen by the Convention or the subject be postponed to another occasion. The Chairman found the meeting hard to control from the beginning, and the first important issue raised was the right of the Provincial Executive to appoint its members as members of the Convention.   Disputes as to credentials, therefore, occupied the attention of the 110 delegates present for hours, and the speeches were interspersed with opinions for and against the adoption of party lines.   Finally a vote of 69 to 41 declared that the Provincial Executive and the Editors of Liberal newspapers appointed by that body were not entitled to membership in the Convention.

Senator Templeman and his friends at once retired, and this left the meeting largely in the hands of those who favoured party lines and were supporters of Mr. Martin.   Mr. G. R. Maxwell, M.P., was at once chosen Chairman and elected President of the Provincial Liberal Association.   Sir Wilfrid Laurier was appointed Hon. President and the meeting broke up for the first day after a speech from Mr. Martin, in which he repudiated the rumours that he was at variance with the Dominion Government.   " I do not say that I have always agreed with what the Dominion Government have done.   I do not say that I intend to in the future, but, in saying so publicly, I defy any man to prove that I have at any time in any way assisted the Conservative party.   As long as I am in Provincial politics I shall take my stand on a question in opposition to the Government at Ottawa if the matter is in the interests of the people of British Columbia.   Party is only a means to an end."   Meanwhile the Victoria delegation and Senator Templeman's friends had returned home.   To the Vancouver *Province* of February 7th, Mr. E. V. Bodwell, K.C., declared that " the action taken by this new Convention is not binding on any one, and we will take no notice of it whatever."   Editorially, the same paper strongly supported the Provincial Executive in its right, as claimed, to a place in the Convention called by its fiat ; termed the action of the opposing element a political conspiracy ; declared that the body in question was now without authority or legal existence ; and expressed the belief that the Liberals of the Province were in a more disorganized condition than ever before.   On the following day the Convention decided by 65 to 25 to proceed with the election of a Liberal leader and Mr. Joseph Martin was chosen by a vote of 47 to 43 of which latter total Mr. W. W. B. McInnes, M.P.P., received 17, Mr. John C. Brown 8, Mr. G. R. Maxwell, M.P., 4, and the rest scattering.   Mr. Martin spoke at some length in response to the selection and stated that the Dominion Government had offered him high positions which he had declined.   Meanwhile, a Resolution had been carried unanimously in favour of introducing party lines into Provincial politics.   Others urged that Mr. Maxwell be taken into the Dominion Cabinet and expressed confidence in Sir Wilfrid Laurier. Officers of the Provincial Liberal Association were then declared elected including the Dominion Premier as Hon. President, Mr. G. R. Maxwell, M.P., as President and Messrs. Stuart Henderson, Richard Hall, M.P.P., J. C. Brown, ex-M.P.P., and S. S. Taylor as Vice-Presidents.   The platform chosen may be summarized as follows :

Immediate redistribution of seats in the Legislature with special consideration for outlying districts.

Government ownership of public services and utilities.

Any future railway aid to be given in cash only and with security for Government control of rates.

Immediate construction of the Coast-Kootenay Railway, the Cariboo Railway, a line from Alberni to the East coast, a road in the Northern part of the Province and the Vernon-Midway line.

Legislation to make dyking areas available for early cultivation.

-　Protection of mining interests against combines and trusts—even to the point of building smelters and refineries if necessary.

The stopping of Oriental immigration and an appeal to Liberals throughout Canada to help in the matter.

Approval of compulsory arbitration so as to prevent strikes and lockouts.

Taxation of privileges rather than industry and no addition to Provincial Debt except for public works properly chargeable to capital.

Retaining Provincial resources as an asset of the people and greater care in alienating the public domain.

Construction and maintenance of roads in mining and agricultural districts.

On February 11th a letter signed by Mr. Martin as "Liberal Leader for British Columbia" appeared in the papers, defending the proceedings of the Convention and declaring that its decisions were arrived at by 93 delegates out of the original 117 present at one part of the proceedings. There were many protests, however, against this view in addition to those of Senator Templeman and Mr. Bodwell. Mr. G. O. Buchanan, of Nelson, and Dr. Sinclair, of Vancouver, protested publicly, and on February 19th the Victoria Liberal Association, with 250 members present, passed a Resolution almost unanimously expressing repudiation of the "so-called Liberal Convention" in appointing Mr. Martin Leader of the party, and declaring that "we hereby express no confidence in him as such." The Vancouver *World* approved of the "party lines" declaration, while the *Province* and the Victoria *Times* repudiated the whole affair. The Ladysmith *Leader* of February 12th declared that the Convention had done nobly, and that the party was now led by "a man of splendid ability, indomitable courage and boundless energy."

As the Labour organizations have greater political influence in British Columbia than elsewhere in Canada, their proceedings and opinions are of some importance. In the Victoria *Colonist* of February 2nd appeared a strong letter from Mr. J. H. Watson, Provincial Vice-President of the Dominion Trades Congress, advocating national Canadian unions and separation from United States affiliations. In all the elections of the year and in discussions of mining interests and taxation the Labour question was prominent. On April 14th to 17th a Labour Convention was held at Kamloops, with 63 delegates present. Mr. J. A. Baker, of Slocan, a Socialist, was chosen chairman, and it was decided to form an organization called the Provincial Progressive Party. A series of Resolutions were passed including one which declared that non-payment of wages should be made a criminal offence, and another which pledged support to only those candidates

Labour Convention and Opinions

who gave the Convention which nominated them a signed and undated resignation of the seat, if elected, for use by a majority of the respective Conventions.   Mr. Christopher Foley, of Rossland, was elected President of the new party's organization, and its platform included the following principles :

Gradual shifting of all taxes from the producers to the land.

Government ownership of railways and means of communication.

Government establishment and operation of smelters and refineries.

Woman franchise and abolition of all property qualifications for public office.

No taxation of farms, improvements, implements, stock, and the assessment of wild lands at prices asked by speculators.

Lands to be held by actual settlers, and ten per cent. of all public lands to to be set apart for educational purposes.

Education to be free, secular, and compulsory up to 16 years, and text books, meals and clothing to be supplied out of public funds when necessary.

Compulsory arbitration of labour disputes and absolute restriction of Oriental immigration.

Pulp-land leases to contain a reforesting condition and the reservation from sale or lease of a certain part of all known coal areas for the future establishment of state-owned coal mines.

Municipal control of the liquor traffic ; the right to a Referendum in all cases of valuable subsidies or franchises ; and compulsory free transportation on all railways, etc., for Judges and members of the Legislature.

Election day to be a public holiday with four hours free from service for each employee.

Of this new organization the press spoke very cautiously.   The Sandon *Paystreak*, in characteristic style, declared, on April 19th, that it was going into politics to clean up the mess at Victoria, and prophesied for it eight or ten members in the future Legislature. Under date of May 2nd a Manifesto was issued, proclaiming its policy as that of progressive reform, denouncing existing parties, declaring Provincial resources to have been given over to the corporations, and urging organization in every locality.   It was signed by Mr. Foley, its other officers, and Mr. J. D. McNiven, Secretary-Treasurer at Victoria.   Speaking to this latter branch of the party on September 12th, Mr. Foley defended Mr. Ralph Smith from various attacks.   On November 7th the Hon. T. R. McInnes, formerly Lieutenant-Governor, accepted the post of Hon. President, and on December 12th Mr. Foley announced his retirement from the Presidency.

During the year agitation amongst the Conservatives for the inauguration of straight party lines in Provincial politics took form and shape and finally it was decided to hold a **Conservative Convention in British Columbia** Convention at Revelstoke on September 13th.   At this juncture Mr. Charles Wilson, K.C., of Vancouver, was the Leader of the party in the Province; Mr. Robert McBride, a strong Conservative, was Leader of the Opposition in the Legislature ; and Lieut.-Col. E. G. Prior, a prospective Premier, was Minister of Mines and a one-time member of the Conservative Government at Ottawa. Besides these three, Mr. F. L. Carter-Cotton, proprietor of the

Vancouver *News-Advertiser* and a strong opponent of the Dunsmuir Government, was thought a possibility for selection as the party leader under new conditions.

When the meeting took place, Mr. R. L. Borden, the Dominion Conservative Leader, was present and addressed the Convention. Each of the others defined their positions, and finally Mr. Wilson was re-elected Provincial Leader; Mr. John Houston, M.P.P., was chosen President of the Provincial Conservative Association in succession to Mr. McBride; and Messrs. A. S. Goodeve, J. R. Seymour, T. S. Annandale and A. E. McPhillips, M.P.P., were selected as Vice-Presidents with Mr. F. S. Barnard as Treasurer. A Resolution was passed declaring that "the stability of government and beneficial legislation can best be secured by the introduction of party lines in local elections and that such a course be adopted." Ex-Premier C. A. Semlin dissented. The following is a summary of the announced clauses in the party platform:

Active aid to the construction of trails in undeveloped sections and to the building of Provincial trunk roads of public necessity.

Government ownership of railways wherever possible and Provincial control of rates, with the right of purchase, in all bonused lines.

Active state aid in the development of agriculture.

Taxation of metalliferous mines on the basis of percentage of net profits.

Government ownership of telephone systems.

Government reservation of a portion of all coal areas granted or sold in the future with a view to the possible establishment of state-owned mines.

A reforesting clause in all pulp-land leases.

Perseverance in Legislative efforts to exclude Oriental labour.

Vigorous prosecution of demands on Dominion Government for better terms in subsidies and appropriations.

Increased customs duties on lead and lead products.

Legislation to help in the amicable adjustment of disputes between employers and employees.

The Commissioner of the Yukon Territory at the beginning of the year was the Hon. James H. Ross, formerly a member of the North-West Territories Government. Upon his **Government** retirement to contest the new seat for Ottawa at **and Politics** **in the Yukon** a later date Major Z. T. Wood of the Mounted Police was Acting-Commissioner. Mr. E. C. Senkler was Gold Commissioner at the beginning of the year; J. E. Girouard, Registrar; C. A. Dugas, Judge; H. W. Newlands, Legal Adviser; and Messrs. Nelson and Prudhomme, elected members of the Yukon Council. On January 17th, this body forwarded a Memorial to the Ottawa authorities asking for the following reforms:

1. Representation in the Senate.
2. The addition of five elected members to the present Yukon Council.
3. The division of the Territory into electoral districts and the setting apart of money for election purposes and members' travelling expenses.
4. Control of the liquor traffic in the Yukon.
5. The nomination of an inland revenue officer in the Yukon.
6. The right to establish breweries.
7. The setting apart of a fund for the maintenance of schools.
8. The setting apart of a fund to maintain roads.
9. The right of the Yukon Council to adopt all ordinances relative to Yukon

matters independently of the Ottawa Government, which, however, should retain the power of veto on Yukon statutes.

A week before this date Dawson City had voted upon the question of a municipal government controlled by the people or a Commission appointed by the Territorial Government. The political struggle was a keen one and a large number of Americans took the oath of allegiance in order to vote for popular civic rule. Most of the trading companies and taxpayers voted for a Commission as being possibly the cheapest and most efficient system but they were beaten by 79 majority in a total vote of 687. It was a case of campaigning at 50 degrees below zero. The election for Mayor took place on February 6th and resulted in the choice of Mr. Henry Macaulay. Commissioner Ross made a prolonged visit to Ottawa and the East during the year—leaving Dawson on February 4th. At Winnipeg, on his way to the Capital, he told the *Telegram* of February 25th that it was the intention of the Government to close all dance houses in Dawson. They had already stopped gambling and there would be no "wide-open" policy in the Yukon. He made the following statement as to his views of the much-discussed Treadgold Concession:

In consideration of providing a certain water supply to work the hydraulic and placer mines and to wash out the gold in the Bonanza Creek district, the Treadgold syndicate is to receive some concessions in reverted claims—that is claims abandoned by miners and which have become the property of the Government. Owners of claims are to have the privilege of working their properties with the aid of the Treadgold water supply but must pay a reasonable amount, set by the Government, for this privilege. I consider the scheme a good one.

Partly as a result of this visit to Ottawa, and partly because of other representations, important changes were made by Parliament in the regulations governing Yukon affairs. On April 21st, the Minister of the Interior presented a measure to the House which enacted that, in future, when there was a case of conflict between an order issued by the Governor-General-in-Council and one by the Commissioner of the Yukon the former was to prevail; that the Yukon Council should have the control and regulation of the sale of intoxicating liquors—leaving the control of manufacture in Federal hands; that the number of elective members in the Yukon Council should be increased from two to five and thus make the total five appointed and five elected. On April 23rd Mr. Sifton presented another bill giving the Yukon one representative in the House of Commons with a franchise similar to that of the North-West Territories. At the same time the Minister of Justice introduced a measure fixing the salaries of the two Police Magistrates in the Yukon at $4,000 a year with $1,800 living allowance; providing an additional High Court Judge for the Territory at $5,000 a year; creating a Territorial Court of Appeal to which appeals could be taken from the judgment of a single trial Judge instead of going, as in the past, to the British Columbia Courts; and giving an appeal from this Territorial Court to the Supreme Court of Canada.

Speaking on May 19th to the Vancouver *Province*, on his way home, Mr. Ross stated that the royalty mining charges were to be reduced from 5 to 2½ per cent. and the collection made more certain; that a Federal grant was to be given the Yukon upon lines similar to that given the North-West Territories; that the individual miner's certificate, costing him $10.00 a year, was to be abolished; that five new schools, several new roads, new bridges and other improvements were to be commenced shortly. When the Commissioner reached Dawson on June 4th he was given a great popular welcome home and public reception. A little later, on July 20th, it was announced that Mr. Ross had been taken dangerously ill on the steamer between Dawson and White Horse. The event was widely commented on and the Calgary *Herald* of July 22nd made the following statement: "There are few men—perhaps none—who have done more for the development and welfare of the West than Mr. Ross. A man of diversified gifts, peculiar force of character and a wonderfully pleasing personality, he is respected and liked by all."

Meanwhile Mr. F. C. Wade, K.C., formerly Crown Prosecutor and a pioneer in Yukon affairs, had been visiting England and Eastern Canada and giving lectures and interviews everywhere upon the resources and prospects of the Yukon. He returned to Dawson temporarily, late in the summer and on August 29th was tendered a banquet by his friends. Later on he was thought to be a probable candidate for the new Dominion seat in the Yukon and then a possible appointee to the Commissionership. Finally, Mr. Ross, after recovering from his illness, received the Liberal nomination and contested the election against J. A. Clarke, the Opposition candidate. The *Yukoner* of October 25th asked the people to vote for "Jim" Ross and the following platform:

1. Reduced fees for Miners' Licenses and Recording.
2. Government Aid for Smelter.
3. Free Quartz Test Mill and an Assay office at Dawson.
4. National Ownership of Large Water Rights.
5. Cancellation of Concessions Obtained by Fraud.
6. Wholly Elective Yukon Council.
7. Mining Machinery Duty Free.

The Minister of the Interior announced on September 3rd that when he had completely recovered Mr. Ross would probably enter the Cabinet. Mr. "Joe" Clarke's platform was "complete Provincial powers" for the Yukon and his paper, the *Klondike Miner*, put up a "red hot" fight for its candidate. Mr. Ross was absent during the contest but he accepted the nomination and his friends, including Mr. F. T. Congdon, Crown Prosecutor, fought vigorously in his interests and won on December 2nd by a majority which eventually turned out to be 892. Many prominent Conservatives supported Mr. Ross and it was stated that the gambling element was behind his opponent. As to the result Mr. Ross told the Vancouver *Province* of December 16th that it indicated a victory of the thinking classes over the foreign element.

PUBLIC APPOINTMENTS AND POLITICAL INCIDENTS.

Jan. 8.—Senator Sir W. H. Hingston, M.D., is presented by friends with a portrait of himself painted by Mr. J. Colin Forbes, R.C.A.

"   20.—*Le Journal* (C), of Montreal, attacks Sir Wilfrid Laurier as "a deserter of the autonomy of his country which he sacrifices to the criminal dreams of Imperialism."

"   21.—The Vancouver Board of Trade joins the Bar Association of the City and the City Council in asking for the appointment of Mr. E. P. Davis, K.C., as Chief Justice of the Province.

"   21.—Mr. Frederick Edward Molyneux St. John is appointed Gentleman Usher of the Black Rod at Oshawa.

"   28.—The Hon. George E. Foster addresses a Conservative meeting in Toronto on the National Life of Canada.

"   29.—The Hon. S. N. Parent, M.P.P., Premier of the Province and Mayor of the City is banqueted at Quebec.

Feb. 7.—Dr. James Edwin Robertson (L), ex-M.P.P. and ex-M.P., of Montague, P.E.I., is appointed to the Senate of Canada.

"   7.—Mr. Frederick Liguori Beique (L), K.C., of Montreal, is appointed to the Senate of Canada.

"   7.—Mr. Frederick Pemberton Thompson (L), of Fredericton, N.B., is appointed to the Senate of Canada.

"   7.—The Hon. Charles Edward Church (L), ex-M.P.P., and for nearly 20 years a member of the Provincial Government, is appointed to the Senate of Canada.

"   8.—Mr. James McMullen (L), ex-M.P., is appointed to the Senate of Canada.

"   8.—Mr. William Gibson (L), ex-M.P., is appointed to the Senate of Canada.

"   14.—Mr. F. H. Hale, M.P., is banqueted by his constituents at Woodstock, N.B.

"   20.—For the first time in the history of the Senate the Liberals are recognized as being in practical possession of a majority and are allowed to control the Striking Committee and the consequent Standing Committees of the House.

"   19.—Mr. Justice B. M. Britton is banqueted at Kingston in honour of his recent appointment to the Bench.

"   21.—The following Chairmen of Committees in the House of Commons are elected :

Public Accounts—D. C. Fraser.
Banking and Commerce—Archibald Campbell.
Railway and Canals—C. S. Hyman.
Private Bills—M. K. Cowan.
Privileges and Elections—F. B. Wade, K.C.
Standing Orders—T. B. Flint.
Expiring Laws—H. J. Logan.
Agriculture and Colonization—J. H. Legris.

"   21.—Mr. R. L. Borden, K.C., M.P., Leader of the Conservative Party in Canada, addresses the Canadian Club of Toronto on constitutional development.

"   22.—The Hon. Thomas Horace McGuire is promoted to the Chief Justice of the North-West Territories.

"   25.—An Address is presented to the Hon. James G. Stevens, Judge of the Charlotte, N.B., County Court, on the anniversary of his 80th birthday.

Mar. 6.—The Hon. James Emile Pierre Prendergast, ex-M.P.P., and Judge of the Winnipeg County Court, is appointed to the Supreme Court of the Territories.

"   7.—Mr. Henry Corby, ex-M.P., is entertained at a Conservative banquet in Belleville with Sir Mackenzie Bowell as Chairman.

"   8.—Mr. Gordon Hunter, K.C., of Vancouver, is appointed Chief Justice of British Columbia in succession to the late Hon. A. J. McColl.

Mar. 25.—The Hon. Thomas Robertson, M.P.P., Speaker of the Nova Scotia Legislature, is presented with an Address and purse of money by his fellow-members of the House in recognition of his courtesy and ability.

April 7.—The appointment is announced of Mr. R. E. Kingsford as second Police Magistrate of Toronto.

" 22.—It is announced at a meeting in Ottawa that $1,600 has been subscribed toward a memorial to the late Nicholas Flood Davin, K.C., and Mr. Charles Magee is elected President of the Committee with Mr. Henry J. Morgan as Secretary.

" 25.—The Liberal Senators, headed by the Hon. David Wark, present Lady Laurier with an Address and a diamond tiara.

" 28.—An Ottawa Order-in-Council appoints Messrs. F. W. G. Haultain, M.P.P., and A. L. Sifton, M.P.P., of the Territorial Government to be King's Counsel.

May 6.—The Conservative Members of the Senate tender a banquet to the Hon. Sir Mackenzie Bowell, late Premier of Canada, and present Leader of their party in that House.

" 7.—A banquet at Montreal is tendered to Dr. J. P. Rottot of Laval, Dr. D. C. McCallum of McGill, and Sir W. H. Hingston, M.D., in honour of their golden Jubilee in the Medical profession.

" 15.—An Address, expressing personal admiration and party loyalty, is presented to Sir Wilfrid Laurier by the Liberal Members of Parliament at Ottawa together with a handsome portrait of himself painted by Mr. J. Colin Forbes, R.C.A. Graceful tribute is paid the Premier by Mr. R. L. Borden.

" 20.—The selection of Prof. Henry Taylor Bovey, LL.D., of McGill University, Montreal, as a Fellow of the Royal Society of London is announced.

" 27.—A number of appointments as King's Counsel are announced by the Ontario Government as follows :

George Kennedy, M.A., LL.D., Toronto.
George Smith Holmstead, Toronto.
James S. Cartwright, M.A., Toronto.
Verschoyle Cronyn, LL.B., London.
John Wesley Kerr, Cobourg.
David William Dumble, Peterborough.
Edward George Mallouch, Perth.
James Henry Burritt, Pembroke.
John Andrew Paterson, M.A., Toronto.
William Henry McFadden, LL.B., Brampton.
Alfred Servos Ball, Woodstock.
Edwin Perry Clement, Berlin.
George Edmison, Peterboro.
Hamilton Cassels, Toronto.
Isidore Frederick Hellmuth, Toronto.
Thomas Graves Meredith, Toronto.
James Carruthers Hegler, Ingersoll.
Thomas Rollo Slaght, Simcoe.
William Barton Northrup, M.P., Belleville.
John Cowan, Sarnia.
James Haverson, Toronto.
Malcolm Græme Cameron, Goderich.
Francis Egerton Hodgins, Toronto.
Michael James Gorman, LL.B., Ottawa.
Charles Edward Hewson, Barrie.
Daniel E. McLean, Ottawa.
William Proudfoot, Goderich.

Alfred Henry Clarke, LL.B., Windsor.
Peter Duncan Crerar, M.A., Hamilton.
James Bicknell, Toronto.
Alexander Monro Grier, Toronto.
James Alexander Hutcheson, Brockville.
Henry Herbert Collier, B.A., St. Catharines.
William Hume Blake, B.A., Toronto.
William Hugh Wardrope, Hamilton.
Edward Cornelius Stanbury Huycke, Cobourg.
Henry Smith Osler, B.A., Toronto.
Thomas Cowper Robinette, B.A., LL.B., Toronto.
Herbert Edward Irwin, B.A., Toronto.
Frances Alexander Anglin, B.A., Toronto.
Robert James McLaughlin, Lindsay.
Hugh Guthrie, M.P., Guelph.
Ronald David Gunn, Orillia.
Thomas Mulvey, B.A., Toronto.
Mahlon Kitchen Cowan, M.P., Windsor.
Alexander Grant McKay, B.A., Owen Sound.
Newton Wesley Rowell, Toronto.
Louis Vincent McBrady, Toronto.
Leighton Goldie McCarthy, M.P., Toronto.

June 6.—Mr. R. F. Green, M.P.P., Opposition Whip in the British Columbia Legislature, is presented with an Address and gold watch by his party.

" 7.—A farewell banquet is given at Rossland to the Hon. T. Mayne Daly, ex-M.P., upon his leaving for Winnipeg.

" 9.—Chief Justice Sir Henry Strong is sworn in as Administrator of the Government during the absence of the Governor-General at the Coronation.

" 9.—The appointment of Mr. Henri Cesairé Breille St. Pierre, K.C., to the Superior Court of Quebec, is announced in succession to Judge Bélanger resigned.

" 17.—It is announced that Senator Sir W. H. Hingston of Montreal, Senator J. P. B. Casgrain of Montreal, Mr. F. T. Frost, ex-M.P., of Smith's Falls and Police Magistrate George O'Keefe of Ottawa are appointed by the Dominion Government to be Members of the Ottawa Improvement Commission.

July 27.—It is announced by cable that H.R.H. the Duke of Connaught, Grand Master of the Masons, has appointed Mr. J. Ross Robertson of Toronto a Past Grand Junior Warden of England in recognition of his services to Masonry.

Aug. 9.—A banquet is tendered Lieut.-Col. the Hon. E. G. Prior, Minister of Mines, at Rossland, B.C., and speeches are made strongly urging a reduction or abolition of the 2 per cent. tax on the mining industry.

Sept. 15.—The Hon. Charles Fitzpatrick is banqueted in Winnipeg by the Catholic Club of that City.

Oct. 2.—Mr. James Fife is appointed Chief Inspector of Weights and Measures in the Inland Revenue Department.

" 7.—Sir Frederick Borden, M.P., Minister of Militia and Defence, is banqueted at Canning, N.S.

" 30.—Judgment is given by the Supreme Court of Manitoba sustaining Mr. D. A. Stewart (L) in his seat for Lisgar and dismissing the petition of Mr. R. L. Richardson.

Nov. 11.—Mr. F. W. Harcourt is appointed Official Guardian of the Province of Ontario in succession to Dr. John Hoskin, K.C., resigned.

" 17.—The Right Hon. Sir Samuel Henry Strong resigns the Chief Justiceship of Canada and is appointed Chief of the Commission to revise and codify the Statutes.

" 17.—The composition of the Commission to revise the Dominion Statutes is announced as being the Right Hon. Sir Henry Strong, Chairman ; E. L. Newcombe, K.C., Deputy Minister of Justice ; A. Power, K.C., of the Department of Justice ; E. R. Cameron, K.C., Registrar of the Supreme Court ; W. E. Roscoe, of Kentville, N.S.; Henry Robertson, of Collingwood, Ont.; Thomas Metcalfe of Winnipeg, and L. P. Sirois, of Quebec. The Secretaries are Charles Murphy, of Ottawa, and Horace St. Louis, of Montreal.

" 17.—The Hon. Sir Henri Elzear Taschereau, Justice of the Supreme Court of Canada, is appointed Chief Justice of Canada.

" 17.—The Hon. John Douglas Armour, Chief Justice of Ontario, is appointed to the Supreme Court of Canada.

" 17.—Mr. Justice Charles Moss, of the Ontario Court of Appeal, is appointed Chief Justice of the High Court of Ontario.

" 17.—Dr. John James Maclaren, K.C., of Toronto, is appointed to the Ontario Court of Appeal.

" 26.—It is announced that Senator Pascal Poirier, of New Brunswick, has been made a member of the French Legion of Honour.

Dec. 10.—Mr. Philip Holt, K.C., of Goderich, is appointed Junior Judge of the County of Huron.

" 11.—The Hon. W. S. Fielding, M.P., Minister of Finance, is banqueted at Halifax.

" 17.—The appointment of Mr. S. J. Jackson, ex-M.P.P. and formerly Speaker of the Manitoba Legislature, as Inspector of Indian Agencies in the Winnipeg District is announced.

Dec. 17.—The ladies of Western Assiniboia present an Address and a gold watch to Mrs. N. F. Davin upon the occasion of her departure to live in Ottawa.

   "   22.—Sir William Mulock, Postmaster-General, is banqueted by the citizens of Meaford, Ont.

   "   22.—The annual banquet of the Dominion Commercial Travellers' Association at Montreal is addressed by the Hon. Messrs. Fitzpatrick, Fisher and Paterson, Mr. R. L. Borden and Hon. J. Israel Tarte.

   "   22.—Mr. Joseph Brunet, (L) M. P. for the St. James' Division of Montreal, is unseated by the Court and declared to be guilty of corrupt practices and therefore disqualified for seven years.

DOMINION BYE-ELECTIONS DURING 1902.

Jan. 8.—Dr. Henri S. Beland (L) is elected to the Commons from Beauce, Que., by acclamation.

   "   15.—Mr. E. Guss Porter (C) is elected to the Commons from West Hastings, Ont., by 501 majority, in succession to Mr. Harry Corby (C) resigned, defeating Mr. J. G. Frost (L).

   "   15.—Mr. Robert Beith (L) is elected to the Commons from West Durham, Ont., by 12 majority over Mr. C. J. Thornton (C) the former member.

   "   15.—Mr. O. Carbonneau (L) is elected to the Commons from L'Islet, Que., by a majority of 21 over Mr. J. E. Caron (Ind. L).

   "   15.—Mr. Melzar Avery (C) is elected to the Commons from Addington, Ont., by 384 majority in succession to the late J. W. Bell (C) and defeating Mr. F. S. Wartman (L).

   "   15.—Alderman Joseph Brunet (L) is elected to the Commons from St. James' Division, Montreal, by 647 majority over Mr. J. G. H. Bergeron (C).

   "   15.—Mr. Donald Farquharson (L) is elected to the Commons from West Queen's, P.E.I., by 475 majority over Mr. A. A. McLean, K.C., and in succession to Sir L. H. Davies.

   "   15.—Mr. Archibald Campbell (L) is elected to the Commons from West York, Ont., by a majority of 111 over Mr. T. F. Wallace.

   "   15.—The Hon. William Harty (L) is elected to the Commons from Kingston, Ont., by a majority of 752 over Mr. J. H. Metcalfe (C).

   "   15.—Mr. J. E. Emile Leonard (C) is elected to the Commons from Laval, Que., by 8 majority over Mr. C. A. Wilson (L).

   "   28.—Mr. George Riley (L) is elected to the Commons from Victoria, B.C., by 419 majority over Mr. F. S. Barnard (C) and in succession to Lieut.-Col. the Hon. E. G. Prior (C).

   "   29.—The Hon. James Sutherland is re-elected member of Parliament for North Oxford, Ont., by acclamation, upon his appointment as Minister of Marine and Fisheries.

   "   29.—Mr. William Power (L) is elected to the Commons in Quebec West by acclamation and in succession to the late Hon. R. R. Dobell.

Feb. 18.—Mr. D. A Stewart (L) elected to the Commons from Lisgar, Manitoba, by 1,016 majority over Mr. R. L. Richardson (Ind.). Mr. J. M. Toombs (C) obtained 1,646 votes.

   "   29.—The Hon. H. G. Carroll (L) is elected to the Commons in Kamouraska, Que., by acclamation, upon appointment as Solicitor-General.

Mar. 26.—Mr. Geo. H. Loy (L) is elected to the Commons from Beauharnois, Que., by 159 majority over Mr. J. G. H. Bergeron (C).

Dec. 2.—Mr. James H. Ross (L) is elected to the Commons from Yukon Territory by a majority of 892 over Mr. Joseph A. Clarke (Ind).

Dec. 3.—Mr. Thomas Christie (L) is elected to the Commons from Argenteuill, Que., by a majority of 191 over Mr. George H. Perley (L) and in succession to the late Dr. Christie (L).

"   3.—Mr. Bowman B. Law (L) is elected to the Commons from Yarmouth, N.S., by a majority of 868 over Mr. Thomas E. Corning (C).

"   9.—The Hon. Raymond Préfontaine, upon appointment as Minister of Marine and Fisheries, is re-elected to the Commons in Maisonneuve by 1,860 majority over Mr. Alfred Labelle (C).

II. RELATIONS WITH THE EMPIRE

The growing closeness of Imperial ties and the importance of Mr. Chamberlain's position in the complex sentiment and system of the Empire made the retirement of Lord Salisbury in July, 1902, an event of great interest to Canada. The comments of the press were many and varied in detail but one underlying idea was almost universal. It seemed to be felt that in the retiring Prime Minister at the seat of Empire, there was a man who embodied in himself the best traditions of British honour, the most careful statecraft of recent times, and the most absolute devotion to duty. He was a statesman whom the most distant peoples of a "far-flung" realm appeared to trust. His successor, the Rt. Hon. Arthur James Balfour, did not possess for Canadians the same striking personality and there were a number of newspapers which expressed a strong belief in the claims of Mr. Chamberlain to the post and voiced his great popularity in Canada. Mr. Balfour was called upon by the King to form a new Government on July 12th and on August 9th its construction was finally announced as complete. The chief changes, besides that of Prime Minister, were caused by the retirement of Sir Michael Hicks-Beach, the Earl of Cadogan, Lord James of Hereford, Sir John Gorst, Mr. Jesse Collings and the Earl of Raglan. The new Cabinet was as follows:

[margin note: Changes in Imperial Administration]

Premier, First Lord of the Treasury
and Lord Privy Seal .... Rt. Hon. A. J. Balfour.
Lord High Chancellor .... Earl of Halsbury.
Lord President of the Council .... Duke of Devonshire.
Secretary of State for Home Affairs .... Rt. Hon. A. Akers-Douglas.
Secretary of State for the Colonies ... Rt. Hon. J. Chamberlain.
Secretary of State for Foreign Affairs .. Marquess of Lansdowne.
Secretary of State for War .... Rt. Hon. St. John Brodrick.
Secretary of State for India .... Lord George Hamilton.
First Lord of the Admiralty .... Earl of Selborne.
Chancellor of the Exchequer .... Rt. Hon. C. T. Ritchie.
Lord Chancellor of Ireland .... Lord Ashbourne.
Chief Secretary for Ireland .... Rt. Hon. George Wyndham.
Secretary for Scotland .... Lord Balfour of Burleigh.
President of the Board of Trade ...... Rt. Hon. G. W. Balfour.
President of the Local Government
Board .... Rt. Hon. W. H. Long.
President of the Board of Agriculture .. Rt. Hon. R. W. Hanbury.
President of the Board of Education .. Marquess of Londonderry.
Postmaster-General .... Rt. Hon. Austen Chamberlain.

Of the officers outside the Cabinet the most important appointments were those of the Earl of Dudley as Lord-Lieutenant of Ireland, and of Lord Cranborne as Under-Secretary of State for Foreign Affairs, with the Earl of Onslow for Colonial Affairs. In Great Britain approval of Mr. Balfour as Premier was very wide-spread amongst Conservatives and Unionists and even with members of the other party. The *Times* declared on July 18th, with much truth, that "rarely has any statesman entered upon the labours and the responsibilities of the Premiership in the enjoyment of a popularity so universal amongst all parties in the State." In this connection Mr. Donald MacMaster, K.C., of Montreal told the *Gazette* on December 19th that, while in England recently, he had found Mr. Balfour widely accepted as "a strong and safe Prime Minister"—not even overshadowed by the personality of the Colonial Secretary, whom he himself considered " the ablest debater who had ever sat in the House of Commons at Westminster." In this general connection should be quoted the tribute paid to Mr. Chamberlain by the new Premier in his first public speech after the change of Government. At Fulham, on July 19th, he referred to Lord Salisbury's satisfaction in leaving Foreign affairs in such a universally peaceful condition, and then dealt with the still more gratifying Colonial relationships of the time as owing much indeed to the personality and policy of Mr. Chamberlain.

It is no disparagement to the many distinguished statesmen who have preceded him in the Colonial Office to say that he has breathed into the Office something of a new spirit, something of a new inspiration, and that not in this country only, not in this country chiefly, but in every Colony throughout our vast and scattered Empire, that centre of Colonial administration in Downing-street is looked at with utterly different eyes from what it was when I first entered political life and for many a long year afterward. That great change is, as I have said, more due to the policy and the personality of the great statesman who rules over that Office than to any other single cause.

There were some appointments or changes in the administrative system of the Empire during the year which might be considered of interest to Canadians. Sir Andrew R. Scoble, Sir John W. Bonser and Sir Arthur Wilson—all distinguished servants of the Crown in India—were appointed members of the Judicial Committee of the Privy Council. A High Court of Justice for the Transvaal was constituted, with Sir James Rose-Innes, K.C., as Chief Justice and Mr. Justice Solomon of Cape Colony, Sir William Smith of Natal, and Mr. J. W. Wessels as his colleagues. Lord Tennyson, on November 26th, was appointed Governor-General of Australia and Vice-Admiral Sir Harry H. Rawson Governor of New South Wales, on January 29th preceding. On June 5th Mr. W. H. Irvine became Premier of Victoria, Australia, and on July 1st Mr. W. H. James, Premier of Western Australia. Two appointments of direct interest to Canada were those of Vice-Admiral Sir Archibald L. Douglas to the command of the North American Squadron early in the year, and Major-General Sir Charles Parsons to that of His Majesty's regular forces in British America. Late in the year there was a rumour that Lord Milner might succeed the Earl of Minto as Governor-General, and what might be termed the Radical press of the Dominion at once protested, on the ground of the very different conditions underlying administration in Canada and in regions like Egypt or South Africa.

7

No event touching Canadian interests or affecting the relations of Canada with the Empire attracted more attention or affected **The Illness of the King** public sentiment more closely than the dramatic and tragic illness of King Edward on the verge of his Coronation. Lengthy despatches in the papers, editorials of sympathetic strain, speeches and sermons and public expressions of sorrow, telegrams and resolutions of loyalty and sympathy from all sorts of institutions and societies and public bodies, marked every stage of His Majesty's sickness—from the time when he was compelled to give way to its influence on June 24th until it was announced on July 5th that he was out of danger. Thereafter, increasing expressions of hope for the postponed Coronation and of gratification at the continued progress toward recovery of the Royal patient marked public opinion throughout Canada. As there were many and varied and contradictory reports of the origin of this historic illness an authoritative statement from the *Lancet* of June 27th may be given here.

On Friday, June 13th, the King was stated to have gone through a particularly arduous day and early in the following morning was attended by Sir Francis Laking, who found him suffering from considerable abdominal discomfort. In the afternoon he felt better and went to Aldershot to fulfil a programme of reviewing troops, etc. There he attended a brilliant tattoo in the evening amid weather conditions which were uncomfortably cold and wet. A distinct revival of the trouble occurred in the early morning following, accompanied by severe pain, and Sir F. Laking at once telegraphed Sir Thomas Barlow. On Sunday, June 15th, the Royal patient had a chilly fit, but on Monday returned to Windsor and bore the journey well. Two days later he was seen by Sir Frederick Treves, who found symptoms of perityphlitis. These, however, gradually disappeared, and on Saturday, the 21st, the King was believed to be on the road to rapid recovery and to be capable of going through with the Coronation ceremonies. Hence the reassuring public statements of Sir Francis Knollys and the *Times*. "Sunday was uneventful. On Monday the King travelled from Windsor to London. Next day the necessity for an operation became clear."

The *Lancet* gave no reason for this sudden change in condition, and it was probably the burden of thought regarding a complicated maze of preparations, combined with the strain of an exciting drive through the cheering London populace, which acted upon a system enfeebled by the first attack, and not yet entirely free from pain— although under normal conditions on the way to recovery. "At ten o'clock Tuesday morning (24th) the urgency of an operation was explained to His Majesty. Recognizing that his ardent hope that the Coronation arrangements might not be upset must be disappointed, he cheerfully resigned himself to the inevitable. Before the actual decision upon an operation was arrived at Sir Frederick Treves took the advice of two other sergeant-surgeons to the King, Lord Lister and Sir Thomas Smith. They, as well as Sir Thomas

Barlow and Sir Francis Laking, came to the unanimous conclusion that no course but an operation was possible in all the circumstances. To delay would, in fact, be to allow His Majesty to risk his life."

Following the operation the course of the disease seems to have been steadily towards recovery, and without serious complications of any kind. But in the press and the public mind there were many mutations of hope and fear, varied reports and rumors, until, on June 28th, it was announced by the physicians that immediate danger had passed. On July 2nd it was stated that the wound had commenced to heal, and on the 13th His Majesty was taken to his yacht for a prolonged and quiet cruise off Cowes. Such are the barest details of an event which carried the feelings of a great and wide-spread people through varied phases of shock and sorrow and sympathy.

To a close observer it would almost seem as if the King had received in 1902 a couple of Coronations—one through illness in the hearts of an anxious people, the other through forms of stately splendour in Westminster Abbey.

His Majesty's Coronation

Before the tragic incident of June, Canadian papers had teemed with pen pictures of the Sovereign, with appreciation of the greatness of the realm over which he had come to rule, with hope for a future worthy of the Imperial trappings of his Coronation celebration. Upon this subject the Toronto *Globe* of June 21st contained an exceptionally eloquent editorial. Addresses of loyal congratulation poured into the authorities for transmission to the Colonial Office, and Legislatures, cities, public organizations and institutions, expressed their feelings of Imperial pride and Canadian patriotism. That of Montreal, dated June, 1902, and signed by Mayor Cochrane and City Clerk L. O. David was of interest as representing two races and speaking of the British Empire as exhibiting "a striking example of authority respected and liberty obeyed, of a wise monarchy that shares all the advantages of a reasonable democracy."

Then came the postponement of the Coronation and a sudden change from the public enthusiasm of celebration to the universal feeling of anxiety and sympathy. Time passed on, the King recovered, and the Coronation took place amidst scenes of subdued splendour and with varied incidents of Imperial interest. The celebrations of the day in Canada were marked and general though not as much so as the first preparations would have made possible. All the large centres showed their loyal pleasure in some way or another and perhaps the most significant was to be found in the very general attendance at special religious services of thanksgiving. On August 7th, the day before the great event, His Majesty issued the following Address:

To My People,—On the eve of my Coronation, an event which I look upon as one of the most solemn and most important in my life, I am anxious to express to my people at home and in the Colonies and India, my heartfelt appreciation of the deep sympathy they have manifested towards me during the time my life was in such imminent danger. The postponement of the ceremony, owing to my illness, caused, I fear, much inconvenience and trouble to all those who intended to celebrate it, but their disappointment was borne by them with admirable patience and temper. The prayers of my people for my recovery were heard, and I now offer up my deepest gratitude to Divine Providence for having preserved my life and given me strength to fulfil the important duties which devolve upon me as Sovereign of this great Empire.

Amongst those present at the historic function, from Canada, were Lord Minto, the Governor-General, Sir Wilfrid and Lady Laurier—the former wearing a robe of blue velvet over his Privy Council uniform—Mr. W. S. and Miss Fielding, Sir W. Mulock, Sir Frederick Borden, Mr. and Mrs. William Paterson, Lord Strathcona and Lord Mount Stephen, Lady Macdonald of Earnscliffe, the various Provincial Premiers, and Sir Charles and Lady Tupper. A description of the Coronation itself would be apart from the scope of this work but a few words from Canadian papers as to its significance may be added here. The Vancouver *World* of August 9th described the King as now setting forth upon his journey into history as "no mere puppet or name, but by the free consent and assurance of his people by all the seven seas, the archetype of their greatness and destiny." "Under him," said the Edmonton *Post* of the same date, "monarchical institutions will be preserved and strengthened." The King now "reigns in the hearts and affections of his people," declared the Kingston *Whig*. Let the words of *Le Journal* of Montreal, on August 8th, conclude these references:

The severe illness from which he suffered furnished the King an opportunity to appreciate the devotion of his people to his person and the universal acclamation that greeted his recovery added more lustre to his Crown than the homage of courtiers. As they shared the grief his Catholic subjects will also take their large share in the rejoicings of this date and the chanting of the *Te Deum* in the churches of French Canada will make the gratitude known to one and all.

During the greater part of the year the subject most universally discussed in Canada was that of the Coronation, with its accompaniments of elaborate preparation, world-wide expectancy, tragical postponement, and ultimate realization. Bound up with it also were the visits of Canadian Premiers and leaders to the Motherland; the Conferences held there upon many important subjects; the hospitalities tendered to Canadians upon a far-reaching and splendid scale. The Royal invitation, specially extended to the Premier of Canada, made him the guest of the British nation during a specified period, with headquarters at the Hotel Cecil in company with the Premiers of Australia, New Zealand, Cape Colony, Natal and Newfoundland, and certain appointed representatives of the Crown Colonies and the Indian Empire. Various references were made in the Canadian House of Commons to Sir Wilfrid Laurier's acceptance of this invitation and following the announcement of that fact at the opening

Canada and the Coronation

The Hon. Sir William Mulock, K.C.M.G., M.A., K.C., M.P.
Canadian Postmaster-General and Minister of Labour.

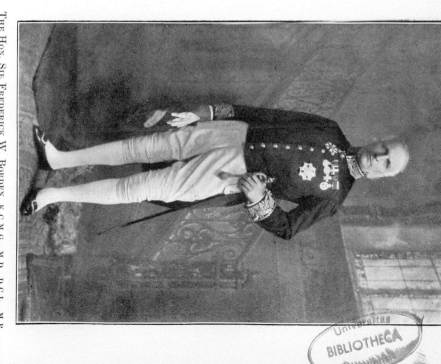

The Hon. Sir Frederick W. Borden, K.C.M.G., M.D., D.C.L., M.P.
Canadian Minister of Militia and Defence.

of Parliament. Speaking on February 14th, the Premier dealt with existing conditions in this connection :

We in Canada live under monarchical conditions, and we are satisfied with our lot. I remember a time when I was much younger than I am to-day, when it was a subject of discussion, rather more academical than practical, whether monarchical government or republican government was the preferable. All such discussions have become obsolete ; in fact, they have disappeared ; and the reason is that we have learned in the last century that there may be as much liberty under a monarchy as under a republic, and that there can sometimes be as much tyranny under a pure democracy as under a despotism. We, in Canada, have the blessing of living under British monarchical institutions, and we appreciate them to the full.

The Premiers of all the Provinces of Canada were also invited to be present at the Coronation, though not as guests at the expense of the nation, and in June the Hon. G. W. Ross, Prime Minister of Ontario; the Hon. G. H. Murray, of Nova Scotia; the Hon. L. J. Tweedie, of New Brunswick; the Hon. Arthur Peters, of Prince Edward Island ; the Hon. R. P. Roblin, of Manitoba; the Hon. F. W. G. Haultain, of the Territories ; and the Hon. James Dunsmuir, of British Columbia ; crossed the Atlantic for this purpose. The Hon. Mr. Parent, of Quebec, declined the Royal invitation, and was represented by Mr. H. T. Duffy, Provincial Treasurer. In Australia, the State Premiers disliked the idea of not being upon an equality with the Commonwealth Prime Minister, and remained at home.

Amongst the Royal invitations issued for the event the Knights Grand Cross of St. Michael and St. George were included and in this category Lord Minto, Lord Strathcona, Sir Charles Tupper, Sir Wilfrid Laurier, Sir Richard Cartwright and Sir Oliver Mowat found a place—although the last two were unable to accept. For the visiting Premiers and Colonial visitors of importance an immense series of entertainments were arranged—partly by the British Empire League, partly as official hospitalities, partly by municipal and personal initiative. The postponement of the Coronation naturally interfered with some of them but as it was the King's express wish that it should not do so, his desire was in the main realized.

These events included Luncheons by the Lord Mayor of Leeds and the Lord Provost of Edinburgh ; a Ball at the Scottish capital and a Banquet by the Lord Provost of Glasgow ; a Banquet and Reception by the Lord Mayor of Manchester ; a Luncheon by the Lord Mayor of Liverpool, and a Banquet by the Chamber of Commerce ; a Reception by the Mayor of Stafford and a visit to the Earl of Harrowby at Sandon Hall ; a Royal Garden party at Windsor and a Reception by Lord and Lady Lansdowne ; a visit to Mr. W. H. Grenfell, M.P., at Taplow Court and a Reception by Mr. and Mrs. Beerbohm Tree at Her Majesty's and by Sir Henry Irving at the Lyceum ; a Luncheon by Mr. Wilfrid and Lady Anne Blunt ; a Ball by the British Empire League and the Empire Coronation Banquet with Mr. Chamberlain as Chairman ; Dinners by the

Prince and Princess of Wales, Mr. and Mrs. Chamberlain, Sir Gilbert Parker, M.P., and Mr. R. A. Yerburgh, M.P., President of the Navy League; a Banquet by the National Liberal Club and a Reception by Lord and Lady Strathcona.

This is not a complete list but it sufficiently illustrates the almost boundless hospitality of the occasion. Sir Wilfrid Laurier, as the chief Canadian representative, had a veritable multitude of engagements and was only able to attend a proportion of them but the other Dominion Ministers in England and the Provincial Premiers assisted him in this respect. While the Conference of Empire Premiers was proceeding the Premiers of the Canadian Provinces also met together upon several occasions and discussed matters of local importance such as the Fishery claims upon the Dominion Government and the desire for better financial terms. The conclusion of these informal discussions was, no doubt, made apparent at the ensuing Conference at Quebec.

Meantime, Canada had been very prominent in the events of the time—partly because of the political discussions, partly because of its military Contingent and partly through the Canadian Arch of wheat which had been erected in Whitehall, opposite the Horse-Guards. It was placed at one of the best points along the proposed route of the Royal procession and was under the auspices of the Canadian Minister of the Interior and the High Commissioner in London. Emblematic of Canadian agricultural resources it was over 50 feet high and bore the words "Canada: the future granary of the Empire," emblazoned across the front. Millions of people saw it, other millions heard of it, and the British press found it a text for innumerable articles upon the Dominion and its resources.

A not un-interesting incident of the Coronation was the King's Honour List. It was lengthy and representative of every interest in the United Kingdom and the Empire. Canada was complimented by its Governor-General, the Earl of Minto, G.C.M.G., being called to the Privy Council; by its most representative author in the Motherland, Mr. Gilbert Parker, D.C.L., M.P., being knighted; by the dignity of K.C.M.G. bestowed upon the Hon. William Mulock, K.C., M.P., Postmaster-General, the Hon. Frederick William Borden, M.D., M.P., Minister of Militia and Defence and the Hon. Daniel Hunter McMillan, Lieut.-Governor of Manitoba; by the knighthood given to the Hon. Henri Elzear Taschereau, Judge, and soon to be Chief Justice, of its Supreme Court and to the Hon. Robert Boak, M.L.C., for 20 years the greatly respected President of the Legislative Council of Nova Scotia; and by the honour of C.M.G. granted to Lieut.-Colonel Frederick White, Comptroller of the North-West Mounted Police, Lieut.-Colonel Arthur Percy Sherwood, Commissioner of Police in Canada, and Mr. Robert Harris, President of the Royal Canadian Academy. The inevitable omissions from such a list caused some slight criticism and the claims of Messrs. Fielding, Blair and Tarte were mentioned by some of the papers. But there

were few expressions of anything except approval as to the honours
actually conferred and it was said in certain quarters that Mr. Fielding had declined a title.

In March, 1902, it was announced that the King desired an
escort of troops at the Coronation which should be representative
of all parts of the Empire and the intimation was
accepted by Canada as well as other British countries.
The Toronto *Globe* of April 1st was not quite sure as
to the advisability of a military display on such
occasions. "The ideal of the Empire after all, is
peace, and particularly is this the ideal of the Colonies." Yet this
might be a time when a display of force would be potent for
peace and, in any case, it would be ungracious to decline. Shortly
afterwards it was announced that Lieut.-Colonel H. M. Pellatt of
Toronto would command the Infantry Contingent with Lieut.-
Colonel A. T. Thompson, M.P., as second. A luncheon was given
at Ottawa on April 15th by the Hon. Mr. Mulock in their honour
and in Toronto on May 28th Colonel Pellatt was dined by the
officers of his Regiment, the Queen's Own Rifles. He stated
upon this occasion that he intended to take the bugle band of the
Regiment to England (it was understood at his own expense) in
order to promote interest in Canada by giving the London people
some specially good music.

The strength of the whole force as finally announced on June
13th was 580 officers and men of whom it was stated that about
200 had served in South Africa. In the end there were 657 in the
Contingent. Lieut.-Colonel R. E. W. Turner, V.C., D.S.O., com-
manded the Cavalry, and the other officers included Majors H. A.
Panet, J. A. Northup, W. Forrester, H. M. Davison, G. W. Stephens,
Jr., and H. J. Mackie; Surgeon-Majors E. Fiset and M. C. Curry;
Captains R. M. Courtney, P. P. H. Ramsay, E. Laliberte, F. A.
Howard, C. K. Fraser, E. A. Dunlop and E. W. B. Morrison;
Lieutenants H. R. Emmerson, A. W. Mackenzie and E. Lemieux;
and Inspector F. L. Cartwright. The troops assembled at Levis,
near Quebec, and were reviewed on June 6th by Major-General
O'Grady-Haly, when a silk flag was presented to them by Mrs. S.
Nordheimer, Mrs. J. I. Davidson and other Toronto ladies on
behalf of the Daughters of the Empire. The Contingent sailed
on June 7th in the *Parisian*, on board of which were also the
Governor-General, Sir Robert Bond of Newfoundland, Premiers
Tweedie, Murray and Peters, Dr. G. R. Parkin and Principal
Peterson of McGill.

The troops were welcomed in Liverpool on June 16th and on
the following day were established at the Alexandra Palace, near
London, with some 2,000 other soldiers from all parts of the world.
The Colonial forces were under the supreme command of H.R.H.
the Duke of Connaught and with him were associated Major-
Generals T. A. Cook, W. H. MacKinnon and Sir Henry Trotter.
The chief staff officers were Lieut.-Colonels A. P. Penton of New

The
Coronation
Contingent
from Canada

Zealand and J. Lyons Biggar of Canada. Various steps were taken to entertain the military visitors and a Committee headed by the Duke of Abercorn and Earl Grey worked hard in this connection. Thousands of free seats were arranged at the theatres, special performances were given at some of them and expeditions were planned and carried out to Woolwich Arsenal, Windsor Castle and other places of interest. A great military tattoo was arranged for the Colonial troops on June 21st but failed somewhat owing to the immense crowds who came to share in the welcome. As a result of this a small charge for admission to the grounds was inaugurated and caused, incidentally, a silly cable canard that Canadian soldiers were being made a "circus attraction" in London.

On June 26th the Hon. R. P. Roblin entertained the men from his Province at a banquet. Dominion Day saw a memorable review of the Colonial troops by the Prince of Wales and Queen Alexandra, accompanied by a number of Royal guests and ladies, by F. M. Earl Roberts, and with one of the most brilliant cavalcades which even London had ever seen. It was described by the correspondent of the Winnipeg *Free Press* as being the most brilliant scene of this remarkable season. Colonel Pellatt commanded the Canadian troops on parade. The Canadian Contingent, in connection with the postponed Coronation, struck camp at Alexandra Palace on July 3rd in order to return home and arrived in the afternoon at Liverpool over 600 strong. There they were entertained by the Lord Mayor at luncheon and along their route to the *Tunisian* were accorded most enthusiastic cheering from large crowds of spectators. The ship reached Quebec on July 12th and Colonel Pellatt there issued an order of thanks for the support given him, appreciation of the discipline and conduct of the soldiers and warmest wishes for future and individual success.

A regrettable feature of this expedition to be guests of the Motherland at a great Imperial function occurred in the complaints made in certain papers and by a few special correspondents as to incidents of alleged ill-treatment. Capt. E. W. B. Morrison complained in the Ottawa *Citizen* of the junior British officers, and the Toronto *Telegram* had special cables denouncing the War Office for "muddling" things, alleging trouble between Canadian representatives and the authorities regarding the place of the troops in the expected Royal procession, and similar charges. In the final analysis the main trouble seemed to lie in a surprising development of wet weather, which caused some discomfort for a time.

Lieut-Colonel James Mason, of Toronto, published an effective reply to these allegations in a number of leading Canadian papers, and Colonel Pellatt, in an interview on July 14th, emphasized the miserable character of the weather, expressed regret that the Canadian Contingent was the only one which did not stay for the deferred Coronation, and declared that the sole ground for complaint

LIEUT.-COLONEL H. M. PELLATT
Commanding the Infantry and the Contingent.

LIEUT.-COLONEL R. E. W. TURNER, V.C., D.S.O.
Commanding the Cavalry and the Royal Escort.

was in the distance of the camp from the city.   Colonel Thompson was more emphatic, and told the *Mail and Empire* on the following day that this "silly gossip" gave the officers much pain "after England had done her very best for us in the way of hospitality." The only drawbacks were the weather, the distance from London, and the King's illness, none of which could be helped.   He totally denied the stories of friction and other incidents and defended the British officers and the authorities.

On July 18th Sir Frederick Borden telegraphed to the Militia Department for an officer and thirteen mounted men to form part of the Colonial escort of the King at the deferred event.   Lieut.- Colonel Turner, as commander of the mounted part of the first Contingent, was selected for the command in this case.   These troops took part in succeeding functions, including the Coronation procession and the Review by the King on August 12th.   Four days later Lieut.-Colonel Lyons Biggar, who had been acting as staff officer for all the Colonial troops, issued a letter of earnest thanks to those who had contributed in varied ways to their enter- tainment and, under date of September 23rd, Mr. Chamberlain wrote to Lord Minto, expressing the thanks of His Majesty's Gov- ernment for the sending of the original Contingent, appreciation of its presence in the country, regret at its inability to stay until August 8th, and the hope that its members had borne away a pleasant recollection of their visit.

In a communication addressed to the Governor-General of Canada, on December 27th, 1901, Mr. Chamberlain conveyed a

Initiation and Scope of the Coronation Conference formal intimation of the Coronation having been fixed for June 26th following, and an expression of the King's desire that the Premier of Canada should be present and be a guest of the Government, together with his wife, for a fortnight from the time of arrival.

On January 23rd, 1902, the Colonial Secretary cabled Lord Minto as follows : "It is proposed by His Majesty's Government to take advantage of the presence of the Premiers at the Coronation to discuss with them the questions of political relations between the Mother Country and the Colonies, Imperial defence, commercial relations of the Empire, and other matters of general interest. Should your Ministers desire to submit definite proposals or resolu- tions on any of the above questions, or should they wish to suggest any further subject for discussion, I should be glad to be informed of the purport by cable, in order that the other Governments can be communicated with."   The period of three weeks after the Corona- tion was suggested as that during which the Premiers should remain as His Majesty's guests.   Under date of February 3rd, Lord Minto replied, accepting the invitation for Sir Wilfrid and Lady Laurier, and dealing with matters of policy as follows :

Referring to the several questions mentioned in your despatch of 23rd January, the only one which, in the opinion of my Ministers, gives promise of useful discussion, is that of the commercial relations between the various sections of the Empire. The political relations now existing between the Mother Country and the great self-governing Colonies, and particularly Canada, are regarded by my Ministers as entirely satisfactory, with the exception of a few minor details ; and they do not anticipate that in the varying conditions of the Colonies there can be any scheme of defence applicable to all. In the opinion of my Ministers there is thus but a limited range of subjects upon which the contemplated Conference can be productive of useful action. Nevertheless my Ministers recognize the desirability of taking advantage of every opportunity for the discussion, by the public men of the Mother Country and the Colonies, of questions of Imperial interest, and Canada's representative will be prepared to give respectful consideration to any proposals that may be submitted by His Majesty's Government or by the representatives of other Colonies.

This important correspondence was laid before the Canadian House of Commons on March 11th. Meanwhile, earlier in the year, Sir Wilfrid Laurier had communicated with Mr. Edmund Barton, the Premier of Australia, and suggested that the representatives of the Commonwealth and the Dominion at the Conference might usefully discuss the following subjects : (1) Trade relations between the two countries; (2) a fast mail service; (3) a better steamer service between Vancouver and Australia and the establishment of a line from Australia to a Canadian port on the Atlantic *via* South Africa; (4) the effect on the Pacific Cable scheme of any Australian concessions to the Eastern Extension Company. On February 13th the Governor-General stated in his speech at the opening of Parliament that "the Governments of Australia and New Zealand have accepted the invitation of my Government to attend a Conference in London in June for the consideration of trade, transportation, cable, and other matters of Intercolonial concern, and it is hoped that the meeting will lead to the extension of Canadian trade with those important portions of His Majesty's dominions." Finally, a couple of months later, the following official statement of the subjects to be discussed at the Conference was issued by the Colonial Office:

Suggested by the Colonial Office : (1) Political relations between the Mother Country and the Colonies ; (2) Imperial defence ; (3) Commercial relations within the Empire ; (4) Relations of Australia and New Zealand to the islands of the Pacific ; (5) Other matters of general interest.

Suggested by Cape Colony and Natal : Naturalization laws.

Suggested by New Zealand : (1) Preferential Colonial tariffs on British manufactures, carried on British ships, to the Colonies ; (2) Reduction of duties on Colonial produce now taxable ; (3) Imperial Army reserve for service outside of the Colonies in case of emergency ; (4) Increase of Australian Auxiliary Squadron on the lines of the existing arrangements ; (5) Australian, New Zealand and Canadian mail services ; (6) Future government of South Africa, together with the admission of professional Colonials to practice there ; (7) Periodical Colonial Conferences.

Suggested by the Commonwealth : (1) Army and navy supply contracts ; (2) Ocean cables and purchase thereof ; (3) Imperial Court of Appeal ; (4) Mutual protection of patents ; (5) Loss of most favoured nation treatment if preference is given to British manufactures ; (6) Imperial stamp charge on Colonial bonds.

Mr. R. L. Borden, Leader of the Conservative Opposition, brought this subject up in the House of Commons on May 12th.

The Conference Discussed in Parliament He read the correspondence between Mr. Chamberlain and Lord Minto; deprecated as discourteous the action of the Government in declining to discuss Imperial defence; declared that of the three possible futures before the country—independence, annexation or present conditions—he preferred the last and believed that it would be the permanent one; and pointed to advantages which Canada had long received from its protection by the British naval and military forces. He then, at considerable length, discussed the existing Preferential tariff and the various proposals for Preferential trade in its wider sense; quoted the Premier's statement in the Session of 1901 that Preferential trade throughout the Empire could not be discussed without premising the abolition of the Protective tariff in Canada; and argued from this and other utterances that the Conference could have no useful result under present conditions of government in the Dominion. He concluded by asking for an authoritative statement as to the policy of the Government in connection with the coming Conference.

We want to know whether the Government, while retaining for Canada the full control of all her public moneys and her system of defence, is prepared to discuss with the Imperial authorities a system of Imperial defence. We want to know whether the Prime Minister proposes, as he did in 1897, and as the Minister of Agriculture did in 1901, to tell the Government and the people of the Mother Country that Canada desires no preference in the British markets. We want to know whether the Government are yet fully seized of the fact that the British Government have adopted a policy with regard to duties on breadstuffs which the Right Hon. gentleman and his colleagues have repeatedly declared during the last five or six years was absolutely impossible of adoption by the Mother Country in the near future.

In his reply Sir Wilfrid Laurier deprecated the idea of any discourtesy, and pointed out that the subjects referred to would all be discussed apart from his Government's expression of opinion as to the value of such discussion. As to Imperial defence, especially, both he and his colleagues felt that no useful purpose could be served by debating it. "If it be intended simply to discuss what part Canada is prepared to take in her own defence, what share of the burden must fall upon us as being responsible for the safety of the land in which we were born and to which we owe our allegiance, in which all our hopes and affections are centered, certainly we are always prepared to discuss that subject. Nor do I believe that we need any prompting on that subject, or that our attention should be specially called to it." But this was not Imperial defence as now much mooted. "There is a school abroad, there is a school in England and in Canada, a school which is perhaps represented on the floor of this Parliament, which wants to bring Canada into the vortex of militarism which is the curse and the blight of Europe. I am not prepared to endorse any such policy."

Turning to the subject of a Preferential trade arrangement the Premier referred to the Protectionist views of the Opposition and the incompatibility of a further preference to Great Britain, under an arrangement for a return preference, with the high tariff ideas of the Conservative party. He defended the Preferential clause in the existing tariff; stated that he was going to England at the invitation of the Imperial Government to discuss general Imperial relations; and declared that he had the intention of "trying, if possible, to secure preferential treatment for the goods of Canada in the British market."

In the early stages of the discussion regarding the proposed Coronation Conference there were a variety of suggestions made and opinions expressed—apart from the debates in Parliament. In the Demerara *Argosy* of March 1st, Mr. Robert Munro, President of the Canadian Manufacturers' Association, explained the objects of that body and declared that its chief aim was to bring all British countries into closer union. " This we hope to gradually accomplish on a Preferential tariff basis. We have made direct representations to Australia and New Zealand on this subject and they are looking forward with much interest to the discussion to take place between the Premiers of Canada, Australia and New Zealand at the forthcoming Coronation." Speaking at Aberdeen, Scotland, on April 9th, Lord Strathcona and Mount Royal referred to the necessity for united action in the improvement of the army and navy of the Empire, and for the consideration of trade questions without regard to hard and fast ideas of free trade or protection. He mentioned the coming Coronation Conference with gratification, and added: "There will be great disappointment, I am sure, if the result of the Conference does not provide, if not a definite settlement, at any rate for the formation of some understanding on which the policy of the different parts of the King's domains in regard to these matters can be based and carried out to the advantage of the whole English-speaking community."

In the *Daily News*, London, of the same date, Mr. Goldwin Smith had a letter deprecating the value of any such consideration of these subjects. He stated that two-fifths of the population of Canada were French and not British; that nine-tenths of this element was opposed to the aid given in South Africa; that American miners and adventurers and farmers were flocking into the North-West and British Columbia and would ultimately prevail; that the Canadian Provinces were largely separated by barriers of nature from each other, with little interchange of population or trade; and that a "factitious militarism" had been created in Canada by Imperial titles and social allurements. "No Imperial Zollverein can tear Canada away, commercially or industrially, from the Continent of which nature has made her a part." What was the use of Conferences ? "You may struggle against nature and for a time partly thwart her, but in the end she will have her way." On April 10th, at a meeting of the Toronto branch of the British Empire League, Resolutions were passed in favour of making use of the forthcoming Conference in order to obtain "a full expression by the representatives of the Colonies of their views for the promotion of closer relations," and to promote a cheap cable service and fast line of steamers between Canada and Great Britain. Four days later the Victoria branch in British Columbia declared that the Colonial Premiers while attending the Conference should also find opportunity to speak throughout the United Kingdom in favour of an Empire policy of unity. At the meeting of the Executive Committee of the Canadian Manufacturers' Association on May 15th, a number of suggestions were made for consideration by the Conference which may be summarized as follows:

1. The direction of British capital and emigration to the Colonies rather than to Foreign countries.

2. Colonial contribution towards Imperial defence.

3. A preferential tariff for the Empire ; lower duties on British goods at all British ports ; special attention to this point in coming tariff arrangements in South Africa.

4. No more clauses in treaties limiting or hampering relations between the countries of the Empire.

5. A fast Atlantic service and encouragement to shipping in British vessels.

6. An all-British Cable connecting all parts of the Empire.

7. The adoption of decimal currency, the metric system of weights and measures and a universal gauge for defining the thickness of metals.

8. Supplementing the present Consular service by the establishment and recognition of Inter-Colonial commercial Consuls.

9. An Imperial postage system for papers, magazines and parcels as well as letters.

10. Preference in contracts to British subjects wherever possible.

11. An Imperial Commission to visit and report upon the resources of all parts of the Empire.

Meanwhile, at the annual meeting of the British Empire League in Canada, held at Ottawa on February 20th, Lieut.-Colonel George T. Denison, the President, referred at some length to the coming Conference and urged its consideration of a special duty of 5 to 10 per cent. imposed at every port in the British Empire on all Foreign goods—the proceeds to constitute a fund for common defence. A Resolution moved by the Hon. J. Israel Tarte, M.P., and seconded by Mr. B. Russell, M.P., was carried unanimously and expressed "profound satisfaction" at the calling of the Conference and the hope and confidence that its deliberations and results would promote and safeguard British and Colonial interests.

On June 3rd the annual Report of Mr. John C. Gass, Grand Master of the Grand Black Chapter (Orange) of British America, was read at the Niagara Falls meeting and expressed pride in the early advocacy of Imperial Federation by Orangemen and the hope that this coming Conference would consolidate the unity of the Empire. Speaking to the *Mail and Empire,* on June 6th, Premier Tweedie, of New Brunswick, referred to the coming gathering and declared that "it is very difficult to say exactly what will be the result. There is even a question whether closer relations will be of benefit to Canada." On July 1st Sir Charles Tupper spoke clearly upon the subject at the Dominion Day banquet in London : " The Colonial Conference which was now being held was fraught with deep importance to the Empire, and no one took a deeper interest in the result than he did. Statesmen in every part of the Empire desired to draw closer the bonds joining them to the Mother Country, and to make them indissoluble, and the best means of doing that, in his opinion, was the adoption of mutual Preferential trade."

The first meeting of the Colonial, or Coronation Conference, of 1902, was held on June 30th. Mr. Chamberlain delivered his inaugural address and Sir John Anderson of the Colonial **Proceedings** Office acted as permanent Secretary. Sir Wilfrid **of the** Laurier, Premier of Canada, Sir Edmund Barton, **Conference** Premier of Australia, Mr. R. J. Seddon, Premier of New Zealand, Sir Robert Bond, Premier of Newfoundland, Sir Gordon Sprigg, Premier of Cape Colony, and Sir A. H. Hime, Premier of Natal, were present as they were at most of the subsequent meetings. The Colonial Secretary's speech, as eventually made public in the *Proceedings*, was an elaborate review of Imperial conditions. There were, he declared, three avenues of approach to the question of how to confirm that unity "upon which the security and the very existence of the Empire depended"—political relations, some form of commercial union and the problem of defence. As to the first he believed existing difficulties would be overcome by time and by a growing sense of common interest and common dangers. But the demand for closer political union must come from the Colonies. He referred to the celebrated phrase of Sir Wilfrid Laurier : " If you want our aid call us to your Councils." This he answered as follows :

Gentlemen, we do want your aid. We do require your assistance in the administration of the vast Empire which is yours as well as ours. The weary Titan staggers under the too vast orb of its fate. We have borne the burden for many years. We think it is time that our children should assist us to support it and whenever you make the request to us be sure that we shall hasten gladly to call you to our Councils. If you are prepared at any time to take any share, any proportionate share, in the burdens of the Empire, we are prepared to meet you with any proposal for giving to you a corresponding voice in the policy of the Empire.

As to method and form he seemed to favour a Council of the Empire evolving gradually into defined scope and work. Meanwhile, periodical Conferences might be held. Turning to the second subject he frankly declared that " our first object is free trade within the Empire." By this, however, he meant no interference with tariffs imposed for revenue purposes but simply the abolition of the protective incidence through excise duties. But if unable to adopt free interchange "how far," he asked, " can you approach it " ? Upon the question of Imperial defence he pointed out that in the present year the naval and military expenditure of the United Kingdom was at the rate of 29s., 3d. per head, while that of Canada was 2s. and of the other Colonies in proportion.   It was not a fair distribution of the burdens and "now that the Colonies are rich and powerful I think it is inconsistent with their dignity as nations that they should leave the Mother Country to bear the whole, or almost the whole of the expense."   He concluded by pointing to the privileges of Empire and declaring that they also involved obligations.

On July 4th, the second meeting was held and questions of defence considered with Lord Selborne and Mr. St. John Brodrick also in attendance.   The former, as First Lord of the Admiralty, urged that naval action should be taken along combined lines and not as a series of isolated systems.   He pointed out that the total trade of the United Kingdom was £877,450,000 and that of the external Empire £327,500,000—all protected by British expenditure.   The Secretary for War pressed the point of having a special military force organized in each country for Imperial service and this was supported, to some extent, by the representatives of New Zealand, Cape Colony and Natal.   Those of Canada and Australia, however, favoured the local defence system and the Canadian Ministers submitted a Memorandum, giving their reasons for preferring to stay within this limited circle of responsibility.   They wished, however, to do it "in co-operation with the Imperial authorities and under the advice of experienced Imperial officers so far as this is consistent with the principle of local self-government which has proved so great a factor in the promotion of Imperial unity."

Mr. Chamberlain's accident delayed the meetings after this, but on July 18th the Conference once more assembled with the Colonial Secretary in the chair.   Mr. G. W. Balfour, President of the Board of Trade, Sir Robert Giffen, the Earl of Dudley and Messrs. Fielding and Paterson of Canada, were present by invitation.   At this and succeeding meetings various subjects were discussed and different authorities, or Departmental heads, or Colonial statesmen, invited to assist on special occasions.   On July 25th Sir John Forrest of Australia, and Sir Frederick Borden of Canada, joined in the discussion of defence questions with Mr. Brodrick and Lord Selborne.   On August 5th, Messrs. Fielding, Paterson, Borden and Mulock were present, with the Canadian Premier, as were also Mr. Arnold-Forster, M.P., Lord Stanley, M.P., Sir George Murray, of the Post Office, Mr. Brodrick, and others.   The tenth and concluding meeting of the Conference was held on August 11th with all the Premiers present—excepting Sir Gordon Sprigg, who was represented by Mr. T. E. Fuller—and Lord Selborne, Sir John Forrest, Sir Alfred Bateman, Mr. G. W. Balfour, Messrs. Paterson and Fielding, together with Lord Onslow and Sir Montague Ommaney of the Colonial Office, who had been officially present at all meetings.

The practical and direct issue of the Conference was the passage of a number of Resolutions and the making of some specified agreements; the indirect result was a great increase in the **Resolutions of the Conference** knowledge of responsible statesmen at home and in the Colonies as to the requirements of the Empire and as to the lines along which the interests of closer unity or concerted action might in the future be developed. The first Resolution passed was as follows:

That it would be to the advantage of the Empire if Conferences were held, as far as practicable, at intervals not exceeding four years, at which questions of common interest affecting the relations of the Mother Country and His Majesty's Dominions over the Seas could be discussed and considered as between the Secretary of State for the Colonies and the Prime Ministers of the self-governing Colonies. The Secretary of State for the Colonies is requested to arrange for such Conferences after communication with Prime Ministers of the respective Colonies. In case of any emergency arising upon which a special Conference may have been deemed necessary, the next ordinary Conference to be held not sooner than three years thereafter.

Upon the subject of Imperial naval defence, Canada refused to do anything definite. Australia agreed to increase its present contribution to £200,000 a year towards the cost of an improved Australasian Squadron and the establishment of a branch of the Royal Naval Reserve. New Zealand, for the same objects, increased its contribution to £40,000 a year; Cape Colony increased its existing contribution toward the general maintenance of the Navy to £50,000 per annum; Natal agreed to contribute £35,000 per annum to the same service; and Newfoundland agreed to grant £3,000 a year towards the maintenance of a branch of the Royal Naval Reserve of not less than six hundred men, and to give a capital sum of £1,800 for fitting up and preparing a drill ship. All these contributions were promised, of course, subject to the approval of the respective Parliaments. A series of Resolutions in the following terms were also passed:

1. That so far as may be consistent with the confidential negotiation of treaties with Foreign Powers, the views of the Colonies affected should be obtained in order that they may be in a better position to give adhesion to such treaties.

2. That the Prime Ministers of self-governing Colonies suggest that the question of the allotment of the Naval and Military Cadets to the Dominions beyond the Seas be taken into consideration by the Naval and Military Authorities, with a view to increasing the number of commissions to be offered; that consistent with ensuring suitable candidates, as far as practicable, greater facilities than now obtained should be given to enable young Colonists to enter the Navy and the Army.

3. That in all Government contracts, whether in the case of the Colonial or the Imperial Governments, it is desirable that, as far as practicable, the products of the Empire should be preferred to the products of foreign countries. With a view to promoting this result, it is suggested that where such contracts cannot be filled in the country in which the supplies are required, the fullest practicable notice of the requirements and of the conditions of tender should be given both in the Colonies and the United Kingdom, and that this notice should be communicated through official channels as well as through the press.

4. That it is desirable that in view of the great extension of foreign subsidies to shipping, the position of the mail services between different parts of the Empire should be reviewed by the respective Goverments. In all new contracts, provisions should be inserted to prevent excessive freight charges, or any preference in favour of foreigners, and to ensure that such of the steamers as may be suitable shall be at the service of His Majesty's Government in war time as cruisers or transports.

5. That it is desirable that the attention of the Governments of the Colonies and the United Kingdom should be called to the present state of navigation laws in the Empire, and in other countries, and to the advisability of refusing the privileges of coastwise trade, including trade between the Mother Country and its Colonies and Possessions, and between one Colony or Possession and another, to countries in which the corresponding trade is confined to ships of their own nationality ; and also the laws affecting shipping, with a view of seeing whether any other steps should be taken to promote Imperial trade in British vessels.

6. That it is advisable to adopt the metric system of weights and measures for use within the Empire, and the Prime Ministers urge the Governments represented at this Conference to give consideration to the question of its early adoption.

7. That it would tend to the encouragement of inventions if some system for the mutual protection of patents in the various parts of the Empire could be devised. That the Secretary of State be asked to enter into communication with the several Governments in the first instance and invite their suggestions to this end.

8. That it is desirable that in future agreements as to cable communications, a clause should, wherever practicable, be inserted, reserving to the Government or Governments concerned the right of purchasing on equitable terms, and after due notice, all or any of the cables to which the agreements relate.

9. That it is advisable to adopt the principle of cheap postage between the different parts of the British Empire on all newspapers and periodicals published therein, and the Prime Ministers desire to draw the attention of His Majesty's Government to the question of a reduction in the outgoing rate. They consider that each Government should be allowed to determine the amount to which it may reduce such rate, and the time for such reduction going into effect.

10. That in arranging for the administration of the Transvaal and the Orange River Colony it is desirable that provision should be made that duly qualified members of the learned and skilled professions now admitted and hereafter to be admitted to practise in the self-governing Colonies be allowed to practise within the newly acquired territories on condition of reciprocal treatment in the Colonies concerned.

Upon the much discussed subject of improving and helping Imperial trade the Colonies represented at the Conference made certain promises for recommendation to their respective Parliaments. Canada undertook to improve the existing Preference of 33⅓ per cent. by an additional preference on lists of selected articles, given in three different ways—by further reducing duties in favour of the United Kingdom, by raising the duties upon foreign imports, and by imposing duties on certain foreign imports now on the free list. Australia promised an undefined preference. New Zealand pledged a general preference of 10 per cent or an equivalent by lists of selected articles along the lines laid down by Canada. Cape Colony and Natal promised a preference of 25 per cent. or its equivalent on dutiable goods, other than specially rated articles, to be given by increasing the duties on foreign imports. The following general Resolutions were passed in this connection :

8

1. That this Conference recognizes that the principle of Preferential trade between the United Kingdom and His Majesty's Dominions beyond the Seas would stimulate and facilitate mutual commercial intercourse, and would, by promoting the development of the resources and industries of the several parts, strengthen the Empire.

2. That this Conference recognizes that, in the present circumstances of the Colonies, it is not practicable to adopt a general system of free trade as between the Mother Country and the British Dominions beyond the Seas.

3. That with a view, however, to promoting the increase of trade within the Empire, it is desirable that those Colonies which have not already adopted such a policy should, as far as their circumstances permit, give substantial preferential treatment to the products and manufactures of the United Kingdom.

4. That the Prime Ministers of the Colonies respectfully urge on His Majesty's Government the expediency of granting in the United Kingdom preferential treatment to the products and manufactures of the Colonies, either by exemption from or reduction of duties now or hereafter imposed.

5. That the Prime Ministers present at the Conference undertake to submit to their respective Governments at the earliest opportunity the principles of this Resolution, and to request them to take such measures as may be necessary to give effect to it.

The comments upon the result of the Conference by some of Canada's public men were interesting. The Hon. R. P. Roblin told the Winnipeg *Telegram* of August 6th that he was greatly disappointed. "The golden opportunity is, I am afraid, being thrown away. The people of Great Britain are in a particularly generous mood towards us. The greatest of all Colonial Secretaries, Mr. Chamberlain, the most powerful man in Great Britain, is at the helm. The British people have every confidence in him and are prepared to follow his lead. Canada, which ought to, and is looked upon to lead, stands halting and shifting, either without any policy or with such a vacillating and indifferent one that confidence is lost and our representatives seem afraid to act." The Hon. G. W. Ross expressed to the Toronto *Globe* of August 24th his belief that while the Conference might not bear "immediate fruit in every particular in which Canadians are interested" yet it would ultimately, in Mr. Chamberlain's words, "produce considerable results." Mr. Goldwin Smith told the Toronto *News* of November 5th that Sir Wilfrid Laurier had, in this case, accurately diagnosed public opinion in Canada.

Lieut.-Colonel G. T. Denison, in the *Globe* of November 7th, expressed the belief that Canada's representatives had made every effort to procure a Preference in the British market. Upon the other chief issue he agreed with the Premier. "On the question of defence I personally think that, at any rate until we have representation in some Imperial body and a full voice in the management of affairs, it would be inadvisable for Canada to be asked to spend money on defence in any other way than under the direction of our Government, and by the hands of our own officers." Sir William Mulock expressed the following general opinion in the same paper two days later: "All who took part in the Conference were strongly of the opinion that it had served a splendid purpose in having afforded an opportunity for the interchange of views on matters of Imperial concern and of considering the lines on which important advances are to be made in the promotion of closer relations, political, commercial and social, between all parts of the Empire." Principal Peterson of McGill University, Montreal, elaborated different views in the *Star* of November 30th. "The general impression in England is that the Canadian delegates went to the Imperial Conference to put a drag on it and that they succeeded in doing so."

The press of Canada was naturally somewhat influenced in its comments by political feeling. The Conservative papers generally described the Conference as a failure and blamed Sir Wilfrid Laurier entirely for the result. The Toronto *World* and *Mail and Empire*, the Charlottetown *Examiner*, the Quebec *Chronicle* and the Halifax *Herald* presented this view strongly. Canada was declared to have been effaced. Many of the Liberal papers took the opposite line and expressed admiration of Sir Wilfrid Laurier's caution, of his aversion to military responsibilities, of his love for liberty and constitutionalism, of his influence in promoting sound views of Imperial unity. The public were apparently content to let matters take their own way whilst organized activity in favour of a different course to that of the Premier was mainly confined to the work of the Navy League.

There were many expressions of opinion in Great Britain during the year regarding the Conference and in the press, for a time, it was a daily subject of discussion. In pre-siding at the annual banquet of the Royal Colonial Institute on April 30th, Earl Grey expressed his hope that the proceedings would be public and "urged that the Colonies should be allowed a direct voice in the control of Imperial affairs coupled with contributory obligations to the Imperial power." At the annual meeting of the British Empire League on July 7th, the Duke of Devonshire presided and spoke at length upon Imperial topics. It would be attempted, he thought, at the Conference, to keep the questions of defence and commercial and political relations apart. "In my opinion," he proceeded, "it will be found that they are inseparable and that, in the main, they will be governed by what seems to be the first and fundamental question—namely that of Imperial defence." As to commercial issues, he had no doubt that the solution would come eventually from the workings of economic laws. He believed they would present no obstacle to the consummation all must desire—"that of free-trade, or the nearest approach to free-trade, within every portion of the Empire."

Speaking as Chairman of the Empire Coronation Banquet on July 11th, the Earl of Onslow, G.C.M.G., Under-Secretary for the Colonies, declared that the Conference had only one object and that was the drawing closer of the bonds of Empire. "It can be promoted in various ways—by improving our political relations, by greater commercial facilities and by the more equal bearing of the common burden of Imperial defence." He spoke of the English people as confirmed free-traders but admitted that changed commercial conditions now prevailed. He regarded the seas as the pathway of the Empire and the policing of them as a somewhat excessive burden to be borne by the Motherland alone—a cost of $155,000,000 last year as against $1,100,000 contributed by the rest of the British realms. This, he hoped, the Conference would help to remedy. At a function held in London, on August 1st, in honour of Mr. Chamberlain and Lord Kitchener, the Colonial Secretary spoke as follows:

> If we move slowly, we move surely. I for one have absolute confidence in the future. All our children are invited to this great partnership of Empire, and I believe that as they grow—and they are growing quickly—to the full stature of nationhood, as they enter more completely into the glorious privileges of our common heritage, we shall not find them either blind or backward to the necessity of sharing, in an even greater degree, the obligations which Empire entails. I believe that this Conference we are holding will lead to considerable results. I believe that it will mark a considerable advance. If that be so, I think we may look forward with confidence to the future.

In the *Standard* of August 16th Mr. T. E. Fuller, Agent-General for Cape Colony, expressed the belief that the Conference would draw the countries concerned closer together and that the promised naval contributions, though small in extent, were important in principle. On December 11th, Lord Onslow presided at a meeting of the Council of the British Empire League, when a Resolution was passed which stated that: "This Council regards with satisfaction the outcome of the recent Conference as a substantial and practical contribution towards the closer union of the Empire," and congratulated the League itself on having so many of its expressed views accepted by the Empire's representatives on that occasion. In his speech Lord Onslow referred to the proceedings and conclusions of the Conference and declared that, as a whole, while not, perhaps, realizing some sanguine expectations, " it has had the effect of softening down and bringing to a clearer sense of proportion the great subjects which occupy the attention of statesmen in England and in the Colonies." The net result had been that "we have travelled a very long way on the road and have become agreed as to what is best for the future of this great Empire."

In the press discussions, meanwhile, the opinions of the Canadian Premier found considerable space, and Mr. I. N. Ford, the well-known correspondent of the Toronto *Globe* and New York *Tribune* endeavoured to voice these general views from time to time. On July 19th he cabled that Sir Wilfrid Laurier was " striving to find the line of least resistance within the range of existing tariff arrangements for grain and wine." On August 12th he wired the following opinion as to the Canadian Premier : " He will not discuss the work of the Imperial Conference, but it is an open secret that he has exerted a decisive influence in keeping the Colonies out of what he calls the vortex of European armaments. There was, without a doubt, vigorous effort on the part of Mr. Chamberlain to concentrate attention on this subject as the most available ground for common action, but there has been a complete failure to commit the Colonies to a costly policy for the military and naval defence of the Empire." This view Mr. Ford repeated again on August 14th, when he referred to the proposal for Colonial contributions to the defence of the Empire as having been rejected "owing mainly to the firmness of Sir Wilfrid Laurier." He had "talked less than Mr. Seddon," but had "exerted a decisive influence."

Various Liberal newspapers took this view, and Mr. W. T. Stead in his *Review of Reviews* for August put the matter with characteristic vigour: "Sir Wilfrid Laurier was dominated from first to last by a passionate determination to oppose to the uttermost every proposal which tended to drag Canada into the vortex of militarism. The result was that the Ministerial proposals were rejected and Sir Wilfrid Laurier has given the death-blow to one of the most dangerous delusions that ever gained possession of our people." The Conference was elaborately dealt with in the *Quarterly Review* for July and in the *Fortnightly* for August. The *Daily Chronicle* of August 2nd did not expect much practical result from the gathering. "But its chief good will be to maintain and develop the practice of discussion and consultation on subjects of common interest between the statesmen in different parts of the Empire." The *Daily News*, a Radical paper whose point of view is embodied in a statement on July 8th that "most Canadians fully endorse the 'no precedent' principle of Mr. Tarte," had many articles upon the Conference, and on August 13th declared that the result of its deliberations had "proved the most serious check to Imperialism that has yet taken place."

The Prime Minister of Canada and Lady Laurier sailed from New York on June 14th to attend the Coronation and Messrs. Fielding, Mulock and Paterson left on the same day **Sir Wilfrid** from Montreal. A week later the Premier received a **Laurier in** **Great Britain** cordial welcome at Liverpool and on June 22nd took up his quarters at the Hotel Cecil as a guest of the Crown. The first important function of a public character attended by Sir Wilfrid was the Dominion Day Dinner—an event of unusual distinction. There were 520 guests present with Lord Strathcona in the chair and on either side of him the Dukes of Argyll and Abercorn, the Earls of Minto, Dundonald and Aberdeen, Lord Kelvin, Lord Mount Stephen, Messrs. Fielding, Borden, Paterson and Mulock, Sir Charles Tupper, Hon. G. W. Ross, Sir Gilbert Parker, Hon. J. H. Turner and other representatives of Canada and various parts of the Empire, including Mr. Seddon and Sir Edmund Barton.

In his speech the Canadian Premier declared that his country was in name a colony but in reality a nation with a nation's history. "It was the brightest gem in the Crown of the British Empire" and recent events had shown that there, as elsewhere, when one spot in the Empire was touched the response came from all its parts. At the Constitutional Club, on July 7th, a Dinner was given presided over by the Duke of Marlborough. After speaking of the loyalty and unity and power of the Empire, its position as a galaxy of free nations, and the influence of allegiance to the Sovereign as a preservative of union, Sir Wilfrid proceeded as follows:

Shall the British Empire be maintained on the line on which it was created, or shall new departures be taken? Perhaps there are some, perhaps there are many, who believe that the British Empire must be maintained by war measures. For my part I believe that it can be well defended by the arts of peace. You are the one nation in Europe which never would be carried away by militarism. You are the one nation in Europe which, whilst other nations were bled white to create and maintain armies, resolved that no standing army should be created by the British Parliament. You are the one nation in Europe which has founded an Empire by the arts of peace far more than by the arts of war.

The greatest of these gatherings, however, was the Empire Coronation Banquet, held at the Guildhall on July 11th with 650 guests, and with the Earl of Onslow acting as chairman through the enforced absence of Mr. Chamberlain in consequence of his regretted accident of a short time before. It was one of the most brilliant scenes in Imperial history. Amongst those present were Sir Wilfrid Laurier and the Premiers of Australia, Cape Colony, Natal and Newfoundland, the Marquess of Lansdowne, the Earl of Minto, Earl Cromer, Sir Charles Tupper, Lord Strathcona, Sir Pertab Singh and the Maharajahs of Kolhapur, Bikaner and Cooch-Behar, King Lewanika of Barotseland, Lord Grenfell, Lord Kelvin, the Lord Chancellor, Sir John Forrest, Sir Reginald Wingate, Sirdar of the Soudan, Sir Howard Vincent M.P., Sir F. Borden, Sir W. Mulock and Messrs. Fielding and Paterson. Lord Onslow delivered a careful speech in which he dealt with the Conference and present hopes for closer union; referred to the naval and military forces of the Empire as being always ready to join in defending Colonial territory from foreign attack; and declared that if the Colonies asked for admission to Imperial Councils they would " be astonished at the alacrity of our response."

The Canadian Premier followed and described the British Empire as " an instrument of good government and a charter of freedom." It was now in a most prosperous and united state. To him it seemed " evident that no condition exists for any organic change." There were some who would take " an unwilling people and launch them into the unknown." But this was opposed to the character of the British race and the genius of British history. The lesson to be drawn from the past and the present was that " it would be a fatal mistake to try and force events." Sir Edmund Barton, to a considerable extent endorsed these views, and urged a natural evolution arising out of feelings of affection. He hoped much from the future, promised some small share in the cost of Empire defence from Australia and hinted at a voluntary fiscal preference. Speeches also followed from the Maharajah of

Kolhapur and Sir J. Gordon Sprigg. On July 14th the National Liberal Club dined the Colonial Premiers. Lord Carrington was Chairman and with him were Sir H. Campbell-Bannerman, M.P., the Liberal Leader, Sir Edward Grey, M.P., Sir William Harcourt, M.P., and Sir Charles Dilke, M.P.

Sir William Harcourt, in speaking, eulogized the Premier of Canada in unusually strong terms and quoted with high approval from what he termed his "peace speech" at the Constitutional Club. Sir Wilfrid in his reply described the giving of responsible government to the Colonies as the greatest of all modern reforms. "The devolution of legislative power has been the bond of union of the British Empire." Sir E. Barton, Mr. Seddon and Sir H. Campbell-Bannerman also spoke. The next function attended by Sir Wilfrid Laurier was a banquet given by the Canada Club on July 16th, presided over by Lord Strathcona, and attended by the Lord Mayor of London, the Earl of Derby, Sir E. Barton, Lord Ashbourne, Sir Robert Bond and a number of Canadian Ministers or visitors. In his speech the Canadian Premier referred to the difference of political conditions in 1837 and now, and then dealt with the material interests of the Dominion.

It was not probable, but certain, that Canada would become the granary of Great Britain. There was sufficient corn land in Canada to feed the whole of Great Britain and of Europe. The one thing they wanted at the present time was population. They had a population of five millions. They had room, they had lands, to give homes and shelter to 100,000,000 at least, and he hoped that at no distant date they would have a population of a hundred millions. When he came to England and saw the distressed condition of many of the people, it was a matter of some surprise to him that no greater efforts were made by the people of England to send over the surplus population to the vast lands of western Canada.

On July 26th the Colonial Premiers visited Edinburgh, received the freedom of the City, were given the Hon. degree of LL.D. at the University and a banquet by the Corporation. At the latter function Sir Wilfrid Laurier spoke at some length, followed by Sir E. Barton, Mr. Seddon and Sir Albert Hime. He told the large gathering present that they should enlarge their patriotism to take in the whole Empire without losing, however, their local pride and love of country. He dealt with Cecil Rhodes and declared that he made one serious mistake—that of being impatient. "Empires, as they knew by experience and the teaching of history, were not built up in a day nor in a generation. To build up an empire, conquest was only a preliminary step, discovery was only a preliminary step. To build up an empire they must conquer the hearts and the intelligences of the people of the empire, and when that had been done, as it had been done already, they had laid down the solid foundations and the stability of such an empire."

After a visit to the continent Sir Wilfrid Laurier sailed from Liverpool for home on October 7th. During this last day in England, he was accompanied by Lord Strathcona and Mr. Fielding and the time was spent in opening the new Produce Exchange of Liverpool, visiting various institutions there and being entertained by the Lord Mayor and Corporation at luncheon. During the day he made seven speeches and at the opening ceremonies he spoke at length. "Canadians were British subjects," he declared, "and were just as proud of the title as the people of the Mother Country. They found that the name of British subject was a passport all over the world as he had recently learned in a short visit to the Continent; and he did not know any title that could be borne with greater pride." He eulogized Canada, spoke again of building up the Empire by the arts of peace, pleaded for more emigration to the Dominion and stated that Canadians, like themselves, were a free people owing no allegiance but that to the King. In addressing a deputation at the Chamber of Commerce he defined the two bonds of Imperial unity as being loyalty to the King and liberty in constitutional action.

Sir Wilfrid Laurier reached Rimouski on October 16th, and was received by some of the Dominion and Provincial Ministers, by Senator Dandurand and others. After a cordial wel-

The Premier's Return to Canada

come here he took the train to Quebec and found the "ancient capital" gay with flags, bright with electric lights and crowded with applauding people. At the drill-hall an Address was presented in the presence of 3,000 persons by Mayor the Hon. S. N. Parent which, in well-phrased words, welcomed the Premier back from his mission as the representative of Canada at a ceremony "solemn and sacred to every loyal subject of the Empire." It described him as having been overwhelmed with marks of attention, honoured by expressions of praise and duly appreciated for his dignity, tact and eloquence. A beautiful tribute to Lady Laurier's grace, distinction and virtues closed the document. Sir Wilfrid's reply was very brief, and regretted that he could not accept the advice as to repose.

There were varied rumours in this latter connection and many expressions in despatches and speeches as to the Premier's health. It was known that he did not want any celebrations over his return which would involve exertion and speeches and he had already curtailed most imposing preparations in Montreal. The welcome there took place on October 18th and in the presence of a large crowd Mayor Cochrane read an Address on the balcony of the Place Viger Hotel. It spoke of the brilliant manner in which Sir Wilfrid had represented Canada upon a great occasion and maintained the position of his country amongst the illustrious men of Great Britain. "We are not ignorant of the fact that in your solicitude for the best interests of your country you sacrificed the pleasures of the rest which the state of your health required." A reference was also made to the Coronation Conference "where your utterances and your counsel exercised a preponderating influence."

The Board of Trade presented an Address dealing mainly with

the Conference. It expressed the hope that in discussing the future welfare of the Empire " you made it clear to the Conference that Canadians are ready to do their duty at all times to uphold in the Empire the position of Canada as its premier Colony." The Irish Catholics and La Chambre de Commerce presented Addresses as well as the Montreal Reform Club. The latter congratulated the Premier upon having at the Conference asserted " the absolute, complete and incontrovertible autonomy of the Dominion." In reply Sir Wilfrid spoke briefly and referred to his love for the sun and soil of Canada. " I have seen the green fields of England, visited the fertile plains of France, climbed the beautiful mountains of Switzerland and enjoyed the blue sky of Italy ; but there was no land and no sun like that of Canada."

There were many references in private and public to the Premier's apparent ill-health and emaciation, but it was declared to be due to a rigorous course of dieting advised by physicians in London and Paris. It was officially stated that there was no organic disease and that only rest was necessary, although Sir Wilfrid himself expressed great anxiety to get back to Ottawa and to work. He reached the Capital on the 10th, was enthusiastically welcomed by the crowds and presented at the City Hall by Mayor Fred. Cook with an Address which referred to the Premier's known desire to beautify and dignify Ottawa, to the conspicuous place he had maintained at the Coronation and to the necessity of repose after his strenuous labours abroad. In a somewhat lengthy reply Sir Wilfrid intimated that in the event of political accidents he would still retain his abode in Ottawa and continue his efforts to improve its civic position. His travels had made him more of a Canadian than ever. His health was again pretty good and he hoped equal to the work before him. " There is no repose for me. I come back to work." He spoke of the character and personality of the King as being dear to the hearts of his people and the Coronation as an event which could never be erased from his memory. In connection with the rumours and statements as to ill-health, Senator Gibson was interviewed on the same day and declared that personal neglect and over-work were the causes of a condition which should have had rest in England instead of three months of severe strain. However, diet and rest were all that were now necessary. A short time after this the Premier left for Virginia Hot Springs, in the South, and spent some weeks in complete retirement.

An important gathering of business and commercial men was held in the Parliament Buildings at Toronto on June 4th and the two following days. It met under the auspices and **Conference** initiative of the Toronto Board of Trade and its **of Canadian** officers—Mr. A. E. Ames, President; Messrs. J. F. **Boards** Ellis and J. D. Allan, Vice-Presidents; and Mr. **of Trade** Paul Jarvis, Secretary. The following Canadian Boards of Trade or Chambers of Commerce were represented by delegates :

ONTARIO.

Barrie	Goderich	Orillia	St. Catharines
Berlin	Guelph	Oshawa	St. Thomas
Bobcaygeon	Hamilton	Ottawa	Stratford
Brantford	Ingersoll	Owen Sound	Strathroy
Chatham	Kingston	Paris	Thorold
Clinton	Lindsay	Peterborough	Toronto
Collingwood	London	Petrolia	Wiarton
Deseronto	Meaford	Port Arthur	Walkerton
Elmira	Mitchell	Sault Ste. Marie	Windsor
Fort William	Niagara Falls	Smith's Falls	Woodstock
Galt	Oakville	Southampton	

QUEBEC.

Chicoutimi	Granby	Quebec	St. Hyacinthe
Drummondville	Marieville	Sherbrooke	Three Rivers
Gaspé	Montreal	Sorel	Valleyfield

MARITIME PROVINCES.

Halifax   North Sydney   St. John   St. Stephen's   Yarmouth

WESTERN PROVINCES.

Portage la Prairie Victoria   Brandon   Nelson
Rossland   Winnipeg   Calgary

President Ames of the Toronto Board was selected as Chairman, and Mr. Jarvis was appointed Secretary of the Conference. In his opening address Mr. Ames referred briefly to the end of the War, to the coming Coronation of the King, to the elements of supremacy and success which existed within the British Empire. " It remains, in order that the position of the Empire shall be maintained and advanced, that the elements of prosperity, which are all available in large measure, shall be recognized, shall be studied, and shall be safe-guarded and that there shall be intelligent co-operation amongst the countries interested. I believe that no one expects that the delegates have come to this Conference with the idea of trying to turn things upside down and trying to have employed any but methods of natural evolution. I take it, however, that the coming together of such an influential body means that you consider that the best method of dealing with problems is not to shirk their discussion, and that nowadays it does not do to drift. I think there is also underlying this assemblage the feeling that the brightest day which the British Empire can have will be when Great Britain and the other self-governing countries of the Empire all combine in realizing that united, in every sense, they stand ; and divided, in any important sense, they fall." Following the opening ceremonies a number of Resolutions from various Boards of Trade were received, debated and dealt with. Kingston, Orillia and Montreal submitted motions as to Imperial newspaper rates; Montreal, Toronto, Barrie, Berlin, British Columbia, Brandon, Vancouver, Galt, St. Hyacinthe, Orillia, Ottawa, Bracebridge and Valleyfield, together with La Chambre de Commerce of Montreal, proposed Resolutions on Trade relations within the Empire ; Brantford upon the Cattle embargo question; Ottawa and Kingston upon the Cable to Australia; Toronto, Peterborough and Pembroke urged the establishment of a Commercial depot in London; St. Hyacinthe, Valleyfield and La Chambre de Commerce of Montreal proposed Commercial Consular agencies for Canada; Halifax, Barrie, Collingwood, Vancouver, Toronto and British Columbia urged an Atlantic fast steamship line; Nelson, and British Columbia wanted a duty on lead; Montreal, Barrie, St. Hyacinthe, Kingston, Valleyfield, Toronto, Vancouver and British Columbia suggested different lines of action upon Imperial defence; Toronto dealt with Copyright and Sault Ste. Marie with Canadian mineral resources; Valleyfield and La Chambre de Commerce of Montreal presented Resolutions upon Inter-Colonial trade relations, the Metric System and Postal and Telegraph communications; Barrie, St. Hyacinthe and Vancouver joined in the last-mentioned matter; Kingston urged the encouragement of ship-building; Vancouver and Goderich wanted a Canadian Insolvency law; Toronto and Vancouver asked for the Metric System. The many and lengthy Resolutions passed may be summarized as in favour of the following proposals:

Lowering of postal rates upon newspapers and periodicals between Great Britain, Canada and the Empire.

An Imperial preferential trade arrangement; a Colonial preference under the terms of the Corn tax; a Royal Commission from all parts of the Empire to evolve a practical preferential trade plan.

Limitation of the existing Canadian preference on British goods to 20 per cent. when coming *via* United States ports.

Removal of the British cattle embargo.

Extension of the state-owned cable system between Canada and Australia right around the Empire.

Establishment of a Commercial depot in London.

Imperial recognition of Colonial commercial agents in Foreign countries.

Establishment of a fast Atlantic line with speed as the only consideration in selecting call and terminal ports.

A subsidized Cargo steam service to South Africa and Australia.

A re-adjustment of the tariff so as to encourage the mining, smelting and refining of lead.

Participation in the cost of Imperial defence and an annual appropriation by the Dominion Government for this purpose.

The recognition of alleged Canadian rights in the Copyright matter.

Subsidies to approved mineral colonization railways.

The establishment of a Railway Commission.

Continued deepening of the St. Lawrence channel and Government aid to ship-building industries.

The forming of an Insolvency Act by a gathering of commercial men under Government auspices.

Government assistance in the building up and equipment of Canadian national ports.

Tariff alterations to meet the fiscal discriminations of certain Foreign countries.

Dominion and Provincial Government aid in obtaining additional railway facilities, deeper waterways, longer navigation, extended harbours and increased shipping tonnage.

Encouragement of Colonization.

Establishment of the Metric System of Weights and Measures, and abolition of the unjust discrimination in Marine insurance against Canadian ports.

The chief subjects of discussion were the Resolutions dealing with Imperial trade relations and Imperial defence. Upon the former question Messrs. George E. Drummond, W. F. Cockshutt of Brantford, W. F. Hatheway of St. John, C. A. Young of Winnipeg, D. R. Wilkie of Toronto, J. X. Perrault of Montreal, A. E. Kemp, M.P., of Toronto, George Robertson, M.P.P., of St. John, M. C. Ellis of Toronto and W. Sanford Evans of Winnipeg made notable speeches. Upon the latter Messrs. Alexander McFee of Montreal Robert Munro of Montreal, Haughton Lennox, M.P., of Barrie, H. J. Wickham of Toronto, D. Masson of Montreal, W. F. Cockshutt of Brantford, Andrew Pattullo, M.P.P., of Woodstock, Thomas Macfarlane of Ottawa, Hon. J. D. Rolland of Montreal, A. E. Ames of Toronto, and W. F. Hatheway of St. John spoke at length. There were many amendments to the Defence Resolution and very diverse views expressed. It was finally carried by 40 to 32 votes.

On the evening of June 5th, a banquet was held, with President Ames in the chair, and with Hon. J. Israel Tarte, M.P., Hon. George W. Ross, Hon. William Mulock, M.P., and Hon. Donald Morison of Newfoundland amongst the speakers and guests. On June 11th the various Resolutions passed by the Conference were presented to the Prime Minister at Ottawa by a deputation headed by Mr. A. E. Ames. In his reply Sir Wilfrid Laurier referred to the Defence discussion, and declared himself " more interested in the trade question than that of war." He also drew attention to the fact that no reference was made by the Resolutions to the return which Canada was to give for a British Preference.

The value, or otherwise, of the Preferential clause in Canada's tariff was largely discussed during 1902. The Conservative press and speakers endeavoured to prove that it was a useless preference to the Motherland and yet injurious to Canadian industries. Various selected lists of articles were published in which it was apparently shown that Canadian imports from the United States had increased at the expense of Great Britain. One of these, in the *Canadian Manufacturer* of October 3rd, gave 100 articles of manufacture in which the import from the Republic under the general tariff totalled $10,306,584 and from the Motherland, under the Preference, $18,747. On April 14th, the Manitoba *Free Press* pointed out, on the other hand, that, since the Preference was granted, imports from Great Britain had increased from $29,412,188 in 1897 to $43,018,164 in 1901, and Canadian exports to Great Britain from $77,227,502 to $105,328,956. As a result of the Preferential tariff " every retail dealer in Great Britain finds that the name Canadian is the best of recommendations to his customers." The Montreal *Herald* of May 6th described it as having enabled the Government to lower duties and taxation and accepted Sir R. J. Cartwright's reference to it as " a flank movement against protection " successfully undertaken after many frontal attacks had failed.

The
Canadian
Tariff
Preference

In the House of Commons criticism and defence were frequent during the Session. Mr. W. R. Brock (C) on March 20th described it as beginning to pinch us hard. " We would like to get rid of it" but he believed that to be "an impossibility and injudicious and unwise at the present time." Mr. L. P. Demers (L) on April 3rd defended it as only fair and just to England. Mr. W. B. Northrup (C) four days later said: "If we owe anything to the Mother Country let us all contribute to the paying of it and not lay the whole burden upon those who happen to be in business, and to be injured by the tariff." Mr. James Clancy (C) on April 8th, declared that " there is not one redeeming feature in the Preferential tariff so far as any benefit to the people of Canada is concerned." On May 12th, the Premier dealt with the subject. "As we could not obtain an Imperial preference we thought we would give a Preference ourselves. Why did we do that ? Because it was our best measure of tariff reform. And it has served its purpose well. It may not have accomplished all that we hoped ; nevertheless, the results are there and show for themselves—one of them being that our trade with Great Britain has almost doubled within five years."

A study of this subject appeared in the London *Times* of June 28th. The writer pointed out that between 1871-2 and 1896-7 the percentage of Canadian imports supplied by Great Britain had fallen from 58·5 per cent. to 26·4, while that supplied by the United States had increased from 33·1 per cent. to 60·2. "During the year 1900-1, in spite of the Preferential rebate of from one-quarter to one-third of the duties, the British imports fell to 24·8 per cent., and those of the United States increased slightly to 60·9 per cent." He concluded that Sir Michael Hicks-Beach "was right when he said that the Preferential tariff had not been of much advantage to our trade." Mr. John Charlton, M.P., (L) in his *Globe* article of July 12th took a very similar view :

Our own discrimination in favour of Great Britain for the last two years has been 33⅓ per cent. This is beautifully sentimental, but absurdly barren of practical results of a desirable character. It has embarrassed certain lines of our manufacturing interests, and has brought not the slightest return in the form of trade concessions from Great Britain.

Supporting the charge that this Preference was hurting certain industries the *Mail and Empire*, of August 16th, stated that in 1895 the total cotton importations were $2,835,448 and in 1902 $5,007,870, while in woollens the figures were respectively $5,914,-340 and $8,257,813. Another phase of the question was Australia's promise *via* Sir Edmund Barton to follow Canada's example and give Great Britain a preference in its tariff. In a letter to the Halifax *Chronicle*, during October, Mr. Harold Cox, Secretary of the Cobden Club, claimed that during the past five years Canadian imports from Germany had increased 31 per cent., from the United States 93 per cent., from France 102 per cent., from Belgium 421 per cent. and from Great Britain 23 per cent. In addressing the

Coronation Conference in August Mr. Chamberlain uttered the following opinion as to the Preferential tariff:

I have to say to you that while I cannot but gratefully acknowledge the intention of the proposal and its sentimental value as a proof of good will and affection, yet its substantial results have been altogether disappointing to us, and I think they must have been equally disappointing to its promoters.

On November 18th the Toronto *Globe* took a list of articles in which imports from the United States were larger than from Great Britain and claimed that owing to natural causes no possible tariff could have made any difference.   Speaking at Hochelaga on November 27th Mr. F. D. Monk, M.P., declared that many Canadian industries were being ruined by the Preference and instanced iron, collars and shirts.   According to the Montreal *Star* report he then demanded its abolition.   England did not want it and Canada was injured by it.   At Hamilton on December 26th Sir William Mulock took a very different view of the subject.   He spoke of the electrical effect of the Preference upon the British public mind, the consequent inflow of money and immigrants to Canada, the prosperity of the farmers through increased sales to Great Britain and the alleged intention of the Conservative party to abolish the Preference if they got a chance.

The entire range of questions connected with the fiscal position of the Empire and its individual countries was discussed as a result of the British Budget of 1902.   It was known **The British** beforehand that new taxes had to be imposed and **Tax on** that the War was causing a huge deficit.   Mr. **Breadstuffs** Chamberlain was supposed to be in favour of some system of incidental protection for Empire products, while a popular belief existed that the Chancellor of the Exchequer was strongly opposed to such views and that there existed a distinct cleavage in the Cabinet upon this question.   At a meeting in London of the United Empire Trade League on March 5th, Sir Howard Vincent, M.P., moved the following motion, which was carried unanimously:

This meeting urges upon His Majesty's Government and the Imperial Parliament, that, from a financial, manufacturing and agricultural point of view, a thorough re-consideration of the existing fiscal system of the United Kingdom is essential before the presentation of the coming Budget, having regard to the constant growth of expenditure and the yearly increasing pressure of direct taxation.   It further declares that the true direction of reform lies in the development of commercial intercourse upon a preferential basis between the various portions of the British Empire, and in giving a Customs advantage in Great Britain and Ireland to all products of the Empire.

On April 14th, Sir Michael Hicks-Beach presented his Budget in the House of Commons.   The estimated deficit was £45,000,500 and a total expenditure of £193,000,000 of which the Army and Navy took £100,000,000.   He proposed to increase the income tax and the stamp duties and to impose a duty of 3d. per cwt. on imported corn, including wheat, oats, rye and other grains, and 5 per cent. on flour, malt, sago, starch, arrowroot, etc.   These items would, he thought, produce £5,000,000 of new revenue and the rest

would be borrowed.   He claimed that there was no question of protection in the matter and that it was a re-imposition of the old
registration duty, which had for a long time been retained by Mr.
Gladstone himself.   Sir W. Harcourt promptly denounced the corn
tax as increasing the price of bread and as falling chiefly upon the
poor of the country, and this was the general line taken by the
Opposition.   The vote on the preliminary Resolutions was 254 to
135.   Defended by the Conservatives as consistent with precedent
and free-trade practice, the press soon took party issue upon the
subject ; bye-elections were fought upon it and Parliament discussed
it—first as a tax on bread and then as an opening for fiscal
arrangements within the Empire.   To the *Daily News* of April
15th, the tax was a reversal of " the great policy of free food."
Another generation had come up which knew not the miseries of
protection and the dear loaf.   " Must it learn these things by sad
experience and by the salt tears of want ? "   In the Commons, on
May 12th, the subject was discussed at length and the Imperial
issue raised by Sir Henry Fowler in the following words :

If this policy was to prevail how were they going to deal with the Colonies ?
At the present moment Canada had made very great concessions to us.   She had
made us preferential rates.   We had met them by saying it was against our
policy to impose protective duties.   We could not say that now.   Canada
would say to us, 'Why cannot you put us on the same footing as Great Britain ?'
This proposal of the Government might be the commencement of a great
zollverein of the British Empire.   Australia, in regard to meat, would advance
the same argument as Canada.

On June 9th, Sir Michael Hicks-Beach dealt with this subject
and declared that the proper course was to be found in such tariff
arrangements within the Empire as would broaden the free-trade
area.   He had not discussed the matter with any Colonial representatives and had proposed the duty as a purely revenue one.   He
then continued : " Cannot we try so to consider the commercial
relations between us that we may make trade freer than it is now
and that without necessarily injuring any Foreign country at all ?
I know that some persons have suggested that you should impose
duties as against Foreign nations in order to give an advantage to
our Colonies.   That is not the policy of His Majesty's Government."
The corn tax was to be " a part of our permanent system of taxation."   Other speakers seemed to fear this possible preference, however, and Sir Edward Grey, a Liberal leader of the Rosebery wing,
declared that " if they had preferential duties against the world
between themselves and the Colonies it was absolutely certain that
this country would have to pay an increased price for the whole of
its food and raw material and the hazard and risk to which their
great export trade would be exposed was such as could not be
measured by any possible balance."
The discussion was resumed on June 15th when Mr. John Morley
declared that the basis of all these Imperial tariff projects was the
substitution of Colonial for Foreign products in the United
Kingdom.   This, in his opinion, would mean (1) a rise in the price

of raw material; (2) a rise in the cost of manufacture; (3) a consequent handicap in neutral markets; (4) playing ducks and drakes with a great Foreign trade for the sake of a small Colonial one; (5) a fiscal machinery which would seriously injure all trade and commerce.   The policy of free imports had created the present pleasant relations with the Colonies but such a series of bargains as was now proposed would soon destroy this harmony.   Mr. H. H. Asquith repeated a former argument as to this corn tax removing the chief answer to Colonial advocates of Preferential trade and continued as follows:

It will be impossible now to say to the Colonies, in answer to any proposals they may put forward, that there is no tax upon our tariff which is not for revenue alone, and that we could not depart from our principles, however we value their sacrifices and their loyalty.   That cannot be said now with any logic.   What are you going to say to the Canadian exporter of wheat or flour ?   The new corn tax will discriminate against him and in favour of the producer here.   You will have no answer to the Canadian who said that ours was not a free-trade system.   It discriminates not only against the Colonies, but against foreigners.   That is a serious state of things, because it deprives this country of an unanswerable argument with which we might have met the proposals of the Colonies.   That in itself is enough to condemn the Clause.   I submit that it would be a bad bargain for the Colonies themselves, a bad bargain for the Mother Country, and a bad bargain for the Empire if a diversion of trade was purchased at the cost of endangering the position of the United Kingdom as, to a large extent, the workshop, the market, and the clearing-house for the industrial world.

In his reply the Chancellor of the Exchequer expressly repudiated any intention of granting a preference to the Colonies, declared that such a system could only be maintained under high duties and referred to his past policy in respect to Colonial wines and sugars. Meanwhile, the subject had become a very live issue in the country and was supposed to have been the cause of some heavy Government defeats in bye-elections.   At Bristol, on May 14th, the Council of the National Liberal Federation passed a Resolution on the subject.   "The Council strenuously protests against the proposed tax on imported corn, flour, and other breadstuffs as a deplorable reversal of the policy of free-trade."   After the duty had been in operation for some time the London *Times* of September 16th quoted various local prices of bread and declared that they were "practically identical" with those ruling before its imposition. Speaking at Aberdeen on May 20th, Mr. James Bryce, M.P., declared that if the new school of fiscal thought had proposed free-trade within the Empire all would welcome it, subject to the necessary duty on alcoholic liquors for British revenue purposes.   But the Colonies desired to still maintain an elaborate tariff system and to ask Great Britain to impose duties on various products in their interests.   This would involve higher prices; and "we shall no longer be free to raise or lower our customs duties as we think best because we shall be bound by a group of treaties with the several Colonies."

Sir H. Campbell-Bannerman followed up this assertion of his

colleague by stating at Darlington, on May 24th, that it was impossible to imagine the Colonies taking the place in trade of Foreign countries, and by declaring the whole project a "fantastic policy" for which, however, the bread tax was a prelude. At Leeds, on May 30th, Lord Rosebery took much the same line as Mr. Bryce and, after expressing his belief that the Colonial Secretary was trying to form an Imperial Customs Union, spoke of his own Imperial ideals and expressed the fear that the project involved would hand over the control of the British fiscal system to the Colonies. If there were counter-balancing advantages to this he would like to hear them. "My mind is open and I shall wait to hear." About this time Mr. Harold Cox, Secretary of the Cobden Club, wrote to the press declaring that the corn tax had been imposed "in order to pave the way for an Imperial preferential tariff," and to tax the food of the British people at home "in order to increase the profits of Canadian corn growers." Major-General J. Wimburn Laurie, C.M.G., M.P., speaking to the Toronto *Globe* on November 21st expressed the belief that the tax had originally been imposed with the intention of favouring the Colonies. He thought the great difficulty was in the British feeling that the Colonies could not give them enough food even if they antagonized Foreign countries in order to help them do so.

Meanwhile, Canada has been discussing this new tax with much earnestness. The Toronto Board of Trade on February 12th passed a unanimous Resolution, expressing the hope that such a duty would be imposed and a preference granted to the Colonies and the belief that such a measure would be a great aid to closer union. On April 8th the Winnipeg Board of Trade passed a similar motion, and on May 19th, at a special meeting, that of Montreal referred to the recently imposed tax and asked the Canadian Government "to urge most strongly on the Government of Great Britain the necessity and advisability of granting free entry to the agricultural products of Canada and the other Colonies while maintaining duties on importations from all Foreign countries." In the House of Commons, on April 15th, Mr. W. F. Maclean drew attention to the subject and declared that if the Government had expressed a willingness to aid Great Britain in the matter of defence the exemption of Canada from this tax would have followed. The discussion was shared in by the Premier, Dr. Sproule, Mr. R. L. Borden, Hon. Mr. Fielding, Hon. Mr. Sifton and others.

Upon the same date the Toronto *News* interviewed a number of Canadians upon the subject. Dr. G. R. Parkin, C.M.G., thought the Budget speech marked "another great stage in the progress of national evolution." It would compel hard thinking upon questions of defence and tariff. Professor Mavor stated that if the preference were given it would be only two cents a bushel. The Hon. G. W. Ross believed the new tax would pave the way to a Preferential system. Sir Wilfrid Laurier hoped that it would

9

help in laying a basis for negotiations at the coming Conference. Mr. Alexander McFee, President of the Montreal Board of Trade, believed the tax would place Canadian farmers in the North-West, particularly, at a disadvantage as compared with the United States farmer, owing to Canadians having to accept any price they could get for their wheat. Mr. J. Castell Hopkins did not believe a preference would result unless the Colonial Governments took definite action. "It seems to me impossible to settle the issue except upon the broad ground that Britain wants organized Colonial aid in the defence of the Empire, while the Colonies want organized commercial advantages in the British market." The subject was very widely discussed in the press but without any common ground of opinion being visible.

The problem of supplying Great Britain with food products from within the Empire, and thus making her independent of Foreign countries, was forcibly presented by Lieut.-Col. George T. Denison, of Toronto, upon various occasions during 1902, as well as in the preceding year. In 1901 the United Kingdom produced 6,755,000 quarters of wheat, and imported 16,296,222 quarters, together with 22,575,230 cwt. of flour. According to values the chief British imports in 1901 were as follows :

The Food Supply Question

Grain and Flour	£61,241,027	Animals	£9,400,033
Dead Meat	39,987,806	Fruits and Hops	8,082,568
Sugar	19,507,037	Cheese	6,227,277
Butter	21,853,687	Eggs	5,495,776
Tea	9,487,793	Seeds	1,872,858

It was claimed by English writers such as Mr. H. W. Wilson, that this £190,000,000 worth of food products would, in the case of serious war, increase greatly in price, even if the seas were kept free for its transport ; that insurance rates would rise as well as wages in the merchant service ; that raw materials for manufacture would consequently increase in cost, and freights would be greatly enhanced. In the *North American Review*, June, 1902, Mr. J. D. Whelpley pointed out another alleged danger. "If the United States were suddenly to stop all present regular exportations of meat and breadstuffs to the United Kingdom, the first effect would be an enormous rise in prices throughout Europe, and it would be but a few weeks before the English people would be threatened by dire famine, with no possible relief in sight so long as commercial relations with the United States were suspended."

He concluded that upon their capacity to supply food to Great Britain depended the power of the United States far more than upon industrial production. "To enable production to keep pace with the growing appetite of the world, and to prevent the United States from losing its control of the great food supply necessary to satisfy this appetite, is even a more statesmanlike policy than to devote all time and energy to the building of great cities, and the creation of industrial armies to be fed from abroad—to be, perhaps, dependent

at intervals upon an enemy for daily bread." The following figures
from the British Agricultural Returns for 1901, give the total production of the United Kingdom :

BUSHELS.		TONS.	
Wheat	53,927,729	Potatoes	7,042,416
Barley	67,643,186	Turnips	25,298,482
Oats	161,174,532	Mangolds	9,228,053
Beans	6,154,369		
Peas	4,018,797		

Colonel Denison's view of this subject was expressed in a
number of his speeches. At Ottawa, on February 20th, he declared
the food supply of England to be her point of gravest danger in
war-time. " She who in the Napoleonic wars was able to feed her
own people from her own productions, now only provides about
5,500,000 quarters of wheat out of the 20,000,000 which she con-
sumes. An embargo on all foods of all kinds by Russia and the
United States, or in the United States alone, might soon force
Great Britain to sue for peace on any terms and this without
fighting." In various English papers, in the *Nineteenth Century
and After* for June, and in addresses before a number of Chambers
of Commerce, he urged his policy of an Empire tax for defence
purposes on Foreign products and other considerations which may
be summed up from an interview in the *Pall Mall Gazette*, May 12th :

We believe that even with an overwhelming Navy you might be reduced to
submission by a hostile combination of foreign food-producing countries. We
feel, therefore, that it would be a sheer waste of money for us to pay for ships,
troops and coaling-stations, while taking no precautions to secure adequate
supplies of food. Our belief is that this preferential tax would serve not only
to enlarge the food supply in England itself, but would enable Canada and other
Colonies to add substantially to their capacity for furnishing you with corn and
other agricultural products. It would go a long way towards enabling the
Empire to provision itself from its own resources. It is therefore the most
effective military, as well as commercial, measure that could be devised.

Apart from the Budget discussions and the food supply question
there were many references in Great Britain to the idea of an
Empire tariff during the year. The Liberal, and
Preferential   especially the Radical, press described it as a sort of
Trade in
Great Britain   Chamberlain-Jingo scheme to revive protection and
tax the people's bread. Mr. H. W. Massingham, the
clever Parliamentary writer on the *Daily News*, told that paper on
February 15th that the Colonial Secretary had long been preparing
the lines of Imperial Federation and that there was only one path
along which such an experiment could travel.

That is the path of Protection, or, as it will probably be called, of an
Imperial tariff. If the more adventurous Colonies, who are now beginning to
discover what splendid spoil may lie in the reversal of our historic commercial
policy, desire to obtain some new substantial advantage from an Imperial connection, that can only be on the basis of a preferential treatment of Colonial as
against Foreign goods.

This particular paper denounced the idea vigorously at every
possible opening. In the *Standard* of July 11th, July 19th and

August 5th Lord Masham—the Mr. Cunliffe Lister of other days
and a well-known protectionist—had letters advocating his favourite
policy with an Imperial addition.   He went to the point of declaring
that it was no use placing a duty on corn or other Foreign products
unless it was high enough to give the British markets to the
Colonies.   The *Spectator* and the *Speaker*, both Radical and free-
trade journals, and the former often quoted in the Canadian press,
opposed this as well as other Imperial projects very strongly.
Speaking at the Royal Colonial Institute, on June 11th, with the
Earl of Jersey in the chair, Mr. Archibald R. Colquhoun, the well-
known traveller and writer, supported a policy of moderate duties
upon Foreign corn, meat, wool and sugar and proceeded as follows :

> The trend of public opinion would seem to be in favour of a certain degree
> of preferential treatment within the Empire, and the feeling grew, certainly in
> the oversea dominions, that the Empire was so composed that it could, to a
> great extent, soon be made self-supporting.   It was quite clear that the Colo-
> nies were going to have a powerful and increasing influence on our Councils,
> whether represented or not, and participation in power must be accompanied
> by participation in representation, by responsibility for the common welfare.
> The initial step might be the creation of an Imperial Council, distinct from
> Parliament.

At the Conference of the National Union of Conservative Associations of Great Britain, on October 15th, Sir Howard Vincent, M.P.,
spoke at length on this subject, referred to the protectionist
Resolution passed in 1887, described the importation in 1901 of
£110,000,000 of foreign food, stated the excess of imports over
exports as now £175,000,000 against £81,000,000 in 1886 and moved
the following motion : " That the Conference rejoices in the progress towards the realization of the views expressed in the Resolution of the Oxford Conference of 1887, and reaffirms that in their
adoption lie the manufacturing, agricultural and labour interests
of the United Kingdom.   It particularly urges upon His Majesty's
Government to carry out to the full the views enunciated by the
recent Colonial Conference on the subject of preferential trade
between all parts of the British Empire."   It passed, with one dissentient.   The *Morning Post* of September 5th, supported this
policy and declared that "the idea will grow ; it must come if we
are to survive."

Resolutions were passed during the year by the Boards of Trade
at Toronto, Orillia, St. John, Winnipeg, Vancouver, etc., asking for
Preferential tariff arrangements within the Empire.
Preferential Trade Opinions in Canada That of Montreal was carried with one dissentient
voice on February 20th, as follows : " Resolved, that
this meeting is of opinion that Great Britain can serve
best her own interests and those of her Colonies by
adopting such change in her fiscal policy as will give the products
of her Colonies a preference in her markets as against the products
of Foreign countries it being believed that such preference would
stimulate trade and develop Colonial enterprises, and, moreover,
serve to make the Colonies attractive, not only to a large number

of British subjects emigrating annually from the British Isles, but also to the surplus population of other countries, and at the same time benefit Great Britain by largely freeing her from dependence upon Foreign countries for her food supplies."

Mr. Alexander McNeill, ex-M.P., who visited Great Britain and had addressed meetings at Aberdeen, Glasgow and Belfast returned home in March and told the Tara *Leader* of March 20th, that he had found this proposal received with a surprising degree of favour. The Presidents of the Chambers of Commerce in Aberdeen and Belfast were both favourable. " The feeling of a very large majority of educated people (outside of a certain circle in London) is that so-called free-trade has been carried too far." Sir Charles Tupper, on his way to England, told the St. John *Gazette* of April 5th, that Australia, New Zealand and other Colonies were in favour of the policy and it only remained for Sir Wilfrid Laurier to press the matter to an issue.

On April 16th Messrs. Alexander McNeill, ex-M.P., and J. M. Clark, K.C., addressed a meeting at Owen Sound upon the subject. In the St. John *Globe* of May 16th an important letter appeared written by Mr. W. Frank Hatheway, analyzing the statistics and nature of the scheme.   He stated that in 1900 the United Kingdom imported from Foreign countries 58,500,000 cwt. of wheat, 20,200,-000 cwt. of flour, 17,000,000 cwt. of barley and 19,600,000 cwt. of oats, as against a total import from the Colonies in all these products of 13,000,000 cwt.   Of British exports he pointed out that in 1900 the United States, France, Germany and Russia took £118,100,000, or 33 per cent. of the whole, while Canada, Australasia, India and South Africa took £84,100,000, or 24 per cent. The imports totalled respectively £245,000,000, or 47 per cent., and £89,000,000, or 17 per cent.   Was this fair to the Empire, he asked ? Mr. John Charlton, M.P., was interviewed in London, England, on May 30th, by the *Standard*, and favoured the increase of the present Canadian Preference to 40 per cent. upon a re-adjusted tariff, if Great Britain would reciprocate to a reasonable extent.

Mr. R. P. Roblin, Premier of Manitoba, was interviewed by the *Pall Mall Gazette* on May 22nd, and declared that in view of Foreign hostility to England and Colonial sympathy for her, the Colonies should be given a preference in her markets.   The reward would soon come to both.   " Canada alone has illimitable possibilities in the way of agricultural production.   She could easily produce within five years all the breadstuffs, the beef and the dairy products now imported into Great Britain.   All that is wanted is a small preferential duty."   On June 13th an interview at Ottawa between a deputation accompanied by Mr. Robert Munro, President of the Canadian Manufacturers' Association, and the Premier, evoked an expression of opinion from the former which was a subject of dispute in its exact terms.   Mr. Munro claimed to have stated that if the Canadian tariff scale was raised so as to equal approximately that of Germany or the United States, " we could give the British manufacturers a 50 per cent advantage" in return for a preference in the British market.   On June 18th the Toronto *Globe* reviewed the whole project editorially and with elaboration.   Summed up its conclusions may be put as follows :

1. Canada would rejoice in a British tariff preference given freely and without Colonial coercion.

2. Canada is too rich in natural wealth and possible industrial greatness to clamour for fiscal doles from even the Motherland.

3. There should be no Canadian alliance with any British political party in order to help to obtain such a preference.

4. The only safe line to approach the question on either side is by the preferential remission of taxation.

5. Canadian revenue requirements and the safety of its industries prevent the adoption of Mr. Chamberlain's policy of free-trade within the Empire.

6. The natural desire of Great Britain is to manufacture for the Colonies, and the natural wish of the latter is to manufacture for themselves.

7. A tax on Foreign grain and food products in favour of the Colonies is desired by the latter, while the Liberal party at home is absolutely opposed to it.

8. Many Canadians seek to re-establish protection in Great Britain ; many in England want to inaugurate free-trade in the Colonies.

9. The present Canadian preference is a fair basis upon which to ask a British preference in the new corn duties.

10. Canada has done much of late for the Empire and has failed to even obtain a relief in the cattle restrictions imposed by Great Britain.

11. The heavily-burdened British tax-payer should not be taxed for the defence of this young, rich and prosperous country, and Great Britain should be relieved of all military expenses in Canada.

12. Cheaper and better transportation agencies constitute an important mutual ground in both defence and commerce.

Speaking on July 7th, in London, the Hon. G. W. Ross pointed out that while British exports under free-trade in the last ten years had increased £1,000,000 those of the United States under protection had risen £85,000,000.   As to certain recent proposals : "Canada cannot afford to agree to free-trade with the Empire just now nor at any future period within the reach of human foresight." To the *Globe* of July 12th Mr. John Charlton, M.P., contributed a lengthy study of the Preferential trade project.   He did not think much of the Canadian Preference, declared any possible tariff reduction given by Canada as practically useless to Great Britain, considered any British tariff preference for the Empire as unlikely in fact and unreasonable in prospect, deprecated "Imperial spread-eagleism," and denounced Colonel Denison's scheme as "an amusing fad," opposed Imperial defence contributions and advocated Reciprocity with the United States.

Interviewed by the Winnipeg *Telegram*, of September 1st, Sir Mackenzie Bowell, Conservative leader in the Senate, said : "I believe the time is rapidly approaching when the British Colonies will be able to give England its food supply, and the English policy should be to encourage its dependencies so as to make itself independent of other countries in times of difficulty."   At the Coronation Conference the Canadian Ministers urged the exemption of Canada from the British corn-tax in return for the existing

Canadian Preference and offered to practically increase that Preference. Speaking to the Commercial Travellers' Association in Toronto on December 26th President M. C. Ellis referred to the difficulties in the way of Preferential Trade, but declared that much greater obstacles in other matters had been overcome and that success would come in this when statesmen set their minds to the task.

Intimately associated with the fiscal movements of the year, both in Great Britain and Canada, was the campaign conducted by Lieut.-Colonel George T. Denison of Toronto in favour **Colonel** of the policy propounded in the following Resolution **Denison's** passed at a meeting addressed by him in London, **Fiscal** Ontario, on January 24th: "This meeting is of the **Campaign** opinion that a special duty of five to ten per cent. should be imposed at every port in the British Possessions on all Foreign goods, the proceeds to be devoted to Imperial defence." In his speech Colonel Denison declared that such a policy would give Canada a preference in every market of the Empire, England's manufacturers a considerable help in the Colonies and the British people an increased wheat area and safe food supply in case of trouble with the United States or Russia.

At the annual meeting in Ottawa of the British Empire League Colonel Denison presided and in a careful speech went over the whole ground of commerce and defence. He pointed out that in 1881-1890 the imports of the United Kingdom had been £3,947,000,000, and in 1891-1900, £4,461,000,000—an increase of £514,000,000. In the same period, respectively, the exports had increased from £2,970,000,000 to £3,005,000,000, or only £35,000,000. He strongly urged his proposed system of combined aid to trade and defence and declared that it would well pay the British workingman to reduce the tax on his tea and tobacco in favour of a tax on Foreign wheat. At the Toronto branch meeting of the League on April 10th a Resolution similar to that of London was passed on motion of Mr. A. E. Ames.

Meanwhile, Colonel Denison had made arrangements to personally press this subject upon the attention of the people of Great Britain and in doing so was given every assistance by the British Empire League of the Motherland without, however, the assumption of any responsibility by that body for the views of their Canadian President. Shortly after his arrival, on April 30th, he addressed the annual banquet of the Royal Colonial Institute in London, and stated that he was there as the representative of the British Empire League in Canada to ask consideration by the public in general and the pending Conference in particular for the proposal already outlined. It was not for protection or free-trade but for the defence of common interests. On May 6th he addressed the Council of the British Empire League in London. Before the Newspaper Press Society in London on May 7th, with Lord Tweedmouth and Mr. Asquith present amongst many others, he urged his views. " He proposed to tax the ports of the Empire for the purpose of raising a war tax for common defence. That was a proposition to which Canada would agree." An interview followed in the Pall Mall *Gazette* of May 12th, and a letter in the *Morning Post* and the Bristol *Times*. At a meeting of the Liverpool Chamber of Commerce on May 23rd, with Sir Alfred Jones in the chair, Colonel Denison outlined his policy and declared that the Canadian people had been thinking of it a good deal and were in favour of it. Comment and criticism were, of course, soon stirred up by his outspoken advocacy of a new policy—new since its tentative and almost forgotten promulgation by Mr. J. H. Hofmeyr, of Cape Colony, in 1887. The London *Daily News* of May 22nd denounced the Canadian visitor as an "Empire wrecker," and on June 18th had the following caustic criticism :

Colonel Denison's ten per cent. on foreign commodities will, in the first place, cost Great Britain £41,000,000 a year, whilst the self-governing Colonies will have to pay £3,500,000 as their part of the scheme of duties. But this is not all. The enhanced price of Colonial produce will mean another ten per cent. on everything we import from Australia and Canada—or eleven millions a year transferred from the pockets of Englishmen to Colonials. The net result is, therefore, represented by a loss to this country of £53,000,000 a year, whilst the Colonies, in return for the duty of three and one half millions which they would put on against the foreigner, will receive eleven millions from the Mother Country.

On June 2nd Colonel Denison addressed the Chamber of Commerce at Tunbridge Wells ; on June 4th he spoke in Glasgow and on the following day at Paisley ; on June 6th he addressed a meeting at Edinburgh, and the Chamber of Commerce at Leith ; on June 10th he spoke at the Royal Colonial Institute ; on June 11th he addressed the Bristol Chamber of Commerce and four days later the London Chamber of Commerce. Opposition to his views was not confined to the Radical press. In the Commons on June 10th Sir William Harcourt attacked the scheme as " a policy of pure and simple protection." To the London correspondent of the Toronto *Globe* the Hon. Dr. Borden, Canadian Minister of Militia, made the following statement on June 13th : "Without reference to the merits or disadvantages of the zollverein policies advocated by Colonel Denison, I have this to say, that he does not represent Canada or the Dominion Ministry, but himself alone. He has no authority to speak for Canada." In the *Times* of June 17th Sir Robert Giffin, the statistical expert, strongly deprecated Colonel Denison's policy. According to the figures which he adduced a ten per cent. import duty around the Empire would take from the United Kingdom £41,400,000, from India £1,800,000, from Australia £1,100,000, from Natal and the Cape £500,000, from Canada and Newfoundland £2,400,000.

The effect of any such tax on the trade of the United Kingdom would be nothing short of infinite disaster. The attempt to levy it would drive away our *entrepot* trade which we retain with great difficulty, as it is, or we should have to make costly arrangements to let the trade go on, if it could, under bond.

Our whole manufacturing for export would also be crippled and for the most part destroyed by a charge of anything like ten per cent. on its raw materials.

To this Colonel Denison replied four days later. As the nominal expenditure of Canada upon defence is £400,000 his policy would involve an increase of £2,000,000. As that of Great Britain is about £41,000,000 it would involve no increase there whatever. A large country with sparse population and without a development of two thousand years could hardly be expected to contribute at the same ratio as the United Kingdom. His plan would give the British manufacturers a preference in the markets of 360,000,000 people; would turn emigration from the building up of Foreign countries to the same work within the Empire; would ensure the safety of the British people's food supply. As to trade in bond there would be no more difficulty at Singapore and Hong-Kong than there was now between Canada and the United States. The matter of raw material might be arranged by a system of rebates. A large portion of the duty would be paid by foreigners and the whole scheme was simply a re-arrangement of taxation for the good of the Empire.

Colonel Denison returned to Toronto on June 21st, and was interviewed in the papers of the following day. The only new point evoked was the statement that at all the meetings addressed he had read a Resolution passed by the Executive of the British Empire League in Canada as being the authority and cause for his presence. He had not claimed to represent Canada and in this connection he strongly denounced Sir Fredrick Borden's repudiation of his views in London. On October 20th, the Colonel was tendered a banquet at the National Club, Toronto, with Mr. J. F. Ellis in the chair and the Hon. G. W. Ross and Hon. J. Israel Tarte amongst the guests. He gave a history of his mission, its objects and progress. The Premier of Ontario warmly eulogized Colonel Denison's work in Great Britain and Mr. Tarte declared (*Globe* report) that "the best way to serve the British Empire is to build up a British nation here" through a thoroughly Canadian tariff.

The question of Imperial Defence is so many-sided that certain initial figures are necessary to its consideration and these were supplied in two pamphlets issued during the year— one written by Mr. F. Blake Crafton, of Halifax, Canada, and the other by Mr. H. B. Bignold, of New South Wales, Australia. In the former it was stated that the Royal Navy protects the commerce of the Empire amounting to £949,000,000 for the United Kingdom and £256,000,000 for the self-governing Colonies, at a cost of £28,479,000 to the Motherland and £220,000 to the Colonies. The revenue of the former was £130 000,000 and the latter £54,000,000; the population of the United Kingdom was 41,000,000 and of the Colonies 10,500,000. Mr. Bignold put the matter in a little different way and took the ordinary defence expenditure—military and naval—of the Empire as follows:

Defence of the Empire

UNITED KINGDOM.

Army (est. 1899-1900)	£23,822,333
Navy (est 1899-1900)	27,578,039
	£51,400,372

SELF-GOVERNING COLONIES.

	Imperial	Local
Cape Colony	£30,000	£220,000
Natal	6,837	60,186
Canada	Nil	491,736
Australia	126,000	587,000
		1,521,759

Total	£52,922,131

The proposals submitted by the War Office to the Coronation Conference suggested special Colonial organization for the defence of the Empire and in the Memorandum on the subject it was said on the authority of the General Officer Commanding in Canada that there was at present no adequate trained force in case of war with the United States which could hold the Canadian frontier until troops arrived from England. The following were the suggestions made in detail: Australia—Two mounted brigades, one infantry brigade; approximate strength, 9,000 men. New Zealand—One mounted brigade, two infantry battalions; approximate strength, 3,000. Canada—One brigade division field artillery, one infantry brigade; approximate strength, 3,000.

At the annual meeting of the British Empire League, on July 7th, the Duke of Devonshire was very frank in discussing a common defence of common interests. "That question is one which our Colonies must at no distant time consider, either in the event of their desiring, as I believe they do desire, that the present British Empire should remain inviolate, or in the other contingency which they do not desire, of having, as great independent States, to provide for their own security." Speaking in Toronto on January 31st Dr. G. R. Parkin, C.M.G., declared that British commerce presented the greatest loot ever offered to the cupidity of the world and that Canada was the only country on earth which did not pay anything for naval defence. He urged payment of the expenses of all Canadian Contingents sent to South Africa.

At the annual meeting of the British Empire League in Ottawa on February 20th Colonel G. T. Denison summed up the question from his standpoint. Under nominal conditions Canada pays forty cents per head for defence, Great Britain $5.40 per head and the United States about the same. If Canada paid in the same proportion for defence as Great Britain it would cost her $16,000,000; if in the same proportion as the people of the United States it would be $28,000,000; if in proportion to her export trade as compared with Great Britain $21,000,000; if in proportion to her mercantile tonnage, $15,000,000. In Montreal, on February 27th, Dr. Parkin spoke on Imperial Federation and took lines similar to those of his preceding Toronto speech. Letters were published in March written during the preceding autumn between the Hon. G. W. Ross and Lord Avebury. Upon the question of defence the Ontario Premier declared that the matter could only be solved as part of the fiscal problem and by the encouragement of emigration to the Colonies.

In submitting measures for the defence of the Empire for public consideration, I think we have very nearly reached the point at which it may be assumed that the Colonies are in duty bound to share the burden of maintaining the Army and Navy of the Empire. While it is so clear that we enjoy material advantages for the protection of our commerce and for maintaining the integrity of the Empire, it follows, as a matter of course, that we should not repudiate the obligations which these advantages impose.

There was, however, the fact to consider that Canada had no part in the Foreign policy of the Empire and that Colonial development and commerce had come in the main without Imperial aid. At a banquet in Toronto on March 17th, Colonel Denison argued that if our Imperial relations were so satisfactory as Sir Wilfrid Laurier contended we should pay something to preserve them and instanced the Behring Sea incident of 1890, and the prompt protection given by Great Britain. To the *Globe*, on March 21st, the Colonel wrote a letter and pointed out that Canada had an overflowing treasury and Great Britain a tax-rate under which the people were groaning— the latter as a result of defending Empire interests. The Dominion Government had done " excellent work for Imperial unity " and he hoped they would now carry it further. At Hamilton on April 23rd, Dr. Parkin urged the discussion of defence questions at the coming Conference and added that " Canadian soldiers were not afraid of bullets and Canadian statesmen should not be afraid of ballots." He took the same line of advocacy at the Canadian Club, Toronto, on May 2nd. He suggested that Canada should assume the burden and cost of Imperial expenses at Halifax, St. John, Sydney and Esquimault and train a hundred thousand men to ride and shoot. Lieut.-Colonel James Mason, of Toronto, was interviewed by the *Telegram* on May 13th, and expressed strong disagreement with the Premier's views of Canada's obligations and position. He thought Canadians, as a whole, were prepared to go a long way to maintain the *prestige* and power of Great Britain. He considered that Canada's existence and freedom depended upon such a result and was prepared to go far in furnishing troops and money to aid England whenever necessary. Speaking on May 18th, the Rev. J. Pitt Lewis, of Toronto, also warmly urged Canadian aid in this connection. The Montreal Board of Trade discussed the question on May 13th and passed the following Resolution by a large majority : " That it is the duty of this Dominion, as an important division of the Empire, to share in the cost of the general defence of said Empire, and therefore, that an annual appropriation should be provided in the Dominion budget for this purpose to be expended as the Dominion Government may direct." Mr. Edgar Judge expressed himself, in speaking to the motion, an admirer of Sir Wilfrid Laurier, but thought that he did not represent the people in his views upon this subject.

In the London *Standard* on May 30th, Mr. J. Charlton, M.P., deprecated external military aid on the part of Canada and thought she had enough to do guarding her own frontier line. Writing in the *Empire Review* for June, Lord Strathcona dealt with this question and expressed the belief that Canadian expenditures upon railways, telegraphs, harbours, steam and cable communications, local defence and Militia expenses were, in some sort, contributions to Imperial defence interests. The question of naval contribution involved the whole problem of Imperial unity and representation. " There seems no reason, however, why there should not be greater cohesion between the military forces in the Colonies and those at home. They certainly ought to form part of the machinery on which the Empire could implicitly rely in times of trouble and difficulty." At the Board of Trade Conference, Toronto, in June a Resolution was passed in favour of a cash contribution to Imperial defence, after prolonged discussion. A very different motion was carried on June 19th at a mass-meeting of 5,000 French-Canadians in Drummondville, representing some 93 townships and addressed by Mr. H. Bourassa, M.P., and others. It was almost identical in form with the words of the circular calling the meeting, as follows :

Seeing that the yellow press and the fanatics have organized a campaign for the triumph of their anti-national idea, that is to say, for the sacrifice of the resources of our country in favour of militarism and raising soldiers and sending them to the four quarters of the globe for the defence of the Empire, instead of employing its resources for the development of its wealth ; Seeing that they endeavour by their clamour to prevent the voice of sound public opinion from being heard ; Seeing that it is our duty as citizens to protest against these actions, whose aim is to sacrifice Canada for the glory of the Empire, and whose success would be the last blow to our influence as a nationality ; Seeing that the future of our country is threatened ; Therefore the French-Canadians of Drummondville invite the citizens of all the parishes of Nicolet to protest against the Imperial campaign and to adopt resolutions approving the position taken by Sir Wilfrid Laurier in his reply to the Secretary of the Colonies, that is to say, no contribution to the wars of England.

Speaking upon this subject at an Orange demonstration at Brockville, on July 12th, Mr. W. Galbraith, Deputy Grand Master of the Order in British America, strongly deprecated the Premier's refusal to discuss it at the coming Conference. He believed public opinion, when the question was understood, would be just as unanimous as it was about the first Contingent to the War. He wanted a scientific system of Imperial defence. " Have we men to sacrifice and no money ? Are men less valuable than gold ? " On June 23rd the Hon. R. P. Roblin addressed the North Staffordshire Chamber of Commerce and concluded in the following terms : " The time must come when the people of the great Dominion of Canada, of the Cape, and of the Commonwealth of Australia, would have to face the question and recognize that they are part and parcel of the British Empire, and that they must formulate some scheme by which they could assist the Mother Country in maintaining a fleet which should be the fleet of the Empire, and make it a *sine qua non* that the command of the sea should be ours." The Earl of Minto discussed the subject at some length at the Barton banquet in Montreal, on September 8th. It was, he thought, common ground. "Surely if the Motherland is pledged to support her young dependencies to her last man, may she not fairly claim some care for the efficiency of their military organization?" The recent war had, perhaps, unduly enhanced in public opinion the value of irregular troops to the disparagement of organization and discipline. He paid high tribute to Colonial courage in South Africa, but urged greater efficiency for home organization.

In my opinion that efficiency can best be obtained by strict recognition of the assumption that our Colonial forces should be territorial armies for the defence of their own possessions ; that they should be the garrisons of those parts of the Empire to which they belong ; but that they should be garrisons upon whose commanders, upon whose organizations and upon whose efficiency His Majesty's Government may justifiably rely, when our field armies are called upon to face the stress of war.

On November 21st Mr. J. P. Whitney, K.C., M.P.P., the Conservative Leader in Ontario, said at a Toronto banquet that the present condition was anomalous and inconsistent and could not last. "Whatever scheme may be decided on we will not haggle about names and shall be ready and proud to take up our share of the burdens of the great Empire of which we form a part. When the time comes no such bogey as 'the vortex of European militarism' shall have any perils for us."

Apart from the important debate of May 12th, on the Coronation Conference, in which Sir Wilfrid Laurier declined to enter "the vortex of European militarism," there were various references to this subject in the 1902 Session of Parliament. On March 25th Mr. A. E. Kemp (C) took strong ground for sharing in the defensive system of the Empire. He favoured the gradual building up of a Canadian Navy. On April 2nd Mr. J. R. Lavell (C) spoke in a similar strain. "There is no doubt in my mind that Canada should bear her share in the expenses of Imperial defence." Mr. L. P. Demers (L) defended Imperialism on the following day against the view of many French-Canadians, and described it as an arrangement amongst members of a family. "It stands to reason that if we want the Empire to defend and protect us it is our duty to offer England our assistance and to stand by her in her hour of distress." But this should always be a voluntary action. Mr. F. B. Wade (L) referred, on April 7th, to the burdens of Great Britain, and thought the time was not far distant when Canada would say: "We wish to share a portion of this burden; we wish to have a voice in controlling the destiny of the Empire and its policy toward other

nations." On April 8th Mr. Rodolphe Lemieux (L) took strong
ground against Imperialism, and gave the following table of alleged
contributions to the Empire by Canada :

Surrender of territory embracing Maine, Wisconsin, Oregon, etc., 300,000,000 acres at $1 per acre......	$300,000,000
Building of the Intercolonial Railway.................	30,000,000
Expenditure incurred through the Fenian Raid........	2,000,000
African Contingents...............................	2,000,000
Purchase of the North-West........................	1,500,000
Building of the C. P. R.............................	100,000,000
Expenditure on Militia since 1867...................	35,000,000
	$470,500,000

Sir Wilfrid Laurier discussed the subject on April 15th, and,
after twitting Mr. Borden and the Opposition with being afraid
to suggest any policy as against his own negative one, proceeded as follows : " In our own estimation and, I believe, in the
estimation of the Canadian people at large, the relations which
to-day bind Canada to the Motherland cannot be improved, at least
I do not see how." The Hon. J. G. Haggart, on May 12th, deprecated the idea of not discussing defence at the Conference, and
declared that the first object and hope of the British founders of
Canadian institutions had been to make and keep Canada a part of
the Empire. Its chief interest was in the fleet and the issue of a
great war might be decided a thousand miles away from Canadian
shores.

The leading papers of Canada devoted considerable attention to
this subject of defence during the year. The Montreal *Star* of
February 13th wrote characteristically of what it
The Press
and Empire
Defence
considered the difference between our professions and
our action. " As a matter of fact we are vitally interested. Our national existence is at stake. The day
Britain abandons Imperialism she abandons us. We can afford as
little as the loyal South Africans to see a pro-Boer party triumph.
And we should say so." The *Mail and Empire,* on March 14th,
pointed to the enormous past expenditure by Great Britain upon
Empire defence, and proceeded as follows :

We are bound to concede that in the past we have enjoyed great advantages,
for which we have been called upon to bear only a trifling part of the cost, and
in which we ought soon to participate, in some shape or other, much more
generously. That, we believe, is the conviction of the vast majority of Canadians. Imperial defence is not a matter that ;can be flippantly thrust
aside by a shallow objection. It is as essential to us as it is to any part of the
Empire, and it is as warmly supported by the loyal people here as by Britons
anywhere.

The Montreal *Herald* took very much the same ground as its
Conservative opponent just quoted. While objecting to details of
suggested schemes it considered the assumption of Imperial responsibilities at Esquimault and Halifax as the next step. On April
4th it treated the matter as follows, after declaring closer Imperial

relations the wish of a majority of the Canadian people: "So long as Canada is connected with the Mother Country, so long as it enjoys the protection of Britain's fleet and Britain's army, so long must it bear a share of the burdens of the Empire. To refrain from so doing would be to play the craven's part and to ignore the primary responsibilities of nationhood." The Regina *West* of April 2nd declared that Canada should pay its share; the Nelson *News* of April 27th urged better local organization for Imperial aid; the Halifax *Herald* of May 5th asked that the questions of defence and commerce be taken up together as constituting the line of least resistance.

The Toronto *Globe* had many editorials on the subject. On March 20th, it urged moderation in discussing it and caution in dealing with it and defended the Premier's position by quoting Sir Charles Tupper's well-known views. On April 2nd it reviewed various plans and concluded that "generally speaking, some voluntary action by the Colonies would be better than a formal agreement." There should be no bargaining in the matter and, perhaps, the maintenance of fortifications on the sea-coasts might be one of the means of action. On June 6th the ground was taken that Canada should be able to attend to and pay for the cost of its own land defence and that its Parliament should control the expenditure. Presumably this did not mean the elimination of British aid in war-time. Transportation was also said to be an important factor in defence and there was room in this respect for development. On June 18th it was stated that Great Britain and Canada should each attend to its own defence as a permanent condition but "each should exhaust its resources for the other in case its integrity were assailed by any hostile combination."

An important double-columned editorial appeared on June 12th in *La Patrie*, the Montreal organ of Mr. Tarte. The subject was discussed very moderately and the conclusion reached that, while there was some justification for Canada making a contribution yet it would be better to spend the money along lines of material development. The subject should not be considered from a racial standpoint. And then the paper continued: "Those who, in good faith, and with the most praiseworthy motives. believe that we ought to contribute to the defence of the Empire, that is to say, enter into the European orb, are they very sure that they are not preparing for to-morrow dangerous discontents? The augmentation of our annual expenses for Imperial and military ends means the necessary increase of taxes and public charges." This would mean taxation without representation and could not but be unpopular. Meanwhile, history taught us that young nations grow as do young generations. "The sons separate from their parents or become their associates." The London *Advertiser* of June 6th favoured the assumption of local defences and later on the protection of coasts and the maintenance of naval bases. The Halifax *Chronicle* upheld in several articles the idea of a circle of sister nations each looking out for its own defence and the support of a common cause in time of war. No direct contribution to army or navy could be tolerated but (March 26th) " Canada's clear and immediate duty is to provide adequately for her own defence by land and measurably by sea." The Winnipeg *Telegram*, of September 13th, supported action such as that of Australia, contribution towards naval defence and the early organization of a naval Militia.

There were special discussions during the year as to the question of Colonial or Canadian contributions to the Imperial Navy. In the Imperial House of Commons on February 21st Mr. T. Lough proposed a motion declaring that " the growing expenditure on the naval defences of the Empire imposes, under the existing conditions, an undue burden on the tax-payers of the United Kingdom." He spoke of the 230 per cent. increase in this outlay during ten years and of rich Colonies contributing £156,000 to the amount while Ireland's share was nearly £3,000,000. It was negatived by 124 to 54 after Mr. H. H. Asquith had made a strong speech declaring that " the measure of naval expenditure is to be found in the needs of the Empire." On June 20th Rear-Admiral Sir John Colomb made the following statement :

Canada and the British Navy

He feared that in the Colonies the people were no more educated as to Naval requirements than the people were in this country twenty or twenty-five years ago. The proposition had even been laid down that no system of defence could be devised which would be applicable to all the Colonies alike. That was true as to Military defence ; it was false as to Naval defence. Our Naval security on the seas was the one thing in which all the parts of the Empire had a common interest.

An interesting article upon this subject by Lieutenant L. H. Hordern, R.N., appeared in the *Empire Review* of August and at the Coronation Conference, during the same month, several important Memoranda were submitted upon the general question. Lord Selborne's conclusions as to the results of the meeting in this respect were that an increase in commissioned men-of-war would follow, that the Australasian Squadron would be greatly improved, that the Admiralty was deeply grateful for the confidence shown in the unconditional grants by Cape Colony and Natal and that much good was hoped from the organization of naval brigades and reserves—especially in Australasia. In this connection there was some keen criticism in the press of Great Britain as to Canada's failure to participate with the other Colonies, but none of it was as pronounced as the statements of the Australian Premier at Victoria and Vancouver quoted elsewhere.

During the year the Imperial Federation (Defence) Committee published a pamphlet giving varied reasons for Colonial aid to the Navy. They may be summarized under the heads of protection to sea-coasts, guarding of commerce, the burden borne by Great Britain for a hundred years in this connection, the increase in expenditure (£19,000,000 in ten years) made necessary by an enlarged Empire and added Colonial wealth, the fact that every

British emigrant to the Colonies is a lessening of tax-paying strength at home, and the position of 41,000,000 free people carrying the burden for eleven millions equally free and prosperous.

On June 12th the Council of the British Empire League passed a Resolution in favour of Colonial branches of the Royal Navy Reserve and the annual Report of the League Executive in Canada on February 1st urged the same policy.   On April 18th the Victoria Board of Trade passed unanimously a Resolution endorsing the idea.   At a banquet in Toronto on April 23rd Mr. H. J. Wickham, Secretary of the Navy League, spoke at length upon Canada's duty towards the question of Naval defence and advocated a policy of subsidized ship-building and organization of Naval reserves. The Kingston Board of Trade unanimously passed the following Resolution on May 14th :

That Canada should not only acknowledge the substantial benefit received, but should also make some material contribution towards the cost of its protection, and that for this purpose it would be advisable to adopt at least two methods of giving assistance, viz., (1) the establishment of Naval reserves, and (2) the annual appropriation of a sum of money in the Dominion budget as a contribution towards the actual cost of maintaining the Navy.

At a banquet to Lord Dundonald in Montreal, on November 19th, the Hon. Mr. Prefontaine, Minister of Marine, said that he " hoped the time would soon come when Canada would organize at least the nucleus of a Navy and believed that if Parliament took such a step it would meet with the endorsation of all Canadians." Somewhat similar ground was taken by Sir F. W. Borden, Minister of Militia, at an Ottawa meeting on November 24th.   He stated that the Government fully recognized the duty of Canada to be in a position to bear its fair share of Imperial defence.   But the difficulty lay in the question of control.   " We are ready to do everything that will assist in forming the nucleus of a Navy in this country."   Meanwhile, the Navy League had been doing a good deal of missionary work in this connection and its annual Report issued in London, in April, described the Canadian Preferential tariff as an indirect gift to Great Britain of £400,000 annually.

The Victoria and Vancouver branches were especially active and through their influence a Resolution was passed by the Provincial Legislature on June 20th which referred to the extensive sea-boards of Canada, the benefit received from past naval protection, the undignified position held by the Dominion in the matter at present and declared that " the time has now arrived when Canada should assume her fair share of the cost of the naval protection afforded."   Reserves for the Royal Navy were stated to be the most practicable immediate step.   On April 11th, the Toronto branch of the League issued a Memorandum for submission to the Canadian Government which chiefly urged British-Canadian subsidies to a fleet of merchant steamers on the Atlantic, suitable for auxiliaries in war-time, and the organization of a naval Militia in Canada.   In the *Globe* of November 29th, Mr. H. J. Wickham urged these suggestions again and opposed the idea of a separate

10

Navy, claiming that Britain's greatest need was men for the ships she already had.

Meanwhile Mr. H. F. Wyatt had come to Canada on behalf of the British Navy League and had organized a number of branches including Montreal on November 3rd, with Senator Drummond as President; Kingston on November 14th; Ottawa on November 24th, with Sir Sandford Fleming as President; St. John on November 28th, with Mr. James F. Robertson, Mayor White, Mr. W. M. Jarvis and Mr. Justice Barker amongst its officers; Halifax on December 5th, with Lieut.-Governor the Hon. A. G. Jones as President and Mr. John F. Stairs, Sir M. B. Daly and the Hon. William Ross, M.P., amongst its officers; Sydney on December 13th and Quebec on December 30th. Summerside and Charlottetown, Prince Edward Island, were also organized. Amongst the officers of the Quebec branch were Mr. William Power, M.P., the Hon. Richard Turner, M.L.C., the Hon. P. B. Casgrain and Lieut.-Colonel O. C. C. Pelletier.

During this work Mr. Wyatt addressed a large number of meetings. His most clearly defined project was the organization of a trained Naval Militia under Government control and his strongest argument was that the British Empire depended for its safety upon supremacy at sea. The meeting of the Montreal Chambre de Commerce on October 30th, was notable for a vehement protest from Mr. J. H. Perrault against "crushing Canada under the burden of militarism." The Monroe Doctrine, in his opinion, was ample protection to Canada and if England did not help us the United States would. At the St. John meeting, the following Resolution was passed unanimously :

Resolved, That this meeting is of the opinion that Canada should take a share in the naval defence of the Empire and considers that this particular object can easily be effected without violating the principles on the one hand of Canadian autonomy or on the other hand of that unity of control and solidarity of the Imperial Navy which is essential to victory in war.

At Sydney Dr. G. R. Parkin also spoke and declared that he would much rather see Canada outside the Empire than holding a contemptible and dependent place within it. At Quebec the following motion was passed: "This meeting approves of the proposed creation by the Dominion Government of a Canadian naval force, and expresses the earnest hope that in its future development the principle of Canadian autonomy may be reconciled with that of the strategic unity of the Imperial Navy and of the integrity of the latter as a single force."

The visit of the Prime Minister of Australia to Canada was both an interesting and important incident. He went upon his Coronation mission with clearly defined objects as outlined at a banquet in Melbourne on May 5th. They embraced the principle that it was not yet time to exact permanent representation in Imperial Councils; that the defence of Australian shores should be assumed together with a share in the maintenance of the Navy; that the

Sir Edmund Barton in Canada

THE RT. HON. SIR EDMUND BARTON, G.C.M.G., K.C., M.P.

Prime Minister and Representative of Australia at the Coronation Conference.
A guest of the Canadian people during the year.

question of Preferential trade should be carefully considered; that a share in the Empire's heritage was theirs and should include some share of its responsibilities. In his many speeches in Great Britain and his work at the Conference Sir Edmund Barton upheld his reputation as a sane, loyal and able statesman. After the Coronation and the Conference were over he returned home *via* Canada and, accompanied by Sir John Forrest, Federal Minister of Defence, and Mr. Austin Chapman, M.P. The party arrived in Toronto on September 3rd, and first attended a Luncheon at the Industrial Exhibition, presided over by Mr. W. K. McNaught. An Address was presented, speeches made and the Exhibition inspected.

In the evening a representative banquet was given by the Board of Trade to the Australian Premier, with Mr. A. E. Ames presiding, Sir John Forrest, the Hon. G. W. Ross and Mr. J. P. Whitney as the other speakers. Sir Edmund Barton made a ringing Imperialist speech. He urged a Canadian news service in place of the existing American system; described Colonial freedom as the result of Empire development and as something equally cherished by British statesmen; defended the Australian idea of contributing to the Navy as a duty and a benefit; advocated cheaper newspaper postage within the Empire; and spoke confidently of the progress of Imperial sentiment and policy. On September 5th he visited Quebec and two days later was banqueted in Montreal by the Board of Trade, with Mr. Alexander McFee in the chair. H. E. the Earl of Minto, Lieut.-Governor Sir L. A. Jetté of Quebec, Hon. Messrs. Tarte and Fisher and Mr. George E. Drummond were the other speakers in addition to the visitors.

Sir Edmund was welcomed at Ottawa on September 10th by various members of the Government and leading citizens and, with the members of his party, including Lady Barton and Lady Forrest, drove to the City Hall, where Mayor Fred. Cook presented an Address and the Premier delivered a speech. On the 12th the party left for the West after the two statesmen had received an Address from the Board of Trade, presented by Mr. John Coates, its President. They reached Winnipeg on the 14th and the Australian Premier was lunched by the Lieutenant-Governor at Government House and entertained by Hon. Robert Rogers. In an interview with the *Free Press* Sir Edmund expressed a strong wish for the establishment of a fast Atlantic line. Three days days later he reached Vancouver and on the following evening was banqueted by the Board of Trade. President W. H. Malkin was in the chair and the speakers included Mr. R. G. Tatlow, M.P.P., Rear-Admiral Bickford, Mr. F. Carter-Cotton, Sir John Forrest, Sir James Fairfax of Sydney, Mr. Bell-Irving and Sir Charles Hibbert Tupper, M.P. Upon the question of Canada and Imperial defence Sir Edmund spoke more frankly than elsewhere.

I would like to remind you that you have two Imperial squadrons on the coasts of Canada, one at your eastern station and one at your western. We

Australians, who propose to pay something towards the Navy, have only one.
If it is right for us to make some contribution then are you helping us, or are
you helping the cause of Empire, by being at the same time the most populous
and the most reluctant to assist of all the great nations of the Empire?

To this view Sir C. H. Tupper took strong exception. On the
19th Sir Edmund was entertained by the Victoria Board of
Trade, and spoke at length on the ties of Empire and once more
dealt with the question of defence, urging Canada to join with
Australia in its policy of contribution. "Now, I want to know if
there is any reason why you should not? It is not a good reason
to say that on account of the interests involved the United Kingdom would have to give you the protection of the British navy
anyhow. That would not be a good reason, because nothing that
is mean can be, and I am sure your people do not and will not
support the withholding of the contribution upon any such ground
as that." If he failed to obtain Parliamentary sanction in Australia for his proposals it would be partly due to Canada's not joining
hands in the policy. He again urged a Canadian news service and
promised to help in trying to obtain a British tariff preference
despite his not having received Canadian aid in the Navy matter.
From Victoria Sir Edmund Barton and his party sailed for home.

As the discussion of Imperial problems in which Canada is interested, or concerned, cannot be adequately followed without knowing
what has been thought and felt in Great Britain during
the year, it will be useful to quote a few more of the
utterances of the period by British statesmen or public
bodies. Under date of January 10th, the Hon. T. A.
Brassey (son of Lord Brassey, and a Parliamentary
candidate upon one occasion), addressed a letter to Liberal agents
and Secretaries of Liberal Associations throughout Great Britain,
describing the work which he and others had done during several
months past in addressing Liberal meetings in favour of a Federal
government for the Empire and the Kingdom. He stated that a
Resolution, which follows, had been unanimously carried at all the
meetings, and claimed, therefore, that "we are justified in describing
the policy advocated as one on which all Liberals can unite." The
following were the terms of the Resolution :

*British
Statesmen
and Empire
Questions*

That this meeting, regarding the congestion of business in the House of
Commons as a fatal obstacle to progress in social and domestic legislation, is of
opinion that this obstacle can best be overcome by the establishment of local
Legislatures in the several countries of the United Kingdom, each having power
to deal with its own internal affairs, leaving to the existing Imperial Parliament
the management of those matters which affect the United Kingdom as a whole,
and of all Imperial business. It is further of opinion that the Colonies should
be invited to send representatives to the Imperial Parliament as soon as they
desire to share with the Mother Country the burdens of Empire.

On February 13th, Mr. Chamberlain was presented at the Guildhall with an Address, contained in a solid gold casket, as a tribute
by the City of London to his administration of the Colonial Office,
which had, in the opinion of the Lord Mayor and Council, "welded
together His Majesty's dominions beyond the seas." In his speech

the Colonial Secretary reviewed the record of the war, described the policy of the Government as being the maintenance of British authority in South Africa and the general unity of the Empire, and proceeded as follows: "The community of sentiment which animates the British race throughout the world has at last found material expression. We know now that the honour and the interests of the Empire are recognized as not in the care of this country alone. Shoulder to shoulder, all for each and each for all, we stand united before the world, and our children have shown that they are not unwilling to share with us the obligations as well as the dignity of our Empire. It is a last step toward consolidation, the value of which cannot be over-estimated. It has been the aspiration of our ancestors; it has been striven for by patriotic statesmen of all parties; and now that it is within measure of practical accomplishment, it is fraught with measures of incalculable importance in the coming years. These new nations are rising like stars above the horizon, and we hope and believe that they will run their orbits in harmony with our own."

Speaking on February 19th, at Leicester, to the National Liberal Federation, Sir Henry Campbell-Bannerman, the Liberal leader in the House of Commons, gave his definition of Imperialism. It had an innocuous and reputable meaning as implying a desire and endeavour to promote, defend and strengthen the common interests of the Empire. But there was another kind of thing covered by this name:

It magnifies the executive power, it acts upon the passions of the people, it conciliates them in classes and in localities by lavish expenditure, it occupies men's minds with display and amusement, it inspires a thirst for military glory, it captures the electorate by false assertions and illusory promises, and then, having by these means obtained a plebiscite and used electoral forms in the servile Parliament thus created, it crushes opposition and extinguishes liberty.

The Earl of Selborne criticized this definition at Oxford on February 22nd, and described Sir Henry as "looking with suspicion and dislike on the whole stream of Imperial sentiment which had permeated the Empire" and been so largely the creation of men like Seeley, Gordon and Kipling. Speaking in London on May 7th, Lord Salisbury delivered a weighty speech, which carefully analyzed existing conditions. In the multiplication and preservation of Colonial liberties he saw peace, satisfaction and deep affection conserved for future generations. Recent events and sympathetic developments had added immensely to the stability of the Imperial structure and the strength of its rulers in the world. Great care was needed in the future, however, in order not to alienate these sentiments or anticipate events too rapidly. The natural play of forces and organizations should be allowed full operation amongst the "vehement races" of the Empire. "There is nothing more dangerous than to force a decision before a decision is ready, and therefore to produce feelings of discontent, feelings of difficulty which, if we will only avoid, will of themselves bring about the results we desire."

On May 12th the Liberal League, of which Lord Rosebery was President and Mr. H. H. Asquith, Sir H. H. Fowler and Sir Edward Grey, Vice-Presidents, issued a Manifesto, which declared that the organization considered Naval supremacy on the seas essential to the security of British realms, appreciated and accepted to the full the duties of our "free, unaggressive, tolerant Empire," and would further every substantial attempt to cement its unity.   On July 31st Lord Rosebery addressed a League banquet in London.   He declared that the great mass of the Liberal party now looked upon the Empire as a serious trust of which they welcomed the responsibilities and which they regarded as "the most fruitful instrument yet devised for the practical realization of liberty and justice."   At Addington, on September 20th, Mr. Balfour, the Prime Minister, defined the element of localism, which in every large Empire must be a possible danger, but might also by its variations of belief be a source of freshness and activity in public life.   " The difficulty is to touch that happy mean by which the subordinate patriotism may exist, may flourish, may grow exceedingly, and yet may never be allowed for one moment to interfere with the larger patriotism which is the essence of the life of every great Empire."

At the commencement of 1902 the long projected Cable line between Canada and Australia was well under way and the **Completion of the Pacific Cable** sustained labours of Sir Sandford Fleming through 25 years of agitation and work were approaching the period of completion and reward.   On March 25th Sir Joseph G. Ward, Postmaster-General of New Zealand telegraphed the Hon. Mr. Mulock and Sir S. Fleming that the first section of the Cable—connecting Australia and New Zealand—had been just completed.   He hoped the end of the year would see the lines at Vancouver and thus form "another important link in the chain which binds together the whole of the British Empire."   Mr. Mulock wired his congratulations and declared that the final event must have a "far-reaching effect upon the commercial and political life of the Empire."   In discussing the position of the Eastern Extension Company in Australia, on April 16th, Sir J. G. Ward urged caution in any Government arrangements with this rival line.   "The probability is that before 20 years have passed Australia will be the joint owner with Great Britain, Canada, India and New Zealand of the whole of the Cables serving these countries."

First proposed by Sir Sandford Fleming in 1874 and approved by Sir John Macdonald and Lord Beaconsfield; meeting with intense opposition from rival Cable lines and advocated from time to time by various Canadian statesmen, including especially Sir Charles Tupper; finally commenced under the special auspices of Mr. Chamberlain, Sir Wilfrid Laurier, Sir Edmund Barton and Mr. Seddon; running some 8,000 nautical miles from Doubtless Bay, Queensland, to Bamfield Creek, British Columbia, and costing £1,795,000; the Pacific Cable was opened on October 31st for the business of the Empire.   The first message despatched was by Sir Sandford Fleming which promptly girdled the earth from Ottawa back to Ottawa and was addressed by himself to the Governor-General.   Messages ensued from Mr. Chamberlain to Lord Minto and to Lord Tennyson in Australia followed with suitable replies. The first-named despatch expressed the congratulations of the Imperial Government and added : "They feel confident that the spirit of co-operation between the Mother Country and the Colonies which initiated the enterprise will gather additional strength from its successful accomplishment."   Sir William Mulock sent a special message to Mr. Chamberlain describing the event as a realization of inter-Imperial policy and a step towards a system of state-owned cables around the Empire.   Various cables were also interchanged between Sir Wilfrid Laurier and other British and Colonial authorities.

Celebrations were held at Victoria and Vancouver.   At a Board of Trade luncheon in the latter place speeches were made in which stress was laid upon the services of Mr. F. Carter-Cotton who, when a member of the Provincial Government, had at a critical period come forward and offered $2,000,000 on behalf of his Province towards the construction of the work.   In Victoria Mayor Hayward presided over a public meeting at which addresses were delivered by Bishop Cridge, the Lieutenant-Governor, Rev. E. S. Rowe, Hon. D. M. Eberts, Mr. A. E. McPhillips, M.P.P., Senator Macdonald and Mr. R. Hall, M.P.P.   During the next few days Sir Sandford Fleming received a multitude of telegrams.   On November 6th Sir W. Mulock was notified by the Pacific Cable Board that the rate per word from points in Canada to all points in New Zealand or Australia was to be 2s. 4d. with every word counted, as against the old rate of $1.50 and the latter one of 99 cents.   The press comments on the subject were many and in them all great credit was given Sir S. Fleming.   As the Halifax *Herald* put it the Empire built the Cable but he got the Empire to work.   The Toronto *Globe* of October 31st added this comment : " Not only was it a Canadian who conceived the project, but it can be said without boasting that but for the resolution and vigilance of the Canadian Government it would have been wrecked by those who fought it with almost equal skill and determination."   At the end of the year Sir Charles Tupper had a long and important letter in the London *Times* dealing with the action of the Canadian Government in the matter from time to time.

The question of high postal rates on newspapers and periodicals between Great Britain and Canada and the consequent flooding of

Postal Rates Within the Empire the Canadian market with cheap and often injurious American journals was somewhat frequently discussed during the year.   Resolutions in favour of lower rates were passed by the Boards of Trade at Kingston, Orillia and Montreal and by the Inland Board of British Columbia and confirmed on June 4th by the Conference of Canadian Boards of Trade, which decided that "in the highest interests of Canada, Great Britain and the Empire, the postage on newspapers and periodicals should be lowered to the domestic rate as has been done in the case of letters."

Meanwhile, the Canadian Press Association had dealt with the matter, after listening to an address from Mr. E. B. Bigger on February 27th, by passing a Resolution expressing pleasure at the support given in Great Britain to views previously urged by the Association and declaring that from the experience of another year and the increased information available "we are more than ever convinced that the political and business interests of Canada and the Empire would be much advanced by an increased exchange of newspapers and periodicals within the Empire." An official declaration of the Government's opinions was asked for. On April 22nd the British Columbia Legislature unanimously passed a Resolution, on motion of Mr. H. Dallas Helmcken, describing the present impossibility of British journals competing with those of the United States in Canada and urging that the great Imperial importance of the issue be placed before the coming Conference in London. On June 5th, at the Council of the British Empire League in London, the following Resolution was passed unanimously:

That this Council urges upon the attention of His Majesty's Government the very serious grievance inflicted upon both British and Canadian newspaper and magazine proprietors and traders by the maintenance of a rate of postage eight times that charged United States periodicals entering Canada; with the result that Canada is flooded with United States literature whilst British periodicals are virtually excluded by the prohibitory rates.

In the London *Spectator* of August 2nd appeared a letter from Mr. Angus McMurchy of Toronto strongly urging action in this matter and which was endorsed by that paper to a considerable extent. A Resolution in this connection was passed by the Coronation Conference and on November 11th Sir William Mulock wrote an English correspondent that the reason American editions of English magazines, with United States advertisements, etc., circulated so widely in Canada was because of this high postage. "The remedy rests entirely with the Imperial Government," as under the Postal Union, "each country retains to its own use all the postage collected in such country."

The possibility of Canada and Newfoundland at last coming together, after various efforts at union, was widely discussed during **Newfoundland** 1902. The discussion was precipitated largely by **And Union** the resignation of Mr. Justice Donald Morison from **With Canada** the bench of the Island in order to re-enter politics with Confederation as his platform. This occurred at the end of April and was followed by the visit of himself and District Court Judge Seymour—who held the same views—to Ottawa and other Canadian cities. To the Toronto *Mail and Empire* of May 12th Mr. Morison said that the Island had a debt of $20,000,000; that its tariff was higher than Canada's; that it was a country of great resources in timber, pulp-wood and minerals; that Confederation would develop its industries, extend its railway facilities and settle the French shore question in a year.

On June 5th, Mr. Morison addressed, at some length, the banquet held at Toronto in connection with the Board of Trade Conference. He explained that of the Island's debt, $14,000,000 was for railways and the balance for public works and that it would have to be assumed by Canada; that its population was $218,000; its revenues, $2,000,000 and its imports and exports each about $8,000,000. Upon his return he said to the St. John's *News* of June 16th: "As you know I have always been in favour of closer political and commercial relations with Canada if satisfactory terms could be arranged. Both countries have something to gain by a fair bargain and so far as I can see nothing to lose. Every year the arguments for union grow stronger and it seems to me only a question of time when the two countries must come together." At Toronto, on May 30th, Mr. C. H. Hutchings, Deputy Minister of Justice in Newfoundland, spoke and expressed his belief that the Island would benefit by union with Canada and would some day come in. The Hon. A. B. Morine, Opposition Leader in the Island, was interviewed at Montreal by the Toronto *Globe* on June 20th. He deprecated Sir Robert Bond's devotion to the American treaty policy, and declared that terms of union could easily be arranged at the Coronation Conference. He then made the following statement:

In sentiment I am in favour of Confederation, and am positive that it is bound to come, and would come in the near future if satisfactory terms could be arranged. This, as far as I have been able to see, is the attitude of the greater number of the people. But such a movement, if it is to be carried out successfully, must be taken up by the Government party. It is more than a mere party question; it is a national one.

The Premier of Newfoundland spoke at the Canada Club banquet in London, on July 16th, and made some remarks in this connection which were widely commented upon. The question of Confederation was, he said, only a matter of terms. "If the terms are advantageous to the people of Newfoundland, I shall feel it my duty to lay the proposal before my people and, if necessary, exert myself to bring the confederation about. We are not jealous of Canada." Speaking to the Winnipeg *Telegram* on September 5th, the Hon. G. W. Gushue, Minister of Public Works in the Bond Government, declared that "Confederation will have to come sooner or later and perhaps it would be better for it to take place while Newfoundland is prosperous." In an interview at Montreal on October 21st, Sir Robert Bond said:

Confederation is not, with us, a live issue at present. It has been discussed, of course, but it is not a question with which we are immediately concerned. I might say, indeed, that the hostility of the Canadian press, or at least a portion of it, has tended to set this matter back in the minds of the people. I do not mean that the Canadian press has been hostile to the idea of Confederation but it has been hostile to certain trade questions and arrangements and undoubtedly the result of that has been to put people out of favour with the idea of Confederation.

Meanwhile the Island Premier had negotiated his Reciprocity arrangement with the United States and, although its acceptance still hung fire in the Senate at the end of the year, it was felt in many quarters that its success would greatly set back the Canadian Union policy.   Mr. P. T. McGrath, the well-known Newfoundland editor and correspondent of the Halifax *Chronicle*, told that paper on November 15th that if the Treaty became operative it would assuredly shelve Confederation.   "The ingrained hostility of a large section of our people to union with Canada will be accentuated by the prospect of our receiving free-trade with the United States. Practical considerations are paramount, and the first of these is that by Reciprocity we shall be able to secure a market for much of our fishery products among the people of the United States whereas Confederation, whatever else it might do, would not afford us an extra market for a quintal of cod."

Mr. A. B. Morine was interviewed by the St. John *Sun* on December 9th and, after some references to his recent bye-election victories, declared that Confederation was not in any way an issue; that many leading men opposed the policy as tending to detach them from England; that there was no relation between Reciprocity sentiment and annexation because the former was a purely business matter; that there was no leaning towards Americanism in the Island.   " The better informed classes, having no trade interests, are in favour of union with Canada if adequate terms can be given."

The passing away of the Marquess of Dufferin and Ava on February 12th, removed one of the brightest and most brilliant figures in modern Canadian history.   His speeches at a pivotal period did much to promote unity in the new Dominion, and afterwards became classics in its literature; his statecraft moulded many constitutional elements in the early stages of Confederation; his voice and influence were always prominent factors in the presentation of Canadian resources to the British world ; his name and memory helped to lay the foundation of modern Imperialism.   Speaking on the day following Lord Dufferin's death, Sir Charles Tupper referred to the former Governor-General's conduct of important political issues, and added: " His personal influence, while at the head of affairs in Canada, was of the utmost value to the country.   He never interfered unduly in affairs of state, but he seemed to possess many of the characteristics which made the late Queen so exceptional a ruler.   He knew that it was not his province to dictate or direct, but his wise and statesmanlike bearing made it possible for him to exercise a very real influence on the destinies of the Dominion." The leading British papers laid stress upon the Empire character of his work—the *Standard* declaring that " he was amongst those who first conceived and propagated the sentiment of Imperial unity, and will rank among the master builders of our Empire."   The *Times*

Death of
Lord
Dufferin

stated that "his work, though few heard of it at the time, was of vast consequence to the solidarity of the Empire and to the permanent happiness of the Canadian people."

As soon as the news reached Ottawa the Canadian Government cabled to Lady Dufferin an expression of popular regret and sympathy, and the reply, dated at Clandeboye on February 14th, declared that "my husband loved Canada and was ever grateful for the kindness and affection shown him by her people." The press of the Dominion was most appreciative in its comments upon the event. The Montreal *Gazette* described him as the ablest of Canada's Governors-General. " His eloquence did much to persuade Canadians of the greatness of the land that had just fallen into their possession, and so gave them confidence to go forward with the schemes to make its resources available." The Halifax *Herald* declared that in Canada " he is remembered as the most brilliant Governor-General we ever had, and his administration here was simply beyond criticism." The St. John *Sun* thought that "of the eight gentlemen who have represented the British Sovereign at Ottawa, the most brilliant and also the most competent was unquestionably the third in succession. Perhaps we shall never have his like again, for there is hardly his equal among the present generation of British diplomatists." The Manitoba *Free Press* described him as an Empire-builder, and spoke of his wisdom, his tact and his brilliancy. "But he also served the Empire in a way still more valuable ; as none knew better than the Canadian people. He proved himself a devoted and far-seeing Imperial statesman by the consummately able manner in which he stimulated the feeling of Canadianism and of strong attachment to the Empire among the people of this Dominion." The Guelph *Herald* declared that " it is impossible to measure the influence exerted by Lord Dufferin in Canada. The dominant tone of his public utterances was national self-reliance."

In the Canadian Parliament various references were made to the departed statesman. Mr. R. L. Borden, on February 14th, pointed out that his period of administration had been one of much party passion but that now everyone recognized the justice and honesty of his course. " He filled a great place in the Empire and did for Canada much in that from the first he was inspired with a supreme confidence in the future of this country, and more than that was possessed with the same confidence that absolute legislative independence will tend to bring about closer ties between this country and the Empire." The Prime Minister made the following reference : " Lord Dufferin was a statesman of Imperial mind. There was nothing shackled about it. He moved on broad lines. Whatever the subject he had to deal with he could rise above all boundaries and divisions of creed and race, or any of the other considerations which divide men. On every question he soared to the highest possible level."

Amongst the important speeches of the year upon subjects connected with the Imperial relations of Canada was that of Mr.

Canadian Speeches on the Empire

A. E. Ames at the annual meeting of the Toronto Board of Trade in which he said, " I thoroughly believe that this is universally taken for granted that the British Empire as it now stands, stands so forever "; those of the Hon. Charles Fitzpatrick, Minister of Justice and Hon. George E. Foster, at Hamilton on April 3rd; those of the Hon. Mr. Foster and Mr. J. Douglas Hazen, M.P.P., at St. John on April 21st; that of the Hon. Mr. Foster to St. George's Society in Montreal two days later; those of Mr. R. L. Borden, M.P., Mr. J. S. Willison and Dr. G. R. Parkin at Hamilton on April 23rd; that of Mr. H. Bourassa, M.P., in Montreal on April 27th; that of the Hon. Mr. Foster and Professor William Clark in Toronto on November 10th in connection with the King's birthday; that of the Hon. Clifford Sifton, Minister of the Interior, at Boston on November 21st and at London, Ont., on December 1st.

IMPERIAL EVENTS OF CANADIAN CONCERN.*

Feb. 19.—At the meeting of the National Liberal Federation in Leicester the following Resolution is presented as coming from six Liberal or Radical Associations but is voted down after a strongly favourable speech from the Hon. T. A. Brassey :

" That this Association, regarding the congestion of business in the House of Commons as a fatal obstacle to progress in social and domestic legislation, is of opinion that this obstacle can best be overcome by the establishment of local Legislatures in the several countries of the United Kingdom, each having power to deal with its own internal affairs, leaving to the existing Imperial Parliament the management of those matters which affect the United Kingdom as a whole, and that the Colonies should be invited to send representatives to the Imperial Parliament as soon as they desire to share with the Mother Country the burdens of Empire."

Feb. 25.—In the House of Commons the Right Hon. J. W. Mellor presents petitions, against making any change in the Royal Declaration, from 98,765 persons in the Colony of Victoria, 284,647 in England, New Zealand, Canada and the West Indies, 36,000 in Scotland, 16,000 in Ireland, and 6,870 in Wales.

May.   —An important article in the *Empire Review* by Mr. Watson Griffin, of Toronto, deals with the subject of an " Imperial Alliance."

May 15.—Mr. Chamberlain thanks the Canadian Government for the assistance voted by Parliament to the Island of St. Vincent in connection with the volcanic eruptions in the West Indies.

June.   —This month's number of the *Nineteenth Century and After* contains an article by Lieut.-Col. George T. Denison, of Toronto, on Imperialism in Canada.

June 3.—The Hong-Kong Contingent for the Coronation arrives at Victoria and thence passes through Canada to the Atlantic Coast.

June 13.—The Canadian team for Bisley sails for England with Lieut.-Col. J. H. Burland, of Montreal, in command.

July 7.—An accident to Mr. Chamberlain, while driving along Whitehall, causes a sensation and delays Colonial discussions at the Conference.

July 8.—The Argonaut Crew of Canada win the second heat at Henley for the

---

* Not elsewhere referred to.

Grand Challenge Cup against University College, Oxford, but on the following day are beaten by Third Trinity, Cambridge. The Argonauts were composed of Messrs. J. Cooper Mason, Joseph Wright, D. R. Mackenzie, H. Duggan, A. H. E. Kent, E. A. Hamber, R. G. Parmenter, T. Hardisty and N. Bastedo (Coxswain).

July 14.—A measure passes its 3rd reading in the House of Lords and receives the King's assent under which the Imperial Institute is transferred to the nation in accordance with the terms of a special meeting of its Executive held on December 21st, 1901, and presided over by the Prince of Wales. On January 1st, 1903, it is to become a Department of the Board of Trade.

Sept. 28.—The *Aurania* arrives at Halifax with the 5th Royal Garrison Regiment commanded by Lieut.-Col. H. M. Hatchell, D.S.O., and relieves the Royal Canadians of their special garrison duties. The latter regiment is disbanded by the Canadian authorities.

Oct. —A number of British journalists visit Canada and travel from the Atlantic to the Pacific, including representatives of the London *Chronicle* and *Telegraph*, the Glasgow *Herald* and Leeds *Mercury*, the London *Mail*, *News* and *Daily Express*, and the Liverpool *Post*.

Oct. 27.—It is announced that Mr. Chamberlain will make a tour of South Africa, leaving at the end of November and returning about the 1st March.

Nov. —A number of Delegates from the London Chamber of Commerce, including Sir Albert Rollit, M.P., F. Faithful Begg, ex-M.P., Sir Vincent Kennett-Barrington, Lieut.-Gen. J. W. Laurie, M.P., H. C. Richards, K.C., M.P., and others, visit Canada and are banqueted at Montreal, Ottawa, Toronto and other places.

Nov. 7.—The Earl and Countess of Aberdeen celebrate their silver wedding at Haddo and receive a great number of congratulatory telegrams.

Nov. 8.—Sir Richard J. Cartwright, G.C.M.G., M.P., is appointed a Member of the Imperial Privy Council.

CANADIAN EVENTS OF IMPERIAL CONCERN.

Jan. 22.—A public meeting is held at Halifax to protest against offensive phrases used in the Royal Declaration. It is presided over by Archbishop O'Brien and addressed by His Grace, Sir M. B. Daly, Mr. Justice Meagher, Senator L. G. Power and the Hon. William Chisholm, M.L.C.

Mar. 11.—The Grand Orange Lodge of Quebec passes a Resolution deploring the recent efforts of Messrs. Redmond, McHugh and O'Donnell to "stir up sedition, strife and treason" in Canada, as well as the action of the Prime Minister in attending certain festivities in their honour.

Mar. 13.—A debate takes place in the Quebec Legislature on the question of limiting appeals to the Imperial Privy Council.

April 20.—At a public meeting in Ottawa the United Irish League is addressed by Senator Sullivan, Hon. J. Costigan, M.P., and others and passes a Resolution denouncing " the unparalleled folly and tyranny of the British Government in bringing on a peaceable people the horrors of coercion."

May 6.—Parliament votes a final sum for expenses of the Royal Tour in 1901— $358,000 in addition to $120,000 the preceding year. Sir Donald Mackenzie Wallace states in his *Web of Empire* about this time that the Prince and Princess of Wales on this Tour travelled 50,718 miles, received 544 addresses, inspected 62,174 troops, entertained on the *Ophir* 525 persons and shook hands with 35,000 people.

Oct. 12.—A number of Boer Delegates sent by the Imperial authorities, on the advice of Lord Milner to study Canadian farming, arrive at Quebec. They subsequently travel through to the Pacific Coast.

Dec.   1.—A public meeting in Toronto is addressed by the Hon. Edward
        Blake, K.C., M.P., and Mr. Joseph Devlin, M.P.   Upon motion of
        Senator McHugh and Mr. Peter Ryan, the following Resolution is
        passed :
              " As citizens of this contented, because self-governing Dominion,
        we protest against the present enforcement of the Irish coercion
        laws, which are alien to our experience of British citizenship.   We
        call upon the representatives of the Canadian people in the
        Legislative bodies to give renewed expression to the opinion of
        Canada in favour of Home Rule and against coercion."
Dec.   2.—Under the local auspices of the United Irish League the Hon.
        Edward Blake, and Mr. Devlin address a large audience in Montreal
        and on the following day speak at Ottawa.

III.—CANADA AND THE WAR

Early in 1901 the Canadian volunteers for the South African Constabulary, to the total number of 1,208, left for the seat of war under the nominal command of Colonel S. B. Steele, C.B., M.V.O., and the temporary command of Captain P. Fall, of Lord Strathcona's Horse. On November 25th the Colonial Secretary telegraphed the Governor-General of Canada that the Imperial Government would gratefully accept the offer of another Contingent*, of not less than 600 men, to be organized upon similar lines to the Imperial Yeomanry. Action was at once taken by the Militia Department, and the force eventually increased to 900 men, while authority was obtained to add to the 2nd Regiment, Canadian Mounted Rifles—as it was finally named—a Field Hospital Company. Orders were issued for the organization of this latter body on January 3rd, 1902. The services of eight Nursing Sisters were also offered and accepted. The officers of the 2nd C. M. R. were Colonel T. D. B. Evans, C.B., in command, and Major W. Hamilton Merritt, second in command. Lieut.-Col. G. W. Cameron was Major, and the Captains included Major R. G. E. Leckie,† Major J. F. Macdonald; Captains P. E. Thacker, J. D. Moodie and J. H. Elmsley; Lieutenants J. Edwards Leckie, D.S.O., I. R. Snider and F. Church. The Lieutenants were as follows: A. F. Ashmead, R. F. Markham, Bruce Carruthers, Guy Kirkpatrick, W. R. Marshall, S. J. A. Demers, C. R. Tryon, A. D. Reford, E. P. Clarkson, G. B. Mackay, G. W. M. Farrell, F. Homer Dixon, J. D. Graham, J. W. Allan, H. Hiam, A. H. Gault, H. J. Lambkin, H. G. Brunton, W. Rodden. C. P. B. Simpson, J. C. Richards, R. H. Ryan, T. Callaghan, H. S. Douglas, H. F. W. Fishwick, E. Blake Allan and W. J. Loudon. ‡

Captain Church was Adjutant; the Medical Officers were Surgeon-Captain J. A. Devine and Surgeon-Lieut.-Colonel H. R. Duff; the Veterinary Officers were Lieutenant R. Riddell and A. E. James; the Quartermaster was Lieutenant J. Graham, and the Paymaster, Lieutenant R. H. Moir. The names of these officers were submitted to the Secretary of State for War for approval, and they were given temporary rank in the Army whilst serving in South Africa from January 14th, 1902. Lieut.-Col. A. N. Worthington, A.M.S., commanded the 10th Canadian Field Hospital Army Medical Corps with Major G. Carleton Jones, A.M.S., and Lieutenants J. A. Roberts, H. E. Tremayne and P. Weatherbe as the other officers. Part of this force sailed for Cape Town on January 14th on the troopship *Manhattan*; part on the *Victorian* on January 28th; and a small

---

*This was largely owing to the personal initiative and offer of Major W. Hamilton Merritt, of Toronto.

† The rank here given is the rank of the officer in the Militia Service.

‡ Major H. J. Woodside was appointed later as a Lieutenant (unattached).

remainder on the *Parthenia* on March 25th. The first-named boat arrived at Durban on February 18th, and the second on February 25th. On March 1st the Regiment was inspected by Lord Kitchener, and was afterwards attached to Colonel Cookson's column in the division commanded by Major-General Walter Kitchener. The following were the chief events in which it participated :

(1) The night ride of forty-five miles to Witpoort Ridge, followed by the drive at daybreak next morning—the Regiment covering eighty-five miles in twenty-three hours.

(2) The operations ending with the Battle of Boschbult, near Hart's River, on March 31.

(3) The drive commencing April 10, culminating with the attack of the Boers on General Kekewich's column and their defeat with heavy losses.

(4) The drive from Driekuil to Klerksdorp on April 14th and 15th.

(5) The operations between April 23 and May 2, west of Klerksdorp, in which a large amount of the standing crops of the enemy were taken or destroyed.

(6) The drive commencing May 5, and ending May 23, to Vryburg, in Cape Colony and return, resulting in large captures of prisoners and stock.

The 2nd C. M. R. sailed from Cape Town on June 27th for Halifax where they arrived on July 22nd. The officers and men received a most cordial welcome in the different parts of the Dominion to which they returned. Meanwhile, on March 29th, the Imperial Government had signified their willingness to accept the service of 2,000 more men and on April 7th Mr. Chamberlain telegraphed that the most convenient form would be four organized units or regiments. Orders for recruiting were at once issued and a large number of men offered—greatly in excess of those required. The commanding officer of the 3rd Regiment C. M. R., as finally announced, was Lieut.-Col. V. A. S. Williams with Major D. I. V. Eaton as second in command, and Captains W. Henderson, S. A. Mackenzie, W. W. Nasmyth, E. C. Arnoldi, and C. T. Van Straubenzie. Those in command of the 4th C. M. R. were Lieut.-Col. T. dit L. Boulanger with Major F. A. O'Farrell as second, and Captains J. E. G. Boulton, W. C. Good, O. L. Pope, T. Dunning and E. F. Mackie, D.S.O. Those in command of the 5th C. M. R. were Lieut.-Col. A. C. Macdonell, D.S.O., with Major E. A. C. Hosmer as second and Captains C. H. Rogers, F. J. Clark, A. W. Strange, D'Arcy Strickland and F. H. Bagley. Those in command of the 6th C. M. R. were Lieut.-Col. J. D. Irving with Lieut.-Col. W. D. Gordon as second and Captains G. B. Motherwell, F. B. Ross, J. M. Caines, A. S. A. M. Adamson and F. F. Uniacke.

The establishment of each Regiment was 509 officers and men and 539 horses. The troops sailed from Canada in three transports—the *Cestrian* on May 8th, the *Winifredian* on May 17th, and the *Corinthian* on May 23rd. They arrived in South Africa

COLONEL T. D. B. EVANS, C.B.
Commanding 2nd C.M.R.

LIEUT.-COLONEL J. D. IRVING
Commanding 6th C.M.R.

LIEUT.-COLONEL T. dit L. BOULANGER
Commanding 4th C.M.R.

LIEUT.-COLONEL GEO. W. CAMERON, D.S.O.
2nd Canadian Mounted Rifles.

THE END OF THE SOUTH AFRICAN WAR.

too late, by a very short interval of time, to take part in the hostilities and were shortly afterwards at sea again on the way home. The *Cestrian* reached Halifax on July 29th, having on board the headquarters and main body of the four Regiments and the remainder arrived on the *Lake Erie* from England on September 13th. Officers and men alike expressed great regret at not seeing active service. Meanwhile, in connection with the despatch of these forces the question of payment had been raised in certain quarters and protests made against the Mother Country being allowed to pay the soldiers instead of it being done by their own Government. Upon this point the most vigorous language was used by the Rev. Dr. Armstrong Black, of Toronto, the Very Rev. Principal Grant, c.m.g., of Kingston, the Rev. Dr. S. D. Rose, of Ottawa, and Dr. G. R. Parkin. The last-mentioned wrote the Toronto *Globe* of March 20th as follows:

I believe the day is not far off when this country will be heartily ashamed of the niggardly attitude it has taken in the matter of paying for the brave fellows we have lately sent to fight and die for the nation's cause in South Africa. If this attitude represents the real and permanent feeling of the Canadian people many of us may be compelled to change deeply cherished views. I for one would prefer that Canada should be outside the Empire rather than holding a contemptible position within it.

Second only in popular interest to Paardeburg was the Battle of Boschbult, or Hart's River, which occurred on March 31st, 1902. Colonel Evans, in his report of the incident, describes the movements of the British force of 2,000 men with whom were his troops, the 2nd C. M. R.; the attack of some 2,500 Boers; and the preliminary skirmish in which Lieut. T. Callaghan and his party of 60 men lost two killed and nine wounded; the arrival of the whole force at Boschbult Farm with the exception of Lieut. Bruce Carruthers and a rear guard of 21 men who remained behind—the commander, it was stated, sending into camp for orders. The official account then proceeded as follows:

The Hart's River Fight

Several hundred Boers swept down on this post on the right, stampeding the Mounted Infantry, who galloped through the line occupied by our men. Lieut. Carruthers, assisted by Sergt. Perry, Corp. Wilkinson, Lance-Corp. Bond and Private McCall, kept his men in hand, dismounted them and formed in a half moon shape to face the Boers. Sergt. Hodgins, whose men were being swept off in the stampede, rallied about ten of them and dismounted to meet the attack. The splendid stand made by Lieut. Carruther's party, without cover of any kind and against overwhelming odds, was well worthy of the best traditions of Canada and the whole Empire. Before their ammunition was exhausted, 17 out of the 21 were either killed or wounded. Sergt. Perry, although badly wounded, fought until he was killed. Corp. Wilkinson, shot twice through the arm and body, continued fighting till he was shot through the eye. He then threw the bolt of his rifle into the long grass to render it useless to the enemy. Private Evans, although mortally wounded through the bowels, exhausted his ammunition, secured another bandolier, used it up, and, as the Boers were making their final rush, he broke his rifle rendering it useless. Private Evans died shortly after being brought into camp. Private Minchin, although wounded in six places, fired his last shot when the Boers were only 25 yards off, and threw his rifle bolt into the grass.

11

Colonel Evans then gives the Regimental losses for the day as 8 men killed, 3 officers and 39 men wounded and 7 missing. According to Army Orders of April 21st, P. H. Kelly, J. C. Bond and G. McBeth were made Corporals for distinguished gallantry in the field and J. A. Wilkinson a Sergeant for the same reason, while Sergts. J. C. Perry and H. A. Lee and Private C. N. Evans were mentioned for gallantry and good service in action. The papers of the time teemed with accounts of the fight. Nor were these reports limited to the Canadian press. The London *Standard* of April 9th described the incident as the stand of a few men against 600 Boers, quoted Lieut. Carruthers as shouting to his men " No surrender," and called every man of the force a hero. Of the commander it spoke as having his clothes perforated with bullets and added that : " When he was taken prisoner some of the Boers wanted to shoot him there and then ; but they ultimately thought better of it, saying that he was too brave a man to die in that way." Lord Kitchener's official report was as follows :

The heaviest loss in this engagement fell upon the Canadian Mounted Rifles, who, in this their first fight of importance since landing, displayed the utmost bravery and determination. Lieut. Bruce Carruthers, of the Regiment, especially distinguished himself. Being in command of a detachment of the rear guard when coming into camp, he remained out in a position of observavation, in which he eventually found himself isolated and surrounded by a large body of the enemy. Rejecting all idea of surrender, however, his small patrol of 21 men fought stubbornly on to the end, no less than six of their number being killed and twelve wounded. There have been few finer instances of heroism in the whole course of the campaign.

Amongst the wounded were Lieuts. R. H. Ryan, R. F. Markham, G. B. Mackey and W. J. Loudon, and of those killed were Corp. A. W. Sherritt of London, Private C. N. Evans of Port Hope, John Campbell Perry of Galt, W. P. K. Milligan, of Peterborough and Corp. W. A. Knisley, who had previously won the Distinguished Service Medal. On April 5th Mr. Chamberlain cabled the Governor-General as follows : " I congratulate Dominion on heroic conduct of Canadian Rifles in action with De la Rey. Deeply regret heavy casualties, and desire to express heartfelt sympathy with relatives of those who have given their lives to maintain splendid traditions of Canadian valour." Two days later Lord Roberts telegraphed His Excellency an appreciation of " the splendid stand made by the Canadian Mounted Rifles " and his regret at their heavy losses. In the House of Commons at Ottawa, on April 4th, Dr. Borden, Minister of Militia, read aloud the news and in doing so made the simple comment that " Canadians are maintaining the reputation that they have already earned in South Africa and they continue to prefer death to surrender." In the New Brunswick Legislature on April 5th and in a myriad other places of meeting or public discussion in Canada similar expressions of sorrow at the losses and pride in the conduct of the troops was heard. No summary is possible here of the press comments.

Private correspondents sent many letters home about this

engagement. Lieut. E. P. Palmer described Lieut. Carruthers as having 14 bullet holes in his clothes. Trooper H. S. Kingdon eulogized greatly the cool bravery of Surgeon-Major Devine. In the *Times*, on May 26th, appeared a letter from Sir Cavendish Boyle, Governor of Newfoundland, eulogizing the brave deed of Charles Napier Evans and in a speech at Kingston on June 19th Sir Richard Cartwright declared that "no soldier in the annals of history has shown greater bravery" than Lieut. Carruthers. Meanwhile that gentleman had returned home and told the Halifax *Herald* on July 23rd that he had only done what any other Canadian would do. Two days later he and Surgeon-Lieut.-Col. H. R. Duff were presented by the citizens of Kingston with Swords of Honour. On October 31st a portrait of the late C. N. Evans was unveiled in the High School at Port Hope by the Minister of Militia, who read a letter written by the young man to his father shortly before his death in which the following words occurred : " We can only hope for a safe and victorious trip. Many a good man has died for the old flag, and why should not I ? If parents had not given their sons, and sons had not given themselves, to the British Empire, it would not to-day be the proud dictator of the world."

On January 9th, 1902, Captain J. Edwardes Leckie, D.S.O., was presented with his Order at Halifax by the Lieutenant-Governor in the presence of a large and distinguished gathering.

Final Canadian War Honours It was stated in March that a number of the officers of Lord Strathcona's Horse were to be granted honorary rank in the Army with the right to wear the uniform of their Corps. The Hon. Lieutenant-Colonel was Lieut.-Colonel S. B. Steele, C.B., M.V.O., and the Hon. Majors were Majors R. Belcher, C.M.G., R. C. Laurie, A. M. Jarvis, C.M.G., A. E. Snyder, D. M. Howard and G. W. Cameron, D.S.O. The others were complimented in the order of their rank. At Ottawa, on April 2nd, Captain E. W. B. Morrison, D.S.O., was presented with his Order by the Governor-General with due ceremony. Major Henry Bertram Stairs, D.S.O., of Halifax, received the same honour on May 6th, at the hands of the Lieutenant-Governor while Major J. Cooper Mason, D.S.O., was decorated at the Armouries in Toronto, on May 16th, by Major-General O'Grady-Haly, C.B., D.S.O., in the presence of the Toronto Regiments and a large gathering of citizens.

In a supplementary despatch from F. M. Earl Roberts, dated 1st March, 1902, Surgeon-Lieut.-Colonel E. Fiset, M.D., and Captain H. E. Burstall were mentioned for services worthy of recognition while reference was made to the scarves worked by the late Queen Victoria as gifts of honour for distribution to the four most distinguished private soldiers from the South African, Canadian, Australian and New Zealand Colonies. That for Canada was given to Private, afterwards Lieutenant, Richard Rowland Thompson for " gallant conduct in the field." Lord Kitchener's despatch of June 23rd, contained a number of references to Canadians. Lieut.-

Colonel Sir E. P. C. Girouard, K.C.M.G., D.S.O., he described as "my principal adviser in all the numerous and intricate questions pertaining to railway administration in South Africa. He is an officer of brilliant ability." Major H. C. Nanton, R.E., was said to have "satisfactorily carried out his work in connection with armoured trains." Others mentioned were Lieut.-Colonel T. D. B. Evans, C.B., Captain T. H. Callaghan, Lieut. R. H. Ryan, Lieut. F. Church, Sergeants D. C. Forster Bliss and M. Docherty, together with Major Charles Ross, D.S.O., Captains A. McMillan and T. H. A. Williams, Sergeant-Major R. J. Stallwood, Sergt. G. Saunders and Private A. Chesworth, of the Canadian Scouts, and Captains H. G. Von Hugel and J. H. de P. Casgrain, of British Regiments.

On June 26th, Capt. Bingham Alexander Turner and Capt. Robert Kellock Scott, of Winnipeg, were given the D.S.O. Major Joseph Alfred Hudon was also gazetted a C.M.G., and a little later it was announced that Sir Percy Girouard had accepted the civil post of Commissioner of Railways in South Africa. On October 31st various honours were announced on account of South African services and amongst them was the D.S.O. bestowed upon Surgeon-Lieut-Colonel E. Fiset, M.D., Surgeon-Major J. A. Devine, M.D., and Captain A. McMillan with Sergeants R. J. Stallwood, D. C. Forest Bliss and J. G. Dale of the Canadian Scouts, or Canadian Rifles. It was also given to Majors H. G. Joly de Lotbinière, R.E. and G. M. Kirkpatrick, R.E. In November, Nursing Sister, Miss Georgina Pope, was granted the Royal Red Cross.

Speaking in Toronto on January 3rd, 1902, the Hon. Dr. Montague dealt with his recent Australian visit and said, in connection with the War: "I may tell you I met no boy from Queensland, or New South Wales, or Tasmania, or Victoria, or New Zealand, who did not feel that it was the event of his life to have met his Canadian fellow-patriots on the distant fields of South Africa, and to have witnessed the bravery and heroism that the Canadian boys displayed." On June 29th, the Montreal Board of Trade unanimously passed the following Resolution :

That this Board has watched with intense interest the conduct of the Boer War, forced on the Empire by the insulting ultimatum of Kruger, and with remembrance of the brutal treatment of the Johannesburg refugees and the vandalism of Boer invaders in Natal, expresses its admiration of the patience, endurance and unparalleled clemency of our troops in the enemy's country, and the kind treatment of the prisoners everywhere, and deprecates the malevolent feeling shown by a jealous Continental European press, from which we had expected, if not a remembrance of past services, at least a truthful and just criticism.

Writing to a Scotch correspondent on March 17th Mr. Goldwin Smith (*Daily News*, April 2nd) declared that were he in England he would heartily support Sir H. Campbell-Bannerman in his efforts to "efface the hideous memories of the War and relieve us of a burden of world-wide odium such as no nation, however mighty, can afford to bear." Upon the character and standing of

Canadian troops Major-General Lord Dundonald sent to Canada the following expression of opinion on April 3rd: "The Canadians who served under me in South Africa were men from the tops of their heads to the soles of their feet, or to be more explicit, there are persons with rifles and men with rifles. When a General has men under him with rifles he knows what he can do and what risks he can take." Sir James Graham, M.P., Mayor of Sydney, Australia, told the Toronto *News* on April 8th that his people "rejoiced in the heroism of the splendid troops which Canada has sent to the front and hope that Canadians reciprocate the feeling in some degree of pride at the behaviour and courage of their Australian kinsfolk." A curious comment of another kind came from a newspaper which, later on, obtained considerable notoriety for other reasons—the Sandon *Paystreak* of April 12th:

We take the flower of our Canadian manhood from useful toil on the specious plea of patriotism. We ship them off to the other side of the world to fight against men with whom we have no quarrel, whom we do not even know, the merits of whose case we do not understand. When our boys pillage and burn and slay we laud their gallantry.

Speaking to the Toronto Militia on May 11th, at Massey Hall, the Rev. Dr. Armstrong Black declared this War to be "the justest, the sanest, and the humanest ever fought by Great Britain." He paid a high tribute to Charles Napier Evans and urged Canada to continue upon the path of Imperial destiny. On June 5th the Toronto *Globe* reviewed the conduct of Canadians at the front with pronounced pride and pleasure.

The Colonies and India contributed 111,000 men out of the 448,435 troops who were sent to or raised in South Africa from
August 1st, 1899, to May 31st, 1902. From India came

British Appreciation of Colonial Aid
18,534 men; from the various Colonies, 30,328 men; and from South Africa itself, 52,414 men. There was an abundance of expressed appreciation in Great Britain for this aid, by official words, by press editorials, by popular demonstrations and in the speeches of statesmen. On January 11th, 1902, dealing only with the year under review, Mr. Chamberlain, in the course of a speech at Birmingham, said:

This war has enabled the British Empire to find itself; it has united the British race throughout the world, and it has shown to all whom it may concern, that if ever again we have, as we have done in the past, to fight for our very existence against a world in arms, we shall not be alone. We shall be supported by the sons of Britain in every quarter of the globe. I say that hardly any sacrifice can be too great for such a result. Fifty years ago, twenty years ago, —I am not certain I could not put it later—none would have ventured to predict that in a struggle in a distant part of the Empire, in the cause in which they had no direct, no personal interest, the great nations of Canada and Australia, the people of New Zealand, would have come to our help, would have furnished us with an army of 20,000 men fit to stand beside the best troops in the world, that they would send these men to fight for their King and for the unity of the Empire of which they form a part; and, believe me, if the peril were greater, if we were indeed in serious danger, I believe is hardly any limit which could be placed upon the assistance which would be afforded to us

by these sister nations across the sea, these nations who have learnt to feel
that they are joint heirs with us of all the glories and the traditions of the
Motherland, and who will never in the future leave her in the lurch.

The importance of this help was felt in the final days of the
struggle as affecting future British policy in South Africa, and this
feeling Lord Salisbury expressed at a London banquet on February
5th, in the following terms : " You must consider the feelings and
the interests of the loyal men in South Africa who have borne so
much and risked so much for the sake of the Empire to which they
belong.   And when you have fully regarded their feelings you
must bear in mind that all the constituent parts of the Empire are
looking upon the work you are carrying through, and it depends
on whether the result is such as they can admire, or whether it
gives them any opportunity for the existence of that emotion—it
must depend on that—whether the result of this very trying three
or four years that we have passed through will tend to strengthen
the great Empire to which we belong, and to extend and increase
the devotion which has grown with every year among the various
Colonies of the Crown."

Speaking at Leicester on March 19th the Earl of Selborne, First
Lord of the Admiralty, declared that " the British Empire had
become a fact in the sense that all the Colonies had come forward
to claim, not only the privileges of British citizenship, but its
responsibilities and its duties.   Who would have dreamt sixteen
years ago that New Zealand would have been sending her tenth
contingent to the field of battle ?   Did not every pulse beat when
we read that news ?   We were unimaginative and phlegmatic by
nature, and it required a war like this to make us understand
what our warmer brothers across the sea had never failed to recognize."   At a banquet in London, on May 23rd, Mr. St. John Brodrick,
Secretary of State for War, spoke as follows:—" Before the war
broke out, as Sir F. Treves had remarked, the auxiliary forces were
to a large degree national forces, but it was not too much to say
that the forces which three years ago were national had now become Imperial, because they had fought side by side with those
who had come from beyond the seas to help us, and whose services
we had no power to command.   The dream of Colonial Federation,
which so many statesmen had entertained for so many years, had
been made a reality by the Boer War.   It was realized at last that
it was possible to look upon the Empire not merely as a machine,
under an ambitious Sovereign or an ambitious statesman, but as an
Association in which with mutual support and confidence those
who were bound together, under one Crown, had come together for
purposes in which all were interested."

On June 6th, Mr. Chamberlain at the Colonial Troops' Club
pointed out that the self-governing Colonies had contributed to
the War a larger force than was the British Army at Waterloo
and proceeded as follows : " We owe a great debt to them for

their moral as well as for their material assistance. They saw, with a keeness of instinct which was not surpassed by even the most patriotic of Englishmen at home, the magnitude of the issues at stake. They know now that this War, terrible as have been its sacrifices, has at least saved the Empire from a great danger, has confirmed and established our dominion in South Africa, and has strengthened the bonds of union as could in no other way have been accomplished. These are great results." Speaking at a banquet in London, on August 1st, the Colonial Secretary referred to the War as having been a revelation to the world of new strength in the British Empire. But the fact involved new obligations and "that common impulse of sacrifice and devotion which have cemented our union in blood and tears must not be suffered to weaken."

At Welbeck, on August 5th, Lord Kitchener said in this connection that from "every part of the Empire large numbers came to serve with us in this struggle and I can assure you that this service was most notable and most valuable." The Duke of Devonshire, addressing the British Empire League on July 7th, pointed out the instinctive recognition by the Colonies of the Imperial character of this conflict. "It was the knowledge that this quarrel was regarded by them as an Imperial quarrel which did most to stimulate us to fresh exertions." On June 6th the formal recognition of these services took place in the House of Commons by a formal vote of thanks moved by Mr. Balfour, seconded by Sir H. Campbell-Bannerman and carried by 382 to 42. After a reference to the Home forces the Resolution proceeded as follows:

That the thanks of this House be given to the officers, warrant officers, non-commissioned officers and men of His Majesty's Colonial and Indian Forces, for their co-operation with His Majesty's Imperial Forces, and for the energy and gallantry with which they executed the services they were called upon to perform during the prolonged campaign in South Africa ; that this House doth acknowledge and highly approve the gallantry, discipline, and good conduct displayed by His Majesty's Colonial and Indian Forces, and doth also acknowledge the cordial good feeling which animated all His Majesty's Forces.

There was no reference to the War in the Speech from the Throne at Ottawa on February 14th, and in reply to an inquiry from

Parliament and the War

Mr. R. L. Borden as to the reason for this omission, the Premier replied by quoting his statement in the previous Session that the War was practically over and was now merely a guerilla contest; pointed out that there was no appropriation for the sending of new contingents; and declared that those who went were simply volunteers recruited through Canadian machinery for Imperial purposes. "There was nothing to announce to Parliament in that. It was not Parliamentary action. It was simply the same thing which took place last year in the case of the South African Constabulary." On April 23rd Mr. John Charlton presented the following motion to the House:

This House is of the opinion that British supremacy should be maintained and firmly established in South Africa, to which end Canada has cheerfully contributed men and money. Having in view the effect of a policy of magnanimity and mercy at the cession of Canada, and at the close of the Civil War in the United States, and for other reasons, this House is also of the opinion that in the interest of peace and future tranquility, harmony and homogeneity in South Africa, the broadest policy of magnanimity and mercy may be extended to a brave foe now opposing British arms, upon condition of submission to British control. And upon this opinion, humbly presented with the prayerful hope that it may aid in securing a favourable and an honourable settlement of South African difficulties, this House invokes the considerate judgment of His Gracious Majesty the King.

In the course of his speech Mr. Charlton professed the strongest personal loyalty, spoke of the unselfish character of Canadian aid to the Motherland in the War, declared that no end to the struggle could be considered except the absolute dominion of Great Britain in South Africa, and referred to the subjugation of the Boer as a great military achievement. He believed that the conflict could now be ended and peace promoted by the exercise of magnanimity. " Severity will retard peace and leave endless hate to fester in the heart of every Boer in that country." He thought that no distinction in the discussion of peace terms should be made between Cape rebels and Boer belligerents. The examples of Canada after the Rebellion of 1837, and the United States after its Civil War were cited as causes for the proffer of magnanimous terms in South Africa.

Mr. Henri Bourassa seconded the Resolution. He declared British supremacy an essential in South Africa, but believed that the best way to establish it was by " respect for minorities and generosity to foes in war." From the first, of course, he had opposed Canadian interference in the conflict, but from the moment Parliament had taken action in that direction Canada had " acquired the right of saying what should be its result." He described it as " a cruel and unfortunate war," denounced the South African colonists who wanted their pound of flesh in the final settlement, expressed strong opposition to any policy of unconditional surrender, and concluded with the hope that South Africa would, through conciliation, some day have what we possess in Canada where "British rule in its general and higher spirit and manifestation is a good rule."

Sir Wilfrid Laurier expressed general agreement with the terms of the Resolution but considered it inopportune and injudicious. He thought it better to leave the settlement with those who now had it in hand and to not make an intervention which might be fatal to the peace they were all hoping for. Dr. Sproule followed in a protest against this and other attempts to advise the Imperial Parliament. It was in very bad taste. Speeches followed from Messrs. D. Monet, S. Hughes, T. Oliver, A. E. Kemp, Jabel Robinson and L. P. Demers, and the Resolution was then withdrawn at the Premier's request.

The Terms of Peace were signed at Pretoria at 11 o'clock on the night of May 31st, 1902, by Lord Kitchener and Lord Milner, representing the British Government; Messrs. M. T. Steyn and J. Brebner and General C. R. De Wet, General C. Olivier and Judge J. B. M. Herzog, acting as the Government of the Orange Free State; and Messrs. S. W. Burger, F. W. Reitz and Generals Louis Botha, De la Rey and Lucas Meyer, acting as the Government of the South African Republic.   Up to that date the British casualties reported had been 518 officers and 5,256 non-commissioned officers and men killed; 183 officers and 1,835 non-commissioned officers and men died of wounds; 1,851 officers and 20,978 non-commissioned officers and men wounded; and 383 officers and 9,170 non-commissioned officers and men missing or captured by the enemy from time to time—a total casualty list in action of 2,752 officers and 35,404 non-commissioned officers and men.   Besides this list, however, 5 officers and 97* men died in captivity, and 339 officers and 12,911 men died of disease, while 27 officers and 771 men met accidental deaths.   Those invalided home numbered 3,116 officers and 72,314 men, of whom the great majority recovered and rejoined for duty. According to the *Daily Express*, of London, in a carefully-compiled table, the War cost the United Kingdom four lives for every 9,000 of its population, and the Colonies three lives for every 9,000 of their population.   The following figures exclude the Yeomanry and Artillery from the Empire forces:—

The End of the South African War

Country.	Killed and Died of Wounds.	Wounded.	Died of Disease and Accidents.	Total Killed and Wounded.
South Africa	1,395	3,402	1,796	4,797
Australia	286	654	280	940
New Zealand	76	201	106	277
Canada	92	285	91	377
India, etc..................	9	18	7	27
Wales	161	512	375	573
Ireland....................	679	2,045	794	2,724
Scotland	824	2,434	908	3,258
England	3,215	10,066	6,448	13,281
Total..................	6,737	19,617	10,805	26,254
Total for United Kingdom, including Yeomanry, etc ..	5,900	17,786	11,493	23,472
Total for Colonies	1,858	4,560	2,280	6,478

A Parliamentary return of a later date gave the total number of all the British forces killed during the period of the war as 5,774; the wounded as 22,829; and those who died of wounds and disease as 16,168.   Another official statement placed the South African garrison on August 18th, 1899, at 9,940 and on October 11th, when the war began, at 22,486.   The total number of troops sent to and raised in South Africa from August 1st, 1899, to May 31st,

---

* Note.—Non-commissioned officers are included with the men in these figures.

1902, was 448,435. Of these forces it is of interest to note that the Australasian contribution was stated by the Sydney *Mail* of June 7th to be, approximately, 22,316. India sent 18,534 men. Canada raised a force of 8,372 men of all ranks including the Battalion which relieved the Leinster Regiment at Halifax. South Africa contributed 52,414 men. At the Coronation Conference official figures were submitted as to expenditure in connection with the War. That of Great Britain was £222,974,000 or £5 7s. 2d. per head of the population and the following table indicated the relative character of the Colonial contributions:

Colony.	No. per 1,000 of Population.	Cost per Head.	No. of Men Sent.
Canada....................	1⅔	2s. 4d.	8,400
New South Wales...............	4⅕	5s. 9d.	6,208
Victoria	3⅓	2s. 3d.	3,897
Queensland..................	6	8s. 7d.	2,903
South Australia...............	4	4s. 6d.	1,494
West Australia...............	6⅓	5s. 8d.	1,165
Tasmania...................	4⅔	4s. 6d.	796
New Zealand.................	8	8s. 8d.	6,000

A supplementary Report on the Canadian Contingents was issued at Ottawa under date of November 24th and gave the total force which went to South Africa as 7,368. Of these 224 died of disease or were killed and 252 were wounded. The names of Major A. L. Howard and some 20 others who had ceased to belong to Canadian corps at the time of their death were not included in these totals. On June 13th it was announced at Ottawa that up to the 5th of the month Canada had supplied food stuffs for the Imperial War Office totalling 195,600 tons of hay, 125,815 sacks of flour, 40,776 cases of beef, 11,743 cases of jam and 294,772 bags of oats—valued as a whole at $7,500,000. In Montreal, on July 24th, Lieut.-Colonel Dent stated to the *Star* that the work of the British Remount Commission was now completed in Canada although 500 horses a year would continue to be purchased there. For War purposes, from April 1st, 1901, to July 1902, they had bought 7,715 horses in Ontario, 2,225 in Quebec, 115 in the Maritime Provinces, or a total of 10,941 horses, with an expenditure of $1,618,066.

The annual Report of the Canadian Patriotic Fund up to 31st May showed total receipts of $338,498 of which the Dominion gave $312,429 and Great Britain $22,534. The expenditures had been $194,546, relieving 912 cases. Meanwhile, in connection with the close of the War, Lord Kitchener announced on June 23rd that 11,166 armed burghers had surrendered in the Transvaal, 6,455 in Orange River and 3,635 in Cape Colony. The signing of the Terms of Peace had already been marked by a cable of congratulation from Lord Minto to Mr. Chamberlain, on June 2nd, stating that "My Ministers hasten to offer His Majesty the King the humble and loyal congratulations of the people of Canada on the restoration of peace" and by another to Lord Kitchener. On the same day

MAJOR H. B. STAIRS, D.S.O.
Of Halifax.

CHARLES NAPIER EVANS
The Hero of Hart's River.

MAJOR R. K. SCOTT, D.S.O.
Of Winnipeg.

MAJOR J. COOPER MASON, D.S.O.
Of Toronto.

THE END OF THE SOUTH AFRICAN WAR.

His Majesty issued the following Message to the people of the Empire :

The King has received the welcome news of the cessation of hostilities in South Africa with infinite satisfaction and trusts that Peace may be speedily followed by the restoration of prosperity in his new Dominions, and that the feelings necessarily engendered by War will give place to the earnest co-operation of all His Majesty's South African subjects in promoting the welfare of their common country.

There was hardly a discordant note in Canadian press comments regarding the news of peace in South Africa and the terms upon which it had been negotiated. Belief in the justice of **Canadian** the British cause, expectation of future progress and **Opinion on** prosperity for the new Colonies, approval of Canadian **the Peace** participation in the War, pride in the deeds of Canadian soldiers, congratulations to the King on having a peaceful Empire for his Coronation, eulogies of Mr. Chamberlain, praises for the bravery of the Boers, and expressed belief in the value of the War as an Empire unifying influence filled columns of editorial expression. There were a few depreciatory remarks regarding the War Office administration of affairs and some criticism of the pro-Boers in England but as a whole the tone of comment was hearty and enthusiastic from Halifax to Vancouver.

Personal opinion was everywhere strongly expressed. As Lieut.-Governor A. G. Jones, of Nova Scotia, put it in the Halifax *Herald* of June 2nd : " Our gallant sons who cheerfully volunteered for service have stood side by side with Imperial legions and in the hour of trial have not been found wanting in discipline, endurance or courage." The Hon. Mr. Tarte expressed to the Montreal *Star* great pleasure at the news and the belief that, from what he knew of the King's ability, His Majesty must have had much influence in the settlement. Resolutions were passed in various Legislatures and by many public bodies. Speaking in Toronto on June 5th, the Hon. Mr. Mulock said, that in his opinion, Canada should forever retain its connection with the Empire and continued : " Recent events in South Africa have testified to the world that in her hour of need Great Britain's sons beyond the seas know of no sacrifice too great for the maintenance of the integrity and honour of the British Empire. The war is over, and peace reigns, and it has left the Empire more united in its people, more powerful, and more respected among the nations of the earth than at any time in Britain's history." In the *Weekly Sun*, of August 20th, appeared a characteristic comment from Mr. Goldwin Smith stating that " the day is not far distant at which the Canadian farmer will be sorry that he has been betrayed by the arts of the politicians and their confederates in the press into depriving his fellows in the Transvaal of their independence."

CLOSING INCIDENTS OF THE WAR

Jan. 21.—Dr. Harbottle, of Burford, Ont., is sentenced to one year in the Central Prison for attempting to shoot H. Stuart of that place. The cause of the incident is a long-continued series of petty persecutions aimed at Dr. Harbottle for expressing pro-Boer opinions. On May 1st it is announced that the Governor-General has pardoned the prisoner.

Feb. 18.—The Lieut.-Governor of British Columbia unveils at Victoria a Memorial Tablet to Capt. M. G. Blanchard and other soldiers of the Province who had fallen in South Africa.

Mar. 5.—It is announced that the Colonial Secretary desires the services of 40 Canadian female teachers to proceed to South Africa and that he has also obtained the appointment of Principal Mullin of the New Brunswick Normal School to a similar position in the Transvaal.

Mar. 22.—Lieut. Leveret Beverley Webster, of the King's Own Royal Lancaster Regiment, and son of Mr. Barclay Webster, K.C., of Kentville, Nova Scotia, dies in London after a prolonged service at the front.

Mar. 23.—A Tablet is unveiled in St. Bartholomew's Church, Ottawa, to the memory of Archibald, Earl of Ava, the eldest son of Lord Dufferin, by H. E. the Earl of Minto.

April 6.—A Memorial Tablet is unveiled at Calgary in honour of Lieut. T. W. Chalmers and other Western men killed during the War.

April 9.—The Countess of Minto issues an appeal for the organization of a Fund to erect Memorials over the graves of Canadians in South Africa. On December 12th it is stated that $5,591 has been subscribed.

April 20.—Major Archibald J. Boyd, son of Sir John Boyd, of Toronto, dies in South Africa of enteric fever.

Aug. 6.—A Monument erected at Ottawa through the subscriptions of 30,000 children and in honour of those from the vicinity who served and fell in South Africa is unveiled by Lord Dundonald, who is followed in a patriotic speech by Mayor Cook.

Aug. 8.—The corner stone of a Memorial at St. John to those from New Brunswick who died at the front is laid by Mayor White.

Sept. 1.—Major-General the Earl of Dundonald pays high tribute in a speech at Toronto to Canadian valour at Hart's River.

Sept. 2.—Distinguished Service Medals are presented by Colonel Montizambert, D.O.C., at Ottawa, to Sergeant-Major Gimblett and Trooper L. W. Mulloy.

Sept. 11.—It is announced that a Royal Commission of Inquiry into the operations of the War has been appointed with the Earl of Elgin, K.G., as Chairman, and Viscount Esher, Sir George Taubman-Goldie, Field Marshal Sir Henry W. Norman, Admiral Sir John O. Hopkins, Sir John Edge, K.C., and Sir John Jackson as members. Later on, Lord Strathcona and Mount Royal and Sir F. M. Darley, Chief Justice of New South Wales, are added.

Sept. 19.—A Monument at Granby, P.Q., is unveiled by Colonel, Lord Aylmer in honour of Shefford County soldiers who served and died at the front.

Nov. 11.—Under this date a despatch is received from Mr. Chamberlain stating that through a strict and necessary rule laid down by the War Office, and applying to Imperial and Australian, as well as other troops, no medal or war gratuity can be given to the members of the 3rd, 4th 5th and 6th C.M.R. who landed in South Africa after the close of the War.

IV.—RELATIONS WITH FOREIGN COUNTRIES

The Alaskan question was discussed in the press and by publicists during 1902, although no serious developments arose. Speaking in the House of Commons on February 11th, 1901, Sir **The Alaskan** Wilfrid Laurier had declared that the Americans have **Boundary** "taken such an attitude and such a course, and we **Question** have also taken such an attitude, that it seems almost impossible to reconcile the two opposing views." He hoped, however, that if an honourable settlement could not be reached an honourable compromise might still be effected. In the meantime, and in view of the further complications which might arise at any moment from fresh discoveries of gold, " we have agreed on a provisional boundary which will serve as a boundary so long as the question remains unsettled, and that provisional boundary has been settled by geographers of the two countries." In answer to an inquiry from Mr. R. L. Borden, the Premier stated that the agreement was " in the nature of a compromise between the respective positions taken by the two parties." On April 16th, in the course of a discussion upon Yukon matters, in Committee, Mr. Sifton, Minister of the Interior, made the following statement regarding international arrangements and the position at the moment :

> As to the portion of the territory which lies contiguous to Alaska, there is a provisional boundary line agreed to between the two Governments, and that line, wherever necessary, has been laid down upon the ground by Commissioners appointed by the parties. Our Commissioner and the Commissioner of the United States went up last season and laid out the boundary line at the only place practically necessary, that is, across the Dalton trail to Pyramid Harbour. Under the terms of the provisional arrangement, the summit of the White Pass, the pass through which the Railway runs, and the summit of the Chilkoot Pass, which was also used by travellers before the Railway was opened, are considered to be the provisional boundary line. They are fixed by agreement. So, we have at all the passes where travel is possible, a fixed provisional boundary line, and there can be no difficulty about administration.

In the House of Commons on February 14th, 1902, Mr. Borden pointed out that the longer the Americans remained in provisional occupation of any territory in this connection the harder it would be to dispossess them. The Premier replied in the following terms : " I agree with the hon. gentleman that the longer this matter is deferred the greater will become the difficulty of settling it. I agree with him that the longer the settlement is deferred the more difficult it will be to recover possession of whatever Canadian territory may be occupied by American settlers. I have to say to my hon. friend that we have pressed as much as we could ; nay, more I may say, that we have pressed in season and out of season, on the Imperial authorites to bring that matter to a close."

In the *American Review of Reviews* for March following, Dr. Albert Shaw, its editor, had an important article upon this subject

—important as showing the extreme view-point of an educated and influential American. He went over some well-worn arguments in favour of annexation and then declared that Canada not only had no case but was not even justified in pressing its claims. The United States would never give up their territory. In the Canadian House of Commons the subject was more or less discussed during the Session. On March 7th Mr. H. Bourassa paid a high tribute to the late Lord Herschell in connection with his duties on the Joint High Commission and referred to the "ability, zeal and devotedness" displayed by him in the cause of Canada. Sir Richard Cartwright, two days before had said much the same thing—especially with regard to the Alaskan dispute. Referring to existing negotiations the Prime Minister, on February 19th, described Canada's view as being very much like that of Great Britain. He wanted a practicable and peaceable solution. "I hope we have not come to this that we want Great Britain to go to war with the United States, if, may be, negotiations are continued a little longer than we wish them to be on a matter of long-pending difficulty. We want to preserve good relations with our friends and neighbours to the south of us even though on some occasions our patience is sorely tried." On June 15th the New York *Herald* published an interview with the Canadian Premier in which he was represented as declaring the Alaskan question to be "full of danger" and expressing an urgent wish for arbitration. Doubt was afterwards thrown on the accuracy of the interview but, meanwhile, the remarks were widely quoted and commented on.

The Hon. Clifford Sifton, Minister of the Interior, delivered an elaborate address upon this subject at Lindsay, on June 20th, from the standpoint of history, record and treaties—Toronto *Globe* of June 28th—and for which he received cordial thanks from various British Columbia journals. In the *National Review* for August appeared an article by Mr. A. Maurice Low which was curiously borne out by subsequent events. He described President Roosevelt's view as being entirely opposed to arbitration and strong in the belief that the Canadian claim was a recent and unjust one due to the finding of gold. He said there was only one mode of settlement which the U.S. Senate would accept—a tribunal composed of three Judges on each side and the decision to be final and binding on both parties. During the same month a singularly able statement of the Canadian case was made by Mr. Thomas Hodgins, K.C., of Toronto, in the *Contemporary Review*. He traced the subject historically and diplomatically and the following quotation may be given here:

The admission of British Columbia into the Dominion in 1871 caused Canada to become a party to the Alaska boundary dispute ; and ever since 1872 urgent and almost yearly requests have been made by the British and Canadian Governments to the Government of the United States for an expeditious settlement of the disputed line of demarcation between the newly-joined Province and the Territory of Alaska. The passive resistance of the United States to these requests is inexplicable unless on the unattractive assumption that the unsanc-

THE DISPUTED TERRITORY ON THE BOUNDARIES OF BRITISH COLUMBIA
AND ALASKA.

Specially prepared by Thomas Hodgins, Esq., M.A., K.C., Judge of the Admiralty
Court of Ontario.

tioned occupation by the United States of British-Canadian territory and the national insistence in defending that occupation, must ultimately, as in former boundary disputes, assure a diplomatic triumph over Great Britain and secure to the Republic a further concession of Canadian territory for the enlargement of Alaska.

Among the numerous American critics of this article was the New York *Evening Post* and to it Mr. Hodgins replied at some length in a letter of which a copy appeared in the Toronto *Mail* of October 11th. In the Toronto *Globe* of October 7th, an editorial quoted various American authorities such as Secretaries of State Blaine, Foster and Fish as giving contradictory interpretations of the very Treaty which Canada asked to have impartially dealt with by arbitration and which the United States now maintained was above all misapprehension because of its perfect clearness. Speaking at Northampton, Mass., on October 16th, Senator Henry Cabot Lodge dealt with the question and declared that " a more manufactured and baseless claim " than that of England was never set up. He proceeded as follows :

If we should yield to it there is not a portion of our northern boundary which England could not attack. President McKinley refused, as a matter of course, to admit any such claim, and President Roosevelt refuses to recognize it, as any patriotic American would. Mr. Gaston, the Democratic candidate for Governor, says that the strip of frigid territory should not be allowed to interfere with reciprocal arrangements. This is the first time within my knowledge that any American public man has proposed to surrender the soil of the United States to Great Britain for any reason whatever.

He added that American miners were there and American interests were concerned and no such territory could ever be given up to a Foreign power. On November 22nd a letter appeared in the New York *Tribune* from Mr. F. C. T. O'Hara of Ottawa, dealing with this question and signed as Secretary of the Dominion Minister of Trade and Commerce. It was really a personal communication and the latter portion of the signature was afterwards stated by the writer to be entirely unauthorized by him. He referred to alleged difficulties which Canada had met with in getting Great Britain to guard its diplomatic interests in past negotiations with the United States, accused the Americans of playing an " ungenerous waiting game," quoted Mr. Grover Cleveland's articles in the *Century* of June and July, 1901, as frequently supporting Canadian contentions and added : " The day must come when a settlement must take place and Canada cannot stand by and see herself despoiled of territory which she firmly and honestly believes is part of her rightful domain." At the Detroit Reciprocity Convention on December 10th, following, Senator McMullen created a mild sensation by declaring that the Alaskan boundary question must be settled before the trade issue was disposed of.

We, of Canada, believe that you have got much territory in the North-West belonging to us. Canada is willing and anxious to leave it to arbitration before a proper tribunal. Settle this question honourably and then we will come together with you. But without that settlement Reciprocity is out of the question.

On March 1st, Prof. McGregor Young spoke at Toronto University upon the Monroe Doctrine and foreshadowed a struggle between Germany and the United States regarding the matter. On March 30th, Mr. T. St. John Gaffney wrote the New York *Sun*, suggesting that the British employment of Canadian troops in South Africa was an infraction of the Doctrine in its vital and fundamental principle of "American paramountcy over this Continent." During the same month the Hon. David Mills, of the Supreme Court of Canada, had an elaborate study of the subject in the *Empire Review*. He described the Americans as practically claiming the sovereignty of the Continent ; the Monroe Doctrine as " an emanation of the manifest destiny dream;" the complacent belief of the American people in their own superiority ; the fact that in Canada there was an average of one murder yearly to 500,000 of its population and in the United States one to every 7,700; the antagonism of Europe to a policy which would eventually involve the Powers in a " species of degrading vassalage " if generally accepted. Speaking at Proctor, Vermont, on September 1st, following, President Roosevelt dealt with this question, advocated a strong Navy to compel respect for United States rights, and continued :

The Monroe Doctrine and Canada

We believe in the Doctrine not as a means of aggression at all. It does not mean that we are aggressive towards any Power. It means merely that as the biggest Power on this Continent we remain steadfastly true to the principle first formulated under the Presidency of Monroe that this Continent must not be treated as a subject for political colonization by any European Power. It is a doctrine of peace, a doctrine to secure a chance on this Continent for the United States here to develop peaceably along their own lines.

English and Canadian papers took the ground very generally that no exception could be taken to this definition so long as it was maintained as outlined. But, as the Toronto *Mail* put it on September 8th, " if ever it were made the excuse for an attempt to exercise control or authority in this hemisphere over countries independent of the United States, the Monroe Doctrine would be intolerable." Arguing on the other hand, however, Mr. I. N. Ford, the London correspondent of the New York *Tribune* and Toronto *Globe*, claimed on September 2nd, that the first Venezuelan affair had changed matters. "Logically, there was no escape from the conclusion that the British Foreign Office had committed itself irrevocably to moral support of an American protectorate over the two Western Continents." The New York *American* followed this up by declaring that " you shall not come " was the negative form of the positive injunction " you must go." England, it was added, should look out for herself. The German-British embroglio in Venezuela ensued and created a wide American discussion of the subject with occasional Canadian echoes. The President's Message on December 2nd, declared, in this connection, that " the Monroe Doctrine should be treated as the cardinal feature of American

Foreign policy." On December 19th the Canadian Society of New York, held a banquet presided over by Dr. James Douglass and addressed by Sir F. W. Borden, Canadian Minister of Militia. He declared that the United States had taught Canada self-reliance and referred to the question under review as follows :

The Monroe Doctrine is a good thing for the American Continent. England has the same amount of land on it now as she had when it was promulgated. Some of her best statesmen favoured it then. It is a guarantee of no coercion, and of freedom and liberty. The Monroe Doctrine is as much in favour of Canadian integrity as it is of the integrity of any other part of the American Continent.

The Reciprocity arrangement negotiated between Sir Robert Bond and Mr. John Hay, with the good offices of Sir M. H. Herbert, The United the British Ambassador, included, was signed at States and Washington by the two latter on November 8th, Newfoundland 1902. By its terms United States fishing vessels Treaty were given the same privileges in the purchase of bait as those of the Island and were allowed to touch, trade and procure supplies in Newfoundland. American agricultural implements and machinery for specified purposes, mining and other machinery, printing presses, paper, types, ink, etc., and salt in bulk were to be admitted free. Certain specified rates of duty were to be charged and not exceeded upon flour, pork, bacon, smoked beef and sausage coming from the United States. In return the following clause was contained in the Treaty :

Codfish, cod oil, seal oil, whale oil, unmanufactured whalebone, sealskins, herrings, salmon, trout, and salmon-trout, lobsters, cod does, tongues and sounds, being the produce of the fisheries carried on by the fishermen of Newfoundland, and ores of metals the product of Newfoundland mines, and slates from the quarries, untrimmed, shall be admitted to the United States free of duty. Also all packages in which the said fish and oils may be exported shall be admitted free of duty. It is understood, however, that the unsalted or fresh codfish are not included in the provisions of this Article.

The Treaty was to operate for five years and further until 12 months' notice of abrogation by either party. The Ottawa Government did not apparently interfere and on one side it was claimed that Canadian interests were not affected, while on the other hand it was stated that the arrangement would indefinitely defer Confederation with Newfoundland and prevent the Island from giving British or Canadian goods any fiscal preference. Mr. P. T. McGrath, in the Halifax *Chronicle* of December 26th, put the Island case thus: "It has no discriminating action against Canada; it simply enables us to grant the American fishermen the same privileges in our waters which the Canadians enjoy, with this difference, that whereas the Canadians, as fellow-subjects, give no return for the concession, the Americans will have to grant us free entry for our fish to their own markets." Meanwhile, it was pointed out that Canada's tariff had always been liberal towards Newfoundland and that, in fact, every natural product of the Island was now admitted free.

Interviewed at Sydney, N.S., on December 21st the Hon. A. B. Morine, Opposition Leader in Newfoundland, spoke as follows: " Personally I was opposed to any arrangement which surrenders the control of our bait and other fish facilities. I think the true policy of the Colony should be to monopolize these for the extension of our own fisheries. I do not, however, believe that the Treaty will meet with the approval of the United States Senate." Meantime, on July 30th, a letter from Sir Wilfrid Laurier had been made public at Ottawa addressed to Mr. F. W. Thompson of the Ogilvie Mills and containing the following assurance :

With reference to the proposed Bond-Hay Treaty, I may tell you that in the event of this Treaty going into operation, no discrimination will be made against Canada, and Canadian products will have from Newfoundland the same treatment as accorded to similar American products. This point is settled. So you can go on with your efforts to take hold of that market, and I am very grateful for what information you have given me.

Opposition at once developed in the New England States and Senator Lodge of Massachusetts soon came out against the terms of the Treaty, as tending to injure American fishermen. Approximately, there were said to be some 31,000 men in those States who would suffer in some degree if Newfoundland fish were allowed free into American markets. Up to the close of the year the Treaty was still " hung up " in the United States Senate.

Prior to his departure for Canada from London Sir Wilfrid Laurier in August had paid a visit to Jersey, accompanied by Lady Laurier and Sir Gilbert and Lady Parker and thence **The Canadian** had left for Paris where he arrived on August 19th. **Premier** **Abroad** He was met by a representative of the Foreign Office, by Mr. Hector Fabre, c.M.G., the Canadian representative there, and by the Hon. W. S. Fielding and other Canadians. Various incidents followed including a luncheon with President Loubet, a conference with M. Delcassè, Minister of Foreign Affairs, a luncheon given by the latter in honour of Sir Wilfrid, a banquet given by the Canadians in Paris and an alleged interview of some length in *Le Journal* of August 22nd. This was telegraphed everywhere and dealt with the relations of Canada, France and Britain. The Premier was stated to have described the United States as a huge melting-pot in which the French language and institutions of Canada would disappear if they were annexed. He did not think that the French language would be overpowered under present conditions. He hoped to improve the commercial relations of France and Canada through a reduction in the tariff and was now negotiating to that end.

This interview created wide comment and was not repudiated until some time later. On August 27th Sir Wilfrid Laurier went to Lille as a guest at the Exhibition which was being held in that industrial centre and was accompanied by Mr. Hector Fabre, Mr. Fielding, Sir W. Mulock and Senator William Gibson. After the formal welcome and tour through the buildings, the Canadian

Premier made a brief speech. "If I am proud of being English, I preserve no less my pride in my French descent." At a banquet in the evening, presided over by M. Dujardin, President of the Exhibition Committee, reference was made to French pleasure in the fact that Canada had once been French territory and that the veins of her children were still rich in French blood. In his reply Sir Wilfrid expressed a hope for better commercial relations, invited French emigration to Canada and concluded as follows:

We have been parted by events and by the fate of arms, but we do not forget that we descend from a chivalrous nation, and should remain chivalrous. Although British subjects, we have a veneration for France, and under the *ægis* of the traditions of England we emphatically express it. That sentiment honours France which has inspired it, Canada which has preserved it, and England which has respected it.

At Paris, on September 1st, the Canadian banquet was held with a number of distinguished Frenchmen joining as hosts of the occasion. M. Ribot, the late Premier, was in the chair supported by men like M. Jules Siegfried, M. Jules Claretie and 200 others of both nationalities. In his speech, Sir Wilfrid declared that Canadians desired better trade relations with France and eulogized the beautiful climate, boundless resources and free institutions of his own country. "They had civil liberty, political liberty and religious liberty." As a consequence they were naturally attached to the Empire and friendly with the Anglo-Saxon people who formed a part of Canada's population. They were proud of their French origin still, however, and would like greater fraternity with republican France. From Paris Sir Wilfrid and Lady Laurier, accompanied by Senator Gibson, went after this event to Geneva, Genoa, Rome, Florence and Turin and thence back to Genoa and Paris, to Liverpool and home to Canada.

The principal Canadian speaker and writer upon Continental commercial relations during 1902 was Mr. John Charlton, M.P., who had been one of the members of the Quebec and Washington Conference of a couple of years before. In the January *Forum*, of New York, he elaborated the view that Canada had passed the period when absolute free trade with the Republic was possible; that it was looking forward to the time when its population would be a hundred millions; that freedom of exchange in natural products and the imposition of various revenue duties was the most advantageous system; that if American duties were not reduced in some reasonable form Canadians would be driven to adopt the American tariff against the United States. He summarized a mass of statistical and other data as follows:

Mr. Charlton on Relations with the United States

(1) The Canadian tariff rates are less than one-half those of the United States. (2) The Canadian exports of farm produce to the United States are only one-third as much as in 1866. (3) Canadian imports from the United States are now over four times what they were in 1866. (4) Canadian imports from Great Britain have increased less than 10 per cent. since 1866. (6) Canada buys three times as much from the United States as she sells to that country,

leaving out of account the precious metals. (7) Without including raw cotton Canada buys from the United States two and a half times the amount of farm products that she sells to that country. (8) Canada buys, at least, $10,000,000 more manufactures from the United States than from all the rest of the world. (9) Canada finds her chief market for farm products in Great Britain. (10) Of the total imports of Canada 63 per cent. comes from the United States. (11) Canada gives the United States a free list of $56,884,000, or 73 per cent. of her entire free list. Included in the free list from the United States are $39,000,000 of free farm products, free forest products and free manufactures. (12) Canada receives, practically, no free list from the United States except the precious metals.

On February 24th Mr. Charlton introduced the following motion in the House of Commons: " That this House is of the opinion that Canadian import duties should be arranged upon the principle of reciprocity in trade conditions so far as may be consistent with Canadian interests; that a rebate of not less than 40 per cent. of the amount of duties imposed should be made upon dutiable imports from nations or countries admitting Canadian natural products into their markets free of duty; and that the scale of Canadian duties should be sufficiently high to avoid inflicting injury upon Canadian interests in cases where a rebate of 40 per cent. or more shall be made under the conditions aforesaid." In his speech he expressed grave concern over the slow increase of Canadian population— 1,689,111 in the 30 years from 1871 to 1901 as against 5,671,569 of an increase in the United States during the period 1790-1820, or 47 per cent. for Canada and 141 per cent. for the young Republic He declared that 3,000,000 persons of Canadian birth, or descent in the first and second generations, were now in the United States while the Dominion could easily support 100,000,000 souls. He quoted various figures to prove that the natural tendency of trade was toward the United States and not Great Britain; argued at length along the Continental or geographical line of thought as it seemed to him related to the Commercial question; spoke of addresses which he had given on the subject in 1901 at Boston, New York, Detroit, Buffalo and other American centres; disclaimed any advocacy beyond that of Reciprocity in natural products; quoted a large number of agricultural products of which Canada imported more from the United States than she exported; stated that, in 1901, the import of manufactured goods from Great Britain was $714,000 less than in 1900 despite the Preference while that from the United States was $2,700,000 more and the free imports were, respectively, $11,118,000 and $53,549,000 from Great Britain and the United States.

He declared the American tariff to be very unfair; in order to make the Americans just he would offer the inducements suggested in his motion. If they were refused then would be the time to resort to a higher tariff. As it was conditions were intolerable. The motion was subsequently withdrawn. On March 20th Mr. Charlton again dealt with the subject in the House of Commons. Meanwhile, on June 18th, he had addressed the Marquette Club in Chicago and declared that Canada must have reciprocity of trade or of tariffs.

In the New York *Independent* during March, Mr. Charlton had a long and vigorous article in answer to the Hon. J. W. Foster. He declared Commercial Union impossible at present and for all time to come if the existing United States tariff were maintained much longer; described again the condition of affairs and Canada as " the best customer of the United States in finished products "; and spoke of a future in which the North-West would have 50,000,-000 souls and its people have turned sorrowfully away from the United States and put up their wall of high protection. On April 8th, he spoke to the Ottawa Board of Trade on this subject and in the New York *Outlook* during September had an article presenting similar views. According to his figures the balance of trade with Great Britain in 1902 was $60,141,000 in favour of Canada and that with the United States $77,527,000 against Canada.

Mr. Charlton was interviewed by the Toronto *Globe* on September 16th as to Mr. Tarte's tariff advocacy and declared that free trade in natural products was the ideal for both countries. But we should not wait forever. " On the contrary, he deemed it advisable to meet present conditions by suitable tariff regulations and to apply speedily the process of Legislative strangulation to the importation of at least $45,000,000 annually of American manufactures, if justice was denied us. He would hesitate to avow himself a protectionist, but he did assert without hesitation, that he was in favour of self-protection." In the Ottawa *Events* of September 20th he published an elaborate article along the same line of thought, and another in *National Reciprocity* of Chicago for October. In December he spoke at length at the Detroit Convention.

Various other meetings were held and many articles written in the United States during 1902 in favour of Reciprocity with

American Advocacy of Reciprocity

Canada, though the subject was but slightly discussed in the Dominion. The Minneapolis *Times*, the New York *Commercial-Advertiser*, the Boston *Herald*, the Minneapolis *Journal*, the Boston *Advertiser*, the DesMoines *Leader* and the New York *Journal of Commerce* were a few of the more prominent papers favouring the policy. The last mentioned declared the feeling along the border States and New England to be strongly favourable. The Boston Chamber of Commerce and those of Richmond and Atlanta passed Resolutions supporting it. The Massachusetts Legislature discussed, on March 27th, a long Resolution in favour of Reciprocity but did not pass it.

On April 8th, the Canadian Club at Boston held its annual banquet with this subject as the basis of lengthy speeches by Senator J. V. Ellis of New Brunswick, and the Hon. J. W. Longley of Nova Scotia. The latter traced the history of Reciprocity movements in Canada, the hostile fiscal attitude of the United States and the gradual drawing away of Canada into a position of independence and indifference. The conclusion he had come to was that the time had probably passed for Reciprocity although the Canadian Government were still willing to discuss the question if assured by developments that it would be done fairly and fully. In the St. John *Globe* of May 14th, Mr. W. Frank Hatheway published a study of the question, in which he traced the effect of American exclusion of Canadian products and American competition in Canada with similar products of the Canadian farm.

The Toronto *Mail and Empire* of July 16th, summed up the situation in these words : " If the United States desires freer trade, let Congress cut the tariff. If it does not, let Parliament raise the tariff." Speaking at a gathering in Boston on September 27th, Senator Henry Cabot Lodge rather deprecated the idea of Reciprocity. It would give the Canadians a market of 80,000,000 people in exchange for one of about 7,000,000. At Chelsea, Mass., on October 30th, the Hon. W: H. Moody, Secretary of the Navy, stated that " the balance of trade with Canada is constantly in our favour and it would seem as if we had no reasonable ground for complaint." A just and well-considered Reciprocity treaty would, however, find him an " ardent supporter." On October 16th Senator Lodge dealt with the subject again during a Massachusetts election and mixed it up with the Alaskan question in the following words :

While Canada insists on its manufactured and baseless claims to our territory, I do not care whether it is in Alaska or whether it is in Maine, there will be no Reciprocity treaty made with her. Let her abandon this preposterous claim and the Republican party, in pursuance of their policy of many years, will make a Reciprocity treaty with her at once.

At Boston, on November 25th, the Massachussetts State Board of Trade passed a Resolution in favour of re-convening the Joint High Commission and of an agreement with Canada " on the basis of equitable concessions and a reciprocal trade." Mr. Theadore M. Knappen, of the Minneapolis *Journal*, was in Toronto on November 29th, and told the *Globe* that eight Congressmen from Minnesota out of nine were in favour of Reciprocity. In his message to Congress on December 2nd, President Roosevelt approved strongly of the making of Reciprocity treaties and spoke as follows : " One way in which the re-adjustment sought can be reached is by Reciprocity treaties. It is greatly to be desired that such treaties may be adopted. They can be used to widen our markets and to give greater field for the activities of our producers on the one hand and on the other hand to secure in practical shape the lowering of duties when they are no longer needed for protection among our own people ; or when the minimum of damage done may be disregarded for the sake of the maximum of good accomplished." Speaking to the Toronto *Star*, on December 19th, Sir William Mulock deprecated any kind of unfair Reciprocity and thought that Canada should not follow " any will-o-the-wisp idea of better markets in the United States " but maintain its present policy of cultivating markets elsewhere.

Under the auspices of the National Reciprocity League of the United States a Convention was opened at Detroit on December **The Detroit** 10th for the international discussion of Reciprocity. **Reciprocity** A hundred delegates were present from the Northern **Convention** tier of States and several from Canada. Mr. F. B. Smith, President of the Detroit Board of Trade, Mayor Maybury of Detroit, the Hon. Eugene Hay of Minneapolis, and Governor A. B. Cummins of Iowa, addressed the meeting. The last-named defined protection as a means of holding the home market and reciprocity as a means of capturing other markets. In this connection "every student of the subject knows we can make a treaty with Canada that will give us more work to do in the United States than we have now." Mr. Charlton, M.P., followed with a long array of statistics and an appeal for reciprocity in natural products. "The call is with the United States. Canada has definitely and deliberately retired from the position of taking the initiative."

Senator James McMullen and Mr. R. F. Sutherland, M.P., were two other Canadian speakers. The former said that the Alaskan boundary question must be settled before Reciprocity could be arranged and the latter hoped for a more conciliatory American attitude although the people of Canada were beginning to feel that they could do without United States trade. On the following day Mr. Eugene M. Foss of Boston, and Congressman John Lind of Minnesota, were the chief speakers. The former said that it would be wise to treat Canada commercially as a State of the Union and then, with the Newfoundland Treaty accepted they would hold the key of the future. "If Canada does raise her tariff against us now many of our New England mills and factories must close down." Resolutions were unanimously passed approving "liberal and fair trade relations" with all the world, and the terms of the Bond-Hay Treaty regarding Newfoundland, together with the following:

Resolved, That it is the sense of this Convention that the Government of the United States should take immediate steps to secure closer and more advantageous trade relations with Canada, and that reciprocal relations, beneficial to both countries, should preferably follow the general lines of the removal by both countries of the duties on natural products of each, and such mutual extensions of the free list and reductions and changes of the duties on manufactured products of both, as will give to each as low a rate of duty as is given to any other country. Accordingly we earnestly urge upon Congress that action to this end be taken at once, either by re-convening the Joint High Commission for the sole purpose of negotiating a reciprocal treaty with Canada, or by adopting such other methods as to Congress may seem best.

Senator James McMullen was banqueted at Mount Forest on April 2nd and in his speech referred to the effects upon Canada of **Some** the McKinley and Dingley tariffs. "We had become **Continental** independent, had surmounted all the trade difficulties **Tariff** which surrounded us, and he hoped, when the Govern-**Considerations** ment revised the tariff, it would act towards the United States according to the treatment which they had accorded to us." On April 18th Mr. John Charlton called the attention of the House of Commons to the continued export of nickel matte from Canada to the United States where it was admitted free but a heavy duty imposed upon Canadian refined ore.   He asked why Americans should be allowed to build up a lucrative business at the expense of Canada and demanded an export duty upon the raw material.   The Canadian Club of Boston was addressed on November 21st by the Hon. Clifford Sifton and Hon. H. A. McKeown of New Brunswick.   The latter referred to international trade conditions as follows :

We set ourselves to the task of industrial and trade up-building with all the energy of a strong and determined people.   The conditions of trade within the nation are now such that the highest possible reward for toil can be secured ; and while we shall not place a bar in the way of our advancement by the vain hope of retaliation, yet in every relationship Canada shall seek her own interest; in every bargain which we make we shall expect to receive and shall receive full value for every concession which we may give.

Meanwhile, the Hon. Mr. Tarte had been conducting his campaign for higher duties and his speech at Peterborough, on June 19th, indicated his reasons and his view of the Americans in this connection: " They made us understand we were not as big as they were; we knew that, but we were happier than they ; we did not have to face the difficulties they had of industrial troubles and the existence of a great negro population.   We were a homogeneous people, a cheerful people, an energetic people, good neighbours.   At times we would be glad to see them a little more amenable to reason.   They had raised a 60 per cent. tariff wall and then slaughtered our market."

From the West came the appeal of the Edmonton *Post* on August 30th to abandon the position of hewers of wood and drawers of water to the American manufacturers.   " If they want to work up our raw products they can only do so on Canadian soil."   The Toronto *Globe* of October 6th took the ground that Canada should arrange its tariff " simply to further its own interests " and without regard to American policy.   On December 22nd extracts were published at Washington from the Report of Mr. James Boyle, United States Consul at Liverpool, in which he drew attention to the great prominence which Canada was now having in Great Britain and then added: " Let there be no mistake.   Canada is very much in earnest in the competitive struggle going on and it would be very unwise to dismiss the matter of Canadian competition as a bugaboo.   During the past year greater efforts than ever, both in Canada and Great Britain, have been made to make this competition stronger.   The latest scheme is to sell Canadian products to the British consumer without the intervention of middlemen."

Though not in any sense a public question in Canada the idea of annexation is always an issue in the opinion of many Americans and is therefore of importance in discussing current conditions.   Addressing a New York business gathering on January 22nd the Hon. Charles A. Gardiner declared American relations with Canada to be the most important of their external interests, recited what he called

Annexation Utterances of the Year

historic reasons for the annexation of Canada, spoke of the reviving earth-hunger and territorial requirements of his people and concluded as follows: "The grandest achievement of the new century will be the political union of the Anglo-Saxon people on this continent. What more ennobling conception can stir our civic duty and patriotic ambition. So far as in us lies, let us in our day consummate the union of the United States and Canada into the freest, most enlightened, most powerful sovereignty ever organized among men."

At Chicago, on March 8th, ex-Congressman J. T. Lentz of Ohio told an Irish gathering that it was time for the United States to finally take control of Canada. "If it is good policy, if it is correct morality for Great Britain to prevent the development and growth of republican governments in South Africa then the time is ripe for the United States to prevent the growth and development of monarchical institutions in North America." The banquet of the Canadian Club at Boston on April 8th was notable for a speech by Mr. Osborne Howes of that city who took occasion to discuss trade relations from the standpoint of "manifest destiny." In his opinion annexation was "predetermined and inevitable." The Canadians living in the United States, the Americans pouring into Canada, the common interests of trade, the inherited resemblances of life and language and literature were given as his reasons. Vigorous protests were expressed by Senator Ellis of St. John and Hon. J. W. Longley of Halifax. The latter declared that not one per cent. of the population of Canada was prepared to give the question a minute's consideration and then added:

I have myself already given it full consideration, and I have risked my position as a Canadian public man by demanding the full and free right to discuss the question. Nevertheless, sir, the stages of political development in every country are guided by incidents and events that are almost intangible and yet of overwhelming potency. The trend of events during the last eight or ten years in Canada has been unquestionably in the direction of Imperialism; in other words, in the direction of throwing all the power and force of the Canadian people into the maintenance and upholding of the great Empire to which we belong.

In the St. John *Globe* of May 14th Mr. W. Frank Hatheway expressed a belief, backed by various figures and arguments, that the "mighty dollar" would, unless counter influences soon came into play, make Canadian farmers "break down the political bars and allow us to be absorbed into the Union." Later in the year the Springfield *Republican* sent a special correspondent to look into these questions in Canada. He wrote from Toronto on October 23rd that "neither the Anglo-Canadian nor the French-Canadian looks for closer relations with America" and that the two countries were really drawing further apart. At a New York banquet on November 11th Archbishop Ireland dwelt upon the growth of the Republic and concluded as follows: "I do not want to be bellicose, but I say this for myself: As sure as fate, although you and I may not see it, the starry banner will wave mistress over all the territory from the Gulf to Hudson's Bay. There will be no conquest, no war. The hearts across the border are already beating with love for us and commerce and agriculture are calling for espousals." Speaking at a banquet in St. Paul, given to the Minnesota Congressmen on November 15th, Senator Moses E. Clapp used the following language :

With this situation in view, it is easy to foresee the manifest destiny of the Dominion of Canada. There is no doubt that in the future, possibly within the lives of some here present, the United States will ultimately include the regions that stretch from the boundaries of the northern States to the Arctic Sea. It will be then that St. Paul will be the seat of Empire, the capital of the greatest nation of the earth. One-third of the population of Canada is American born, and the stream of immigration is increasing year by year. The peaceful invasion is going quietly on. We will acquire the Dominion by the process of assimilation and not by conquest. There is no power on earth that can prevent the union of that country with our own.

In its issue of November 21st the Halifax *Chronicle* declared that there should be half a million men maintained capable of bearing arms in the Dominion. " It might prove the turning point in some American political crisis which would be almost as gratifying to honourable Americans as to ourselves." This was written in connection with a letter from A. W. Cobb, of Boston, who quoted Senator Lodge as repudiating the views of the Boston *Herald* which maintained the following lines permanently at the head of its editorial column : " Our greatest duty. The thought of every public man, year in and year out, should be directed to this our greatest national, economic, political and military safety, the acquisition of Canada." To that paper in November Mr. R. R. McLeod, formerly of Halifax, wrote a long letter analyzing the idea and denouncing the policy of annexation.

INCIDENTS IN THE FOREIGN RELATIONS OF CANADA*

Jan. 18.—At a banquet of the New York Press Club some difference of opinion takes place between Congressman William Sulzer and Mr. Gilbert Parker, M.P.

Feb. 10.—Mr. J. W. Ivey, United States Collector of Customs at Sitka, issues an order to his deputy at Skagway, practically taking over the duties of the Canadian officers at that port. At the same time he issues orders at Unalaska instructing a refusal of port privileges to all Canadian sealing vessels.

Feb. 21.—The Quebec *Telegraph* states that seven members of the present United States Congress are Canadians—Senators James McMillan, Jacob H. Gallinger, J. H. Willard and Thomas Kearns, and Congressmen J. T. McCleary, J. A. Hughes and William Connell.

Feb. 26.—Collector of Customs Ivey is superseded at Sitka and wires the Secretary of the United States Treasury about his Skagway order and the Canadian officials that : " I have sent the concern—bag, baggage, flag and other paraphernalia flying out of the country."

Mar. 4.—It is announced at Quebec that the Sons of the Revolution in Massachussetts have withdrawn their application to erect a monument in Quebec to General Montgomery.

*Not elsewhere referred to.

Mar. 24.—The 48th Highlanders of Toronto, under command of Lieut.-Colonel W. C. Macdonald, are welcomed at New York and parade before Lieut.-Governor Odell at the Madison Square Tournament of the Military Athletic League.   Four days later they are reviewed by the Hon. Dr. Borden.

May 24.—The Right Hon. Lord Pauncefote of Preston, G.C.B., G.C.M.G., British Ambassador at Washington since 1888, dies at the Embassy.

May 30.—It is announced that the Hon. Michael Henry Herbert, C.B., will succeed Lord Pauncefote as British Ambassador at Washington. On June 26th he is created a K.C.M.G.

June 10.—Ottawa is visited by 58 Freemasons from Detroit.

June 11.—Upon motion of Mr. H. Dallas Helmcken, K.C., the following Resolution is unanimously passed by the British Columbia Legislature :

"Whereas, British subjects have faithfully observed the regulations made pursuant to the Award dated the 15th of August, 1893, for the proper protection and preservation of the fur seal in the Behring Sea ; and, whereas, it is announced that the Government of the United States have lately passed an Act, in effect that unless *modus vivendi* prohibiting the killing of seals be secured at the opening of the pelagic season for 1902, authority will be given to kill all the male and female seals with the exception of 10,000 females and 1,000 males ; and, whereas, the exercise of such presumed authority is contrary to the finding of the Behring Sea tribunal, and a direct violation of the spirit of the agreement entered into between the Governments of Great Britain and the United States, and an unwarrantable interference with and infringement upon the undoubted rights of British subjects ;

"Be it therefore resolved, that this House would view with regret the commission of such act, and in the opinion of this House an humble address be presented to His Honour the Lieutenant-Governor-in-Council to communicate with the Dominion Government protesting against such action, and urging that all proper steps be taken to bring this matter to the attention of the Imperial Government."

Aug. 10.—New York papers devote unprecedented space to the King's Coronation and " God Save the King " is sung in various theatres.

Aug. 11. The British Societies of Massachusetts join in celebrating the Coronation and hold an important banquet in Boston.

Aug. 14.—Prince Tsai Chen, Envoy of the Chinese Emperor to the Coronation, reaches Ottawa on his way through Canada.

Aug. 30.—The decisions of the German Customs authorities to require certificates of origin in the case of " American " grain is supposed to be for the purpose of collecting the retaliatory duty upon Canadian wheat in connection with the Preferential tariff of Canada.   It is expected to prevent Americans from mixing Canadian and United States wheat for the German market.

Sept. 1.—The 10th National Guard of Albany, New York, and the Hong-Kong Coronation Contingent are reviewed at Ottawa by H.E. the Governor-General of Canada.   Lord Minto concludes a brief address as follows : " It has been very impressive to see United States troops and British troops side by side on the field.   I only hope that, not only on parade, but always in the field, they will be shoulder to shoulder."

Sept. 22.—President Roosevelt reviews a Canadian Regiment, the 21st Essex Fusiliers, at Detroit in the presence of a great concourse of people. Lieut.-Colonel N. A. Bartlett, of Windsor, commanded and there were 288 men under arms.

Sept. 22.—A despatch from Ottawa states that the United States Government has decided to add 25 cents a ton duty on ground wood-pulp and 35 cents a ton on unbleached sulphite and soda pulp.   It is supposed to be an enforcement of the Dingley Act and retaliation for the

Ontario and Quebec pulp legislation which the Supreme Court of Canada had declared not to be export duties but which the American Government considered to be the same thing.

Oct. 26.—At a legal banquet in Montreal, Chief Justice Alton B. Parker, of the New York Court of Appeal, delivers an address.

Nov. 30.—His Highness Somditch, Crown Prince of Siam, reaches Vancouver on his way accross Canada from attending the Coronation and studying European institutions.

Dec. 20.—It is announced that Messrs. Mackenzie & Mann, of Toronto, have received a large concession along the Orinoco in Venezuela. It is said to be rich in gold, rubber and asphalt.

V.—THE CANADIAN MILITIA

The second annual statement submitted, under date of December 31st, 1901, by Major-General R. H. O'Grady-Haly, C.B., D.S.O., was an elaborate description of the Militia conditions of Canada as seen by him. He thought the difficulty in obtaining recruits for the Permanent Force was due partly to its small proportions and partly to the general prosperity of the country, and consequent demand for labour. The remedy would be in a re-adjustment of the rates of pay so as to bring the general enrolment of the soldier more on a footing with the current rate of wages. An addition in numbers to the Cavalry School at Toronto was recommended. A similar small increase was urged in the Field Artillery and the Garrison Artillery for the purpose of promoting their general efficiency. He also recommended that each of the Infantry Schools should consist of two complete companies, and thus enable the instructional work of the Force in connection with the general Militia to be carried out more efficiently. "The foregoing recommendations would entail an increase in the Permanent Force of about 18 officers and 462 'other ranks' and, consequently, clause 28 of the Militia Act would require to be amended so as to provide for the maintenance of Permanent troops not exceeding 1,500 men; but I submit that the enormous increase in the wealth and responsibilities of the Dominion since the Act was passed more than warrants such an increase." The country would, he believed, then possess an effective force of highly trained troops which, under existing conditions, it could not have.

He deprecated the continuance of the Provisional Schools for young city officers as having a prejudicial effect on the standard of efficiency, and urged a reform in the system under which examinations for promotion were conducted. In connection with his inspection of the Camps of Instruction, the Major-General praised the rural corps for their zeal, intelligence, cleanliness and discipline and thought as much was accomplished in the way of training as existing conditions would permit of. "But I can only repeat that in nine working days it is absolutely impossible to impart more than the mere rudiments of a soldier's training. Officers and men, I feel sure, do their very best, but I can only reiterate what I said in my last Report, 'that the troops can never be made even fairly fit to take the field with the limited period of annual drill which they receive under existing arrangements.'" Especially was this the case when fully 60 per cent. of the men were raw recruits. The most serious drawback against which the Militia of Canada had to contend was declared, however, to be the wastage of men from the rural corps and the apparent indifference of captains of companies

189

to the necessity of retaining their men for a reasonable period, or to that of enforcing the law against deserters. He urgently recommended an increase in the statutory drill period to 28 days, and a scale of graduated pay in direct ratio to the length of training. Half the present force properly trained would be better than 40,000 troops on paper. The city corps were described as well drilled and equipped and of good physique. Their efficiency in the use of the rifle was declared to be fair, but, owing to the limited space in a drill-hall, their knowledge of scouting, outpost duties, hasty entrenchments and other details of practical warfare was necessarily meagre.

According to figures furnished the Minister of Militia and Defence for his annual Report, dated March 12th, 1902, and supplied by Colonel Lord Aylmer, Adjutant-General, the Statistics of the Militia regimental establishment of the Active Militia on December 31st, 1901, was 38,090 officers, non-commissioned officers and men ; the number ordered to drill during the year was 35,437 ; and the total number trained or partly trained was 30,262. The total number of officers and men participating in the Royal Review by the Duke of Cornwall and York at Quebec was 3,546; at Toronto, 10,801 ; at Halifax, 3,766. The total vote for Militia services in the year ending June 30th, 1901, was $3,097,752, with pensions for the North-West Rebellion, the Fenian Raids and the troubles of 1837, amounting to $21,240 additional. The total revenue was $85,470, which included $22,035 from the Royal Military College at Kingston. The following table shows the chief items of expenditure :

General Officer, Adjutant-General and Quartermaster-General	$ 10,480
Pay of Staff, Permanent Corps and Active Militia	355,135
Halifax Provisional Garrison	349,870
Yukon Contingent	14,321
Annual drill of the Militia	454,357
Salaries of Civil employees	86,494
Military properties, etc.	302,830
Warlike and other stores	85,170
Clothing and necessaries	209,656
Provisions, Supplies and Remounts	121,790
Royal Military College	72,520
Transport and Freight	39,823
Grants in aid of Artillery, Rifle and other Associations	36,035
Government Cartridge Factory	110,783
Defences of Esquimault, B.C.	128,140
Arms, Ammunition and Defences	131,551
Special Service in South Africa	558,810
Miscellaneous	330,056

During the year, according to Col. D. A. Macdonald, Chief Superintendent of Military Stores, 719 rifles and a million and a-half cartridges were issued to newly organized Rifle Associations. Over 12,000 new helmets were issued, and 572,000 rounds of ammunition.

An important debate upon the condition of the Militia took place in the House of Commons on April 10th.   Lieut.-Col, the Hon.

Militia Reform in Parliament
David Tisdale, introduced the general subject of reform by strongly endorsing the recommendations made by Major-Gen. O'Grady-Haly in his annual Report. He drew attention to the historical foundation of the Militia in the response of 24,000 men who volunteered in one day at the time of the Trent affair; described the present system in its three branches of the Permanent Force of 1,000 men, the Active Militia or Volunteers and the Sedentary Militia or Reserves; and quoted largely and approvingly from the Report of the G.O.C.   In his reply, the Minister of Militia agreed with much of the praise bestowed upon the Major-General's views, and declared that he had been given and should always have a perfectly free hand in expressing opinions and making suggestions.   The proposal to increase the Permanent Force to 1,500 men was a wise one, and at the next Session of Parliament he would ask for a re-enactment of the Militia Act which would enable this and other changes to be effected.   He did not think it possible to get the 35,000 members of the Militia together every year for 28 days as recommended, or even for 21 days, but he believed that once in every three years something of the sort might be practicable.   Dr. Borden then referred to the Major-General's suggestion as to a Militia Reserve, and made an announcement which was really a declaration of public policy :

I may tell the House that at this very moment the suggestion which the General has made is being carried into effect.   It is one which will involve very little additional expense, because the extra men who will be required for the purpose of increasing the number up to somewhere near a total strength of 100,000 can all be interested in the Militia by being brought into the Rifle Associations, for which provision was made at the last Session of Parliament.   I hope in this way, without any great increase in the annual expenditure, that we shall be able to have what will practically amount to a trebling of the present force of men who will be almost as effective as the 35,000 which we have now.   At any rate, it will be composed of men who will have had experience in the art of rifle shooting.

The Minister hoped in the near future to have an improved cartridge for the force, and to greatly encourage the practice of shooting.   The Government was largely increasing the capacity of the arsenal at Quebec, and expected to raise its annual output from 2,000,000 to 7,000,000 rounds.   He referred to the adoption of the Sir Charles Ross rifle, on the recommendation of a Committee composed of Colonels Otter, Hughes, Gibson and others, and to the organization of an Army Service Corps.

In February, 1902, there were rumours that Major-General the Earl of Dundonald, C.B., C.V.O., who had so distinguished himself in

The Appointment of Lord Dundonald
South Africa and at the same time been so popular with his men, might be appointed to the command of the Canadian Militia when Major-General O'Grady-Haly's time was up on June 30th.   On April 9th it was announced by the War Office that no change would be made

until July 1st when Lord Dundonald would take over the appointment. It was noted in this connection that the 7th Earl of Dundonald had been killed at the seige of Louisbourg while Admiral Sir Alexander Cochrane and Admiral the 10th Earl of Dundonald had both served in command of the North American station.

On June 12th Major-General O'Grady-Haly issued his farewell to the Militia force, expressed pride in his association with them for a time and declared that in war and peace they had proved themselves " worthy to share in the best traditions of the British Army." In the press of the Dominion, for the first time on record, there was practical unanimity of approval regarding the administration of affairs by a departing G. O. C. There was a similarly general desire to welcome the new Commander—except in one or two Radical papers which could see no good in a British officer. Prior to leaving England Lord Dundonald was interviewed by the *Morning Post* of July 12th. He expressed himself as opposed to British garrisons in the Colonies as promoting neglect in local defence and mistrust of local power. Nor did he place much value upon the interchange of regiments between the countries of the Empire. The commands should be interchangeable.

" The present arrangement," he added, " by which the chief command in some of our large self-governing Colonies is always in the hands of a British officer cannot be perpetuated, as these are rapidly rising nations in wealth, importance and armament. If it were known that a career in the Imperial Army would always be open without favour to Colonial officers of proved ability, the armies of our kinsfolk beyond the seas would be strengthened, professional spirit stimulated and better men attracted to the service." The new General Officer commanding the Militia arrived at Montreal on July 25th and was welcomed by Colonel Lord Aylmer and a large gathering of officers. In the evening he reached Ottawa and was received by a guard of honour, a salvo of thirteen guns and the cheers of some thousands of people. His first duty was the issuing of a general order, on July 26th, welcoming home from South Africa the officers and men of the Canadian Mounted Rifles.

The new G.O.C. became popular from his first appearance in Canada and soon had many engagements outside of the strict duties of his office. The first was the unveiling of a monu-

Lord Dundonald's Work and Opinions

ment to Ottawa soldiers in the late war which took place on August 6th. After a reference to its erection by the gifts of 30,000 children and to the honour due to volunteers who had given up their lives for the Empire, Lord Dundonald continued as follows: " The blood of these men has cemented the Empire with links of iron, and Canada may be assured that, if ever she were attacked, the sons of Natal and the Cape, and the sons of the other places throughout the

MAJOR-GENERAL, THE EARL OF DUNDONALD, C.B., C.V.O.,
Appointed in 1902 to Command the Militia of Canada.

Empire, would stream across the seas to help her, just as she had done in sending her sons to South Africa."

On September 1st he came to Toronto to open the Industrial Exhibition. The first function of the visit was a luncheon at the Exhibition with Mr. W. K. McNaught in the chair and a brief speech from the guest, who paid special tribute to Strathcona's Horse and to an incident where six of the men in that corps gave up their lives rather than surrender. "It was easy to be a General if one had men like that." Then followed the opening ceremonies, the presentation of an Address and a reply which was tactful in phrase and warm in its praise of Canadian troops, especially those who had fought at Hart's River. "If a small people such as the Canadians had their troops well organized, well armed, well led and well equipped, no force or nation could conquer the Dominion. Should trouble ever come, however, the men of the Empire would spring to the aid of Canada." In the evening Lord Dundonald was dined at the National Club, with Mr. J. F. Ellis in the chair, and addresses by Senator Gibson, Professor Clark, Dr. G. R. Parkin, Lord Aylmer and others.

He made certain very clear statements. "I have come to this country to consider the matter of how to make and maintain an efficient military force composed of men who are not paid for their services." There were some things essential : (1) thoroughly trained officers ; (2) officers with brains ; (3) promotion for merit and not through favour or affection ; (4) efficient riflemen. On the evening of September 2nd Lieut.-Colonel H. M. Pellatt gave a large military dinner for Lord Dundonald and in his speech expressed the hope that their guest might be heartily supported in making "needed changes and improvements in the Militia." In his reply Lord Dundonald referred to the necessity of rifle shooting for the cavalry and to the desirability of efficient camps of instruction. Meanwhile, the G.O.C. had been formally welcomed in the afternoon by the Scotchmen of Toronto with an Address and the skirl of bagpipes.

Following this visit Lord Dundonald made a tour of inspection through the Maritime Provinces, and on November 19th was banqueted at Montreal by the local garrison. Lieut.-Colonel W. D. Gordon, D.O.C., presided and the General spoke in both English and French. Meanwhile there were various comments in the press. The majority were complimentary and friendly to the ideas expressed in these speeches while a fairly persistent minority were represented by the following editorial paragraph in the Montreal *Herald* of September 4th :

Dundonald apparently shares a delusion dear to Hutton. He seems to think the people of Canada are concerned about being in readiness for war, or that if they are not they are to blame and should be stirred up. Any man who thinks that way—and all European soldiers do—fails to grasp the essential distinction between Europe and North America. With Europe war is a condition. With us it is a theory.

13

One of the first plans carried out by the new G.O.C. was the holding of three Camps of Instruction for officers and non-commissioned officers. At Niagara, between September 23rd and October 4th, nearly all the Regiments of Ontario were represented and the main object was instruction in the infantry drill, which recent events in South Africa had completely changed in character, and in rifle shooting. Some 2,400 were present and there was much musketry practice and company drill as well as a series of lectures on outposts, advance guard duties, etc. Colonel Lawrence Buchan, C.M.G., was in command of the Camp and Lord Dundonald was present during a part of the period. In his address to the troops on September 24th, the G.O.C. told them that they would be drilled in the main features of a soldier's education—the elements of trenching and of general field work. The Divisional Commanders were Lieut.-Col. J. Peters, D.O.C., No. 1 District, Lieut.-Col. J. Mason, R.O., and Lieut.-Col. W. D. Gordon, D.O.C., No. 3 District. At the Three Rivers' Camp, which was held from September 16th to September 27th, Lieut.-Col. O. C. C. Pelletier, D.O.C., No. 7, was Divisional Commander. At the Sussex, N.B., Camp Lieut.-Col. J. D. Irving, D.O.C., No. 9, was in command of the Division. Lord Dundonald also visited and inspected these latter Camps. The Brigade Commanders were as follows :

The Camps of Instruction

Niagara—

1st Infantry Brigade, Lieut.-Col. C. S. Ellis.
2nd   "   "   Lieut.-Col. A. H. Macdonald.
3rd   "   "   Lieut.-Col. J. M. Delamere.
4th   "   "   Lieut.-Col. T. H. Lloyd.
5th   "   "   Lieut.-Col. W. E. Hodgins.
6th   "   "   Lieut.-Col. John Hughes.

Three Rivers—

7th Infantry Brigade, Lieut.-Col. H. Prevost.
8th   "   "   Lieut.-Col. E. B. Worthington.
10th   "   "   Lieut.-Col. P. Landry.
11th   "   "   Lieut.-Col. G. T. A. Evanturel.

Sussex—

12th Infantry Brigade, Lieut.-Col. H. McLean.
14th   "   "   Lieut.-Col. B. A. Weston.

It was announced on February 27th that General, H. R. H. the Prince of Wales, K.G., had accepted the position of Hon. Colonel of the 43rd Regiment Duke of Cornwall's Own Rifles, Ottawa. On May 1st, Lieutenant-Colonels Frank King, J. Davidson, R. Costigan, T. dit L. Boulanger W. G. Hurdman and R. L. Maltby were placed on the Regimental List of the Field Artillery with the rank indicated. On June 1st Lieut.-Col. G. Rolt White was appointed D.O.C.

Militia Changes and Promotions

of No. 8 District. Meanwhile, on May 15th, Lieut.-Colonel C. C. Sewell, M.D., A.M.S., was promoted Colonel, and Surgeon-Lieut.-Colonel G. S. Ryerson, M.D., A.M.S., was promoted to Hon. Colonel. On November 1st Surgeon-Lieut.-Colonel H. R. Duff, M.D., became Principal Medical Officer of District No. 4, Lieut.-Colonel A. N. Worthington, M.D., A.M.S., of Districts No. 5 and 6, and Major G. C. Jones, M.D., A.M.S., of District No. 9. The following changes occurred during the year in the command of Regiments:

Jan. 18.—Lieut.-Colonel J. A. McGillivray succeeds Lieut.-Colonel J. E. Farwell in command of the 34th, Ontario, Regiment.
Feb. 2.—Lieut.-Colonel John B. McPhee succeeds Lieut.-Colonel J. Ward in the 35th, Simcoe, Foresters.
Feb. 8.—Lieut.-Colonel William R. Stevens succeeds Lieut.-Colonel J. W. Harkom in the 54th, Richmond, Regiment.
Feb. 22.—Lieut-Colonel J. W. Little succeeds Lieut.-Colonel A. M. Smith in the 7th Fusiliers, of London.
Mar. 12.—Lieut.-Colonel Daniel Stewart succeeds Lieut-Colonel T. S. McLeod in the 82nd (Charlottetown) Regiment.
Mar. 22.—Lieut-Colonel Francis S. McKay succeeds Lieut.-Colonel A. E. D. Labelle in the 65th, Mount Royal, Rifles, of Montreal.
April 1.—Lieut.-Colonel J. F. Kenward succeeds Lieut.-Colonel C. S. Ellis in the 27th (Lambton) Regiment.
April 8. —Lieut.-Colonel A. F. McRae succeeds Lieut-Colonel J. N. Bethune in the 94th (Victoria) Regiment.
May 2.—Lieut Colonel C. A. Andrews is appointed to command the 75th (Lunenburg) Regiment.
June 11.—Lieut-Colonel George A. Stimson succeeds Lieut-Colonel John Bruce in the 10th, Royal Grenadiers, Toronto.
June 23.—Lieut.-Colonel Bedford Harper succeeds Lieut.-Colonel J. M. Baird in the 74th (Sussex, N.B.) Regiment.
July 18 Lieut.-Colonel Noble A. Bartlett succeeds Lieut.-Colonel J. G. Guillot in the 21st, Essex, Fusileers.
Sept. 2.—Lieut-Colonel Edward T. Sturdee succeeds Lieut-Colonel H. H. McLean in the 62nd, St. John, Fusiliers.
Sept. 18.—Lieut.-Colonel J. W. Millar succeeds Lieut.-Colonel E. B. Edwards in the 57th, Peterborough Rangers.
Oct. 30.—Lieut.-Colonel T. J. de M. Taschereau succeeds Lieut.-Colonel A. Chabot in the 92nd (Dorchester) Regiment.
Nov. 26.—Lieut.-Colonel E. D. Cameron is appointed to the command of the 38th, Dufferin Rifles, of Brantford.
Dec. 2.—Lieut.-Colonel J. A. Morin is appointed to command the newly-organized Regiment, No. 17, of St. Levis, Quebec.

Militia Orders of January 1st and February 1st, 1902, gave long lists of officers to whom had been awarded the Colonial (Auxiliary Forces) Officers' Decoration, and on February 2nd it was announced that another lengthy list of recommendations for the same honour had been made. On February 1st it was announced that Major T. dit L. Boulanger was to be Brevet Lieut.-Colonel, and also Major S. J. A. Denision C.M.G., for services in South Africa, and Captain J. Cooper Mason, D.S.O., to be Major in recognition of similar services. On April 16th it was announced that Major G. W. Stephens, Jr., had succeeded Major R. Costigan in command of the Montreal Field Battery. On August 26th the Militia Department received a

British war medal, ribbon and clasp for presentation to Lieut-Colonel T. dit L. Boulanger, the only Canadian officer who had served in the Chinese war.

The annual statement of the Department of Militia and Defence for the year ending June 30th, 1902, showed a revenue of $43,564, pensions paid amounting to $21,178 and expenditures of an Imperial nature totalling $474,703— including defences of Esquimault, $122,432, special service, South Africa, $97,310 and Halifax Provisional Garrison $254,961. The total expenditures were $2,947,375, which included, besides the items just mentioned, $224,736 on arms and ammunition, $207,614 on Dominion Arsenal, $81,912 on the Royal Military College, $129,694 on provisions and supplies for the Permanent Force, $224,805 on clothing and necessaries for the Permanent Force and Active Militia, $343,506 on military properties, $529,625 on the Annual Drill, and $270,028 on the pay of the Permanent Force.

The Militia Report for 1902

Colonel D. A. Macdonald, Chief Superintendent of Military Stores, reported 1,630,204 issues of small arm ammunition to Rifle Associations during the year. Colonel Lord Aylmer, Adjutant-General, reported 1,905 officers and 20,902 non-commissioned officers and men as the authorized Establishment called out for training in 1902. Of these, 881 officers and 6,932 non-commissioned officers and men received 12 days' training in District Camps. At Local Headquarters out of an authorized Establishment of 1,001 officers and 12,216 non-commissioned officers and men called out, 799 of the former and 10,685 of the latter were trained during the year. In the Report of the Department for 1902 were also included an official record of the 1st Canadian Coronation Contingent, by Lieut.-Colonel H. M. Pellatt, and of the 2nd Contingent, or special Royal escort, of thirteen men, by Lieut.-Colonel R. E. W. Turner, v.c., d.s.o. The Royal Military College was dealt with briefly, Lieut.-Colonel R. N. R. Reade, the Commandant, approving the drill, gymnastics, signaling, rifle shooting and gun drill, but criticizing as entirely inadequate the riding instructions.

The new General Officer Commanding presented his first Report to the Minister of Militia and Defence, under date of December 31st, 1902. He enclosed a special document, which was not published, containing " a broad scheme for the improvement of the Militia." He added that " if the proposals contained in it are carried out they will in my opinion conduce to the greater efficiency of the Militia." Lord Dundonald then dealt with the events of the half year in which he had commanded the Militia ; referred to the Camps of Instruction, to which he had devoted 25 days of personal supervision and training in practical work ; declared that the officers and men picked up the new methods and tactical exercises very quickly ; and stated his intention in future to omit marches past and ceremonial and " convert the camps practically into schools

Lord Dundonald's First Recommendations

of instruction for fitting the soldier to take the field with not one item in the programme that does not make for fighting efficiency." He described general conditions as follows—with the summarized statement that there did not yet exist the "trained framework needed to make a citizen army efficient in time of war:"

Though the Rural Militia contains a large proportion of earnest, self-sacri-ficing officers and men, it does not satisfy the requirements of a national defence force. Nominally it is a body of men who engage to serve for a period of three years. As a matter of fact it consists and always has consisted of a number of regiments which are almost recruited afresh every time they are called out for training. Large numbers of entirely raw men enlist before the particular training and are perhaps never seen afterwards, no real effort being made to compel them to fulfil their engagement, owing to powers of compulsion being quite inadequate for the purpose. Consequently it is impossible to carry instruction beyond the most elementary stages. Such a system is unduly expensive and ineffective from a military point of view. So small is the rate of pay, and so unsatisfactory have been the conditions of training, that the best men do not enter the Militia as they might. From this it follows that the non-commissioned officers also are to a large extent insufficiently qualified for their posts, nor can they command ready obedience from the soldier when, as in many cases, they are quite ignorant of the very rudiments of their duties.

MILITIA AND DEFENCE INCIDENTS

Feb. 3.—Lieut.-Colonel Lawrence Buchan, C.M.G., commanding the Royal Canadian Regiment, lectures before the Canadian Military Institute Toronto, on "With the Infantry in South Africa."

Feb. 27.—At the meeting of the Dominion Artillery Association in Ottawa the Hon. Dr. Borden makes the following statement:
"There should be a force in Canada able to take the field at a moment's notice. His aim had been to have the conditions in time of peace the same as in war time. The experience in South Africa had many salutary lessons ; that was why every branch of the service had been represented there. The money and blood spent on the voldt had been paid ten times in the valuable lessons there learned of active warfare."

Mar. 4.—It is announced that Vice-Admiral Sir Archibald Lucius Douglas, K.C.B.—a native of Quebec—will succeed Admiral Sir Frederick Bedford in command of the North-American Station.

Mar. 19.—A new Drill-Hall is opened at Vancouver by Lieut.-Colonel C. A. Worsnop of the Duke of Connaught's Own Rifles.

Mar. 22.—Lieut.-Colonel R. N. R. Reade, Commandant of the Royal Military College, Kingston, lectures at the Toronto Armouries upon "Intel-ligence and Information in War."

April 14.—Lieut.-Colonel Sam Hughes presents, discusses and finally withdraws the following Resolution in the House of Commons:
"That in the opinion of this House the system of training citizens of Canada for the positions of officers in the active Militia should be such as would furnish the greatest number of properly qualified persons in each regimental district necessarily required, upon a war basis, at the least possible cost consistent with efficiency ; and that all needless hindrances, customs and expense in the way of any and every citizen obtaining such military education shall be removed."

April 18.—Major-General Sir Charles Parsons, K.C.M.G., arrives at Halifax to assume command of the Imperial Forces in Canada.

May   5.—The Hon. Dr. Borden, Minister of Militia, opens new Armouries at Brockville.

June 11.—Captain A. E. Rastrick of the Southern Nigerian Regiment and formerly an officer in the Haldimand (Ontario) Rifles, dies in London, England, from hydrophobia.

June 17.—Mr. Justice Langelier renders judgment in the celebrated case under which Lieut.-Colonel J. P. Cooke of the Prince of Wales Fusiliers, Montreal, claimed $1,000 damages from Lieut.-Colonel F. M. Cole, acting D.O.C., on the ground that the latter, during certain labour troubles at Valleyfield and while in command of the local troops, had him arrested for refusing to parade the men of his Regiment. Judgment is given in favour of the plaintiff for $100 and costs.

June 19.—Five graduates of the Royal Military College are recommended for commissions in the Imperial Army and Diplomas of graduation are awarded to 17 Cadets.

June 20.—A Militia Order provides for the division of the Queen's Own Regiment of Toronto into two battalions under the command of Lieut.-Colonel Pellatt ; makes the Royal Grenadiers and Highlanders of that city of uniform strength—568 in all ranks ; gives Montreal and Ottawa each a Company of Engineers; allows the Permanent Corps slight increases in strength ; and makes various minor changes in the Militia.

July　1.—The Hon. S. A. Fisher, M.P., unveils a monument at Eccles' Hill in memory of the local battle and resistance to Fenian raids in 1870.

July　4.—Major-General Sir Charles Parsons reviews the Hong-Kong Contingent for the Coronation, at Vancouver.

October.—The current number of Queen's Quarterly, Kingston, contains a study of conditions in the Canadian Militia, by Mr. C. F. Hamilton of Toronto.

Oct. 31.—The War Office announces the promotion of Captain R. K. Scott, D.S.O., son of Lieut.-Colonel Thomas Scott of Winnipeg, to the Brevet rank of Major.

Nov.　3.—An Ontario branch of the Incorporated Soldiers' and Sailors' Help Society is organized in Toronto, with the Lieutenant-Governor as President, and Hon. O. Lambart, Mr. Justice Street, Colonel W. D. Otter, C.B., Col. G. A. Sweny, Commander A. W. Whish, R.N., Lieut.-Colonel the Hon. J. M. Gibson, Colonel L. Buchan, C.M.G., and Lieut.-Colonel J. Mason as Vice-Presidents.

Nov. 24.—The Hon. G. W. Ross, Premier of Ontario, unveils a monument in Toronto to the British and Canadian soldiers who fell in the War of 1812.

Nov. 29.—The Garrison Club of Quebec gives a banquet in honour of Sir F. W. Borden, Minister of Militia, with Lieut.-Colonel O. C. C. Pelletier in the chair.

VI.—DOMINION AND PROVINCIAL FINANCES

On March 17th, the Hon. W. S. Fielding, Minister of Finance, presented his sixth annual statement to the House of Commons. He had no changes in the tariff to announce, and The Dominion Budget of 1902 stated that machinery and structural iron for beet-sugar factories would remain free of duty for another year from April 1st. He estimated the revenue for the fiscal year, ending June 30th, 1902, at $56,800,000, the expenditure at $51,000,000, the surplus at $5,800,000, and the addition to the Debt of the Dominion at about $6,000,000. He was able to say that his expression of belief in his last Budget speech that the country had about reached the crest of the wave of business prosperity had been proven incorrect by the activities and progress of the past year. The revenue had been greater than his estimate, and larger than that of the year 1899-1900, as the following table showed:—

	Year ending June 30, 1900.	Year ending June 30, 1901.	Increase.
Customs	$28,374,147	$28,425,284	$ 51,136
Excise	9,868,075	10,318,266	450,190
Post Office	3,205,535	3,441,504	235,969
Railways	4,774,162	5,213,381	439,219
Lands	1,388,023	1,517,319	129,295
Miscellaneous	3,420,050	3,598,945	178,895
	$51,029,992	$52,514,699	$1,484,704

Mr. Fielding drew special attention to the Post Office returns in this connection. There was an increased revenue of $235,969, and total receipts from the Department of $3,441,504. But the expenditure was $3,939,446, showing a deficit of $489,941. He claimed, however, that the deficits had once been as high as $800,000, and that in the meantime Mr. Mulock had not only reduced the amount, but had cut the British postage in two and reduced the Canadian postage one-third. In railways he described the condition as noteworthy. From total receipts of $3,140,678 in 1896, when the Laurier Government took office, the amount had risen in 1901 to $5,213,381. The total expenditure on Consolidated Fund account, or permanent expense account, was $46,866,367, as against $42,975,279 in the preceding year. In legislation there had been an increase of $342,424; in arts, agriculture and statistics—which included the Census—the increase was $235,645; in militia there was an increase of $215,495; in railways and canals—chiefly the working expenses of the Intercolonial Railway—the increase was $1,133,660; in public works the increase was $1,096,743; in the Government of the North-West Territories $150,177; and in the Post Office $173,431. Adding to this Consolidated Fund expenditure, however, the Capital account expenditures, such as additional

199

or special payments to railways, canals, public works, and the South African War, the total was $57,982,866, as against $52,717,466 in 1899-1900. For railways on Capital account there was an expenditure in 1901 of $3,914,010; for canals, $2,360,569; for public works, $1,006,983; for Dominion lands, $269,060; for militia, $135,884; for the Canadian Pacific Railway, $8,978. The total was $7,695,488, or an increase altogether of $226,645 over similar extra expenditures in 1900. The net Public Debt was described by the Minister as having been $268,480,003 on June 30th, 1901, as against $265,493,806 in the previous year. In the five preceding years, he added, the increase had been $9,982,570, or an average of $1,996,514, as compared with an average of $6,563,075 in the preceding eighteen years. The exact increase for 1900-1901 was $2,986,196. The situation as presented by the Minister may be summed up for the fiscal year 1901 in the following table:

Consolidated Fund expenditure.....................	$46,866,367
Capital expenditure on railways, public works, etc...	7,695,488
Special expenditures, South Africa and railway subsidies.....................................	3,421,010
Total expenditure..........................	$57,982,865
Consolidated Fund revenue.......................	$52,514,701
Applied to Sinking Fund.........................	2,480,336
Refund, N.W.T. Rebellion........................	1,632
Added to Public Debt............................	2,986,196
Total.....................................	$57,982,865

During his speech Mr. Fielding pointed out that a temporary loan of $6,000,000 would mature in London on July 1st, and would require re-arrangement. The present rate of interest was 3½ per cent. He then dealt at length with the general condition and prosperity of the country. Mr. R. L. Borden followed in denunciation of the Government for their increasing expenditures, additions to the indebtedness of Canada, and failure to keep promises of retrenchment. From 1892 to 1896 the expenditure had been $210,708,819; from 1897 to 1901 it was $250,550,005. During the same years taxation had risen from a total of $138,606,054 to that of $170,168,924. He concluded by moving a Resolution along tariff lines, which, after prolonged discussion, was defeated by the normal party majority. On May 5th Mr. Fielding presented to the House a Resolution empowering the Government to borrow $15,000,000, if required, for loan renewals or special purposes, and this was, of course, granted. On May 13th Mr. R. L. Borden presented a Resolution describing the increased expenditures of the Government and the increasing additions to the Debt, and concluding as follows:

That this House desires to place on record the opinion that the expenditures for the year ending June 30th, 1902, and the proposed expenditure for the year ending June 30th, 1903, are excessive and extravagant, and regrets that the Government, with the exceptionally large revenue at its command, has not only failed to reduce but has largely increased the Public Debt, and has incurred capital expenditure for which the country does not receive and cannot expect any adequate return.

After discussion the motion was lost by 84 to 41 votes. According to the Public Accounts as presented to the Minister of Finance by Mr. J. M. Courtney, C.M.G., Deputy Minister, on December 10th, 1902, the receipts for the year ending June 30th, 1902, on Consolidated Fund account were $58,050,790 and the expenditures $50,-759,391, leaving a surplus of $7,291,398. The expenditures chargeable to Capital account included $7,217,528 upon railways (of which the Intercolonial received $4,626,841) and $2,190,125 on public works. Summarized, as above for 1901, the situation for the fiscal year 1902 was as follows :

Consolidated Fund expenditure.....................	$50,759,391
Capital expenditure on railways, public works, etc..	10,078,636
Special expenditures on South Africa, railway subsidies and iron and steel bounties...............	3,132,769
Total expenditures........................	$63,970,796
Consolidated Fund revenue...............	$58,050,790
Applied to Sinking Fund..........................	2,569,380
Refund to N.W.T. Rebellion......................	1,541
Added to Public Debt...........................	3,349,085
Total..................................	$63,970,796

The Premier and Provincial Treasurer of Ontario delivered his third annual Budget speech in the Legislature on January 22nd, 1902. The Hon. Mr. Ross reviewed the financial **The Ontario** policy of the Liberal Governments of the past 30 years, **Financial** described the expenditure of $113,000,000 during that **Statement** period, and claimed that, although $27,000,000 had been collected in that time from woods and forests, yet many more millions had been returned directly to the people in refunds and subsidies. In replying for the Opposition, Lieut.-Col. A. J. Matheson denied the existence of a surplus, and claimed that the Province was in debt $4,900,000 above all available assets. The Treasurer's figures were of special importance at this Session, as they were largely used by Government supporters in the ensuing election campaign. He stated that the revenue from liquor licenses in 1871 was $58,558, and that in the year ending December 31st, 1901, it was $376,372. From woods and forests the receipts were $215,973 in 1871, $1,479,847 in 1901, and a total of $27,720,965. He claimed that the expenditure of this sum was not a wasting of capital, as the Opposition alleged, because since 1867 the Province had spent upon public buildings and works $11,249,778 ; in subsidizing railways $8,304,901 ; on colonization and mining roads $3,528,339 ; on surveys $3,591,352 ; and on rivers, lakes and bridges $1,160,620—a total of $27,834,991. " The wealth of the forest has simply been transmuted into public utilities."

He took great credit to the Government for their saw-log legislation of 1890 by which the export of logs to United States mills for manufacture had been stopped, and he pointed out the benefits of their policy of setting apart forest reserves to the extent of some 2,500,000 acres. He stated that since Confederation in 1867 they had received $3,814,588 interest on investments ; that the Government had encouraged the railways of the Province by adding 2,219 miles (since 1871) at a total cost of $10,058,942; that during the same period $3,492,410 had been spent upon colonization roads, $4,407,546 upon asylums, $1,307,880 upon penal institutions. $1,399,542 upon educational institutions, $541,565 upon agricultural institutions, and $1,502,682 upon the new Parliament Buildings. With some minor sums these items made a total of $9,986,026 which had been spent upon public institutions and special interests. Since 1867 the Government of Ontario had also expended $10,796,-784 upon the administration of justice, $3,692,361 upon hospitals, $19,640,246 upon education—a total of $53,555,666 altogether. Out of this sum he claimed $50,773,821 to the credit of the existing Liberal Administration. Turning to the actual receipts for the year 1901 the Treasurer stated that they had exceeded the estimates by $640,511. They were given as follows :

Subsidy from Dominion	$1,116,872	80
Specific Dominion Grant	80,000	00
Interest due by Dominion Government	142,414	48
Interest on Investments	46,760	93
Crown Lands Department, including Woods and Forests	1,634,724	42
Law Stamps	55,747	95
Licenses	376,372	83
Education Department	57,379	78
Secretary's Department	88,157	09
Fisheries' Department	35,887	24
Supplementary Revenue Act	237,506	83
Succession Duties	366,581	96
Public Institutions	97,735	75
Casual Revenues	92,655	07
Miscellaneous	37,246	79
Total	$4,466,043	92

The expenditures included civil government $281,135, legislation $134,138, administration of justice $416,042, education, $782,193, maintenance of public institutions $833,163, agriculture $209,858, hospitals and charities $192,280, repairs and maintenance $91,681, public buildings $194,607, public works $60,847, colonization roads $138,801, Crown lands $179,008, railway aid certificates $96,209, annuities $102,900. With miscellaneous items the total was $4,038,834.49, as against receipts of $4,466,043.92. The balance in banks on January 1st, 1901, was $1,033,546.31 and on December 31st, $1,468,492.99. The estimated receipts for 1902 were $4,075,872.80 and the estimated expenditures $4,004,228.92. The Assets of the Province, as on December 31st, 1901, were stated by the Treasurer to include $220,898.05 of direct investments, $6,212,497.34 of funds held by the Dominion, and bank balances of $1,468,497.34—a total of $7,901,888.38. The Liabilities were given as $1,819,804.86 due to the Dominion, $1,688,691.64 as the present value of railway certificates, $1,822,099.17 as the present value of annuities—a total of $5,330,595.67. This statement left a surplus of $2,571,292.71 to the credit of the Province.

The Opposition claimed that this surplus was a mere matter of book-keeping; that the annuities and railway certificates should not be taken at their present value but at the sum payable by the Province at maturity of the obligation, or a total of $5,870,040.95. This latter sum was stated to be more nearly the Debt of Ontario. As to the surplus of revenue over expenditure, it was claimed to be due to the sale of timber limits, which amount should not be placed to the credit of revenue but of capital. Deducting this $517,000, there was really a deficit. Such was the view of Lieut.-Colonel A. J. Matheson, the Conservative financial critic.

The Hon. H. T. Duffy, Provincial Treasurer of Quebec, delivered his financial statement in the Assembly on March 12th. The ordinary receipts for the year ending June 30th, **Finances of** 1901, were given as $4,563,432 and the expenditures **Quebec** as $4,516,257—leaving a surplus of $47,175. The total receipts from all sources, including trust funds and sales of inscribed stock, were $4,816,218; and the total expenditures, including railway subsidies, Quebec Bridge, trust funds and redemption of debt, were $4,756,002. This left a net surplus of $60,215. The estimated ordinary receipts had been exceeded by $384,000 and the estimated ordinary expenditure by $268,000.

The Treasurer spoke at some length of the Government's success in financial matters and claimed that they had turned a succession of serious deficits into a surplus; had changed a rising indebtedness into a diminishing one; had kept public buildings in first-class condition; had aided education in poor municipalities and furnished pupils with free maps and text-books; had done repairs on 803 miles of road and built or repaired 15,000 feet of bridges and culverts; and had gained $300,000 from the Dominion on account of the Common School Fund. The Hon. E. J. Flynn, in criticising the Budget speech for the Opposition, declared that the sum of $403,197 received and credited to revenue by the Treasurer was really part of the capital of the Province as being the product of timber sales during the year from Crown lands. If this amount were deducted it would turn the alleged surplus into a deficit of $331,857 which he claimed to be the actual condition of affairs. On March 21st the Opposition Leader moved, seconded by the Hon. L. P. Pelletier, that:

This House is ready to vote the Supplies to His Majesty but regrets to state that the Budget speech of the Honourable the Treasurer is not satisfactory either as regards the marshalling of the figures or the true financial situation, while it is also supremely unjust towards the (preceding) Conservative Administrations.

On August 30th, 1902, an official statement was issued stating the receipts and expenditures for the fiscal year ending June 30th, 1902. It gave the ordinary receipts as $4,515,169 and the expenditures as $4,490,677—showing a surplus of $24,492. The total receipts, including trust funds, etc., were $4,612,008 and the total expenditures of all kinds $4,653,718. The receipts included $1,279,105 from the Dominion; $1,291,111 from lands, mines and fisheries; $254,282 from the administration of justice; $681,229 from hotel and shop licenses; $231,695 from direct taxes on commercial corporations; $222,763 from the Succession duties; and $300,056 from interest on the price of the Q. M. O. and O. Railway. The total expenditures were as follows:

Public Debt	$1,542,140 79
Legislation	207,720 63
Civil Government	271,891 19
Administration of Justice	580,980 23
Public Instruction	455,184 79
Public Works and Buildings	119,693 26
Agriculture	217,358 69
Lands, Mines and Fisheries	204,043 83
Colonization	112,540 00
Lunatic Asylums	353,825 00
Charges on Revenue	122,609 45
Miscellaneous Services	124,556 79
Sundries	341,173 94
Total	$4,653,718 59

The Funded Debt of the Province was given as $34,934,870 with a sinking fund invested of $10,100,142, or a net Debt of $24,834,728. There were some temporary loans and indebtedness outstanding which increased this sum to a total of $25,975,516.

In presenting his Budget speech, on March 19th, to the House of Assembly, the Hon. Mr. Tweedie, as Provincial Treasurer, first

New
Brunswick
Finances

defended the general policy of the Government in connection with lumber, mining and railway interests and declared that if average revenues had increased so had expenditures upon public purposes. He instanced the increase between 1882 and 1901 of the average yearly expenditure upon agriculture as being $9,832, upon education as $36,362, upon roads and bridges and other public works as $10,539, and upon the care of the insane as $14,928, over the annual average of the preceding fifteen years. For the fiscal year 1900 the net Public Debt was described as being $2,851,086, and for 1901 as $2,776,264. The transactions of the latter year which caused this decrease of $74,822 were described as follows:

The Debt was increased by a deficit between the ordinary receipts and expenditures of $30,999; on subsidy account, $14,500; bonds issued to wharves and the grain elevator, St. John, $2,500; over-expenditure Lunatic Asylum in 1901, $14,419; over-expenditure by Board of Works, $88,895; steel bridges, $34,192; interest Equity Court deposit, $37; open account, $29,542. This latter sum included $15,487 for expenses of the Eastern Extension arbitration. The total increase of Debt was $215,086, but the Debt was decreased as follows: Award of arbitration on Eastern Extension, $281,821; added to sinking funds, $6,752; outstanding coupons paid off, $1,334.

The total receipts for the year ending October 31st, 1901, were $1,031,267, including the Eastern Extension payment and $200,320 for timber and other licenses. The expenditure was $910,346. Mr. Tweedie concluded his speech by stating his hope of receiving over $2,000,000 from the claims against the Dominion in connection with the Halifax Fisheries Award, and his expectation that the Dominion Government would "treat the Province fairly" in the better terms movement, which was later on to reach a head at the Quebec Conference of 1902. Mr. Douglas Hazen, on behalf of the Opposition, deprecated an alleged large and steady increase in the controllable expenditures of the Province. If they were not cut down some form of direct taxation would, he declared, have to follow. Messrs. J. K. Flemming and O. M. Melanson for the Opposition and the Hon. Mr. Pugsley for the Government also spoke at length.

At the close of 1902 the receipts and expenditures for the fiscal year ending October 31st were announced. The former included the Dominion subsidies of $495,311; the territorial revenue, or license fees of various kinds, of $184,761; the taxes on incorporated companies of $26,336; the Succession duties of $16,935; and proceeds of Provincial debentures amounting to $250,000. With sundry small items the total was $1,102,423. The chief items of expenditure, totalling $1,095,637, during the year were as follows:

Administration of Justice.......................... $	18,937 02
Agriculture......................................	27,089 89
Contingencies, including contingencies of Legislature	16,621 82
Education.......................................	201,480 54
Executive Government............................	31,005 29
Eastern Extension expenses	11,728 00
Game protection.................................	11,914 90
Health, smallpox................................	18,927 57
Interest not chargeable to special funds............	132,147 22
Legislative Assembly.............................	20,739 20
Lunatic Asylum..................................	54,419 94
Public Printing.................................	13,396 97
Public Works, ordinary expenditure................	191,350 00
Public Works, extraordinary expenditure..........	150,000 00
Public Works, on account of permanent bridges....	100,000 00
Royal Reception.................................	24,670 30
Miscellaneous...................................	68,208 51
Total	$1,095,637 17

The Nova Scotia financial statement was presented to the House of Assembly at Halifax, on March 19th, by the Hon. Mr. Longley.

Finances of Nova Scotia   The estimates for the year ending September 30th, 1902, included ordinary receipts of $1,052,106 and expenditures of $1,047,920, as against the estimate for the preceding year of $1,034,096 for revenue and $1,026,965 for expenditure. The actual ordinary receipts for the year ending September 30th, 1901, had been $1,090,230 and the ordinary expenditures $1,088,927. The actual total receipts from all sources for that year were $1,843,995, made up as follows: Crown lands, $91,603; Fees, Provincial Secretary's Office, $7,458; Mines, $437,-726; Public Charities, $61,671; Dominion of Canada subsidy, $432,806; Succession duties, $45,566; Bank of British North America re Provincial charter, $75,000; Eastern Extension Railway refund from Dominion authorities, $671,836; and the balance in small sums from various sources. The expenditures were as follows:

Agriculture	$ 36,719	Public Works	$ 42,978
Criminal Prosecutions	6,286	Salaries	20,600
Crown Lands	30,598	Sinking Fund	10,966
Debenture Interest	146,680	Steamboats, etc.	42,178
Education	256,886	Succession Duties	9,348
Eastern Extension Arbitra-		Road Grants	117,644
tion	10,065	Special Loan, Bank of B. N.	
Interest	18,468	America	225,000
Legislative expenses	52,208	N. S. Hospital Annex	7,000
Mines	36,438	Bridges	130,694
Miscellaneous	56,350	Railways	163,000
Provincial Engineer's Office	16,000	Smaller Bridges	32,582
Public Printing	14,926	Miscellaneous	32,178
Public Charities	138,347		

Total $1,654,139

The Assets of the Province on September 30th, 1901, were stated as $1,368,654, of which $1,056,128 was a Dominion of Canada indebtedness to the Province, dating from before Confederation. The Liabilities included $2,043,500 of Provincial debentures payable in Halifax and $1,727,666 payable in London.

The Hon. Mr. Peters, Premier and Treasurer, delivered his Budget speech at Charlottetown on April 8th. The first portion con-

Prince Edward Island Finances

sisted of appreciative remarks concerning his predecessor, the Hon. Mr. Farquarson, and an analysis of alleged Conservative opposition to various measures of progress proposed or carried out in recent years by the Government. He then quoted various items of expenditure as illustrating the economy practised by Liberal Administrations in the Island and referred with pride to other items in which there were increases—such as the expenditure upon education which had grown from a yearly average of $106,292 under Conservative rule to $124,203 under that of his party. He placed the Public Debt at $642,177 of which the Liberals were responsible for $471,177. Since they attained power in 1892 $359,155 had been expended on Capital account and charged to this indebtedness while the balance had been spent upon the Prince of Wales College, the Insane Asylum, etc.

The Opposition critics, including the Hon. Daniel Gordon, the Leader of the party, claimed that this Debt was a floating liability really amounting, with certain unpaid accounts, to over $700,000; that $220,980 was due to the Banks and $176,998 was in the form of temporary loans—liable to be called in for payment at a moment's notice. The revenues had been stated by Mr. Peters at

$309,445 for the year ending December 31st, 1901, but the Opposition contended that $25,014 of this amount were proceeds of a sale of debentures and were not revenue at all. The expenditures were $330,632 and this left a deficit according to the Government of $20,000 and according to the Opposition of $45,000. The revenue included $196,931 from Dominion subsidies; $64,922 from special taxes—land, income, road, commercial travellers and corporations; $17,317 from various fees; and $5,258 from public lands.

The chief items of ordinary expenditure were $17,524 upon justice, $128,288 upon education, $23,436 upon the Hospital for Insane, $24,803 upon interest, $20,322 upon ferries and steamers, $18,969 upon roads and $20,783 upon bridges. With miscellaneous sums this made a total of $310,326 to which was added an expenditure of $20,306 on Capital account. Mr. J. A. Matheson, on April 14th, replied to the Treasurer and claimed that the Conservatives while in power from 1880 to 1890 spent an annual average of $275,787 and that from 1892 to 1901, inclusive, the Liberals averaged $312,774. During the first term of ten years a total of $2,727,863 was expended and in the second period $3,127,741—an increase of $399,877. The estimates for 1902 had, meanwhile, been given as $318,811 for revenue, as against $284,431 estimated for 1901. The expenditures were placed at $312,792 as compared with $315,326 in the preceding year. The increase in the expected receipts was mainly in the $15,000 additional Dominion subsidy and in large returns from the road and income tax.

The Budget speech of the Hon. J. A. Davidson, Treasurer of Manitoba, was delivered on February 4th, 1902. He first described the Assets of the Province as being $28,130,128, in-

Budget and Finances of Manitoba cluding $3,578,941 in Dominion Government Capital account and $314,853 in the same account which, however, the Federal authorities had not yet admitted as due by them to the Province; $99,259 in advances by the Province to municipalities; $850,104 as the value of public buildings owned by the Province; 7,700,000 acres of Provincial land at $3.00 an acre and worth a total of $23,100,000; $41,065, on drainage districts interest account and $145,903, cash on hand. The direct Liabilities consisted of Provincial debentures valued at $4,040,013. Deducting this from the total Assets it left a surplus of $24,090,115. He pointed out that there were also indirect assets and liabilities which balanced each other and were made up of guarantees on bonds of the South Western Colonization and Canadain Northern Railways and drainage district debentures.

The receipts for the year ending December 31st, 1901, were $1,008,653 in Consolidated revenue account—including $483,687 from Dominion subsidies, $22,915 from interest on School Lands' Fund, $85,495 from land titles' fees, $29,667 from liquor licenses, $36,732 from interest, $120,566 from Provincial lands, $46,595 from lunatic asylums, $43,900 from municipalities' tax, $31,608 from corporation taxes and $32,111 from railway taxes. Besides this total,

certain Open Ledger accounts realized for interest, etc., $65,828; while Trust accounts of various kinds brought in $305,368—a total revenue from all sources of $1,379,850. As to expenditures the total was $1,287,886, including all accounts and with a cash balance on hand of $664,624, as against $572,660 on the preceding 31st of December. The expenditures were as follows:

Legislation...................................... $	34,113 42
Executive Council	4,148 92
Treasury Department	36,708 74
Treasury Department (Special)..................	217,790 26
Provincial Secretary's Department..............	8,135 41
Education	158,997 54
Agriculture and Immigration....................	133,721 38
Attorney-General's Department.	142,821 18
Attorney-General's Department (Litigation *re* Liquor Act).................................	11,153 55
Provincial Lands Department.	19,099 72
Railway Commissioner's Department.............	10,757 45
Public Works' Department:	
(*a*) Miscellaneous..........................	56,589 03
(*b*) Charitable Institutions..................	112,350 13
(*c*) Aid to Municipalities	36,943 90
Municipal Commissioner........................	4,920 00
Open Ledger Accounts..........................	134,064 82
Trust Accounts................................	165,571 08
Total...................................	$1,287,886 53

Mr. Davidson, in the course of his speech, explained the uses to which the $500,000 loan of the preceding year had been put. The expenditures in this connection included $238,146 upon what he called the Greenway Government deficit; $54,812 expended on public buildings; $14,472 upon foundations of the Parliament Buildings; $17,772 on railway bonuses; $7,775 given to Souris branch railway; $1,996 upon land refunds; $7,417 as interest on Emerson and Minnedosa loans; $32,420 upon drainage debenture interest; $4,592 upon Half-breed mortgages; $31,276 upon seed grain loans; and $21,636 on land surveys—a total of $442,310. The Hon. Mr. Greenway and Mr. R. H. Myers criticized the Treasurer's statement at length on behalf of the Opposition. The estimates for 1902 were presented to the Assembly by Mr. Davidson on the same day. The proposed expenditures totalled $1,288,868 and the revenue was placed at $1,490,613—leaving an estimated surplus of $201,745.

The sums voted by the Assembly of the North-West Territories for the year ending December 31st, 1902, included $53,851.94 for civil government, $23,275 for legislation, $13,200 for **Financial Position of the Territories** the administration of justice, $260,000 for public works, $204,000 for education, $22,350 for agriculture and statistics, $16,098 for hospitals, charities and public health and $44,450 for miscellaneous purposes—a total of $637,224.94. The Budget speech was delivered in the Assembly at Regina on April 15th by the Hon. Arthur L. Sifton,.

who complained very strongly of the "totally inadequate" grant of $357,000 a year which the Dominion Government gave to meet these expenditures.

Speaking in the House of Commons at Ottawa, three days later, as to this vote of $357,979 for the Territories, Mr. Walter Scott of Regina went back to the year 1899 when the Parliamentary grant had been $283,000 and the expenditures $414,000. Since then the local revenues had, he said, increased from $30,000 or $40,000 a year to $80,000 or $90,000—mostly derived from a small land tax. In 1901 the sum asked for the Territorial Government was $600,000 and they received $357,000. They had consequently anticipated the next year's revenue by over $175,000 and it was in his opinion obvious that a larger grant was now imperative. Immigrants were pouring in and increased demands of all kinds were being made upon the Territorial Government. Messrs. T. Oliver and J. M. Douglas warmly supported an addition to the Subsidy. Others spoke and the Minister of the Interior followed. He referred to an understanding in 1896 with the Territorial Executive that the increase then given in the grant would be sufficient for some years; to the special assistance given in connection with the floods of 1901; and stated that the Government were considering the question of an increased amount for the current year. If decided upon it would appear in the supplementary estimates. It subsequently did so to the amount of $100,000.

The Hon. J. D. Prentice, Minister of Finance, delivered his Budget speech in the Legislature at Victoria on April 28th. He paid a graceful tribute to his predecessor, the Hon. J. H. Turner, and then stated the receipts for the year ending June 30th, 1901 as $1,605,920 and the expenditure, $2,407,492. The deficit therefore, was $801,572, from which might properly be deducted $119 671 put aside for sinking fund investment and redemption of debentures. The Government's overdraft at that date was $871,171 and on June 30th, 1902 it was $1,658,000. The times had been unfavourable for a loan, the Treasurer explained, and it had not been attempted. The receipts and expenditure of the Province for the fiscal year 1901-2 and the estimates for 1902-3 were as follows :

Finances of British Columbia

Receipts.	1901-2.	Estimates. 1902-3.
Dominion Subsidies	$284,151 05	$305,968 05
Land Sales	120,000 00	80,000 00
Land Revenues	37,000 00	37,000 00
Timber Royalties, etc.	85,000 00	80,000 00
" Leases	80,000 00	110,000 00
Free Miners' Certificates.	130,000 00	100,000 00
Mining Receipts	200,000 00	175,000 00
Licenses	70,000 00	80,000 00
Real Property Tax	125,000 00	210,000 00
Personal "	75,000 00	140,000 00
Wild Land "	55,000 00	130,000 00
Income "	35,000 00	55,000 00

14

Receipts.	1901–2.	Estimates. 1902–3.
Revenue Tax	200,000 00	150,000 00
Mineral ,,	80,000 00	130,000 00
Fines, Law Stamps, and Probate Fees	40,000 00	40,000 00
Registry Fees	110,000 00	80,000 00
Chinese Act (Refund)	135,000 00	40,000 00
Fisheries		35,000 00
Succession Duty	100,000 00	20,000 00
Coal Royalties, etc.	95,000 00	130,000 00
Miscellaneous	84,600 00	94,600 00
Total	$2,140,751 05	$2,222,568 05

Expenditures.	1901–2.	Estimates. 1902–3.
Public Debt	$411,440 31	$493,140 31
Civil Government	253,980 00	263,280 00
Administration of Justice	231,132 00	232,012 00
Legislation	41,325 00	44,195 00
Public Institutions	124,380 00	128,590 00
Hospitals and Charities	87,300 00	74,800 00
Education	369,537 00	412,140 00
Public Works	804,641 10	662,200 00
Miscellaneous	152,100 24	175,770 00
Total	$2,475,835 65	$2,486,127 31

The Minister proceeded to point out that the Government had authority under various Acts to borrow an aggregate sum of $1,878,952 but that this was entirely insufficient and they would ask for larger powers. He spoke of the claims they had made upon the Dominion Government for " better terms " and their hopes of obtaining something in connection with the Fisheries question. As to the wealth and assets of the Province they were undoubted and he described the total as $340,000,000. This estimate included $18,000,000 as the value of industrial interests, $65,500,000 as that of railways and telegraphs, $50,000,000 as that of mines and smelters, $58,000,000 for municipal assessments, $40,000,000 for Provincial assessments, and $65,000,000 for timber leases, etc.

The principal critics of this speech were Messrs. R. G. Tatlow and Dennis Murphy. The former deprecated certain serious mistakes in estimates of revenue and expenditure and placed the actual deficit for the 18 months, ending December 31st, 1901, at $1,226,650. Mr. Prentice had stated the Public Debt of the Province at $6,407,-757, or $36.38 per head. Mr. Tatlow added together existing loans, debentures, Bank overdrafts, etc., and made out a Debt of $11,-000,000 with $5,000,000 more authorized by the Legislature. Mr. Murphy estimated the interest-bearing Debt, when the new Loan was floated, at $10,249,986. He accused the Government of " an utter lack of candour" in presenting their estimates, of needlessly increasing the civil list, of having wasted money in appropriations for party purposes and of having " by their every act demonstrated that to them office was everything and the interests of the country nothing." On November 12th, 1902, a British Columbia loan of $3,500,000 was floated in London and underwritten at 92 per cent.

On February 13th, 1902, the Commissioners appointed during the preceding year to investigate the condition and laws regarding assessments and municipal taxation in Ontario made their final Report. The Commission was composed of Judges Maclennan and MacMahon. Messrs. D. R. Wilkie, K. W. McKay, A. Pratt, M. J. Butler and T. H. Macpherson. They went into the whole subject with elaboration and concluded that " in Ontario, as everywhere else, the direct taxation of personal property generally fails to reach the new kinds of property or wealth which modern civilization has produced." The existing taxes of this kind should be abolished and the only feasible substitutes were thought to be: (1) An improved and more general income tax and (2) a tax on the occupiers of land based on the rental value. The single-tax policy was not only too radical a measure but it was impossible as well as unprecedented. Various recommendations were made and a Bill submitted for the Government to utilize; though nothing was really done in the matter. The following table shows the relative assessments in Ontario cities during the year 1899 :

The Ontario Assessment Commission

City.	Real Property.	Personal Property and Income.	Total.
Belleville	$3,567,026	$276,550	$3,843,576
Brantford	6,444,815	667,440	7,112,255
Chatham	3,340,515	198,983	3,539,498
Guelph	3,476,830	324,500	3,801,330
Hamilton	23,402,810	3,924,090	27,326,900
Kingston	6,757,945	1,070,264	7,828,209
London	14,620,274	2,464,153	17,084,427
Ottawa	21,921,815	1,783,075	23,704,890
St. Catharines	3,729,295	704,250	4,433,545
St. Thomas	3,987,435	506,268	4,493,703
Stratford	3,785,980	268,870	4,054,850
Toronto	114,303,002	12,986,160	127,289,162
Windsor	5,104,425	208,600	5,313,025

MISCELLANEOUS FINANCIAL INCIDENTS

Jan. 30.—The total assessment of the City of Ottawa is announced as $27,420,-740, and the exempted property is valued at $16,337,150, of which the Government owns or leases $10,134,850.

Feb. 5.—Mr. H. J. Pettypiece delivers an elaborate speech in the Ontario Legislature on taxation and assessment. The following extract indicates his point of view :

" If the assessment of railway property in Ontario bore the same relation to the capital invested as does the assessment of farm property to capital invested, the total assessment of the railways would be $225,000,000 instead of $14,000,000 as now, and if the railways on that assessment paid the same rate of taxation as does the farm property in the Province, they would pay in taxes $2,300,000 instead of $300,000, as at present."

Mar. 12.—A Special Committee of the Halifax City Council and Board of Trade, with Alderman R. T. MacIlreith as Chairman, submit a Report recommending that Government property shall be subject to taxation and that, while certain charitable institutions should be exempt, all church and educational lands shall be taxed.

April 9.—The Premier of Prince Edward Island presents a measure to the Legislature increasing the tax on outside Banks doing business in the Province to $1,000, and on local Banks to $500.

May 3.—It is announced that the City of Charlottetown will follow the example of the Provincial Government and tax all " transient traders " in its midst.   All commercial travellers, therefore, became liable to a tax of $300 from the City, in addition to the Government's $20 imposition.   Three days later, however, the Provincial Supreme Court decided by unanimous judgment that the Provincial taxation of resident agents was unconstitutional and at variance with the Federal character of Canadian institutions.

June 1.—The total assessment of the City of Toronto is stated at $128,954,144 for the year 1901, of which $114,836,084 is real property and the balance personal property and taxable income.   The exemptions are $23,428,893.

June 1.—The Municipal statistics issued by the Ontario Government state the total assessment of the Province at $835,697,607, the total taxes imposed for all purposes as $13,341,355 and the rate of taxation per head as $6.58.   The assessment value of townships is $458,811,926, in towns $99,921,377, in villages $29,849,933, and in cities $247,114,371.

June 7.—The Financial Committee of the City Council of Montreal place the property exemptions from taxation in 1901 at $38,254,130, including Catholic churches and benevolent societies at $13,500,770, Protestant churches and societies at $6,716,880, and corporations at $11,718,680.

Sept. 10.—The Ontario Municipal Association meets at Brockville and various speakers severely criticize the assessment laws of the Province—including especially Mayor Henry, of Kincardine.

Oct. 24.—The assessable property of Winnipeg, according to the City Comptroller's Report for the fiscal year 1902, is $28,615,810, as against $19,286,405 in 1886.   Of this the personal property is $4,676,950 and the real property $23,938,860.

VII.—TRANSPORTATION INTERESTS

There were in Canada, on June 30th, 1902, railways having a mileage of 18,867 and lines under construction embracing 766 miles.* Their ordinary share capital, paid up, was The Railway Interests of Canada $328,135,066; their preference share capital was $132,266,796; their bonded debt issued was $425,-949,488 and sold $404,806,846; the Dominion aid received by way of loans had amounted to $15,964,258 and by bonuses $162,057,927; the Provincial aid given had been $4,648,956 by loan, $31,580,836 by bonus and $300,000 by subscription to bonds; the assistance from municipalities, paid up, was $16,465,604; the total paid-up capital was $1,098,852,206.

According to the Report of the Deputy Minister of Railways—Mr. Collingwood Schrieber, C.M.G.—that Department expended on railways in 1901-2 the sum of $13,407,152. The revenue from railways was $5,918,990 The total Government expenditure upon railways in Canada up to June 30th, 1902, was $258,860,655. During the fiscal year there were 1,328 persons injured on, or by, Canadian railways. At the close of the same year there were 558 miles of electric railways—including street railways—of which the paid-up capital amounted to $41,593,063, the gross earnings to $6,486,438, the working expenses to $3,802,855 and the number of passengers to 137,681,402.

The gross earnings of steam railways for the year ending June 30th, 1902, were $83,666,503, of which $22,600,090 came from passenger traffic and $53,000,072 from freight. The operating expenses included $12,959,574 on maintenance and buildings, $18,904,364 on working and repairs to cars, $5,264,591 on working and repairs to engines and $20,274,701 on general expenses. The freight carried included 18,164,357 barrels of flour, 203,119,138 bushels of grain, 4,012,195 head of live stock, 5,414,396 tons of lumber, 1,578,047 tons of firewood and 6,168,420 tons of manu-factured goods—making, with miscellaneous articles, a total of 42,376,527 tons of freight.

The question of establishing a Government Commission for the oversight and control of railways in certain specified directions Railway Commission Proposals came to a head during 1902. Early in the year there was made public the special Report of Mr. S. J. McLean, M.A., Ph.D., who for three years had been studying the history of the subject and the practical application of railway rates in Canada and of railway regulations generally. The conclusions only can be dealt with here. Upon the existing system of oversight by the Railway Committee of the Privy Council at Ottawa he reported that the dual function of

---

*The Annual Report of the Department of Railways and Canals.

being both political and administrative was a serious difficulty; that there was no migratory organization for investigating grievances; that distances were usually too great to enable complainants to appear before it; that there was a lack of technical training in those who had to deal with the subject. He urged the appointment of a Railway Commission of three members for the purpose of regulating the railways under general powers of supervision as given by the British North America Act. The Commission should have the following powers:

1. All regulative authority in regard to rates, preferences, discriminations, rebates, etc., now possessed by the Railway Committee.

2. Supervision of through rates and routes and the obtaining of equal facilities of shipment for all.

3. Regulative control of traffic agreements, supervision of crossings and safety appliances, control of stock and bond issues and advisory power over Parliamentary bills.

4. Power to act as arbitrator in disputes, to answer Parliamentary questions *re* railway legislation and policy, to make investigations under Parliamentary sanction and to enforce the provisions of Acts under which the railways operate.

On April 9th, the Hon. A. G. Blair introduced a measure to appoint such a Commission, or rather to pave the way for its appointment through the passing of a similar bill at the next Session of Parliament. Under the terms of this proposal the Railway Committee of the Privy Council was to be abolished and its powers and duties transferred to a Board of Railway Commissioners. In his speech the Minister of Railways stated that it was proposed to divide the work of the railways into three classes— 1st, ordinary traffic; 2nd, commodity traffic; 3rd, competitive traffic. In the first and largest class the Commission would have power to sanction what rates should be charged. In the second class the Commission would have power to fix a maximum and minimum rate and the Company to have right of choice between the two. In the third case, where conditions were constantly changing, no arbitrary rule could be laid down but the Commission would be given power to pass upon the rate presented to it by the Company. After discussion the measure was ultimately withdrawn.

The operations of the Government lines created some attention during the year. The total cost for building and equipment up to

The Inter-Colonial Railway June 30th, 1901, was $63,640,028 and during the following year $4,670,590 was added to this sum— including $293,000 for improving the ferry service at the Strait of Canso, $111,299 to improve accommodation at St. John, $71,928 for the same purpose at Halifax, $77,609 for similar purposes at Sydney, $75,341 for the same object at Levis, $93,431 to strengthen bridges, $188,190 for steel rails, etc., $157,998 for additional sidings, $135,049 for engine houses, $2,066,879 for rolling stock, $952,528 *re* the Eastern Railway Extension matter in Nova Scotia and New Brunswick.

The gross earnings of the Railway, with its 1,333 miles of operated road, were $5,671,385 in 1901-2 and the working expenses $5,574,563. The passenger traffic realized $1,770,941, that of freight $3,644,513 and that from mails and express $255,931—an all-round increase over the previous year of $199,150. The number of passengers carried was 2,186,226 and the amount of freight 2,385,-816 tons. The working expenses increased $114,140 over those of 1899-1900. The gross earnings of the Windsor branch line were $49,604 during 1901-2 and one-third of this was paid to the Government by the lessees of the road.

Early in January, 1902, the Halifax Board of Trade sent out a circular letter expressing certain views and representing certain criticisms of the Intercolonial management. It was stated that the I.C.R. had practically no western connection; that, though efficient within a local area, its failure in connection with traffic originating west of Montreal was conspicuous; that elevators and terminal facilities remained unused; that local business men were suffering severe losses through its arrangements. Three suggestions were considered—an independent Commission, an extension west to Georgian Bay, and the acquisition of the I.C.R. by the C.P.R. The last proposal was strongly favoured. On April 24th the Hon. Mr. Blair spoke at length in the Commons upon the condition and management of this Railway. He stated that the earnings had increased since 1896 from three to five millions; that the present Government had spent $7,000,000 in improvements upon the road; that deficits had been steadily reduced and politics excluded from its management. As to the future he was very hopeful:

I am not one of those who think that the I.C.R. has either reached the limit of its progress or that it has ceased to be an important factor in the business of this country. I have looked forward and still look forward to the time when there will be important extensions of the I.C.R. When we reached Montreal that was regarded by me as the first step in the onward march of progress, but I do not think it ought to be the policy of the Government in the future to stop there, but that when the proper time comes we should carry that road forward to another point westward and then perhaps still farther westward. I have always felt that when the time was ripe one of the best things that could be done in the interest of this country would be to extend that road from Montreal to the Georgian Bay.

The Canadian mileage of the Canadian Pacific Railway System on June 30th, 1902, was 8,646. On January 26th, it was announced that the Dominion Government had approved of the C.P.R. increasing its ordinary share capital by $19,500,-000 for certain specific purposes and, on February 10th, Sir T. G. Shaughnessy issued a statement to the shareholders showing (as follows) the objects which the Directors had in view for this expenditure:

The
Canadian
Pacific
Railway

Locomotive cars and other equipment..............$10,000,000
Enlargement of construction and repair shops....... 2,000,000
Improvements of grade, allignment and track........ 6,500,000
Additional grain elevators, terminals, sidings, etc..... 4,000,000

Total.....................................$22,500,000

To make up the difference it was proposed that $3,000,000 be appropriated from the surplus earnings fund. A special meeting of the shareholders was held in Montreal on March 27th with Sir William Van Horne in the chair. In moving the Resolution authorizing the increase of stock, etc., Sir Thomas Shaughnessy referred to the great development of business and stated that this money would "ensure greater convenience for the public and a marked reduction in the cost of moving traffic." It was carried unanimously and the policy was generally approved in business circles everywhere. In Toronto, Messrs. W. R. Brock, M.P., A. E. Ames, W. D. Matthews, D. R. Wilkie and E. B. Osler, M.P., were interviewed and all spoke of the matter as an evidence of national prosperity and a production which made increased facilities necessary.

In the House of Commons, on April 17th, the Minister of Justice introduced and eventually put through a measure giving legal permission for this action and providing that the new stock was not to be sold below par; that it must be employed for improvements and upon rolling stock; and that the increase was not to militate against the Government's right to reduce tolls when the Company should earn a profit of ten per cent. upon its actual construction capital. Meanwhile, on February 5th, it was stated that a five-year contract had been entered into with the Imperial Government by which the C.P.R. was to carry troops when required, as well as mails and stores, to and from the East and to receive an annual subsidy of $300,000, of which the Dominion contributed $75,000. In April the Ottawa, Northern and Western Railway, owning 151 miles of road and the Inter-Provincial bridge at Ottawa, was acquired by the C.P.R.

During the same month there were heavy sales of C.P.R. stock in New York and much speculation as to the cause. By the end of May it was stated in the press that over 90,000 shares, valued at $11,000,000 had changed hands at a price varying from 116 to 139. On April 28th the Toronto *World* entered into an elaborate analysis of the equities and property controlled by the C.P.R. Company and concluded that its $65,000,000 of common stock was really worth 341, as against the current price of 129. The large sales of the stock aroused some alarm as to its possibly passing into American hands but the Directors did not appear to share the feeling and it was pointed out that a majority of the Board had to be British under the charter. On May 6th it was announced that 10 extensions, or branches, in the West were to be shortly commenced or had been recently completed—comprising altogether 371 miles of road—together with 42 miles in British Columbia. At the same time a number of rate reductions in Manitoba and the Territories were announced.

On June 1st Mr. E. H. McHenry, formerly Chief Engineer of the Northern Pacific, assumed charge of the same position on the C.P.R. and a month later Mr. George McLaren Brown became

Reaping Wheat on a Manitoba Farm near the Canadian Pacific Railway.

Superintendent of the Sleeping and Dining Car service. As a result of various Resolutions passed by the Winnipeg and other Western Boards of Trade asking for a substantial rate reduction, and equality in this respect with the Canadian Northern Railway, Sir T. G. Shaughnessy on November 5th wrote at length to President Russell of the Winnipeg Board. He did not consider the Company in any way bound to reduce its rates because a competitor had obtained privileges from the Provincial Government in return for which the C.P.R. might have been willing to grant such reductions. He stated that the farmers were getting the same price for wheat even where the railway rates were higher. He also declared that the farmers of the Canadian West had a lower scale of grain rates than those of corresponding districts in the United States. The Annual Report of the Canadian Pacific Railway for the year ending June 30th, 1902 showed the following balance sheet:

ASSETS.

Cost of Railway and Equipment	$230,072,641.33
Ocean, Lake and River Steamships	3,996,377.89
Acquired Securities (Held)	39,818,943.45
Hotels, buildings and properties	1,785,411.99
Deferred payments on Land Sales	7,025,254.28
Advances to new Lines	2,154,473.31
Material and Supplies on hand	4,450,526.98
Station and Traffic balances	3,207,939.97
Miscellaneous Securities and Advances	1,678,182.14
Other Items	1,086,797.89
Cash on Hand	15,227,691.47
Total*	$310,504,240.70

LIABILITIES.

Capital Stock	$ 65,000,000.00
Payments on Subscription to new Stock	7,624,162.00
Four per cent. Preference Stock	31,171,000.00
Consolidated Debenture Stock	63,532,415.86
Mortgage Bonds	47,238,086.33
Land Grant Bonds	16,430,000.00
Current Accounts, Pay Rolls and Traffic Balances	5,911,699.72
Interest on Funded Debt, etc	1,780,565.71
Cash Subsidies from Governments and Municipalities	29,969,688.07
Proceeds of Land Sales	27,660,988.13
Surplus Earnings Account	14,185,634.88
Total	$310,504,240.70

The business of the fiscal year showed gross earnings of $37,-503,053, working expenses of $23,417,141 and a surplus—after adding certain interest sums and deducting some fixed charges—of $7,709,913. From this was paid the two half-yearly dividends of 2 per cent. on Preference stock and 2½ on Ordinary stock and amounting to a total of $4,496,840. The earnings from passengers

---

* NOTE.—In addition to these Assets the Company own 14,680,101 acres of land in Manitoba and the Territories and 3,922,922 acres in British Columbia.

were $9,359,522 and from freight $24,199,428. Of the expenses $5,361,067 went to the conducting of transportation, $5,634,497 to the maintenance of way and structures, $7,387,065 to motive power, and $1,868,045 to the maintenances of cars. On June 30th, 1902, the C.P.R. had 745 locomotives, 842 passenger, baggage, dining and sleeping cars, and 21,159 freight and cattle cars. The freight carried during the year was 8,769,934 tons and the passengers numbered 4,796,746. The freight included 52,719,706 bushels of grain, 4,921,993 barrels of flour and 1,033,569,377 feet of lumber.

The above Report was presented at the annual meeting in Montreal, on October 1st, when President Shaughnessy explained the Fast Line tender, spoke of the increasing volume of traffic and declared that the Company had " barely entered upon the threshold of the expansion and success that the future has in store for it." The policy of the Directors was approved by formal Resolutions and the following were re-elected to the Board : Lord Strathcona and Mount Royal, Sir W. C. VanHorne, Mr. R. B. Angus, Mr. E. B. Osler, M.P., Mr. W. D. Matthews, Mr. George R. Harris, Sir Sandford Fleming, Mr. Thomas Skinner, Mr. Charles R. Hosmer and Sir T. G. Shaughnessy. Sir William VanHorne was re-elected Chairman of the Board of Directors and Sir T. G. Shaughnessy President of the Company, with an Executive Committee composed of Lord Strathcona, Mr. Angus, Mr. Osler, and the Chairman and President. Late in the year a careful plan of superannuation for officers and permanent employees of the road was announced.

The Canadian part of the Grand Trunk System on June 30th, 1902, had 3,157 miles in operation. Its ordinary share capital, paid-up, was $109,362,375, its preference share capital was $89,244,198, its bonded debt $93,401,597. The total of Dominion Government loans which it had received was $15,142,633 and the total cost of the Railway and rolling stock was placed by the annual Report of the Minister of Railways and Canals at $334,702,310. The Statements of the Grand Trunk Railway Company for the half-years ending December 31st, 1901, and June 30th, 1902, showed gross receipts of £2,569,804 and £2,377,201, respectively, with working expenses of £1,757,154 and £1,603,612—leaving net traffic receipts of £812,650 and £773,589. To these latter amounts certain other sums were added which increased the respective total revenue receipts to £908,846 and £875,175.

Deducting charges for interest the sums of £299,161 and £255,635 were left as available for the payment of dividends. The gross receipts from passenger traffic in the half-years were, respectively, £834,662 and £601,469; from mails and express £125,072 and £106,314; from freight and live stock £1,539,457 and £1,597,954; from miscellaneous sources £70,614 and £71,464— a total of £2,569,805 and £2,377,201, or $24,735,030 for the 12 months. The number of passengers carried was 4,446,614 and 3,525,855 and the tons of freight and live stock were, respectively,

5,466,424 and 5,675,338. On maintenance of way and structures £496,987 and £242,466 were spent; on maintenance of equipment £317,935 and £436,063; in conducting transportation £847,985 and £853,633; on general expenses and taxes £94,248 and £71,450.

Four per cent. debenture stock to the amount of £411,003 was issued during the half-year of 1902 as part provision for the repayment of £522,200 Northern Railway five per cent. bonds; while £85,600 of Montreal and Champlain bonds were repaid. Sir Charles Rivers Wilson, the President, concluded his statement of October 31st by saying that "the cost of operation has been reduced, increased dividends are available for distribution, and additions to capital have been maintained within the most reasonable limits." The doubling of the track between Toronto and Montreal was also nearly completed—only 21¼ miles remaining of single track.

Of the chief associated lines the Grand Trunk Western Railway, in the periods under review, showed gross receipts of £442,503 and £464,654 with working expenses of £371,902 and £098,375. The passengers numbered, during the 12 months, 1,346,106 and the freight carried was 2,440,212 tons. The Detroit, Grand Haven and Milwaukee Line had gross receipts of £124,179 and £108,005 with working expenses of £85,069 and £85,578, respectively, during the half-years, and the passengers carried during the 12 months were 711,301 in number and the freight 780,730 tons.

Taking the figures of the Grand Trunk Railway for the *calendar* years of 1901 and 1902 they showed an increase in the passengers carried of from 7,652,055 to 8,213,506; in the tons of freight and live stock from 11,080,037 to 11,823,868; in the earnings per train mile from 65·52 d. to 70·23 d. The receipts and expenditures were as follows:

Receipts	1901	1902
Passengers.	£1,386,779	£1,446,186
Mails and Express	226,531	248,050
Freight and Live Stock	3,100,713	3,353,442
Miscellaneous	143,577	141,401
	£4,857,600	£5,189,079

Expenditures	1901	1902
Maintenance of Way and Structures..	£ 720,829	£ 800,968
Maintenance of Equipment	661,937	746,483
Conducting Transportation	1,753,240	1,859,349
General Expenses	118,533	120,740
Taxes	47,227	50,893
	£3,301,766	£3,578,433

Late in December, 1901, Mr. Charles M. Hays had again taken charge as 2nd Vice-President and General Manager of the Grand Trunk Railway System, and on January 8th, following, he arrived in Montreal to assume his duties. A little later he also succeeded Mr. G. B. Reeve as Director and Chairman of the Central Vermont Railway. On March 31st Mr. F. H. McGuigan was appointed

Manager of the Grand Trunk System with charge of the maintenance of way and transportation departments. In the middle of the year the handsome new offices of the Company in Montreal were occupied and opened. The Directors of the Railway on and after June 30th, 1902, were Sir Charles Rivers Wilson, G.C.M.G., C.B., President, Colonel F. Firebrace, R.E., Sir H. M. Jackson, Bart., Lord Welby of Allington, G.C.B., Sir W. Lawrence Young, Bart., and Messrs. Joseph Price, George Allen, J. A. Clutton-Brock, Alexander Hubbard, L. J. Seargeant and A. W. Smithers.

An announcement was made on November 24th, which aroused much interest in the public mind of Canada. It was a formal statement from Mr. Charles M. Hays that his Board of Directors had been considering for some time, and were ready to go ahead with, a line of railway extending from North Bay, or Gravenhurst, on the G.T.R., through what is known as New Ontario and on through Manitoba, Saskatchewan, Assiniboia and Alberta *via* Peace River or Pine River Pass through British Columbia, to either Bute Inlet or Port Simpson on the Pacific Coast. The road was to be constructed and operated as a separate corporation under the name of "The Grand Trunk Pacific Railway Company" and would be of the most up-to-date character in its construction, equipment and facilities. Mr. Hays then continued :

The Grand Trunk Pacific Project

No one who has been studying the wonderful developments that have taken place in the North-West during the past few years can fail to be deeply impressed with the growth of this extensive and rich territory, and our Directors feel, that in view of the apparent need for additional railway facilities and in order to guarantee to the present Grand Trunk System direct connection with that very important and growing section of Canada, the only wise policy is to take active steps towards this extension, which, I may add, will be commenced as soon as the necessary legislation has been obtained from the Government.

In reply to many speculations as to the policy of his Company in the matter of subsidies, Mr. Hays told the press on November 30th that " anyone who thinks that the Company will not apply to Parliament for aid is greatly mistaken "—Toronto *Globe* of December 1st. According to a reported interview in the Winnipeg *Tribune* on December 2nd, Mr. F. M. Morse, 3rd Vice-President of the G.T.R., told its Vancouver correspondent that his road would ask for subsidies from the different Governments concerned and would " expect the same treatment from a subsidy standpoint as had been meted out to the Canadian Pacific." On December 1st, Mr. Hays was again interviewed in Montreal and repeated the statement that Government aid would be asked. The *Canada Gazette*, of December 20th, contained the formal application for a charter along the lines already mentioned and including also power to construct and operate branches to Winnipeg, Calgary, Regina and other points, to amalgamate, lease, or otherwise acquire, or connect with any railway in Canada, and to do a transportation, mining, franchise, land securities and general construction business of the widest and most varied character.

According to Mr. Hays in the Montreal *Star* of November 24th, the route was to follow very largely that originally laid down by Sir Sandford Fleming, C.E., for the C.P.R. and approved by the Government of Mr. Mackenzie. A steamship line on the Pacific would probably be necessary, the capitalization would be from $75,000,000 to $100,000,000, and about five years would be required for construction. Public opinion upon the announcement was congratulatory in its expression from Halifax to Vancouver; although the question of possible subsidies disturbed some minds and some papers. The Minister of Railways told the press that he had known of the project for some time and believed that the development of the West would afford ample traffic for three trans-continental roads and would fully warrant the G.T.R. in this undertaking to build 2,500 miles of railway. He thought that $25,000 a mile would be a fair average of cost. No assurances had been given the Company as to subsidies. Sir Thomas Shaughnessy told the *Globe* of November 25th that it was a "very big contract." The C.P.R. now operated 6,000 miles of rail in the West and yet there was plenty of room for more lines. As to Government aid "the conditions have changed enormously since the pioneer road was constructed and circumstances which then made Government co-operation absolutely essential no longer exist."

Sir S. Fleming was interviewed by the Montreal *Star* on November 26th and declared that this project would not compete with other lines, that it should run from Quebec to Port Simpson, that it would open up the rich lands of the Peace River, and that it ought to be followed by a continuation of the Intercolonial across the continent as suggested by the Hon. Mr. Blair. Senator L. J. Forget, of Montreal, stated to the *Globe* on November 25th that the great point in this announcement was the confidence shown in the future of the West. The construction of this new line "is the best thing that could happen to Canada." Settlement would follow and the volume of business be increased even to the C.P.R.

In Toronto, Mr. William Mackenzie told the *Globe* that this project would not effect the C.N.R. Their Eastern extension would commence soon and they held the right of way in British Columbia through the Peace River, Pine River or Yellowhead Passes. Mr. W. R. Brock, M.P., described the plan as "an inestimable boon to Canada," and Mr. W. D. Matthews declared that the only difficulty was that of obtaining settlers. The C.P.R. and C.N.R. had not yet nearly filled up the country through which they passed. Meanwhile, Western opinion in many directions might be described as jubilant—with occasional shadows cast by the subsidy problem. The Winnipeg Board of Trade, after discussing the question at two meetings, with the chances of Winnipeg being somewhat side-tracked, declared (on January 2nd, 1903) that it welcomed the projected line but was not yet prepared

to express an opinion as to the question of granting Government
aid for its construction. The Calgary Board of Trade on December
4th did not limit its expressions of pleasure at a statement of
Messrs. Morse and Wainwright that their city would be built into
by the new road.

Sir Charles Tupper, on December 7th, was interviewed in
Montreal and declared that it would be easier to secure the
required capital for the new line without Government assistance
than it had been twenty years ago for the C.P.R. to do with all
possible backing from the Government. The Victoria Board of
Trade, on December 12th, recommended the project to the
assistance of the Dominion and Provincial Governments. Premier
Roblin of Manitoba took very different ground in a Montreal
interview on December 18th:

> Speaking for the people of Manitoba—and I might even say for the people
> of the North-West—I would say that they would greatly oppose any proposal
> to grant a land or cash subsidy to the Grand Trunk Pacific Railway project.
> The most that they would agree to would be that the Dominion Government
> should guarantee the bonds of the Railway.

The Quebec Board also objected strongly and at great length,
on December 4th, to any subsidy being given on the ground of
Quebec interests in the Trans-Canada project. The Toronto *Globe*
in discussing the matter on November 25th and 26th, expressed
strong faith in the financial profits of the project, pleasure in the
public benefits coming from the expenditure of a hundred millions
in the West and belief in the aid which its construction would
give to the development of Northern Ontario, to the convenience
of the farmers of Manitoba, to the opening up of wheat and coal
resources in the Territories, and to the mining interests of central
and northern British Columbia. But care should be taken in the
matter of subsidies and an eastern ocean terminus in Canada should
be absolutely assured.

This projected trans-continental line was proposed as a purely
Canadian road running from Quebec to Port Simpson and touching
at James Bay. It was claimed during the year by its
The Trans-   promoters that it ran too far north to compete with
Canada Rail- the C.P.R.; that through being 300 to 500 miles dis-
way Project   tant from the international boundary and in touch
with navigation at Hudson's Bay it would, in the event of war,
prove a great Imperial factor and highway; that from Quebec to
the Coast *via* Trans-Canada would be 2,830 miles as compared with
3,407 miles by the Grand Trunk project and 3,078 miles by the
C.P.R.; that the saving in distance and gradients would enable the
Railway to save the Manitoba farmer 7 cents per bushel on the
present cost of transportation; that Sir Sandford Fleming and Sir
W. C. Van Horne had described the proposed route as the best for a
new trans-continental line; that the wheat and timber lands of
Northern Quebec, the possibilities of the Hudson's Bay country, the
minerals of Northern Ontario, the rich wheat lands of the Peace

River, would all be developed by its construction; that its steel rails and steel bridges—with which the whole road was to be fitted—would help a great Canadian industry by being purchased in Canada.

The promoter of the project was Colonel George Earl Church, Vice-President of the Royal Geographical Society (an American living in London), and his first ideas were stated as derived from a study of the route as a military element in the Imperial situation. Authorization was finally obtained from the Quebec Legislature, so far as that Province was concerned, and in 1901 the Dominion Government granted a subsidy of $3,200 per mile, or $192,000, in aid of the first 60 miles of the Railway. Negotiations were opened in 1902 for the acquisition of the Quebec and Lake St. John Railway and a charter was obtained from the Dominion Parliament. Early in October an Executive Committee composed as follows was appointed at Quebec from amongst the Provisional Directors: Ald. George Tanguay, M.P.P., J. T. Ross, Gaspard Le Moine, J. G. Scott, William Price, Lieut.-Col. B. A. Scott and William Shaw. A provisional contract was also executed with Colonel Church for the construction of the road from Roberval to near James Bay—a distance of 400 miles.

On October 26th a meeting of 400 Mayors, Councillors and delegates from the two Counties of St. John and that of Chicoutimi was held at Chicoutimi. After addresses from the Hon. Charles Langelier and Mr. Tanguay, M.P.P., and an appeal from the latter for the taking of $100,000 of stock in the enterprise, Resolutions were passed asking the County Councils to submit the question of aid to the rate-payers and declaring that "the said Railway is of the greatest importance to Canada and especially to the Saguenay district, its proposed route offering the shortest, most level and best outlet for the products of Manitoba and the North-West to the seaboard and should be adopted by the Government for the new railway which has now become necessary for carrying such products to Canadian ports." Speaking at the Laval banquet on October 27th the Hon. L. P. Pelletier, M.P.P., eulogized the project as Canadian and opposed that of the G.T.R. as meaning the building up of American ports. On November 28th a meeting was held at Quebec with Mr. George Tanguay, M.P.P., in the chair and the Hon. Jules Tessier, M.P.P., and Hon. N. Garneau, M.L.C., present, with many others of the original charter members of the Company. A discussion took place regarding the action of the Grand Trunk and upon this point the Chairman said:

The position thus created is especially exasperating as the Trans-Canada had a short time ago given a provisional contract for the first 400 miles of its railway in this Province, and the financial negotiations for the whole line are now in a very forward state. As the Grand Trunk have no charter whatever for any Western line, it seems a pretty cool proceeding for them to be issuing maps showing that they intend to build a line on precisely the location—for the portion from Lake Winnipeg to Port Simpson—granted by Parliament last Session to the Trans-Canada.

The Quebec Board of Trade met on December 4th to consider

the matter and was addressed by Mr. Tanguay, its President, J. G. Scott, O. E. Talbot, M.P., Senator Landry, S. E. Gourlay, M.P., and others. Strong Resolutions were passed denouncing the action of the G.T.R., pointing out the Canadian character of their own project and its steady progress, and protesting against any Government aid to rival operations. Upon the following day a deputation from the Board waited on Premier Parent to present a special Resolution asking a Provincial grant of 20,000 acres per mile, or 8,000,000 acres, for the line from Roberval to James Bay. If granted, President Tanguay pointed out, they could then go to the Dominion for help. The Hon. Mr. Parent, in reply, stated that within two weeks his Government had declined $1.50 an acre for 25,000,000 acres in the northern country from which this free grant was now asked and had refused on the ground of the offer being inadequate. While personally in sympathy with the project of the deputation nothing could, he said, be done until the Commission of Inquiry into land grants, etc., appointed at the preceding Session, had reported to the Government. The action of the Quebec Board was followed by Resolutions along the same line by other Provincial Boards and Councils.

The Canadian Northern System under the control of Messrs. William Mackenzie and D. D. Mann comprised on June 30th, 1902, 1,248 miles of completed road, and included the Lake **The Canadian Northern Railway** Manitoba Railway and Canal Company's Line, the Winnipeg Great Northern, the Manitoba and South-Eastern, the Ontario and Rainy River and the Port Arthur, Duluth and Western, together with the leased lines of the Northern Pacific and the Portage and North-Western. The two latter comprised 355 miles. The first train over the C.N.R. from Port Arthur to Winnipeg arrived at the Manitoba capital on January 1st, 1902. Meanwhile, Messrs. Mackenzie and Mann had obtained powers for the construction of railway lines from Quebec through to the Coast and during the year had made arrangements with the British Columbia Government for a road across that Province into Victoria *via* Bute Inlet and a ferry service. When completed the approximate length of the Railway from Winnipeg to Victoria was placed at 1,544 miles.

In the Manitoba Legislature, on January 25th, Premier Roblin stated that the road from Port Arthur would be open for public business on February 1st; that the people of Manitoba now had a competitive line running for 1,200 miles through various parts of the Province completely under their control as to rates; that the Government having power to fix these rates had done so at two cents a hundred pounds cheaper than those now existing. Mr. Thomas Greenway contended in reply that the rates were not low enough; that the C.N.R. could not greatly relieve the situation because of the lack of elevators for the grain; and that the Government's liability of millions incurred in their guarantees for this road would prevent the aiding of other lines for years. The succeeding policy of the Railway and the Government was one of reduction in various directions. On February 15th the rate on general merchandize, live stock and farmers' produce was lowered. On March 10th the rate on lumber from Port Arthur and Rainy River was reduced one cent per cwt. On April 1st there was a general reduction of rates.

It was announced at Toronto on March 17th that Messrs. W. Mackenzie, D. D. Mann, Z. A. Lash, K.C., and a couple of others, had been incorporated as Mackenzie, Mann & Company, Limited, with a share capital of $5,000,000 and head offices at the City of Toronto. On October 16th it was stated that Mr. D. B. Hanna, who had been General Superintendent of the Railway since its inception, had been appointed 3rd Vice-President and Comptroller with headquarters in Toronto. A handsome presentation was made to him on November 11th by the citizens of Winnipeg. Mr. E. A. James, Superintendent of Transportation on the C.P.R., succeeded to his position and assumed charge on October 26th.

In the Montreal *Witness,* of November 5th, Mr. Mackenzie discussed the plans of his Company. They would shortly have 1,500 miles in operation and would handle 15,000,000 bushels of wheat this season, as against 10,000,000 last season. They would also have elevator accommodation very shortly for six or seven millions. As to their trans-continental ambitions they proposed going along quietly and steadily and making each section, as completed, pay its way. "We can see the completion of this system to the Coast as an accomplished fact," he said, after a reference to the British Columbia subsidies for a portion of the route.* Speaking to the Toronto *Star* of November 28th, in reference to certain rumours, Mr. B. E. Walker, General Manager of the Canadian Bank of Commerce, made the following statement:

> In reference to the phase of the matter in which I am most concerned, I might say that the Canadian Bank of Commerce has not a more satisfactory connection than that of Mackenzie, Mann and Co. and the Canadian Northern Railway; that the Railway has been built thus far without any financial stress whatever; that the bonds arising from the enterprise are selling to our entire satisfaction; that the enterprise itself is long past any doubt as to its financial basis; that the Bank has not now, and never has had, any right or desire to influence the owners of the Canadian Northern Railway to dispose of the road —the Bank's true interest in any event being the reverse of this.

In connection with the steady construction of the line west through the Territories, Messrs. Mann and Hanna were at Edmonton on November 29th, and the former told the Town Council that through its low bonded indebtedness the road would be able to haul freight much more cheaply than any line in the Western States or Western Canada. Speaking at Brandon on December 13th, Premier Roblin of Manitoba stated that the C.N.R. had constructed under the present Government, or were con-

---

*For the projects and interests of Messrs. Mackenzie and Mann in British Columbia, see page 74.

15

structing, 330 miles of new railway and quoted elaborate tables to show the substantial reductions in freight rates which that line had carried out. At Montreal on December 22nd, Mr. D. D. Mann told the press that Mr. Mackenzie and he intended to build a transcontinental line; that extensions would be pushed as rapidly as capital could be secured and be probably completed across the continent within six years; that no lines which they owned would be sold to either the G.T.R. or the C.P.R.; that Mr. Mackenzie and he controlled 85 per cent. of the stock of the Railway and meant to hold on to their property; that they were making a large profit, with a surplus of $800,000 per annum over running expenses and interest. In Winnipeg, on December 30th, Mr. Mackenzie stated that the proposed Grand Trunk Pacific would not effect their policy in the least. As to their eastward extension he said : " We have had survey parties out locating a route since last Session and we intend to take in all the centres of population, including Ottawa, Montreal, Quebec and Toronto."

Apart from the Tariff probably the most general subject of controversial discussion in the Dominion during the year was that of Transportation in one or other of its varied phases. Before the

General Transportation Questions

St. John Board of Trade, on February 7th, Mr. Louis Coste, C.E., of Ottawa, declared that Canada was not deriving the benefit it should from a total expenditure on railways and canals of $465,000,000. " I will continue to say so as long as I see one pound of Canadian freight shipped from a port of the United States." He advocated French River improvement at a cost of $5,000,000 and Intercolonial extension to North Bay. In the House of Commons on February 17th Mr. H. Bourassa moved a Resolution, seconded by Mr. A. W. Puttee (which was subsequently withdrawn), in the following terms :

That the time has come when a railway policy should be framed by which the people of this country could expect some return from the enormous sacrifices they have made in order to further the development of their avenues of trade, and especially in preventing our railway systems from falling under the control of foreign railway corporations.

At a banquet given by the Montreal Reform Club on March 16th, the Hon. Charles Fitzpatrick, Minister of Justice, spoke at length upon this question as being the most important of the hour. How to carry the grain of the West *via* the great lakes to the sea and upon Canadian cars and vessels, and how to divert traffic from United States cities and ports to Montreal and Canadian channels was the problem he wished to solve. " We are the most formidable competitors of the United States in the world's markets, yet we are dependent, in large measure, for the outlet of our products upon their good will." Lower transportation charges, removal of the insurance discrimination against the St. Lawrence, and improvements in the latter route, were his remedies for the situation. At Winnipeg, on September 26th, Mr. Fitzpatrick spoke of the vast treasure house around him which was waiting to be opened, up and declared that future improvements in the St. Lawrence route would enable Canada to carry on the bosom of its national river not only its own produce but the lion's share of the traffic between Duluth and Chicago.

In the House of Commons on May 7th Mr. A. F. Maclaren (C) moved an amendment on the supply motion that "it is both expedient and indispensable that the Government shall at once inaugurate such a policy in connection with our waterways and the ship-building industry as will speedily lead to the completion of a Canadian system of both inland and ocean transportation." After a discussion in which Mr. Tarte spoke at length the motion was negatived by 43 to 93 votes. In this general connection the Toronto *Globe* had a good deal to say during the year. On May 19th it declared transportation to be the " the greatest of Imperial questions as it is the greatest of national questions." On December 24th it dealt with the matter of subsidizing a new trans-continental line—*apropos* of the Grand Trunk and Canadian Northern plans as follows :

Both enterprises announce that they are looking for public aid. One of them has already for a portion of its road been liberally bonused. There is a well-defined and a growing sentiment against the further bonusing of railways. One thing absolutely certain is that we will not at the present moment undertake to subsidize two trans-continental railways. We are interested in both enterprises ; hope to see them both realized, but will not subsidize them both. Our sympathies would be very quickly transferred, however, to that road which proposed to carry out its plans without public aid.

The Maritime Board of Trade meeting, at Sydney on August 20th, and with 100 delegates present, passed a Resolution in favour of the further protection and equipment of Canadian waterways and ports and the carrying of Canadian trade over Canadian routes and through Canadian sea-ports. On October 9th the Hon. A. G. Blair was at Vancouver and in addressing the Liberal Association there dealt with the need for more railways, the propriety of all possible Government aid, the impossibility of doing without another trans-continental line and the fact that many present would live to see three or four running through Canada. "The ideal condition for Canada from a railway point of view would have been that the Government should have traversed this continent with a Government railway. I am not so sure that the idea is fanciful or chimerical even now. I dream sometimes of a prolongation by water and rail of the Government system which we know as the Intercolonial Railway." He did not believe this policy at all impracticable and with fair and moderate rates thought that such a line would control the situation in the interest of the people.

Meanwhile, the Hon. Mr. Tarte had inaugurated his tariff and transportation campaign. At Montreal on February 9th he spoke of a possible Government acquisition of the C.P.R. and urged

Quebec as a winter terminus for the Fast Line; at Toronto on June 5th he demanded transportation through Canadian channels, in Canadian ships, over Canadian soil and through Canadian harbours; at Fort William on July 24th he announced that contracts had just been given for deepening the Kaministiquia and dredging the harbour at Port Arthur; at Midland on August 6th he promised to recommend the deepening of the harbour to 22 feet. After a month's tour of the harbours, channels and towns around the great lakes and including Collingwood, Owen Sound, Sault Ste. Marie and various American cities, he told the Ottawa *Citizen* of August 9th that all the harbours of that region must be deepened to 22 feet. At St. John, N. B. on August 13th he promised to recommend a new wharf to his colleagues and ordered plans to be made; at Bowmanville on August 27th he urged free expenditures upon transportation; at Orillia, on September 19th, he declared that he had come to "preach the gospel of transportation" and the spending of all the money needed to carry Canadian trade through Canadian hands and routes; at the Montreal Board of Trade on October 14th he pointed to the 2,000 American bottoms on the great lakes as against the 24 belonging to Canada.

In Winnipeg, on October 15th, Dr. T. S. Sproule, M.P., told the *Telegram* that his solution of the question in the West was a Hudson's Bay Railway. In British Columbia Mr. John Houston, M.P.P., of Nelson gave an open letter to the press on December 23rd in which he proposed an issue by the Province of land-scrip for 25,000,000 acres at $1.00 per acre—the proceeds to be used in constructing railways through undeveloped portions of the Province. Speaking at Winnipeg on December 16th the Hon. Thomas Greenway declared transportation the problem of the day, and, apparently, an insoluble one owing to the immense increasing possibilities of production. He urged the building of a Hudson's Bay Railway and the construction of a direct line to Duluth. The position of the West with its increased production in 1903 would, he thought, be intolerable.

The total Government expenditure by Canada on its canals and waterways up to June 30th, 1902, was $102,484,545 and its total
Canals and Waterways of Canada revenue therefrom $13,017,756. During the fiscal year 1901-2, the expenditure of the Department of Railways and Canals on the latter was $2,978,770 and the revenues therefrom $300,413. In the season of 1901 the quantity of wheat and other grains shipped down the St. Lawrence Canals to Montreal continued to show a decline—from 604,200 tons in 1897 to 295,928 tons in 1900 and 203,316 in 1901. The total traffic on the Canadian Sault Ste. Marie Canal during 1901 was 2,820,394 tons; on the Welland 620,209 tons; on the St. Lawrence Canals, 1,208,296 tons; on the minor Canals 1,016,360.

The freight passing up Canadian canals and between Canadian ports in 1901 was 340,805 tons, and down, 1,686,094 tons; up and down from Canadian to United States ports it was 469,680 tons; up and down from United States ports to United States ports it was 2,308,900 tons; up and down from United States ports to Canadian ports it was 859,880 tons. The total number of tons going up was 1,294,173 and down 4,371,086, and the amount of tolls collected was $244,055. The whole subject of Canadian waterways, rates, ports, commerce, etc., was discussed in the House of Commons on March 7th, as a result of a motion presented by Mr. A. F. Maclaren.

On December 31st, 1901, there were 6,792 sailing ships and steamers on the registry books of the Dominion with a gross steam tonnage of 298,421 and a net tonnage of steamers and sailing ships of 664,483. The registered tonnage showed a slight increase over 1900 but a marked and steady decline from the 869,624 tons of 1894. The shipping tonnage (net) of the chief countries of the world* in that year was as follows:

Canadian Shipping Interests

British Empire	10,304,388	France	961,259
United States....	2,318,876	Italy............	947,079
Germany........	2,106,885	Russia..........	850,695
Norway.........	1,393,096	Canada ,........	664,483

The number of Canadian vessels, steam and sail, passing up and down Canadian canals in the season of 1901 was 20,860 and the tonnage 3,980,264. The number of Canadian vessels entered *inwards* from sea in Canada with cargo, during the year ending June, 30th, 1902, was 2,786 and the tonnage 453,258.† Those in ballast numbered 2,909 with a tonnage of 475,915. Entered *outwards* they numbered, with cargo, 3,780 and had a tonnage of 791,938; in ballast the number was 1,938 with a tonnage of 216,116. The Canadian vessels (steam) trading on the Inland waters and arriving at Canadian ports during the fiscal year, 1902, were 9,303 with a tonnage of 3,480,020 and crews numbering 188,180; the sailing vessels numbered 1,693 with a tonnage of 365,219 and crews numbering 8,086.

The British or Canadian vessels employed in the coasting trade of Canada during the fiscal year 1902 (arrived and departed) numbered 64,679 with a tonnage of 7,055,512 and with crews numbering 262,138; the Foreign vessels numbered 743 with a tonnage of 151,495 and crews numbering 4,628. The vessels built in Canada during the year (steam and sail) numbered 260, with a tonnage of 28,288; those registered numbered 316 with tonnage of 34,236; those sold to other countries numbered 27 with a tonnage of 11,360 and a value of $235,865. The total tonnage of all vessels of all countries entering inwards and outward (sea-going and Inland navigation) was 30,025,404 and the tonnage of all vessels employed in the coasting trade was 40,700,907.

---

* Annual Report of the Marine Department, 1902.
† Trade and Navigation Returns, 1902.

One of the most important matters which developed during the year in connection with Canadian interests abroad, was the position of the Atlantic Steamship Companies and the influence of Mr. J. Pierpont Morgan's combinations. Since 1894 there had been a consolidation of the former concerns for the purpose of maintaining higher passenger and steerage rates. In a general way the British Isles had been given to the Cunard, White Star, American, Dominion and Allan Steamship Companies, while the German, Holland and French Lines controlled rates from the Continent. The Elder, Dempster Company and its subsequent acquisition, the Beaver Line, had remained out of this arrangement, however. As bearing upon later developments and the operations of Mr. Morgan, certain statistics of the chief international Steamship Companies in 1901, compiled from the Liverpool *Journal of Commerce*, may be given here:

Canada and the Atlantic Steamship Combine

British Companies	Vessels	Tons
Elder, Dempster & Co	120	382,560
British India S. N. Company	120	378,770
Peninsula and Oriental Co	58	313,343
F. Leyland & Co.	55	242,781
Union-Castle Line	41	222,613
White Star Line	25	212,403
Wilson Line	89	189,818
Ocean S. S. Company (Holt Line)	41	165,143
Clan Line	46	164,487
Allan Line	36	152,367
Lamport & Holt Line	47	149,712
Harrison Line	31	146,625
Anchor Line	41	132,540
Maclay & McIntyre	51	126,917
Cunard Line	26	126,332
Dominion Line	13	105,430
Johnston Line	24	100,460
R. Ropner	36	100,426
Royal Mail S. P. Co	28	88,205
J. Westoll	38	88,306
Bucknall Bros	23	83,207
	989	3,672,445

The principal German Lines were the Hamburg-American, with 202 vessels of 541,085 tons; the North German Lloyds, with 111 vessels of 454,936 tons; and the Hansa Line, with 57 vessels of 157,037 tons— a total of 370 vessels of 1,153,058 tonnage. The chief French lines were the Messageries Maratimes, with 62 vessels of 246,277 tons; the Compagnie Générale Transatlantic, with 59 vessels of 183,243 tons; and the Chargeurs Réunis, with 26 vessels of 81,149 tons—a total of 147 vessels of 510,669 tonnage. The United States had the American Line (formerly the Inman and Red Star Line), with 25 vessels of 167,105 tons, and the Atlantic Transport Company, with its 17 vessels of 123,000 tonnage. Japan boasted the Nippon Yusen Kaisha, with 69 ships of 218,361 tons;

Italy had the General S. N. Company, with 102 vessels of 205,104 tonnage; Austria had the Austrian Lloyd, with 68 vessels of 169,436 tons ; and Spain possessed the Cis Transatlantica, with 23 vessels of 88,453 tons.

Towards the end of April it was announced that Mr. Morgan had organized a shipping combination, which included the White Star, the Dominion, the Leyland, the Atlantic Transport, the American and the Red Star Lines. Of these the White Star, Dominion and Leyland Lines were British, the others American. The agreement between the Companies was made public on May 9th, and constituted what was to be known as the International Mercantile Marine Company. It was afterwards stated that the Hamburg-American and North German Lloyd Lines had agreed to contribute a portion of their dividends to the International in return for a six per cent. payment annually on $5,000,000 capital. This was intended to prevent rate-cutting and competition expenses. On October 2nd the new Company was incorporated at Trenton, New Jersey, with a capital of $120,000,000, of which half was to be in Preference stock with a 6 per cent. cumulative dividend; and with authority to issue 4½ per cent. bonds to the amount of $75,000,000. Mr. C. A. Griscom, of New York, was President, and the British Committee consisted of Sir Clinton Dawkins, the Right Hon. W. J. Pirrie, and Messrs. J. Bruce Ismay, Henry Wilding and C. F. Torrey. Mr. Charles Steele, a member of the Executive, told the American press on the above date that the majority of Directors would be American, and that the stock was all subscribed.

The combination thus formed, according to the New York *Journal of Commerce*, consisted of 118 ships, with a tonnage of 881,562, while the affiliated German lines had 376 ships of 1,224,178 tons. Alarm was very freely expressed in Canada as to its effects upon Canadian interests. The original 'Conference of shipping interests had not been over-friendly to emigration to the Dominion, and the Elder-Dempster and Beaver Lines had already suffered considerably because they had kept out of the arrangement. It was soon stated that under the new combination the position was much worse and had taken the character of a practical boycott against the interests friendly to Canada. There was a good deal of exaggeration in this and other rumours, and the Hon. W. S. Fielding was interviewed in London by the *Daily News* of September 20th upon the situation. He did not think there was any ground for alarm, denied that his Government was trying to organize a British combination, and stated that all they wanted was to meet great commercial and industrial development in Canada by obtaining a faster shipping service to and from European markets.

Meanwhile the matter had been dealt with in England in many quarters as a very serious one involving considerations of subsidy, service in war-time and transfer of national authority. The White Star Line had three vessels receiving a yearly subsidy of

£27,000 to act in war-time as armed cruisers and were under contract as to five others. Upon this point Mr. W. J. Pirrie, in a statement issued early in May, declared that the Line in question had "given an undertaking that the vessels at present held at the disposition of the Admirality shall remain so during the unexpired period of the contract." He did not see any reason why the arrangement should not be renewed. The Cunard Company on September 30th announced an arrangement with the Government by which they remained out of the Combine and would be for twenty years a purely British concern. "Under no circumstances shall the management be in the hands of, or the shares, or vessels of the Company be held by other than British subjects." On the same day Mr. Gerald Balfour stated that the Government had arranged with the International Company that British companies in the Combine were to remain British in constitution, management and flag.

On January 4th, 1889, at a banquet in Toronto, the Hon. George E. Foster, Minister of Finance, had announced that the Dominion Government were about to establish a Fast Atlantic **The Fast** Steamship Service. On June 6th, 1902, the scheme **Atlantic** was still being discussed, and at a banquet in the same **Line Project** city in honour of the Canadian Boards of Trade Conference, the Hon. J. Israel Tarte, Minister of Public Works, made the following pronouncement :

We must have transportation—transportation through Canadian channels, in Canadian bottoms, over Canadian railways. We must have Canadian boats and harbours. We must have a Canadian policy on land and sea. We must have no foreign domination, no foreign organization of railways and steamship lines on this continent. I am glad that at your Conference you dealt with the great question of transportation on broad lines. We will have a Fast Line of steamers—Canadian and British, I hope. We will have it in such a way as not to be in the reach of Morgan and his associates.

Between these two speeches there had been thirteen years of fitful effort and constant failure to establish the much-discussed Fast Line project. In 1901, Sir Christopher Furness had visited Canada and expressed himself as strongly favourable to the proposal, and Lord Strathcona had upon several public occasions urged the carrying out of the scheme. In the *Nineteenth Century* of January, 1902, Mr. Edwin C. Burgis had an article pointing out that in the days of sailing vessels Canadian clippers had beaten the Americans across the Atlantic. He denounced the St. Lawrence route as dangerous and slow ; and urged Sydney as the only available port of call for a Fast Line. Comparing the amount of time which might be saved in travelling from Liverpool to Toronto *via* Sydney instead of New York, Mr. Burgis calculated it at 20 hours and 45 minutes. To the landing-place at St. John, *via* Sydney instead of New York, the saving would be 55 hours, 13 minutes. Speaking to the Halifax *Chronicle* of January 27th, upon his return from England, Captain J. A. Farquhar, who had taken a great interest in the project for years, declared that steamship men were really beginning to take the matter up, and that the proposal of a medium service was losing ground in favour of one equal to the best running out of New York. This, he said, was the view of Lord Strathcona, who also " believed that the summer terminus of the line in Canada should be a Cape Breton port, and the winter terminus Halifax."

From this time on, in connection with the Morgan combine plans and the Coronation Conference, the question came continuously before the public. Tho Toronto *Globe* of May 19th, pointed out that we now had Canadian production and large systems of land transportation. "Nothing is wanting to complete the chain but Canadian or British transportation by sea." On June 2nd, Mr. E. S. Clouston, General Manager of the Bank of Montreal, in addressing the shareholders said : " There are indications that the recent consolidation of Atlantic steamship lines by an American Syndicate will compel Canada, in self defence, to take up the question of a fast Atlantic service and, if we wish to secure immigration, retain the traffic properly belonging to our own ports, and safeguard the interests of our commerce we must see that the Service, both passenger and freight, is second to none in speed and equipment." The Toronto *Globe* followed this utterance up with several strong editorials—notably on June 6th and June 9th. On the latter date it said : " If there is to be a shifting of shipping interests across the Atlantic why should it not be to Canada, building up Canadian ports and having Canadian farm products carried in British ships ? " At the Boards of Trade Conference on June 5th, Resolutions in favour of a Fast Line were presented from the Boards of Halifax, Barrie, Vancouver, Toronto, Montreal and British Columbia, and it was resolved by the Conference as follows :

1. That the establishment of a Fast Atlantic Steamship Line from a Canadian port to a port in Great Britain would assist trade in the Dominion, would increase our export trade, especially in perishable products, would add greatly to the volume of passenger travel through Canadian channels, would give an impetus to ship-building in Canada and would, with the aid of our trans-continental railways, bind the different portions of the Empire more closely together. II. That speed should be the first consideration in the selection of the ports of call and terminal ports and that the conduct of the enterprise should be under the control of the Dominion Government. III. That our representatives at the London Conference be respectfully asked to seek financial support and co-operation from the Imperial Government towards an undertaking of such importance to Canada and the Empire.

On the same day in London the Executive of the British Empire League passed a Resolution declaring that the time had come when this matter must be seriously considered, and urging Imperial co-operation with Canada in its settlement. Before a Committee of the British House of Commons, on July 23rd, Senator Drummond, of Montreal, testified as to the importance of the project to Canada, the Empire, and to trade. " Unless the ships were first-class in every respect, they would serve no useful purpose. They would require a sea-going speed of 22 knots on the average." The Canadian Government, he thought, should go as high as £200,000 per annum in subsidies. At a meeting of the Corn Exchange of Montreal, on July 30th, a Resolution was passed by 15 to 7, which favoured a Fast Line if the steamers were as swift as the best sailing from New York; with Quebec and Montreal as the summer terminals and Halifax or St. John as the winter terminus. " But this Association does not favour the subsidizing of freight steamers, nor the granting of a subsidy to a line of steamers under the control of any railway or combination of railways."

On the preceding day the Montreal Board of Trade passed a Resolution, by 32 to 15 votes, that such a service should have a speed of at least 23 knots, urging the same ports as in the Corn Exchange motion, and pressing for improvements in the St. Lawrence navigation. At Halifax, on August 14th, the Canadian Manufacturers' Association recommended the granting of a reasonable subsidy and Government control over the freight rates. On August 21st the Maritime Board of Trade passed a long Resolution in favour of immediate action in the granting of any necessary subsidy, declaring speed a most vital consideration, and urging that the port chosen be the one nearest to Europe and best suited for large ships at all seasons of the year. Another meeting of the Montreal Board, held in conjunction with La Chambre de Commerce, on August 25th, urged speedy action and, in order to avoid any hampering influence, declared that the contract made would be satisfactory if it simply provided that the summer terminal port should be " on the River St. Lawrence as near to the heart of the country as conditions will admit."

This vexed question of ports of call and terminals came in for much discussion. On October 7th the St. John Board of Trade urged that City as a proper terminal port in winter. At Montreal, on September 1st, Sir Robert Bond, Premier of Newfoundland, was interviewed, and urged an Island port for this purpose. The Line should be as swift as possible, and only for passengers, mails and express goods. The Sydney Daily Post, on August 1st, declared that place " the destined port, the port that must be selected sooner or later." Senator Drummond was interviewed at Montreal on August 25th, and strongly favoured Halifax as an all-year round terminal port. Premier Murray, of Nova Scotia, said four days before this that Halifax would be the winter terminal, Quebec the summer one, and Sydney a port of call.

Meanwhile, the Hon. Mr. Tarte and La Patrie, of Montreal, had been favouring Quebec, and Mr. W. Wainwright, of the Grand Trunk, and Mr. R. Prefontaine, M.P., had been urging Montreal as the rational and national terminal point. Under date of October 4th the Halifax Board of Trade issued a circular letter, urging the claims of that port. On October 23rd the same Board held a massmeeting, addressed by President George S. Campbell, Benjamin

Russell, M.P., Wm. Roche, M.P., Senator Josiah Wood, A. C. Bell, M.P.,
Premier Murray and F. B. Wade, M.P. Resolutions were passed
urging that the speed of the steamers be equal to the swiftest
running out of New York, and declaring Halifax to have the
strongest claims as the Western terminus of the Line.

Meanwhile the Canadian Pacific Railway Company had tendered
for the proposed Service. On July 24th Sir Thomas Shaughnessy,
President of the Railway, stated at Montreal that his
Company had tendered for a fast Atlantic steamship
service, that the offer was engaging the attention of
the Imperial and Canadian Governments and that it
would be considered at the pending Coronation Conference. He
believed that the Company could give a satisfactory service and
stated that the tender included passengers and freight. Mr. D. W.
Campbell, Manager in Montreal of the Elder-Dempster Company,
was interviewed by the Toronto *Globe* as to this action and stated
that large negotiations had been going on in London for some time
with a view to meeting the Morgan combine; that the Canadian
Ministers had been anxious for a proposal from the Elder-Dempster
people and the Allan Line; and that they had submitted one
covering projected lines to England, to the Cape and to Australia.
He believed the Atlantic Line should be one of 18 knots. Any
higher speed would not pay.

The comments in London were very favourable to the C.P.R.
tender which it was understood covered a weekly fast service
between a St. Lawrence port and 'Liverpool in the summer and
Halifax and Liverpool in the winter combined with a good freight
service and the expectation of a yearly subsidy of $1,500,000. The
Times of July 25th referred to the previous good work of the C.P.R.
as an Imperial factor and declared that this action of the Company
would constitute an even greater service to Imperial interests.
Opinions varied in Canada. The Toronto *Globe* of July 28th protested against such a subsidy unless some Government control of
rates and charges accompanied it. Montreal shipping men naturally
criticized this possible development of heavily subsidized opposition
and were led in doing so by Mr. D. A. P. Watt and Mr. Robert
Reford. Interviewed at Montreal on September 19th, Mr. H. A.
Allan of the Allan Line, opposed the C.P.R. proposals, stated that a
shipping combination had been formed in London which intended
to run a fleet of 40 to 60 freight steamers from Quebec and Montreal
in summer and Portland and St. John in winter, and declared that a
20-knot service was sufficient.

At a mass-meeting in Halifax on October 23rd Mr. Peter Innes,
President of the King's County Board of Trade, urged the acceptance of the C.P.R. tender because (1) the financial standing and
capacity of the Company were unquestioned; (2) it would be
conducted on business principles and successful lines; (3) modern
improvements would be maintained in speed, construction and
equipment; (4) a large ocean traffic from its railways would be at

The C.P.R.
and the
Fast Line

once available.   Meanwhile, on October 1st the annual meeting of
C.P.R. shareholders took place in Montreal and power was given
the Directors to act along the lines of the tender which they now
announced as follows :

The Company offered, subject to certain traffic arrangements, to establish a
weekly service of 20-knot steamships between Liverpool and a St. Lawrence port
during the summer months, Halifax to be the Canadian port during the winter
months, for a subsidy of £265,000 sterling per anuum during the first ten
years, with a graduated reduction in the amount of subsidy during each of the
following periods of five years, the ships to be most modern in every respect,
and to be built especially for the route.   In addition to this, the Company
signified its willingness to furnish a fleet of modern freight steamers of ten
thousand tons' capacity each, sailing at a speed of about 12 to 13 knots per
hour, serving Canadian ports.

MISCELLANEOUS TRANSPORTATION INCIDENTS

Jan. 15.—The Hon. F. R. Latchford introduces in the Ontario Legislature
and eventually carries through a measure appointing a Commission
to construct and operate a railway of from 90 to 100 miles from
North Bay to Lake Temiscamingue.   Adjacent ungranted lands, in
tiers of townships not to exceed 20,000 acres per mile, are set apart
for expense of construction.

Jan. 28.—It is announced that Dr. W. Seward Webb, representing great
railway interests in the United States, has obtained a three months'
option on the Canada Atlantic System at a price of $11,000,000.

Feb. 15.—The new rates on the White Pass and Yukon Railway arranged
between President S. H. Graves and the Hon. A. G. Blair show
marked reductions as follows ·

Class.	Old.	New.
No. 1, per 100 lbs	$2.85	$1.90
No. 2, " " "	2.84	1.66
No. 3, " " "	2.82	1.42
No. 4, " " "	2.80	1.19
No. 5, " " "	2.75	.95
No. 6, " " "	2.74	.90
No. 7, " " "	2.73	.75
No. 8, " " "	2.72	.73
No. 9, " " "	2.71	.73
No. 10, " " "	2.70	.70

Feb. 27.—Mr. P. J. Loughrin writes to the Toronto *Globe* that after having
traversed the region in question for years he believes the proposed
Georgian Bay Canal would cost $300,000,000.

Mar. 11.—Mr. George Y. Wisner of Ottawa, Consulting Engineer to the
Georgian Bay Canal Company, replies to Mr. Loughrin and
estimates the total cost of the project at $80,000,000.

Mar. 15.—The railway subsidies voted by the Ontario Legislature are
announced at its prorogation to total $613,000, of which the chief
items are $150,000 to the Bay of Quinte Railway, $210,000 to the
Irondale, Bancroft & Ottawa, and $95,000 to a portion of the James
Bay Railway—in addition to $285,000 previously voted.

Mar. 26.—Under this date the Council of the Montreal Board of Trade petitions the Governor-General-in-Council for aid " by granting subsidies
or otherwise " in the development of railway facilities in the West ;
for assistance to an enlarged Canadian Marine by giving a subsidy
of one dollar per registered ton per annum for five years on all
vessels of foreign build placed on the Great Lakes and having a

capacity of not less than 1,000 tons burden ; and a similarly conditioned subsidy of two dollars on all vessels so trading and built in Canadian ship-yards.

April 12.—The Grand Forks and Republic (Kettle Valley Line) is opened at Grand Forks, British Columbia.

April 29.—The Great Northern of Canada Consolidated Company with a capital stock of $100,000,000, is incorporated in New Jersey, U.S., in order to operate railways in the North-West and is said to be backed by James J. Hill.

May 12.—The first sod of the Temiscamingue Railway is turned by the Hon. Mr. Latchford.

May 14.—Messrs. Mackenzie and Mann are stated to have acquired the Nova Scotia Central Railway running 74 miles between Middleton and Lunenburg.

May 16.—It is announced by the Toronto *Globe* that lines of railway recently completed or now under construction in Ontario total 2,078 miles.

June 2.—The sale of the Canada Atlantic and Parry Sound Railways to an American syndicate falls through by the lapsing of the option and the financial troubles of Dr. Webb and his friends.

Aug. 2.—Mr. James J. Hill, the American Railway magnate, speaks to the Board of Trade at Grand Forks, B.C., and states that though he once owned one tenth of the C.P.R. stock he does not now possess a share.

Oct. 6.—It is announced that the Great Northern Railway through a St. Paul contracting firm, has acquired the Victoria Terminal and Sydney Railway system in British Columbia.

Oct. 28.—After many months of struggle the Vancouver, Victoria and Eastern Railway is granted permission by the Railway Commission at Ottawa to construct certain branch lines in British Columbia and to cross the Kettle River Railway.

Nov. 26.—A letter is published in Montreal from the Hon. Mr. Prefontaine outlining his proposed policy in the Marine and Fisheries Department and promising to complete the equipment of the Port of Montreal "in the most efficient and permanent manner."

Dec. 10.—The Montreal Board of Trade pass an unanimous Resolution declaring Western transportation facilities inadequate ; expressing pleasure at the proposed G. T. R. Pacific extension ; declaring that there is ample room for such a railway ; congratulating the G. T. R. upon the double-tracking of its line ; and urging " a constant endeavour to develop its eastern terminal business entirely within Canadian territory."

VIII.—AGRICULTURE IN CANADA

A most important and authoritative reference to Canadian agricultural conditions was presented by the Hon. S. A. Fisher, M.P.,

Agricultural Conditions and Trade

Minister of Agriculture, in his annual Report for the fiscal year ending October 31st, 1902. He used the following explicit words: "I am happy to be able again to congratulate the country on a most prosperous agricultural year. Notwithstanding the enormous crop which our North-West produced last year, it has been exceeded in the present season, and I can venture again to prophesy that in the years to come it will constantly increase in a most marvellous manner. The agricultural production of Eastern Canada has been full to overflowing this year. Butter and cheese have been produced and exported in much larger quantities than ever known before, while the prices have been so high that the value of the exports is much the greatest in the history of our country. The pork industry has also been stimulated by the very high prices and, although the increase in quantity is not so very great, the increase in value is most satisfactory. Poultry and egg production have been again much stimulated. The only difficulty in fact in regard to these products is that the buyers cannot find in Canada enough to meet their demands. This may also be said of our hog products. It is indeed a fact that this year in Canada farmers could have sold far more than they had to sell, at prices which were uniformly profitable; the only difficulty that has appeared in our agriculture being the lack of labour to produce what we could sell and to develop an increased area of productive fields." Hardly less interesting is the ensuing table of Canadian agricultural exports for 1896 and for the two years 1901 and 1902:

	1896	1901	1902
Wheat	$5,771,521	$6,871,939	$18,688,092
Flour	718,433	4,015,226	3,968,850
Oats	273,861	2,490,521	2,052,559
Oatmeal	364,655	467,807	344,332
Peas	1,299,491	2,674,712	1,805,718
Cattle	7,082,542	9,064,562	10,663,819
Sheep and lambs	2,151,283	1,625,702	1,483,526
Cheese	13,956,571	20,696,951	19,686,291
Butter	1,052,089	3,295,663	5,660,541
Pork, bacon and hams	4,446,884	11,829,820	12,457,863
Poultry	18,992	141,518	238,047
Eggs	807,086	1,691,640	1,733,242
Fruits	1,716,278	2,006,235	1,922,304
Total	$39,659,686	$66,872,296	$80,705,184

In 1901 official figures gave the value of farm lands in Ontario as $585,354,294, that of buildings as $226,575,228, that of implements as $59,897,513, that of live stock as $129,496,261—a total of $1,001,323,296 as against $974,814,931 in the preceding year. The sales of live stock in 1901 amounted to $46,592,103 in value. The creameries in the Province at the end of 1901 numbered 286 with a production valued at $1,798,264. The cheese factories numbered 1,167 with a production of 134,942,517 lbs., valued at $9.09 per 100 lbs. The area of assessed land in the Province was then 23,636,178 acres of which 13,436,482 were cleared, 6,715,872 were woodland and 3,483,824 acres were swamp, marsh or wasteland. The crops for 1901 were as follows:

Ontario Agricultural Interests

Product, 1901.	Acres.	Bushels.	Value.
Fall Wheat	911,587	15,943,229	$10,538,474
Spring Wheat	358,048	5,498,751	3,673,166
Barley	637,201	16,761,076	7,542,484
Oats	2,408,264	78,334,490	28,357,085
Peas	602,724	10,089,173	6,588,230
Beans	53,688	824,122	1,030,153
Rye	158,236	2,545,268	1,254,817
Buckwheat	88,266	1,757,071	850,422
Corn	521,855	27,197,619	14,157,508
Potatoes	154,155	18,116,637	7,717,687
Carrots	9,221	3,199,967	399,996
Mangel-wurzels	61,095	29,683,324	2,374,666
Turnips	145,909	68,287,467	6,828,747
		Tons.	
Hay and Clover	2,557,263	4,632,317	37,012,213

The total acreage therefore was 8,667,512 and the market value of the crops $128,325,648. There were 2,777,983 acres of pasture land in the Province, 346,915 acres of orchard and garden, 12,227 acres of vineyard, and 6,777,935 apple trees, of 15 years and over, producing 14,430,650 bushels of apples. On July 1st, 1901, there were 620,343 horses in Ontario valued at $50,038,465. During the year 50,755 were sold for $4,347,582, or an average value of $86. The cattle on July 1st numbered 2,507,620 and were worth $59,527,119. Those sold or slaughtered during the year numbered 610,880 valued at $20,286,936—an average of $33.21. Sheep numbered 1,761,799, worth $7,772,793. Those sold or slaughtered during the year numbered 729,148, worth $3,103,513.

Hogs numbered 1,491,885 and were valued at $9,298,712. Those sold or slaughtered during the year numbered 1,973,405 valued at $17,548,490, or an average of $8.89. Poultry numbered 9,745,236 valued at $2,859,172. Those sold or killed in the year were valued at $1,305,555. The value of the wool clip was $781,769 and that of the colonies of bees in the Province was $1,114,099. In the following year, on July 1st, 1902, the live stock in the Province, included 626,106 horses, 1,715,513 sheep, 2,562,584 cattle, 1,684,635 hogs and 9,762,808 poultry. The table which follows gives the estimated crop of Ontario for 1902 as contained in Bulletin 81 of the Department of Agriculture :

Product, 1902.	Acres.	Bushels.	Yield per Acre.
Fall Wheat	748,592	20,033,669	26·8
Spring Wheat	303,115	6,048,024	20·0
Barley	661,622	21,890,602	33·1
Oats	2,500,758	106,431,439	42·6
Peas	532,639	7,664,679	14·4
Beans	53,964	670,633	12·4
Rye	189,318	3,509,332	18·5
Buckwheat	93,324	1,911,683	20·5
Potatoes	144,733	12,942,502	89·0
Carrots	8,625	3,227,161	374·0
Mangel-wurzels	76,553	39,140,924	511·0
Turnips	136,725	71,740,204	525·0
Corn for husking (in the ear)	371,959	20,512,194	55·1
		Tons.	
Corn for silo and fodder (green)	209,859	2,611,334	12·44
Hay and Clover	2,646,202	4,955,438	1·87

A prominent feature in agricultural development for a number of years past has been the Ontario College at Guelph. When the institution was opened in 1874 it had 28 students ; in 1901 there were 359. The training—under the guidance of Dr. James Mills, President of the College since 1879—includes chemistry, dairying, veterinary science, physics, English, biology and mathematics. Amongst the students in 1901 taking the general course were 222 from Ontario and 27, scattering, from amongst the other Provinces, while England, Jamaica, the United States and the Argentine Republic had respectively 7, 3, 4, and 14 representatives. As to results, the Toronto *Globe* of March 31st, 1902, pointed out that " 70 per cent. of the graduates of the College are engaged in farming, dairying, etc., in Ontario ; so that the Province is not spending its money to train young men to develop and enrich another country."

Closely associated with the College and the Model Farm is the Guelph Fat Stock Show, which has become an established institution. At its annual banquet, on December 11th, the Hon. John Dryden, M.P.P., the Hon. Sidney A. Fisher, M.P., Mr. J. P. Whitney, M.P.P., Dr. R. A. Pyne, M.P.P., and others were amongst the speakers, and President Mills declared that the Ontario Government did not give him enough money to keep his best teachers from going away to United States institutions. He wanted to obtain $35,000 right away for a bacteriological laboratory and isolation stable. On December 10th His Excellency the Governor-General had visited the College, and spoken at a banquet in the evening, with Dr. Mills in the chair. Lord Minto expressed a hope that the time was not far distant when the Dominion Government would grant the Ontario Agricultural College $40,000 a year, and a similar sum to proposed Colleges in the Maritime Provinces and Manitoba.

The prospects and progress of Manitoba and the North-West, in regard to their crops, were subjects of vital interest throughout Canada during the year. The production of 1901 had been phenomenal, and it was hoped that the product of 1902 would exceed it. According to the Official Bulletin, issued at Winnipeg on December 12th of the former year, the area under wheat had been 2,011,835 acres; the average yield per acre was 25 bushels and the total yield 50,502,085. Under oats there was an area of 689,951 acres, with an average yield of 40 bushels, and a total yield of 27,796,588 bushels. Under barley the area was 191,009 acres, with an average yield of 34 bushels, and a total product of $6,536,155. In flax, rye and peas the total production was 345,030 bushels, and the acreage 24,564. The total grain crop of the Province, with its 35,000 farmers, had been 85,179,858 bushels. In potatoes there was an acreage of 24,429, an average yield of 196 bushels to the acre and a total production of 4,797,433 bushels. In roots the area under crop was 10,214 acres, the average yield 286 bushels, and the total yield 2,925,362 bushels. The farmers of the Province sold during 1901, 77,220 turkeys, 33,940 geese and 306,365 chickens. They erected new buildings to the value of $1,434,880, and broke in 149,305 acres of new land for the crop of 1902.

On June 12th of this latter year the Provincial Department of Agriculture issued another Bulletin in which it was stated that 2,039,940 acres were under wheat, 725,060 acres under oats, 329,790 acres under barley, 41,200 acres under flax and 18,845 acres under rye, peas, corn and bran. Potatoes were planted in 22,005 acres, and roots in 12,175 acres—a total of 3,189,015 in all crops, against 2,961,409 in 1901, and 2,122,500 in 1900. The live stock fattened during the winter were stated at 9,908, and the milch cows at 119,835 in number. Dairying was described in the Bulletin as steadily increasing in popular attention, and lists were given of 28 creameries and 37 cheese factories in the Province. The prospect of crops all through Manitoba was reported as excellent. It may be added that on July 1st, 1901, there were in the Province 142,080 horses, 263,168 cattle, 22,900 sheep and 94,680 swine. Of Provincial lands available for sale at figures ranging from $2.50 to $6.50 per acre, there were in the beginning of the following year some 2,000,000 acres.

The question of transporting the heavy crop of 1901 was a serious one even up to the time when it became necessary to think of moving the next year's crop. The elevator capacity of the Province was large and increasing, but certainly not yet up to requirements. The Canadian Pacific Railway had an elevator capacity at its terminals of 6,400,000 bushels, on its main line of 2,843,400, bushels, and on its branches of 4,574.500 bushels. The Canadian Northern Railway had at its terminals a capacity of 1,500,000 bushels, on its main line of 467,500 bushels, and on its branches of 1,610,400 bushels. The only other difficulties in connection with

16

this crop of 1901 were the absence of sufficient permanent labourers
and an insufficiency of machinery. Meanwhile, no consideration of
storage or transportation and no trouble with wind or weather
affected the crop of 1902. Once more the records were broken, and
the following official figures tell the story of production:

Product.	Total yield in bushels.	Average yield to acre.
Wheat	53,077,267	26·0
Oats	34,478,160	47·5
Barley	11,848,422	35·0
Flax	564,440	13·7
Rye	49,900	19·5
Peas	34,154	21·4
Total	100,052,343	

The production of potatoes was 3,459,325 bushels and of roots
3,230,995; that of butter was 3,915,875 lbs. valued at $636,160;
that of cheese 1,093,653 lbs. worth $111,443. During the year, as
reported by a Government Bulletin on December 16th, 1902, the
farmers of the Province sold 83,905 turkeys, 34,270 geese and
363,020 chickens. They erected $2,228,875 worth of farm buildings
and possessed at the close of the year 146,591 horses, 282,343 cattle,
20,518 sheep, and 95,598 pigs. The cattle trade of the Province
was almost entirely in yearlings, not purchased, as formerly, by the
United States dealers, but shipped into the neighbouring Territories.
In 1898 20,000 of this class had been sold to the States and 9,500
to the Territories. In 1902 the figures were reversed to 25 to the
States and 20,000 to the Territories. Meantime, the export of beef
cattle had decreased from 12,525 to 4,000 head.

There was more than the usual trouble in August and September in obtaining farm hands to harvest the mass of golden grain.
The number required was placed at 20,000 but despite cheap excursions and wide advertisement in the East only about 12,000 were
obtained. The weather was splendid and the work of some 1,800
threshing machines was over by December 1st while the autumn
work showed 1,730,995 acres prepared for the crop of 1903. The
value of the total crop grown by the 35,000 farmers in Manitoba
in 1901 had been $39,368,051; that of the 38,000 farmers of 1902
was over $44,000,000—as shown in the following table:

Wheat	$30,254,042	Chickens	$ 90,775
Oats	7,254,042	Eggs	100,000
Barley	2,962,105	Dairy Products	747,603
Flax	564,440	Cattle (exported)	168,000
Rye	19,960	Stockers	300,000
Peas	17,077	Hogs (sold)	420,000
Potatoes	864,831		
Roots	323,099		$44,099,682
Geese	13,708		

The average income, per farmer, over and above living expenses
was, therefore, $1,170, or double that of 1892, and 41 per cent.

greater than that given by the Census returns of 1900 for the
farmers of the United States. Yet the area of 3,000,000 acres
under crop was only a fraction of the total area of 23,000,000 acres
of cultivable land available in the Province. This immense crop
for a few people to raise and the stream of money which it promised
to the country, added to that which had come from the crop of 1901,
produced wide prosperity and much outside comment. The Canadian Arch at the Coronation spoke Canadian pride in this future
" granary of the Empire " and Canadian public men were not
behind-hand in referring to it.

To the London *Telegraph* on May 28th Lord Strathcona
observed : " I should say that in 10, or at the outside 15, years the
Dominion will be capable of producing all the breadstuffs required
by the Mother Country." To the *Daily News* of June 14th Hon.
R. P. Roblin spoke of the production of 1901 and the 20,000,000
acres still awaiting cultivation. " This done, we can, independent
of those nations that are hostile in sentiment and fact produce the
wheat and breadstuffs that are necessary to feed this great Motherland ot ours." At the Canada Club dinner in London, on July
16th, Sir Wilfrid Laurier declared that " There is absolute certainty
that Canada will be the granary of Great Britain. At the present
time there is in Canada an ocean of ripening grain of a quality
unsurpassed in the world and, as for quantity, in a few years there
will be enough to feed the whole of Great Britain, nay, the whole
of Europe."

Visitors to the West were unstinted in their expressions of
admiration for the country. Writing home to Sir John See on
August 6th Sir F. M. Darley, Chief Justice of New South Wales,
said that he had been much struck by the prosperity of Canada
and by the appearance of Manitoba where " the whole country
was under wheat." Mr. R. L. Borden, M.P., after his tour of the
West, told the Winnipeg *Tribune* of October 6th that he was going
back to be " an immigration agent " and with his Canadian patriotism broadened and greater than ever, and more comprehensive in
scope. Interviewed in Montreal upon his return from the West,
on September 30th, Sir W. C. Van Horne described the agricultural
scenes he had witnessed as magnificent. " Indeed, I regard them
as matchless. I have never seen anything to equal them and there
are marked evidences of prosperity in every section." The English
journalists who toured Canada during the autumn wrote reports
to their papers of the strongest kind and no doubt did much to
promote the ensuing immigration. One word of warning was
heard in a statement by Mr. B. E. Walker, General Manager of the
Canadian Bank of Commerce, who drew attention at his annual
meeting on November 30th to the great scarcity of farm labour
which, " had it not been for a most favourable autumn, would have
entailed an enormous loss." Farmers were strongly advised to
provide more granaries for themselves.

According to the Census returns of 1901 only 6,569,064 acres, out of a land surface of 187,932,617 acres, in the Territories of Alberta, Assiniboia and Saskatchewan were occupied **Agricultural** as farms. Of this 93·22 per cent. was owned by the **Production** occupier and 24·31 per cent. was improved. In 1891 **In the** the area under crop was 194,773 acres and in 1901 it **Territories** was 649,073, or an increase of 333 per cent. The total value of farms and lots in 1901 was placed at $79,090,340 including $44,803,361 for land and buildings, $28,225,323 for live stock, $6,061,656 for implements and machinery. The sum of $13,389,665 was credited to crops and animal products. The 158,000 population of the Territories possessed, in 1901, 186,462 horses, 591,739 cattle, 154,152 sheep, 515,125 hens and chickens and 73,926 swine.

According to the estimate of production issued by the Territorial Government, on September 1st, 1902, the crop of that year was 14,649,500 bushels of wheat as compared with 12,808,447 bushels in 1901 ; 10,725,500 bushels of oats as against 9,716,132 bushels in 1901 ; and 795,100 bushels of barley as compared with 736,749 bushels in 1901. About the same date Mr. Hugh McKellar, Deputy Minister of Agriculture in Manitoba, issued a statement giving the total land area of Manitoba and the Territories as 230,823,040 acres and the following computation of desirable farm lands in this total :

Manitoba	23,000,000
Assiniboia	19,000,000
Saskatchewan	17,000,000
Alberta	16,000,000
Total	75,000,000

Of this amount it was estimated that 20,000,000 acres in Manitoba and 10,000,000 acres in the Territories had become homesteads or been sold by the Dominion Government and interested Railways. During the year ending June 30, 1902, 2,573,120 acres of Government land were homesteaded, and 2,126,880 acres of railway lands sold. At the present rate of settlement and sale and production Mr. McKellar computed the crop in the Province and Territories ten years hence at 350,000,000 bushels of wheat, 200,000,000 bushels of oats, and 50,000,000 bushels of barley. And then only 20,000,-000 acres out of the 75,000,000 available would be cropped !

Returning to actual production, the North-West creameries in 1901 showed a product of 672,393 lbs. of butter valued at $129,483, with 1,345 patrons. The Secretary of the Western Stock Farmers' Association in April, 1902, stated the shipment of live stock from Alberta in 1901 at 45,390 head, and at the annual meeting of the Territorial Horse-Breeders' Association at Calgary, on May 16th, the Secretary estimated the number of horses in the Territories at 90,000 for Alberta, 45,000 for Assiniboia, and 15,000 for Saskatchewan. Speaking to the St. John *Telegraph* on December

APPLE ORCHARD AT COLDSTREAM RANCH, IN BRITISH COLUMBIA.

6th, Lieut.-Col. H. W. A. Chambre, of Winnipeg, embodied Western opinion in this connection in the following statement :

Why, the West is the greatest country under the sun and Eastern Canadians don't seem to realize it. It has been demonstrated that wheat can be grown successfully 800 miles north of the international boundary, in the Peace River district, and from that to the international line the country is one immense farm with greater wheat crops per acre and better farming results generally than any other locality can show.

At the Pacific Coast agriculture is rather an important possibility than a subject of large present consequence. Out of 236,922,177 acres of land surface, according to the Census of 1901, only 0·63 per cent. was occupied as farms and lots. Yet the value of farm lands and buildings in 1901 was $26,001,377, of implements and machinery $1,201,196, of live stock $6,184,313 and of crops and animal products $6,664,369—a total of $40,051,255. The production of wheat was 368,419 bushels, of barley 73,790 bushels, of oats 1,441,566 bushels, of hay 170,187 tons, of potatoes 956,126, of hops 299,717 and of various field roots 635,988 bushels. By values the horses in the Province were worth $2,074,528, cattle $3,452,033, sheep $164,679, swine $271,327, poultry $209,747, field crops $3,100,577, fruits and vegetables $435,794, live stock (sold during the year) $1,202,607, dairy products $1,159,993, and eggs $426,629.

Agriculture and Fruit in British Columbia

In a Report published early in 1902—the first since 1896—Mr. J. R. Anderson, Deputy Minister of Agriculture in British Columbia, expressed regret at the absence of statistical data in this connection; pointed to various improvements in agricultural methods; referred to the very large increase in agricultural imports from the United States—from $2,362,298 in 1896 to $5,497,809 in 1900; and spoke of the Provincial production of horned-cattle as a profitable one, the swine industry as capable of a great expansion and poultry breeding as the most remunerative branch of local agriculture. At the Royal Colonial Institute, London, on February 11th, the Hon. J. H. Turner, Agent-General for the Province, made the following statement in this connection :

Another very important resource is the agricultural land, and this is intimately connected with mining, inasmuch as mining communities are the best customers for the product of the farm, orchard or garden. A very few years ago British Columbia was looked upon as a mining country, but with no prospect for agriculture ; it is now found that the very finest grain and the choicest fruits can be produced there. Probably the wheat-growing section, for profit, is limited, still one district—the Okanagan—has three very fine flour mills of most modern construction, working steadily and sending large quantities of flour to Victoria, Vancouver and other points. But as a whole the Province is more suited for stock-raising in some sections, in others for fruit-growing and mixed farming, in others again for mixed farming, fruit and dairying.

At the meeting of the Dairymen and Live Stock Association in Victoria, on February 27th, Mr. G. H. Hadwen in his Secretarial report urging the breeding of horses, the cultivation of a poultry trade and the encouragement of swine-raising. Two days before this the Central Farmers' Institute passed a Resolution urging Government aid in establishing cold-storage stations and Government action in the obtaining of cheaper binder twine; asked power to form Mutual fire insurance Associations and advocated the placing of nature studies upon the compulsory school list of subjects.

In the Report of the Victoria, B.C., Board of Trade for 1902, there appeared a special statement by the Hon. J. D. Prentice, Minister of Agriculture, which declared conditions in that regard to be most favourable, the demand to be increasing much faster than the production and the prices going steadily higher. Dairying interests were, he stated, being rapidly developed through co-operation and private creamery plants, condensed milk was becoming a profitable industry, the prices for light hogs were decidedly remunerative, higher rates were being offered for mutton, egg production was proving very profitable, horse-breeding was in a healthy condition and the demand for horses active, while fruit-growing was being greatly aided by improved methods of shipment and cheaper freight rates.

Fruit raising proved a profitable industry in 1902. In the previous year there were 436,644 apple trees in the Province and 88,943 plum trees, and the total yield of fruit was 344,390 bushels. A feature of the development of 1902 was the large profit which the Earl of Aberdeen was understood to have made out of his property in the Okanagan region. The market, rapidly growing in extent and value, which Manitoba and the Territories were opening out to fruit-growers, was the subject of a special Report at the meeting of the Provincial Fruit Growers' Association on January 23rd. The President pointed out a difficulty which they had, in his opinion, to face in the following terms:

A great drawback to fruit-growing in the Upper Country, I believe to be due to the indifference of the present land-holders. Notwithstanding the knowledge of having climate and soil second to none for fruit, they have grown wealthy and lazy and do not care to branch out. As soon as sub-division takes place and some more live fruit growers go in there and cut up a lot of those large ranges into fruit farms then, and not until then, will the soil and climate of the Upper Country tell of its value in horticulture.

The Province of Nova Scotia, according to the Census of 1901, has a land area of 13,483,671 acres, of which 37·68 per cent is occupied as farms and lots. The value of farm lands and buildings in 1901 was placed at $58,752,384, of implements and machinery at $3,208,899, of live stock at $10,603,624, and of crops and animal products at $16,305,555—a total value of $88,870,462. There were 1,975,575 apple trees in the Province, and the total yield of all fruit trees was 2,131,045 bushels. The wheat production of 1901 was 248,476 bushels, that of barley 181,085 bushels, that of oats, 2,347,598 bushels, that of buckwheat 196,498 bushels. Hay showed a production of 658,330 tons, potatoes 4,394,413 bushels, and other field roots 2,074,806 bushels. There were 316,174 cattle in the Province

Agriculture in Nova Scotia

285,244 sheep and 45,405 swine. According to value the horses of the Province were placed at $3,854,382, the cattle at $5,381,824, sheep at $757,278, swine at $387,380, poultry at $218,223, total field crops at $8,584,956, fruits and vegetables at $1,407,369, live stock, sold during 1901, at $1,427,777, and dairy products at $2,885,997.

The agricultural societies in Nova Scotia numbered 151 in 1901, with 8,500 members, paying subscriptions of $10,771, and with a Government grant of $10,000. Special attention was paid during the year to dairying, and official reports of operations, published on April 5th, 1902, showed a production of 316,180 lbs. of cheese, worth $30,087, and of 542,626 lbs. of butter, valued at $53,222. In his annual Report the Provincial Secretary of Agriculture stated that the farmers were giving more attention to the raising of horses. The question of establishing a Maritime College of Agriculture was considerably discussed during the year, and a long debate upon the subject took place in the Legislature on March 18th.

The Census of 1901 afforded means of ascertaining agricultural conditions in the Island Province, as well as in Nova Scotia, which were not before available. Out of a land area of 1,397,991 acres, 85·44 per cent. was occupied as farms and lots, almost the whole of it in an improved state. The value of farm lands and buildings in 1901 was $23,118,946, of implements and machinery $2,628,787, of live stock $4,878,980, and of crops and animal products $7,467,663 —a total value of $38,094,376. The number of apple trees in the Province was 202,910, and the yield of all fruit trees was 184,487 bushels. Wheat showed a production of 738,679 bushels, barley 105,625 bushels, oats 4,561,097 bushels, hay 168,326 tons, potatoes 4,986,633 bushels, and various field roots 3,932,591 bushels. According to values the horses on the Island were worth $2,147,935, cattle $1,843,197, sheep $384,790, swine $355,373, poultry $147,159, fruits and vegetables $4,641,947, live stock (sold during the year) $678,217, dairy products $1,111,614, eggs $248,423. Writing in May, 1902, as to the dairying conditions of the Island, Mr. John Anderson told the *Maritime Farmer* that its people were at last convinced that they had the best dairy country in the world—" the conditions being unequalled, plenty of clear, pure water, a soil to produce abundance of rich, succulent food, pasturage continuously good from May to November, a moderately warm summer, with cool, pleasant nights."

Prince Edward Island Agriculture

MISCELLANEOUS AGRICULTURAL INTERESTS

Jan.   9.—The Hon. Mr. Fisher, Minister of Agriculture, warns farmers at a meeting of the Eastern Dairymen's Association that the cheese industry is in a rather serious condition. Of the $4,000,000 decrease in cheese exports during 1901, half was due to decrease in quality of the product. "There was no reason in the world why Canadian cheese should sell at four cents less per pound in England than the domestic article."

Jan. 28.—At the annual meeting of the Farmers' and Dairymen's Association of New Brunswick, Commissioner of Agriculture, the Hon. L. P. Farris, makes the following statement as to Provincial crop production in 1901 :

	Acres.	Bushels.	Bushels per acre.
Wheat	26,010	478,886	18·4
Oats	184,114	4,999,992	26·8
Barley	4,396	99,540	22·6
Buckwheat	70,114	1,479,477	21·1
Potatoes	77,525	4,077,478	108·6
Turnips	7,633	2,098,940	275·1

Jan. 28.—A Resolution is passed unanimously by the New Brunswick Farmers' and Dairymen's Association in favour of Provincial co-operation with Nova Scotia in the proposed establishment of a Maritime College of Agriculture.

Feb.   1.—Mr. John Gunion Rutherford, v.s., is appointed Chief Veterinary Inspector for the Dominion in succession to Dr. Duncan McEachran, resigned.

Feb.   5.—At the annual meeting of the Dominion Grange in Toronto, opinions are expressed in favour of a Federal Railway Commission; the placing of railway lands under legislation similar to that of drainage lands; the total destruction of barberry bushes; and the further encouragement of agricultural education and of the Guelph College.

Feb. 19.—In the House of Commons the Minister of Agriculture declares that there is practically no chance of the British embargo against the landing of live cattle being raised at present or for some time to come. It applied to all countries.

April 5.—The Halifax *Herald* places the production of the three Maritime Provinces in cheese, during 1901, at 39,434,305 lbs., valued at $4,094,240.

April 12.—The land sales of the Canada and North-West Company for 1901 are stated at 121,082 acres and $629,040 in value, as against 71,109 acres for $387,712 in 1900. The Canadian Pacific Railway sales are stated at 399,808 acres for $1,262,224 as against $268,699 for $860,006 in 1900.

May   2.—A Conference of Dominion dairy experts at Ottawa reaches the following conclusion :

"That it would tend to secure a better and more uniform quality of dairy products to have all cheese factories and creameries organized into groups or syndicates consisting of from 15 to 30 factories, each group being under the supervision of a competent instructor, and that these groups should be centralized under one authority in each Province, and short courses of instruction be held in the dairy schools for farmers' sons so as to ensure cheese and butter being manufactured only in factories that are free from sanitary defects, and possessed of well-constructed and cleansed rooms, pure water, good drainage, and clean utensils and surroundings."

May 20.—Mr. George Finley O'Halloran is appointed Deputy Minister of Agriculture.

June 10.—At Edmonton, N.W.T., under the initiative of Mr. John T. Moore, delegates from various towns meet and pass a strong Resolution, demanding from the Dominion Government aid in building roads in the Territories.

July 24.—Mr. Theodore M. Knapp, of Minneapolis, tells the United States Bankers' Association at Washington that "within ten years Western Canada will be producing annually 250,000,000 bushels of wheat."

Aug. 31.—At the opening of the Provincial Exhibition of New Brunswick, at St. John, Lieut.-Governor, the Hon. J. B. Snowball, makes the following comment on existing conditions :

"He deplored the small quantity of wheat raised. In the Province there are, thanks to the efforts of the Provincial Government, 21 up-to-date flour mills, with an aggregate capacity of 500 barrels a day. The Province raises 500,000 bushels of wheat annually, or equal to 274 barrels of flour a day, but little over half the capacity of the mills. The daily consumption of flour in the Province is 2,000 barrels, and it would require 60 more mills, all run at their full capacity, to supply our wants and stop a drain of $6,900 per day going out of the Province for flour."

Sept. 6.—An organization is formed in Toronto under the auspices of Mr. Goldwin Smith and Mr. W. L. Smith, Editor of the *Farmers' Sun*, called the Ontario Farmers' Association. The latter gentleman acts as Secretary and Mr. C. A. Mallory, of Cobourg, is appointed Chairman.

Oct. 7.— In a speech at Montreal the Hon. C. Fitzpatrick, Minister of Justice, pays the following tribute to a great Canadian interest :

"Our agricultural resources are almost unlimited. In Eastern Canada our farmers can grow almost everything which will flourish in the temperate zone in Europe and much else besides. In southern Ontario we have miles of vineyards, and peaches are grown by the acre. In the West, each settler seems lord of a farm bounded only by the horizon, and of which the plough furrows are measured by the league ; and the former roaming grounds of the buffalo have already become one of the great wheat belts of the world."

Oct. 9.—At a meeting of the Winnipeg Board of Trade Resolutions are read which had been passed by the Boards of Trade at Virden, Rapid City, Portage La Prairie, Stonewall, Emerson, Deloraine, Neepawa, Melita, Souris, Moosomin, Brandon, and a number of Municipalties protesting against C.P.R. freight rates. A similar Resolution passes the Winnipeg Board.

Oct. 29. Professor J. W. Robertson tells the Winnipeg *Free Press* that Sir W. C. Macdonald has now founded 20 Institutes for Manual Training and that 7,000 boys are being instructed. He declares that farmers in all parts of the country are enjoying prosperity.

Nov. 6.—A branch of the Ontario Farmers' Association is organized at West Lorne for the County of Elgin and a Resolution passed expressing alarm at the efforts of manufacturers to increase the import duties on agricultural implements.

Nov. 28.—The British Board of Agriculture closes the ports of the United Kingdom against the importation of cattle and sheep from Maine, New Hampshire, Vermont, Massachussetts, Connecticut and Rhode Island on account of the prevalence of the dreaded foot and mouth disease. This is applied to Canadian and other animals passing over railways in those States to the seaboard.

Nov. 30.—The Dominion Government follows the Imperial example and places an embargo against the importation of cattle, sheep, etc., coming from the New England States and also against the passage of animals through the State of Maine from one part of Canada to another.

Dec.   6.—In connection with Canadian shipments through Maine and t..c
protests evoked by their stoppage the Minister of Agriculture en-
deavours unsuccessfully to obtain the approval of the British authorities to a lifting of that part of the embargo.   Mr. Fisher makes the
following statement :
"Without such direct approval it was strongly felt that if the
permission were given for Canadian cattle to pass through one of the
States which the Imperial Government had quarantined it would lay
the Canadian Government open to the accusation on the part of the
Imperial authorities that we had not been taking the necessary pre-
caution to ensure that no disease could come to Great Britain
through our ports." *

Dec. 12.—The Premier of Manitoba announces at Brandon that his Government will establish a Provincial School of Agriculture.

Dec. 18.—The North-West Grain Dealers' Association issues a circular stating
that of a total Western crop of 64,000,000 bushels of wheat about
13,000,000 bushels are being held for seed and local mills, 36,300,000
bushels have been carried by the railways to terminal points or
marketed, and about 14,000,000 remain to be transported.

Dec. 29.—Referring to Mr. Hanbury's determination to maintain the exclusion
of Canadian live cattle—or rather not to make an exception in their
favour—the Winnipeg *Free Press* terms it really a Protective measure
and adds : "Mr. Hanbury knows perfectly well that in over a million
Canadian cattle slaughtered in Great Britain since the introduction
of the embargo not one case of disease has been found.

Dec. 31.—It is announced that the C.P.R. land sales for 1902 have totalled
2,420,440 acres at a figure of $8,140,245.   The sales of the North-
West Land Company are reported as 516,000 acres for $2,520,000.

---

* At the time of writing, March 17th, 1903, the general embargo is still maintained, but on
February 7th an Order-in-Council admitted animals through the State of Maine in bonded, sealed cars,
via the C.P.R.

IX. TRADE AND COMMERCE

The aggregate trade of Canada increased during the year ending June 30th, 1902 by $37,000,000 and since 1895 by $199,500,000. The total imports rose from $190,415,525 in 1901 to $212,270,158 in 1902; the total exports from $196,-487,632 to $211,640,286; the total trade from $386,-903,157 to $423,910,444. The increase in this trade as compared with that of other countries and limited to merchandise only was shown in his annual Report to June 30th, 1902 by Mr. W. G. Parmelee, Deputy Minister of Trade and Commerce. According to his figures the trade of Canada increased between 1895 and 1901 by 96·05 per cent.; that of Japan by 89·06 per cent.; that of Australia by 62·21 per cent.; that of the United States by 48·08 per cent.; that of the Netherlands by 43·80 per cent.; that of Italy by 39·01 per cent.; that of Germany by 32·45 per cent.; that of Belgium by 32·08 per cent.; that of the Argentine Republic by 30·91 per cent.; that of the United Kingdom by 24·77 per cent. The Dominion therefore headed the list of nations in its proportionate trade development. The general incidence of its trade with the chief countries concerned may be seen in the following table compiled from the *Trade and Navigation Returns*:

The General Trade of Canada

Trade with*	1895.	1901.	1902.
Great Britain	$92,988,727	$148,347,120	$166,526,283
United States	95,932,197	182,867,238	192,012,434
France	2,920,456	6,979,352	8,061,042
Germany	5,421,135	9,162,957	13,515,747
Holland	384,164	984,840	1,195,856
Belgium	693,019	6,634,592	4,156,049
Newfoundland	3,065,046	2,886,067	3,498,482
Spain	436,580	897,893	856,793
Portugal	115,921	181,707	234,874
Italy	415,919	642,424	963,641
West Indies	8,681,622	4,707,677	5,472,747
South America	1,610,470	2,567,278	3,440,987
China and Japan	2,906,574	3,149,591	2,555,462
Switzerland	260,040	603,397	780,183
All other Countries	3,059,444	7,113,487	11,161,301
	$218,891,314	$377,725,620	$414,431,881

The chief imports into Canada (merchandise only) in the fiscal year 1902 included living animals $1,986,341; books $1,668,159; breadstuffs $11,731,268; carriages, etc. $1,430,364; coal, coke, etc. $14,150,653; cordage, twine, etc. $1,973,206; cotton and manufac-

* Imports entered for consumption only.

tures of, $13,715,612 ; drugs, dyes, etc. $5,536,729 ; earthenware and China $1,227,986 ; electric apparatus $1,373,022 ; fancy articles $2,224,946 ; fish and fish products $1,154,524 ; flax, hemp, jute, etc. $4,359,907 ; fruits $4,396,929 ; furs and manufactures of, $2,967,-099 ; glass and manufactures of, $1,932,539 ; gutta-percha, India-rubber, etc. $2,431,304 ; hats, caps and bonnets $2,030,357 ; hides and skins $5,086,052 ; leather and manufactures of, $1,804,762 ; metals, minerals and manufactures of, $41,610,579 ; oils $2,408,565 ; paper and manufactures of, $1,942,795 ; provisions $2,550,712 ; settlers' effects $4,580,481 ; seeds and roots $2,443,293 ; silks and manufactures of, $4,539,706 ; spirits and wines $2,146,276 ; sugar, molasses, etc. $9,102,258 ; tea $2,977,129 ; tobacco and manufactures of, $2,490,476 ; woods and manufactures of, $5,899,440 ; wool and manufactures of, $12,623,107.

The chief exports (merchandise only) were living animals $14,106,916 ; breadstuffs $37,415,883 ; coal, charcoal, etc. $5,127,445 ; cotton and manufactures of, $1,226,679 ; drugs, dyes, etc. $1,081,-931 ; fish and fish products $13,567,142 ; fruits $1,980,518 ; furs and manufactures of, $2,373,539 ; hay $4,415,324 ; hides and skins $1,737,230 ; leather and manufactures of, $2,319,763 ; metals, minerals and manufactures of, $34,796,920 ; provisions $41,463,488 ; seeds $2,337,793 ; settlers' effects $1,592,845 ; vegetables $1,005,051 ; wood and manufactures of, $35,234,203.* The following table gives the general distribution of Canadian exports in the year ending June 30th, 1902 :

Articles.	To British Empire.	To Other Countries.
Produce of the Mine	$1,231,018	$33,860,210
Produce of the Fisheries	7,882,497	6,304,573
Produce of the Forest	14,862,115	17,268,798
Animals and their Produce	54,056,728	5,773,424
Agricultural Products	40,236,515	7,305,328
Manufactures	10,713,625	10,121,783
Miscellaneous Articles	54,152	300,098
Bullion and Coin	33,970	1,635,452
Total	$129,070,620	$82,569,666

Of Canadian imports in 1902 from the British Empire—chiefly Great Britain—$37,294,421 were dutiable, $16,736,969 were free, $6,467,674 came in under the general tariff and $30,635,889 under the Preferential clause. Of imports from Foreign countries—chiefly the United States, France and Germany—$90,660,860 were dutiable and $67,577,908 free. The duties collected under the general tariff were $26,696,301 and under the Preferential clause $5,729,230. The trade of Canada and the duty collected on imports, by Provinces, was as follows :

---

* NOTE.—Only items exceeding $1,000,000 are given in these figures. The table which follow includes $8,156,611 of Foreign produce in the Empire column and $7,463,912 in the other.

Provinces.	Total Exports.	Total Imports.	Duty.
Ontario	$48,597,480	$86,232,560	$12,577,342 63
Quebec...............	91,057,201	82,014,443	11,675,114 40
Nova Scotia	14,978,222	12,510,752	2,069,988 91
New Brunswick.	17,657,751	7,307,271	1,255,788 47
Manitoba.............	4,896,149	8,659,028	1,563,740 32
British Columbia......	18,385,335	10,391,256	2,354,404 78
Prince Edward Island..	801,013	643,829	150,266 74
North-West Territories.	1,183,648	2,491,237	252,144 28
Yukon Territory	14,083,487	2,019,782	526,741 78
Total.............	$211,640,286	$212,270,158	$32,425,532 31

Various comparative figures were quoted during the year besides those of Mr. Parmalee already given. The Department of Trade and Commerce, in its monthly statement for February, stated the increase of imports into Canada between 1890 and 1900, at 58·16 per cent., and that of exports from Canada at 105·71 per cent. The Australian increase during that period in imports was 17·91 per cent., and in exports 56·82; the United States increase in imports, 4·29 per cent., and in exports 73·43 per cent. ; the British increase in imports 24·33 per cent., and in exports 7·96 per cent. Other countries showed much smaller increases. The official monthly summary of commerce in the United States, for August 1902, placed Canada as first of all countries in the percentage growth of its exports between 1891 and 1901 and fourth in that of its imports—Cape Colony, Egypt and the Argentine Republic being those in advance of the Dominion.

British imports from within the Empire increased between 1891 and 1901 from £99,464,718 to £105,573,706 and from Foreign

Trade with Great Britain countries the figures were, respectively, £335,976,546 and £416,416,492. The exports to British countries rose during that period from £93,338,119 to £113,118,-364 and to Foreign countries from £215,775,599 to £234,745,904. The total trade, therefore, increased from £744,554,-982 to £869,854,466. The distribution of British import trade as between the competitive products of Canada and the United States may be seen in the following table :

Products, 1901.	From Canada	From United States.
Cattle......................	£1,484,860	£ 7,324,154
Sheep......................	99,506	463,519
Horses.	46,737	659,299
Bacon and Hams..............	1,226,331	13,465,667
Beef (fresh)	40,503	6,761,587
Butter......................	1,008,002	689,164
Cheese......................	3,697,660	1,274,061
Wheat......................	2,216,049	13,475,541
Barley......................	122,762	872,694
Oats.	317,488	1,185,928
Wheat and Flour.,.............	628,611	8,698,249
Eggs.......................	255,956	125,643
Hay.	165,904	338,640

Products, 1901.	From Canada.	From United States.
Apples.	305,953	487,884
Fish.	690,454	836,177
Paper.	115,997	517,070
Pulp-wood.	312,356	91,491
Skins and Furs.	360,602	618,535
Wood and Timber.	4,607,316	4,289,474

The exports from Great Britain to Canada of articles, the produce and manufacture of the United Kingdom, totalled in 1901 £7,785,472 as against £18,393,883 to the United States, while those of Foreign and Colonial merchandize were to Canada £1,465,054 and to the United States £19,257,267. During the year 1902, as in previous periods, Lord Strathcona did much to develop trade between the Dominion and Great Britain. His office as High Commissioner was always open to the public for purposes of information and on January 25th, he wrote to the press detailing the recent progress of Canada and offering every facility to those who desired aid in the initiation of trade arrangements. On November 1st, he wrote a similar letter recapitulating statistics of progress and prosperity and promising help to all who would apply. On March 15th his annual Report was presented to the Dominion Government. He spoke of the cattle trade as now well established ; of the quality of Canadian animals as not so good as it should be ; of the rare appearance of Canadian beef, as such, for sale in shops ; of the disadvantage—which he was trying to remove—of Canadian beef being excluded from Army contracts ; and then referred to the following much-discussed matter :

The free entry of Canadian cattle into the United Kingdom remains very much where it was. There is no immediate prospect of Canadian cattle being admitted into the United Kingdom, except for slaughter at the port of landing, for some time. In fact it cannot be done without new legislation in view of the Act of 1896, which applies to all countries. It is some satisfaction to know that the Board of Agriculture seem to hold no longer the view that pleuro-pneumonia has existed in Canada, and that they are prepared to give a clean bill of health to the Dominion in this respect. At the same time, however, they state that they are debarred, by the existing legislation, from extending to Canadian cattle the treatment they formerly received, with so much advantage to the two countries, of free entry into the United Kingdom.

The trade in horses, he declared, would never be what it should until more attention was paid in Canada to breeding. He referred to Canada as ranking after the United States and the Argentine in supplying wheat to Great Britain, and declared that local grain merchants would prefer to buy their grain from Canada if other things were equal. Canadian oats, he said, were not popular. He drew attention to the inclusion of Canadian exports *via* New York in United States returns, and spoke of immense possibilities in the butter trade. With cold storage and a more steady export the apple trade should become much more profitable. There were great openings for trade in condensed milk and in poultry. Reference was made to the value of the Canadian exhibits at Glasgow, Wolverhampton and Cork, aud in the Royal Exchange, London.

Meanwhile, Mr. Harrison Watson, Curator of the Canadian Section in the Imperial Institute, had reported, on March 1st, that greatly increased interest was being shown in the resources and possibilities of the Dominion—" an almost sudden prominence which Canada has assumed in the public intelligence." Speaking to the Toronto *Mail* on August 22nd, after a visit to England, Mr. A. F. Maclaren, M.P., stated that Russia was making a determined effort to capture the British dairy market. Canada should be more aggressive and commercial agents should be appointed in each of the chief cities. And then he added :

I think Canada can obtain a sentimental preference if she keeps her goods to the fore. Five years ago the English business man did not care a button whether he dealt with Canadians or Americans. In fact, the latter enjoyed the greater *prestige*. Now all that is changed ; all things being equal, the Englishman is anxious to buy from Canadians in preference to Americans.

On January 23rd, the Hon. Dr. W. H. Montague, a member of the Canadian Government in 1894-96, addressed the Canadian Manufacturers' Association at a banquet in Hamilton, presided over by Mr. Cyrus A. Birge. The speaker, who had paid a lengthy visit to Australia in the preceding year, dwelt first upon the general conditions of trade in that country, the shipping of some 21,000,000 tons entering and clearing at its ports, the commerce of over $400,000,000, the private wealth of the people estimated at $4,395,000,000, the bank deposits of $511,000,000, and its gold output of $70,000,000. He praised very highly the freezing plants and cold storage facilities of Australia, and pointed out that recent figures indicated that in a total of 425,000,000 pounds of frozen meat annually imported into England, Australia and New Zealand sent about 72,000,000 pounds, the United States 308,000,000 pounds, and Canada only 10,000,000 pounds. Now, he thought, was the time for the Dominion to wake up and take advantage of the national developments going on in the Island Continent. " In the first place the Colonies are ablaze with the spirit of loyal devotion to the Motherland and to one another. In the next place the Australian Commonwealth is in the formative period ; old lines are being wiped away, new lines of trade are being laid down, and it is much easier to enter the field successfully now than to attempt to do so when the lines of commerce, so hard to disturb when once they have been established, have been taken. Again, we are about to construct the Pacific Cable. And, finally, we have reached a time when the trade poliicies of the Empire are undergoing a revolution." After a reference to the British tax upon food imports, he urged an effort to compete with the United States in some of the $30,000,000 worth of manufactured goods which that country now sent to Australia, and which he analyzed in the following table :

Agricultural implements $1,000,000
Carriages and Bicycles 1,457,000
Clocks and Watches 298,000
Patent medicines....................................... 333,900
Cottons 694,000
Canned fish 463,000
Rubber goods 8,455,900
Boots and Shoes 2,000,000
Oils, etc.. 2,000,000
Paper (chiefly printing)............................... 2,250,000
Manufactures of Tobacco 2,300,000
Wood and manufactures of.............................. 2,400,000
Iron and Steel 200,000
Other goods, including apparels, woollens, etc............. 5,000,000

Most of these products, Dr. Montague thought, could be profit-ably exported by Canada if new tariff conditions did not prevent. Upon this point, however, he was hopeful. "During the seven or eight months which I spent in Australia, I had specially good opportunities of finding out what the sentiment of the Australian people is with regard to a tariff preference for Canada, and I think I am quite within the mark when I say that with proper handling that preference can be got. The people themselves are strongly in favour of trade with Canada." Wherever he had spoken this idea of a mutual preference had been received with cheers, and the Australians believed that two countries which could fight together should also trade together.

He then gave in detail the articles and products which Canada could sell to the Australians and including spades, forks, axes, plated ware, sewing machines, cream separators, paper products, onions, oatmeal, lumber, India rubber goods, boots and shoes and other leather goods, sauces, hosiery, cotton goods, wearing apparel, beer, carriages, bicycles, furniture, lumber, carpets, hardware, organs, pianos, varnishes, collars and cuffs, ties, steel products, tobacco, malt, etc. From Australia Canada could take hides, wool, fruits, raw sugar, hardwoods and wines. In the Commonwealth, if success were to follow, however, we must have more commercial agents, more warerooms, more advertising, more visiting business men and lower tariffs.

The considerations thus presented were reiterated in different ways and added to from time to time in his monthly Reports by Mr. J. S. Larke, Canadian Commissioner in Australia.

Trade Relations With Australia He frequently laid stress upon the necessity for promptness in correspondence, better arrangements for packing and careful supervision of all shipments going *via* New York. During the year the continued drought in Australia caused much distress and disturbance in fin-ancial and commercial matters. In his August letter to the Trade and Commerce Department Mr. Larke stated that Canadian butter was unknown there but that there was a profitable opening for it. The wheat harvest was going to be very poor and he asked for samples of Manitoba grain. But despite this and various public intimations he found no advantage taken in Canada of the demand. On November 4th he wrote of a profitable market for barley and peas, of opportunities for the sale of frozen hogs and poultry, of the openings for apples and potatoes. His letter of December 1st contained the following statement:

I have previously pointed out the possibilities of Canadian trade with Western Australia. There are yearly imported over thirty million dollars worth of goods and the bulk of the lines we have not yet touched. The imports from the United States amounted to three million dollars and were more than double those of the previous year. The direct ships from New York, with low freight rates, are the chief cause of this rapid expansion. With similar advantages Canada could have supplied flour, meals, oats, canned fruits and vegetables, bacon and hams, plaster and timber from the Eastern Provinces, besides general manufactures. Under the common tariff and its prosperous developments Western Australia is the most promising field for Canadian enterprise just now.

The imports of Canada from the Commonwealth and New Zealand in the fiscal year 1902 were only $157,237 and the exports (merchandise) $2,940,247. The latter included breadstuffs $235,-199; carriages, etc. $315,134; cotton and manufactures of, $492,-995; fish and products of, $199,336; metals, minerals and manufactures of, $852,185; wood and manufactures of, $438,376. It may be added that the total exports of Australia in 1896 were $277,956,000 and in 1900 $354,066,551 while the imports rose from $269,596,000 to $336,844,440.

Meanwhile various utterances had been made in the direction of encouraging trade between the Commonwealth and the Dominion. On February 26th, the Victoria Board of Trade reported through a special Committee that " we have been impressed by the fact that a very large business is carried on between the Australian and other Colonies and the United States; much of which might under a system of inter-Imperial trade be diverted to Canada." Frozen mutton might, they thought, replace the import of sheep in British Columbia from the United States and Australian butter replace that now bought in California. British Columbia timber, fish and iron should find a ready market in Australia. Canned salmon and frozen fresh fish might also be supplied. The members of the Committee were Messrs. C. H. Lugrin, D. R. Ker, A. G. McCandless, R. Seabrook, and the Hon. E. G. Prior.

On March 26th the correspondence connected with the Hon. Mr. Mulock's visit to Australia in 1901 was presented to Parliament. The Postmaster-General had apparently found strong evidence of a desire to promote closer trade relations with Canada and declared that the Australian Premier was particularly anxious in this connection. Sir Edmund Barton, during the summer of 1902 in London and later on during his visit to Canada certainly indicated that this was the case. Under date of February 10th Mr. D. H. Ross, a Canadian living at Sydney, N. S. W., wrote a long letter to Sir Richard Cartwright dealing with existing trade conditions. He stated that the new Commonwealth tariff was, as a whole, lower than the various preceding tariffs of the Colonies; that the Imperial feeling was very strong in Australia and might well be taken

17

advantage of by Canadian merchants; that a line of steamers running between Canada, Australia and South Africa was imperatively required and regularity of shipment essential; that the best lines of trade open to Canada were furniture, boots and shoes, agricultural implements, carriages and waggons, steel rails and fish plates.

During the year various prominent Australians visited Canada, including Chief Justice Sir F. M. Darley, of New South Wales, and the Prime Minister, Sir Edmund Barton.* On June 14th, the Hon. William Knox, M.P., and the Hon. Edward Miller, M.L.C., of Melbourne, were at Victoria and addressed the Board of Trade. To the Winnipeg *Telegram*, on June 18th, Mr. Knox stated that Canadian merchants and manufacturers were " gradually exploiting the markets of Australia and New Zealand," and were becoming more and more successful. Sir James Fairfax, of the Sydney *Herald*, and Sir John Forrest, the Commonwealth Minister of Defence, were not so sanguine upon this subject during their visits. To the Toronto *Star* of September 3rd the latter said : " Trade between Australia and Canada? Well, what have you got here that we haven't got? Wheat? Why, we raise some of the finest wheat you ever saw. Apples? Some of our apples are world-beaters. So it is with grapes and plums and peaches, pears and other kinds of fruits. We do not raise much corn in Western Australia, but in Queensland it is raised quite extensively."

On March 1st, 1902, Mr. James Cumming, Canadian Trade Commissioner in South Africa for some time, submitted a formal Report at Ottawa as to existing conditions. He told **Trade with** the Minister of Trade and Commerce that the great **South** difficulty was lack of direct transport. " American **Africa** exporters have bought Canadian goods and shipped by way of New York considerable quantities of our timber, lumber, doors, dressed lumber, ploughs, furniture, split peas, biscuits, etc. From Great Britain, our asbestos, bacon, canned salmon, cheese, agricultural implements, etc., are being shipped more or less." He described the demand for all kinds of lumber as enormous, and stated that the Americans were taking Canadian raw material, dressing it for this market and making large profits.

Amongst the products in which Canadians could find the best and most really profitable openings were Portland cement, furniture of all kinds, pianos and organs, agricultural implements, windmills, carriages and other vehicles, bicycles, harness, boots and shoes, wheat, biscuits and confectionery, butter (if sent in steamers with refrigerator cold storage), plants, and canned fruits. He added that, though protectionist in opinion, there was considerable feeling amongst the people in favour of a fiscal preference to Canadian goods and, in any case, there would be a sympathetic reception given to them.

Mr. James G. Jardine was appointed early in March as Commercial Agent for Canada in South Africa, with headquarters at

Cape Town, and, under date of June 12th, reported to the Minister from Durban, Natal, that there were many complaints as to American and German goods. "English merchants here stand by British manufacturers chiefly because their goods open up exactly as samples shown." Prices were, he stated, enormously high, and the demand in many lines which Canada could supply was growing steadily. Commercial travellers were badly needed and could be profitably sent from Canada. "South Africa is pre-eminently an importing country and must of necessity be for many years to come, and has an abundance of gold, diamonds and copper to pay for her purchases."

From Johannesburg, on August 25th, Mr. Jardine wrote that, with the proposed direct steamship service, a ready sale at high prices should be assumed for most of the products already mentioned as being wanted. As to the future, there would be demands for $130,000,000 worth of mining machinery, for much and varied agricultural machinery, for steel rails and sleepers, for passenger and flat cars. He thought Canada should share in these openings. In Johannesburg alone, he reported on October 10th, there would be $30,000,000 spent during the next few years on draining, water installation, electric tramways and buildings. English and American methods must be adopted, and he recommended resident Canadian agents at the chief centres.

It may be stated here that the trade of Cape Colony increased from $95,767,902 of imports in 1900 to $116,761,217 in 1901, and from $39,651,994 of exports to $52,916,595 in the same years. The imports from Great Britain in 1901 were $69,100,574, from Australasia $19,838,665, from the United States $9,350,263, from Germany $3,920,684, and from Canada $25,214. Most of the exports went to Great Britain and $6,399 to Canada. Animals, food, drinks and narcotics made up $35,243,052 of the imports, and textile fabrics, dress, etc., $24,653,769. The total imports of Natal in 1901 were $49,482,826, and the total exports $24,918,000. The chief imports of the two Colonies are included in the following figures:

Products.	Natal.	Cape Colony.
Ale, Beer, &c.	$324,831	$1,080,054
Agricultural Implements.	......	461,093
Apparel and Slops.	2,600,197	4,367,702
Butter.	......	1,655,684
Cabinet-ware.	606,284	......
Coal, Coke, &c.	......	1,788,986
Corn, Grain and Flour.	1,339,526	6,152,707
Haberdashery and Millinery.	3,108,316	7,109,786
Cotton Manufactures.	......	5,818,679
Hardware, Cutlery, &c.	1,363,975	4,394,497
Leather and manufactures of.	2,096,238	4,238,409
Machinery, &c.	1,713,932	2,619,936
Stores and Provisions.	7,427,920	5,735,877
Rail and Tramway materials.	......	2,912,632
Spirits.	826,569	2,244,092
Wood and Timber.	1,168,360	2,701,272
Woollen Manufactures	469,716	1,922,388

Meanwhile, Canadians had been watching trade as well as war developments in South Africa. In June the Guelph Board of Trade passed a strong Resolution in favour of Government action in promoting commercial interchange between the countries and on August 30th, the Toronto *Globe* published a long letter from Mr. A. F. McIntyre, K.C., of Cornwall, who in 1901 had visited the Cape. Wheat, flour and bacon, apples and pears, butter and cheese, poultry and eggs, boots and shoes, implements and furniture, were specially referred to by him as constituting a big possible demand on Canada if requirements of freight and speed and packing were properly met.

During the summer Sir William Mulock entered into arrangements in London for the starting of a direct steam service to South Africa and, on August 26th, a contract between the Imperial and Canadian Governments and the Elder-Dempster and Furness Lines was made public in Canada. The vessels were to be under the British flag, have cold storage accommodation and be furnished with electric light. The contract was for five years, the vessels were to also carry the mails, the rates were to be moderate and subject to approval by the Dominion Government, additional steamers were to be supplied if needed and the Canadian subsidy was to be £30,000. On September 18th, Sir William Mulock addressed the Canadian Manufacturers' Association in Toronto upon this subject and, later on, it was announced that the first steamer sailing under this arrangement, *The Ontarian*, had reached Cape Town on November 21st laden to the hatches with Canadian goods. On November 12th the Ottawa Board of Trade passed a warm Resolution of thanks to the Postmaster-General for his services to the country and the Empire in this regard and also in connection with his support of the Pacific Cable policy.

Canadian trade with the historic Islands of the West Indies hardly held its own during the past decade. In 1892 the exports from Canada were $3,546,559 and in 1902 they had **Canada and the British West Indies** decreased to $3,298,912, while the imports were, respectively, $4,092,287 and $2,173,835. Meanwhile, Canadian Agents in Trinidad, St. Kitts and Jamaica had done much vigorous work, and a total sum of about $1,000,000 had been expended by the Dominion in subsidies to steamers. Early in 1902 Mr. Robert Munro, President of the Canadian Manufacturers' Association, accompanied by its Assistant-Secretary, Mr. J. F. M. Stewart, visited Bermuda, St. Lucia, Antigua, St. Kitts, Dominica, Montserratt, St. Vincent, Barbadoes, Trinidad, British Guiana, Turks' Island and Jamaica (islands with a total area of 116,299 square miles and a total population of 1,563,212), and prepared an exhaustive Report, which was made public in *Industrial Canada* for June.

In nearly every important line of product the United States was found to be Canada's chief competitor. Bermuda showed this in the relative imports from the two countries of box material, butter, cheese, flour and lumber; Barbadoes in its bacon, biscuits, flour and fish imports; Trinidad in its fish, flour, meat and timber imports; British Guiana in its imports of flour, oats, lumber and boots and shoes; Jamaica in its imports of butter, flour, biscuits and boots and shoes. The conclusions come to were that sentiment would help Canadian trade considerably if it were given a chance; that the boats of the Pickford and Black Line had done good service, but were not sufficiently swift to permit of meeting United States competition; that the matter of freight rates should be carefully inquired into; that the steam service to Jamaica was little more than a name, and that even the addition of the new three weeks' service from St. John would be unsatisfactory, the boats being small and the rates in excess of those from New York; that the Association should appoint special representatives in Bermuda, Trinidad, Jamaica and Demerara; that more care should be taken in packing goods and greater rapidity in filling orders.

Meanwhile, on April 30th, Mr. G. Eustace Burke, the Canadian Agent in Jamaica, referred, in his report to Ottawa, to the inauguration of the Canada-Jamaica Steamship Service between St. John, N.B., and Jamaica. He said it had made a plucky and energetic beginning, and hoped for permanent good to trade from its operations. He reported that the Reciprocity Convention with the United States had not been ratified by Congress and was "all but dead." Of the Island's imports—according to customs returns—the United Kingdom sent 45 per cent., the United States 43 per cent., and Canada 8 per cent. On May 13th he quoted from the Report of a Committee which had met the recent Canadian visitors and which asked why bananas could not be given a Canadian preference. Out of 600,000 bunches consumed in a year in the Dominion only 12,600 had come from Jamaica. So with oranges, coffee and unrefined sugar. On the other hand the Island imported 148,816 barrels of flour annually, of which only 15 barrels came from Canada. Transportation facilities of a direct and efficient character were urged as the only solution of the matter.

In his Report to the Canadian Government of conditions at Trinidad and Tobago, Mr. Edgar Tripp, on June 6th, pointed out that those Islands took $155,241 worth of flour from the United States and $12,726 from Canada, and other things in proportion. Canadian products were, however, gaining ground. In sugar, asphalt and cocoa there was ample room for larger imports by Canada from Trinidad. Meanwhile, there was a good deal of talk in different Islands of the West Indian group as to closer political relations with Canada helping in the other matter of commercial expansion, and, on September 6th, a representative meeting of planters in Jamaica passed Resolutions deploring the condition of the sugar industry and demanding federation with the Dominion as a means of retrieving the situation. There were other evidences during the year of a growth of feeling in this connection, and the visit of Messrs. Munro and Stewart did something to help it as well as to advance trade and give information about Canada. It may be added that in 1902

Canada sent to the British West Indies $250,128 worth of grain, $136,279 of flour, $969,328 of fish and their products, $100,784 of provisions and $172,816 of wood and wood manufactures. The chief import from there was sugar and molasses to the value of $1,189,879.

Though part of Canada, the Yukon Territory is so separated by conditions and distance from the other Provinces that its commercial interests have a separate concern and bearing and are generally discussed from that standpoint. By the joint freight tariff issued on April 12th, and arranged between the White Pass and Yukon transportation interests and the Alaska Steamship Association, rates were lowered to the Yukon from 20 to 33 1/3 per cent. and a pronounced step was taken in promoting trade with Canadian Pacific ports and business houses. On March 21st Mr. F. C. Wade, K.C., lately Crown Prosecutor in the Territory, lectured before the Canadian Club, Toronto, and dealt at some length with Canadian trade interests there and the successful competition of Americans in obtaining business. In flour, bacon, tea, preserves, butter, cheese, canned goods, rubber goods, miners' boots, shovels, picks, and steel candlesticks, there was room, he declared, for an ample increase in supplies from other parts of Canada in place of their being obtained from United States outfitters in Seattle.

Trade with the Yukon

Other reports during the year indicated, however, that this condition was changing and that Canadians had acquired control of two-thirds of the trade. This was the statement of Mr. George Anderson who, during the summer visited the Yukon as a special Trade Commissioner appointed by the Dominion Government. He gave the figures of Canadian goods landed in Skaguay and forwarded during the 12 months from June 30th, 1901, to June 30th, 1902, as $3,109,187 and the Foreign goods as $1,192,361. He analyzed this trade carefully and described the following articles as being chiefly purchased from the United States—beer and ale, butter, boots and shoes (about half the supply), ready-made clothing, candles, doors and sashes (about half the supply), eggs, felt boots and shoes, iron pipe, frozen poultry, oats, oils, potatoes, rope, rubber boots, sugar, hams and bacon, and tobacco. In nearly all these lines he thought Canadians could capture the market if they tried.

About the same time that Mr. Anderson was in the Yukon Mr. S. Morley Wickett, Ph.D., visited it on behalf of the Canadian Manufacturers' Association. He prepared an exhaustive Report which was published in the October *Industrial Canada*. His opinion as to trade conditions was that a fair estimate would be the crediting of 60 per cent. of the imported goods to Canada. In the following lines he thought there was room for a profitable increase —mining machinery and boilers; waggons, carriages and sleighs; candles, soap and lubricating oils; electric apparatus and rubber boots; ready-made clothing and woollen under-clothing; hams, bacon, poultry and games ; canned meats, lard, butter, eggs and beer. The best quality in commodities and great care in packing and shipment were, however, required.

Canadian trade relations with the United States continued of an important character during 1902—the most so after those with the Empire.* There was a total increase in the inter-**Trade with** change of merchandise between the countries of some **the United** nine millions in the two years, 1901 and 1902. But **States** United States trade in general did not increase. From the countries of the British Empire its imports in the fiscal year 1901 were $258,463,917 and in 1902 they had risen to $290,632,142. The exports to British countries, however, decreased from $820,552,307 to $745,865,355. From other countries its imports were $564,209,-099 in 1901 and $612,694,929 in 1902 ; while its exports to those countries decreased from $667,203,250 to $635,854,046. The increase in the total imports was therefore $80,000,000 and the decrease in the exports $106,000,000—a total net decrease in trade of $26,000,000. The chief items in the trade of Canada with the United States in 1902 may be seen in the following table :

Exports to United States.

Animals (living)........	$2,535,493
Grain, Flour, etc,, ...	651,181
Coal and Charcoal.......	4,564,433
Drugs, Dyes, etc........	747,415
Fish and Fish Products...	4,146,803
Furs and Manufactures of.	683,241
Hay....................	504,247
Hides, Skins, etc........	1,701,442
Copper.................	2,649,650
Gold Quartz, etc.........	19,677,074
Silver Ore.............	2,055,428
Iron, Steel and Manufactures of..............	2,460,528
Other Metals and Minerals	2,901,427
Seeds..................	370,306
Settlers' Effects..........	1,502,265
Stone and Manufactures of	593,695
Vegetables.............	594,535
Wood and Manufactures of	16,723,229

Imports from United States.

Animals (living).........	$1,832,777
Books, Pamphlets, etc....	1,184,098
Wheat.................	7,217,137
Other Grains...........	3,186,752
Carriages..	1,356,891
Cordage, Rope and Twine.	1,683,772
Cement	588,510
Coal, Coke, etc..........	13,956,842

Cotton and Manufactures of	$7,651,447
Flax, Hemp, Jute, etc....	745,500
Drugs, Dyes, etc.	3,041,991
Electric Apparatus.......	1,350,505
Fancy Goods............	389,990
Fish and Fish Products. ..	486,298
Fruits (dried)...........	766,133
Fruits (green)...........	1,924,176
Furs and Manufactures of..	1,179,318
Glass and Manufactures of	523,820
Gutta-Percha and India Rubber...............	2,153,423
Jewellery................	519,403
Copper and Manufactures of	1,255,224
Leather and Manufactures of....................	1,466,382
Hides and Skins..........	2,174,764
Brass and Manufactures of	944,052
Agricultural Implements..	2,634,384
Other Iron and Steel Manufactures...............	22,353,043
Oils....................	1,865,732
Tin and Manufactures of..	494,742
Paints and Colours.	560,461
Paper and Manufactures of	1,473,666
Provisions...............	2,466,281
Sugar, Molasses, etc......	915,063
Wood and Manufactures of	5,656,270
Settlers' Effects..........	3,751,363
Seeds, etc...............	1,748,580
Tobacco	2,005,153

The imports into Canada from the United States increased from $119,306,775 in 1901 to $129,794,147 in 1902. Of this increase

---

* Note.—Various statistics in this connection will also be found on Pages 179-81 in connection with the Reciprocity Question.

$6,099,439 was in dutiable goods and $4,387,933 in free goods. In 1902 the total import of dutiable goods from the Republic was $68,922,500 and of free goods $60,871,647. Meanwhile, the total exports to the United States from Canada had slightly decreased, from $72,382,230 in 1901 to $71,197,684 in 1902.

The trade of the Dominion with Germany is a growing one. In 1892 the exports to that country were $942,698 and in 1902 they were $2,692,578 while the imports rose from $5,583,-

Canadian Trade with Germany 530 to $10,823,169. The chief items of the Canadian import list from Germany in the fiscal year 1902, were as follows:

Cotton and Manufactures of	$243,819	Metals and Minerals and	
Drugs, Dyes, etc........	360,484	Manufactures of........	$2,055,798
Earthenware, etc........	202,482	Paints and Colours.	233,334
Fancy Goods............	392,363	Silk and Manufactures of.	363,126
Furs and Manufactures of.	800,684	Sugar, Molasses, etc......	3,655,570
Glass and Manufactures of	300,425	Wool and Manufactures of	884,016

The total of dutiable goods imported was $9,175,383 and of free goods (merchandise only) $1,744,611. In the exports to Germany there were only three large items—breadstuffs $1,046,506, metals, minerals, etc., $565,295 and seeds $729,879. During the year there was more or less discussion of Germany's action in placing Canada under its maximum tariff on account of the Preference to Great Britain. On March 6th the subject was discussed in the House of Commons on a motion by Mr. F. D. Monk asking for correspondence between the Governments concerned. The Premier replied that informal negotiations were still proceeding and that the papers could not be produced. The motion was voted down by 51 majority. The subject was dealt with in its May number by *Industrial Canada* and the conclusion stated that "the German maximum tariff is of narrow significance to Canadian manufacturers for it affects only three or four lines of manufactured goods and most of them very slightly." American competition, it was added, was the danger-point in Germany and, with very similar goods they had so far badly beaten Canadian manufacturers in that market. It was very different with grains, wood, lumber, timber, provisions and animals. Here, it was pointed out, the discrimination between the maximum and treaty tariff—the United States being under the latter—was very marked and averaged a third higher in the maxi mum rate.

X.—MINERAL RESOURCES AND PRODUCTION

The total production of Minerals in Canada in the fiscal year 1901 was $66,712,708 and in 1902 it was $64,970,732.* The Mineral exports, according to the Report of the Trade and Commerce Department, were $24,580,266 in 1900, $40,367,683 in 1901, and $34,947,574 in 1902. Of the last total coal constituted $4,867,088, of which nearly the whole went to the United States; copper and copper ore $2,990,312,of which the most went to the same market; asbestus $1,131,202, of which two-thirds went to the United States ; gypsum $273,335, lead $889,318, mica $242,310, nickel $834,513, of which the bulk went to the Republic; gold $19,668,015 and silver $2,055,428, of which the whole went to the United States ; and a miscellaneous mineral total of $2,000,000, which was also exported to the Republic. The production of Minerals in the fiscal years 1901 and 1902 were respectively as follows :

The Mineral Production of Canada

METALLIC.

Product.	Value, 1901.	Value, 1902.
Copper	$6,096,581	$4,553,695
Gold	24,128,503	20,741,245
Iron ore (exports)	762,284	1,065,019
Pig Iron from Canadian ore	1,212,113	1,043,011
Lead	2,249,387	935,870
Nickel	4,594,523	5,025,903
Silver	3,265,354	2,280,957
Zinc	....	8,068
Miscellaneous	457	....
Total	$42,309,202	$35,653,768

NON-METALLIC.

Arsenic	$41,676	$48,000
Asbestus and asbestic	1,259,759	1,203,452
Coal	12,006,565	15,538,611
Coke	1,228,225	1,538,930
Corundum	53,115	84,468
Graphite	38,780	28,300
Grindstones	45,690	48,400
Gypsum	340,148	356,317
Limestone for flux	183,162	218,809
Mica	160,000	400,000
Mineral Water	100,000	100,000
Natural Gas	339,476	195,992
Petroleum	1,008,275	934,740
Pyrites	130,544	138,939
Salt	262,328	288,581
Miscellaneous	107,502	121,555
	$17,304,245	$21,245,094

NOTE.—Official figures "subject to revision" but constituting "a very close approximation " to the final returns.

265

STRUCTURAL MATERIALS AND CLAY PRODUCTS.

Cement, natural rock..............	$94,415	$91,870
Cement, Portland................	565,615	1,028,618
Granite.........................	155,000	170,000
Pottery.........................	200,000	200,000
Sands and gravels (exports)........	117,465	119,120
Sewer pipe......................	248,115	294,465
Slate...........................	9,980	19,200
Terra-cotta, pressed brick, etc......	278,671	348,597
Building material, including bricks, building stone, lime, tiles, etc....	5,130,000	5,500,000
Total structural material and clay products...............	$6,799,261	$7,771,870
Total all other non-metallic....	17,304,245	21,245,094
Total non-metallic............	$24,103,506	$29,016,964
Total metallic................	42,309,202	35,653,768
Estimated value of mineral products not returned..................	300,000	300,000
Total Minerals	$66,712,708	$64,970,732

In reporting these summaries, Mr. Elfric Drew Ingall, of the Geological Survey Department, pointed out in 1901 that, leaving the Yukon out of consideration, the permanent metal mining industries of the country showed an increase of nearly 37 per cent. despite a reduction of over 20 per cent, in the value of lead production. In 1902 he stated that the falling-off in production amounted to 2·61 per cent. and was due not only to the decrease in the Yukon output but also to the lower values of metallic minerals, outside of nickel. As to the distribution of Minerals, in the chief items of production, gold in 1901 was 36·17 per cent. of the whole, and in 1902 it was 31·92 per cent. Coal rose during the same years from 17·99 per cent. to 23·92 per cent. There were no other marked changes. Canada, it may be added, imported in 1902 1,652,451 tons of anthracite coal (free), valued at $7,021,939, and 3,247,256 tons of bituminous coal (dutiable), valued at $6,020,129.*

In this connection there occurred the most marked industrial development of 1901 and 1902 in the Dominion of Canada. During

Canadia.ı
Iron
Resources

170 years the iron and steel industry had maintained a fluctuating and feeble existence in Canada, largely because it was not believed that iron ore and coal were anywhere in juxtaposition. In a Report to the American Government, which was made public on June 17th, 1902, the United States Consul-General at Montreal, Mr. John L. Bittinger, made the following statement: "A country that has vast deposits of iron ore has a solid foundation for commercial ascendency. Few countries have more iron ore than the Dominion of Canada. It has also coal, and the immense value of these deposits has only been fully appreciated within the last few years." He proceeded to describe the ore bed of British Columbia, of Northern Ontario, and of the islands in Hudson's Bay, off the coast of Ungava

as all being contiguous to coal beds, and declared that the Canadian Iron Furnace Company and the Cramp-Ontario Steel Company obtained their coal at a freight of $1.97 per ton, which was $1.28 lower than the Pittsburg standard, while at Sydney the Dominion Iron and Steel Company saved $2.45 per ton on pig-iron as compared with Pittsburg, and $2.00 a ton on freight for export. In the May number of *Industrial Canada*, the organ of the Canadian Manufacturers' Association, these facts were also accentuated. " Investigation has shown that in all the four districts of Canada that can boast of iron ore supplies the assemblage of the raw materials for iron and steel furnaces can be made at a lower cost than at Pittsburg, the cheapest centre in the United States."

These four divisions of iron ore territory include the region in British Columbia marked by the Crow's Nest coal developments ; the large and pure beds of iron ore on the northern shore of Lake Superior illustrated by the Helen Mine, now being worked by Mr. F. H. Clergue ; another Ontario section of great promise which can draw its coal from the Canadian Lake region or the Connelsville district in the United States ; and the iron beds of Nova Scotia in close proximity to immense quantities of coal which have been estimated as showing 220,000,000 tons in sight. Great Britain sells about this much per annum, yet Nova Scotia, with billions of tons of coal under its soil, has only had a total output so far of 55,000,-000 tons. The Helen Iron Mine is in the same range as the famous ore beds of Michigan and Minnesota, and is said to assay 58 per cent. of pure iron, with an estimated production in sight of 30,000,-000 tons of ore. Within 35 miles of this mine, and all in the Michipicoton Range, are other undeveloped properties of great mineral wealth, from which the Clergue Companies expect to ship 3,000,000 tons of iron a year before very long. To quote once more from *Industrial Canada :* " Our opportunities to supply both export and domestic trade are unparalleled, for have we not ore on both the east and west coasts for Foreign lands and on lake coasts, in the centre of the Continent, for our home trade. What more can we ask for ? If Canada does not become a greater producer of iron and steel it will be because Canadians have neither the energy nor the capital to develop their resources. But they are now recognizing their opportunity and are grasping it."

Steady progress was shown in the development of the Mining interests of Ontario during 1901-2. On March 4th of the latter year the official Report of the Bureau of Mines, prepared by

Ontario Mines and Minerals Mr. Thomas W. Gibson, Director, was submitted to the Lieutenant-Governor, and was made public in August following. The production of the four years preceding the 1st of January, 1902, was as follows :

Year	Total Production of Minerals	Metallic Output	Per cent.	Non-Metallic Output	Per cent.
1898	$7,235,877	$1,689,002	23	$5,546,875	77
1899	8,416,673	2,055,492	24	6,361,081	76
1900	9,298,624	2,565,286	28	6,733,338	72
1901	11,831,086	5,016,734	42	6,814,352	58

In 1901, therefore, the total production showed an increase of $4,595,209 in value over that of 1898, or 63 per cent.; while the metallic products increased by $3,327,732, or 191 per cent. Of this latter output in 1901, copper contributed 11 per cent., nickel 37, and pig-iron 33 per cent. Gold, silver, iron ore and steel were small in comparison. During the year under consideration the mining business maintained its position in the formation of joint stock companies under Provincial charters. The number of such concerns incorporated was 47, with a nominal capital of $27,716,000, while 13 companies of foreign origin took out licenses to sell stock and hold real estate in the Province, with a nominal capital of $12,-250,000—a total of 60 companies and aggregate nominal capital of $39,966,000, as compared with 57 companies and a total capital of $42,403,999 in 1900. Upon this point Mr. Gibson made the following comment : " It is a somewhat remarkable fact that metalliferous mining in this Province is almost wholly carried on by companies whose share capital is in the hands of people living in Great Britain or the United States. In nickel and copper this is true without exception ; in gold it is all but true, and so also in iron. There is no objection whatever to English and American capital finding employment in our mining industry ; on the contrary capital is the industry's crying need, and is made heartily welcome from whatever source it comes—neither sentiment nor the laws of the country discriminating between funds of home and foreign origin. But in this, the formative stage of the business, it is matter for regret that the people of Ontario invest so little money in legitimate mining enterprises in their own Province, and are allowing the control of what promises to be one of the most important factors in the country's development to pass into the hands of others." The following table shows the Mineral production and industrial accompaniments in 1901 :

Product.	Value.	Employees.	Wages.
Gold	$ 244,443	585	$ 287,409
Silver	84,830	65	29,500
Copper	589,080		
Nickel	1,859,970	2,284	1,045,889
Iron Ore	174,428	360	231,039
Pig-iron	1,701,703		
Steel	347,280	580	274,554
Zinc Ore	15,000	10	6,287
Total Metallic	$5,016,734	3,884	$1,874,678
Tile, Drain	$ 251,374		
Brick, Common	1,530,460	3,318	752,184
Brick, Paving	37,000	40	20,000
Brick, Pressed	104,394	172	45,816
Building Stone	850,000	1,800	600,000
Carbide of Calcium	168,792	83	40,788
Cement, Natural Rock	107,625	89	35,460
Cement, Portland	563,255	460	190,536
Corundum	53,115	68	30,406
Lime	550,000	775	210,000
Mica	39,780	83	6,280

Product.	Value.	Employees.	Wages.
Natural Gas...	$ 342,183	129	$ 59,140
Pottery..................	193,950	213	81,720
Petroleum	1,467,940	351	161,042
Salt......................	323,058	189	67,024
Sewer Pipe..............	147,948	81	33,096
Miscellaneous...........	103,478	100	24,984
Total Non-Metallic........	$6,814,352	7,951	$2,358,476
Add Metallic.............	5,016,734	3,884	1,874,678
	$11,831,086	11,835	$4,233,154

There was a slight decrease during the year in the production of gold and a marked increase in that of nickel—25 per cent. in quantity and 145 per cent. in value. In 1897 the latter product was valued at $359,651 and in 1901 it was over five times as much. The bulk of the nickel-copper business at Sudbury had been done by the Canadian Copper Company and, early in 1902, a consolidation of the interests of that concern with other properties in Ontario and New Caledonia and with refining works in the United States was effected into the International Nickel Company with $12,000,000 common, $12,000,000 preferred stock, and $10,000,000 worth of bonds.* The production of iron ore was three times that of the preceding year and the shipments from the Helen Mine alone totalled 258,755 tons. Yet Ontario iron mines were handicapped by the long land haul to the smelting plants and by the United States duty of 40 cents a ton. Stone, lime and brick showed a marked advance of $340,000 in value. In cements there was a slight decrease and petroleum showed over $400,000 of a decrease.

The Report of the Ontario Bureau of Mines for 1902 showed a production for that year of $13,577,440 or an increase of $1,746,354 in value. There was a gain of 19 per cent. over 1901. The metallic products were $6,285,259 and the non-metallic $7,292,181. There was marked development in the nickel industry, in the production of iron ore, and in the steel and cement industries. The following figures illustrate the condition of production :

	1902.	Increase.
Copper..	$ 686,043	$ 96,963
Iron Ore	518,445	344,017
Nickel.......................	2,210,961	350,991
Steel........................	1,610,031	1,262,751
Stone.	1,020,000	170,000
Cement.......................	967,010	296,136
Lime.........................	617,000	67,000
Petroleum Products............	1,600,000	132,060

	1902.	Decrease.
Gold........................	229,828	14,615
Carbide of Calcium............	89,420	79,372
Brick, common................	1,411,000	119,460
Natural Gas..................	189,238	152,945
Tile, Drain	199,000	32,374
Mica.	101,600	61,820

* The *Engineering and Mining Journal*, New York, April 5th, 1902.

On February 11th, 1902, the Hon. J. H. Turner, Agent-General for British Columbia, addressed the Royal Colonial Institute in
London, and dealt at length with the great Mineral
Mines and Mining in British Columbia　resources of his Province. " It is known that nearly the whole of Kootenay and a great part of Yale, Lillooet and the Cariboo District are practically all rich in minerals, and that these territories alone contain some millions of acres. But following up the mountain ranges to the extreme north, some 600 miles, you still find minerals in paying quantities all the way, and Cassiar, Omenica and Atlin Districts are now attracting much attention in the far northern part of the Province." He referred to the vast unexplored regions of the Mainland and to the coal mines in Vancouver Island, which produced the best coal mined on the shores of the Pacific, shipped a million and a half tons annually and supported the beautiful towns of Ladysmith and Nanaimo. Then followed a reference to recent developments :

On the Mainland the enormous coal deposits at Crow's Nest Pass were only opened about three years since ; this coal produces the finest quality of coke and is so accessible to the smelters of Southern British Columbia that it is supplied at about $8 or $9 per ton, whereas they were paying $16 to $17 until the Crow's Nest ovens were started. The out-turn of this mine was about 1,000 tons a day last year, and is now, I am informed, 2,000 ; and in a year or two, on completion of a short railway now building, will reach 5,000 tons a day. A competent local manager states that the mine is capable of turning out 15,000 tons a day. There are other deposits at Similkameen, Nicola and Kamloops, on the Mainland, and a very large field of fine quality on Queen Charlotte Island, on the route of steamers to Alaska, but none of these are being developed. There is also in the Province an abundance of fine granite, marble limestone and building stones of various kinds.

The total mineral production of British Columbia up to and including 1901 was $172,241,988. To this general total, placer gold mining contributed $63,554,543 and coal $52,652,930. In 1898 the production was $10,906,861, in 1899 $12,393,131, in 1900 $16,344,-751, and in 1901 $20,086,780. The increase in production in 1898 was $4\frac{1}{3}$ per cent. ; in 1899, $13\frac{2}{3}$ per cent. ; in 1900, $31\frac{1}{4}$ per cent. ; and in 1901 23 per cent—a fairly steady ratio. Of the coal produced in the Province during 1901, 413,705 tons were sold for consumption in Canada, 895,197 for use in the United States, and 18,966 in other countries. Of coke, 80,154 tons were sold in Canada and 47,379 tons went to the United States. As in coal, so it was with gold, the output of 1901 was the greatest on record. The percentage of increase over 1900 in the latter product was $11\frac{4}{5}$. So it was in silver and copper, the latter increasing its product by 175 per cent. The annual Report of Mr. W. F. Robertson, Provincial Mineralogist, for the year ending December 31st, 1901, gave the following table of production :

Product.	1900.	1901.
Gold, placer........................	$1,278,724	$ 970,100
Gold, lode.........................	3,453,381	4,348,603
Silver.............................	2,309,200	2,884,745
Copper............................	1,615,289	4,446,963
Lead.............................	2,691,887	2,002,733
Coal..............................	4,318,785	4,380,993
Coke..............................	425,745	635,405
Other Minerals	251,740	417,238
Total......................	$16,344,751	$20,086,780

In his Report Mr. Robertson stated the number of mines shipping ore in 1901 as being 119, of which 78 shipped over 100 tons each. The number of men employed by them was 3,948. Excluding Yukon Territory, British Columbia produced in that year 82 per cent. of the silver, 67 per cent. of the copper and 96 per cent. of the lead produced in the Dominion. Conditions were described as unsatisfactory during the year in the Atlin District, because of friction between individual miners and large hydraulic companies. In East Kootenay the chief advance was in Crow's Nest Collieries. The Slocan and other districts had suffered from the silver-lead situation. Yale, the Boundary, and the Trail or Rossland districts were said to be fairly satisfactory in general developments.

Speaking to the Nelson *Miner*, on August 5th, Mr. J. J. Hill, the American railway magnate, used the following language as to one great mineral interest of the Province : " We have been waiting a long time to see if the Rossland Camp would prove permanent. We are now satisfied, in view of the showing of the *Le Roi* and other mines, that the camp is permanent, and are prepared to take the matter up in detail with a view to doing everything possible in our power to enable the mines to utilize the great deposits of low grade ore that we are satisfied they contain." On September 10th Mr. Edmund B. Kirby addressed a meeting of the Canadian Mining Institute at Nelson and gave an estimate of the value of Provincial industries as $27,000,000, divided as follows :

Industry.	Probable Annual Production.	Per Cent.
Metal Mining	$15,070,382	55·1
Coal Mining.........................	5,016,398	18·3
Fisheries	3,065,900	11·2
Lumbering	1,690,000	6·2
Agricultural and Miscellaneous	2,520,000	9·2
	$27,362,680	100·

He claimed that the actual taxes of every kind were 20 per cent. of everything produced while the taxation on the mining industry was probably 30 per cent. of its product. The Governments were doing much to injure this great industry ; they could yet do much to help it. In the Nelson *News* of October 1st, Mr. Nicolai C. Schou of Vancouver, undertook to correct Mr. Kirby's figures and gave his estimate as $20,100,000 for Mining, $7,300,000 for Fisheries, $4,500,000 for Lumbering, $8,060,000 for Agriculture and $9,000,000 for Miscellaneous Industries—a total of $48,960,000.

A meeting was held at Rossland on November 27th which, after addresses from Mr. C. V. Jenkins and Mr. Smith Curtis, M.P.P., passed a long Resolution asking for a Dominion bonus of $7.50 a ton on metallic lead and zinc, the diversion of the refined lead bounty to the producer of the lead ore, the modification of the duties on mining machinery and supplies and the imposition of revenue duties on lead and zinc and their products. A few days before, on November 21st, Messrs. William Thompson and Smith Curtis had addressed the Rossland Liberal Association along the same lines and the latter's speech was widely commented on. Interviewed by the Vancouver *World* on December 13th Mr. C. H. Mackintosh, ex-M.P., of Rossland, expressed the following opinions :

> The reduced cost of treatment at the smelters will be an enormous factor in the development of the country contiguous to Rossland. Four years ago the smelting charges at the Northport smelter were $8.50 per ton, while now the same class of ore is being treated for $3.75 and as soon as the amount of coke that is required can be obtained the cost will be reduced to $3. There are a dozen mines in Rossland that can produce any amount of $8 to $11 ore, and many of the ores are self-fluxing. I believe that there are great probabilities for the construction of a customs smelter at Rossland for the treatment of these immense deposits of ore.

Official statistics in the early stages of production and in a country like the Klondike are necessarily incomplete but they none-the-less afford, in this case, a vivid picture of progress. In 1897 the mines of the Yukon produced $2,500,000 worth of gold; $10,000,000 in 1898; $16,000,000 in 1899; $22,275,000 in 1900 ; and $18,000,000 in 1901. The total product, since statistics were kept in the matter, was therefore $70,313,513. Speaking to the Montreal *Star* on March 31st, 1902, Commissioner J. H. Ross stated that the production for the current year would be very much the same, as far as could be estimated, as in 1901 :

Mines and Mining in the Yukon

> That is to say between $15,000,000 and $17,000,000. Of this there is no reason why at least $13,000,000 should not find its way into Canadian banks. Last year the Canadian Bank of Commerce alone received $8,000,000. There is not any doubt now that the Yukon has proved a valuable asset to the Dominion for in the past year a surplus of $750,000 was obtained. I really believe that quite as many fortunes have been made in Dawson as out in the mines. Merchants and real estate men have, of course, made the most. Men are obtaining, in yearly rentals, as much as they paid for their properties. Then, the population is increasing rapidly.

According to advices received by the Victoria, B.C., *Times* on November 28th, following, the actual value of the Yukon output in 1902 did not much exceed $12,000,000. The " season " was from May 1st to November 1st and during that time the valuation of the gold exported and upon which the Government collected royalty, was $11,945,299. Instead of $15 for each ounce, however, at which the Government rated the gold, the public value was placed at $16, which would have made the export $12,741,000. In his annual Report to the Minister of the Interior, Commissioner Ross on June 30th had, meanwhile, described the progress of the Territory as "very satisfactory." Great development had taken place in quartz mining but it was still too soon to say "whether the vast deposits of quartz and conglomerate can be worked at a profit." He seemed, however, to be hopeful of the final result. Hydraulic mining was stated to have a great future before it though the initial expenses would be heavy. Coal mines had been found—two of them easily accessible from Dawson. As to general conditions Mr. Ross wrote as follows:

For a short time the production of gold may decrease, but this will be succeeded by a period of greater development, until the production of the country is placed upon a permanent basis when the Yukon will cease to be an ephemeral placer-mining camp, and become a steady producer of minerals. The reason for the above statement is that the methods of mining are changing. Experiment has shown that by the introduction of improved machinery great savings can be made in the working of claims, and large owners are investing heavily in plants which will revolutionize the mining industry of this country. Instead of the pick and shovel being the chief implement of labour, we now have the steam shovel and the dredge, which can handle vast amounts of dirt at an expense far below the old methods, rendering of immense value large tracts of country which before could not be worked at all. It will take considerable time before this change can be generally introduced, and many rich claims will remain practically unworked until the owners can introduce these improved methods.

Meanwhile various matters had occurred of import to Yukon mining interests. In February considerable excitement was created by the Treadgold Concession matter. Through an arrangement of December 7th, 1901, it was understood that the Dominion Government had given to a British Syndicate, represented by Mr. A. N. C. Treadgold, titles in fee to all lapsed claims on the Hunker, Bear, Bonanza and Eldorado Creeks. Local misapprehension as to the creation of a great mining monopoly was increased from American sources, and highly coloured despatches were sent out to the press of Canada and the United States. At Ottawa, on February 18th, the Hon. R. W. Scott, who was acting for Mr. Sifton, declared that there was nothing to cause alarm. The main object of the grant was the utilization of sections of mining lands not at present accessible owing to their situation above water level. There was, he said, no monopoly, and the miners were fully protected. A mass meeting, however, was held at Dawson, presided over by Mayor Macaulay, which entered a vigorous protest in the matter, and on February 14th the local Liberal Club wired Commissioner Ross, who was on his way to Ottawa, asking him to protect Yukon interests and to have certain obnoxious clauses cancelled. Some amendments in Council had meanwhile been made, and on February 20th Mr. Ross dealt with the subject in the Vancouver *Province* as follows:

Owing to the fact that there are many claims on creeks in the Klondike region which cannot be successfully worked at present on account of poor water

18

supply, the owners can but await the time when some powerful financial corporation or syndicate provides a generous water supply. That is what the Treadgold Syndicate have contracted with the Government to do, and in return for their cash outlay the Government will allow them to work inaccessible bench claims, the titles to which have lapsed or which the owners do not care to work. Owners of claims have the privilege of working their properties with the aid of the Treadgold water, for which they must pay a reasonable sum to the Syndicate, the amount being set by the Government, so that no imposition on the part of the Syndicate will take place. That is the question as I understand it, and such being the case the Concession cannot but be a source of great benefit to the whole region.

Following upon the visit of Mr. Ross to Ottawa the Concession was, however, reconsidered, and a new Order-in-Council adopted, in which the privileges were very much restricted in scope and limit of time. With the beginning of the season of 1902 the new royalty of $2\frac{1}{2}$ per cent. replaced the old one of 5 per cent., and new methods of collection were also adopted. Meantime the Commissioner of the Yukon had not been the only visitor to the East. Mr. F. C. Wade, K.C., formerly Crown Prosecutor, delivered a number of addresses on mining matters in the Territory, beginning with one at the Canadian Institute, Toronto, on February 10th. On February 22nd he spoke at Toronto University on the same subject and described the procession of gold areas and mining camps through British Columbia and into the Klondike and thence into Alaska. He was most optimistic in both addresses as to the future of quartz mining in that country. On March 21st Mr. Wade delivered an elaborate lecture before the Canadian Club, Toronto, and spoke of the Yukon Territory as having an area of 198,000 miles, of which the Klondike only included 800 miles. He then proceeded as follows :

The mileage of creeks actually operated in the Yukon does not go over fifty miles. Professor McConnell, Mr. Miers and others who have visited the country agree that there is no reason for imagining that the gold area will not extend to almost all the creeks in the Yukon, and when I tell you that only fifty miles have been worked and that there are seven thousand miles of creeks in the Yukon, almost all of which are unprospected, you can have some idea of the future which lies before that country.

In London, England, early in June, Mr. Wade gave a lengthy interview to *The Commerce* upon the development of this region. He described the Americans as getting the plums in the progress indicated, and urged British investment in what he believed to be great resources of gold quartz mining. A very different view of matters was given by Mr. George H. Hees, of Toronto, who paid a visit to the country during the early summer, and reported in *Industrial Canada* for August that, despite the work of thousands of prospectors, no new gold discovery of importance had been made for a year, while the old creeks were being gradually worked out and the total production was steadily declining. "The hope of the Klondike now is in the discovery of gold-bearing quartz of sufficient richness to pay to work. So far no such quartz has been discovered." This statement created considerable comment. To the Manitoba *Free Press* of August 11th Mr. F. C. Wade stated that Mr. R. G. McConnell, of the Geological Survey, was authority for the belief that placer gold might be discovered over many of the large creek areas yet remaining unworked; that he himself considered much of the prospecting referred to by Mr. Hees as entirely unreliable; that the local confidence of miners and public alike controverted these pessimistic views:

When one finds men of as wide business as any on the continent, and hundreds of intelligent and competent mining men all over the gold-producing districts bringing in boilers and machinery to such an extent that for months the streets are obstructed by them, and hastening to erect plants upon their claims; when steady, calculated business methods supersede the former make-shift ways; when mine owner after mine owner declares that already in sight is dust to occupy years in working; and when it is recognized that although Eldorados are not struck every day, or more than once in a lifetime, yet daily there are being disclosed enormous tracts of good paying ground; and when in addition there is every indication and prospect of early development of quartz mining, it is not difficult to find justification for the wealth which is found here, wherever one turns, in the resources of the country.

Speaking to the Toronto *Mail* of August 12th, Judge C. D. Macaulay of Dawson, said: " I agree with Mr. Wade that the Yukon country is only on the eve of development and I cannot but consider that Mr. Hees' impressions are entirely erroneous." He was, however, uncertain as to the permanent paying value of the gold quartz discoveries and declared that time and experience could alone prove the point. In the same paper four days later Mr. H. D. Hulme of Dawson, expressed agreement with Judge Macaulay, declared Mr. Hees to be incorrect in his assumptions and stated that he knew of no claim or claims in the Dawson district which had yet been worked out. On August 15th Mr. E. C. Hawkins, General Manager of the Klondike Mines Railway Company, deprecated in the Toronto *World* any statement as to the decline of production in that region. He believed it had a very bright future before it and stated that on Dominion Creek alone there were 40 miles of ground to be worked yet while cheaper methods would develop many places not now workable. On Stewart Creek, he said, Mr. William Ogilvie had asserted that placer diggings would yet produce $15,000,000 per annum. Major H. J. Woodside of Dawson, spoke in a similar strain to the Ottawa *Free Press* of September 4th. Mr. Hees replied to his critics in the Toronto *Globe* of August 21st, as follows:

I knew that the one who should write of the conditions as they appeared to me would invite criticisms, and probably become unpopular. But having no stock to sell or depress, having no schemes to promote, not holding a Government job, nor wanting one, having no axes of any kind whatever to grind, and having paid my own expenses, and believing I might possibly save many a poor fellow from going to a place already over-crowded, I concluded to show the other side. I was very careful to quote the highest authorities for my statement. For the reduction of business houses I referred to Bradstreet. For differing with Mr. Wade that only 50 miles of the Klondike had been worked or prospected and that there were 7,000 miles of creeks that had hardly been prospected, I quoted Governor Ross, who told me the statement was misleading, and should not have been made.

Meanwhile, the Ottawa Government had appointed Mr. George Anderson of Toronto, as a special Trade Commissioner, to visit the Yukon and investigate existing conditions. Under date of October 1st, his Report was made public and, after analyzing prices and trade prospects proceeded to discuss mining conditions. He spoke of bituminous coal of good quality as having been found at various points and as being mined at three places. That produced at White Horse had been tested on the White Pass Railway and found equal in quality to the Comox coal of Vancouver Island. He reported 8,065 men engaged in actual mining and apart from prospectors. As to mining conditions he agreed practically with previous official statements. "That the production has fallen off during the past two years there is not the slightest doubt, but with improved methods in mining operations now being rapidly introduced, it is expected that the next few years will prove more fruitful. Practical miners have every confidence in the district and from the number of claims that daily are being recorded, there must be a large area unprospected and undeveloped. It is true there are claims in a state of suspended animation that may again be profitably operated. The question of quartz mining, which would certainly give permanency to the camp, is yet in the balance. Samples of quartz have been brought into Dawson and the assay value would indicate that it can be worked to great advantage."

About the same time Mr. S. Morley Wickett was in the Yukon as the special representative of the Canadian Manufacturer's Association. In his Report, as published in October, he stated the gold bearing sands to be of immense area and the belief that, though their output might fluctuate, the camp would remain an important one for many years. While the yields were not so striking as in the early years, the cost of production had fallen fully 50 per cent. since 1899. As to quartz mining prospects he referred to the opening up of different locations, the confidence of local men in the future, the fine specimens of gold quartz which had been found, and the ore bodies discovered in the White Horse country containing " an extremely high percentage of copper and a fair percentage of gold." But of the future prospects in this respect " no one can even yet speak with assurance." In the Toronto *Globe* of October 4th Mr. Wade, after his return from England, again took up the statements made by Mr. Hees and produced various arguments and proofs in rebuttal. At Vancouver on October 25th, Mr. William Ogilvie told the *World* that he looked forward confidently to the future of the Yukon. " It is just on the threshold of its development and prosperity." In his annual Report dated November 15th, Mr. J. A. Smart, Deputy Minister of the Interior, dealt with this general subject, endorsed the conclusions of Commissioner Ross, quoted Mr. Morley Wickett's views with approval and referred to his own recent visit to the Yukon. He summarized the position as to placer and quartz mining as follows:

I found that the persons holding the larger claims, known as hydraulic concessions, are at present very few in number. A great many of the larger leaseholds have been cancelled owing to the failure of the lessees to comply with the conditions. In fact, a number of hydraulic concessions have been in the last few months thrown open to placer miners and a great many claims have been taken up. It might be mentioned in this connection that a great deal of the land taken up for hydraulic mining was formerly covered by placer claims which were abandoned as not sufficiently rich to pay for working, but which have been found profitable since the introduction of better methods and improved machinery.

The discovery and development of quartz mines in various parts of the country will assuredly add much to the permanency of the mining industry, and in view of recent developments in this respect the Government would doubtless be justified in taking the proper measures to lend assistance. Indeed, this has already been begun by the letting of a contract for the erection of a quartz mill and Assay Office at Dawson, at which miners can have tests made at a most reasonable cost under the supervision of a reliable and competent Government officer. The purchase of drills for prospecting purposes is also a matter worthy of consideration, as it would result beneficially both to the district and the miners generally.

The total mineral production of the Nova Scotia in the year ending September 30th, 1901, is not given by values in Provincial returns but there were 30,537 ounces of gold; 419,567 tons of iron ore—which is described as including imported ore; 3,625,365 tons of coal; 135,637 tons of gypsum and 65,794 tons of limestone. The total sales of coal during the year were 3,119,335 tons as against 2,997,546 tons in 1900. They were distributed as follows:

Mining
Interests of
Nova Scotia

Destination.	1901	1902
Nova Scotia	863,900	998,814
New Brunswick	406,519	349,994
Prince Edward Island	68,103	53,773
Newfoundland	99,307	105,620
Quebec	934,229	1,017,046
United States	624,273	590,086
Other Countries	1,215	4,002

During the years 1785 to 1900 the coal sales of Nova Scotia had totalled $54,968,043 in value. In the decade 1881 to 1890 they were $13,910,136 as compared with $20,552,536 in 1891-1900. In the output of coal for 1902 a marked increase over 1901 was shown—the Dominion Coal Company producing 3,174,227 tons as against 2,561,783 tons in 1901 and the Acadia, Intercolonial and Cumberland Companies showing very similar progress. Meanwhile the revenues of the Mines Department for the year ending September 30th, 1901, had increased considerably over 1900 and amounted to $437,726—which included Coal royalties of $367,925. On February 26th, 1902, the Nova Scotia Mining Society met in Halifax with President W. L. Libbey in the chair. In his opening address Mr. Libbey reported great increases in the facilities of local coal mines; substantial progress in obtaining the confidence of capitalists in Provincial resources and transportation arrangements; marked progress in systematic and legitimate development work below ground; a fairly plentiful supply of labour in the coal districts and gold areas; and an inadequate supply of technically educated mining men. A report was then presented from the Committee which had been appointed to urge upon the Government suggestions favouring the establishment of a Government Assay Office; the encouragement of technical education and deep mining; improvements in the Departmental reports and sundry minor reforms. They stated that careful consideration had been promised by the Commissioner of Mines. Mr. George W. Stuart was elected President of the Society for the ensuing year and presided over a large meeting held at Halifax on October 8th following. Various addresses were delivered and proposals made. Encouragement to technical education and the Mining Schools was strongly urged and a Committee composed of Messrs. Alex. McNeil, H. S. Poole and Hon. R. Drummond, M.L.C., was appointed to press the matter on the Government.

VARIOUS MINING INTERESTS AND INCIDENTS

Jan. 1.—The report of the Hon. A. T. Dunn, Surveyor-General of New Brunswick, for the fiscal year ending October 31st, 1901, states that a Commission of the Government, composed of Hon. G. F. Hill, Hon. L. P. Farris and himself, had investigated coal conditions in the Counties of Queen's and Lunenburg. He reports as follows :

"The amount of coal in Newcastle coal fields is estimated at not less than 50,000,000 tons, and it may amount to three times as much as that. There is, at all events, enough coal there to last for hundreds of years, and to keep the proposed railway fully employed. Assurances were received from the owners of private coal mines in that district that they would be prepared to greatly increase their output if a railway were constructed, so that there will not be the slightest difficulty in obtaining 150,000 tons a year, which the Act for the construction of the railway requires."

Mar. 6.—The Canadian Mining Institute meets in Montreal and elects H. E. the Governor-General, Sir Wilfrid Laurier, the Hon. Mr. Fielding and the Hon. Mr. Sifton as Patrons ; Dr. A. R. C. Selwyn, C.M.G., of Vancouver, as an Honorary member ; Mr. Charles Fergie, M.E., of Westville, N.S., as President ; Messrs, R. R. Hedley of Nelson, Graham Fraser of New Glasgow, James McArthur of Sudbury, and Dr. F. D. Adams of Montreal as Vice-Presidents ; with Mr. B. T. A. Bell of Ottawa as Secretary, and Mr. J. Stevenson Brown of Montreal as Treasurer.

April 30.—The appointment is announced of Prof. W. G. Miller, of Queen's University, Kingston, to the position of Provincial Geologist and Inspector of Mines in Ontario.

May 19.—A Dominion Order-in-Council is announced, selecting 50,000 acres of coal lands in the vicinity of Morrissey Creek in the Crow's Nest coal fields. The estimated value of this property is very great.

May 22.—A disaster occurs in the Crow's Nest Company's Mine at Coal Creek, near Fernie, B.C., by which ever 100 men lose their lives. A report issued at the end of the year by Messrs. W. F. Robertson, Provincial Mineralogist, F. H. Shepherd and Alex. Faulds declares the the most tenable theory as to the cause of the disaster to be an explosion of gas, or gas and dust, through the lighting of a match or the exposure of light in a safety lamp to which some of the miners had false keys.

May 30 —New regulations are issued by the Dominion Government as to coal
mines under their control in Manitoba, the Territories and British
Columbia, as follows : "Lands containing anthracite coal may be
sold at an upset price of $20 per acre and coal other than anthracite
at an upset price of $10 per acre, or, if the Minister of the Interior
so decides, may be sold by public competition. A royalty at the
rate of ten cents per ton of 2,000 pounds will be collected on the
output of the mine, and the operator must furnish the Government
with sworn returns accounting for the full quantity of coal mined."

June 30.—Dr. Eugene Haanel, Superintendent of Mines, in his Report for the
year ending at date, states the value of the gold deposited at the
Dominion Assay Office, New Westminster, British Columbia, as
$1,153,014.

Aug. 29.—Mr. T. G. Blackstock, Vice-President, informs the *Globe* that a
contract has been made by the War Eagle and Centre Star
Companies for the shipment very shortly of 12,000 tons of high-
grade ore a month, and that they have arranged for a reduction in
the charges of treatment by the smelter. They had not shipped
any ore since the strike of July, 1901, but had had 225 men constantly employed in the mines.

Sept. 30.—The statement to date of the Central Star Mining Company shows
development work for the year of 11,087 tons costing $172,552. In
the preceding year the tonnage had been 80,419 costing $258,340.

Oct. 3.—In connection with the United States coal strike and demands for
coal in the other Provinces Mr. James Dunsmuir, as the controlling
power in Vancouver Island Collieries, is interviewed by the Vancouver *World* and states that he can deliver Comox coal on board the
cars at Vancouver for $3.90 per long ton. "See C.P.R. about freight
rates," he added. The current standard rate was 75 cents a cwt. to
Toronto or Montreal and this would make the coal about $15 a ton
laid down.

Oct. 11.—The Nelson *Tribune* states that the management of the *Le Roi* Mine
of Rossland, has been issuing monthly statements which are "not
only intelligible but show that the mine is making money at the rate
of a million dollars a year." During July it was said to have shipped
16,170 tons at a gross value from the mine of $17.67 a ton. The
expenditure for the month was $51,385. Referring to this and other
statements the paper continues : "If this rate is kept up for 12
months the *Le Roi* will be out of debt and will be paying dividends
that will go far towards restoring the confidence of British investors
in our mines."

Oct. 28.—The Port Arthur *Chronicle* announces an important local silver
mining transaction in the sale of the Canadian shares in the Consolidated Mines Company of Lake Superior, Limited, to Pennsylvania
and Ohio capitalists for $100,000.

Nov. 12.—Mr. George E. Roberts, Director of the Mint at Washington, United
States, reports the world's output of gold and silver for 1901 at
$263,374,700 of the former and $104,999,100 of the latter. The
chief producing countries are given as follows :

Country.	COMMERCIAL VALUE.	
	Gold.	Silver.
United States............	$78,666,700	$33,128,400
Mexico	10,284,800	34,593,900
Canada.................	24,128,500	3,145,600
Africa	9,089,500	......
Australasia..............	76,880,200	7,829,500

Nov. 24.—A meeting of the Nelson Board of Trade passes, unanimously, a
Resolution moved by Mr. John Houston, M.P.P., asking for an increase
in duties on pig-lead and the admission duty free of all mining
machinery and supplies not manufactured in Canada.

Dec. 15.—A banquet is given by the citizens of Rossland to Messrs. William Thompson, M.E., and Bernard Macdonald, M.E., with Mayor Clute in the chair and a notable speech from Mr. Edmund B. Kirby.

Dec. 31.—The Rossland *Miner* gives various statistics as to the position and progress of the Camp. Its production in 1902 is placed at 319,714 tons as compared with 279,133 tons in 1901. The pay-roll of its mines is estimated at $1,120,960 including $677,650 for the two *Le Roi* Mines, $168,397 for *Centre Star* and $123,913 for *War Eagle*.

XI.—FORESTS AND FISHERIES

In a lecture delivered at Montreal on March 22nd, 1902, Prof.
D. P. Penhallow of McGill University referred to the immense
quantity and variety of Canadian forest resources.
The Woods and Forests of Canada Taking spruce alone, the area of its forests commenced
at the eastern extremity of Labrador, passed westward
to Ungava Bay, thence south-westward to Hudson's
Bay, thence to near the mouth of the Coppermine River and found
its greatest northern expansion at the mouth of the Mackenzie.
He quoted Dr. Robert Bell, Director of the Geological Survey, as
estimating the area of these northern forests at 2,500,000 square
miles, in which the black and white spruces were the principal
trees, and were capable of producing 16,500,000 cords of wood.
Speaking a little before this, at the opening of the Quebec Legislature, on February 15th, the Hon. S. N. Parent, Premier of the Province, devoted himself to an account of the great forest resources
of Quebec.

Here, he said, east of the Saguenay, there are water powers and supplies
of wood sufficient for an almost infinite production of pulp and paper. Most
people had but a very imperfect idea of the proportions of the rivers which
water this vast territory. Thus, the Manicougan, whose great falls had been
measured and computed last year, was more considerable than the St. Maurice,
both as regards length and volume of water. Its first falls were capable of
producing 100,000 horse power, and ten miles higher there were other falls
still more extensive. These falls were near both to the sea and to a port that
was equally accessible in winter and summer, and were in the vicinity of practically inexhaustible forests.

In this connection, Mr. J. C. Langelier, in the Report of the
Quebec Commissioner of Lands for 1901-2, had a study of forest
conditions in that Province. On the Manicougan River, with its
immense water powers, he spoke of 4,400,000 acres of forest, yield-
ing at least 2 cords of pulp-wood per acre, or 100,000 tons of pulp
annually for 50 years. The territory watered by the Aux Outardes,
another branch of the St. Lawrence, was stated to have pulp-
wood totaling at least 75,000 tons yearly for 40 years.*

Speaking on October 8th, at a banquet in Montreal, the Hon.
Mr. Fitzpatrick, Minister of Justice, declared that in her vast and
practically inexhaustible forests Canada had a national asset which,
if properly managed, would give her a place apart in the world.
" The progress of scientific discovery has revolutionized the timber
trade. The constantly increasing use of wood-pulp for the manufacture of paper has not only increased the demand for timber, but

---

*NOTE—Some years ago Mr. George Johnson, Dominion Statistician, in an elaborate study of
Canadian forest resources, placed the total area at 1,348,798 square miles, of which Ontario possessed
102,118 ; Quebec 102 117 ; New Brunswick 14,766 ; Nova Scotia 6,464 ; Prince Edward Island 797 ;
Manitoba 25,626 ; British Columbia 285,554 ; and the Territories 696,952 square miles.

has invested with a new value precisely the class of trees which in this Province is now found in the greatest abundance, and which has hitherto been passed over by the lumberman as almost unworthy of his notice." At Boston, on November 22nd, the Hon. Clifford Sifton dealt at length with Canadian resources, and made the following reference to the subject under review:

The spruce forests of Canada, lying for hundreds of miles in the valleys of our rivers, with abundant water power close at hand, will supply the pulp and paper of the world, for the excellent reason that no other country possesses the same inexhaustible supply. The growth of the demand cannot cease, so far as human wisdom is able to discern; and, with the raw material and the power, we have the necessary elements for successful competition. Great paper mills in the United States are largely dependent upon the forests of Canada for their supplies. The transfer of the industry to the place where it can be most economically carried on seems to be one of the changes which natural conditions must very speedily bring about.

The forest resources and production of British Columbia attracted considerable attention during the year. To a Toronto *Globe* correspondent (October 11th) Mr. J. R. Anderson, Deputy Minister of Agriculture, said: "Picture to yourself thousands of trees, Douglas fir predominating, of prodigious size, so close together that it is difficult and often impossible for an animal to go between; limbless, except the tops, through which the rays of the sun scarcely penetrate; the ground carpeted with mosses and ferns and the hush of nature all around you, and you can perhaps form some idea of a forest in British Columbia." The correspondent, himself, was greatly impressed with what he saw, and stated from official information that there were 16,000 square miles of lumber on the Coast, practically untouched and composed chiefly of Douglas fir, cedar and hemlock, while inland, beyond the 52nd parallel, there was an immense area of unexplored forest estimated to contain chiefly balsam and sub-arctic pine There were 80 saw-mills at work in the Province with a capacity of 2,000,000 feet per annum, and a frequent forest yield of something like 500,000 feet of lumber to an acre. "The prospects of the industry are great and the owners of timber limits will reap rich harvests." To the Leeds *Mercury* of October 10th a correspondent who was familiar with this subject wrote a letter, dated a month previously, which most enthusiastically reviewed the saw-mill and other industrial interests connected with forest production in this Province and then continued as follows:

Although the cedars and Douglas firs are the trees of greatest economic importance to British Columbia at present, and the Coast forests where they grow are the only ones likely to be worked for some years to come, they by no means exhaust the forest wealth of this Province. The big trees form a mere littoral fringe—a fringe, however, equal in area to Italy. In the central region between the Cascades in the West and the Rocky Mountains in the East, over an area of 770 miles long and 300 miles broad, is a solid forest of black spruce and white spruce, the greatest preserve for the pulp industry which the world contains.

In the fiscal year ending June 30th, 1902, there was an increase of $2,500,000 in the Canadian export of lumber.* Deals (pine) increased in export from $2,837,828 in 1901 to $3,164,-

Trade in Forest Products 552 in 1902; deals (spruce and other) decreased from $8,174,304 to $7,451,148; deal ends decreased from $681,384 to $472,015; laths, palings and pickets increased from $603,720 to $840,714; logs decreased from $1,055,551 to $565,840; joists and scantling decreased from $387,150 to $367,965; planks and boards rose from $9,380,505 to $12,568,991; staves and headings decreased from $438,973 to $301,047; miscellaneous items decreased from $675,218 to $610,993. The sum total was $22,977,574 in 1901 and $25,540,081 in 1902—of which in the latter year Great Britain took $11,962,723, the United States $11,300,470 and other countries $2,276,888.

In other forest products blocks for pulp-wood were exported in the fiscal year 1901 to the value of $1,397,019 and in 1902 to the value of $1,315,038; shingles were exported, respectively, to the value of $1,145,450 and $1,525,386; shooks (box and other) were, respectively, $376,398 and $370,405; sleepers and railway ties were $152,209 and $182,198; square timber, including birch, elm, oak, white pine, etc., amounted, respectively, to $1,929,945 and $1,767,570; miscellaneous items to $774,203 and $615,558. The total of all forest products exported was $30,009,857 in 1901 and $32,119,429 in 1902. Of the latter amount Great Britain took $14,154,467, the United States $15,517,528 and other countries $2,447,434.†

According to figures given in the Vancouver Board of Trade Report for 1902 the shipments of lumber from British Columbia in the preceding year totalled 65,718,275 feet (board measure) valued at $666,354. Of this the Hastings Saw Mill produced $252,739, the Moodyville Saw Mill $148,103 and the Chemainus $265,512. In East Kootenay during 1902 there was great activity in the erection of saw-mills and the cutting of timber—especially in the Crow's Nest region. The capacity of new mills thus erected was stated in the Nelson *News* of December 24th at 89,000,000 feet. On the Atlantic Coast there was also an increase in business. The well-known annual circular of the J. B. Snowball Company, Ltd., of Chatham, gave, under date of December 31st, the total deal shipments from New Brunswick in 1902 as 451,518,691 feet (superficial) compared with 399,000,000 feet in 1901. A statement of the wood trade of the Province compiled by the St. John *Globe* (January 3rd, 1903,) gave the estimate as 445,682,162 feet (superficial) as against 398,169,548 feet in 1901. The tonnage was stated at 605,598, in 1902, carried in 410 vessels.

---

* NOTE—Trade and Commerce Report, 1902.

† NOTE—The export of wood-pulp in 1902 was $2,046,398 and of other wood manufactures $1,043,445.

In the fiscal year 1900 pulp-wood was exported by Canada to the value of $902,722, in 1901 to the value of $1,397,019 and in 1902 to the value of $1,315,038. This trade in pulp-wood, coupled with the increasing demand in Great Britain and the United States for the product and with the enormous resources which Canada undoubtedly possessed, caused varied Legislative action and popular discussion. The Ontario Government, in connection with its control of estimated pulp-wood resources in New Ontario amounting to 228,000,000 cords, commenced in 1900 to grant concessions for cutting the wood on various large tracts of country in return for an agreement by the concessionaires to expend certain sums of money and employ a certain number of men in the mills which they were to erect. On May 21st, 1902, the London *Advertiser* gave the following figures in this connection :

Pulp-Wood and Legislative Action

Company.	Under Agreement to Expend.	Number of Men to be Employed.	Tons of Pulp per Annum.
Sault Ste. Marie Co..............	$ 400,000	400	42,400
Under Algoma Central Act......	200,000	200	13,250
Sturgeon Falls Co.	1,000,000	240	35,000
Spanish River Co...............	500,000	250	20,000
Nepigon Co.	250,000	200	15,000
Blanche River Co...............	750,000	400	50,000
Keewatin Co....................	1,500,000	500	40,000
Montreal River Co.............	500,000	250	37,500
Totals..................	$5,100,000	2,440	253,150

New agreements at this date had recently been made with three of these concerns and the Montreal River Company contract was an entirely new project. The paper went on to point out that these arrangements only touched the fringe of possible production in the Province; that it would take the Companies under the terms of contract 693 years to cut up to the level of present resources; and that spruce reproduced itself every 20 or 30 years. The subject was one, however, of keen political discussion in and prior to the Provincial elections of 1902. In dealing with the agreement made by the Government with the Montreal River Pulp and Paper Company Mr. J. P. Whitney denounced the concession as a "public crime" and as "developing a state by despoiling it" and claimed that the 1,660 square miles granted under its terms were not even defined as to location. The Hon. Mr. Davis defended the policy of the Government and pointed to the development which had already taken place in different directions as a result. Outside the House Mr. N. W. Rowell, K.C., dealt with the subject from a Government standpoint in several able speeches—one being at Sturgeon Falls on May 17th. The Toronto *Mail* of March 31st claimed that in these transactions no public sale was made, no money paid to the Province, no rental charged. The areas were not defined in the contracts as a rule but the Conservative organ estimated them at a total of 15,660 square miles.   The Government side was presented by the Toronto *Globe* of April 28th as follows :

The right to cut the timber is made conditional upon the investment of capital and the employment of labour.   The average expenditure required from the seven Companies has been $700,000, and the average number of men to be employed is 300,000.*   The industry must be located in the new districts adjacent to the pulp-wood supply, and all the wood cut must be manufactured into pulp at the Companies' own mills.   No right to the soil passes to the Companies ; the land continues open for settlement.   All the concessionaire really gets is the promise of the Government that if he will invest his money in establishing an industry, the Government will sell him wood to keep his industry running for 21 years.   The price remains wholly within the control of the Government.   In the early agreements the price was 20 cents a cord.   In the year 1900 it was fixed at 40 cents, and this may be increased by the Government from time to time, so long as the concessionaires are not compelled to pay more than the general public.   If the Company makes default in carrying out the conditions the concession is forfeited.

In Quebec the subject was found to be one of importance. During 1901 the Quebec Lands Department had reported sales in the previous year of 1,933 square miles of spruce territory at a price of $129,171 and a ground rent of $5,829 annually.   In his Report for 1901 dated 1st February, 1902, the Hon. S. N. Parent, Minister of Lands, etc., went into this subject at some length.   During the year he had deemed it desirable to put up at auction the lease of a large extent of public land and the result of this policy, in June 1901, was the sale of 4,634 square miles of timber limits at a bonus price of $375,947.   By an Order-in-Council of June 1st in that year the Minister pointed out that the extra stumpage on logs for export was changed in the following regulation : "All pulp-wood, 128 cubic feet to the cord, (equivalent to 600 feet board measure) is charged with 65 cents per cord—equal to $1.08 per 1,000 feet, or an additional charge of 43 cents."

Meanwhile, there had been some movement amongst manufacturers favouring the imposition of a Dominion export duty upon pulp-wood going into the United States.   The Ontario Government had put into operation the principle that timber grown on Crown Lands should be manufactured within the Province and this, of course, compelled the lease-holders of timber limits to erect their saw-mills and pulp mills and do their work in Ontario.   The same regulations prevailed in British Columbia.   Under the law in Quebec increased stumpage of 65 cents per cord, as above, had to be paid on pulp-wood for export.   Speaking at the meeting of the Canadian Forestry Association in Ottawa, on March 7th, Mr. D. Lorne McGibbon, Manager of the Laurentide Pulp Company, made a vigorous appeal for an export duty on pulp-wood.   He stated that the United States exacted a duty of $1.67 per ton on mechanical or ground wood-pulp and a duty of $3.33 per ton on sulphite pulp, with a prohibitory duty on paper.   This gave the Americans free raw

---

* NOTE—These are the *Globe's* figures, given as they appeared, though it seems probable that there was a misprint in the number of men.

material and no industrial competition, in this connection, from Canada.

"It certainly seems absurd," he went on, "that Canada should allow her pulp-wood to be exported from the country for a very slight charge and that the American manufacturers who use this wood do not have any competition in the finished product—paper." In a speech before the Canadian Manufacturers' Association at Halifax on August 13th Mr. E. B. Eddy claimed that the forests of Canada were being depleted for the benefit of American manufacturers and objected strongly to the free export of Canadian pulp-wood into the United States while Canadian pulp had to pay a duty of over $3.00 a ton. In this connection a large meeting of pulp and paper manufacturers was held at Montreal on December 2nd under the chairmanship of Mr. Eddy and a Committee was appointed, unanimously, to wait upon the Governments of Quebec and the Dominion and urge the imposition of a moderate export duty upon pulp-wood.

The Canadian Forestry Association held its third annual meeting at Ottawa on March 6th and 7th and reviewed the general position **Preservation** of forests in Canada and the best means of preserving **of Canadian** them from fire and undue depletion, or restoring them, **Forests** to some extent, in localities where this depletion had already occurred. The Report for the year stated that the British Columbia Forestry Association was working earnestly for the preservation of local forests from fire ; that an exhibit of growing trees of different ages had been made at the Winnipeg Industrial Fair and the Western Fair at Brandon for the purpose of encouraging Manitoba farmers in planting trees ; that while the loss of timber upon the Ontario Crown Lands had been slight during the year and the work done on the railway belt in British Columbia effective, a serious loss had occurred from fire in the Temiscamingue region in Quebec ; that in New Brunswick the Government and lumbermen had taken up the work of forest protection with good success ; that in Nova Scotia an agitation had been started along similar lines while in Prince Edward Island the passage of an Act for Forest Fire Prevention had been obtained.

A brief paper from Sir H. G. Joly de Lotbiniére, the veteran friend of Forestry in Canada, was followed by an elaborate one by Mr. Thomas Southworth, of Toronto, on the conditions of Ontario Forestry. He divided the Province into three sections—the first stretching from the confluence of the Ottawa and St. Lawrence around the great Lakes and more or less fully settled; the central division stretching a thousand miles from west of Ottawa to Rat Portage and nearly all in the hands of the Crown—with the great permanent forest of Ontario in its heart ; the northern district, including the region watered by streams flowing into the James Bay and containing a forest belt within its area of at least 288,000,000 cords of spruce which would be subject to immense damage from fire as a result of impending railway development and settlement.

Mr. Southworth pointed out that if fire is kept away the forest perpetuates itself and, in the process of time even waste lands become gradually re-clothed with trees.

He then dealt at length with conditions in the central, or Crown Lands, section. In 1885 the Algonquin National Park had been constituted by the Legislature with 1,109,383 acres kept as a game preserve and, incidentally, as a forest preserve. In 1901 the pine-bearing region around Lake Temigami, with timber amounting to from 3,000 to 5,000 million feet, board measure, had been reserved for Government protection. He hoped for the extension of this system and prophesied a time when 25,000,000 acres of the Crown Forest of Ontario would be reserved for the permanent use and revenue of the people. Already, and with the wastefulness of the moment, $1,000,000 a year was reaped in revenues from a small part of these great forest lands. "The composition of this vast forest is such as to make it the most valuable in the whole world. While it contains a large quantity of spruce and birch (the paper and furniture wood *par excellence*) it is the natural habitat of the most valuable tree of them all—the lordly white pine."

In the discussion which followed Mr. J. R. Booth, of Ottawa, drew attention to the allowing of settlers in a forest region essentially unfitted for agricultural purposes. In the recent Kippewa fire—to his knowledge caused by settlers—"more timber was burnt than all the settlers in forty years would pay for." Mr. Hiram Robinson expressed the belief that the recent Temiscamingue fire, in which at least 200,000,000 feet of timber had been destroyed, was started by fishermen—not settlers. In an ensuing paper Mr. R. H. Campbell dealt in detail with the forest fires of 1901 throughout the Dominion. He urged (1) an effective law with adequate penalties; (2) proper advertisement of the law by local posters, etc.; (3) enforcement of the law; (4) education of public opinion as to the value of forests; (5) warning to hunters by Game Associations as to the danger and injury of fires; (6) clearing of strips along all railways; (7) the appointment of more fire wardens and the further setting apart of timber reservations.

Papers were also read by Prof. John Macoun of the Geological Survey on "Discovery in the West"; by Dr. William Saunders upon the Western work of the Experimental Farms in promoting tree planting on the prairies; by Mr. Norman M. Ross upon general Forestry work in the North-West; by the Rev. Father Burke upon Forestry interests in Prince Edward Island; by Mr. D. Lorne McGibbon upon the Pulp Industry of Canada; by Mr. Austin Cary, on the management of pulp-wood forests; by Mr. E. G. Joly de Lotbiniére upon the danger threatening Crown Land forests in Quebec owing to the cutting of pulp-wood under existing regulations. Mr. Joly claimed that the existing dues on pulp-wood for export were utterly inadequate and urged the prohibition of export as the only way of averting destruction to a great Provincial interest. Mr. J. R. Anderson, of British Columbia, read a paper on

Preservation of the Forests, and the meeting adjourned after electing
the Governor-General as Patron, the Lieut.-Governor of British
Columbia as Hon. President, Mr. William Little, of Westmount,
Quebec, as President, Mr. Hiram Robinson, of Ottawa, as Vice-
President, and Mr. E. Stewart, of Ottawa, as Secretary.

Under date of January 24th, 1902, the annual Report of Mr.
Thomas Southworth, Director of Forestry in Ontario, was issued.
He dealt with the general work of his Department, with many of
the subjects referred to in his paper before the Association meeting
at Ottawa, and analyzed at length the woodland area of the settled
part of the Province.   He described six counties as having over
25 per cent. of woodland or forest area—Stormont, Glengarry, Russell, Renfrew, Haliburton (54·72 per cent.) and Hastings; ten counties as having less than 25 and over 20 per cent. ; sixteen counties as
having less than 20 and more than 10 per cent.; eleven counties as
having less than 10 per cent. of woodland.   He summed up the
situation as follows :

On the basis of these returns, as well as from other sources of information,
it is evident that in much of the older settled portion of the Province the proper
proportion of wooded to cleared land no longer exists, and evidence is not wanting that we have begun seriously to feel the effects of over-clearance.   Farmers
are now noting the disadvantage of having no forests to stop the sweep of the
winds, owing to which the snow is blown off the fields in winter and the moisture
quickly evaporated in the summer, while the melted snow and rain at all seasons
run rapidly off the surface instead of being gradually absorbed into the soil.
While many of the farmers already realize the damage to agriculture caused by
over-clearance, few have made any attempt to improve the condition of affairs
by replanting or by adequately preserving their existing wood lots.   To most
farmers the raising of a crop of trees from the seed or from seedling trees seems
a long and hopeless undertaking.   They fail to see that long before the trees
have reached maturity, or even a mercantile size, their presence on the farm in
the earlier stage of growth will contribute largely to bring about improved
conditions in providing a shelter from the winds.   Aside from the apparently
unprofitable nature of tree-planting, the fact that woodland is liable to be
assessed and taxed higher than if the land remained waste, or poor pasture land,
is a deterrent factor, preventing the increased woodland acreage.

The total production or yield of Canadian Fisheries, in the year
1901, was $25,737,153, an increase of $4,179,514 over the previous
year, which had shown no marked difference over the
yield of the preceding six years.   In 1893 it had been
$20,686,661.   According to the Report of the Depart-
ment of Marine and Fisheries for 1902 the total
production of the Fisheries from 1870 to 1901, inclusive, was
$527,383,820, and the yield of 1901 was $3,000,000 ahead of any
preceding year.   By Provinces, Ontario produced $1,428,078, Que-
bec $2,174,459, Nova Scotia $7,980,548, New Brunswick $4,193,264,
Manitoba and the Territories $958,410, British Columbia, $7,942,-
771, and Prince Edward Island $1,050,623.   The chief items in this
production were as follows :

The
Fisheries
of Canada

Cod	$4,039,394	Lobsters	$3,245,881
Herring	1,865,394	Salmon	7,221,387
Mackerel	1,372,459	Haddock	782,163
Hake	304,292	Pollock	227,218
Trout	663,642	Whitefish	783,465
Smelts	483,874	Sardines	562,965
Oysters	179,488	Pike	172,941
Halibut	394,021	Sturgeon	133,264
Pickerel	339,686	Fur seal skins	366,330

Nova Scotia contributed the bulk of the mackerel, cod and lobsters; New Brunswick did well in herring, cod, lobsters, smelts and sardines; British Columbia gave nearly all the salmon to the total; Quebec produced some cod, salmon, herring and lobsters; and Prince Edward Island did best in lobsters. The bulk of the fresh water fish came from Ontario and the North-West.

The Fishing industry as a whole in the fiscal year 1901 employed 9,148 fishermen in vessels, 69,142 men in boats and 15,315 men in the lobster canneries. The number of boats used was 38,186, valued at $1,212,297, and of vessels 1,231, valued at $2,417,680. The gill nets and seines were valued at $2,312,187, the value of the lobster plant was placed at $1,388,907, the value of the pound and trap nets, etc., used was $880,508 and the approximate worth of freezers, ice and smoke houses, etc., was $3,279,721. The total value, therefore, of the industry was $11,491,300 and to it might very well be added that of the salmon canning interests of British Columbia with 77 establishments valued at $1,500,000 and employing 18,941 persons.

The sealing fleet of the latter Province consisted in 1901 of 39 schooners, 139 boats and 226 canoes valued at $370,000 and manned by 900 sailors and hunters. It may be added that the Canadian exports of fish and fish products in the fiscal year 1902 were $13,567,142 as compared with $10,680,739 in 1901, while the imports for home consumption were $1,055,025 in value. The amount paid out by the Dominion Government in Fishing bounties during 1901-2 was $155,942; in Fisheries protection $152,723; on Fish-breeding $79,891; and to the various Provinces and miscellaneous purposes a sum which, with the amounts specified, totalled $549,569. The chief payments to and receipts from the Provinces included $23,813 to New Brunswick and $11,658 from that Province; $32,618 to Nova Scotia and $6,084 from the Province; $18,560 to British Columbia and $41,178 from the Province. As to the bounties, Nova Scotia in 1901 received $101,024 or a total of $2,019,040 since the system commenced in 1882; New Brunswick received $13,420 or a total of $304,596; Prince Edward Island $8,335 or a total of $207,855; and Quebec $33,161 or a total of $624,620. During 1902 there were 271,401,000 fry distributed from the various Fish hatcheries of the Dominion as against 203,540,000 in the previous year. Much good work was done in fish culture and other directions during the year by Prof. Edward E. Prince, Federal Commissioner of Fisheries.

19

The salmon pack in the Pacific Province varies greatly from year to year. In 1900 the number of cans was 585,413 ; in 1901 it was 1,236,156. According to the statement of the Fraser River Canners' Association, issued at the close of 1902, the total for that year was 625,982 cans. The British Columbia sealing fleet in 1901 had a total catch of 24,422 seals as against 35,523 in 1900. The boats in the business numbered 139, the vessels 39 and the canoes 226. In the crews were 443 white men and 465 Indians, while the value of the seal-skins was $562,845 in 1901 and $441,825 in 1900. It may be added that the capital invested in British Columbia Fisheries in 1901 was $2,965,682 and in the fur sealing $394,400 ; while the fishermen, cannery employees, vessel men and seal hunters totalled 20,354 in number. In April, 1902, in this Province, Mr. J. P. Babcock who, late in 1901 had been appointed Provincial Fisheries Commissioner, issued a Report dealing with the salmon interests of the Pacific Coast and urging the establishment of a large hatchery at Seaton Lake.*

According to the Report of the Dominion Department of Fisheries for 1902 the value of the capital invested in the Lake fishery interests of Ontario in 1901 was $749,071 and the men employed numbered 2,802 with 101 tugs and 1,299 boats. Of the fish caught and valued at a total of $1,428,078, trout figured at a valuation of $554,426, whitefish $249,670, herring $165,394, pickerel $152,702, sturgeon $34,085, caviare $19,777 and pike $74,250. The Report for 1901 of Mr. S. T. Bastedo, Deputy Commissioner of Fisheries in Ontario, was issued in the following year and stated that licenses to fish with 2,410,627 fathoms of gill net and various other methods had been issued; that employment during the year was given to the number of men and tugs and boats and capital mentioned above; that the aggregate catch was 27,428,375 lbs. and its estimated value $1,428,078. Upon the value and condition of these inland fisheries Mr. Bastedo reported as follows :

> They are becoming more important each year, not only on account of the large and valuable amount of food which they furnish, but to a much greater extent from the fact that they are a drawing attraction to tourists who come to spend their summer or vacation with us, enticed hither by the excellent fishing to be had in the fresh water lakes, rivers, and streams with which the Province abounds, and by our cool, healthful climate and gorgeous scenery ; and this source of profit will no doubt increase in the future as new districts are opened up, and become more accessible. It is interesting to contemplate the vast amount of revenue which the citizens of this Province will derive from such visitors even a few years hence, if our inland waters are stocked with good varieties of game fish, such as trout, bass and maskinonge, and other varieties as we may be able to introduce them. And, of course, the more and better attractions of this kind we have to offer the greater the number of people who will come. It is estimated that $10,000,000 annually are left in Maine by tourists visiting that State. But with the increase of tourist travel, and the growth of the summer resort business our rivers and lakes have been subjected to incessant fishing, and for this reason and owing also not a little, no doubt, to

*Note—Published in full in *Victoria Colonist*, April 16th, 1902.

the successful operations of the poacher in years past, in many places game fish are practically extinct. To restore these waters, therefore, and to anticipate the drain which will naturally follow the annnally increasing number of visitors, the work of re-stocking appeared to the Government to be one which should be undertaken immediately and prosecuted with vigour.

The event of the year in connection with British Columbia Fishery interests was the appointment, under a Dominion Order-in-Council dated January 24, 1902, of a Commission **British Columbia Salmon Commission** to investigate the proper protection and future conditions of the Salmon Fisheries of the Province. The Chairman of the Commission was Prof. E. E. Prince, of Ottawa, and the other members were Messrs. Aulay Morrison, M.P., and George R. Maxwell, M.P. Upon the death of the last-mentioned gentleman, Mr. George Riley, M.P., of Victoria, was appointed his successor. The first meeting was held at Vancouver on January 24th, and the last on February 5th. Sittings were had at Vancouver, New Westminster, Victoria and Nanaimo, and fishermen, canners, merchants, fish dealers and official representatives of various public bodies were heard. Many memorials, statements and petitions were submitted and seventy witnesses examined. On January 31st, the Commission met the Vancouver Board of Trade in conference and on February 4th the Mayor and a number of leading Victoria citizens presented considerations affecting the better protection of the salmon rivers, the more efficient supervision of trout fisheries and the encouragement of sporting facilities. On this latter date the Report which follows was passed by the Victoria Board of Trade and, as it was closely associated with the discussions of the Commission, may be given here :

That the Fisheries Committee of the Victoria Board of Trade consider it absolutely necessary, in view of the great development of the canning industry on Puget Sound and the consequent competition through their cheaper methods of taking salmon, that permission be granted British subjects to operate traps, purse and drag seines, and gill nets of unlimited length, on Vancouver and adjacent islands in the waters south of the 49th parallel ; also that in the event of these privileges being granted, and the great importance of the industry, it is desirable that a separate "fishing district" should be established covering the above territory. We are also strongly of the opinion that exclusive fishing privileges should not be granted parties who have no capital invested and are not in any way connected with the industry either as fishermen or canners.

The information furnished the Commission was very conflicting. The question of changing the system of salmon catching from the use of nets to that of traps (after the American style) was the chief subject of discussion. On January 28th a number of witnesses were examined—nearly all being practically connected with the Fisheries. It was stated in the evidence that on the American side men employed on the traps got from $50 to $100 a month and board ; that ten traps would employ one hundred men, each trap cost from $10,000 to $16,000 and its operation cost $750 a month ; that the cost of seining licenses was too high ; that traps were more economical than nets from the canners' standpoint ; that cheaper fish obtained through adoption of traps was the only salvation of the industry from American competition; that, on the other hand, traps would very soon deplete the Fisheries to a ruinous extent and that gill nets were the only proper means of catching fish while preserving the Fisheries; that there were too few white fishermen and that Japanese were necessary to the industry, while it was also contended that the latter prevented white employment and should be dispensed with.

On January 29th, at New Westminster, Mr. R. Mackie, President of the Local Fisherman's Union, presented the following opinions as those of his organization, and claimed that they embodied the views of the Fraser River fishermen as a whole : " (1) That the weekly closing for seine fishing be the same as for gill nets at present; (2) that licenses to fish, purse or drag seines, be granted to all Provincial voters among the fishermen, and to Indians ; (3) that an unlimited length of nets be used outside the sand heads ; (4) that we don't want any traps in British Columbia waters under any circumstances ; (5) that no fishing licenses whatever be granted to any canneryman." On the following day the opinions of the cannerymen were elaborately presented in a statement, or memorial, signed by Alexander Ewen, H. Bell-Irving, W. McPherson, J. A. Russell, John Wallace, C. A. McDonald and R. J. Ker, acting as a Committee of the Salmon Canners of the Province. It may be summarized as follows :

1. Experience has shown the artificial propagation of salmon to be not only beneficial but absolutely necessary in British Columbia waters.

2. The revenue derived from fishing licenses should be devoted to the enforcement of regulations, the erection and maintenance of hatcheries, the clearing of spawning grounds, the removing of log jams, and to other matters tending to foster and conserve the industry.

3. A non-political local Fishing Board, composed of experienced men, should be appointed to make by-laws and regulations for the conservation of the fish supply and to act in a general advisory capacity under Government control.

4. If this were done then the present license fees should be reduced and the Fishing Board empowered to levy an assessment on all salmon packed or cured in British Columbia, the revenue to be used for conservation purposes.

5. Valuable and exclusive fishing privileges should not be granted to parties who have invested no capital in the industry and are in no way connected with it. In order to remedy this evil seining licenses should be granted along the entire coast of the Province to all British subjects entitled, under present regulations, to receive gill net licenses. The close season should be the same as for gill net fishing, and for this latter purpose certain specified waters were suggested for reservation.

6. Trap fishing was declared to be " the most scientific method of catching salmon in certain waters," and, under proper regulations, not prejudicial to the conservation of the fish supply. " In view of the competition forced on the British Columbia industry by Puget Sound and Alaska packers, it would appear that trap-fishing is inevitable. It is an open question, however, whether canners and fishermen would suffer more from this competition or from trap licenses being granted outside of those presently engaged in the business."

7. The construction of hatcheries on the Fraser, Thompson, Skeena and Naas Rivers and River's Inlet should be carried out.

8. An early settlement of questions of relative interest in or control over the Fisheries, as between the Dominion and Provincial Governments, should be arranged.

9. Existing regulations regarding gill net licences should be maintained, while those for obtaining fishermen's licenses were declared entirely equitable and satisfactory if properly carried out. The Fisheries should remain open to all British subjects and not be confined to the Provincial Voters' Lists.*

10. Proper and more adequate protection should be accorded fishermen who, having paid for their licenses, desired to follow their calling in a peaceable manner and were prevented from doing so in the past two seasons by the "lawlessness, intimidation and violence which prevailed on the Gulf during the fishermen's strikes."

11. The great value of the Province's deep-sea Fisheries was pointed out and their exploitation by American fishermen for the benefit of United States interests strongly deprecated.

During Mr. Bell-Irving's evidence he stated that the amount of money invested by gill-net fishermen in gear-boats, etc., was $18,000 for Indians, $92,000 for whites and $128,000 for Japs. He declared the latter to be the most steady and industrious fishermen. His figures were not accepted by representatives of the fishermen who were present. Mr. R. J. Ker, the Manager for R. P. Rithet and Company's large cannery interests, urged, on February 2nd, the adoption or trial of traps, seines, drag-nets, etc., in place of gill nets and in order to cheapen production and meet the American competition which was steadily increasing. "There was always an uncertainty in traps, but the fact that Americans could sell at seventeen shillings in the London market showed that they were getting fish cheaper than the Canadian canners. If traps were allowed on the Canadian side, in a few years it would considerably affect the American catch. At present the American canners get the fish before they strike the Fraser River. If our traps were here ahead of them, the Canadians would get the fish before they struck the American trap."

The testimony as a whole varied greatly but the fishermen generally seemed to prefer the existing system of gill net fishing as most likely to conserve their individual employment and the canners wanted traps, etc., in order to cheapen their production. Upon the point of American competition Mr. C. F. Todd stated on February 4th that Canada only took about 30,000 cans a year from the Fraser River canneries; that the bulk of their product had to meet the cheaply caught fish of Alaska and Puget Sound in Foreign or British markets; that 700,000 cans of British Columbia salmon of last year's product remained unsold and that none of the canneries had made any money since 1897. Yet the large United States concerns were making money freely; the Alaska Packing Company had paid last year a dividend of 12½ per cent.; and a new organization had just been effected in San Francisco with $23,000,000 capital. In Alaska, he added, they used purse seines entirely. At the last meeting, on February 5th, the Secretary of the Japanese Society of Steveston stated that the Japs had $150,000 invested in this business and that 3,000 of them were employed on the Fraser with 1,500 licenses.

---

* NOTE—An indirect means of excluding the Japanese.

The lack of unanimity and varied differences of opinion made the subject a difficult one for the Commission to deal with, but on March 4th the Commissioners, with one exception, signed an interim Report and presented it to the Minister of Marine and Fisheries. It reviewed the problems concerned and the evidence given but deferred recommendations or suggestions until fuller consideration could be given. Owing to Mr. Maxwell's illness and death and other causes the final Report was delayed and had not been issued at the end of the year. It may be added that the subject of Provincial control over the foreshore Fisheries, and the question of traps and seines, were discussed in the British Columbia Legislature on April 23rd and May 7th. Mr. Dallas Helmcken, K.C., drew attention, especially, on the latter date, to the aid given American fishing interests by the use of traps and then referred to the following matter:

One feature of the problem, which was most serious and required the most careful consideration, was to guard the trap fishing grounds from the United States canners, who were prepared to expend large sums of money to secure a monopoly of the business. Matters should be so arranged as to shut out all chance of our Fisheries falling into the hands of aliens and preserve them for our own people.

XII.—MANUFACTURING INDUSTRIES

General Industrial Conditions

There was marked progress of an industrial character in Canada during the year. In the export of manufactured goods there had been a steady increase from $11,706,707 in the fiscal year 1899 to $18,462,970 in 1902. The imports of free goods—manufactured and partially manufactured—were $32,494,013 and included binding twine $1,507,344, cotton wool and waste $5,864,089, drugs, dyes and chemicals $3,598,247, gutta-percha, etc., $1,655,967, and metals $13,423,351. The table* which follows gives the chief dutiable imports of manufactured products during the fiscal year, 1902, and the exports from Canada of Canadian manufactured goods:

MANUFACTURED PRODUCTS.

Imports for Consumption.		Exports.	
Carriages, Railway Cars, etc.	$1,421,265	Agricultural Implements..	$1,814,730
Cement.	863,646	Carriages, Waggons, etc ..	480,739
Cottons.	7,392,977	Cottons.	903,595
Curtains	477,762	Cordage, etc.	250,397
Electric Apparatus	1,266,810	Drugs, Chemicals, etc....	621,137
Fancy Goods	2,218,708	Explosives	248,434
Flax, Hemp, Jute, etc....	1,979,710	Household Effects.	1,538,186
Furniture.	487,749	Iron and Steel and manu-	
Furs.	1,060,521	factures of.	2,460,781
Glass.	1,938,808	Leather.	2,301,963
Hats, Caps, etc.	1,730,723	Lime and Cement.	113,269
Iron and Steel and manu-		Liquors.	398,236
factures of.	24,072,141	Musical Instruments.	465,818
Leather	1,810,261	Oil Cake.	205,793
Paper.	1,945,786	Furniture.	279,260
Silk	4,183,926	Wood Pulp.	2,046,398
Wool and manufactures of.	10,946,856	Wood (other).	1,133,445

The Iron and Steel Industry in Canada

Apart from the special industries at Sydney, New Glasgow and Sault Ste. Marie, there was much general progress in the iron and steel industry during 1902. It had started with the following encouragement from bounties per ton granted by the Dominion Government:

	On Pig Iron.		On Steel
	From Native Ore.	From Foreign Ore.	
To April 21, 1902	$3.00	$2.00	$3.00
April 21, 1902, to July 1, 1903	2.70	1.80	2.70
July 1, 1903, to July 1, 1904	2.25	1.50	2.25
July 1, 1904, to July 1, 1905	1.65	1.10	1.65
July 1, 1905, to July 1, 1906	1.05	.70	1.05
July 1, 1906, to July 1, 1907	.60	.40	.60

For 1901 the Canadian Furnace Company of Three Rivers had received $16,614, the Midland Iron Works $59,169, the Deseronto

---

*The details of the exports are compiled from the Trade and Commerce Reports, 1902, and those of the imports from the *Trade and Navigation* Returns, 1902—both official.

Iron Company $27,468, the Dominion Iron and Steel Company of Sydney $55,287, the Hamilton Iron and Steel Company $12,455, and the Nova Scotia Iron and Steel Company $66,711. Since 1884 the amount of bounties paid on pig iron had been $1,724,394. For iron puddled bars the Hamilton Steel and Iron Company received $16,703, with $28,310 for steel ingots, while the Nova Scotia Steel Company received $71,746 for the latter. In the fiscal year 1902 the figures were greatly increased and bounties were claimed upon 413,039 tons of iron and steel while $791,089 was actually paid by the Government. The tariff, it was claimed, did not afford sufficient protection against American manufacturers in many cases. Out of 800,000 tons of iron and its products consumed annually in Canada, it was pointed out, only about 30 per cent. was yet produced in native furnaces. Barb and galvanized wire mill-owners, particularly, asked for a higher tariff, while it was claimed that the making of steel rails at the Sault, the construction of a steel rail mill at Sydney, and developments in the making of structural steel at New Glasgow, Hamilton and Collingwood, combined to render a duty upon the importation of steel rails for railways necessary, as well as a higher tariff upon structural steel products.

Of the general iron and steel interests in the country, the Canada Iron Furnace Company made marked progress during the year. Its Managing Director was Mr. George E. Drummond, and its Radnor Forges Furnace in the Three Rivers district, Quebec, possessed a capacity of 10,000 tons of pig-iron, while its Midland Furnace was credited with 45,000 tons capacity. The Hamilton Steel and Iron Company, Limited, with the Hon. A. T. Wood as President, and Mr. C. S. Wilcox as General Manager, was stated in May, 1902, to have 900 men employed, and to possess a capacity of 65,000 gross tons of pig-iron, 18,000 tons of steel ingots, 12,000 tons of steel bars and 100,000 kegs of cut nails. The Cramp Steel Company, Limited, of Collingwood, was organized in 1901 and during the succeeding year proceeded in the construction of several buildings with a capacity of 75,000 tons of pig-iron, 100,000 tons of steel ingots, blooms, etc., and 200,000 tons of finished products. Other interests which showed progress during the year were the Deseronto Iron Company with a capacity for 11,000 tons of Lake Superior charcoal and pig-iron for malleable castings and car wheels; the Grantham Iron Works of Drummondville, Quebec, with a yearly output of 5,000 tons of car-wheel iron; and the Canada Foundry Company of Toronto with large new buildings.

In his annual Report to the United States during the middle of 1902, Consul-General J. L. Bittinger, at Montreal, paid tribute to Canadian progress in this connection. He pointed out that the annual capacity of the 18 rolling mills and steel works in Canada was 301,400 gross tons of ingots and castings and 981,900 tons of rolled products. The production of pig-iron was rapidly increasing but there was still a wide difference between the home product of

244,000 tons in 1901 and the home consumption of 800,000 tons. Of Ontario production Mr. T. W. Gibson spoke at length in his Report for the Bureau of Mines, issued during 1902. He referred to the pig-iron and steel product of $2,048,983 and stated that 194,510 tons of ore had been smelted, of which 109,109 tons were from Ontario mines.

The Consolidated Lake Superior Company of Sault Ste. Marie, Ontario, which has become popularly known as the Clergue Syndicate, and whose controlling spirit is Mr. Francis H. Clergue, was originally incorporated as the American Lake Superior Power Company on April 17, 1897. Its charter was changed to the present title on July 7, 1898, and amended in 1899 and 1901. The capital comprises $82,000,000 common stock, of a par value of $100, and of which on April 30, 1902, $68,000,000 had been issued; and $35,000,000 7 per cent. non-cumulative preferred stock of a par value of $100 of which at the same date $20,000,000 had been issued. The head office is at Philadelphia, the Canadian offices at Sault Ste. Marie, and $20,000,000 are stated to have been already spent upon the works and development at the latter point. Mr. E. V. Douglas, of Philadelphia, was President at the beginning of 1902; Mr. F. H. Clergue, Vice-President and General Manager; and Mr. F. S. Lewis, Treasurer. The concerns controlled by this corporation, through stock ownership, include the Lake Superior Power Company (Ontario charter), with a capital stock of $500,000 preferred and $1,500,000 common; the Michigan, Lake Superior and Power Company (Michigan charter), with a capital stock of $500,000 and a bonded debt of $3,500,000; the Sault Ste. Marie Pulp and Paper Company (Ontario charter), with a capital stock of $750,000 preferred and $1,250,000 common stock; the Tagona Water and Light Company (Ontario charter), with a capital stock of $200,000 and a bonded debt of $100,000.

The Syndicate possseses varied assets. The lands and water power rights at Sault Ste. Marie, Michigan, are stated as sufficient for the development and operation of mechanical power to the amount of 60,000 horse power, while those on the Canadian side are estimated at 100,000 horse power. One-half of the former are leased at a yearly rental of $200,000 to the Union Carbide Company, of New York and Chicago, for 25 years. There are pulp mills on the Canadian side producing over 100 tons per day, and yielding an annual net profit of about $150,000—according to the *Canadian Mining Review* of July 31, 1902. There are machine shops and a foundry equipped for the manufacture of pulp and paper mill, hydraulic mining, smelting and electrical machinery. The nickel mines owned by the Company in the Sudbury region are reported as having very rich ore, and the manufacture of nickel steel was commenced during the year. The Helen Iron Mine needs no description here, and a Company controlled by the Clergue interests was organized in 1899 to construct a railroad to the

Michipicoten district. A sulphite paper mill was completed in 1902 for the manufacture of long fibre pulp. A sulphuric acid plant for manufacturing sulphuric acid from the sulphur of the Sudbury ores, and a laboratory for testing, chemically and electrically, various raw materials and products have also been established. Water and light are supplied by the concern to the Ontario town of Sault Ste. Marie, and by contract with the Provincial Government the Company own a grant of timber equal to the growth upon 1,000 square miles of virgin forest. Its new steel industry is carried on by the Algoma Steel Company, Limited, with Mr. F. H. Clergue as President, and with a capacity for 380,000 tons per annum of pig-iron, 245,000 tons of coke, 200,000 tons of steel ingots, and 180,000 tons of finished product.

On March 2nd, 1902, Mr. Clergue and the gentlemen already mentioned, together with Mr. W. P. Douglas of Philadelphia and Mr. H. C. Hamilton of the Sault, figured in the incorporation of the Algoma Tube Works, Limited, with a share capital of $30,000,000 and headquarters at the Sault. Its object was the manufacture of metallic tubes. On April 11th following Premier Ross of Ontario visited the Clergue industries and found some 7,000 persons engaged in them. A new enterprise was inaugurated on May 5th as the Canadian Rolling Stock Company, Limited, with a share capital of $2,000,000, Directors similar to the others already mentioned, and for the purpose of constructing and dealing in all kinds of railway supplies and rolling stock. Meanwhile, on February 15th, the Algoma Steel Company had produced what was claimed to be the first steel manufactured from Canadian pig-iron by the Bessemer process, and was announced as the preliminary stage in a production of steel rails, for which the plant was in process of installation. At a Board of Trade banquet in Sault Ste. Marie, on March 27th, it was stated by the Auditor of the Clergue Companies that the local pay-roll for the past month had been $120,000, with $50,000 more disbursed at the mines and along the railway for wages. The money paid for material ran from $500,000 to $900,000 a month. The condensed balance sheet of the Company, as announced for June 30th, 1902, was as follows:

ASSETS.

Subsidiary Companies.........................		$93,060,309 76
Current Assets—		
Algoma Central and Hudson's Bay Railway Company.....................	$ 63,132 99	
Algoma Commercial Company, Limited..	798,301 73	
Algoma Steel Company, Limited.......	1,034,910 32	
Lake Superior Power Company........	369,334 85	
Tagona Water and Light Company......	36,868 63	
Sault Ste. Marie Pulp and Paper Co....	207,733 13	
Total of inventories................	$2,510,281 65	
Accounts receivable.................	4,040,710 04	
Cash..............................	376,353 05	
		6,927,344 74
Total.....................................		$99,987,654 50

ONTARIO WORKS
OF THE CONSOLIDATED
LAKE SUPERIOR
SAULT STE MARIE ———— COMPANY

LIABILITIES.

Capital stock of the Consolidated Lake Superior Company :
  Preferred....................... .... $23,547,250 00
  Common 70,151,800 00
                                              ———————— $93,699,050 00
Preferred stock instalment receipts :
  Amount received from purchasers of stock........... 1,849,300 00
Current liabilities—
  Vouchers, bills and accounts payable................. ...... 3,342,496 30
  Profits and loss of the Consolidated Lake Superior and
    subsidiary Companies........................... 1,096,808 20
                                                            ————————
  Total....................................... $99,987,654 50

On October 25th the great water power Canal of the Michigan and
Lake Superior Power Company was opened at the American Sault Ste.
Marie and turned over to Mr. Clergue and the Consolidated Power
Company with due ceremony. A banquet was held in the evening
with addresses from Mr. Clergue and the Hon. J. Israel Tarte. The
former referred to this new enterprise as having cost $6,000,000,
as possessing power which would cost $2,000,000 a year if supplied
by coal, and as being sufficient to grind flour to feed 100,000,000
people. He believed the whole 60,000 horse power of the new
canal would be disposed of within two years, and by that time
another canal on the Canadian side would be almost completed.
He concluded by deprecating the fiscal conduct of the United States
towards Canada. Mr. Tarte took strong ground along this line,
and declared that he was preaching " the gospel of an aggressive
policy." He told the Americans present that Canada accepted $250,-
000 for pulp-wood which was taken away and made in the United
States into a product worth $50,000,000. He then declared, accord-
ing to the Sault *Star* of October 30th, that there was going to be
a big export duty on pulp, and added : " I went out of office just to
fight along this line." He also urged a duty of $10 a ton on steel
rails.

To Mr. Clergue and his interests the matter of importing steel
rails and the tariff thereon was, of course, an important one during
the year. Speaking at Ottawa, on November 20th, to the Toronto
Globe correspondent, he described the situation from his point of
view. " The German market," he said, " is protected by a duty of
between $6 and $7 a ton. Consequently, if you were to buy rails
in Germany for use in that country, the price would be from $30
to $32 a ton. The usual freight on these rails from the German port
to Montreal would be $3 more, and from Montreal to Port Arthur
another $3, or a total of about $38 per ton. Now, Messrs. Mackenzie & Mann are reported to have purchased their rails for $27 a
ton, delivered at Port Arthur. We cannot afford to produce rails
at that figure." At Montreal, on November 28th, he said that
Canada was able for the first time in its history to furnish the
entire supplies for the construction of a trans-continental railway.
The output of his iron mines at the Sault was now 1,000 tons a day
and all that was needed was more protection.

Following this it was stated on December 9th that the steel rails mill at the Sault had been closed down temporarily after filling orders to something over 30,000 tons. By this action 500 men were thrown out of employment. It was said that the cause of the stoppage was partly German competition and partly because home Companies like the Canadian Northern Railway would not patronize a local industry. To this Mr. William Mackenzie replied—Toronto *World* of December 11th—by stating that in March, 1902, a contract had been placed with the Clergue concern for 10,000 tons of rail but that the delivery of some 2,500 tons of the order had been done under conditions very unsatisfactory to the Railway and therefore additional orders had been given elsewhere.

On December 11th a panic took place in the price of the common stock of the Consolidated interests at the Sault and it ran down from 35 to almost nothing. Three days later Mr. Clergue issued a statement declaring that there was no adequate cause for the "slump" and it was at, the same time, announced from other official quarters that a loan of $3,000,000 had been arranged in Philadelphia to cover all immediate necessities of the concern. Meantime Mr. F. S. Lewis who, in October, had succeeded the late E. V. Clergue as President, resigned his position and Mr. Theodore C. Search of Philadelphia, Vice-President, acted temporarily in his place. On December 20th Mr. Clergue stated that $8,000,000 were now available for the continuance of the Company's operations. A week before this the Ontario Government had announced that the Clergue tender for constructing steel rails for the Temiscamingue Railway had been accepted at a figure of $32 per ton of 2,240 lbs., delivered at North Bay.* On December 23rd the Toronto *Globe* gave a careful study of the finances of the varied Sault interests of Mr. Clergue by a special correspondent and the following extract may be quoted here:

The common stock is made up of $28,000,000 acquired in exchange for $14,000,000 of the original Consolidated Lake Superior common stock ; $28,000,-000 acquired in exchange for $14,000,000 of the Ontario Lake Superior Company common stock ; and $14,151,800 stock issued for the acquisition of the Algoma Steel Company. For the last-named purpose a balance of $11,848,200 remains to be issued, making $82,000,000 in all of common stock. Since June 30th $2,000,-213,650 of preferred stock has been issued, leaving $9,239,100 still to be received from purchasers of preferred stock, in instalments, for completing construction and providing working capital which, when paid in, will complete the total preferred capital stock, authorized, of $35,000,000.

The general income account shows the Lake Superior Power Company, which disposed of so much Helen ore, to have been the bread-winner last year, with a net income from operation of $619,104. The Railway came next, with $382,084, and the Algoma Commercial Company, with its lumber and logging operations, came third with $301,986. From the pulp mills came $77,548 and from the water and light service $47,411, making a total net income from operation of $1,428,136. From this was paid preferred dividends of $1,115,403 and general expenses, $20,103, leaving a surplus of $292,628. This, added to $380,-424 cash subsidy on the Railway, and $423,735 from profit and loss of the previous year, left $1,096,808 to the credit of profit and loss on June 30th last.

---

* NOTE—The Company afterwards withdrew from this contract.

The progress of the Sydney industrial concerns during 1902 was of national importance.   Beginning in 1891 with a capital of $15,-000,000, the Iron and Steel Company found a local

The Domin-ion Iron and Coal Companies population of 2,500.   In 1902 the city had 10,000 people within its bounds, while the Company employed some 4,000 men, and its balance sheet of April 30th, in that year, showed property valued amongst its assets at $29,419,534.   Other assets in this statement included cash on hand, $97,983; accounts receivable, $591,198; product on hand, $590,793; raw material on hand, $600,983; warehouse material on hand, $296,849.   The total assets were $31,597,385.   The liabilities reached the same figure and included $8,000,000 in bonds, $15,000,000 in common stock, $5,000,000 in preferred stock, $2,589,550 in notes payable, $955,396 in accounts payable, and $52,441 as a reserve for replacement.   In the Director's statement submitted to the shareholders on June 12th, the acting-President, Senator Mackay of Montreal, referred to their construction of new piers, installment of compressing machinery in the coke ovens' plant, the construction of open-hearth steel furnaces, the starting of the rolling mill, the work done upon a steel rail mill, and the construction of a large machine shop.   He stated the present production of coke at an average of 1,000 tons per day, the four blast furnaces as having a capacity of 1,000 tons per day, the output of steel for week ending May 31st, 1902, as having been 1,800 tons, and the production of the rolling mill, between February and June 1st, as 14,000 tons.   His summary of property included the following statement:

The principal supply of ore is from the Company's mine at Bell Island, Newfoundland, about 400 miles from Sydney, where there is an immense deposit of red hematite.   This mine has been equipped with modern machinery and shipping piers capable of handling about 5,000 tons of ore per day.   In addition to this mine, the Company has acquired, for the purpose of obtaining the necessary furnace mixtures, several mining leases in the Province of Nova Scotia, and for the purpose of making sulphuric acid, a pyrites mine on the coast of Labrador.   Some of these properties are now being developed.   The Company owns a property of remarkably pure marble from which a very large supply of limestone can be procured.   This quarry is situated in the Bras d'Or Lakes, about 60 miles by water from Sydney.   There is also a dolomite quarry at George's River, 14 miles by rail from Sydney, and from which open-hearth furnace lining is obtained.

In concluding his report, Senator Mackay added that since the financial statement had been prepared 50,000 shares of common stock had been underwritten at $60 per share, and that by July 11th this $3,000,000 (less commission) would be available for reduction of debt, and further improvements.   The estimated expense in production at these works has been frequently published.   It has been stated on reasonable authority that the cost of mining and loading the ore on vessels at Bell Island would not be more than 50 cents per long ton for several years to come, and then not more than from 80 cents to $1.00; that the freightage to Sydney would range from 35 cents to 45 cents; that a safe total average would be $1.10 per ton for ore running about 54 per cent. in iron. Coal was stated to be available at the furnace at not more than $1.25 per ton.

Meanwhile, on the same day, the Dominion Coal Company held its annual meeting with Mr. James Ross, Vice-President, in the chair. The Report stated the output at 2,651,263 tons for the fiscal year ending February 28th as compared with 2,044,877 tons in 1901; 1,739,374 tons in 1900; and 1,295,543 tons in 1899. The total output from 1895 to 1902, inclusive, had been 12,067,982 tons. During this increased business the Company had found large additions to the mining plant necessary as well as additional railway and equipment, shipping piers, buildings, etc. The coal areas owned by the concern were stated to have an extent of 140 square miles with known seams of over three feet in thickness and of 1,500 million tons capacity. They had two large piers at Sydney with a capacity of 10,000 tons in 24 hours and two others at the Louisbourg terminus. They owned five steamships, two tugs and five barges, 1,200 houses at Sydney Mines and various stores. The balance sheet of the Company on February 28th, 1902, was as follows:

ASSETS.

Property account as per last Report...	$21,333,163 86	
Less written off for Depreciation......	122,374 77	
Add Capital Expenditure during year..	960,344 35	
		$22,171,133 44
Cash in Banks and Offices.........................		327,355 36
Accounts receivable..............................		632,344 29
Coal on hand		196,289 80
New Supplies in Stores and Warehouses		518,114 74
Insurance paid in Advance		25,451 41
Interest paid in Advance		2,308 05
Steamship Hire paid in Advance...................		14,072 79
Cash in New England Trust Co. for Sinking Fund....		134,547 05
Total.....................................		$24,021,616 93

LIABILITIES.

Capital Stock, Common..............	$15,000,000 00	
Capital Stock, Preferred	3,000,000 00	
First Mortgage Bonds...............	2,704,500 00	
Hochelaga Mortgage................	22,000 00	
Cape Breton Real Estate Debentures..	289,391 75	
Dominion Rolling Stock Debentures ..	289,391 75	
		$21,305,283 50
Accrued Dividend January-February..	$ 40,000 00	
Unpaid Royalty	37,589 50	
Accounts Payable	161,941 50	
Notes Payable.....................	840,000 00	
		1,079,531 00
Special Reserve		106,277 25
Surplus—		
Balance from previous years......	$592,843 74	
For Current year.	937,681 44	
		1,530,525 18
Total.....................................		$24,021,616 93

The surplus earnings of the Company in the fiscal year 1902 had been $937,681, while $122,939 had been deposited in the sinking fund for redemption of bonds.   The net proceeds from sales, etc., were $1,551,880 as compared with $687,254 in 1901.   The bonded indebtedness was now $2,589,500.   At these meetings the Directors were selected, and those of the Dominion Iron and Steel Company were re-elected as follows: H. M. Whitney of Boston; Sir W. C. Van Horne, Hon. R. Mackay, James Ross, R. B. Angus and Hon. L. J. Forget of Montreal; Hon. George A. Cox and Elias Rogers of Toronto; Hon. David McKeen, W. B. Ross and B. F. Pearson of Halifax; J. S. MacLennan of Sydney; H. F. Dimock, A. H. Paget and F. S. Pearson of New York.   The Directors of the Dominion Coal Company were chosen as follows: Lord Strathcona, R. B. Angus, H. F. Dimock, Senator Forget, Senator McKeen, J. S. Mac-Lennan, F. S. Pearson, James Ross, W. B. Ross, Sir W. C. Van Horne, H. M. Whitney and Senator Cox.   Of the now affiliated Companies Mr. James Ross was elected President and Senators George A. Cox and L. J. Forget Vice-Presidents.

Prior to this time several important events had occurred as well as the partial amalgamation of the two concerns.   On February 17th Mr. A. J. Moxham announced his retirement from the position of General Manager of the Dominion Iron and Steel Company, and Mr. James Ross assumed the position of Managing Director until the retirement of Mr. Whitney from the Presidency and the acquisition of practical control over this and the Coal Company by their Canadian Directors made him President.   Mr. David Baker had been appointed General Manager under Mr. Ross.   On March 2nd it was announced that the Iron and Steel Company had decided to issue an additional common stock of $10,000,000, and that amount had already been underwritten by a syndicate of Canadian banks.   In the Nova Scotia Legislature on March 5th, Attorney-General Longley moved the second reading of a measure giving necessary powers to the Company in this connection and it passed the House in due course.   One of the financial features of this period was the rapid speculative advance in the prices of Dominion Steel and Dominion Coal stock, one estimate giving the enhanced value over the same date in 1901 at $1,140,000 for the former and $2,550,000 for the latter.*

Speaking to the Vancouver *Province* on April 8th, Mr. Frederic Nicholls, a Toronto capitalist, expressed his belief that the Maritime Provinces were " destined to become one of the greatest manufacturing centres on the continent," and then added : "The Dominion Iron and Steel Works at Sydney have alone expended in the vicinity of $16,000,000, and this industry is immense and far-reaching in its results."   On April 14th the Directors of the Dominion Iron and Steel and Dominion Coal Companies met in Montreal and dealt with the option of leasing the Coal Company which the other concern had held for some time—under conditions which included the payment of the fixed charges of the Coal Company, a 6 per cent. dividend on the common stock, an allowance of $25,000 a year for expenses, a royalty of 15 cents per ton on coal taken out in excess of 3,500,000 tons in any one year, assumption of all debts and liabilities (including an immediate payment of about $2,000,000) and the exclusion of certain valuable Coal properties from the arrangement. An agreement was finally and unanimously come to along the following lines:

(1) The present agreement to be modified so as to make it include all the properties and assets of the Coal Company, including its $1,530,000 surplus earnings. (2) The Coal Company to pay off its bonds and preferred stock by the issue of $5,000,000 common stock at 120 to its common shareholders, thereby increasing its total capital to $20,000,000. (3) The Steel Company to be relieved from the obligation to provide $600,000 forfeit money, and to pay the Coal Company a rental equal to 8 per cent. on its $20,000,000 capital stock.

This arrangement—which was afterwards approved at the annual meeting of the shareholders—was announced as so improving the position of the Steel Company that they would only ask for $5,000,000 of new stock instead of the larger sum originally intended. On the following day Mr. Ross stated that Mr. H. M. Whitney had resigned the Presidency of the Steel Company but would remain in charge until the annual meeting. On May 1st a special meeting was held and the issue of 50,000 new shares of common stock formally authorized. The purchasers of this stock were nearly all Canadians and included Lord Strathcona 1,000 shares, Mr. Ross 5,000, Senator Forget 5,000, Senator MacKay 2,500, Mr. R. B. Angus 1,000 and Mr. B. F. Pearson 1,000 shares.

Following these incidents of the union of the Companies and the annual meetings marked progress was shown in both concerns. Speaking to the press at Montreal on August 15th Senator Forget referred to the great activity prevailing at Sydney where the Coal mines were producing 12,000 tons a day of excellent coal and the Steel works, which had not commenced operations when he last visited them in September, 1901, were now producing 12,000 tons a month. The Coal Company was employing 26 vessels between Sydney, Montreal and Boston and the two concerns had more than 10,000 men in their employ. In November an important re-arrangement of an old contract made with the New England Gas and Coke Company of Boston, during the early days of the Coal Company by Mr. Whitney, was effected. After various fruitless negotiations Mr. Ross and Mr. Cornelius Shields, General Manager of the Coal Company, had decided to break the existing contract and it was announced on November 21st that shipments to Boston had been stopped. A week later the re-arranged contract was announced by which coal was to be supplied to the Boston concern at $1.95 for five years instead of at $1.90 for 20 years.

At a meeting of the Dominion Iron and Steel Company on December 18th it was decided not to proceed with the erection, as originally proposed, of a mill for the construction of steel rails, on

the ground of the limited available market. But it was stated
that the mill, when completed about May, 1903, would be devoted
to the manufacture of structural and other kinds of steel for which
there was better protection and a larger market. The official returns
of production issued by this Company for the year ending December
31st, 1902, showed 298,654 tons of iron ore mined at Bell Island;
27,499 tons imported from Spain, 24,978 tons imported from the
United States and 12,989 tons from Sweden and Cuba; 204,040
tons of limestone quarried by the Company, locally; and products
of 338,230 tons of pig-iron and 86,424 tons of steel billets and slabs.

There was a preliminary development during 1902 in the building of steel ships in Canada and a most pronounced movement in
various directions looking to the extension of the
Steel Ship-
Building,
Projects and
Interests
industry through Government and other public aid.
In an open letter to the Minister of Customs, dated
January 7th, Mr. John Bertram of Toronto, pointed to
the difficulty of Canadian competition with British-
built vessels fully equipped, coming in free of duty, when the local
manufacturer had to pay duty upon every item entering into the
construction of his ship with only a small and quiet inadequate
amount allowed as a drawback. After dealing with American
methods in the coasting trade, Mr. Bertram proceeded as follows:

First, Canadian ship-builders should be placed on a footing of equality
with British ship-builders. How this should be done is within the purview of
the policy of the present Government. A beginning has been made already by
granting a small drawback on new tonnage, and it only requires to go a step
further and make it such an amount as would equalize conditions between ship-
builders here and in Great Britain. Second, there seems no other way of
stopping our sharp and ingenious friends on the other side of the Lakes from
having us at a disadvantage except by strictly carrying out our own law with
regard to coasting regulations; and further, by taking a leaf out of their own
book and forbidding the registration of any American-built vessel in a Canadian
port.

At Halifax, on January 21st, President George S. Campbell of
the Board of Trade in his annual address referred to the encouragements which were being given locally to this industry, and
continued: "As steel of excellent quality is now being manufactured at Sydney, it seems to be only a question of time when ship-
building will again become an important Provincial industry."
Speaking to the Montreal *Star*, on February 8th, Mr. G. B. Hunter,
a well-known Newcastle-on Tyne ship-builder, stated that he had
been investigating possibilities in Canada, declared the importation
of steel plates and bars a heavy handicap to the industry, mentioned the probability of an early establishment of a steel ship-
building plant in Nova Scotia, and concluded by saying that there
was a great future for the industry in Canada. "From the nature
of things steel ship-building can be done in Canada cheaper than
anywhere else in the world. No country will in the future be able
to compete with Canada—neither England nor Germany nor the
United States."

20

On March 17th, Mr. Hunter announced in Halifax his willingness to take up and put through the matter of a steel ship-yard on the shores of Halifax Harbour if proper assistance were given him. Mayor Hamilton, in an interview with *The Herald*, strongly approved of the proposal and urged the immediate granting of the $100,000 previously voted by the city to help such an enterprise. A week later the City Council passed Resolutions approving once more the bonus of $100,000 which had been voted by the rate-payers, stating its willingness to discuss an increase in the subsidy if necessary, but declaring that the placing of the plant outside of City limits should be subject to another plebiscite. The Halifax Board of Trade followed up this action on April 17th with a lengthy Resolution, unanimously passed, of which the following clauses are the most important:

This Board notes with appreciation the wide-spread interest shown in the question of increased Canadian-built tonnage.

This Board is convinced that the building, owning and operating of a strictly Canadian merchant marine fleet, adequate to the transportation of our rapidly increasing exports, is essential to the continued prosperity of this Dominion as a whole.

That the people of Canada possess all the elements of maritime ascendancy, as no other country controls more valuable navigation, waterways, finer harbours, or greater extent of coast-line, all presenting unrivalled opportunities for marine traffic.

That this Board is of opinion that the Federal Government of Canada should encourage the building of modern steel ships in this Dominion sufficiently to place the industry on a parity at least with foreign competition.

That apart from any precedent, we believe that the establishment and operation of large ship-building plants in the different Provinces of this Dominion will be of direct and very material benefit to every Canadian interest. It will give employment to the better class of our native artisans (who now too generally seek their livelihood in the United States), increase our population, enlarge our home market for all kinds of agricultural products, and widen and quicken the domestic demand for all sorts of manufactured goods.

That every Province and Territory of the Dominion would be directly benefited by this industry; Ontario, Quebec, New Brunswick, Nova Scotia and British Columbia by the immediate impetus to business from the establishment of large works on the shores of their lakes, rivers or oceans, and Manitoba and the Territories by improved facilities and consequent cheapening of transportation for their products.

Be it Resolved, therefore, that in order to encourage the investment of capital and labour in this industry, this Board recommends that the Government at Ottawa pass a measure granting assistance to steel ship-building in Canada, which shall be sufficient in amount to place Canada on a parity at least with our chief competitors, and extend over a term of years long enough to fairly establish this industry, so that it may hold its way against outside competition.

And further, this Board would press upon the Government the imperative necessity for immediate action in this matter, particularly on account of the disastrous lack of Canadian tonnage on the great lakes for the movement of the grain crops of the North-West. We consider it a serious reflection on our commercial standing as a nation that such a large proportion of the products of our great North-West should be carried in Foreign bottoms and through Foreign channels.

Mr. Hunter wanted the offered City bonus of $100,000 and either another similar amount from Halifax, or permission to utilize the $100,000 offered by the neighbouring town of Dartmouth, together with the $100,000 promised by the Provincial Government. On April 30th the rate-payers of Halifax voted $200,000 subsidy toward the erection of a plant on Halifax Harbour. Meanwhile the Winnipeg Board of Trade on April 8th had passed a Resolution very similar in terms to that of Halifax and declaring that "the building, owning and operating of a Canadian merchant marine fleet, both on the ocean and inland lakes, adequate for the transportation of Canadian imports and exports, is a prime essential of the continued prosperity of the Dominion." The Toronto Board, on April 21st, passed Resolutions in favour of the application to Foreign-built ships of the same regulations as to registration which the said Foreign countries applied to Canadian ships and asking the Dominion Government "to make such increase in the rebates now allowed, and provide such other suitable allowance as would place Canadian builders on an even basis with British builders and bring such increase into effect at the earliest possible moment so as to facilitate the establishment of ship-yards of sufficient capacity to meet the rapidly growing demands made by the products of Western Canada, and in order that the carrying trade of Canada both on ocean and inland waters may be retained in Canadian hands."

The Dominion Government was urged on April 30th, by a delegation which waited on Sir R. Cartwright and Messrs. Sutherland and Mulock, to grant aid to the steel ship-building industry on the basis of $3 a ton for lake-built ships and 10 per cent. on the cost of construction for ocean-going and passenger steamers of Canadian registry with a tonnage of 1,000 or over. The Polson, Bertram and Collingwood Companies of Ontario were represented as were the prospective interests of the Maritime Provinces by Messrs. E. M. McDonald, M.P.P., and H. Crowe of Halifax. A Committee of House of Commons members was also organized with Mr. Wm. Roche as Chairman and they urged similar proposals upon the Premier and Mr. Fielding. Sir Wilfrid Laurier replied in a letter to Mr. Roche on May 12th to the effect that the matter would have "sympathetic consideration" and be inquired into after the close of the Session.

Meantime the Collingwood Ship-building Company of which Mr. John J. Long was President, had been making substantial progress in extending and increasing their plant and in building a handsome screw steamship for the Northern Navigation Company. The *Huronic* with a freight capacity of 3,200 tons and a passenger capacity of 300 was launched on May 24th amid due ceremony. Mr. Long, in his speech at a Collingwood Luncheon, referred to the recent increase of their authorized capital to $2,000,000, stated that $550,000 was issued and paid up and that $300,000 of new capital was required. They wanted to remodel the dry-dock, build a first-class machine shop and erect foundry and boiler shops. On August 22nd the Toronto *Mail* announced that the new issue had all been taken up. The Toronto *Globe* of August 9th stated that the Company had two more large steamships on hand and were steadily employing some 900 men in their works while the Cramp Steel Company were erecting elaborate and substantial buildings which would, in time, manufacture ship plates and other material essential or important to the neighbouring ship-building Company.

Early in June the Boards of Trade Conference in Toronto passed a Resolution in favour of Government assistance to the ship-building industries of the country and about the same time the *Record* and the *Post* of Sydney, C.B., started an agitation for the establishment of a local plant. The latter declared on July 17th that it would make the town a great industrial and distributing centre with a harbour full of steamers and railways alive with rushing cars. On August 5th a mass-meeting of rate-payers was held and a Resolution passed in favour of granting a civic bonus of $250,000 to such an industry. The day after, however, Mr. James Ross of the Dominion Steel and Coal Companies of Sydney, was interviewed in Montreal. He declared that his Directors had not yet considered such a matter and that expert opinion was divided as to its possibilities of success. He concluded as follows :

Ever since I became connected with the Dominion Iron and Steel Company I have given the subject much attention and, without wishing in any way to discourage those who are interested in the project, I hardly think the present time is a proper one to install such a plant in Canada. The undertaking is a gigantic one, and yet is one in which every large steel company is greatly interested. Events may happen in the near future which will change my opinion on the subject, but my present view is the result of careful investigation, made both at Sydney and Halifax.

At the meeting of the Maritime Board of Trade in Sydney, on August 21st, a Resolution was unanimously passed in favour of Dominion aid to the industry in the form of a tonnage bounty sufficiently large to enable Canadian builders to compete with outsiders, and extended over a term of years, so as to ensure the permanent establishment of the industry. Speaking to the press in Montreal, on September 24th, the Hon. G. H. Murray of Nova Scotia said that his Government was anxious to aid steel shipbuilding, and that he was about to visit the Bertram works in Toronto with a view to learning more of its possibilities. No definite arrangements had yet been made in his Province with any Company.

GENERAL INDUSTRIAL INTERESTS

Jan. 1.—The Nova Scotia Steel and Coal Company, Limited, claim that their coal areas in Cape Breton contain 216,000,000 tons of coal. According to their statement for the year ending December 31st, 1901, they had during that period mined and disposed of 350,000 tons of iron ore, 238,000 tons of coal and 26,000 tons of limestone and dolimite, and produced 52,000 tons of pig-iron and steel ingots. Meantime a coal-washing plant and coke-ovens at Sydney Mines had been completed, a coal-shipping pier at North Sydney commenced and a contract entered into for a new 200-ton blast furnace. The profits for the year are stated at $508,936, with dividends paid of $205,000.

Feb.   1.—The Hon. S. N. Parent, Premier of Quebec, reports as Minister of
Lands and Mines that there are 28 pulp and paper mills in the Province which have been in operation for a year or more, or are now
ready to commence work, and that 12 others are in course of construction and will shortly be in operation.

Feb. 14.—Speaking in the Nova Scotia Legislative Council, the Hon. David
McCurdy refers to the important industrial undertakings at Sydney,
which, he believed, when completed would be beyond the competition of anything of the kind on the Continent. "In the near future
we will become the manufacturing centre of the great Dominion if
not of the whole of North America."

Mar.   6.—Statistics published by Mr. George Johnson, Dominion Statistician,
show that the wood-pulp industry of Canada in 1902 was carried on
in 35 mills, with an output of 240,989 tons as compared with 264,600
tons in 1901. The value of the output in 1902 is stated at $4,383,182
and that of the exports at $2,501,664. Of the latter total Great
Britain took $976,102, the United States $1,598,139, and other
countries $17,333.

Mar.   7.—The annual meeting of the Crow's Nest Pass Company, Limited, is
held in Toronto, with Senator George A. Cox in the chair. The
Report shows Assets on December 31st, 1901, of $3,086,415,
invested in mines, real estate, plant, etc.; cash in bank of $115,000 ;
and accounts receivable of $245,285. The liabilities include a paid-up
capital stock of $2,500,000, bills payable of $219,032, accounts payable of $148,151, dividend accrued of $62,500 and amount at credit
of profit and loss $517,017. The President states the production
at 425,457 tons of coal, including 203,061 tons turned into coke
at Fernie ; the expenditure of $2,265,548, of which the pay-roll
amounted to $911,407 ; the employment of 1,312 men at the end of
the year ; the building of 112 new coke ovens ; the sale of coal to
the value of $644,253, and of coke $551,639 ; the delivery to Canadian smelters of 71,684 tons of coal and 137,782 tons of coke ; and
the export to the United States of 90,640 tons of coal and 85,047
tons of coke.

Mar. 26.—Negotiations are completed by which Messrs. C. R. Hosmer and
F. W. Thompson gain control of the W. W. Ogilvie Milling Company. It is therefore reorganized as the Ogilvie Flour Mills
Company, Limited, with the former gentleman as President and the
latter as Managing Director with head-quarters in Montreal. The
Western elevators controlled by the Company number 61 with a
total capacity of 1,737,000 bushels. Mr. Thompson tells the Montreal *Witness* that they propose to make their concern the strongest
flour milling business in the British Empire.

Mar. 29.—A meeting is held in Toronto of the shareholders of the Canada
Cycle and Motor Company with Mr. J. W. Flavelle in the chair.
The latter explains the condition of the business at length, warmly
defends the Directors and states that at a certain stage in the
affairs of the Company Senator Cox, Mr. A. E. Ames and himself
had purchased $160,000 worth of stock in order to protect the situa-
tion and that this they still held. The members of the Board and
their immediate friends now held $1,300,000 out of $2,500,000 worth
of shares. He admitted errors of judgment in the Directorate
caused by sudden changes in the whole character of the business
and greatly increased costs of operation, but deprecated unfair criticisms. The following Resolution was then carried without opposition : "That this meeting, having heard the explanations of the
Chairman and President with entire satisfaction, are of opinion that
whatever mistakes in judgment may have been made there has been,
in our opinion, entire good faith in the action of the Directors in
the inception and management of the Company ; and that it is

desirable in the interests of the shareholders and a matter of justice to the Directors to give them our hearty support and confidence in the future."

April 1.—The formal organization of the International Nickel Company takes place at New York. The concern assumes the capital stock of the Oxford Copper Company, the Canadian Copper Company, the Anglo-American Iron Company, and the Vermillion Mining Company—all of Sudbury, Canada ; the Nickel Corporation of London, the Societie Miniers Caledonienne of New Caledonia and the American Nickel Works of Camden, New Jersey. Mr. Ambrose Monella is elected President and Mr. R. M. Thompson Vice-President.

May 30.—The second reading of a measure moved by Mr. J. F. Garden in the Legislature of British Columbia passes without opposition and provides that all railways given a Provincial subsidy of any kind in the future shall use rails and spikes constructed within the Dominion—provided they can be obtained at the prices current in Great Britain or the United States *plus* the cost of freightage.

July 16.—A meeting of the Directors of the Nova Scotia Steel and Coal Company is held at Montreal with Mr. John F. Stairs, President, in the chair and with Senator Melvin Jones and Robert Jaffray present from Toronto ; R. E. Harris, C. Graham Fraser and J. D. McGregor from Nova Scotia ; and Robert Reford from Montreal. The Managing Director, Mr. Fraser, presents a Report of a most prosperous character for the first six months of the year and speaks of the completed up-to-date shipping pier at North Sydney ; the busy coke ovens at Sydney Mines ; the steel plant at Trenton crowded with orders ; the Company's fleet of ten large freight steamers with an aggregate tonnage of 53,000, all exceptionally busy ; and the foundation at Sydney Mines of what he believes will be a town of 15,000 or 20,000 persons in a few years.

Sept. 29.—The Calgary *Herald* points out that Canada pays $10,000,000 a year for its sugar to other countries and yet could produce unlimited beet sugar at a large profit to its farmers. The soil and climate of Alberta are declared to be better than those of Ontario for the purpose although Berlin, Wallaceburg, Dresden and Wiarton had already started factories with a combined capacity of 2,400 tons daily.

Oct. 2.—At the annual meeting of the Ogilvie Flour Mills Company, Limited, a most satisfactory Report is presented. Mr. Charles R. Hosmer is elected President ; Mr. F. W. Thompson, Vice-President and Managing-Director ; Senator George A. Drummond and Messrs. H. Montague Allan and E. S. Clouston Directors; Shirley Ogilvie, Secretary ; S. A. McMurtry, Treasurer ; and W. A. Black, Western Manager.

Oct. 6.—Mayor Howland of Toronto criticizes the Dominion Coal Company for its stated inability to supply coal to Toronto during the Pennsylvania strikes ; accuses them of being indentified with American mine owners; and suggests the oxpropriation of a portion of Canadian mines for public purposes. General Manager Shields promptly denies these statements and asserts that three-fourths of their product is sold in Canada. The Canals, he states, are not deep enough to send coal to Toronto and in any case they did not have enough on hand at the moment to meet the demand.

Oct. 8.—The Calgary *Herald* continues its beet-sugar campaign and points out that an average factory of this kind costs $500,000, involves the cultivation of 5,000 acres, pays the farmers $225,000, employs 206 workmen and pays $70,000 in wages. It urges action in Calgary, Edmonton and other places.

Oct. 15.—The organization in Toronto is announced of the Canadian Preference League with a Committee composed of Messrs. W. Barclay McMurrich, K.C., Edgar A. Wills, Frank E. Hodgins, K.C., George H. Hees, Wm. Wallace and George H. Roberts and with objects stated in the membership card, as follows :

"I hereby associate myself with the Canadian Preference League, and as a member thereof I pledge myself to give preference, when making purchases, to the products of this country, and to all articles of Canadian manufacture, when the quality is equal and the cost not in excess of the similar foreign products or manufactured articles. I also undertake to give preference to Canadian labour and to this country's educational and financial institution."

Oct. 31.—The annual meeting of the Canada Cycle and Motor Company is held in Toronto with Mr. J. W. Flavelle in the chair and Senator Cox, Senator Melvin Jones and others present. It is stated that "the bottom had fallen out of the bicycle market" followed by decreased sales and lower prices. The importation of cheap wheels from the United States had been injurious during the past year, the European business had proven a disappointment and that of Australasia had shown a satisfactory increase. Various economies and consolidations had been effected during the year. The net amount of "liquid" assets are placed at $1,239,498 and the liabilities to the public at $1,092,927. A reorganization is recommended as soon as present litigation in the Courts is concluded.

Nov. 20.—It is stated that at a meeting held in St. John, N.B., following several other conferences, a reorganization of the Alexander Gibson Railway and Manufacturing Company, Limited, is to take place with a capitalization of $6,000,000 and Provincial Directors consisting of Mr Gibson, Mr. John F. Staus of Halifax, Lieut.-Col. H. H. McLean, K.C., and R. E. Harris, K.C., of Halifax, and others. The properties concerned include the Canadian Eastern Railway, the Gibson Cotton Mill at Marysville, the Gibson lumber lands of 250,000 acres, lumber mills at Marysville, a grist mill, a brickyard and the village of Marysville itself.

Nov. 26.—It is announced that Messrs. William Mackenzie, Fred. Nicholls and H. M. Pellatt have organized a Company to obtain water power from Niagara Falls.

Dec. 5.—The *Canadian Manufacturer* states that the five Portland Cement factories in operation in Canada during 1901 had a yearly capacity of 445,000 barrels ; that in 1902 there were nine in operation with a capacity of 815,000 barrels ; and that the year 1903 would open with a full capacity of 1,515,000 barrels and with four new Companies constructing works of 825,000 barrels capacity.

XIII.—FINANCIAL INTERESTS AND AFFAIRS

The year 1902 was a most prosperous one in Canada. Speaking in London on February 20th, at the annual meeting of the Bank of British North America, Mr. E. A. Hoare, President of the

Business and Financial Conditions
institution, declared that while the Dominion in 1901 had reached the highest mark in her progress "we are inclined to hope that the year upon which we · have now entered may establish another record." The expectation was more than realized and, as the months passed away, the most cautious business man lost any fear of a change in current development.

To the Bank of Montreal shareholders, on June 2nd, Mr. E. S. Clouston, General Manager, spoke as follows: "Generally speaking, the past year has been a prosperous one for Canada, and so far the hand of the commercial barometer still stands at fair. The revenues of the country are large; railway earnings are steadily increasing; farmers are prosperous; the outlook for lumber is improving; and the tide of immigration has set in with greater volume, ensuring to Western Canada and indeed to the whole country, more rapid progress in population and material prosperity. The natural resources of the country are being steadily developed; the output of coal is increasing; and it looks as if we were on the eve of important results in the iron and steel industry." To the Canadian Bankers' Association meeting at Toronto on November 12th, Mr. Clouston in his annual address as President was still more explicit:

The year that has elapsed since our last meeting has witnessed a further remarkable expansion in all branches of Canadian trade and commerce, in which the business of banking has had its due share. It has been a year of no untoward incident in the domain of mercantile affairs. The prosperity enjoyed in bountiful measure since 1897 continues unabated, and no clouds are yet perceptible on the horizon, save perhaps an undue and speculative desire for financial expansion to anticipate the profits that still lie in the future. On the contrary, the signs from which encouragement and hope spring are abundant. A bountiful harvest has been safely gathered, particularly in our North-West, and is rapidly being carried to market, thanks to the liberally increased facilities provided for its transportation. The last returns show that the amount of grain moved to date this year exceeds by nearly forty per cent. the total for a similar period of 1901. Labour is fully employed, manufacturing industries are working well up to their capital, immigration is increasing at a rate which prompts the hope that we are at last succeeding in solving the problem of populating the North-West, new markets for our products are being exploited and old markets enlarged, means of transportation are being supplied and improved. Indeed, were one disposed to dwell on the possibilities of the future in the way of material development and prosperity, the field would afford a vast scope. Railway earnings, clearing house returns, figures of foreign commerce, the failure list, bank statements, in a word, all the tests by which the material conditions of a country are judged, indicate that Canada is experiencing an exceptionally high degree of prosperity.

There was no lack of statistical evidence as to this progress and prosperity. The *Insurance and Finance Chronicle* of Montreal, on November 28th, pointed out that in the preceding five years (fiscal) Canadian trade had increased $166,741,582 or 65 per cent.; the deposits in Canadian chartered banks had grown by $181,812,660 or 84·40 per cent.; the deposits in Government savings banks increased by $9,969,906 or 20·40 per cent.; discounts in banks increased by $141,171,651 or 68 per cent.; the bank notes in circulation increased by $24,348,045 or 58·56 per cent., and Government notes in circulation by $10,845,872 or 46·66 per cent. There were other indications of this prosperity. The Money Orders issued in Canada during 1897 totalled $12,987,230 and in the fiscal year 1902 amounted to $23,549,402. Of this latter total the amount payable in Canada had increased by $7,742,199 and that payable in other countries by $2,819,972. The Orders drawn on Canada rose from $2,245,467 to $3,575,803. Meanwhile, Bradstreet's* showed the following record of business failures for the calendar years 1901 and 1902:

	Assets.		Liabilities.	
PROVINCES.	1901.	1902.	1901.	1902.
Ontario	$1,669,823	$1,136,779	$3,784,451	$2,901,943
Quebec	1,467,930	1,353,300	3,938,804	3,377,980
New Brunswick	720,360	133,775	1,530,250	243,525
Nova Scotia	245,918	133,591	449,564	268,032
Prince Edward Island	49,900	50,615	81,000	124,179
Manitoba	129,320	57,853	334,045	130,340
North-West Territories	103,250	70,585	187,773	118,368
British Columbia	810,450	654,725	1,351,050	1,147,791
Yukon Territory		6,000		16,500
	$5,196,951	$3,597,223	$11,656,937	$8,328,658

The other Agency, Messrs. Dun and Company, gave somewhat different figures. Its total failures for 1901 were 1,341 with assets of $7,686,823 and liabilities of $10,811,671; while for 1902 the number given was 1,101, the assets $7,772,418 and the liabilities $10,934,777. Bank clearings showed marked increases in the large cities. In Montreal the figures were $734,941,608 for 1900 and $889,486,915 for 1901 and a still larger sum in 1902. In the eight cities possessing clearing houses there was an increase of nearly 300 millions in 1901 and, according to figures issued by the Toronto Clearing House on December 31st, 1902, the figures in that City had grown from $513,696,401 in 1900 to $625,271,306 in 1901 and $809,078,559 in 1902. There was a great deal of stock speculation

* NOTE—There are no official statistics of insolvency in Canada and the figures of the two chief continental agencies have to be accepted.

during the year and, according to figures quoted in the Halifax *Mail* of January 5th, 1903, the Montreal Stock Exchange transacted in 1902 ordinary sales of 2,025,128 shares as compared with 1,256,709 shares in 1901; and $7,322,950 sales of bonds at par value as against less than $2,000,000 in the preceding year. In Toronto the early part of the year saw a great advance in the price of stocks and later on a severe depression, including the "slump" of November 14th which will probably go on record in the stock market as " Black Friday." In this connection and as a summary of general conditions, a quotation may be given from the annual address of Mr. B. E. Walker, General Manager of the Canadian Bank of Commerce, on January 13th, 1903 :

As far as we can see, the basis of our largely increased trade is sound. Taking Canada as a whole, the area, yield and money value of our agricultural and pastoral products have increased. The exceptions to such general good fortune, which are almost certain to occur in any year, are less present than we have ever before known to be the case in Canada. No country in this happy condition can fail to go rapidly forward, nor can the general financial position be made weak, except by the one cause which is almost certain to operate adversely in the long run, that is, undue speculation. The increase in the volume of our manufactures, and in the distribution of these and of imported goods, naturally accompanies the increase in the products of agriculture, pastures, mines, forests, etc., but it has been so great as to seem to require a note of warning.

The authorized capital of Canadian chartered banks on January 31st, 1902, was $76,326,666 and on December 31st, 1902, $83,332,566. The paid-up capital rose during the **Banking** same period from $67,621,011 to $72,795,440; the **Progress** reserve fund from $37,483,053 to $44,517,681; the **in 1902** notes in circulation from $48,586,529 to $60,574,144; the public deposits (in Canada) from $232,856,622 to $370,108,368; and the total liabilities from $439,734,790 to $499,508,534. Similarly the total assets increased from $550,875,792 to $625,388,209.* Of these latter sums the specie held by the banks on January 31st, was $11,843,574 and on December 31st, $12,892,235; the Dominion notes were stated at $21,891,097 and $24,730,575 respectively; the balances due by agencies or banks outside of Canada increased from $18,778,485 to $22,718,448; the Dominion, Provincial, Municipal, Colonial or Foreign securities held were valued respectively at $24,357,179 and $24,335,406; the railway and other bonds, debentures, stocks, etc., held increased from $33,167,297 to $36,925,800; the call and short loans on stocks and bonds in Canada rose from $38,079,718 to $51,385,890 and, outside of Canada, amounted to $44,189,514 on January 31st, and to $43,704,054 on December 31st. The current loans in Canada were $287,722,080 at the former date and $322,879,089 at the latter, while the current loans outside of Canada rose from $28,719,992 to $34,131,237. The following table is a condensed summary of the individual position of the chartered banks of Canada on December 31st, 1902 :

---

*Note—Official figures issued by Mr. J. M. Courtney, c.m.g., Deputy Minister of Finance.

Name.	Total Assets.	Total Liabilities.	Paid-up Capital.	Reserve Fund.	Call and Short Loans.	Current Loans.	Notes in Circulation.	Deposits on Demand.	Deposits on Notice.	Specie and Dominion Notes held.
Bank of Montreal	$123,618,710	$102,613,948	$12,000,000	$8,400,000	$7,187,304	$68,296,306	$9,588,070	$22,981,294	$40,524,891	$6,076,474
Bank of New Brunswick	4,810,628	3,536,065	500,000	750,000	789,320	2,453,767	477,331	676,616	2,234,835	355,930
Quebec Bank	13,672,816	10,103,765	2,500,000	800,000	3,347,391	7,114,453	2,164,403	3,123,725	4,318,945	828,947
Bank of Nova Scotia	27,658,558	22,560,802	2,000,000	3,000,000	5,869,069	11,680,547	1,903,834	5,555,678	11,392,984	3,285,230
St. Stephen's Bank	823,038	464,897	200,000	45,000		515,210	129,400	103,776	212,106	26,534
Bank of British North America	38,426,290	28,785,549	4,866,566	1,776,333	7,732,658	17,457,691	2,963,626	5,121,701	7,993,909	2,048,432
Bank of Toronto	23,741,434	18,368,919	2,500,300	2,600,000	2,944,240	14,052,328	2,312,991	4,969,459	10,515,039	2,049,484
Molson's Bank	24,772,241	19,680,412	2,500,300	2,250,000	2,804,931	15,502,524	2,316,575	5,122,708	11,796,918	1,271,819
Eastern Townships Bank	12,444,408	9,068,412	1,998,330	1,200,000	570,101	8,382,154	1,485,730	1,361,483	6,058,143	301,474
Union Bank of Halifax	9,394,813	7,203,235	1,205,300	775,000	450,898	6,247,307	1,104,736	968,115	4,029,260	721,830
Ontario Bank	13,608,546	11,477,498	1,500,900	425,000	804,514	9,633,727	1,383,968	2,736,694	6,624,947	486,300
Banque Nationale	8,895,571	6,813,376	1,498,524	350,000	516,139	7,055,129	1,432,874	1,266,261	3,877,018	282,433
Merchants' Bank of Canada	38,370,465	29,565,735	6,000,000	2,700,000	7,698,732	16,702,671	5,157,035	6,529,043	16,046,277	1,921,585
Banque Provinciale du Canada	3,662,894	2,779,919	819,214		640,732	1,743,092	237,637	574,885	861,183	53,323
People's Bank of Halifax	4,409,056	3,324,166	700,000	280,000	122,248	3,576,515	657,744	111,715	1,953,375	241,900
People's Bank of New Brunswick	973,520	598,806	180,000	160,000	75,000	765,042	161,123	52,729	298,503	28,180
Bank of Yarmouth	877,091	502,393	300,000	50,000		683,396	74,129	359,925		49,029
Union Bank of Canada	17,120,795	13,979,400	2,244,800	650,000	702,272	14,190,443	2,198,692	4,322,957	6,637,168	761,040
Canadian Bank of Commerce	72,293,497	61,654,404	8,000,000	2,500,000	967,834	44,758,296	6,928,005	14,597,237	31,791,927	2,661,620
Exchange Bank of Yarmouth	719,718	387,612	266,596	50,000		435,167	28,035		194,283	16,179
Royal Bank of Canada	21,929,968	16,789,343	2,481,000	2,500,000	790,755	11,145,743	1,920,713	3,129,962	9,405,863	1,836,834
Dominion Bank	32,611,338	26,028,566	2,917,468	2,917,468	861,003	18,327,999	2,596,441	7,174,160	15,645,742	2,879,982
Merchants' Bank of P. E. I.	1,787,752	1,274,804	300,013	205,000		1,515,040	278,682	515,303	457,682	51,251
Halifax Banking Company	6,025,680	4,990,680	600,000	525,000	311,415	3,854,173	560,475	827,439	3,158,353	623,990
Bank of Hamilton	22,520,807	18,686,516	2,000,000	1,600,000	2,409,013	14,252,043	1,825,590	4,568,206	10,916,812	1,364,822
Standard Bank of Canada	13,952,273	12,017,677	1,000,000	850,000	1,109,973	8,023,774	886,925	2,920,086	7,539,120	724,120
Banque de St. Jean	768,405	473,409	263,417	10,000		510,328	141,373	33,473	278,714	17,457
Banque d'Hochelaga	12,981,047	9,840,355	1,989,800	950,000	1,389,026	8,118,638	1,683,658	2,251,637	5,417,282	731,033
Banque de St. Hyacinthe	1,787,445	1,321,502	328,865	75,000	15,913	1,536,615	252,580	61,803	1,002,290	23,838
Bank of Ottawa	17,701,606	13,691,441	2,000,000	1,865,000	1,577,164	11,380,907	1,804,901	2,806,845	8,911,123	1,221,132
Imperial Bank of Canada	28,422,875	22,603,354	2,985,394	2,495,087	4,447,422	14,689,089	2,628,291	7,227,838	12,381,124	3,372,983
Western Bank of Canada	3,852,488	3,204,599	434,889	150,000		2,027,195	388,195	455,019	2,361,076	57,575
Traders' Bank of Canada	13,896,576	11,943,872	1,500,000	350,000	2,313,875	7,876,862	1,428,225	2,373,103	7,847,666	751,883
Sovereign Bank of Canada	4,730,113	3,189,003	1,263,764	263,793	1,587,257	1,885,762	873,365	992,769	1,148,865	255,621
Metropolitan Bank	2,225,747	224,050	1,000,000	1,000,000	1,253,473	459,393	38,330	111,108	24,611	242,546
	$625,388,209	$499,508,534	$72,795,440	$44,517,681	$95,289,944	$357,010,326	$60,574,144	$115,880,499	$254,217,869	$37,622,810

Several incidents of import to the banking system of Canada occurred during the year. In January it was announced that the Sovereign Bank of Canada, which had obtained a charter at the preceding Session of Parliament, would shortly enter the financial field with an authorized capital stock of $2,000,000, issued at a premium of 25 per cent. and with Mr. Duncan M. Stewart, lately Inspector of the Royal Bank of Canada, as General Manager. The new institution was formally organized and opened for business on April 23rd with the following Directors: Messrs. H. S. Holt and James Carruthers of Montreal; A. A. Allan, Archibald Campbell, M.P., Randolph Macdonald and John Pugsley of Toronto; Senator Peter McLaren of Perth and Senator McMillan of Alexandria; Henry R. Wilson of New York. Mr. H. S. Holt was elected President and Messrs. Macdonald and Carruthers, Vice-Presidents. Branches were announced as about to be opened in Montreal, Amherstburg, Perth, St. Catharines and Stouffville and the paid-up capital, according to the official statement for May 31st, following, was $740,711 with a reserve fund of $110,000.

Toward the close of the year the Metropolitan Bank was organized under somewhat exceptional circumstances. The principal promoter was Mr. A. E. Ames, President of the Toronto Board of Trade, and the capital stock was announced at $1,000,000 with the shares placed at 100 per cent. premium. On September 8th, it was stated that application had been received for $1,400,000 of the issue and the public was allowed to subscribe for the remaining $600,000 on September 15th—which they did to considerably over the amount offered. The organization meeting of the new institution was held in Toronto on October 24th, when Mr. Ames was elected President and the Rev. R. H. Warden, D.D., Vice-President. The remaining Directors were Messrs. T. Bradshaw, Chester D. Massey and S. J. Moore. On November 17th the Bank was opened with Mr. F. W. Baillie as General Manager and a little later Mr. W. D. Ross of the Finance Department, Ottawa, became Assistant General Manager. The official figures for November 30th, showed a paid-up capital stock of $702,975 and a reserve fund of the same amount.

Meanwhile, in general banking matters, Mr. H. C. McLeod, General Manager of the Bank of Nova Scotia, had been advocating certain changes in the Banking Act and these were summarized by the Halifax *Mail* of April 9th as including (1) the requirement that all banks should, under heavy penalties, be compelled to hold specie and Dominion notes to the extent of 15 per cent. of their combined deposits and circulation; (2) the privilege to banks of increasing their circulation beyond the amount of their paid-up capital—which is the present limit—by depositing specie or Dominion notes with the Dominion Government equal in amount to such proposed increase; (3) the Government inspection of all banks and rigid supervision of bank circulation. On November 13th, the Canadian Bankers' Association met in Toronto with

Mr. Duncan Coulson acting as Chairman in the absence of the President, Mr. E. S. Clouston.

An address, however, from the latter was read which reviewed the conditions of the year at some length. He referred to the remarkable expansion of the period in all branches of trade and commerce as well as in banking; mentioned the increase of Canadian bank assets in the past decade from $291,000,000 to $610,000,000, of notes in circulation from $33,000,000 to $56,000,000, of deposits from $166,000,000 to $359,000,000; pointed out that the limit of note circulation under the Bank Act was nearly reached but strongly deprecated the suggestion that the rest or reserve account might be made a basis for additional circulation; opposed the proposal to issue notes, after depositing a similar sum with the Government, as interfering with the general elasticity of the system; and seemed to consider increased capital as the best and safest way to meet the situation. The following officers of the Association were elected: Hon. Presidents, Lord Strathcona and Mount Royal and Mr. George Hague; President, Mr. E. S. Clouston of Montreal; Vice-Presidents, Messrs. D. Coulson of Toronto, H. Stikeman and M. J. A. Prendergast of Montreal, and George Burn of Ottawa. Toward the close of the year the Union Bank of Canada absorbed the Commercial Bank of Windsor, N.S. The latter institution had seven branches—all in Nova Scotia—and, according to its last statement to the Government on September 30th, had a paid-up capital of $350,000, a reserve fund of $25,000, notes in circulation of $323,846, deposits of $961,466, current loans of $1,239,764 and total assets of $1,688,140; with total liabilities of $1,304,170.

The most prominent incident of Canadian banking progress in 1902 was, perhaps, the very large number of new branches opened for the purpose of meeting the enlarged and increasing requirements of the country and of business. On the 1st of January, 1902, there were 747 branches of Canadian banks in Canada. During the year 120 were added to this total. The Bank of Montreal opened at Raymond, N.W.T., and at Paris and Collingwood, Ont. The Canadian Bank of Commerce opened at Ladysmith, B.C.; at Carman, Dauphin, Elgin, Gilbert Plains, Grandview, Neepawa, Swan River and Treherne in Manitoba; at Calgary, Edmonton, Medicine Hat and Moosomin in the North-West Territories; and at Wiarton, Ont. The Imperial Bank of Canada opened at North Bay, Ont., Cranbrook and Victoria, B.C., and at Metaskiwin, Manitoba.

The new branches of the Bank of Hamilton were at Brantford, Teeswater, Hagersville, Niagara Falls (South) Hamilton (West End) Dunnville and Midland—all in Ontario; at Roland, Minnedosa, Winnipeg, (Grain Exchange branch) Miami and Gladstone in Manitoba; and at Saskatoon, N.W.T., and Kamloops, B.C. The Merchants Bank of Canada opened during the year at Crediton, Creemore, Lancaster, Little Current and Meaford, in Ontario, with sub-agencies at Lansdowne and Wheatley; and at Carnduff,

Leduc, Macgregor, Morris, Oak Lake and Whitewood in Manitoba and the Territories. The Ontario Bank opened a new branch at Collingwood, Ont., and another at the corner of Yonge and Carlton Streets in Toronto. The Bank of Toronto opened at Creemore, Elmvale, Millbrook, Oakville, Sudbury and Thornbury in Ontario and at Gaspé Basin in Quebec. The Dominion Bank opened another branch in Toronto and one at London, Ont., as well as at Brandon, Boissevain and Deloraine in Manitoba and at Grenfell, N.W.T. Besides its acquisition of the Commercial Bank of Windsor in Nova Scotia, the Union Bank of Canada devoted much attention to the West and during 1902 opened branches at Altona, Birtle, Cypress River, Rapid City, Russell and Shoal Lake in Manitoba and at Arcola, Cardston, Didsbury, Edmonton, Fort Saskatchewan, Frank, High River, Lumsden, Medicine Hat, Okatoks, Oxbow, Qu'Appelle, Sintaluta, Wapella and Wolseley in the Territories.

The Standard Bank of Canada opened a new branch in Toronto and others at Lucan, Beaverton, Orono and Parkhill—all in Ontario. The Bank of Nova Scotia opened at Granville, Ferry, Parrsboro' and Sydney Mines in Nova Scotia ; at Port Elgin in New Brunswick ; and at Hamilton in Ontario. The Traders' Bank of Canada opened offices at Rodney, Lakefield, Prescott, Schomberg and Woodstock in Ontario. Then there were the two new institutions. The Metropolitan Bank opened three branches in Toronto, besides the main office, and also at Milton, Ont. The Sovereign Bank of Canada opened at Amherstburg, Crediton, Milverton, Mount Albert, Newmarket, Ottawa, Perth, St. Catharines, Stirling, Stouffville, Unionville and Clinton—all in Ontario; and at Montreal, Sutton and Waterloo in Quebec.

At the close of the year 1900 there were in Canada 97 Companies classified officially as Loan Companies or Building Societies.

The Loan Companies of Canada They possessed assets* of $152,640,265, which included current loans on real estate of $112,685,625, other loans of $10,733,599, cash in hand and in banks of $5,730,107, and property valued at $29,221,042. The liabilities included a paid-up capital of $48,894,491, a reserve fund of $10,290,381, deposits of $19,959,462, debentures payable in Canada of $15,044,231, debentures payable elsewhere of $35,650,417, and various liabilities of $22,801,282. The dividends declared in 1900 amounted to $2,415,049, the money loaned was $26,087,251, the amount received from borrowers was $29,621,335, the interest paid and accrued amounted to $3,543,110, and the value of the real estate under mortgage was $190,992,476.

Ontario, as a Province, was the chief centre of this business, however, and on June 2nd, 1902, Mr. J. Howard Hunter, Registrar of Loan Corporations, issued his Report for the year ending December 31st, 1901. The abstract of his statement, which follows, includes statistics of the Loan Companies having some terminating

---

* NOTE—The latest figures for all Canada and the only ones available are these from the Statistical Year Book of 1901.

Mr. James Ross

Mr. A. E. Ames

stock, or all terminating stock, as well as the main element in the
subject—those Companies which possess only permanent stock. It
also includes Loaning Land Companies and Trusts Companies:

ASSETS.

Debts secured by mortgages of land...........	$103,385,529	67
Interest....................................	2,291,585	78
Debts secured by—		
1. Debentures and Debenture Stock..........	3,247,801	02
2. Government Securities...................	935,076	86
3. Shareholders' Stock.....................	923,240	58
4. Other Stocks, bonds and securities........	15,310,216	00
Office Premiums............................	2,117,937	57
Freehold Land..............................	7,010,006	75
Office Furniture.............................	86,928	08
Cash.......................................	4,089,761	49
Miscellaneous..............................	1,084,167	07
Trust Securities............................	15,129,914	14
Total..................................	$155,612,165	01

LIABILITIES.

To Shareholders—		
Permanent Stock (paid-up)...................	$26,578,895	11
Permanent Stock (partly paid-up).............	16,755,044	32
Terminating Stock (paid-up)	271,674	33
Terminating Stock (prepaid)	1,316,320	91
Terminating Stock (instalment)...............	3,914,192	57
Reserve Fund.	10,317,861	75
Dividends declared and unpaid................	902,768	51
Contingent Fund...........................	811,219	24
Unappropriated Profits.......................	680,615	65
Profits on Terminating Stock.................	434,570	38
Miscellaneous..............................	236,500	60
To the Public—		
Deposits...................................	19,892,496	65
Interest on Deposits........................	247,197	32
Debentures payable in Canada	16,879,498	94
Debentures payable elsewhere.................	35,015,011	30
Debenture Stock	3,321,149	58
Interest on Debentures......................	496,734	87
Due on incomplete Loans....................	356,048	65
Owing to Banks.	440,336	31
Contingent Liabilities.......................	15,158,138	96
Miscellaneous..............................	1,585,889	06
Total..................................	$155,612,165	01

The total amount of Life Insurance in force in Canada at the
end of 1901 was $463,769,034, or an increase of $32,699,188 over
the previous year. It was divided amongst the
Companies as follows: Canadian $284,684,621, or
an increase of $17,533,535; British $40,216,186, or
an increase of $730,842; and American $138,868,227,
or an increase of $14,434,811. There was a total insurance effected of
$73,899,228 as against $68,896,092 in 1900 and including $38,298,747
for Canadian Companies as compared with $38,545,949 in 1900;

*Life
Insurance
in Canada*

$3,059,043 for the British Companies as against $3,717,997 in 1900; and $32,541,438 for the American Companies as compared with $26,632,146 in 1900. This latter increase was due to the Metropolitan Life taking over the risks of La Canadienne, a concern doing an industrial insurance business in Quebec. It may be added that the special forms of insurance included in these general Life figures cover the industrial policies of the London Life and the Metropolitan, the thrift policies of the Sun Life, the monthly policies of the Excelsior Life and the provident policies of the North American.

The premium income in 1901 of the Canadian Companies was $9,133,891, of the British Companies $1,346,666 and of the American concerns $4,709,298—a total of $15,189,854. The assets in Canada of British Life Companies in 1901 were $24,500,867 and the liabilities $13,409,496; the assets of American Life Companies in Canada were $29,835,015 and the liabilities $27,280,467. The total income of the former was $2,365,482 and of the latter $5,732,232. The expenditures of the former in Canada were $1,236,478 and of the latter $4,189,295. The following table gives miscellaneous facts regarding Canadian Life Companies in 1901:

ASSETS.

Real Estate	$5,128,108
Loans on Real Estate	19,065,310
Loans on Collaterals	3,890,222
Cash Loans and Premium Obligations	6,437,681
Stocks and Bonds and Debentures	27,064,633
Cash in hand, Bills Receivable, Outstanding Premiums, etc.	4,596,160
	$66,182,114

LIABILITIES.

Unsettled Claims	$ 579,392
Net Re-insurance Reserve	59,211,836
Sundries	559,641
	$60,350,869

SUNDRIES.

Surplus of Assets over Liabilities	$5,831,245
Capital Stock paid-up	3,189,097
Net Premium Income in 1901	10,891,454
Total Income	13,866,753
Payments to Policy-holders	4,890,754
Total Expenditures	8,281,653

The official statistics for the year ending December 31st, 1901, showed 38 Fire Insurance Companies doing business in Canada— 21 British, 9 Canadian and 8 American. The cash received for premiums during the year was $9,650,348 and the amount paid for losses $6,774,956. The rate of the losses to premiums was, therefore, 70·20 as compared with 93·31 in 1900. Since 1869 the total premiums received had been $166,443,890 and the losses paid $116,187,297—

Fire
Insurance
in Canada

an average ratio of losses to premiums amounting to 69·81 per cent. per annum. During this period the Canadian Companies received $37,952,772 and paid in losses $26,568,096 ; the British received $110,260,764 and paid in losses $76,964,154 ; the American Companies received $18,230,354 and paid out $12,655,047. The following table illustrates the business of these Companies during 1901 :

Particulars.	Canadian Companies.	British Companies.	American Companies.
Gross amount of risks taken during the year..................	$170,894,095	$542,142,232	$108,486,527
Gross cash received for Premiums	2,400,305	7,583,192	1,574,946
Rate of Premium per cent. of Risk	1·45	1·41	1·44
Net Cash paid for Losses........	1,009,898	4,889,192	875,865
Net Cash received for Premiums..	1,727,410	6,595,447	1,327,491
Net amount at Risk Dec. 31, 1901	221,756,637	694,491,228	122,439,754

The total of all risks taken and renewed during the year was $821,522,854 ; the total premiums charged were $11,688,957 ; the total cash paid for losses was $6,774,956 ; and the total net cash received for premiums was $9,650,348. The income of Canadian Companies in 1901 was $6,286,942 from premiums, and the total income was $6,469,140. The expenditures were $6,304,161, including $4,065,778 in losses paid, $2,032,419 in general expenses, and $205,964 in dividends to shareholders.

There were four Companies doing a combined Fire and Marine Insurance business in Canada during 1901—the British-American, the Western, the Ætna, and the Insurance Company of North America. But the net cash received for premiums during the year was only $31,113, and the gross amount of policies, new and renewed, $9,561,027. There was the usual discussion from time to time as to the St. Lawrence route and the marine rates of a discriminating character imposed by British Companies. On January 21st the Halifax Board of Trade considered this subject in its annual Report from a local point of view. "Your Council has been unable to do anything more than continue to protest against the unjust discrimination against this port in connection with Marine Insurance. To place this fine open port on the same footing with the intricate navigation of the St. Lawrence is so manifestly unjust that it cannot be defended. If the ordinary business principle of making the premium correspond to the risks were applied, Halifax should have as favourable rates as any port on the Atlantic seaboard." The general standpoint was reviewed by Sir William Mulock, at a luncheon given in London, on July 13, by Lloyds' Register of Shipping, in the following terms :

Miscellaneous Insurance Interests

They felt in Canada that they did not get full justice from those who were interested in Marine Insurance, with the discrimination of nearly 100 per cent. against their waterways. Whatever views were held in this country, it was the determination of the people of Canada that Canadian produce should find its way to the markets of the world through British ports. Would it be out of the way for him to suggest that a Committee of Lloyds' should wait on the Canadian

21

representatives and point out where they could by any expenditure of money
or otherwise improve the navigation of their waters, so that Canadian trade
should not be handicapped as it was at present ? In the past month of June
there came from Canadian ports a very much larger quantity of wheat than
from the Port of New York, and that was but a commencement of what would
occur in the future.

Canadian Companies doing business of an Accident, Guarantee,
Plate-Glass, Burglary Guarantee and Steam Boiler Insurance character in Canada had total assets on December 31st, 1901, of
$1,760,604, of which $1,254,047 was invested in stocks, bonds and
debentures. Their liabilities were stated at $458,245 and their
paid-up capital stock at $680,865. The net cash received from
premiums in the year was $620,044, and the expenditures were
$580,443. The Guarantee Companies had policies in force of
$23,878,369 and the Accident Companies of $11,881,818.

On September 10th, 1902, Mr. J. Howard Hunter, Provincial
Inspector of Insurance, presented his Report for the calendar year
Fire and Life 1901 to the Attorney-General of Ontario. There were
Insurance only three Life Insurance Companies under Provin-
in Ontario cial jurisdiction, and they had assets of $332,703,
liabilities of $203,469, and carried risks amounting to
$3,836,313. Similarly, there were only three joint-stock Fire Insur-
ance Companies, with assets of $304,472, liabilities of $201,596, and
risks totaling $11,092,364. The Cash-Mutual Fire Insurance Com-
panies numbered ten on December 31st, 1901 ; possessed real estate
worth $85,730, mortgages, bonds, etc., worth $440,760, and cash in
offices $219,947 ; held unassessed premium notes of $953,977 ; and
possessed other assets making a total of $1,883,990. Their liabilities
included unpaid losses (afterwards discharged) of $25,922, unearned
premiums of $340,522, and capital stock, paid-up, of $100,104. The
net amount at risk was $93,630,146. The receipts for the year
were $961,367, including $466,892 as premiums on cash system and
$340,811 as fixed payments ; while the expenditures were $916,206,
including $123,499 as commission, etc., $512,385 paid out for losses.
and 101,442 paid for re-insurance.

The position of the 85 Purely-Mutual Fire Insurance Companies
of the Province on December 31st, 1901, showed assets of $4,909,905,
which included cash on hand of $217,000 and an unassessed pre-
mium note capital of $4,577,451. The total liabilities were $43,170,
the number of policies in force was 102,051, and the net amount of
risks $142,878,557. The receipts for 1901 were $364,771 and the
expenditures $304,199. The new business taken during 1901 was
$63,474,624, the premium notes were $2,481,009 in amount, and the
surplus of general assets over liabilities was stated at $6,321,267.
These were farmers' organizations for mutual insurance and so far,
in Ontario, seem to have been fairly successful and popular. The
Life Insurance or Benefit Societies of a Fraternal nature acting
under Provincial charter showed the following statistics on December 31st, 1901 :

Total membership	244,316
Insurance Certificates in force.................	809,939
Total amount of Insurance	$1,339,882,487
No. of Claims matured in Ontario during 1901 ...	1,227
Amount of Benefits paid in Ontario during 1901..	$1,684,273
Assets in Ontario at date	3,207,563
Liabilities in Ontario at date..................	226,107
Total Assets (anywhere)......................	9,094,459
Total Liabilities (anywhere)	1,520,430

The statistics in 1901 of sick and funeral benefits in some 86 Societies of a benefit and fraternal character in Ontario showed a membership of 63,140 ; the death of 1,059 during the year and the payment of $42,062 in funeral benefits ; the sickness of 16,727 members during a total period of 80,690 weeks; the payment as sick benefits of the sum of $320,237, for medical attendance of $52,338, and for special relief of $9,966 ; total assets of $1,501,883 and total liabilities of $85,393.

GENERAL FINANCIAL INTERESTS

Jan. 17.—The vacancy in the management of the Canada Permanent and Western Canada Mortgage Corporation caused by the death of Mr. Walter S. Lee is filled by the appointment of the 1st Vice-President, Mr. J. Herbert Mason, to be Managing Director.

Feb. 4.—Mr. Thomas Rodman Merritt is elected President of the Imperial Bank of Canada in succession to the late H. S. Howland and Mr. D. R. Wilkie, General Manager, is elected Vice-President in addition to his other post. In this latter connection, the *Globe* comments as follows : "This demand for his services in two important positions attests to the confidence and appreciation of the Directors. He deserves the reputation he enjoys of being one of the most prudent, sagacious and progressive bankers in Canada."

Feb. 27.—The annual meeting of the Canada Life Assurance Company is held in Toronto with the President, Senator George A. Cox, in the chair. During the year 1901, 3,659 policies were issued representing risks of $7,761,131. The death claims paid were $1,163,098, the net premium income was $2,476,251 and that from investments was $1,041,365. The total Assets on December 31st, 1901, were $24,504,790—an increase of $1,856,586. The total Liabilities deducted left a surplus on policy-holders' account of $1,348,706.

Feb. 28.—Mr. Justice Lavergne gives judgment at Montreal against the Mutual Reserve Fund Life Association of New York in a case in which the Hon. A. R. Angers, ex-Lieut.-Governor of Quebec, demanded the return of certain moneys on the ground of having been deceived as to the amounts which would have to be paid on two policies of $10,000 each, taken out in the Mutual Reserve. The Company denied any deception and claimed that the contracts were made under full knowledge as to conditions. Judgment is given on the stated ground of "misrepresentations and concealments" as to the rates exacted and payments to be met and all premiums collected are ordered to be repaid to Mr. Angers.

April 30.—The annual statement of the Bank of Montreal for the year ending at this date gives Assets of $114,670,653—including Government securities and Railway and other bonds, debentures and stocks, of $6,972,253 ; call and short loans in Great Britain and the United States, $29,220,983 ; current loans and discounts of $63,211,068 ; Government demand notes and specie, $7,125,746. The Liabilities include a capital stock of $12,000,000, a reserve fund of $8,000,000, notes in circulation amounting to $7,007,321, deposits not bearing interest of $22,899,086 and deposits bearing interest totalling $63,926,547. The profits for the year are $1,601,152.

June 4.—At the annual meeting of the Eastern Townships Bank at Sherbrooke the resignation of Mr. R. W. Heneker, D.C.L., President of the institution, is accepted after he had held the position for 28 years. Mr. William Farwell, General Manager, is elected in his place.

June 25.—It is announced that the Hastings Loan and Investment Society of Belleville and the Sun Savings and Loan Company of Toronto are to amalgamate with a capital of $1,000,000 and Mr. W. Pemberton Page as Manager.

July 7.—The annual meeting of the Hudson's Bay Company is held in London and presided over by Lord Strathcona. The proceeds of the sale of furs in England during the year ending March 31st are stated at £263,452—after deducting all charges for insurance, freight, etc. The sales in the Land Department are reported at £217,143 as against £84,588 in the previous year. The profits of the Company are stated at £138,197.

Sept. 16.—The retirement is announced of Mr. J. H. Plummer from the post of Assistant General Manager of the Canadian Bank of Commerce and the appointment of Mr. Alexander Laird, agent of the Bank in New York, to succeed him. Messrs. H. B. Walker and William Gray succeed Mr. Laird in New York.

Sept. 22.—The Treasury Bureau of Statistics at Washington reports the total deposits in the National Banks of the United States as being $2,937,-753,233 ; the deposits in Savings Banks as $2,597,094,580 ; those in State Banks as totalling $1,610,502,246 ; those in Loan and Trust Companies as $1,271,081,174 ; and the deposits in Private Banks as $118,621,903—a total of $8,535,053,136. This indicates, roughly, deposits of about $113 per head in the United States, in various forms, as against $89 in Canada, though the comparisons cannot be made exact.

Nov. 14.—In connection with the winding up of the Manitoba and North-Western Loan Company, which was commenced in 1898, the *Monetary Times* of Toronto states that a stock dividend of 50 per cent., or $375,000, has just been paid the shareholders ; that in the period mentioned lands, mortgages and other securities have been disposed of to the extent of $1,368,000 ; and that enough is now on hand to pay off the rest of the shareholders.

Nov. 28.—The *Insurance and Financial Chronicle* of Montreal draws attention to the fact that while in 1872 the paid-up capital of Canadian Banks was $45,003,435 and the total assets were $144,728,233, in 1902 they were, respectively, $71,137,510 and $616,326,970—a change of percentage in the relation of capital to assets from 31.10 in 1872 to 11.50 per cent. in 1902. It is also pointed out that in the former year the excess of deposits over paid-up capital was $3,954,-047 and in the latter year it was $326,041,382.

Nov. 30.—The annual statement of the Canadian Bank of Commerce to date shows Assets of $72,825,632, including Government bonds, municipal and other securities of $7,483,326, call and short loans of $7,247,-389 and current loans of $46,990,539. The Liabilities include a paid-up capital stock of $8,000,000, a reserve fund of $2,500,000, notes of the Bank in circulation amounting to $7,368,042, deposits not bearing interest of $15,978,891, and deposits bearing interest of $37,944,396. The net profits for the year are $1,028,509.

Dec. 2.—The organization is announced of the Great Western Permanent Loan and Savings Company, with headquarters at Winnipeg and incorporation under the Statutes of Manitoba. Mr. W. T. Alexander is President and Managing Director, and the other Directors are

Messrs. E. S. Popham, M.D., E. D. Martin, James Stewart, E. L.
Taylor, F. H. Alexander and Mayor Arbuthnot of Winnipeg.

Dec. 4.—It is announced that the Home Savings and Loan Company of
Toronto have applied for a Dominion charter as the Home Savings
Bank of Canada, and will start operations in 1903 under the old
management, and with deposits of over $2,500,000, a paid-up capital
of $1,000,000, and a reserve fund of $333,333.

Dec. 10.—At the annual meeting of the Bank of Ottawa, Ottawa, Mr. Charles
Magee announces his retirement from the Presidency, after having
served as Vice-President from the foundation of the Bank in 1874
up to 1892 and since then as President. Mr. George Hay is elected
his successor.

Dec. 10.—The shareholders of the Royal Bank of Canada are informed by
circular that a syndicate of American capitalists has offered to purchase one-half of the un-issued and authorized capital of the Bank,
amounting to 5,000 shares, or a total of $1,250,000. Mr. E. L.
Pease, the General Manager, approves the sale, subject to ratifica-
tion by his shareholders, and states that Marshall Field of Chicago,
J. J. Mitchell, President of the Illinois Trust and Savings Bank,
G. F. Baker, President of the First National Bank, New York, and
representatives of the Armours of Chicago and Blair and Company
of New York are amongst those interested.

Dec. 23.—The judgment of the Superior Court of Quebec in the case of Hon.
A. R. Angers against the Mutual Reserve Fund Life Association of
New York is considered by the Court of Appeal at Montreal and
reversed by unanimous decision. It is held that Mr. Angers should
have understood the terms upon which he insured, and is bound
to abide by them.

Dec. 27.—The organization meeting of the Sovereign Life Assurance Company
is held in Toronto and the Report of the Provisional Directors
accepted. Mr. A. H. Hoover is elected President and Managing
Director, with Messrs. William Dineen of Toronto and R. Shaw Wood
of London as Vice-Presidents. The other Directors are A. F. Web
ster, R. E. Menzie, E. E. Shoppard and J. T. Hornibrook of
Toronto; W. M. German, K.C., M.P., of Welland; John McClelland
of Parry Sound; and James Dixon of Hamilton.

Dec. 31.—The annual statement of the Confederation Life Association shows
Assets of $8,988,986, a premium income during 1902 of $1,139,054,
an interest income of $378,761, payments to policy-holders of
$633,163, policies issued of $3,400,495, cash surplus above all Liabilities of $485,861, and a total insurance in force amounting to
$34,609,831—an increase of $1,457,746 over 1901.

Dec. 31.—The Superintendent of Insurance reports regarding Canadian Companies doing the business of Life insurance upon the Assessment
plan. The one of chief importance is the Independent Order of
Foresters, with total Assets of $5,282,227, which amount includes
$2,762,542 loaned on real estate, $1,297,104 in stocks, bonds and
debentures, and $332,435 as cash in hand. The Liabilities are
stated at $342,141; the assessment income for 1901 at $2,612,717;
the total income at $3,002,485; the total expenditure at $2,356,529,
of which $1,728,775 went to members for insurance payments and
sick and funeral benefits. The amount paid by members in Canada
during the year was $1,005,483 and in other countries $1,628,565;
the amount of certificates new and taken up in Canada was $5,968,-
500 and elsewhere $17,902,500; the total insurance in force was
$83,308,500 in Canada and $133,719,000 abroad.

XIV.—POPULATION AND IMMIGRATION

Details of the Dominion Census taken in 1901, under the auspices of Mr. Archibald Blue and Mr. Thomas Coté, appeared at intervals during 1902. The population of Canada, which numbered 3,635,024 in 1871, 4,324,810 in 1881, and 4,833,239 in 1891, was announced as being 5,371,315 in 1901. The increase in the last decade was, therefore 538,076, and the only Province which showed a decrease was Prince Edward Island—from 109,078 to 103,259. The largest numerical increase was in Quebec, which rose from 1,488,535 to 1,648,898; the largest proportional increase was in the North-West Territories and Yukon, which had grown from 97,934 to 423,298. Ontario increased slightly, from 2,114,321 to 2,182,-947; Nova Scotia from 450,396 to 459,574; New Brunswick from 321,263 to 331,120. Manitoba grew from 152,506 to 255,211, and British Columbia from 98,173 to 178,657. The increase in city and town population was marked all over the country. In 1891 the rural districts totalled 3,296,141 and in 1901, 3,349,516, while the urban growth was from 1,537,098 to 2,021,799. The distribution was as follows:

The Fourth Census of Canada

Province.	Rural 1891.	Rural 1901.	Urban 1891.	Urban 1901.
Manitoba	111,498	184,738	41,008	70,473
Ontario	1,295,323	1,246,969	818,998	935,978
New Brunswick	272,362	253,835	48,901	77,285
Nova Scotia	373,403	330,191	76,993	129,383
Prince Edward Island	94,823	88,304	14,255	14,955
Quebec	988,820	992,667	499,715	656,231
British Columbia	60,945	88,478	37,228	90,179
Territories	98,967	164,334	......	47,315

According to religions or sects there were 157 divisions recorded and classified. There were only five over a hundred thousand in number and they included the Church of England, which showed an increase from 646,059 in 1891, to 680,620 in 1901; the Baptists, who had increased from 302,565 to 316,477; the Methodists, who showed an increase from 847,765 to 916,886; the Presbyterians, who rose in numbers from 755,326 to 842,442; and the Roman Catholics, who had risen from 1,992,017 to 2,229,600 in number. According to sexes and conjugal conditions the population showed a total of 2,460,471 males in 1891 and 2,372,768 females, while in 1901 there were 2,751,708 males and 2,619,607 females. The single or unmarried males in 1891 were 1,601,541, and in 1901, 1,748,582; the single females, respectively, 1,451,851 and 1,564,011. The married males in 1891 were 796,153, and in 1901, 928,952; the married females, respectively, 791,902 and 904,091. The widowed males in 1891 were 62,777, and in 1901, 73,837; the widowed females in 1891 were 129,015 and in 1901, 151,181. The divorced

326

males in 1901 were 337 in number and females 324. There were in the Dominion in 1901, 1,028, 892 houses and 1,070,747 families. According to origins there were 1,260,899 English, 988,721 Irish, 800,154 Scotch and 13,415 others of British origin. Those of French extraction numbered 1,649,371, of German origin 310,501, of Dutch origin 33,845, of Scandinavian extraction 31,042, of Russian origin 28,612, of Austro-Hungarian origin 18,178. There were 10,834 Italians, 16,131 Jews, 34,481 Half-breeds, 93,460 Indians, 22,050 Japanese and Chinese, 17,437 Negroes and the balance varied or unspecified. By nationality, as the Census termed it, there were 5,238,701 Canadians, 40,850 Americans, 19,087 Austro-Hungarians, 19,837 Russians, and 16,375 Chinese. The British-born population, born in Canada, numbered 4,671,815, born in the British Isles 390,019, and born in British Possessions 15,864. The Foreign-born population of Canada numbered 278,449. The population in 1901, which had originally emigrated to the Dominion, was 684,671 in number, of which 405,883 were of British origin.

This important subject attracted much attention during 1902, and the accessions of population through immigration were even more gratifying in this year than in the preceding one.

General Immigration to Canada According to the figures of the new Census, however, the influx from foreign countries had been increasing at a ratio in excess of that from British countries. The figures of population in the Dominion, of Foreign extraction, in 1891 were 157,110, including 80,915 from the United States ; those for 1901 were, respectively, 278,449 and 127,899. The population of British and Colonial birth—outside of Canada—was in 1891, 490,252. In 1901 it had decreased to 405,883. It may be noted, in passing, that the American Census in 1890 showed 678,442 English-speaking Canadians and 302,496 French-speaking Canadians in the United States, while that of 1900 showed 785,958 and 395,297 respectively.

During 1901 the arrivals of steerage passengers from across the Atlantic numbered 6,354, as against 4,983 in 1900, and all through 1901-2 the figures of immigration from the United States steadily increased. Meanwhile, every effort was being made to encourage immigration from Europe to Canada, and the British Returns for the six months ended June 30th, 1902, showed 10,093 persons of English extraction, 1,895 of Scotch, 712 of Irish, and 21,372 of Foreign extraction, who had left England as passengers for Canada. Of course a proportion of these were neither immigrants nor settlers. The total was 34,099 as against 21,920 during the same period in 1901. Under date of September 17th, 1902, the Report of Mr. Frank Pedley, Canadian Superintendent of Immigration,* gave the total figures for the fiscal year 1901 as 49,149 and for that of 1902 as 67,379. Of the former total 11,810 were British, 19,352 Continental

---

* NOTE—In the Report of the Department of the Interior, 1902.

and 17,987 American. In the latter year 17,259 were British, 23,732 Continental and 26,388 American. In 1902 the figures included 1,721 children. Of the Continental immigration in that year 6,550 were Galicians, 2,451 Scandinavians and 3,759 Russians and Finlanders.

According to the Report of Mr. J. Obed Smith, Immigration Commissioner at Winnipeg, dated June 30th, 1902, the arrivals of immigrants at that City in the fiscal year 1900 numbered 31,510, in 1901 32,005, and in 1902 55,261. In the last-mentioned year 10,768 of the total were from Great Britain—an increase of 150 per cent. over 1901; 12,530 were from Eastern Canada and 2,102 were Canadians returning from the United States. Of the 19,570 Americans reaching Winnipeg by rail nearly the whole were described as practical farmers. As to these latter figures Mr. Obed Smith stated that 25 per cent. at least should be added to include immigrants who came over the frontier by waggon, etc., instead of by railway. In Quebec Mr. René Dupont, Secretary of the St. John Repatriation Society, reported to the Interior Department the arrival in that Province of 2,514 new settlers in the year 1901-2 of whom the majority were French-Canadians returning from the United States. Thirteen agents in various parts of the United States reported to Mr. Pedley as to their work in Ohio, Michigan, Indiana, Dakota, Wisconsin, Nebraska, etc., and indicated much activity in the distribution of information.

An indication of the progress in this general connection was to be found in the land sales, etc., which occurred in the West during this period. According to the Report of Mr. J. A. Smart, Deputy Minister of the Interior, submitted to the Hon. Mr. Sifton on November 15th, 1902, the fiscal year recently ended showed sales of 2,201,795 acres, or 1,580,768 acres in excess of 1901. The combined area of land disposed of by the Government under homestead entry, by sale, etc., and by the Railway companies, amounted to 4,954,847 acres. The homestead entries in 1901-2 were 14,633 as against 8,167 in 1900-1. Of these 4,080 were made by Canadians from the States and 4,761 by Americans. Mr. Smart reported in this connection a Departmental correspondence in the past year of 352,748. The per capita cost of settling the immigrants in Canada averaged $7.34 in 1902, or a reduction of $1.00 over the preceding year.

This general increase in immigration created much discussion during the year in its dual aspect of British *versus* Foreign settlement. Upon the propriety of obtaining more settlers for the West there were no differences of opinion, though some protests were heard from Labour Unions as to the importation of industrial workers. In the annual Report of the Victoria, B.C., Board of Trade, the Hon. J. D. Prentice, Provincial Minister of Agriculture, submitted a brief paper dealing with the work of Mr. J. H. Turner in London ; the general need and advantages of British Columbia in connection with immigration ; the agreement made by the Government with

the Kalevan Kansa Colonization Company to settle Malcolm Island
with Finlanders; and their efforts in general to promote immigration. On November 17th the Hon. Clifford Sifton, Minister of the
Interior, addressed a mass-meeting in the Metropolitan Church,
Toronto, upon this subject and the religious and educational work
which increased settlement would make necessary. He declared
that: "The tide of population is only beginning to rise. I am not
one of those who are inclined to undue optimism. I am in the
habit of looking at rosy and exuberant predictions in a somewhat
cold-blooded way; but, having regard to the sources of information
at my disposal, I should not be at all surprised if by the first day
of July, 1905, there were about 750,000 people in Manitoba and the
North-West Territories, and perhaps a million." Referring to the
general prospects of the West, the Minister then added:

I speak as one who has seen the work of the early pioneers and lived
among the people while the capabilities of the soil were being tested. I have
seen the years of hail, wind, drouth, and frost, and in the light of that experience I have no hesitation in saying that in a comparatively short time you may
look to see the people of the West producing upon a scale which will render
them, man for man, one of the richest and most independent agricultural communities in the world. Here, then, we have the situation in a nutshell—a vast
and productive territory becoming quickly occupied by a throng of people who
will be called upon to take up the duties of citizenship almost at once, whose
successful pursuit of agriculture will make them financially independent, and
who in a short time will constitute a most potent factor in the national life of
Canada.

Every effort was made during 1902 to promote the movement
of British emigrants towards Canada instead of to the United
States. By speeches, pamphlets, newspaper letters
Encourage-
ment of British
Emigration
to Canada
and other methods of creating publicity, the natural
prominence of the Dominion owing to current events
of an Imperial character and to its own national
development, was greatly stimulated. The work
done by Mr. W. T. R. Preston in this connection was marked, and
that of the Canadian Department of the Interior was vigorous and
effective. Interviewed on January 16th by the London *Daily News*,
Mr. J. A. Smart, Deputy Minister of the Interior, referred to the splendid crops and prospects of the Canadian North-West and expressed
amazement that in the face of a British country where about 35,000
farmers raised 110,000,000 bushels of food products, the returns
should show that in the past year some 65,000 British subjects went
to live in the United States, and only about 13,000 in Canada. He
referred to the American farmers who were now pouring into the
Dominion, and concluded by saying: "I hope that under an active
propaganda the British emigrant will fully understand and appreciate the advantages that are offered to him in moving to a country
where he will continue to be under British institutions and at the
same time, without question, make more material progress than he
possibly could in any other country in the world."
The question of bringing certain Welsh settlers from Patagonia

created some interest about this time. During 1901 Messrs W. J. Rees and W. L. Griffith had been sent by the Department of the Interior to that country to visit these people and inquire about their proposal to remove to Canada. On February 18th, 1902, a deputation, headed by Sir J. T. Dillwyn-Llewelyn and Mr. Alfred Thomas, M.P., waited upon the Colonial Secretary and asked aid in transporting some 500 Welshmen from Patagonia to the Canadian West. Mr. W. L. Griffith, Canadian Agent in Wales, stated that the Canadian Government would reserve a complete township of 36 square miles, appoint a special staff to accompany and locate the settlers, provide house accommodation for some months and grant a bonus of £1 per head, if the Imperial Government would undertake the transportation. Mr. Chamberlain declined on the ground that for many years the Government had given no aid to emigration to self-governing Colonies, primarily at the wish of Colonies which desired to control the conditions in this connection. He hoped, however, that means would be found to settle these people in Canada and, later on in the day, joined with others in a personal subscription which totalled $7,000. During his speech Mr. Chamberlain made the following observation : "The extraordinary increase of the prosperity of Canada during the last few years is a sufficient indication that industrious men are sure there to find all the social, religious and political surroundings which they naturally desire for themselves and for their children." In comparing the climates of Patagonia and Canada he also made a reference to the "terrible rigour" of the latter. About 200 of these Welshmen eventually succeeded in reaching the West, and on June 30th, Sir Wilfrid Laurier wrote Mr. Griffith, expressing the hope that many others would follow from Wales itself. "No settlers will be more welcome. As some one has said about the Welshman, there is 'a certain blend of optimism and tenacity' in him which is just what is wanted." Meanwhile, at the annual meeting of the Central Farmers' Institute at Victoria, B. C., on February 26th, the following Resolution was passed :

Whereas, the last Census of Canada has been very disappointing to the Government and people of Canada ; and whereas the Dominion Government have started upon an energetic propaganda respecting emigration from the British Isles and elsewhere to Canada ; and whereas the crying need of this Province is early settlement with more people ; therefore be it resolved by the delegates of the Central Farmers' Institute assembled, that the Government of this Province use every endeavour and method possible to induce immigration to this Province.

On March 6th, Mr. James A. Smart returned to Ottawa from his visit to Great Britain, and stated to the Toronto *Globe* correspondent that immigration work in the United Kingdom, as well as on the Continent, was now under the direct supervision of Mr. W. T. R. Preston and quite apart from the work of the High Commissioner's Office. A general re-organization of the work had been made and, amongst other steps taken, 350,000 copies of a publication called *Western Canada* had been mailed to English farmers and labourers. The Deputy-Minister said that the fact which seemed to have most interest and effect upon the people generally in this connection was the influx of settlers from the United States. It was a sort of substantial evidence that what Canadians claimed as to the country was correct. The subject was discussed in the House of Lords on July 25th by Lord Burghclere and the Earl of Onslow, the latter stating that " the fertile lands of the Dominion were being taken up with unexampled rapidity." During the summer and autumn the British journalists visiting Canada wrote many letters home in praise of the country, and the London *Daily News* had a series of glowing letters from a special correspondent. To the Manchester *Guardian* of July 30th Mr. F. W. G. Haultain, Premier of the Territories, contributed a lengthy interview eulogizing the West, its resources and its opportunities.

During the years 1897-1901, some 86,000 settlers from the United States located in Manitoba and the North-West. In 1902 this migration showed evidences of being a considerable movement of population instead of a casual and individual immigration. As the Toronto *Globe* put it on May 31st: " We see the beginning of a movement which will not cease until there are millions where there are now hundreds of thousands in the Canadian West." This referred to the general increase of immigration from all countries, but there were many expressions of doubt during the year as to the effect of a large influx of Americans upon Canadian institutions and the sentiment of the future.

Up to the middle of 1902 the proportion of new settlers in the West was not much over half American, but after that date it was considerably greater. On May 19th the Toronto *World* interviewed a number of citizens upon the subject. It declared as a preliminary that Americans were pouring into the West by tens of thousands, buying land through companies and agents in thousands of acres a day, and preparing to control the factories and trade of the whole region as well as the stock of the Canadian Pacific Railway. Mr. B. E. Walker, General Manager of the Canadian Bank of Commerce, stated that he was not greatly alarmed. " All we want is the population, and let the Americans come, as many as will. If they do bring in American capital to erect factories, it is not at all likely that they will bar Canadian labour." Mr. D. R. Wilkie, General Manager of the Imperial Bank of Canada, spoke upon these points as follows:

The immigration of American farmers, which is so great at present, I consider a decided benefit to the development of the country. As for the idea of American capital erecting factories and employing American labour exclusively, I believe it, for the most part, to be a quite erroneous impression ; but that American capital should gain control of the Canadian Pacific Railway and work in conjunction with other capitalists towards the development of the country for their own exclusive benefit should not be permitted under any circumstances. Every Canadian who is a loyal subject should give this matter his serious consideration and endeavour to make this Railway a national enterprise, with every man, woman and child a shareholder. To sum up the matter, I think that the Canadians are slow to realize the possibilities of the North-West, and until they do so they are giving untold wealth to the Americans, who are fully alive to the situation.

Mr. F. A. Kenaston of St. Paul, who was connected with a large Minnesota agricultural industry and who had just taken over the John Abell Works of Toronto, was also interviewed. He described the immense opening market for agriculural implements in the West; declared that 200,000 Americans would migrate thither during the year; and stated that Minnesota, though the banner wheat State of the Union, had never produced such a crop as had Manitoba in 1901. " The coming great wheatfields are in the Canadian North-West. I believe before very many years you will have a population of 40 or 50 million people in your Western territory." About this time the Toronto *Globe* had sent a special correspondent to investigate this movement and his letters indicated no general fear as to future results from the influx of Americans and nothing but pleasure as to the present position of affairs. On April 29th, his letter described Messrs. Haultain and Sifton at Regina as both stating their belief that there was no political danger though the Premier would not express an opinion in this connection if 50,000 a year were to come in for several successive years. The general belief was that the most of the new comers would very shortly take out naturalization papers. Other letters followed on May 17th, June 20th, 25th, and 28th, September 13th, 25th and 30th, and October 9th, all indicating a rush of investment and population. The existing conditions and elements of future import in this movement were summarized as follows on June 28th :

1. American capitalists seeking an outlet for surplus funds formerly used in land operations at home have invested very largely in Canadian lands, and will advertise them all over the Union.

2. The American pioneers and frontiersmen, who have led the movement of settlement in their own country, from Iowa to Minnesota, and from Minnesota to the Dakotas, have reached the limit of the good land in their own territory, and are coming into Canada in thousands. The reports they are sending back will for many years to come result in increasing immigration from the United States, for the land they are settling upon is admittedly better than that of any of the States west of Iowa.

3. The rush of European immigration into the United States, which was begun when there were vast tracts of free land there, still continues, and cannot be stopped speedily. Many years must elapse before it becomes generally known to European agriculturists emigrating to America that there is no longer room in the Western States. A large part of these belated landseekers will cross the border into Canada and find homes with us.

The discussion continued in various quarters. Early in June the New York *Sun* declared that the new American settlers would " preach annexation from the moment they raise a log cabin and dig a well " and, despite any encouragement to British immigration, it would not be long before the Canadian authorities had " an

outlander question" on their hands.   In this connection the Rev.
Dr. Bryce of Winnipeg—Moderator of the Presbyterian Church in
Canada—after a visit to the Arcola district spoke to the *Free Press*
of July 31st in the following terms : " As to their influence politically and socially, there is one consideration that much modifies
the question.   Probably half of those who enter the country are
expatriated Canadians, or their children, who are returning to
their own land.   These rejoice in their old institutions and freely
express their preference for Canadian laws and customs.   The other
half of the influx are very miscellaneous.   Many of them have
German or Norse blood, some are natural-born Americans.   It is
stated that these express a desire to conform readily to their new
conditions."

To the Montreal *Witness* on September 16th he repeated these
views and declared that there was no danger of the country being
Americanized.   In an interview at Montreal, reported in the Toronto
Mail and Empire of August 28th, the Hon. S. A. Fisher, Minister
of Agriculture, made the statement that " seventy per cent. of the
immigrants who have come into the Canadian North-West from
the United States have been naturalized as British subjects."
Speaking to the press at Montreal on September 30th Sir William
Van Horne expressed the following view of this migration :

The homestead lands immediately along the railway track have been taken
up, but you must remember that the territory is enormous, and that when all the
homestead lands are taken up, the population will be numbered by millions,
and the railway mileage will be increased tenfold.   In Manitoba, I suppose
practically all the homestead lands have been taken up, and practically all the
railroad lands have been sold.   This is also largely true of Eastern Assiniboia,
but as you go further west, of course, the unoccupied areas increase.   I regard
this as a permanent movement.   It is not stimulated by speculation as the
earlier movement was.   The great majority of the people are coming with the
intention of remaining permanently as farmers, and not for the purpose of
buying up lands for an advance.   The greater part of them are people from
Iowa, Minnesota, Nebraska and others of the better western States, who have
been successful, who originally bought their lands very cheaply, or took up
homesteads which they are now able to sell at very high prices, and who are
coming to the Canadian North-West to repeat this operation.

To the Toronto *Globe* correspondent at Ottawa the Hon. C.
Fitzpatrick, Minister of Justice, spoke on the same day about his
recent Western trip and pictured conditions very much as Sir W.
C. Van Horne was doing in Montreal.   He described the Western
people as resourceful and optimistic and spoke of the enormous
yield of grain, the great development in the cattle industry and
the remarkable general progress.   A special correspondent of the
Toronto *World* took a very different view in an elaborate article
which appeared on November 1st.   He analyzed American influence
throughout the West, quoted as a possibility the statement that
either a new Dominion might some day be formed or else annexation
to the United States take place and proceeded as follows : " The
people of the East and of the Motherland simply must have
more confidence and show more interest in the West.   There is

now a nation in the making west of the great lakes, and that nation will have British or American tendencies largely in proportion to the amounts of British or American capital that may be invested in the country. If the Motherland and the East won't help the West with money and men, then depend upon it, in this part of the Empire in the next generation there will be more Yankee-Doodle sung than God Save the King."

Speaking in Toronto, with the Hon. Mr. Sifton, on November 17th, Mr. N. W. Rowell, K.C., referred to Canadian moral responsibilities in this connection. "While these men are among our very best settlers and, if we do our duty, will be among our very best citizens, yet many of them come to us with different ideas of Sabbath observance or respect for law and with different ideas in other material respects from those which we cherish and hold most dear." At the Canadian Club banquet in Boston on November 21st, the Minister of the Interior declared that "an army of hardy and intelligent farmers are trekking to the plains of Manitoba, Assiniboia, Alberta and Saskatchewan. And I am assured that the movement is only beginning." To the London *Commerce*, of November 12th, Sir Gilbert Parker, M.P., said in an interview upon this subject that "if the Canadian Government were not the Government it is and if Canada had not so steadfastly preserved her position for a hundred years against the commercial tyranny and pressure of the United States we might feel rather anxious." As it was, Canada would "rule these American immigrants entirely for their good " and they would necessarily conform to their surroundings and monarchical institutions.

There were many other comments in England and, no doubt, they all helped to swell the growing tide of British emigration to Canada. One only may be quoted here. In the *Fortnightly Review* for November Mr. Archibald S. Hurd had an elaborate and rather alarmist article upon the question of the "Foreign Invasion of Canada." "Must we," he asked, "sit by and watch one of the most promising daughter-lands of the Mother Country being peopled by settlers of alien blood, witness the development of a policy which, if not anti-British is seemingly not pro-British, and risk the political complications which may occur in spite of all the sanguine hopes of the Dominion immigration officials." He urged British emigration to the Dominion instead of to the United States.

On February 27th the Report of the Royal Commission to inquire into Oriental Immigration was presented to Parliament. It

Oriental Immigration and Canadian Interests. was an elaborate study of Chinese and Japanese life, character, and work, in 800 pages of printed matter.* The original appointment of the Commission was on September 21st, 1900, and in the Minute of Council authorizing this action "the representations made by the people and Legislature of British Columbia " in this connection

_____

* NOTE—See also page 80.

were given, and in the conclusions of the Commission were declared to be "substantially true and to urgently call for a remedy." They were as follows:

That the Province is flooded with an undesirable class of people, non-assimilative and most detrimental to the wage-earning classes of the people of the Province, and that this extensive immigration of Orientals is also a menace to the health of the community.

That there is probability of a great disturbance to the economic conditions in the Province and grave injury being caused to the working clases by the large influx of labourers from China, as the standard of living of the masses of the people in that country differs so widely from the standard prevailing in the Province, thus enabling them to work for a much less wage.

That it is in the interests of the Empire that the Pacific Province of the Dominion should be occupied by a large and thoroughly British population rather than by one in which the number of aliens would form a large proportion.

The recommendations of the Commission were that "the further immigration of Chinese into Canada ought to be prohibited; that the most effective and desirable means to attain this end is by treaty supported by legislation; and in the meantime, and until this can be obtained, that the capitation tax should be raised to $500." The Japanese situation was thought to be met in a considerable measure by the action of the Emperor of Japan in prohibiting emigration—though some guarantee of the permanence of the edict was desirable. On March 17th, a deputation from the Trades and Labour Congress of Canada waited on the Dominion Government and, amongst other Resolutions, presented one of protest against the driving of white labourers out of British Columbia by the Orientals and urging a $500 capitation tax. Sir Wilfrid Laurier and the Hon. Mr. Mulock replied briefly. In the House of Commons on March 21st Mr. Ralph Smith made a lengthy speech upon the same subject. At Victoria, B.C., on June 11th, the local School Board, during a discussion of proposals to separate the Chinese and white pupils, were told by Superintendent Eaton that he was informed by the teachers of the City, without exception, that the deportment of the Chinese scholars was either "fair, excellent or very good, and that there was nothing in their character likely to exercise a debasing effect on white children."

Speaking to the Toronto *Mail* of August 25th, on his return from the Coast, the Rev. Professor Cody expressed the opinion that British Columbia could not get along without the Chinese. "In the salmon canneries you find the tireless and industrious Chinaman doing all the distasteful and dirty work. He does it well, too, and does not complain at the nature of his task. In the saw-mills the Celestial is to be found turning the heavy logs, moving the lumber and in other ways bearing the white man's burden. He is the servant; he is also the market gardener. Wherever you find him he is always law-abiding, always civil, and generally honest." It may be added here that the Report of the Interior Department to June 30th, 1902, showed the total immigration of Chinese since 1886 as 35,158, and the immigrants for 1901-2 as 3,587. The collection of fees in this connection was $364,972 and the refund to the Provinces (chiefly British Columbia) was $87,687. The total collected since 1886 was $1,997,914 and the Provincial share of this capitation tax was $484,900. During the years mentioned 14,591 Chinese had taken out certificates of leave or registered for leave of absence.

In reporting to the Superintendent-General of Indian Affairs— the Hon. Clifford Sifton—for the year ending June 30th, 1902, **The Indians** Mr. James A. Smart, the Deputy Sup't. General, stated **of the** that conditions amongst these wards of the nation **Dominion** were, as a whole, satisfactory. There had been during the year 2,500 births and 2,349 deaths, while the fact of the Census enumerators having been able to go beyond treaty limits in their enumeration enabled him to now give more complete and correct statistics as to the number of Indians in the country. The figures were stated as follows :

	1901	1902	Increase	Decrease
Ontario	20,763	20,983	220	....
Quebec	10,865	10,842	....	23
Nova Scotia	2,020	2,067	47	....
New Brunswick	1,655	1,644	....	11
Prince Edward Island	315	316	1	....
British Columbia	24,576	25,500	924	....
Manitoba	6,840	6,754	....	86
North-West Territories	17,927	17,922	....	5
Outside Treaty Limits	14,566	22,084	7,518	....
	99,527	108,112	8,710	125

A good deal of progress was reported in the matter of cattle raising and herding amongst the Indians of the Territories. One tribe, the Blood Indians, were stated by Mr. Smart to own 3,000 head of cattle amongst 176 persons and, through the supervision by officials, more care was being taken in the matter of breeding. Hunting and trapping amongst the Quebec Indians during the year fell off nearly one-half in proceeds—from $50,945 to $101,738. Those along the north shore of Lake Superior and up to Manitoba realized $133,915 from hunting and $70,806 from fishing and were better off than in the previous year. In Manitoba the Indians took in $107,181 from fishing and $68,923 from the chase, while the total return to those in the Territories was $139,366 or an advance of $27,482 in 1901. In British Columbia they did still better and realized $203,491 from game and fur and $451,150 from salmon and other fishing. They earned wages in Canada, as a whole, to the amount of $1,181,760—an increase of $150,000.

Improvement was noted in the building of frame houses, which had commenced in the West and become quite common in British Columbia. Of the 283 schools amongst the Indians 100 were under the auspices of the Roman Catholics, 87 in connection with the Church of England, 41 were Methodist and 14 Presbyterian. The rest were undenomational and the total number of pupils included

5,177 boys and 4,492 girls. These figures did not include those who went to white schools in the more settled communities. The surveyed Indian Lands which were surrendered to the Government during the year numbered 103,461 acres and realized $160,519. At the close of the fiscal year the capital of the Indian Trust Fund was $4,045,945 as against $3,941,393 in 1901. The amount expended upon the Indians in the year from the Consolidated Revenue Fund, under votes by Parliament, was $1,057,130. Upon matters of moral progress Mr. Smart reported as follows:

If abstinence from offence against the laws of the country, and especially from the commission of serious crime, be taken as a criterion, then the morality of the Indians will certainly not suffer from comparison with that of the rest of the community, and during the year they have more than sustained the enviable reputation that they have already earned. In considering other aspects of morality, allowance must be made for the fact that even among bands under missionary and other elevating influences there seem to be still, although not always avowed, a hereditary pagan influence at work. Attachment to old tribal customs is often slumbering, where least suspected, until something occurs to give it expression. Alcoholic intemperance, because of its immediate degrading and impoverishing effect, and on account of provoking and at the same time breaking down the power of resisting other vices, is probably the most dangerous to the Indians. The rarity of serious crimes and the growth of general prosperity are in themselves proof that it has not an extended hold on them. The habitual and moderate use of stimulants common among other classes is, as a consequence of the provisions of the Indian Act relative to intoxicants, almost unknown among the Indians, nor is habitual, excessive indulgence at all common.

According to the Census of 1901 the Indians were divided by religion into 14,472 Anglicans, 1,375 Presbyterians, 11,106 Methodists, 34,735 Roman Catholics and 12,155 Pagans. In Ontario the Indians owned 19,393 acres of cleared or cultivated lands, $36,031 worth of implements and vehicles, $65,747 worth of live stock and poultry, $13,658 worth of general effects, $110,753 worth of household effects—a total real and personal property of $1,476,313. The increased value of Indian agricultural products and industries in Ontario during the fiscal year 1902 was stated by the Indian Department Report at $20,930, the total value of their farm products at $97,335, the wages earned at $174,015, the total income from all sources at $423,614. In Manitoba they held 368,985 acres of cleared land and 19,943 acres of cultivated land, while the figures for British Columbia were, respectively, 140,437 and 1,635 acres. Apart from Ontario, as above, the following table gives certain figures for 1902 of Indian wealth and standing in Canada:

	Value of Implements and Vehicles.	All Real and Personal Property.	Total Income from All Sources.
New Brunswick..........	$5,500	$155,658	$85,681
Prince Edward Island....	810	41,000	18,402
Nova Scotia.............	3,972	114,085	73,787
Manitoba...............	20,940	941,052	328,778
British Columbia........	128,178	6,121,624	1,533,295
Territories.............	187,751	8,238,574	577,085

22

IMMIGRATION INCIDENTS AND INTERESTS

Jan. 16.—The Toronto Trades and Labour Council issues a Memorial on Canada's immigration policy. They declare that enormous sums in past years have been expended upon the "importation of cheap labour"; that agents have been sent to the poorest countries in the world in order to flood the market with men, women and children willing "to work at almost any price"; that many are now tramping the streets in idleness and that the result will be a reduction of wages; but that there is no objection to the coming of suitable immigrants who come without assistance.

Feb. 28.—Mr. R. E. Gosnell, Secretary of the British Columbia Bureau of Immigration, issues a Report dealing with the organization of the Bureau and with local conditions in this connection. As to permanent settlement his conclusions are given as follows : "What the peculiar conditions of the Province suggest as the proper and effective method of settlement is the setting apart of tracts of land, where available, in small holdings for the purposes of fruit, poultry, vegetables, dairying in a small way, and other products of small mixed farming, to which those settlers so inclined could be invited."

Mar. 21.—A farewell banquet is given at Vancouver to the Hon. S. Shimisu, Chief Japanese Consul in Canada, who had won much respect and popularity in the management of a difficult post during some time past. Mayor Neelands presides and in his speech Mr. Shimisu refers to the alliance of "the Empire of the Rising Sun with the Empire where the Sun never Sets."

April 16.—The Hon. Mr. Sifton, Minister of the Interior, introduces a measure in Parliament of which the operative clause is as follows : "The Governor-General may, by a proclamation or order, whichever he considers most expedient, and whenever he deems it necessary, prohibit the landing in Canada of any immigrant or any other passenger who is suffering from any dangerous or infectious disease or malady, whether such immigrant intends to settle in Canada, or only intends to pass through Canada to settle in some other country." On April 29th, he added the proviso that such prohibition might be absolute or might be accompanied by permission to land for a given period of medical treatment.

June 20.—The Western correspondent of the *Globe* speaks of Haslem & Wright of Winnipeg as holding 170,000 acres of land around Halbute; Schwab & Co. of Clear Lake, Minnesota, as having 250,000 acres north and east of Weyburn; the Canadian-American Land Company as holding 201,000 acres at Milestone; and other syndicates as holding similar blocks of land in the Territories which would total altogether some 750,000 acres. On September 4th the same writer describes the Saskatchewan Valley Land Company as buying 1,100,000 acres; while another concern of Mason City, Iowa, is stated to have bought 50,000 acres near Carman, Manitoba.

June 30.—The figures of the import of settlers' effects into Canada help to indicate the growth of immigration. From the United States the total for 1901-2 is reported as $3,751,363 in value as against $2,915,000 in the previous year; and from Great Britain the figures are, respectively, $802,313 and $801,000.

July 8.—In a letter published in the Halifax *Herald*, Mr. Robert H. Upham, President of the Canadian Club of Boston, advises young men and women to stay at home in Canada. Opportunities are declared to be better than in the States. If they must move, however, go to the North-West, and then he adds : "A great many are going there from New England, and it looks as if the prediction of Sir Charles Tupper, made at a dinner of the Canadian Club three years ago, that it would not be long before the tide of immigration will flow from this country toward Canada, is about to be verified."

July 16.—By the Census Bulletin of this date there are stated to have been in Canada in the previous year, 3,279 blind persons, 6,174 deaf and dumb persons, and 16,495 of unsound mind—a total of 25,948. Of this 13,939 were males and 12,019 females, and 21,201 were born in Canada.

July 25.—According to the Census Bulletin of this date there were in the past year 131,580 infants of one year old or under in Canada; 129,485 children of between 5 and 9 years of age; 580,339 persons between 15 and 19 years; 423,385 persons between 25 and 29 years; 331,226 persons between 35 and 39 years; 239,186 persons between 45 and 49 years; 160,671 persons between 55 and 59 years; 105,673 persons between 65 and 69 years; 47,796 persons between 75 and 79 years; 9,838 persons between 85 and 89 years. There were 961 persons of 95 and over.

Oct. 15.—The Summerside *Journal* declares that while much of the country is rejoicing over an inflow of immigrants, Prince Edward Island has to complain of an exodus. "One has but to observe which way the tide of travel is flowing, and to note the class of people who are on the move, to be able to form a pretty good idea of the situation. During the past two or three years, especially, thousands of our young people of both sexes have left the Province in the hope of bettering their fortunes abroad. True, some of them will return and a good many have settled in the Canadian West, but too many of them by far have become permanent residents of the United States, and are lost to Canada for all time to come."

Dec. 27.—Lieut.-Col. Sam Hughes, M.P., of Lindsay, has a long letter in the London *Morning Post*, dealing with Canadian history and progress, urging emigration to the Dominion and concluding as follows: "It will afford me pleasure in the near future to lay before the British public the real facts concerning Canada's North-West, showing why such splendid climate and soil are hers; tracing the effects on North-Western Canada of the Japanese current, just as the North Atlantic Gulf stream ameliorates the climate of North-western Europe. Western Americans, understanding prairie life, have been quicker than others to grasp the great possibilities of Canada's prairies, but Eastern Canada is now in the race. And it will be but a few weeks until the Britisher will be vigorously moving. In every town and shire in the British Isles will be heard the cry, 'To Canada.'"

Dec. 13.—In an elaborate article on Immigration, the Manitoba *Free Press* gives the following table to indicate the European countries from which Canada can best draw an agricultural population:

Name.	Total Population.	Agricultural Population.	Per cent. of Agriculturists.
England and Wales	30,000,000	1,070,000	3·7
Germany	50,000,000	21,000,000	42
Sweden	4,300,000	1,000,000	23·2
Russia, including Finland, Poland and the Caucasus)	108,000,000	48,000,000	44·4
France	38,000,000	18,000,000	47·4
Belgium	6,200,000	3,000,000	48·4
Austro-Hungary	43,000,000	24,000,000	55·8

XV.—RELIGIOUS AND MORAL INTERESTS

According to the Census of 1901 there were 680,620 Anglicans in the Dominion as compared with 646,059 in 1891. The Baptists numbered 316,477 as against 302,565 in the former **General Religious Conditions in Canada** year. The Methodists numbered 916,886 as against 847,765, and the Presbyterians were 842,442 in number as compared with 755,326 in 1891. The Roman Catholics increased from 1,992,017 in 1891 to 2,229,-000 in 1901. The Congregationalists remained stationary at 28,157 in 1891 and 28,293 in 1901; the Jews rose from 6,414 to 16,401; and the Lutherans increased from 63,982 to 92,524. The Roman Catholics possessed in their Church establishment an Apostolic Delegate, 7 Archbishops, 23 Bishops and some 1,500 clergy. The Church of England in Canada had 2 Archbishops, 20 Bishops and about 1,000 clergy. The Methodists had a General Superintendent, 9 Presidents of Conferences and some 1,950 clergy. The Presbyterians possessed in their establishment a Moderator of the General Assembly, 6 Synod Moderators and 1,368 clergy. By Provinces, in 1891 and in 1901, the four principal divisions of Christianity in Canada were as follows:

Provinces.	Methodists 1891.	Methodists 1901.	Roman Catholics 1891.	Roman Catholics 1901.
British Columbia	14,298	25,047	20,843	33,639
Manitoba	28,437	49,936	20,571	35,672
New Brunswick	35,504	35,973	115,961	125,698
Nova Scotia	54,195	57,490	122,452	129,578
Ontario	654,033	666,388	358,300	390,304
Prince Edward Island	13,596	13,402	47,837	45,796
Quebec	39,544	42,014	1,291,709	1,429,260
Territories	8,158	26,636	14,344	39,653

Provinces.	Presbyterians 1891.	Presbyterians 1901.	Church of England 1891.	Church of England 1901.
British Columbia	15,284	34,081	23,619	40,689
Manitoba	39,001	65,348	30,852	44,922
New Brunswick	40,639	39,496	43,095	41,767
Nova Scotia	108,952	106,381	64,410	66,107
Ontario	453,147	477,386	385,999	367,937
Prince Edward Island	33,072	30,750	6,646	5,976
Quebec	52,673	58,013	75,472	81,563
Territories	12,558	30,987	15,966	31,659

The General Assembly of the Presbyterian Church in Canada met at Toronto on June 11th, with the Rev. Dr. R. H. Warden, Moderator, in the chair. It was opened by an elabo- **The Presbyterian General Assembly and Church** rate address from Dr. Warden, covering the history and progress of the Church during the past year.* Reference was first made to the deaths of the Rev. Dr. G. L. McKay of Formosa, Rev. Dr. A. B. Mackay of Montreal, Rev. Dr. Robertson, Rev. Dr. Laing, and Principal

---

* NOTE—The Church year ends on February 28th.

Grant; to the fact that double the $400,000 asked for in connection with the reduction of debts on Church property had been subscribed; to the regrettable falling-off in the members of Christian Endeavour and other young peoples' societies, although they still totalled 26,319; to the increased circulation of Presbyterian papers, now numbering, altogether, 173,187; to the increased endowment of the Aged and Infirm Widows' Fund, now amounting to $252,000, and to the maintenance of the Widows' and Orphans' Fund, now totaling $403,530; to the Home Mission work, in which there were 506 divisions, with 16,474 families and 18,477 communicants; and to the missionaries in this connection labouring amongst the Icelanders, Germans, Swedes, Gallicians, Doukhobors, etc., of the far West, with total contributions from the Church of $122,731 in the past year. The following general summary of the situation was given:

Steady progress has been made in almost every department of the work. In connection with the 58 Presbyteries of the Church there are 1,368 ordained ministers, of whom 1,198 are pastors of congregations, professors in colleges or filling positions to which they have been appointed by the Assembly. There are 783 self-supporting charges, embracing 1,152 congregations, and 203 charges —embracing 370 congregations—aided by the Augmentation Fund. In addition to these, we have 506 home mission fields, with 1,461 stations, at which the Gospel is more or less regularly preached by our missionaries. Our elders number 7,559, our families 118,114 and our communicants 219,470, a net gain of 5,799 to the membership reported a year ago. The number of communicants received during the year on profession of faith was 11,259, an average of seven to each congregation. Not including mission fields, 228 congregations report no conversions during the year—no members received on confession of faith— and in 656 of the other congregations of the Church, where additions were made on confession of faith, the number in no case exceeds six. There is surely ground for humiliation here. Our people contributed last year $1,052,-691 towards the salaries of their ministers and $2,857,489 for all denominational purposes. The value of the property owned by our congregations is a little over ten million dollars, on which there is still an indebtedness of about one million and a half. There are 3,196 Sabbath Schools connected with the Church (an increase of 147 in the number reported the preceding year), with 21,717 teachers and officers and 182,335 scholars. The scholars show an increase of 626 over those reported a year ago. This increase is encouraging, although, according to the recent Dominion Census, there must be a large number of young people of school age in Presbyterian homes not in attendance upon our Sabbath Schools.

Dr. Warden then went on to say that in consequence of a special effort made in the previous year there were now 150 congregations each supporting a Home Missionary, while the American Presbyterian Church of Montreal had assumed the liability for the whole of the missionary work of the Presbytery of Victoria. During the past year 27 churches, 82 manses and 3 school-houses had been built under Church auspices and an active evangelization work carried on in Quebec, where there were now 40 fields, with 85 stations, and a contribution during the year of $26,926 from the Church generally. The Augmented charges were doing well both in contributions from the Church and in self-support, and now numbered 203, with 11,143 families and 19,501 communicants. To Home Missions the people had given $181,778 during the year, and

to Foreign Missions $158,561, of which the women raised $65,000.
He urged, in a general financial connection, that each member of
the Church's congregations should put aside one cent a day, or
$3.65 a year, to Church purposes. It would constitute a total of
$803,000 a year.

But the greatest need of the Church in his opinion was "men
consecrated to the service of Christ." There was a falling off in
those seeking the Ministry and a decrease in the attendance at
Theological Colleges. "Because of death, retirement from service
and other causes, the number of our ministers is reduced by 48
every year. The number of students graduating from the various
Colleges of the Church last year was 46, a number insufficient to
make good the loss sustained, leaving the Church without any men
with which to take possession of new openings in the home field
or to increase the staff of missionaries abroad. Last year, in order
to meet the requirements of our home mission work, upwards of
40 men were brought from the Motherland." After this address
the Rev. Dr. George Bryce of Winnipeg was, by a very large
majority, elected Moderator for the coming year upon motion of
Principal Caven and the Rev. Dr. Murray of Halifax. At the
following day's meeting a letter from Lord Strathcona to Mr. J. K.
Macdonald was read sending a subscription of $20,000 to the Aged
and Infirm Ministers' Fund and a Report was submitted from the
Rev. Dr. Torrance which dealt with the statistical progress of the
Church and gave, amongst other figures, the following table of
comparison:

	1875.	1901.
Congregations	706	1,781
Ministers	579	1,368
Communicants	88,228	219,470
Additions to communicants	8,422	11,259
Church sittings	249,953	601,885
Elders	3,412	7,559
Stipends paid wholly by congregations	$405,192	$1,052,091
Arrears	14,200	11,716
Total contributions for congregational purposes	835,668	2,857,480

In presenting a Report regarding Western progress Dr. Warden
pointed out that while the population had increased 83 per cent.
in ten years the Presbyterian population had increased 187 per
cent. and that this was largely due to the exertions of the late
Dr. Robertson. Since 1881 the Presbyteries there had increased
from 1 to 78, the congregations from 15 to 141, the ministers
from 17 to 247, the communicants from 1,153 to 23,858, the church
buildings and manses from 16 to 475, the contributions from
$20,408 to $632,196. On June 17th the Rev. J. A. Carmichael of
Regina was appointed Superintendent of the Synod of Manitoba
and the North-West, the Rev. Dr. J. C. Herdman, Superintendent
of the Synod of British Columbia, and the Rev. Dr. E. D. McLaren
of Vancouver became General Field Secretary. The Assembly

adjourned on June 19th after deciding to meet in 1903 at Vancouver. The last days of the Session were filled up with various reports and addresses. Principal MacVicar of Montreal presented the statement of the French Evangelization Board showing 64 pastors, colporteurs or teachers at work with an average attendance at service of 2,414 persons, a local contribution of $8,286 in the year and the distribution of 35,804 tracts, etc., together with 2,082 Bibles.

The Sabbath School statistics showed a gain during the year of 147 schools, 517 teachers and officers and 2,968 scholars. The amount raised by these schools during 1901 was $112,110. As to Young Peoples' Societies special recommendations were made and adopted looking to the common name of Presbyterian Guild for all of them and suggesting religious and missionary work as their chief aim. The Century Fund, at date, amounted to $1,600,000 and the Rev. Dr. Campbell in submitting the Report, stated that "there probably never had been a subscription at any time in any Church, or in any body, so fully paid up." A Committee on Church life and work urged more regular religious exercises in the home, a better observance of the Lord's Day, a vigorous advocacy of total abstinence and instruction of the young in the value of temperance, a more careful use of the privileges of citizenship. The representation in the General Assembly was reduced from one minister in four to one in six with the same proportion of elders.

Turning to the year's historical or personal record apart from this meeting, it is found that the first incident of importance in connection with Presbyterianism in Canada was the last official one in the Rev. Dr. Robertson's strenuous life—an appeal dated January, 1902, signed by himself and the Rev. Dr. Warden, asking for financial aid in order to meet the religious demands of the increasing Western population. The document spoke of the excellent work done in the past and the way in which missions and assisted congregations were becoming self-supporting. From Great Britain in the past year £13,579 had come in aid but they should not have to ask it from abroad. For their work in the Kootenay and the Klondike, the Church had been highly commended. "Missionaries have been the saving salt where drinking, carnality and gambling held high carnival. Past success is a potent plea for aggressiveness. The respect in the West for law and order is largely due to missionary effort." Upon this point the Toronto *Globe* dwelt at length in an editorial reference to the record of the Church, on June 16th, and laid stress upon the national character of its work. "The Presbyterian Church is actively, conscientiously, avowedly, engaged in the nationalization of the diverse elements of the population of Western Canada." Following up this comment a further tribute was paid :

The Presbyterian Church has for years made Western Canada the point of a carefully planned and vigorous home mission campaign. The piercing provision of Robertson was backed by the intelligence and cohesion of the

Church, and to-day, at the opening of the great rush into our vacant lands, the Presbyterian Church finds itself in a singularly advantageous position. The proud assertion was made in the present General Assembly that not one little community has been established in our great West, in which, within the first year, the ordinances of religion were not administered by a Presbyterian home missionary. So much for the past. As for the future, it is enough to say that the present General Assembly has given the gravest attention, has evinced the keenest interest, in the problem of the West, as one of its leaders styled the whole complex and magnificent situation, and has taken with an enthusiasm which rose to unanimity a step in organization which many of the commissioners evidently felt to be daring—the trebling of the superintending staff.

Writing on June 14th *The Westminster* dealt with the difficulties before the Church. It needed more men for the Ministry. There was " a distinct lack of competent, equipped, well-qualified men to carry on the work at home and abroad." It needed better training for its ministers, who were now taught much that lacked all rational relevancy to the duties which they would have to discharge. It required more educating in financial matters, in the facts of missions and in the value of forming habits of systematic giving. It needed a more straightforward and direct policy in missionary management. On September 14th the Rev. Dr. E. D. McLaren preached his farewell sermon at Vancouver before taking up the duties to which he had been called by the General Assembly, and on the following evening was given a banquet and presentation by the Masons of the city in remembrance of what M. W. Bro. H. H. Watson described as his " work for the cause of morality and religion during the past 13 years." On September 17th his congregation tendered him a public farewell.

Principal, the Rev. Dr. William Caven, of Knox College, Toronto, celebrated the 50th anniversary of his ordination on Oct. 6th, and was tendered a banquet of a very representative character. Mr. Justice Moss, Vice Chancellor of Toronto University, Chancellor Burwash of Victoria, Chancellor Wallace of McMaster, Principal Sheraton of Wycliffe, President Loudon of Toronto University, Professor Watson, Vice-Principal of Queen's, the Premier of Ontario, Sir Thomas Taylor and the Rev. Dr. Warden were amongst those present and Mr. W. Mortimer Clark, K.C., occupied the chair. In speaking, Principal Caven traced the growth of the Church in Canada, the development of Knox College, the accomplishment of Presbyterian unity, and urged the increasing of spiritual life and the need of earnest practical work in the great West. Of Dr. Caven, in this connection, the Rev. J. A. Macdonald wrote in the *Star* of October 4th that he was " the sanest counsellor and the wisest guide the Church in Canada has in this perilous day of theological transition." Another Presbyterian jubilee was that of the Rev. Dr. Allan Pollok, who for fifty years had been a Minister in the Church and for the past eight years Principal of the Halifax Presbyterian College. The event was celebrated on December 18th by the receipt of an LL.D. degree from Dalhousie University, a presentation cheque of $1,000, a letter of warm congratulation from the Lieut.-Governor of the Province, a public meeting attended by representatives from Queen's University and other institutions, and by the presentation of an Address.

During the year 1902 a good deal of discussion took place in Anglican papers and pulpits as to the cause and character of the

The General Synod and Church of England in Canada

decline in Church growth which the Census had revealed. The *Canadian Churchman* had a series of letters upon the subject which probed the question more or less thoroughly and it was referred to at various Synod meetings. In the *Church Record* of June 2nd a reason was said to lie in the fact that the Service of the Church was not comprehensible and therefore not attractive to the occasional visitor. " Many other reasons could be assigned for the slow growth of the Church. There is, and it is especially felt in the country towns and villages, a certain aloofness of the Church, which is sometimes, and perhaps with reason, attributed to pride and an exclusive spirit." Perhaps another cause might have been found in the disputes between various elements of thought in the Church—well illustrated in the local troubles which were ended by the return of the Rev. F. J. Steen to his duties at Christ Church Cathedral, Montreal, on February 16th. In his sermon on that date he declared he had not modified or changed any of his views, had recanted nothing, withdrawn nothing and made no excuses. Good might, however, come out of the misunderstanding. " Perhaps through it all we shall better appreciate the breadth of the Church of England, and realize more fully than before that we are not a sect that exists for the propagation of one set of ideas, the offspring of some fertile brain, such as even Augustine, or Luther, or Calvin, or Cranmer, or Pusey, or Newman, but that we are the Church Catholic, that embraces or tries to embrace all sides of truth and whose toleration our individual grasp of truth can never exhaust."

He described the ways in which the Church might do its best service to religion and to the people. The first and foremost was a worship which should not only follow the exquisite language of the Prayer-Book but embody personal faith, sincerity and earnest devotion. In the " matchless liturgy " of the Church was given the most perfect form for this worship. The second was in the teaching of the Word of God without fear of modern thought or hostility to its honest phases. The third was in earnest parish work and the organization of Sunday Schools and Church auxiliaries. At the meeting of the Synod of the Diocese of Montreal on March 5th following, and in response to the desire of Archbishop Bond, a Bishop-Coadjutor was selected. Almost unanimously, by 65 votes of the clergy and 49 of the laity as against 22 of the former and 15 of the latter divided amongst twelve names, the Very Rev. James Carmichael, D.D., D.C.L., Dean of Montreal, was chosen for the position. His consecration took place at St. George's Church on April 24th with an elaborate ceremony presided over by the Archbishop of Montreal, assisted by the Bishops of Huron and

Niagara—Dr. Baldwin and Dr. DuMoulin. The sermon was preached by the latter and the Bishops of Toronto, Nova Scotia, Quebec, Ottawa, Algoma, Ontario, Saskatchewan and Calgary and Vermont, U.S.A., were also present.

In Toronto, on June 10th, the Rev. Canon E. A. Welch preached a sermon which attracted considerable attention. He objected strongly to the " hapless name " adopted by the Church in Canada. " It stamps us emphatically as not the Church of the people of this land and, as we have adopted the name of the Church whose life-blood flows in our veins, we have only too faithfully adopted and perpetuated methods many of which have been none too successful even in England." He wanted some name which did not suggest separation from the soil of the country. " We have allowed our grand, historic ancestry, instead of being a great and glorious inspiration, to lay the dead hand of the past upon the warm young life of the present." Canon Welch then referred to the decline in numbers which the Church in Ontario showed through the Census, and blamed it to the lack of adaptability as revealed in the failure of priests and laymen alike to fit very admirable machinery to new times and places. Ineffective teaching in Sunday Schools and inability to properly employ laymen in spiritual work were two matters which he also criticized. Mobility and flexibility in method were strongly urged.

The Niagara Synod was opened on June 11th, with an elaborate address from Bishop DuMoulin. After references to the Coronation and the close of the War, His Lordship proceeded to deprecate what he described as " a very wide departure from Church order which has established itself all over the land "—the introduction of a solo-ist and the singing of a song during the taking of the offertory. He also referred to the poor attendance at morning services, and sug-gested that perhaps Roman Catholic success in this connection might be due to their short and frequent services. The receipts and disbursements of the Diocese for the year were stated at $408,792. The Report submitted on the state of the Church urged larger stipends to the clergy ; dealt with the decrease of general popula-tion in the Diocese of 2 per cent., and of 9 per cent. in its Anglican population ; and described the Sunday Schools as the weakest part of the Diocesan work.

In opening the Diocesan Synod of Nova Scotia, on June 20th, Bishop Courtney delivered an important address, reviewing the current history and condition of the Church. He dealt first with various public events, certain deaths amongst his clergy, the visit which he had paid in 1901 to Australia and Japan, and the proba-ble work of the General Synod. His Lordship stated, in touching on the matter of statistics, that, during the 14 years of his Episco-pate, he had consecrated 73 churches and 41 burial grounds, set off 12 new parishes, ordained 55 deacons and 60 priests, held 1,091 confirmations and confirmed 16,154 persons. He urged at some length the amalgamation of King's College and Dalhousie University, and deprecated the growing tendency to fail in proper observance of the Sabbath. "Putting the matter simply upon the broadest humanitarian grounds, I claim that every workman has a legitimate and inalienable claim to one entire day's rest in every week." Upon the "deplorable leakage" in the Church shown by the Census returns he spoke freely, and his views may be summarized as follows:

1. There is in the community a very general departure from the definiteness of faith which once existed, while materialism and unbelief are wide-spread.

2. The Church has lost many to other denominations—especially in the North-West—through a lack of definite teaching as to the necessity and importance of remaining in her communion.

3. Mixed marriages have caused substantial losses. "A rightly-instructed Churchman would make it a *sine qua non* of marriage that the other party should come into the communion of the Church." If the Church is really a distinct organization, based upon the principles of Apostolic succession and with a true creed essential to salvation, then its adherents should act as if they believed the fact and not as though all churches and creeds were much the same.

4. There is a serious decadence in the Church of the preaching of definite Christian doctrines in relation to practical daily life, backed up and made effectual by the living personal experiences of the preacher.

At Winnipeg, on August 20th, the Synod of Rupert's Land met. in its annual session, and an address, written by Archbishop Machray in England, was read by the Chairman, Bishop Young of Athabasca. His Grace first referred to the generous way in which the great English missionary societies had recently helped to endow the Diocese of Moosonee with £9,000; to the completion of the endowment of the Diocese of Calgary; to the separation of Saskatchewan from the latter Diocese, and the evidences of development shown by the necessity for this new Diocese and that of Keewatin. He then proceeded: "I am sure we all feel that we are at such a crisis in the life of North-West Canada that I may well wish to impress upon you and myself the gravity of the position and the necessity for the most prompt and vigorous action on the part of the Church. The fertile lands of Manitoba and the North-West Territories are receiving large accessions of immigrants. There must be new missions, otherwise we shall drift gradually into the position of a large part of the American Church, ministering only to towns and letting the country go; and to let the country go is to lose hold of large classes in the towns, for it is the country that gradually feeds the towns."

The chief help in the past, he added, had come from England, and the S. P. G. had recently voted further assistance of £8,000 for Western work. It was regrettable that Eastern Canada could do so little in this connection and he hoped the Church there would soon make some special effort to do its duty. "We all know how large an amount is spent every year by members of the Church on social amusements and pleasures—a very little of which would go far to make up our deficiencies." The Archbishop concluded by pointing out that the policy of the C. M. S. and the S. P. C. K., to whom they owed such a debt of gratitude, was the gradual reduction of their grants in the West so as to utilize their means in regions more dependent upon the Church at home. Much would therefore lie upon the Church in Canada for future supervision and work in these Western missions and far-spreading Dioceses. A Resolution was passed by the Synod, after much discussion, which referred to the educational and other common interests affecting the Indians which existed between the Church and other religious bodies in the West, and appointed a Committee, " to seek the co-operation of representatives of the Methodist and Presbyterian Churches of Canada with a view to joint council and united action in dealing with such matters."

On September 3rd the General Synod of the Church of England in Canada opened at Montreal with a sermon in the Cathedral by Archbishop Bond, Metropolitan of Canada, and with the attendance of eighteen Bishops—of whom two were United States representatives—and a large number of clergy and laity. Owing to ill-health Archbishop Machray, Primate of all Canada, was unable to be present and his place was taken by His Grace of Montreal. The former, however, contributed a written address to the proceedings of the Synod which drew earnest attention to the rising and great communities of the West and to the enthusiastic work of the missionary societies of other religious organizations. " But the action of the Church has been weak beyond expression and any appreciable help from the East has been only brought out by spasmodic appeals from needy Dioceses." He urged the establishment of a Canadian Church Missionary Society and forwarded a canon which he had prepared with that object in view. This was afterwards discussed, modified and accepted by the Synod. The Upper House sent on the following day word that they had appointed Chancellor Dunbar, Chancellor J. A. Worrell, K.C., Dr. L. H. Davidson, Dr. Wilson, and Mr. Justice Walkem as members of the Supreme Court of Appeal which was to be constituted by the General Synod and which, on September 12th ensuing, was given power to deal with appeals from any Ecclesiastical Court, Provincial or Diocesan.

Following up in part the recent remarks of Canon Welch a motion was presented to the Synod on September 8th by Dr. J. A. Worrell, K.C., to the following effect: "That, the Upper House concurring, a joint Committee of both Houses be appointed (a) to take such steps as may be necessary to have the Church in the Dominion of Canada designated by a distinctive national name, as in the case of Ireland, South Africa or the United States; (b) to publish an edition of the Book of Common Prayer, with such additions and adaptations as may be required by the needs of the country; (c) to define and limit the title and duties of the various ecclesiastical offices to which clergymen may be appointed by any Bishop in Canada." It was claimed by the mover as to the first part of his Resolution that no organic connection now existed with the Church in England and that so long as the same standard of faith and conduct was possessed a change of name would not affect the existing intimate relations with the Mother Church. "The present name was long, unsuitable, and entirely indefensible and the formation of the General Synod, combining all the Dioceses into a national Church, had done away with all excuse for its use." Canon Welch seconded the motion and declared the name anomalous and prejudicial to the interests of the Church. It made them seem as if they were merely sojourners here.

Judge McDonald of Brockville, strongly opposed any change in the name on grounds of Imperial patriotism and because Parliament would not incorporate them under any national designation. As to the word "Anglican" being adopted he did not see what was to be gained in a popular sense by substituting a Latin for a Saxon name. On motion of Mr. Matthew Wilson, K.C., of Chatham, seconded by Judge Savary of Annapolis, the six months' hoist of the first part of the motion was carried by 37 to 35. The third was defeated by a large majority and the second, in modified and amended form was carried with only two dissentients, after a speech from Mr. Wilson, during which he read a letter from the Archbishop of Canterbury stating that there might be grave danger in a change of name for the Church but that he concurred in an attempt to bring the Prayer-Book into closer harmony with its local environment. One change proposed by the speaker was the introduction of some simple prayers suitable for family worship. The Lower House also passed a Resolution in favour of meeting every three years instead of six as at present. On the following day this was concurred in by the House of Bishops and it was decided to hold the next meeting in Quebec.

Both Houses agreed, after discussion, in prohibiting marriage with a deceased wife's sister or deceased wife's sister's daughter and in ordering the table of prohibited degrees to be placed in the vestry of every church within the jurisdiction of the Synod. It was decided to incorporate the Board of Missions and the residence of the new General Secretary, the Rev. L. Norman Tucker, whose appointment had also been made and ratified, was fixed in Toronto. A Committee was appointed to arrange for the new Canadian edition of the Prayer-Book and a long discussion on Divorce was initiated in the Lower House by the presentation of a motion by Dr. L. H. Davidson, declaring that no clergyman should be allowed to solemnize a marriage between persons, "either of whom shall have been divorced from one who is living at the time." In connection with the Report of the Committee on Statistics the Rev. Provost Macklem of Toronto made the following statement:

Most, if not all, of the Dioceses which have made complete returns show a marked increase in Church population, an increase considerably greater than that in the total Church population of the same districts as shown by the recent Dominion Census. Now, when it is considered that the returns which come into this Synod embrace only that portion of the Church population which is known to the clergy, while the Dominion Census, on the other hand, includes all who themselves claim adherence to our Church, it is plain the larger ratio of increase in Church population, returned by the clergy as compared with the ratio increase in the returns of the Dominion Census, goes to show that of late years a larger proportion than heretofore of the total Church population is known to the clergy and brought within the ministration of the Church. This surely affords more ground for encouragement than the Dominion Census, so disappointing in some respects, does for discouragement. This efficiency of ministration is likely to be increased now that the numbers of the clergy are being increased.

Meanwhile, the discussion of the Divorce question continued for several days at intervals. The Upper House had already taken ground very similar to Dr. Davidson's motion but, after various amendments had been presented and defeated, and speeches of marked ability and learning delivered on different sides of the problem by Judge McDonald, Judge Savary, Principal Whitney of Lennoxville, Mr. N. W. Hoyles, K.C., the Rev. Canon Kittson, Mr. Matthew Wilson, K.C., and others, it was found that the two Houses could not agree nor could the clerical and lay members of the Lower House. On September 12th the General Synod was closed with a Pastoral Letter signed by the Archbishops and Bishops of the Church in Canada. It pointed to the growing greatness of the country, to the established unity of the Canadian Church, to the organization of the new Missionary Society and the appointment of the Rev. Mr. Tucker, to the financial needs and duties of the Church, to the necessity of keeping the Sabbath more earnestly and suitably, to the desirability of a closer popular study of the Scriptures, to the need of better home training for children and a more sanctified home life, to the imperative need of supporting the Sunday Schools. Before this final word to the Church was issued, however, Resolutions had passed authorizing the use of the Revised Version; declaring it the duty of the Church to inaugurate evangelistic and educational work amongst the new settlers in the West; permitting a change in the Confimation service so as to admit persons baptized in other religious bodies; approving the work of the Brotherhood of St. Andrew; appointing a joint Committee to consider and report at the next Session as to a proposed appendix to the Prayer-Book. Some of the minor incidents of the year in connection with the Church—mainly personal—were as follows:

April   3.—Holy Trinity Episcopal Cathedral is consecrated at New West-minister by His Lordship, Bishop Dart.
May   15.—It is announced that the Ven. Lewis Evans, D.C.L., Archdeacon of Montreal, is to succeed Dr. Carmichael as Dean of Montreal ; that the Ven. J. G. Norton, D.D., Archdeacon of St. Andrews, is to succeed Dr. Evans ; that the Rev. Canon John Ker, D.D., is to succeed Dr. Norton ; and that the Rev. J. Gilbert Baylis, D.D., is to be the new Canon of Christ Church Cathedral.
June   1.—The Rev. Canon Alexander Sanson of Trinity Church, Toronto, celebrates his 50th anniversary as Rector of that Church.
June   15.—The Rev. A. H. Baldwin, M.A., celebrates his 30 years of service as Rector of All Saints' Church, Toronto.
July   4.—The jubilee of the ordination of the Ven. Henry Roe, D.D., Arch-deacon of the Diocese of Quebec, is celebrated at Richmond by a large gathering, presided over by the Lord Bishop of Quebec, and marked by the presentation of two illuminated Addresses—one from Bishop's College, Lennoxville.

Aug. 27. The Right Rev. J. H. Lofthouse, D.D., is consecrated at Winnipeg as Bishop of the new Diocese of Keewatin. The Bishop of Athabasca officiates, assisted by the Bishops of Calgary and Saskatchewan, Qu'-Appelle, and Moosomin.

Sept. 28.—The Very Rev. S. P. Matheson, B.D., is formally inducted as Dean of the Diocese of Rupert's Land.

Oct. 28.—On this and succeeding days various formal farewells, presentations of Addresses and public evidences of popular regard, are tendered at Vancouver to the Rev. L. Norman Tucker, M.A., Rector of Christ Church, upon the occasion of his departure to assume charge of the new Church of England Missionary Society.

Nov. 9—The Ven. O. Fortin, B.A., Archdeacon of Winnipeg, celebrates the 27th anniversary of his induction as Rector of Holy Trinity Church.

Dec. 23.—The Most Rev. and Right Hon. Frederick Temple, Archbishop of Canterbury and Primate of all England, passes away in London to the deep regret of many in the daughter Church of the Dominion.

The meeting of the Methodist General Conference at Winnipeg, in September, 1902, was marked by incidents and surroundings of unusual importance. It was opened on September 4th by a masterly address from the Rev. Dr. Carman, General Superintendent of the Church, in which he reviewed at length the progress of Methodism and the religious and moral position of the country. He began be declaring that personal and corporate responsibility, history and experience, connexional loyalty, religious sentiment and national patriotism were all alike impelling them at this time to take full advantage of the rising tide of population and progress in Canada. "If we ever needed Divine direction and help it is to-day. If we ever needed wise and vigorous Church statesmanship it is to-day." Upon the subject of amusements—orthodox or the reverse, questionable or innocent—he dwelt at length. Referring to the prohibition in the Note to the general rules as to dancing, playing cards, etc., he concisely and fairly reviewed the two sides of the discussion, and then expressed his own opinion of the situation as follows:

From my point of view it has appeared to me useless to agitate the Church, weaken her and unnecessarily expose her weakness, on such an issue. If the agitation had been to secure more and better local preachers, more and better class leaders, more open-air preaching or street preaching, more self-denial instead of more self-indulgence, more devotion to Christ and crucifixion of the carnal mind instead of more social gratification and worldly pleasure, more zeal for evangelism instead of more thirst for perishable creature good, Methodistically speaking, I could have understood it. As some that were urging the deletion of the Note might be among the very last themselves to take any advantage of such deletion, one might wonder in what interest, with honest purpose, they were striving. If the question were submitted to the vote of the Methodist membership of the Dominion, can you estimate how small the vote in favour of deletion would be, or how large in favour of retention? If it were submitted to the vote of our Young Peoples' Societies and Epworth Leagues, can you estimate with what energy of decision and what preponderance of votes the prohibition would be upheld and the deletion proposal submerged? I am of the opinion that the majority of our families, not members of the Church, loyal adherents, so far as they take any interest in the matter, prefer the Discipline as it is. Now, why agitate and vex the Church regarding the question?

From this question to that of Prohibition Dr. Carman passed, and, as to the latter, pointed out that all the Conferences of the Church, general and annual, had time and again declared themselves positively and unreservedly in favour of the prohibition of the liquor traffic. They believed it to be antagonistic to every interest of the State : the fruitful source of pauperism, disease, insanity and crime ; the cause of corruption in public government and immorality in private life. The speaker went on to deal with the Prohibition issues in Manitoba and Ontario, to deprecate the carrying of a question of morals into the political arena, to urge the Church, as such, to keep itself clear of political parties in this connection. But they must, he declared, educate the people in temperance principles, reform the drunkard by social organizations and institutions, and strengthen in every possible direction the religious and moral fibre of their people. A statistical review of the progress of the Church during the past four years was also submitted by the speaker, as follows :

	1902.		Increase or Decrease from 1898.
Membership.........................	291,805	Inc.	11,385
Ministers...........................	1,792	Inc.	89
Probationers	238	Dec.	90
Local Preachers.....................	2,248	Dec.	104
Exhorters...........................	1,119	Inc.	88
Class Leaders.......................	6,791	Dec.	518
Number of Sabbath Schools............	3,425	Inc.	80
Number of officers and teachers........	33,396	Inc.	378
Number of scholars..................	272,506	Inc.	2,237
Amounts raised by Sabbath Schools....	$545,261	Inc.	$62,146
Number of Leagues and Young People's Societies	1,809	Dec.	138
Membership of same.................	69,402	Dec.	12,533
Amounts raised by same	$245,017	Dec.	......
Number of churches.................	3,413	Inc.	84
Number of parsonages...............	1,208	Inc.	75
Number of burial grounds............	1,109	Inc.	8
Number of colleges and schools........	22	Inc.	3
Value of churches...................	$11,836,410	Inc.	$539,608
Value of parsonages and furniture......	2,173,544	Inc.	148,843
Value of college and school property....	2,168,164	Inc.	607,127
Value of book and publishing property..	443,351	Inc.	47,815
Total value of church property.........	16,802,438	Inc.	1,372,484
Amount raised for ministers...........	3,276,661	Inc.	120,295
Amount raised for circuit purposes.....	5,932,001	Inc.	1,363,362
Amount raised for all purposes	10,911,271	Inc.	1,634,285
Total church and parsonage debts......	2,520,230	Inc.	392,081

On the following day the Rev. Dr. Walford Green, representing the British Wesleyan Conference, and the Rev. Principal Crawford of the Irish Conference were introduced, and on the 8th inst. delivered addresses full of fraternal feeling and eloquent words. The first-named, in particular, was most effective in his utterances upon the bonds of Empire, the stormy events of recent years, the general progress of Methodism and the historic names and characters of the Church in Canada. On the same day the Rev. J. W. Graham of the St. James' Church, Montreal, described the financial condition which had made it necessary for them to appeal for aid to the Methodists in general. Their debt in 1898 was $622,224, it was now $512,822, and in order to save their buildings they must raise $182,697. Of this amount $132,697 had been subscribed—$50,000 of it by Mr. Chester D. Massey, and $5,000 each by Messrs. A. E. Ames, J. W. Flavelle, T. Eaton, E. R. Wood, and Senator Cox of Toronto. A day was set apart by the Conference for the subject to be presented to every Methodist Church in Canada. Home Missions were then dealt with in a Report presented by the Rev. Dr. W. R. Young, and making certain recommendations, which may be summarized as follows:

1. That increased and more authoritative supervision over Home Mission work should be established.
2. That four Superintendents should be appointed—one for New Ontario, two for Manitoba and the Territories and one for British Columbia.
3. That as the development of population in the West promises to be very rapid the Board of Missions should be authorized to increase the number of local Superintendents of Missions.
4. That a Corresponding Secretary should be appointed to whom these Western Superintendents could report and who should act as a medium between them and the Mission Board and aid, generally, in facilitating their work.
5. That a special Fund be raised to meet these and other expenses connected with the immediate extension of the Home Mission field.

This Report was adopted in its different clauses after an eloquent speech from Mr. N. W. Rowell dealing with the growth of the West and the need for Methodist labour amongst its peoples. In the evening, besides thanking the British delegates for their visit with a standing vote and a motion which described them "as fellow citizens with us of a British Empire federated in fact if not in name," the Conference received a delegation from the Presbyterian Church in Canada composed of the Rev. Dr. Bryce, Moderator of its General Assembly, the Rev. Principal Patrick and the Rev. C. W. Gordon. Each of the speakers urged united action in meeting the great religious needs of the growing West and Principal Patrick vigorously advocated the union of the two denominations as one "national Protestant Church." The question of admitting women to membership in all Church Courts, district meetings and Conferences was discussed at length on September 9th. Those in favour urged that women were fitted and worthy for the position and that the time had come for their admission. Those opposing the proposal did not deny the fitness but took ground upon the point of advisability and expediency. The vote was a tie, of 126 on either side, in a question which required a three-fourth majority to effect any change.

On the following day Prohibition was discussed as a consequence of the Report from the Committee on Temperance recommending the appointment of a Permanent Secretary to act as field agent in the interests of temperance and moral reform. The Rev. C. T.

23

Scott of London presented the proposal and it was supported by Mr. Joseph Gibson, the Rev. W. Kettlewell, and Rev. Dr. E. S. Rowe and opposed by Mr. Joseph Tait and Dr. S. F. Huestis. It carried almost unanimously. Following this was a discussion upon the question of changing the limit of the pastorate from three to four years. The argument on the one side was the friction and dissatisfaction, caused or rendered possible, by the longer time, and the claim that it was not desired by the majority of ministers. On the other hand was the contention of the Rev. F. A. Cassidy that short pastorates meant a "shallow ministry and a fickle membership." After the expression of varied opinions the proposal for a four year term was carried by a large majority.

On Sept. 11th the Rev. Dr. A. Sutherland was elected fraternal delegate to the British Wesleyan and Irish Methodist Churches; the Rev. William Dobson to the Methodist Episcopal Church of the United States ; and the Rev. Principal Sparling of Wesley College, Winnipeg, to the Methodist Episcopal Church South. Delegates from these last two Churches had been received by the Conference a couple days before this. On September 13th and the following day prolonged debate took place on a proposal coming from the Committee on Itinerancy that the term of the General Superintendent should be four instead of eight years. The chief point in favour of the change seemed to be the bringing of the position into more democratic touch with the Church and into harmony with the four year period prevailing in all other appointments or elections at the hands of the General Conference. The main opposing arguments were the fact that the Methodist Episcopal Church had insisted on the eight year term as a compromise for its abandonment of Episcopacy when entering the Union and that the longer period meant more efficient and experienced management. Mr. John T. Moore, Dr. J. J. Maclaren, K.C., Joseph Gibson and the Rev. Dr. J. S. Ross were amongst the supporters of the proposal; the Rev. Dr. J. S. Williamson, Rev. Dr. J. C. Antliff and Joseph Tait opposed it. The vote was 103 for and 105 against.

The most vehement discussion of the whole proceedings took place on the evening of September 15th when Mr. N. W. Rowell, K.C., presented the Report of the Discipline Committee regarding Rule 35 of the Church, which dealt with and prohibited dancing, cardplaying, theatre-going, etc. A large number of memorials had been received by the Committee asking either that the Rule be made admonitory instead of prohibitory, or praying that it be not changed at all. The Committee reported its concurrence in the latter view. A sheaf of amendments was moved and lost—that of the Rev. Dr. S. P. Rose "strongly discountenancing" the specified amusements as "proven by experience to be prejudicial to the highest spiritual life" being defeated by 139 to 74. The Report was finally and almost unanimously adopted. On the following day the General Mission Board was announced as including the Rev. Dr. E. B. Ryckman, Rev. Dr. Leo Gaetz, Rev. Dr. William Briggs, Rev.

Dr. W. R. Young, Rev. Dr. S. F. Huestis, Rev. Dr. T. G. Williams, Senator George A. Cox and Messrs. C. D. Massey, N. W. Rowell, K.C., J. A. M. Aikins, K.C., J. J. Maclaren, K.C., and J. W. Flavelle.

The Board of Management of the Educational Society was then appointed together with the Boards of Regents of Victoria University and Mount Allison University, the Board of Conveners of the Wesleyan Theological College, the Board of Managers of Wesley College and Albert College, the Board of Governors of the Methodist College of St. John's, Newfoundland, the Board of the Ontario Ladies' College and Alma College, and the Board of Directors of the Columbian College. The election of officers resulted in the unanimous choice of the Rev. Albert Carman, D.D., as General Superintendent for another 8 years, of the Rev. Dr. W. Briggs as Book Steward for the Western Section and of the Rev. Dr. S. F. Huestis for the Eastern Section. After several ballots the Rev. G. J. Bond was chosen Editor of the *Christian Guardian*. The Rev. Dr. W. H. Withrow was re-elected Editor of the *Methodist Magazine* and the Sunday-School publications, unanimously, as was the Rev. Dr. Sutherland as General Secretary of Missions and the Rev. Dr. James Henderson as his Associate. The Rev. Dr. James Woodsworth was unanimously elected Corresponding Superintendent of Missions in the West, the Rev. Dr. John Potts as General Secretary of Education, the Rev. A. C. Crews as Secretary of Sunday Schools and Epworth Leagues, the Rev. Dr. E. S. Griffith as Clerical Treasurer. On September 17th the Report of a Committee on Church Union recommending the union of the Methodist, Congregational and Presbyterian Churches was received and accepted and a special Committee appointed to discuss the subject with the bodies named and report at the next General Conference. In the document submitted regret was expressed at previous failures to evolve a comprehensive scheme of union, but the future prospects were described as more hopeful. It proceeded as follows:

Inasmuch as the problem of the unification of several of these denominations appears to present much less serious obstacles, since their relations are already marked by a great degree of spiritual unity, and they have already become closely assimilated in standards and ideals of church life, forms of worship, and ecclesiastical polity ; and since, further, the present conditions of our country and those in immediate prospect demand the most careful economy of the resources of the leading and aggressive evangelical denominations, both in ministers and in money, in order to overtake the religious needs of the people pouring into our new settlements—which economy seems impossible without further organic unity or its equivalent; this General Conference is of the opinion that the time is opportune for a definite practical movement, concentrating attention and aiming at the practical organic union of those denominations already led by Providence into such close fraternal relations ;

And whereas, a definite proposal has been discussed to some extent in the press and elsewhere looking to the ultimate organic union of the Presbyterian, Congregational and Methodist Churches in Canada, this General Conference, in no spirit of exclusiveness towards others not named, declares that it would regard a movement with this object in view with great gratification, believing that the deliberate, friendly discussion of the doctrinal, practical and administrative problems involved, with the purpose of reaching agreement, would not only facilitate the finding and formulation of a Basis of Union, but would also educate the people interested into a deeper spirit of unity, and into that spirit of mutual, reasonable concession on which the successful consummation of such movement ultimately depends ; and this General Conference would further commend this movement to the prayerful interest and sympathy of the Methodist Church in' the devout and earnest hope that, if organic union of the denominations named be achieved, it may be accompanied with great blessings to the Church and to the nation at large, and redound to the greater glory of God.

The further proceedings of the day included the election of the Rev. Dr. S. D. Chown to the new post of General Secretary of Temperance and Moral Reform, the reception of a delegation from the Congregational Union and the presentation of an interesting Report from the Committee on Sociological problems. On September 18th the Rev. John MacLean, Ph.D., was elected Editor of *The Wesleyan* and on the following day the Conference, on motion of Judge Chesley, referred to the prevalence of political corruption, called the attention of the pulpit and of Christian people to the dangers arising from such a condition, condemned the venal and cowardly violation of duties which it involved, urged citizens to free their political parties from suspicion in respect to the sanctity of the ballot, and suggested that time be given in Sunday Schools, in Epworth League meetings, and in Public Schools, on Empire Day, to the discussion of the duties of a citizen. The Committee on Civil Rights reported upon the Order of Precedence question and suggested that it should be based on the numerical strength of the religious bodies as shown by the latest Census. After passing a loyal Address to the King the General Conference then adjourned.

The chief event in connection with the largest distinct religious organization in Canada during the year was the retirement of **The Papal Delegate and Roman Catholic Church** Mgr. Diomede Falconio, D.D., Apostolic Delegate to the Dominion, in order to take up a similar position at Washington. His Excellency had performed his duties for two years with much tact and admirable discretion and when the transfer was announced on October 31st there was a general expression of opinion in this respect amongst all who understand the responsibilities of the post which he had held. On November 16th a farewell Address was presented to Mgr. Falconio by the Ancient Order of Hibernians at Ottawa. In replying he referred to the little he had once known of Canada and the continent at large and spoke of his visits to all the most important points in the Dominion and of his appreciation of its vast proportions and great resources. "I must say that the mere extent of territory, its beauty and richness, would not have impressed my mind so strongly had there not been a corresponding equivalent in the moral and civic virtues of the people. A glance at your numerous institutions of charity, at your colleges and schools, at your magnificent churches, and at the constitution by which you are governed, will suffice to let a foreigner understand in an instant the superiority of your moral and religious character."

His Excellency concluded by expressing the belief that a great future was before a country which had been so signally blessed in such a variety of ways. During the day farewells were said by many distinguished callers—amongst whom was the Premier of Canada—and in the evening an Address was presented by the Canadian branch of the Knights of Columbus. On the following morning Archbishop Duhamel, the Hon. R. W. Scott and Hon. C. Fitz-patrick were present at the station with a large crowd of clergy, students and others to see him off to Toronto where a farewell banquet was to be tendered. This affair was held under the auspices of the Canadian Catholic Union and Mr. Justice McMahon, as its President, occupied the chair. Amongst others present were the Archbishop of Toronto, the Hon. G. W. Ross, Premier of Ontario, Mr. O. A. Howland, C.M.G., Mayor of Toronto, Bishop McEvay of London, Senator McHugh of Lindsay, Vicar-General McCann and Mr. Eugene O'Keefe. The first toast was that of the Pope and then came the toast of the King. In replying to the toast of his own health Mgr. Falconio said little more than an expression of thanks for many kindnesses rendered him in Canada and of admiration for the country and liking for its people. In the course of his speech the Hon. Mr. Ross recognized religious duty as the first which demanded attention and declared that there was no Canadian who did not accept the fundamental rule that "no country can be great unless its institutions are based upon morality and virtue." Canada had endeavoured to lay that foundation and had been aided by a well-directed and tolerant clergy who had worked along the lines of good-will among all races and creeds.

In his own experience of many years as Minister of Education in Ontario he had always found amongst the Roman Catholic clergy the broadest desire to help in revising the curriculum of studies in their Separate Schools and in improving in every possible way the administration and standard of work. Whether in the matter of improved inspection, more systematic study, or better qualified teachers, he declared that he had ever found them ready to progress. Then came the incident of the evening. Mayor Howland, in responding to the Civic toast, held the delicate position of Chief Magistrate in a city noted for its strong Protestantism and of guest at a function where the issue of State and Church had been possibly raised by the place given on the toast list to the Holy Father followed by His Majesty the King. He commenced by a reference to Mgr. Falconio as having come from "the most ancient of capital cities, from the centre of the Church which was the nexus of Christianity and civilization during the dark ages" and as being most welcome in every sense and by all citizens to the capital city of Ontario. He then proceeded as follows:

I have joined with you in drinking the toast of His Holiness, a friend of the British Empire, a friend of the peace of the world, one whose name and fame are respected by all creeds. I would have preferred it should not have been followed by the toast of His Majesty the King. I think it would have been better if the relations between the Church and the State had not thus been expressed in this city and under the British flag. I could not refuse to join with you in drinking the toast of His Most Gracious Majesty. I am sure every Roman Catholic present joined most heartily and loyally in the toast, and I know you meant nothing more than the expression of a sentiment in which I can not altogether disagree with you, that the spiritual is higher than the material. I regret, however, that sometimes the form of expression of a sentiment differs from the essence of the sentiment.

The incident occasioned a good deal of comment. The Toronto *Globe* of November 20th expressed its belief that the almost universal custom of honouring the head of a nation first amongst the toasts at a public banquet should not have been departed from in this instance. Premier Ross, who had not referred to the matter at the Dinner, was interviewed by the *World* on the following day and deprecated any criticism. The expressions regarding Canada and the Empire could not in his opinion have been more earnest. " Loyalty does not depend merely on a matter of precedence and I, for one, would never think of separating myself on a festive occasion—particularly of a quasi-religious character—from my Roman Catholic fellow-citizen because their order of business was different from that which prevails generally at other gatherings." Archbiship O'Connor was also interviewed and described the banquet as essentially a religious affair though it may have placed the Premier of Ontario and the Mayor of Toronto in a slightly awkward position. " As the banquet was a tribute to the representative of the Pope, it seems to be quite proper that the first toast should have been to the Holy Father. The order of the toasts was arranged by a Committee of the Catholic Union. I may say I knew of this order, and could not see that it did violence to any traditions of the Church. There is nothing new in the position of the Church, with reference to the national ruler and the Holy Father's position. It is too well defined to require discussion at this time." On the day of this Toronto banquet it was announced from Rome that Mgr. Donatus Sbarretti, Archbishop of Ephesus, had been appointed Apostolic Delegate to Canada.

Meanwhile, various events of differing degrees of importance had occurred in Church affairs during the year. The Lenten season was marked by a farewell announcement from the venerable Bishop Rogers of Chatham, N.B., who retired from administrative work after 42 years of ecclesiastical labour in a Diocese which had seen many churches, schools and hospitals established under his direction and the number of its priests increased from seven to sixty. On August 8th the full charge of the Diocese was taken over by the Right Rev. T. F. Barry. On February 16th Archbishop O'Brien of Halifax issued a Lenten Pastoral dealing with various doctrines of the Church associated with the season. His Grace referred at length to the existence, the influence and the work of an evil spirit, ever the enemy of the human race. The fact of his power and personality were proven not only by Scripture but by modern experience of the hatred which exists to all things good, to the Gospel of Christ and the laws of God. As to the future the lot of the wicked must be hell and of the good, heaven. "The Catholic Church understands by hell a place where those who die in the service of the devil are eternally punished with him. Apart from its unending duration and everlasting banishment from God, we do not assume to define the nature and intensity of that punishment. In our present state the human mind can form no adequate conception of the joys of heaven, nor of the sufferings of hell. Nor can the language of earth describe the one, or the other. We know, however, that the just in heaven will be supremely happy, the impious in hell utterly miserable." After dealing at length with these and other subjects the Archbishop concluded by saying that denial of a personal devil is usually the first step toward infidelity and disbelief in everlasting punishment the second.

In the death of Bishop Vital Justin Grandin of St. Albert, the Church of the West lost one of its pillars of strength. His successor, Mgr. E. J. Legal, addressed a Pastoral to the clergy of that Diocese early in July which pointed out how the late Bishop had cleared the way for the future. "He fully realized from the beginning the importance of the cause of education, and he has strenuously worked to secure to the Catholic Church the rights that are essential to her influence. He it was who had the first notion of promoting evangelization of the Indian children by means of industrial and boarding schools. For the primary education in civilized centres he has done much also in order to secure the principle of Separate Schools." At Halifax, on August 25th, a Convention was held of the Catholic Mutual Benefit Association. Archbishop O'Brien, in welcoming the gathering, declared that the C. M. B. A. had the highest approval of the Church. The Rev. Father Crinion of Hamilton stated that the Association afforded to Catholics the best form of assurance, that its membership was 17,000, its insurance in force $22,500,000, its reserve fund $130,000, and its total payments to widows and orphans $2,500,000. "It aims also to make its members ideal Catholic citizens, loyal to God, to the State and to the Church." The Hon. M. F. Hackett of Montreal, Grand President of the Association, spoke at some length and declared that "no men in Canada love their country better, love its government and institutions more, than do the Catholics." He urged all members of the Church, everywhere, to join the Association in a union for the moral, intellectual and material benefit of Catholics and for nothing else.

An interesting decision of a semi-religious character was given at Halifax, in the autumn, by Mr. Justice Townshend and announced on October 1st. It dealt with the will of the late Patrick Power who, in 1881, had left a portion of his estate to be "applied in the introduction and support of the Jesuit fathers in the City of Halifax." The Court was now asked as to the application of this money and under the pleadings made had to consider (1) whether it was practicable to now introduce the Jesuit Order in the Province; (2) whether the Jesuits were willing to come; (3) and whether the refusal of the Archbishop to permit of their coming was the sole cause of their not doing so. The decision was that the residue of the estate should now be applied to the charitable and other objects to which the bulk of it had been devoted by the Trustees, under the will, during the past twenty years. On October 29th Vicar-General Bayard of London, delivered an important sermon upon the Church's view of matrimony and divorce. Marriage he defined as both a natural contract and a sacrament; divorce as "a barbarous and iniquitous practice outraging common decency." Marriage could not be dissolved by divorce as "no human law can prevail against the law of Christ." Christian marriage represented an indissoluble union like that of Christ and the Church.

Speaking at Halifax, on November 23rd, to the St. Mary's Young Men's Society Archbishop O'Brien deprecated the modern spirit of flippant consideration of things of a religious character. If he were to himself write a treatise on law or medicine, he would be laughed at because he had neither studied nor practiced in those pursuits. "But when it comes to matters of religion every man seems to think that he has a right to teach and explain even the most hidden truths of God. Hence our modern magazines, our modern novels, are filled with thoughts and suggestions well calculated to teach a merely natural religion and destroy the reign of God in men's hearts. Guard then, and guard intelligently, against the literature of to-day." His Grace described bad reading, in conclusion, as "the modern agent of Satan." At Penetanguishene, on December 11th, a splendid memorial to the heroic Fathers Jean de Brèbéuf and Gabriel Lallement, pioneer missionaries and martyrs of the Order of Jesus, was inaugurated in the form of a church which had been commenced on September 5th, 1886, and was now completed. Archbishop O'Connor performed the ceremonies assisted by the Bishops of London and Peterborough.

The important event of the year in Baptist history was the meeting of the annual Convention at Montreal from October 15th to 21st. The retiring President, Mr. A. McNee, **The Baptist** delivered an address at the opening ceremonies which **and Congre-** reviewed the early work of the denomination in **gational** Canada; hoped for much in the future from their **Churches** College at Acadia in Nova Scotia, the Feller Institute in Quebec, the McMaster, Woodstock, and Moulton Colleges in Ontario and Brandon College in Manitoba; dealt with the individualism which had so long been the basic principle of the denomination and asked if, in this age of consolidation, they were not carrying the spirit of personal independence too far. Had they not been cherishing an ideal which could only be realized under ideal conditions! "Has the Lord's work been hampered and hindered by a spirit that is often called independence of thought when, perhaps, it is more properly too often another name for an abnormal development of self-esteem and selfishness? Does not such a policy result in a measure of weakness and inefficiency on the part of our members and churches?"

Cohesion was as necessary in its way as independence and if the Baptist cause was to be promoted in Canada they must get away from their present system of disjointed weakness. "Liberty to an extreme is an evil. The interests of the aggregate body should prevail." He pleaded in strong terms for a spirit of more pronounced pride in the history of the Baptist order, for more Baptist loyalty and Baptist self-respect and concluded with the following reference to the question of a union of Christian Churches:

Those present may not see the organic union of the leading Protestant denominations in Canada, but we do see evidences of a desire among these denominations for a closer working union, by which the resources and working forces of the denominations may be better conserved and directed. Two of the large denominations have already absorbed other bodies closely related to them in faith and practice. Would it not be well for us, therefore, to anticipate the time when organic Church union might be possible and desirable, and in the meantime strengthen ourselves by making an earnest effort to consolidate all those bodies more or less intimately related to the Baptists, and whose differences are superficial rather than vital.

The officers of the Convention were then chosen. The Rev. J. L. Gilmour, B.D., of Montreal, was elected President, Mr. R. D. Warren of Georgetown, Vice-President, Rev. J. E. Trotter, of St. Catharines, 2nd Vice-President, and the Rev. P. K. Dayfoot, M.A., of Port Hope, Secretary-Treasurer. Reports of Colleges were presented, the Publication Board made its statement showing a small surplus to the good, and the Sunday School Committee reported that they had 36,450 scholars enrolled with an average attendance of 24,998; that the teachers and officers numbered 4,472; that the schools numbered 427 with total contributions of $18,760; that 35 churches reported no schools and that the scholars joining the communion during the year numbered 1,338. The appointment of a General Superintendent of Sunday Schools was urged and, after discussion in the Convention, a motion by Mr. D. E. Thomson, K.C., was carried referring the matter to the Boards concerned in order to take such action as was possible in this direction. On the following day Chancellor Wallace of McMaster University addressed the Convention on Sunday School work and Mr. D. E. Thomson on Educational work.

The Report of the Western Missions' Committee, on October 17th, showed total disbursements of $6,337 and it was stated that in 28 years they had established 98 churches in Manitoba and the North-West with 300 preaching stations. Amongst the churches 14 were German and 6 Scandinavian. In British Columbia, Superintendent P. H. McEwen reported that they had 19 churches of which only 3 were self-supporting. The Board of Home Missions reported 124 pastors and 50 students serving 290 churches and preaching stations, with contributions during the year of

$10,297. A Congregational delegation waited upon the Convention in the evening and addresses were delivered by the Rev. Dr. J. Edgar Hill and the Rev. Hugh Pedley of Montreal and the Rev. Dr. Alfred Rowland of London, England. On October 20th the Convention received the Report of Foreign Missions for the year showing an income of $36,214, of which the Women's Societies gave one-fourth. On the following day a fraternal delegation from the Methodist Church was received and the 66th Report of the Grande Ligne Mission presented. It dealt with the work amongst the French-Canadians and described the success of the Feller Institute with its 73 boys and 55 girls in attendance— of whom 9 were Roman Catholics. The financial statement showed total contributions of $18,786 for mission purposes, a special fund of $40,425 for building purposes and $28,717 at the credit of the Endowment Fund. The Convention then closed and the delegates went to Grande Ligne where the new building connected with the Feller Institute was formally opened. This institution had been founded by Madame Henrietta Feller for the purpose of furthering among the young French-Canadians the missionary work which she had commenced in 1837 with the co-operation of the Rev. Louis Roussy.

The Resolutions passed by the Convention included approval of the Canadian edition of the English *Baptist Hymnal*; concurrence in the work and objects of the Lord's Day Alliance as "of vital importance to the moral and religious life of the nation"; protest against any grants of public money to institutions controlled by religious bodies as "unreasonable, unrighteous and oppressive"; agreement with the recent finding of the Presbyterian General Assembly that the existing Rules of Precedence in State functions were "wanting in courtesy and foreign to the genius of this country"; support by prayer and effort in fufilling the conditions of the Prohibition Referendum in Ontario; regret at the retirement of the Rev. Dr. Thomas from his Toronto pastorate; interest in and sympathy with the Nonconformists of England in their opposition to "the unjust Education Bill," now before the Imperial Parliament, as being "out of all harmony with the spirit of the age." The report on the State of Religion in the two Provinces, which was submitted to the Convention, showed 2,202 baptisms during the year since the preceding Session and a present membership of 43,940. Churches of 100 and more had gained 966 members since 1895-6 and those of less than 100 had gained 2,738. The total expenditure of the Church at home in 1901-2 was $313,845 and abroad $77,020. An important incident in the Baptist annals of 1902 was the retirement of the Rev. Dr. B. D. Thomas from the pastorship of the Jarvis St. Baptist Church in Toronto. It was announced in a letter read from the pulpit on October 12th by the Rev. Dr. Harris. The reason given was simply a belief that after 20 years' service a new and younger man might be expected to do better work for the cause of Christ. Dr.

Thomas expressed the deepest gratitude for all the support that had been given him and at the congregational meeting two days later explained once more that he was not now a young man and that the church demanded the services of one in the prime of manhood and power. Resolutions of regret and appreciation were passed.

The Congregational Union of Ontario and Quebec met at Ottawa on June 5th. The Rev. T. B. Hyde, of Toronto, was elected President and the Rev. Dr. W. H. Warriner, of Montreal, Vice-President. The event of the day was an address by the Rev. Hugh Pedley, B.A., on the Congregationalism of Protest and of Progress. The protest against State supremacy in religious matters had, he declared, been largely successful and now they should turn—in Canada at least—to a larger thought, to a newer consciousness. He made a straight appeal for the closer union of denominations :

We see to-day a world with a great need. We must as Congregationalists fit our organizations to suit the environment, the needs of the people. We must not hold on to any theory of church government simply because it is a theory. Some of the Episcopalians are saying this, and if they felt it under the pressure of a great need, how much more should we who believe we are in a freer atmosphere. The principles of Congregationalism are the right of a man to go into God's presence for himself and the right of that man to come forth from the presence and do all the good he can for the Kingdom of God. Leave us these two principles and we are ready for any adaptation of our organization. The stress we had placed on independency must be transferred into interdependency. To these we must add unity and brotherhood.

A Resolution was unaminously passed in favour of supporting and voting for Prohibition at the coming Referendum in Ontario and delegates were received from the Presbyterian General Assembly. The remarks of the Rev. Dr. Armstrong in this connection upon the links binding the two Churches were warmly received. In place of the Rev. Dr. J. Edgar Hill, whose other duties impelled his resignation, the Rev. J. G. Daly, B.A., was elected Secretary of the Union. At St. John, N.B., on September 11th, the 55th annual session of the Congregational Union of the Maritime Provinces met. The Rev. Churchill Moore was elected Chairman for 1902-3 and the Rev. J. W. Cox, B.A., Secretary. The chief incident which marked the gathering was a paper on Church Union by the Rev. Robert Pegrum of Yarmouth and the ensuing discussion. He argued at some length that uniformity is not essential to unity. The majority of Christians would be satisfied if identity of spirit is reached amongst the various Churches. " We feel that the minds of men are various, their modes and habits of thought, their original capacities and acquired associations infinitely diverse ; and perceiving that the law of the universal system is manifoldness in unity, we have ceased to expect any other oneness for the Church of Christ than that of a sameness of spirit showing itself through diversities of gifts." Christian unity, he declared, had always been one of the prominent principles of Congregationalism. Their Council in the United States had put itself on record in 1895 as favouring the union of allied Churches upon a basis of (1) mutual acquaintance and fellowship; (2) co-operation in foreign and domestic missions; (3) the prevention of rivalries between competing churches in the same field. He then proceeded as follows :

We, as a denomination, have a mission ; and if we can bring the different branches of the Christian Church into visible unity, we shall perform a highly important work. It is especially our business to teach the principles of equality, liberty, fellowship and unity, and to emphasize the words of Christ—"One is your Master, even Christ, and all ye are brethren." Our principles are broad enough to include all believers in the Lord Jesus Christ ; and, therefore, Congregationalists are enabled to labour more naturally and more easily for Christian unity than any other denomination. We have no historic Episcopacy, no exclusive immersion, no close communion, no Wesleyan Discipline, no compulsory creed to stand in our way.

Mr. Pegrum summarized the situation by saying that "a Congregational Church is an ecclesiastical solvent amongst other denominations." The speakers who followed were somewhat fearful of the results of Church Union. One declared that it would mean for Congregationalism nothing but absorption. The Rev. Mr. Morson wanted more denominational spirit rather than less, and deprecated the lack of interest shown by the Mother Church in England. Mrs. M. A. Tupper thought they were not denominational enough and the Rev. Dr. Warriner urged aggressive work pending any possible union of the future. Meanwhile, a well-known Congregationalist minister—the Rev. Hugh Pedley—had been celebrating in Montreal, on May 4th, the 25th anniversary of his work in the Church. Some months later, on October 16th, after having previously declined the honour of D.D. from the Congregational College of Montreal, he presented the Rev. Alfred Rowland, B.A., LL.B., of London, for the degree. On the same day the Congregational Association of Quebec met in Montreal and elected Mr. Pedley Moderator for the ensuing year.

Perhaps the most extraordinary religious or sectarian development in Canadian history occurred during the autumn in the North-West Territories. There had been much discussion during 1902 and the proceeding year as to the advisability, or otherwise, of the Doukhobor settlement and varied and contradictory opinions expressed as to the character of the individual settlers. Speaking to the Toronto *Mail and Empire* on July 19th, the Rev. Dr. John MacLean of Carman, Manitoba, described them as a people with many peculiarities and as widely separated from the genius of Canada. But he considered them to be industrious, tractable, not unintelligent, and likely to some day become useful citizens. "At present they are practically a section of Russia penned in upon the prairie lands. They regard themselves as God's peculiar people, and have exclusive ideas as to their religion and civil rights. In faith they are nearly allied to the Quakers, and their religion dominates their lives to a great extent. They believe in a community of interest, and refuse to own or register lands separately. More than that, they regard the Government registration of marriages, births and deaths as an impious interference with the Almighty, and decline to accede to the demands of the law in this line. Of course they also refuse to fight in any way." Later in the year these people became very restless. They, or certain representatives, asked permission in October, by means of a petition, to remove to British Columbia and were refused any consideration by the Government there. They prepared, signed and despatched a most curious appeal to the Sultan of Turkey asking for some corner in his land where they might live by the labour of their hands, not be compelled to obey laws made by man, and be able to work without having to employ beasts of burden. The document then proceeded as follows:*

We emigrated from Russia to Canada to the number of 7,000 in the years 1898-99. We had heard of Canada as a land of religious freedom, but that appears to have been a misunderstanding. Freedom of conscience does prevail in Canada, but not the freedom of conscience we desired. We believe that God rules our lives and leads us to eternity by His own holy ways. We obey only the commands of the Lord in our hearts, and can obey no other commands or laws. We cannot submit ourselves to the laws or regulations of any State, or be the subjects of any other ruler except God. Our expectation that we should be allowed to live according to our belief in Canada has not been fulfilled. It is true that we are exempted from military service because we cannot bears arms or kill living beings, but they demand that we should become the subjects of Great Britain and not of the Lord. They refuse to give us any land unless we promise to obey all the laws of Canada. We declare before God that this is impossible, and that we would sooner bear any oppression than be false to Him.

Late in October entire settlements became seized with the idea that the second coming of Christ was imminent and that they must all, men, women and children, proceed at once to meet Him. They gathered together in a body of about 1,200 and with infants and cripples and sick persons on stretchers proceeded, with little food and no thought of shelter, to march across the prairies of Assiniboia. Yorkton was reached on October 28th, a prayer meeting held outside the town, the good offices of the citizens refused until, in the case of women and dying infants, it was absolutely forced upon them. According to the correspondent of the Winnipeg *Telegram*, of October 31st, their views were pretty much those of the following statement: "Even if some of our people freeze to death still we will keep on marching. We are going to meet Christ and he will look after us. The Millennium dawn is here." The local immigration officials endeavoured to prevent this particular band from going further, held the women and children in the town, and even brought back the men after a first attempt to continue their journey.

*Note—Translated from the St. Petersburg *Viedomosti* and appearing in the London *Standard* of November 14th.

On October 29th, however, the latter broke away successfully and started once more for Winnipeg. At Salcoats, on October 31st, some 700 of the horde arrived, barefoot, haggard and scantily-clad, but singing lutisly. Much of their clothing had been deliberately discarded in bursts of frenzied fanaticism. And, though suffering greatly from hunger, exhaustion and the cold nights, they stead-fastly continued their march from this point, crossed the border into Manitoba and passed through Binscarth on November 3rd, singing psalms and begging bread alternately. Meanwhile, they had faced an early snow-storm and become the subject of some strong tele-graphic communications between Mr. Roblin, Premier of Manitoba and Mr. Sifton, Minister of the Interior, as to the responsibility for their charge and for the cost and trouble of compelling their return to the deserted settlements. The Minister promptly despatched Mr. Frank Pedley, Superintendent of Immigration, to deal with the matter and he arrived at Winnipeg on November 6th. Meantime, the Doukhobors had passed through Solsgirth, Birtle, Shoal Lake, Strathclair, Newdale and other villages, while the women remain-ing at Yorkton had been taken back to their homes by the authori-ties there. At Minnedosa, on November 7th, the Doukhobor men were met by Mr. Pedley and Mr. C. W. Sears, accompanied by a contingent of North-West Police, and a conference held with the leaders. It was to no effect, however, and two days latter the passively but stubbornly resisting crowd was loaded by force—very much as cattle are driven—into the trains and taken back to their villages. This ended an incident which created much excitement amongst the solitary settlers and small villages of the West and much interest in varied quarters away from the West.

The position of the Dominion in respect to Temperance ques-tions shows it to have the most moderate liquor consumption of any important civilized nation. In 1898 the *per capita* consumption of spirits in the United Kingdom was 1·05 of a gallon; in the United States 0·92 of a gallon; in Canada 0·55 of a gallon.* According to the Report of the Inland Revenue Department of Canada for the fiscal year ending June 30th, 1902, the excise revenue was $11,257,485 as against $10,423,865 in 1901. The chief elements in this taxation and the consumption which it represented were, in 1902, $5,620,613 upon spirits; $3,563,578 upon tobacco; $897,360 upon cigars; and $1,077,809 upon malt. The quantity of spirits produced was 3,234,-147 proof gallons, and the raw material used included 3,432,066 lbs. of malt, 41,397,871 lbs. of Indian corn and 9,449,057 lbs. of rye.

The figures regarding the general position of the liquor traffic in the community can only be obtained in the form of estimates. Mr. F. S. Spence in his *Digest* of the Report of the Canadian Royal Commission of 1892, placed the capital invested in breweries, dis-tilleries and malt houses at $15,588,953; the value of real estate

Side note: Canada and the Liquor Traffic

---

*Mr. H. Bence Jones, B.A., F.S.S., before the Royal Statistical Society of London—April 24th, 1900.

occupied by vendors of liquor at $38,000,000 ; the value of fixtures, etc., connected with the trade, at $21,000,000 ; wages, taxes and payments by brewers and distillers at $5,039,906 ; payments for imported liquors at $1,901,000 ; wages paid by retail and wholesale liquor interests at $10,500,000. The Federal excise licenses, etc., were over $7,000,000 and the Provincial and Municipal licenses $1,350,000—a total of over $100,000,000 invested in the business. The minority Report of the Royal Commission of 1892, estimated the cost of this traffic to Canada at $143,000,000 of which $76,000,-000 was attributed to the " loss of productive labour." In an article contributed to the Toronto *Globe* of March 9th, 1901, the Rev. Dr. Charles A Eaton gave the following statistics of the consumption of alcohol per head of the population (English gallons) in various countries or Colonies :

Country.	Consumption.	Country.	Consumption.
Belgium	2·81	Queensland	1·04
France	2·72	Cape Colony	·95
Italy	2·40	New South Wales	·90
Western Australia	2·27	New Zealand	·73
Germany	2·09	Russia	·60
United Kingdom	2·05	Tasmania	·55
United States	1·16	Canada	·54
Victoria	1·16		

During the year ending June 30th, 1902, the distilleries of Canada manufactured 3,234,147 gallons of liquor, and warehoused 3,668,286 gallons. There remained in the warehouses from the previous year 10,853,570 gallons, and this amount, with the total added as above and with 187,826 gallons imported and 2,592,044 gallons received from other sources, made a general total of 17,301,728 gallons. Nearly the whole of this quantity, or 14,983,304 gallons, was manufactured in Ontario. Of malt there were 72,870,605 lbs. manufactured during the year and warehoused, and of malt liquor 27,623,767 gallons were made. The convictions for drunkenness in Canada numbered 12,727 in 1901 as against 12,215 in the previous year, and included 3,900 for Ontario, 2,973 for Quebec. 1,387 for Nova Scotia, 1,299 for New Brunswick, 834 for Manitoba, 1,232 for British Columbia, 241 for Prince Edward Island, 491 for the Territories, and 370 for the Yukon. The total showed one conviction to every 424 inhabitants.

The country was deeply interested during 1902 in the Prohibition Plebiscites of Ontario and Manitoba, and the figures of preceding votes of the kind may, therefore, be given here for purposes of comparison. The Dominion Plebiscite of September 29th, 1898, showed a vote of 278,380 in favor of Prohibition and 264,693 against, out of a total vote on the lists of 1,236,429. The majority for the proposal in Ontario was 39,214 and in Manitoba 9,441, while Quebec rolled up a majority of 94,324 against it. The previous Provincial Plebiscites had resulted as follows :

PROVINCES.	Date.	VOTES POLLED.		Major-ity for.	Number of Voters on Dominion Electoral List.	Proportion of Votes Polled to Number of Voters on List.
		For	Against.			
Manitoba.............................	July 23, '92	18,637	7,115	11,522	46,609	55·18
Prince Edward Island	Dec. 13, '93	10,585	3,331	7,254	24,065	57·83
Nova Scotia.........................	Mar. 15, '94	43,756	12,355	31,401	111,124	50·49
Ontario	Jan. 1, '94	192,489	110,720	81,769	549,202	55·21

An interesting incident of the year in this connection was the visit to Canada of Earl Grey—brother to Lady Minto and Administrator of Rhodesia in 1896-7—who had been one of the founders of the Public House Trust in England. On March 2nd he addressed a semi-private gathering in Toronto and explained the conditions surrounding temperance questions and work in Great Britain, where "one party was liquor-logged and the other water-bound." He then described his movement as follows:

It was an organization formed to secure all new licenses issued. They went to the license authorities and said: If you are going to grant any new licenses or re-dispose of lapsed licenses, they should be given to us. They then put a trustworthy man in charge, who had no interest in the sale of intoxicants, but received a commission on the sale of soft drinks and edibles. They thus removed the chief evil; it was no longer in the interest of the publican to press his neighbourhood to drink as much as possible. . . . The profit from the liquor traffic in Great Britain reached nearly twenty million pounds. They proposed to put a ring fence around all existing licenses and to acquire in time every single one. The shareholders were restricted to a profit of five per cent., and the net income over and above that figure was applied by a Board of Trustees to works of beneficence.

Writing to the Toronto *Globe*, on March 7th, the Rev. Dr. A. C. Courtice reviewed this policy as propounded by Lord Grey, criticized in the February *Monthly Review* by the Earl of Carlisle and recently endorsed to some extent by Principal Grant, and summed it up as involving "not less drinking but more respectable drinking." He favoured Prohibition as the law of the Province with the exception of those cities which under his proposals might wish to establish a system of Government stores where no drinking would be permitted but where the purest liquors could be purchased in sealed packages for domestic use. Writing in the London *Daily News* of September 26th a special Canadian correspondent had the following interesting summary of conditions in Canada in this regard: "It is a rare thing to see any wine, malt liquor, or other intoxicant on a dinner table in Canada. A good deal of drinking takes place, but not in the open. In England, to drink intoxicants is social orthodoxy; in Canada not to drink intoxicants is social orthodoxy. In England legislation lags behind public opinion on the temperance question. In Canada legislation has got ahead of public opinion on the temperance question. The law in most of the Provinces is so stringent that it is generally disregarded—not openly, but with only a pretense of disguise."

During the years 1901 and 1902 the sentiment of Ontario, Manitoba and Prince Edward Island was more or less affected by this measure, which passed the Manitoba Legislature in 1900. It was to come into operation on June 1st, 1901, but was not then proclaimed, and, after being carried through Canadian Courts to the Judicial Committee of the Privy Council in London, was declared on November 22nd, 1901, to be constitutional. Its terms might be summarized as prohibiting the sale of liquor within the Province except by licensed druggists; prohibiting the keeping or giving away of liquor except in private dwelling houses; permission for its use in mechanical and medicinal purposes and for church services. The most important clause was the following:

Provisions of the Manitoba Prohibition Act

No person shall, within the Province, by himself, his clerk, servant, or agent, expose or keep for sale, directly or indirectly, or upon pretence or upon any device, sell or barter, or, in consideration of the purchase or transfer of any property or thing, or at the time of the transfer of any property or thing, give to any other person any liquor, without having first obtained a druggist's wholesale license or a druggist's retail license, under this Act, authorizing him so to do, and then only as authorized by such license, and as prescribed by this Act.

No person within the Province, by himself, his clerk, servant or agent, shall have or keep or give liquor in any place wheresoever, other than in the private dwelling house in which he resides, without having first obtained a druggist's wholesale license or a druggist's retail license, under this Act, authorizing him so to do, and then only as authorized by such license.

Exception was made in the case of alcohol used for mechanical or scientific purposes up to ten gallons. Clergymen were not to have more than two gallons for sacramental purposes, and the supply kept at hospitals was to be solely for the consumption of patients. Brewers licensed by the Dominion Government were free to store liquor for export in specially constructed warehouses. The consumption of liquor on licensed premises was specially forbidden, and strict provision was made against violation of the Act by societies, clubs or associations. A physician was allowed to prescribe intoxicating liquor for a patient, giving a written order therefor upon a druggist, and for purposes of prescription he might have liquor in his possession not exceeding two quarts. If he prescribed intoxicating liquor not for a medical reason and in order to aid any person in contravening the Act, he was liable to a penalty of not less than $50 or more than $300 for a first offence. Similar provisions were made for dentists and veterinary surgeons. A druggist's wholesale license was to be granted only to a person carrying on exclusively a drug business. The quantity of liquor which could be sold at any one time, to any one person, for mechanical or scientific purposes was restricted to ten gallons and in the case of a physician, or a druggist holding a retail license, to five gallons. Sales of liquor for mechanical or scientific purposes could be made only on production of an affidavit declaring the use to which the liquor was to be put.

The Manitoba Prohibition Act was not put into operation during 1901, though subject to proclamation at the hands of the Lieut.-Governor-in-Council. On January 6th, 1902, the **The Prohibition Referendum in Manitoba** Hon. R. P. Roblin, Premier of the Province, was interviewed by the Winnipeg *Telegram* as to the intentions of the Government in this respect. He intimated in reply a desire to know what the Ontario Government was going to do with their Prohibition question; spoke of the importance of co-operation between the two Provinces in any such enactments; and referred to the difficulty of guarding against evasions of the law where serious inter-Provincial differences in legislation existed. And then he continued as follows: " Is there an efficient preponderating sentiment among the people in its favour—a strong popular majority of Manitobans having convictions so decided in its favour, so unyielding, that they will bear down all opposition to its enforcement. This seems to be absolutely necessary, otherwise the Act will become ineffective and a by-word, and in the interest of temperance had better never have been called into existence."

Three days later Mr. Roblin told the same paper that the Government had decided to submit the enforcement of the Act to the vote of the people at the close of the coming Session. On this and the following day various prominent citizens were interviewed. Archbishop Machray, Messrs. W. Georgeson, President of the Board of Trade, F. H. Phippen, E. L. Drewry, J. H. Munson, K.C., the Rev. Father Drummond and Mayor Arbuthnot approved the policy; while Messrs. W. Scott, President of the Labour Party, A. W. Puttee, M.P., Lieut.-Colonel H. W. A. Chambre, Ald. John Russell, the Rev. W. S. Armstrong, the Rev. Dr. Wilson and others were either opposed to a Referendum or thought it unnecessary. Varied and somewhat warm discussions ensued. On January 16th, representatives of the Ministerial Association of Winnipeg and of the Provincial branch of the Dominion Alliance for the Suppression of the Liquor Traffic waited upon the Government, protested against the proposed Referendum and urged the immediate enforcement of the Act. The Rev. Dr. Wilson, Rev. Dr. DuVal, the Rev. Messrs. J. J. Roy, R. P. Bowles, Joseph Hogg and Dr. Stuart spoke more or less strongly upon the subject as well as Messrs. W. Redford Mulock, K.C., and E. L. Taylor. The Premier thanked the deputation but declined to say more just then. In the evening the Dominion Alliance met and passed the following Resolution almost unanimously though after a stormy discussion :

Whereas, this Convention has expressed itself already by unanimous Resolution against the so-called Referendum in the case of the Liquor Act and, whereas, such Referendum has been finally decided on by the Government; therefore, be it resolved that we recommend to the temperance people of this Province that they ignore this Referendum and abstain from polling their votes thereon, and that the Executive Committee be instructed to prepare for distribution a fuller statement of the principles and considerations which have guided us to this conclusion.

This action was approved in a sermon by the Rev. C. W. Gordon (Ralph Connor) on January 19th following and two days later the Premier wrote to a correspondent a letter which was published in the Winnipeg *Tribune* of March 23rd and which contained this expression of opinion regarding the Prohibition Act: "It is no prohibition bill whatever; it is simply a bill providing for free whiskey—liquor without any control by the Government, which any man in the Province can get at any hour and in all quantities that he desires. That being the fact I do not think the endorsement or otherwise of the Act is justification for classing a man a Prohibitionist or otherwise." Meanwhile, the decision of the Dominion Alliance to refrain from action in the premises created marked differences in the temperance ranks. On February 13th Mr. J. K. McLennan, Vice-President of the Alliance, resigned, and in doing so wrote very strongly as to the harm which would follow from a policy of assumed indifference in this connection.

Two days later a meeting of the License Holders' Benefit Association was held, with Mr. E. L. Drewry in the chair, and a long Resolution passed, describing the injury which it was claimed the enforcement of Prohibition would be to individual rights and interests and the loss in trade and real estate values which would follow, and warmly endorsing the proposed Referendum policy of the Government. At the annual Convention of the Royal Templars of Temperance on February 19th some strong speeches were made. The Rev. Mr. Harrison denounced the Government. Mr. Redford Mulock, K.C., as President of the Dominion Alliance, defended the non-intervention policy, strongly criticized the Government, claimed that the Prohibitory legislation had been engineered all through in the interests of the liquor men and urged Prohibitionists to refrain from voting under the Referendum. Mr. J. K. McLennan defended his position and expressed his belief that "work and prayer" would enable them to win despite the announced conditions of the vote. Finally, the meeting by a vote of 61 to 3 endorsed the action of the Dominion Alliance "in resolving to ignore the so-called Referendum."

Meanwhile, on the same day, the Hon. C. H. Campbell, Attorney-General, had introduced in the Legislature a measure referring the enforcement of the Prohibition Act to a popular vote. Under its terms every person on the municipal lists and every British subject over 21 years of age and living for 12 years in the Province was entitled to vote. Practically it was to be manhood suffrage. The date fixed was March 27th and, if the following conditions were complied with, the Prohibition Act would come into force on June 1st following: (1) If 45 per cent. of those on the list vote in favour of the Act; (2) if 60 per cent. on the voters' list vote and 60 per cent. thereof vote in favour; (3) if the vote falls below 60 per cent. then a percentage between 60 per cent. and 66⅔ per cent. to be taken. No reference was made in the measure or in the speech to any question of compensation. On February

26th Mr. Greenway, Leader of the Opposition, and Premier Roblin spoke at length upon the Government proposals.

The former declared the arrangement a fair one and the vote asked an equitable one. It would have been better, though, to have enforced the Act for a year and then asked the people if they wished it sustained. As it was, however, he would not move an amendment as the Government could carry their proposals anyway. He did not think there was any excuse for the proposed inaction of the temperance people and he, himself, proposed to go to the polls and vote for the enforcement of the Act. The Premier, in a long and energetic speech, deprecated the intemperance in language and argument which he said had lately been very pronounced; analyzed previous popular votes in favour of Prohibition and declared the numbers fairly large but the percentage of the population very small; referred to the necessity for a strong public opinion behind such legislation; and expressed his belief that the Act itself would not result in restriction but in free and uncontrolled liquor-drinking. The measure passed in due course after a change in the date of the Referendum to April 2nd.

While it was pending in the House a petition was presented to the Governor-General of Canada and the Lieutenant-Governor of Manitoba signed by W. Redford Mulock, President of the Provincial branch of the Dominion Alliance, and protesting against any reference of the enforcement of the Prohibition Act to the people as "subversive of the principles of representative and responsible government and injurious to the dignity and prerogative of the Crown, if not also *ultra vires* of the British North America Act." Mr. Mulock wrote various letters and made an elaborate statement in support of this request for a veto of the Referendum Bill and on April 23rd the reply of the Hon. Mr. Fitzpatrick, Minister of Justice, was made public. In this document he declared the measure in question thoroughly within the power of the Legislature, deprecated the use of American "precedents" as being entirely inapplicable under the Canadian constitution and declined altogether to advise disallowance or Federal interference in the matter.

Writing to Mr. B. R. Hamilton of Neepawa on January 24th* Mr. Mulock defended vigorously the much-discussed action of the Alliance in refusing to vote or work in the premises; stated that Principal Patrick and the Rev. Dr. Kilpatrick approved the course decided on by their Convention of five or six hundred workers; and claimed that the voting under the Referendum would be a farce and the support obtained by the Liquor men, if unopposed, so small that no Government would dare to repeal the Prohibition Act. A public meeting in Winnipeg, on March 2nd, with Ald. Russell in the chair and addressed by Mr. Mulock, the Rev. Dr. Patrick and others, criticized the Government severely

---

*NOTE—Published in Winnipeg *Telegram* of March 1st.

and endorsed the action of the Alliance.   On the following evening another temperance meeting, presided over by the Hon. J. W. Sifton and addressed by Rev. Professor Riddell, Dr. Beath, Rev. Dr. Pitblado, Mr. E. L. Taylor, the Rev. Dr. Sparling, and Mr. T. E. Greenwood, M.P.P., was equally pronounced in favour of active work and of getting out a full vote under the Referendum.   On March 4th, the Dominion Alliance again met in Winnipeg and passed a unanimous Resolution approving the action of the late Convention and declaring that recent events had confirmed the belief as to "the righteousness and propriety of that position." The Board of Trade, on March 13th, met and passed the following Resolution, moved by Mr. A. M. Nanton, with a vote of 45 in favour and 30 against.

Whereas, a measure, entitled the Liquor (or Prohibition) Act, is about to be submitted to the people, by way of referendum, on April 2 ; and whereas such Act, if enforced, will detrimentally affect the commercial interests of the people of the Province and create a feeling of unrest at a most important period in our history, when a large increase is expected to be added to our population ; and whereas such Act is not a Prohibitory Act, but permits the free importation from the other Provinces and Territories of liquor in any quantity, merely transferring the drinking from licensed hotels to the homes and unlicensed resorts, and will not materially decrease the consumption of liquor in the Province : Resolved, that while expressing no opinion on the general question of the prohibition of the manufacture or of the importation of liquor into the Province yet insomuch as we believe the Liquor Act will fail in its purpose and result in injury instead of good to the commercial and social interests of the people, therefore it should not become law.

A Temperance Convention was held in Winnipeg on March 25th, following, under the call of the Prohibition Campaign League which had been lately organized with Mr. E. L. Taylor as President. It was largely attended and Dr. Beath, who acted as Chairman, declared in his opening speech that he and his friends believed a united effort would carry the Act again.   A long and stormy discussion followed in which politics and Prohibition were pretty well mixed but, finally, a Resolution was unanimously passed deploring the divisions in the temperance ranks, hoping for an early re-union of all workers, and continuing as follows : "In view of the fact that the time before the day of voting is now too brief to restore complete harmony among temperance workers and thus ensure that anything like the full strength of the Prohibition vote will be polled, and in view of the fact that some sincere temperance workers are irrevocably committed to the policy of voting while others equally sincere are irrevocably committed to the policy of not voting, this Convention agrees to recommend the cessation of all further organized effort to influence the vote on April 2nd and that each man be left to the exercise of his individual judgment, irrespective of allegiance to any temperance organization."
About this time also a Manifesto was issued signed by many of the leading Prohibitionists of the Province, including the Rev. Dr. F. B. DuVal, Rev. R. P. Bowles, Rev. C. W. Gordon, Professor Kilpatrick, Rev. Dr. Andrew Stuart, etc.   It denounced the Refer-

endum as subversive of constitutional government, as being promulgated without any popular mandate, as without precedent and as constituting a serious abdication of Legislative power. Following this came a dispute as to voting opportunities under the Referendum. Under date of March 19th Mr. F. H. Phippen sent out a circular stating that any person entitled to vote under the terms of the Referendum was also entitled to vote at any polling sub-division in Manitoba where he might happen to be on April 2nd. In the papers of March 28th Mr. E. L. Taylor wrote making the circular public and denying that there was any legal ground for this statement. Meanwhile the Rev. Dr. W. A. MacKay, President of the Ontario branch of the Dominion Alliance, issued a call to all Prohibitionists to vote in the coming Manitoba Referendum as a matter of duty, and on March 28th Mr. Mulock telegraphed him an expression of regret at this action and of repudiation on the part of the Manitoba Branch. The day before polling Mr. J. S. Ewart, K.C., confirmed Mr. Phippen's view as to the right of voting in a legal opinion which was made public in the following terms:

(1) That all persons are entitled to vote at the coming Referendum who would on such day be entitled to have their names registered anywhere as voters under the Manitoba Election Act. (2) That there is nothing in any of the statutes limiting the exercise of that right to any particular polling place, municipality or electoral division. (3) In my opinion, therefore, a person entitled to be registered anywhere in the Province can, on taking the oath, vote wherever he may happen to be on the day of the poll.

The voting took place on April 2nd, and resulted in a fairly strong expression of opinion against putting the Prohibition Act into force. The vote polled was, under the circumstances, a large one—over 38,000 out of a total possible number of 74,000. In the Provincial elections of 1899 the vote cast had been 47,014 and in the Dominion elections of 1900 it was 41,687. There were now 15,607 persons who voted in favour of enforcing the Prohibition Act and 22,464 against its enforcement. Various charges of unfair voting were made, especially in connection with the alleged right to vote away from the place of residence. The Rev. C. W. Gordon, in commenting upon the result (*Telegram*, April 3rd), declared that the condition of the country roads, the fragmentary vote and disunion of the temperance people, the active work of the liquor men, and the desire of many Conservatives to save the Roblin Government from an awkward position, were the main causes of the result. The Executive of the Provincial branch of the Dominion Alliance met in Winnipeg on April 23rd, following, and passed a series of Resolutions, which may be summarized as follows:

1. The Referendum and the vote thereon were unnecessary and uncalled for, and therefore many people refused to go to the polls.
2. There was a popular impression that the Referendum was simply a means of evading responsibility and, therefore, others declined to vote.
3. Many considered the Referendum an unjustifiable innovation upon our Parliamentary system and, therefore, would not vote.
4. Others believed the statement of the Premier and Attorney-General that the Prohibition Act would not prohibit and, therefore, voted against it,

while many opposed it because the Premier had expressed personal antagonism to it.

5. The temperance vote was only partially polled, while no election in Provincial history had been characterized by "such bribery, personation, perjury and fraud."

Three days later the Government's observations upon the question of Dominion disallowance of the Referendum Act were made public in the form of the letter addressed by the Hon. D. H. McFadden, Provincial Secretary, to the Lieutenant-Governor of Manitoba. The principal point was that preceding Plebiscites had been taken upon the wish of the people to "prohibit the manufacture, sale and importation of liquor" in the Province and that, as the present Act practically did none of these things, it was desirable to test public opinion regarding its enforcement. On May 9th Mr. W. Redford Mulock addressed a communication, which filled a page of the Winnipeg papers of May 12th, to the Minister of Justice, protesting against the legality of the Referendum, quoting various American authorities to show that it should have been disallowed, and making an elaborate constitutional argument to the following effect : (1) That it should have been vetoed because it placed Legislative functions directly in the hands of the people ; (2) because it took responsibility from the Government and the Legislature and cast it on the people themselves ; (3) because it was unprecedented in form and application ; (4) because it infringed on the Royal prerogative by compelling the Crown to proclaim or repeal legislation at the dictation of the people.

On July 4th, following, the Manitoba License Holders' Association met in Winnipeg, with Mr. E. L. Drewry presiding, and passed a Resolution of pleasure at the result of the Referendum ; of satisfaction that the people were not disposed to tolerate "narrow class legislation" ; of protest against the statements that the Referendum Act was so loosely drawn as to permit any kind of loose voting ; and of strong denial that corruption or fraud took place at the hands of the Liquor interests in the election. A couple of months later, on September 29th, the Rev. J. B. Silcox, in an elaborate sermon at Winnipeg on total abstinence, declared that the Premier and his associates had played into the hands of the liquor traffic and that the result had been a "victory for rum." The action should "never be forgotten and never forgiven."

The year opened in Ontario with a wide-spread discussion as to the probable policy and action of the Government regarding the Imperial Privy Council decision admitting the power to prohibit the sale of liquors as a Provincial right. Referring to the possibilities in this connection, the Hon. Mr. Ross had told a deputation on February 13th, 1901, that "the Government would no doubt go as far as the definition of constitutional limitations would allow ;"* and the Prohibitionists now demanded the fulfilment of what they

The
Prohibition
Question in
Ontario

* The Toronto *Globe* report, February 14th, 1901.

termed a pledge.   On January 3rd, 1902, a deputation waited upon the Government representing the Ontario branch of the Dominion Alliance for the Suppression of the Liquor Traffic, and the Ontario section of the Committee on Temperance of the General Conference of the Methodist Church.   Besides the Premier there were six members of the Government present and some fifty members in the delegation, including the Rev. Dr. Carman, Rev. J. C. Speer, Rev. Dr. Chown, Rev. Dr. W. A. McKay, Rev. W. Kettlewell, Mr. F. S. Spence, Rev. Dr. Brethour, Dr. J. J. Maclaren, K.C., Mr. G. F. Marter, M.P.P., Rev. Dr. Parker and Rev. S. Cleaver.   Several short speeches were made, asking for Prohibition, and in reply the Hon. Mr. Ross simply expressed appreciation of the delegates' presence and of the gravity of the situation.   " All you have said will receive my most careful consideration as well as the consideration of my colleagues in the Government."   In the afternoon the deputation held a private conference under the chairmanship of the Rev. Dr. McKay, and passed a Resolution in favour of immediate electoral organization and the following: " That in view of the strong case for prohibitory legislation as again presented to the Government to-day, based upon the facts of the Plebiscite Prohibition majorities, the Government's promises, and the decision of the Privy Council, and in order to strengthen the hands of the Government in carrying such legislation through the House, we request Prohibitionists to petition the Legislature for the enactment of prohibitory legislation to the limit of its jurisdiction."

Speaking on January 14th, at Victoria University, Toronto, Sir James Grant, M.D., of Ottawa, urged education as to the dangers of liquor, and the training of the youthful mind against intoxicants, as being the best remedies for the drinking evil.   " I hope," he said, " you will not assist in promoting a Prohibitory law."   It was unnecessary, could not be enforced and would " stimulate many to drink who would not otherwise have drunk at all."   He spoke of the many evils of over-eating and concluded by declaring alcohol to be of no comparative service to the human frame unless administered as medicine in cases of great nervous depression.   On January 22nd representatives of the Methodist Church and the Dominion Alliance again waited upon the Premier, in order to protest against any possible realization of the rumours that in the proposed Referendum there would be a clause making some specific majority necessary in order to carry the proposed Prohibitory law into operation.   The Rev. Dr. Carman spoke vigorously, and denounced the suggestion as " intolerable and un-British."   The Hon. Mr. Ross promised careful consideration of what had been said.   Four days later 3,000 people met in Massey Hall, Toronto, under the auspices of the Canadian Temperance League, unanimously passed a Resolution protesting against a Referendum or any proposal other than the usual Legislative or electoral majority for the law, and, after reciting the conditions created by the Privy Council decisions, declared that:

It is the duty of the Ontario Government at the present session to avail themselves of this privilege and to enact a law along these lines.   This step we deem not only in the best interest of the Province, but it will also be a fulfilment of promises repeatedly made by the Hon. George W. Ross, Premier of Ontario, and his predecessor, Sir Oliver Mowat—that so soon as this question was definitely settled the Government would be prepared to grant as large a share of Prohibitory legislation as would be legally permissible.   This League enters its protest against any steps that may be taken to apply the principle of the Referendum to such a law as to require that other than a majority vote, as in Provincial elections and legislation in general, shall be necessary to make the law operative.

During this month the Rev. J. A. Macdonald continued in *The Westminster* the advocacy which had earned for him, through his initiative action in the preceding November, the title of "Father of the Referendum." He urged, editorially, a good majority as imperative. "Unless Ontario can poll more that 250,000 votes in favour of Prohibitory legislation, the Province is not ready for such a law, and its enforcement would not be morally salutary." Different interviews given to this paper showed that Principal Caven and Chancellor Wallace were opposed to a bare majority in such a case as being sufficient, that Chancellor Burwash and the Rev. Dr. R. H. Warden wanted two-thirds of all the voters, Principal Sheraton a three-fourths majority of the votes cast, and the Rev. Dr. Potts seventy per cent. of the votes polled. Meantime, on January 23rd, a large deputation of over 1,000 men waited upon the Government to protest against any Prohibitory enactment by the Legislature, and demanding compensation in the event of such a law being passed. The delegation was composed of brewers, distillers, hotel men, etc., from all over the Province, and was presented to the Premier and his associates by Mr. Eugene O'Keefe of Toronto and addressed by Mr. James Haverson, K.C., at length, and by others very briefly. Mr. Haverson made an interesting statistical statement of the position of the liquor interest.

He said there was invested in the distilleries and breweries of the Dominion 15½ millions : in the real estate of the retailers, 38 millions ; in the stock and fixtures, 21 millions ; making 74½ millions of money directly invested in the business.   There was paid by the distillers and brewers to the farmers annually $2,382,000, and to the transportation companies $450,000 ; wages, $1,200,000 ; other outgoings, $1,012,000.   The retailers paid $10,500,000 in wages.   There was an outgoing by the trade of nearly 15½ millions annually.   There was to-day in bond in the Dominion 14 million gallons of spirits, which, with the duty upon it, represented 26½ millions of dollars alone.   The Province of Ontario last year derived in revenue from the liquor trade $629,000, of which $250,000 was paid to the municipalities.   All the distilleries of the country were in this Province, and the largest number of the breweries.   The retail trade of Ontario was more than one-half that of the rest of the Provinces put together.   Not only the liquor trade would be affected, but the banks, the loan companies, and the financial institutions.

The Premier merely promised consideration in his reply. On January 31st, a Prohibition Convention was held at Hamilton and Resolutions passed protesting against any special vote being required under a Referendum and calling upon the Government to enact a Prohibitory law to the full extent of their jurisdiction. A week later, on February 7th, an influential delegation of Toronto financial men waited upon the Government. Mr. J. W. Langmuir headed the party and stated that as representatives of large financial interests they wished to oppose a Prohibitory law as being ineffective and unnecessary. If, however, it was decided to introduce one they hoped the Government would exact a majority of at least two-thirds of the vote cast. Dr. Goldwin Smith declared the Province to be very temperate and intemperance to be steadily losing ground. Indemnity should be guaranteed to the liquor interests. Mr. D. R. Wilkie thought Prohibition would seriously injure the business of the Province and asked for a majority of the voters on the lists as necessary to its enactment. Dr. John Hoskin, K.C., Mr. W. T. White, Lieut.-Col. James Mason and Messrs. Fred. Wyld, R. N. Gooch, G. R. R. Cockburn and J. Herbert Mason, all took strong ground against Prohibition for various reasons of industrial concern, individual liberty, destruction of capital, etc. Four days later the Toronto Board of Trade held a special meeting and passed a Resolution by 56 to 25 which referred to the permanent growth in temperance sentiment, to the general desire for greater restriction in the sale of liquor and then proceeded to "petition the Government of the Province of Ontario that if it should decide to introduce a Prohibition Bill, such Bill should provide for the just payment by the Government for that percentage of value of property which would be confiscated if such Bill should provide for the speedy application of the Act; and that in order to be assured of an efficient public sentiment in favour of the measure, so that its practical enforcement may be insured, the Bill be followed by a Referendum, with the majority necessary to confirm to be either two-thirds of the vote cast or fifty-one per cent. of the duly qualified voters."

The much-discussed proposals were finally presented to the Legislature by the Hon. G. W. Ross in the concrete form of a Bill on February 12th. His speech and those which followed, as well as the votes under which the Referendum came into operation, were all necessarily more or less affected by political considerations which have no place in this immediate connection.* The Premier's speech was an able presentation of the constitutional conditions surrounding a referendum, of the necessity and desirability of having one at this juncture, of his own position as a believer in Prohibition and of the details connected with the proposed legislation. The prohibitory part of the measure was based almost wholly upon the Manitoba Act, the majority was to be a majority of the votes which should be cast at the ensuing general election and the date fixed was October 14th, 1902. Changes were afterward made fixing a majority of the total vote at the elections of 1898 as the basis and the date as December 4th following. The

---

* NOTE—For the votes on the measure see page 46.

second reading of the Bill passed on March 5th by a majority of
13 and was notable for the speech of the Leader of the Opposition.
Mr. Whitney denounced the Premier as going back upon his
temperance record, as trying to fool the Prohibitionists and as
perpetrating a jug-handled scheme for defeating Prohibition itself.
His policy and opinions as then announced may be summarized as
follows: (1) Opposition to the Referendum as unconstitutional and
improper in its application. (2) Opposition to the Prohibitory
measure on its own account and apart from the Referendum. "We
cannot have Prohibition in a Province." (3) In place of these
proposals the advocacy of a decrease in the number of licenses ;
the vigorous maintenance of existing restrictions; the removal of
Commissioners and Inspectors from political influences; the honest
enforcement of the License Law.

The measure finally passed on March 14th but had, meanwhile,
been variously dealt with by the public and the Prohibitionists.
In the Toronto *Star*, of February 13th, Principal Caven described
the Referendum as reasonably fair; the Rev. Dr. Sutherland
declared it "as good a measure as we can expect;" the Rev. Dr.
Potts expressed himself greatly pleased with the whole policy of
the Bill. Dr. J. J. Maclaren, K.C., announced to the Montreal
Witness on the same day full approval of the measure, opposed
any compensation to the liquor interests and thought the law-
abiding character of the Ontario people would render enforcement
of the Act easy. John A. Nicholls, W. W. Buchanan and other
temperance organizers opposed the Referendum part. At Guelph
on February 18th the Grand Councillor of the Royal Templars of
Temperance, Mr. J. A. Austin, expressed bitter disappointment
with the measure and declared it utterly impossible to poll the
required number of votes. A Resolution of "emphatic protest
against such an evasion of responsibility" was passed unanimously.
Similar disapproval was expressed at a meeting in Peterborough
on February 20th.

A stormy meeting of temperance men and members of the
Ontario branch of the Dominion Alliance, to the number of 1,500,
was held in Toronto on February 25th with the Rev. Dr. W. A.
McKay in the chair. In his speech the Chairman denounced the
whole policy of the Government in this connection. The Referendum was "throwing a bone to a dog." Its conditions were "unjust
and unreasonable." Mr. F. S. Spence presented the Report of the
Executive Committee of the Alliance declaring the requirements
of the Bill "difficult, unreasonable and unjust"; expressing regret
that the Government had not carried out their promises; and
protesting against various specific conditions as well as the date for
voting. Then came a storm-cloud of Resolutions and amendments,
a medley of speeches and comments, together with frequent political
thrusts and counter-thrusts. Finally, the adoption of the Report
was carried by a large majority and a deputation appointed to wait
upon the Government. On the following day they were received

by the Premier and his colleagues. After brief speeches from the Rev. Dr. McKay, Mr. A. B. Spence of Collingwood, Mr. C. J. Miller of Orillia and Mrs. Thornley of the W. C. T. U., the Rev. Dr. Carman spoke at some length and with much earnestness. "If the liquor men had the heart of humanity in them, if they would give up crushing hearts, destroying homes and filling the asylums and jails, the temperance people would give up the fight along that line." He protested against the restriction as to voting and the date proposed. In his reply the Premier would promise no change except a reconsideration of the date and referred to the terms of the vote as follows : "We say that a minority of three voters out of every eight can force Prohibition on the other five. Now, I want you to think that over; three men who go out and vote for Prohibition can force it on the other five. Prohibition would then become the law of the land, the Government by proclamation will make it the law of the land, and the Government, if this Government is still in power, will give its whole effort to make it effective. That is as far as we can go, and there is no use holding out any hope that a bare majority of the votes polled will give Prohibition."

Many of the arguments and much of the controversy of this period were directed for or against the principles of the Referendum and the political sides of the issue rather than to consideration of the moral aspects of the Prohibition question. Speaking at Deer Park, Toronto, on March 20th, however, Mr. N. W. Rowell dealt with this latter subject and described the saloon as resting upon (1) the moderate drinking habits of many people; (2) the treating custom which was an outgrowth of this habit; (3) the social life provided for men who have no other opportunities of the sort; (4) the patronage of men addicted to the use of strong drink for its own sake; (5) the resentment felt by many at any interference with what they believed to be their right to take a glass of liquor when wanted. The great body of citizens lay between the extremes represented by the liquor dealers on one side and the Prohibitionists on the other, and the aim of temperance people should be to obtain the support of this large class. On March 25th the Dominion Alliance Executive met in Toronto and passed an appeal to the Prohibitionists of Ontario to prepare for the struggle at the polls in the coming elections. This manifesto may be summarized briefly :

1. It referred to "the terrible drink evil" which had entrenched itself in the "vantage ground of political methods and institutions" and through a united and energetic liquor interest had won a temporary victory.

2. As the "reasonable resquest" of the Convention of February 25th had been refused by the Government and Legislature the only hope now lay in obtaining representatives who would vote honestly for Prohibition principles.

3. The recent Government measure was "a combination of useful Prohibition and unjust requirements." The Prohibitory portion was of the most complete and comprehensive character which Provincial jurisdiction would permit but the conditions of the Referendum were "exceedingly unjust" and in the interests of the liquor traffic.

4. It was necessary to secure the nomination and election of reliable candidates at the general elections regardless of party and pledged to Prohibitory legislation.

5. Acceptance of the Referendum under protest was urged together with concentration of effort and the consecration of every energy to the winning of a great victory for the cause of temperance.

Following up this action and a Resolution passed on March 25th by the Ontario section of the Conference Committee of the Methodist Church, which deprecated the Referendum but urged a large vote for Prohibition, the Rev. Dr. Carman published a vigorous appeal in the *Christian Guardian* of April 2nd addressed to this Committee. He expressed his realization of the present and special need of vigilence and loyalty amongst temperance men and of the "bewildering confusion of selfish and partizan aims and cries." But, while deprecating any unfair conditions in the Referendum, he urged that a big fight should be put up for moral reform and a great effort made "to stay the tide of intemperance, to save our youth from ruin, to protect our social, moral, political, educational and financial interests, to make our industries more secure and productive, to empty police courts and prisons, saloons and hovels, tenements and poor-houses." He pressed for organization and for active work in the election of Prohibition candidates at the coming political contest, for the raising of money to aid in this end, for the final "banishment of the bar" from social life and the path of the people. The Ontario general elections took place on May 29th following. Half-a-dozen Prohibitionists were in the field and, though none were elected as straight candidates, there was little doubt of various constituencies being more or less affected in the net result.

After this event the work of preparation for the issue of December 4th went on quietly and steadily. On June 6th the Congregational Union of Ontario and Quebec, meeting at Ottawa, declined to pronounce upon the Referendum itself, but unanimously recommended " all friends of temperance and Prohibition to accept the Act and cast their votes for it as a first instalment of the legislation which we can never cease to demand on the subject." On July 1st a Prohibition Convention was held in London and the Temperance Legislative League formed, with Mr. George F. Marter, ex-M.P.P., as President, Mr. R. M. Hobson of Guelph as Vice-President, and Mr. Robert Rae of Toronto as Secretary. The Committee consisted of W. W. Buchanan, Rev. Dr. W. A. McKay, Rev. Wm. Kettlewell, Mrs. Thornley and others. The League approved the Prohibition part of the Referendum Act, declared the attached conditions most unfair, and urged earnest work for the carrying of the main principle. A Convention was held in Toronto on July 29th, composed of some 600 members of the Dominion Alliance. The Rev. Dr. McKay delivered his annual address as Chairman. He spoke with directness along lines which the following quotation will indicate and concluded by urging a large vote for Prohibition:

Another year has come and gone, bearing with it more than the usual quota of opportunities, encouragements and discouragements. Some of you think the discouragements have predominated. And yet to-day we sound our trumpet note, not in the minor key, but in the major. No doubt we still see the liquor traffic in full blast in our land, doing its deadly work upon the hearts and homes, the bodies and souls of our people ; we see both our political parties prostrate before it and shamefully corrupted before that power ; and the Church itself in too many places asleep, as if chloroformed by the fumes of strong drink. Repeatedly during the year we have waited upon our Provincial Government and reminded it of the solemn promises, some of them typewritten, given us so frequently and with apparent good faith. With little organization we went into the election in May last ; we made our first fighting record on the political field and we are greatly encouraged by the result. I emphasize that. We opposed no man because he was a Liberal, none because he was a Conservative. We elected some, we defeated others, we changed the result in many places, and we convinced every politician in the land that we were a power in politics that could no longer be ignored or belittled.

Plans for the campaign were promoted and Resolutions passed pressing for electoral action and a united vote, and urging the raising of a fund of $10,000. The Rev. Dr. McKay was re-elected President and Mr. F. S. Spence Secretary, with the following Vice-Presidents : George F. Marter, Rev. Dr. Chown, Rev. Dr. Carman, Senator Vidal, Senator Cox, Hon. J. C. Aikins, Hon. G. W. Ross and Mrs. M. R. Thornley. Mr. R. J. Fleming was elected Treasurer. At the General Conference of the Methodist Church, which opened in Winnipeg on September 3rd, the Rev. Dr. Carman, General Superintendent, spoke vigorously upon various moral questions, and then dealt with that of Prohibition. He congratulated "brave and progressive Manitoba" upon having its initiated legislative action along this line ; regretted that in Ontario as well as in the Prairie Province the question had fallen into the eddyings and surgings of political strife ; claimed, however, that it was too much to expect the Rum power " to quietly retire, yield up their strongholds, abandon their violence, frauds and deceit because we are just beginning to summon their surrender "; and expressed the belief that ultimately the interjection of moral questions into politics would purify the atmosphere and educate both citizens and statesmen. Whatever the result, he believed that the vote on December 4th in Ontario would help to tone up the moral and spiritual fibre of the community.

On October 26th the Prohibition campaign was formally inaugurated in a number of Toronto churches. Dr. J. J. Maclaren, K.C., Mr. S. C. Biggs, K.C., Mr. John A. Patterson, K.C., and others spoke. Dr. Maclaren combated the idea that it was useless to work because they would have to obtain 213,000 votes in favour of Prohibition. "If we get a majority we are on top and will get our way sooner or later." Mr. Biggs dealt with the revenue argument and asked who had paid the $12,500,000 collected in Ontario as revenue during the past twenty-five years. "Was it not the poor men who handed their meagre earnings over the bar ?" As to the compensation, it was not due to those who had so long enjoyed special privileges,

but to the widows and orphans, the wives and children of those
who had been ruined by the traffic. Mr. Paterson declared that
there were 3,000 deaths annually in Ontario as the result of over-
indulgence in strong liquor.

At a Temperance Convention in Guelph on Nov. 6th, Mr.
N. W. Rowell, K.C., declared the saloon a menace to the political
interests of the country because it encouraged corruption; to the
welfare of the State because it created an organized liquor party;
to the business interests of the country because it destroyed productive labour and took many millions of money from business
establishments to throw into the bars; to moral and religious life
because it encouraged criminals and promoted moral irresponsi-
bility. Upon the other hand Dr. Goldwin Smith, in a letter which
appeared in the Toronto *Mail* of Nov. 21st. described Canada as a
remarkably temperate country and deprecated the intemperance of
those who would call down wrath and vengeance on the liquor
sellers. "Surely no cool-headed man, looking to the general habits
of civilized nations, and the undeniable practice of Christ and His
apostles, can pretend to believe that the use of alcoholic liquor is a
crime; and if its use is not a crime, neither can its sale be one.
The liquor trade, instead of being branded as criminal, has been
exceptionally recognized and licensed by the State. Zeal for
temperance need not extinguish our regard for justice." A mass-
meeting was held in Toronto four days later and addressed by a
number of gentlemen in favour of Prohibition. Mr. G. F. Marter
presided and the first speaker was the Hon. G. W. Ross.

He stated that in their legislation upon this subject the Government were anxious for a calm and comprehensive vote of the people.
The question practically was "whether the abolition of the bars
of the Province and the substitution for them of a restrained sale
of intoxicating liquors in our drug stores is going to be an advantage to the community." He hoped everyone would vote in a
matter affecting so closely the homes and happiness of all. Personally, he would vote for Prohibition and he hoped the Government
would be given a decisive mandate in the matter. The Rev. Dr.
Potts followed the Premier and referred to "the lifetime of loyalty"
which Mr. Ross had given to the temperance cause and declared that
if the Act became law vast sums now wasted in drink would go into
channels of legitimate industry. Dr. Oronhyatekha spoke strongly
in favour of Prohibition and referred to the successful operation of
the law affecting Indians in this connection. He believed the
measure under consideration to be "one of the best ever framed
for the suppression of the liquor traffic." Other speakers were
N. W. Rowell, K.C., E. Coatsworth, Jr., and the Rev. J. A. Macdonald.

The *Canadian Baptist*, the *Westminister*, and the *Christian
Guardian* had, meanwhile, maintained a vigorous advocacy of
Prohibition and the first-named paper on Nov. 27th, described the
measure in the following words: "It is a measure of the most
stringent kind against the bar-room and club-room drinking. If

384 THE CANADIAN ANNUAL REVIEW

enforced it will close all bar-rooms and clear out all liquors from club-rooms. The spirits for medicinal, manufacturing and sacramental purposes can only be obtained by the proper parties on regularly obtained certificates, at places licensed to sell for these objects. If bar-rooms can all be closed, it will cut up by the roots nine-tenths of the waste, the temptation, the degradation, the home misery and all the other evils of the liquor traffic." The *Christian Guardian* of Dec. 3rd had a final summary of the situation. No form of legislation, it declared had been absolutely successful in dealing with the liquor traffic. Results in the end depended upon the moral stamina of the people. One of the great evils of the saloon was its influence upon politics and the great difficulty of the license system was its admission of the element of profit as a stimulant to the sale of liquor. The barriers to progress were described as (1) a slight and superficial sense of the evils of the traffic; (2) the craving for stimulants in a hurrying and feverish age; (3) the greed for gain and willingness to make money without regard to social or moral results; (4) business entanglements and social influences; (5) the supposed welfare of political parties.

The day before the voting took place a largely-signed manifesto of representative business men was published in Toronto declaring the Prohibition Act an "unwise and impracticable measure" which would transfer the drinking from " licensed and regulated places to unlicensed and disreputable resorts and to the homes of the people." The signatures included financial and business men and firms such as H. C. Hammond, W. R. Brock, D. Coulson, J. H. Plummer, H. M. Pellatt, J. W. Langmuir, Heintzman & Co., Nordheimer & Co., H. N. Baird, H. D. Warren, R. W. Elliott, G. W. Beardmore, C. Cockshutt, W. T. Murray, John Catto, W. K. George, W. K. McNaught and many others. An analysis on the following day stated that the list included 14 bankers, 14 brokers and 24 barristers. This was the last of a vigorous campaign put up by the liquor interests and those opposed to Prohibition under the direction of Mr. E. Dickie. A pamphlet written by Mr. John Mudie had been widely circulated and this stated that under Prohibition the Municipalities would lose $1,000,000 from their share of license fees; the Provincial Government, $304,676 from the same source; the Province $1,000,000 a year from its share in excise and customs duties on liquor; the people would be taxed $3,650,-000 to pay for the 10,000 detectives necessary to protect the Province from smuggling and illicit sales; while another million a year would be required to pay the interest on the compensation which should be given vested interests—a total cost of $6,104,676 per annum. Some of the lessor incidents of this prolonged contest and agitation may be summarized here:

Feb. 22.—Mr. H. H. Fudger writes to the *Globe* a vigorous letter urging the Methodist Church to remain neutral in the controversy and not to interfere, as a Church, in a question of purely moral reform about which freedom of opinion was imperative.

Feb. 23.—At the Parkdale Congregational Church the Rev. Charles Duff preaches on Prohibition and, after the service, a long Resolution is passed defending the Government in connection with the Referendum and deprecating the views pronounced by the Ontario branch of the Dominion Alliance.

Mar. 6.—In addressing the Licensed Victuallers' Association at Montreal Mr. Laurence A. Wilson, its President, deals with the situation in Ontario, declares the fifty per cent. test a just one in view of the vested interests involved which he places at $75,000,000. The amount which each voter would be taxed to meet this policy should, however, have been placed on the ballot paper. But "we are grateful to Mr. Ross for using his best endeavours to remove this vexing question of Prohibition from the political arena and placing it in a position where the issue can be squarely and fairly fought out."

Mar. 8.—The Rev. C. T. Scott of London publishes an open letter to the Premier criticizing his statment that a Prohibitory law would require a large majority for its proper enforcement. Such a doctrine Mr. Scott contends is calculated to "relax the authority of law and create a sentiment that some laws may be ignored or violated. We cannot regard any wide promulgation of this theory as otherwise than vicious."

Mar. 11.—Mr. J. W. Flavelle, in an interview with the *Mail and Empire*, states his strong desire to control and modify the evils of intemperance; his disbelief, however, in the capacity of Government to enforce Prohibition; his fear that the policy as a whole is impracticable at the present juncture. "I give unequivocal support to Mr. Whitney in the position he has taken that the remedy applicable to the present situation is a further restriction of licenses, and the fearless administration of the law. I believe his position to be honest, sane, and deserving of the support of the country at large."

Mar. 19.—At the meeting in Hamilton of the Grand Council of the Royal Templars of Temperance a Report is presented and adopted which "deplores the bad faith of the Governments of Manitoba and Ontario in evading the fulfilment of distinct and repeated pledges" by means of their Referendums; denounces the action in point as "immoral and inimical to good government"; and recommends the candidacy of Prohibitionists in all constituencies during the coming elections.

April 4.—Mr. F. S. Spence explains the result in Manitoba by stating that the temperance leaders had first denounced the Government and then asked the people to ignore the Referendum. The Provincial branch of the Dominion Alliance had, in particular, issued posters signed by Mr. Redford Mulock, President, which were placarded all over the Province and which called on all Prohibitionists to stay at home on polling day.

Dec. 3.—The Presbytery of Toronto passes a unanimous Resolution declaring that the chief aim of the Prohibition Act is to "abolish the bar-room and the treating system" and urging every elector to come out on the following day and vote for the Act.

The vote resulting from the Referendum was a surprise to many people. The cities and towns as a whole supported Prohibition and Toronto gave 14,747 for it and 13,183 against it. Only London, St. Catharines, Ottawa, Belleville, Stratford and Kingston out of the larger towns and cities returned a majority opposed to Prohibition. As reported on December 5th the incomplete vote stood at 107,502 for and 65,363 against Prohibition and showed that though the Act would not carry yet the popular majority might be large.

Results of the Ontario Referendum

For some days the returns came in slowly and steadily increased the Prohibition support until the final figures showed a total vote for the Act of 199,749, or very nearly the 213,000 required to carry it. The favourable vote in 1894 had been 180,087 and in 1898, 152,337. The negative vote was 104,539 in 1902 as compared with 108,495 and 102,638 in the other years, respectively.

In expressing an opinion upon the result on December 5th, in the early stage of the returns, the Premier said to *The Telegram* that: "Judging by the results of the vote on Prohibition at Toronto and at some other points, as far as we have seen the figures, it would almost appear as if the statement made by the liquor dealers yesterday that the Conservative organizations throughout the country had used their influence to carry the measure in order to embarrass the Government was correct." The Rev. J. A. Macdonald expressed to *The World* perfect satisfaction with the result, believed it to be a severe blow to the bar-rooms, and to have created a situation which might procure a better Act than the one which had been rejected. Secretary F. S. Spence told *The Star* that he was greatly pleased with the figures and that they were proof of the justice of the temperance contention that the law should have gone into force without a vote. The Rev. Dr. Carman told the same paper that it was "a mandate to any and all Governments that the saloon and bar must go." The *Canadian Baptist* of that date, declared the vote to show that a united Temperance party could carry the country and that it must now be organized to do so. The *Christian Guardian* of December 10th was explicit and strong in its statement of opinion :

How can the Legislature of Ontario delay any longer, or escape the solemn responsibility of responding to the will of the people ? If government is to be by the people, and if government is to be for the people, then the course of honest legislation is clear. The present licensed liquor trade cannot remain. If government is to be by the lobbies, and if government is to be for those who have had and still have special and lucrative privileges, then the time-serving, trimming legislators will listen to the clamorous voice of those whose craft is in danger.

On December 9th the Premier of Ontario attended a meeting of the Grand Division of the Sons of Temperance in Toronto and, speaking as a Past Grand Worthy Patriarch of the Association and a member for 40 years, declined to commit the Government to any specific action in the premises. He explained, however, the personal belief that temperance was growing in sentiment and practice every day and expressed the hope that their educational campaign would continue steadily. On the following day the Association passed a Resolution declaring that no expression of opinion had ever been obtained from any free people so strong as was this vote for Prohibition and urging Government and Legislative action. Four days later Senator George A. Cox presided at a Massey Hall meeting of the Canadian Temperance League, and declared that a great protest had been entered against the open bar-room. " It ought to be the aim of temperance leaders to enlist the sympathies of that large class who were with them, this far at least, that the bars must be closed, and seek to secure legislation along those lines." On December 16th the Executive of the Provincial branch of the Dominion Alliance met at Knox Church, with some 200 Temperance workers and a delegation from the Sons of Temperance in attendance and, on motion of the Rev. Dr. Carman, seconded by Principal Caven, passed the following Resolution :

That in view of the recent expression of the electors of the Province of Ontario in favour of the Liquor Act of 1902, we deem it advisable to appoint a deputation to wait on the Government and request them that effect be given to the said vote by the abolition of public bars and the selling of liquor in clubs ; and that the imposition of such restrictions to the traffic shall be most effectual in curtailing its operation and remedying the evil.

The last of the many public discussions in which Principal Grant participated during his strenuous life was upon this problem of Prohibition. He wrote a series of letters to *The Globe* early in 1902 which undoubtedly affected public opinion in some measure and which were the subject of careful consideration and treatment in both press and pulpit—and of frequent quotation during the Referendum campaign in the autumn. On February 4th he took the line, in his first letter, that "sumptuary laws should not be passed save where there is practical unanimity of sentiment "; that under existing conditions and in view of their pledges, the Provincial Government could do nothing else but introduce a Prohibitory measure ; that it would, however, be an "arbitrary stretch of power " to give such a measure legal force without submitting it to electoral opinion ; that everyone who valued the moral life of the Province should vote yea or nay when the issue was placed before him.

Four days later he cleared the ground as to his personal views by declaring that the more varied his experience and the longer his life ; the more impartial his study of conditions under Prohibition enactments and the more mature his reflections on the springs of human action ; "the more convinced am I that the Prohibitionists are on the wrong track and that they have been and are doing more harm than good—especially to the cause of temperance." The very words he declared to be antagonistic. The one meant restraint by force, the other self-restraint. He referred with approval to the severe, but just, rebuke which he described Bishop Potter of New York as lately administering to intemperate Prohibitionists, and then expressed the following definition : " The men who use either malt or fermented or distilled liquor soberly, as all God's gifts should be used ; or the men who, like myself, do not use them as beverages, for one reason or another, but always for a reason which appeals to their own sense of duty and which does not bind anyone else, save in as far as it appeals also to his reason and conscience—these are temperance men." Turning to the application of different laws in this connection Principal Grant concluded that Local Option legislation had been largely successful in both Ontario and Quebec, while the Scott Act had been an admitted failure. The latter was prohibitory in character and it therefore followed, in his opinion, that "Provincial Prohibition would be a greater failure still." He described the failure of the Prohibition enactment of 1856 in New Brunswick and quoted from the evidence of Mr. Justice Hodgson of Prince Edward Island, before the Royal Commission of 1892, as to similar legislation in the Island having proved "an unmixed evil" and the source of perjury, increased drinking, black-mailing, evasion of and contempt for law in general.

In his third letter, on February 12th, he pointed out the desirability of moderate reforms ; the splendid work once done by Temperance organizations in teaching temperance and quietly cultivating a public conscience; the fact that the extremists and Prohibitionists had now obtained control of these Societies ; the danger of confusing the public mind and of dulling the public comprehension of evil by describing liquor drinking, under all and any conditions, as a sin, when it was not ; the fact that Christianity, as embodied in the Scriptures and in Christ's words and example, did not as did Mohammedanism and Buddhism, expressly condemn and forbid the use of liquor ; the evident effect of Prohibition organization and extreme advocacy in compelling the liquor interests to also organize and in making them impervious to pressure for such moderate and possible reforms as General Booth had frequently obtained in Old Country districts through cautious and moderate action. On February 21st the Principal reviewed the three methods now being tried on a large scale for the control or regulation of the liquor traffic and defined them as follows :

The licensing system, which may mean the imposing of a very low or very high tax, and either a large or a small number of places in which the sale is allowed ; Governmental management, the best example of which is, perhaps, the State Dispensary system of South Carolina, which, after a trial of some years, Senator Tillman recently pronounces to be such a success that there are now fewer places in the State where liquor can be bought than in Prohibitory States like Kansas or Maine ; and the Company or Society system, commonly called by the name of the City of Gothenburg, the first place in Sweden in which it was tried, where it has been in operation steadily, though with varying success, since 1865, and whence it has spread all over Scandinavia.

The first was the one generally adopted, but he did not believe it could be permanent. He argued at length that it was natural for men engaged in business to push their trade, to promote drinking, to encourage the sale of their product, to surround the business with all possible and legal allurements. And the higher the license fee the more liquor they must sell to pay it and preserve their profits. "I must live" was as strong an argument with an hotel man or liquor seller as it was with any other father of a family. The chief evils of this system were (1) the introduction of the element of private gain; (2) the inevitable adulteration of liquor; (3) the difficulty of enforcing Sabbath laws or protecting certain persons from its influence; (4) the presence of immoral accessories at some saloons; (5) the encouragement of the stupid habit of treating; 6) allowing the sale of liquor on credit; (7) the formation of an organized liquor party in the state. With many of these evils the Dispensary system would deal effectually, but he deemed it a dangerous law in a country governed under the party plan. The principles, however, which rested at the basis of the Scandinavian or Gothenburg plan fully commended themselves to his judgment; though it could not be established at present in Ontario because both the organized " trade " and the organized Prohibitionists would oppose it.

The last letter appeared on March 2nd, and summarized his views as previously expressed; referred to many vehement letters and criticisms which he had received from deeply earnest advocates of Prohibition; pointed out that these men and women, in their passion for law as a medium of morals, were like those who, in the Middle Ages, " tried to prohibit heresy by external laws "; and strongly deprecated undue interference with the personal liberty which every man so instinctively values. He concluded by urging consideration and adoption of the Gothenburg or Company system, promising his own personal aid in the matter, declaring spiritual and educative forces as better in this connection than politicians and policemen, and giving the following general view of existing conditions:

To establish the Scandinavian system all that is needed, in addition to the present Local Option law, is that power should be conferred on the authorities of towns and cities to hand over the licenses, allowed in each case, to a company consisting of such persons who would undertake the business, not for the sake of profit, but for the public good ; that the shareholders should not derive profit beyond the ordinary rate of interest on the capital invested, and that the profits should be devoted, after equitable consideration of the men formerly engaged in the business, to the municipality, or to the promotion of temperance, and the establishment of reading rooms, coffee houses, and other philanthropic objects. This is the principle of the Gothenburg system, and the fact that no single community, so far as has been learned, which has ever tried it, has afterwards abandoned it, is the best certificate in its favour and a striking contrast to the changes in public opinion and continued legal tinkering in Canada.

Meanwhile, the issues in Ontario and Manitoba had naturally projected the question of Prohibition, in some one or other of its phases, into the public mind of the other Provinces.

Temperance Affairs in the Other Provinces On March 23rd a delegation waited upon the Hon. Mr. Tweedie, Premier of New Brunswick, and presented the petition of 9,369 residents of the Province asking for Prohibition. All the speakers declared the sentiment of the Province to be strongly in favour of such action and the Premier promised careful consideration of the matter. On May 12th the reply of the Government was made public. It expressed recognition of the evil resulting from excessive drinking ; declared that a Prohibitory law might be effective but would have to be backed very strongly by public sentiment; mentioned the failure and repeal of the Provincial enactment of 1855 in this connection; expressed the belief that the Scott Act now in force in nine counties was as stringent a measure as any Prohibitory law could be; and pointed out that the License law in the rest of the Province made local Prohibition possible wherever desired by the people. The conclusion was that the Government did not feel warranted in taking any action at the present time. On the following day the Sons of Temperance of New Brunswick met at Moncton and the Grand Worthy Patriarch, Mr. L. D. P. Tilley, read a report favouring a change of tactics and the education and strengthening of public opinion in support of individual and total abstinence.

In Nova Scotia there was occasional discussion of this subject during the year. On March 26th, in reply to questions in the Legislature, the Hon. J. W. Longley, Attorney-General, read from a letter which he had addressed two days before to Mr. A. M. Bell of Halifax, an extract stating that "for various reasons it would not be expedient to introduce a Provincial Prohibition Act at the present time." At the annual meeting of the Sons of Temperance of Nova Scotia, held in Halifax on October 27th, a membership of 13,068 was reported (an increase of 1,714 over 1901) and the Grand Scribe, Mr. W. S. Sanders, stated that the Order was pressing the pledge of total abstinence at every point. He congratulated the people of Great Britain upon the organization of a similar crusade there under the direction of the National Temperance Society and with a special Committee headed by the Archbishop of Canterbury and including Canon Farrar, Sir Wilfrid Lawson and Mr. W. S. Caine, M.P., with Mr. F. S. Spence of Toronto as representing Canada. He then went on to say : " The issue between us and Gothenburgism, dispensaries, trusts of all kinds, high licenses, etc., is sharp and well defined. All those schemes are designed to perpetuate the traffic. They are intended to remove the effect but leave unimpaired the cause." On November 29th, following, the Halifax *Chronicle* deprecated the extreme ideas of Prohibitionists; declared temperance, or the absence of it, an essentially individual matter; urged that the State cannot make a man sober by legislation; and described the inconsistency and danger of permitting importation of liquor while prohibiting its manufacture and thus placing the source of supply beyond local control. The strong opinions which follow were then expressed :

It is such compulsion that we condemn and have always condemned. In their most advanced legislation Prohibitionists concede the right of the individual to buy liquors. In practice they all know and generally admit that there is a constant demand for liquor which must and will get itself supplied. Yet they refuse to regulate that supply in any way, even with a view to decreasing the demand. They rail at all connected in any way with supply, while relieving as far as they can from responsibility those who create the demand. In other words, temperance effort is now, and for years past has been, entirely misdirected. That is why it has been doing harm rather than good. That is why the liquor trade is becoming more and more demoralized and demoralizing. That is why temperance among us seems to be going backward instead of forward.

In Prince Edward Island this question aroused a certain amount of controversy in 1902, despite the oft-claimed public sentiment in favour of Prohibition. During February a petition was circulated in Charlottetown asking the Legislature to submit the existing Prohibitory law, as applied in the City, to a vote of the people. On April 4th a petition signed by 800 ratepayers was presented to the Assembly by Mr. J. F. Whear. It stated that the citizens were never consulted about the Act which had gone into force on June 1st, 1901 ; that when they had an opportunity they defeated the Scott Act at the polls; that the new law had been a distinct blow to local prosperity and had promoted drunkenness, blackmail, perjury and contempt for law in general ; that a plebiscite should be at once granted in order to let public opinion be expressed. Mr. Whear moved a Resolution in presenting the petition but could not find a seconder, and the matter dropped. It was pointed out in the press on March 6th that since the Act came into force there had been 3,900 convictions and commitments to jail and $2,200 in fines paid under its terms. On April 15th Premier Peters presented to the Legislature two important amendments to the Act with provisions which may be summarized as follows :

1. Legally qualified chemists were to be allowed to sell only ten ounces at one time and upon one prescription, and the liquor could not be drunk on the premises. The penalties were to be $20 for the first and $40 for the second offence.

2. Officers of the law were to be allowed to enter and search suspected houses for liquor which, if found, they could seize and remove. Any one interfering with such action could be fined $100 or imprisoned for 3 months.

In speaking to the measure the Premier declared the Act to be defective at present, stated that a good deal of liquor was still being sold, and that he did not think the law as it stood could be enforced. The Bill finally passed without a division. Two distinct views were taken in the Island as to this general legislation. The *Guardian* of Charlottetown defended it vigorously and declared that both the Prohibitory law in the city and the Scott Act in the rest of the Province had done much to restrict the area of drink. On July 22nd it stated that " both Charlottetown and the Island have less drunkenness because of these laws than they had under the License system." The *Examiner*, on the other hand, and on the same date, declared that the law had been " a lamentable failure." It proceeded to say that " the law was passed to humbug the people of the Province and it has been partially, intermittently and hypocritically prosecuted." Drunkenness was said to have abounded and increased. It may perhaps be added that the former paper was a supporter of the Government and the latter an opponent. At a meeting of the Provincial branch of the Dominion Alliance, on

September 30th following, presided over by Mr. J. K. Ross, all the speakers stated that the law was not enforced and, after listening to the defence of the Government Prosecutor, passed a Resolution in favour of another appointment to that position.

An interesting incident of a temperance nature in Nova Scotia occurred in a letter written to Mayor Crow of Sydney, C.B., by the Manager of the Dominion Iron & Steel Company and made public on October 9th. It protested against existing conditions in that town, where men, "not previously addicted to drinking to excess, have, since coming here, acquired the habit." The results after pay day were said to be of a character calculated to injure the efficiency of the men, affect the life and progress of Sydney, reduce the output of the business and increase the cost of the product. "Good regulations for the sale of liquor" was what the Company asked and not the unlimited and unlicensed sale of intoxicating drinks now carried on under the supposed operation of the Scott Act. In Quebec, the annual meeting of the Provincial branch of the Dominion Alliance was held at Montreal, on February 27th, and Mr. J. H. Carson, the Secretary, stated in his Report that at no time had the liquor party been "more audacious, defiant and aggressive." He stated that strong representations had been made to the Provincial Government asking for a separation of liquor and grocery licenses; for the submission of the question of license or no license to the electors at municipal contests; and for authority to the two Recorders of the city to sit on the Board of License Commissioners. On the same day petitions were presented by Mr. Matthew Hutchinson, M.P.P., to the Quebec House of Assembly from the Provincial W. C. T. U. and the Municipal Reform Association of Montreal, asking for legislation along similar lines, and by the former body demanding the prevention of cigarette sales to any person under 18 years of age.

The number of organizations connected with charitable, moral and religious work which are controlled by women in Canada is **Women's** increasing from year to year. Reference may be made **Work and** here to only one or two of the principal Associations **Societies** as typical of the character and labours of all. **in Canada** The National Council of Women is perhaps the most important in a public sense. Organized by the Countess of Aberdeen during her career in Canada for the purpose of "applying the Golden Rule to society, custom and law" it claims to have aided in promoting manual training and the teaching of domestic science in Public Schools; to have obtained the appointment of women inspectors for factories in Ontario and Quebec, of women on the school boards of New Brunswick, with the right of election to the school boards of British Columbia; to have effected various changes and reforms in the position of women in the prisons and to have organized Boards of Associated Charities in various centres; to have established hospitals, originated the idea of the Victorian Order of Nurses, organized cooking schools and classes for women, and diffused knowledge regarding Sanitary Science; to have checked the circulation of impure literature and encouraged good reading by means of the National Home Reading Union; to have conducted inquiries into the laws affecting the protection of women and children and the care and treatment of aged, poor and feeble-minded persons, and to have made various recommendations in this respect to the authorities; to have looked after the condition and treatment of women immigrants, promoted instruction for women in Art Design and aided in organizing branches of the Red Cross Society during the War.

The annual meeting of this organization for 1902 opened at St. John on July 3rd with the President, Mrs. Robert Thomson, in the chair. Her annual address briefly reviewed the work of the year, deeply regretted the death of Miss Francis E. Murray, deplored the recent retirement of Lady Taylor from the Presidency and pointed to their programme of subjects as evidence of the extent to which women were becoming interested in the welfare of humanity at large. Mrs. J. V. Ellis, President of the Local Council, welcomed the visitors to St. John and a letter was then read from Lady Aberdeen, Advisory President, conveying her greetings to the Council, opposing any change from the system of annual meetings and regretting the resignations of Lady Taylor as President and Miss Teresa F. Wilson as Secretary.

The ninth annual Report was submitted by Miss Wilson, the Corresponding Secretary, and various other Reports were presented and papers read during this and succeeding days. Amongst the former were statements from a Committee on the advisability of a Dominion certificate for teachers; from the Committee on laws for the better protection of women and children; from that on the promotion of industrial and fine arts in Canada; from that on the care of the aged and infirm poor; from the Committee on the question of women as members of School Boards; from that on the spread of pernicious literature; and from Committees on Domestic Science and the care of feeble-minded women. The Local Councils represented at this gathering were those of Toronto, Hamilton, Montreal, Ottawa, London, Winnipeg, Kingston, St. John, Halifax, West Algoma, Victoria and Vancouver Island, Nelson, Vancouver, New Westminster, Regina, Brandon, Rat Portage, Charlottetown and East Pictou—each having a large number of affiliated local Societies.

In the evening of July 4th a public meeting was held, with Mayor White in the chair, for the discussion of Prison Reform questions. Papers were read by Mrs. J. L. Hughes and Mrs. J. K. Barney and the occasion was marked by strong references from Canon Richardson and other local speakers to the jail conditions of the City and by an equally strong protest from Chief Justice Tuck against describing St. John as what it certainly was not in his opinion—"a regular pest house." On the following day Mrs. Robert Thomson was re-elected President and as Vice-Presidents,

Lady Laurier and Lady Taylor were selected while the Provincial Vice-Presidents were chosen as follows: Mrs. Hoodless for Ontario, Madame Dandurand for Quebec, Lady Tilley for New Brunswick, Mrs. R. L. Borden for Nova Scotia, Mrs Anderson for Prince Edward Island, Mrs. McEwen for Manitoba, Mrs. Kate Cummings for the Territories, and Miss Perrin for British Columbia. Mrs. Learmont was elected Treasurer, Mrs. Willoughby Cummings, Corresponding Secretary, and Miss Laidlaw, Recording Secretary. During the session, which lasted for some days, various subjects were discussed including music in the schools, led by Mrs. Torrington, of Toronto; the qualifications and certificates of school teachers and education in general, led by Mrs. Hughes of Toronto; the efficiency of divorce laws and the servant girl question; the dissemination of Art knowledge and the promotion of public interest in the subject; hygienic conditions in the home, domestic science and physical culture; penny savings banks, Government annuities, Life insurance plans for women and other Provident schemes; purity teaching in the Public Schools; the work of the Victorian Order of Nurses and many other collateral topics. Lieut-Governor Snowball formally welcomed the delegates on July 7th and it was decided to refer the matter of yearly or less frequent meetings to a Committee for report in 1903.

Various Local Councils of this organization met during the year. That of St. John was held on January 29th with Mrs. J. V. Ellis in the chair. In the Secretary's statement attention was drawn to the fact that 20 societies were now in affiliation with the Local Council and that in September the $1,000 a year provided as a fund by Lady Aberdeen would cease to be available for National Council work and would necessitate larger local contributions. Mrs. Ellis was re-elected President and a number of reports were received. At Ottawa the Local Council met on February 27th and was addressed at length by Mrs. Willoughby Cummings, of Toronto, who spoke of the useful character of their work—especially in the efforts to have separation effected between the inmates of jails who were criminals and those who were merely paupers. At present five out of seven of the aged inmates of prisons were paupers and not criminals. Care was urged in keeping bad literature out of the hands of children. Mrs. Edward Griffin was elected President and amongst the Vice-Presidents were Lady Laurier, Mrs. E. H. Bronson, and Lady Ritchie. In the Report of the Secretary reference was made to the Local Council's exertions to obtain the school play-grounds for use of children during vacation, to the domestic science classes organized in the city schools and to the efforts they had made for obtaining separate quarters at the Police Station for juvenile offenders. Meetings of Local Councils were also held during the year at Toronto, Montreal, Hamilton, London, Winnipeg, Kingston, Halifax. Victoria Vancouver, Regina, Charlottetown, New Westminster and other places, and considerable activity shown along the lines indicated. At

Whitby, Belleville, Port Hope, Guelph and Berlin provisional officers of new Local Councils were appointed.

The Women's Christian Temperance Union is another important organization in this connection. The Manitoba branch met at Souris on July 1st and two following days with Mrs. Stewart, of Winnipeg, in the chair. In her address the President dealt with the Christian and moral character of their work. Reports were read from various Committees and Mrs. Chisholm, of Winnipeg, was elected President for the ensuing year. Resolutions were passed favouring a policy of "total abstinence for the individual and legal prohibition for the State;" opposing the Gothenburg system as simply transferring liquor profits from the dealer to the Government; expressing the belief that alcohol as a medicine is "almost unnecessary;" declaring the disenfranchisement of women as "contrary to the fundamental principles of our Government and out of harmony with the idea of Christian co-operation for the highest good of humanity"; urging stronger efforts for the enfranchisement of the sex; protesting against liquor being allowed in military canteens; urging the enforcement of the law regarding the carrying of concealed weapons; disapproving the providing of "theatrical and immoral amusements" at the Winnipeg Industrial Fair; discouraging the use of bird-plumage for millinery purposes; advocating the prohibition of the manufacture and sale of cigarettes; warning the public against the "literature and lies" of the Mormon settlers; urging a proper observance on railways and elsewhere of the Lord's Day; condemning the Provincial Government in connection with the Referendum and declaring the result an unjust measure of Prohibition strength in the Province; protesting, with alarm, at the increase of gambling amongst men and women; urging every effort to prevent the circulation of impure literature, the use of coarse posters and the reporting in newspapers of demoralizing stories and incidents.

The British Columbia branch of the Union met at Vancouver on September 2nd and 3rd. Mrs. Gordon Grant in a lengthy address dealt with the temperance work of the W. C. T. U. and the blighting effect of the cigarette on boys and girls. Reference was also made to the morphine habit which the speaker declared to be growing amongst women with alarming rapidity. The Ontario Association met in Toronto on October 30th with Mrs. S. G. E. McKee in the chair. A great welcome was accorded Lady Henry Somerset who attended and briefly addressed the Convention. The Secretary reported that the Union had 190 branches in the Province with 4,952 regular members and 1,154 honorary ones; and 64 Bands of Hope with 3,719 members; that they had held 568 meetings during the year and received $13,888. It was stated that the Minister of Militia had made satisfactory promises as to the regulations regarding liquor in camps and reports were presented regarding rescue homes, work amongst the Indians and sailors and activities in the teaching of domestic science and hygiene. Resolutions were passed congratulating the Prohibitionists who had nominated and voted for special candidates in the late elections; expressing regret at the revelations in recent election trials and declaring that "the man who offers a bribe should be disfranchised for life and the man who takes a bribe should be similarly sentenced for a term of years;" urging the need of women at the polls as a means of purifying politics; and congratulating Methodist women upon the "moral victory" of the recent vote in their General Conference.

On the following day Lady Henry Somerset, World President of the W. C. T. U., addressed a mass-meeting in Toronto under the auspices of the Provincial branch. Mr. Chester D. Massey occupied the chair and Lady Henry paid high tribute to the Canadian soldiers who had helped the Motherland "to bear one another's burden's" and delivered a beautiful eulogy of the late Francis E. Willard. She then turned to the temperance question. "You have heard something of the misery that drink is causing in England. It would be impossible for me even to tell you a one-tenth of what it is doing. When I think about your problems here and ours I realize that yours is comparatively an easy task. I realize that we in the Old Country have got conditions about which you probably know absolutely nothing at all." She urged Canadian women to fight the evil while conditions were comparatively favourable and quoted Lord Rosebery's words: "If you don't govern the liquor traffic it will govern you." Meanwhile, at the Convention, it was stated that the attendance had been unusually large—over 260 in number—and reports or papers were read on cigarette smoking, scientific temperance, social purity and similar subjects. Mrs. McKee was re-elected President and Mrs. May Thornley Vice-President.

During the year ending June 30th, 1902, the average daily population of the Penitentiaries in the Dominion was 1,294 as compared with 1,405 in the preceding fiscal year.*

Crimes and Criminals in Canada
There were 43 pardons, 14 deaths and one escape during the year while 157 were released upon parole. As to this latter point Messrs. Douglas Stewart and G. W. Dawson, Inspectors, stated in their annual Report that the operation of the Parole Act upon the industry and conduct of the convicts had continued to be most salutary. The criminals in the Penitentiaries included 1,106 white men, 49 coloured, 32 Indians, 19 Half-breeds and 8 Mongolians while, as to nationality, 858 were Canadians, 188 from other British countries and 168 from Foreign countries. In their civil condition 743 were single and 388 married; in social habits 165 were abstainers, 619 temperate, and 430 intemperate; in educational matters 230 could not read nor write and 893 could do both; in creed 617 were Roman Catholics, 242 Church of England, 146 Methodist, 103 Presbyterian, 57 Baptist

* NOTE—Report of the Minister of Justice, 1902.

and the rest scattering. The expenditure by the Government in this connection was $417,355 for the year and the receipts $74,136.

On August 13th, 1902, a Report dealing with criminal statistics in the year ending September 30th, preceding, was made public by Mr. George Johnson, Dominion Statistician. The number of charges for indictable offences in the period reviewed was 8,291 as against 8,419 in 1900; the convictions were 5,638 as compared with 5,768; the proportion of convictions to charges was 68 per cent. in 1901. The figures indicated, during the year in question, that there was a decreased ratio of crime to population in Prince Edward Island, New Brunswick, Manitoba, Ontario, the Yukon and British Columbia, while the Territories showed a considerable increase and Nova Scotia and Quebec a slight increase. As to urban crime the statistics were stated to show convictions of 29·80 persons in every 10,000 inhabitants and in rural crime of 2·35 persons in every 10,000. By occupations the returns indicated a decrease in convictions amongst the agricultural, commercial, professional, domestic and labouring classes and an increase in the industrial class. Of the total convictions during 1901 there were 5,338 males and 300 females—a decrease in each case and, amongst the females, a continued proportionate decrease from 7·1 per cent. in 1892 to 5·67 per cent. in 1901. According to Provinces the figures were as follows:

PROVINCES.	NUMBER OF CONVICTIONS.		CONVICTIONS PER 10,000 OF POPULATION.	
	1900.	1901.	1900.	1901.
Ontario	2,769	2,769	12·72	12·68
Quebec	1,487	1,400	9·11	9·64
British Columbia	489	457	29·41	25·57
Nova Scotia	325	329	7·08	7·16
Manitoba	269	202	11·15	7·92
Territories	170	207	11·66	13·02
New Brunswick	137	127	4·15	3·83
Yukon	95	40	35·18	14·69
Prince Edward Island	27	17	2·60	1·64
	5,768	5,638		

There were 18 Asylums for the Insane in the Dominion in 1900-1 and during the year indicated 11,879 persons were treated of whom 6,116 were males and 5,581 females. The deaths during the year numbered 946.* On February 15th, 1902, the Report of the Ontario Inspector of Lunatic Asylums was presented to the Legislature of that Province and showed 4,604 patients in the Asylums on September 30th, 1901, as compared with 4,498 in 1900. He stated the number of patients admitted during the past year to be twenty in excess of the previous year, ending September 30th, 1900. During these years there were admitted 742 and 722, respectively. "It would not be correct, however," he added, "to

Lunatic Asylums and Insanity in Canada

---

* NOTE—Statistical Year Book for 1901.

assume that a reduced number of admissions for the past two years was evidence of a decreased demand for accommodation for, notwithstanding the increased room furnished within the past twelve years by the construction of the Asylums at Mimico and Brockville, and the additional accommodation provided at Kingston and Hamilton, amounting to a total of 1,218 beds, the room was fully occupied." The following table was given and illustrates what appears to be a marked increase in insanity during a period of 40 years in the Province:

	Population of the Province.	Number of insane and idiots officially known.	Ratio of insane to population.
1861	1,396,091	1,631	1 to 856
1871	1,620,851	1,427	1 to 1,136
1881	1,926,922	2,698	1 to 727
1891	2,114,321	4,119	1 to 513
1901	2,182,942	5,880	1 to 371

MISCELLANEOUS RELIGIOUS AND MORAL INCIDENTS

Jan.   1.—The divorces granted by the Dominion Parliament during 1901 are stated to have been 2 in number and by the Courts in the Provinces of Nova Scotia and British Columbia 17 in number—a total since 1867 of 71 granted by Parliament and 229 by the Courts of the two Provinces mentioned and of New Brunswick. These three Provinces, together with Prince Edward Island, which had never availed itself of the privilege, were the only portions of Canada possessing the right to grant divorce in their Courts.

Feb. 11.—The Nova Scotia Branch of the Lord's Day Alliance meets in Halifax with Mr. George Mitchell, M.P.P., in the chair. The Report of the Executive expresses great pleasure at the co-operation with them of the local Trades and Labour Council, deprecates the Sunday excursion of the Minister of Militia to Buffalo at the time of the Exhibition and refers to successful remonstrances presented to the Governor-General against Sunday travelling. Mr. Mitchell is re-elected President and the Rev. J. W. Falconer, B.D., Secretary.

Feb. 22.—Judge N. H. Meagher, of Halifax, writes strongly to the press as to the conditions prevailing in the County Jail at Amherst, N.S.

Feb. 26.—The Quadrennial Convention of the Student Volunteer Movement for Foreign Missions is held in Toronto and lasts until March 2nd. The delegates number 2,955 and represent 22 countries and 465 institutions of higher learning. Mr. John R. Mott presides at the first meeting and the Convention is welcomed by the Lord Bishop of Toronto, Principal Caven and the Rev. Dr. Potts. The President defines the significance of the gathering as follows : "It represented the coming Christian leadership of Canada and the United States. It illustrated the hold Christianity had on the institutions of Higher Education. It made plain the fact that intellectual life was not inconsistent with actual spirituality and practical Christian movements. It embraced the leadership of the aggressive Christianity of the day, and it was a mighty challenge to the anti-missionary spirit of indifference and unbelief which had cast a spell over the continent, owing to the terrible experiences of North China during the last two years ; and lastly it accentuated the oneness of Christianity." The subjects of consideration are the varied elements entering into missionary work all over the world—home and foreign alike.

Feb. 26.—A debate takes place in the House of Commons at Ottawa upon the question of religious precedence at State functions. Sir Wilfrid Laurier states that the matter is under consideration by the Government, that they will be glad of suggestions as to settlement of a very difficult situation, and he intimates that a new table of precedence will be presented to the King for approval.

Feb. 28.—In the Toronto *Globe* the Rev. Dr. A. C. Courtice publishes the fourth of a series of letters replying to the views and statements of Principal Grant on the Prohibition question.

Mar. 6.—Addressing an audience in Toronto the Hon. George E. Foster refers to the visit of Earl Grey to Canada and declares that statesman to be doing what Governments either would not or could not do. "Two great forces combined to keep the liquor traffic a potent agency for evil. They were the insatiable desire for gain on the part of the men in the business and the uncontrollable appetite for liquor on the part of the individual. These great obstacles to progress were, in a measure overcome by Earl Grey's Public-house Trust movement, by which the element of gain was eliminated and the appetite for strong drink not encouraged. The temptation was thus reduced to a minimum, and whatever tended to do this was in his opinion doing a splendid and much needed and meritorious work. He believed there was a field here for similar work, and hoped to see as a result of Earl Grey's mission the organization in Canada of a body of philanthropic men whose aim would be the establishment of such a Trust."

April 19.—Dr. Amelia Yeomans, of Winnipeg, President of the Equal Suffrage Club, addresses an open letter through the press to the women of Manitoba earnestly urging the vote of women as the only way to obtain Prohibition. "Equal suffrage will not bring the Millenium, but it must come before we approach that era. Its great value is not in radical (immediate) results, but that it places us on a natural basis ; once there and all progress will be real, every step a gain, because it will be taken along the highway of manifest, normal, human destiny."

May 2.—At the annual meeting of the Canadian Temperance League in Toronto Mr. J. S. Robertson is re-elected President for the 8th year in succession, and is presented with a handsome walking stick.

May 3.—*The Liberator*, the new organ of Ontario Prohibitionists, makes its first appearance, edited by Mr. W. W. Buchanan.

May 10.—The Report of the Hon. L. J. Tweedie, Premier of New Brunswick, upon his investigation into alleged breaking of the Sabbath in the City of St. John is made public. He states that while the evidence shows clearly that sales of intoxicating liquors, etc., have occasionally occurred on Sunday there was no proof that the Chief of Police knew or had connived in the matter. "I am not, however, satisfied that the policemen on duty were as prompt and vigilant in reporting offenders against the law as they might be—especially in the case of druggists selling soda water."

June 5.—The Manitoba branch of the Dominion Alliance holds a meeting in Winnipeg and listens to addresses from Mr. R. L. Richardson and other members of the Provincial Reform Union urging combined action against both parties at the next general elections. A Committee is appointed to discuss the details and report.

June 6.—The Rev. Dr. E. H. Dewart of Toronto celebrates the jubilee of his service in the Methodist Ministry and preaches an eloquent sermon in the Metropolitan Church of that City.

July 22.—A Dominion Alliance Convention at Winnipeg decides to appoint and constitute a joint Committee with the Political Reform Union, for co-operative action in the ensuing general elections. It is understood, however, that the Union refuses to put a straight Prohibition plank in its platform.

July 22.—The Rev. John Langtry, D.D., of Toronto, starts a somewhat widespread discussion of a sociological character by a letter in the *Mail and Empire* protesting against a recent announcement that the Bank of Montreal had raised the salary limit of marriage for its clerks to $1,500 a year. This he terms "a scandalous and immoral act" and meaning that four-fifths of the clerks can never marry at all. He asks who are the most likely to be honest, faithful employees—those who are struggling for their homes and families or those who fall into the dissolute ways so natural to constrained celibacy ? Banking circles show much interest in the question and various papers discuss it throughout the country. The pulpit as well as the press deals with it and some severe criticism is heard regarding such constraints.

July 27.—Sir Wilfrid Laurier speaks at Edinburgh and makes some interesting remarks of a sociological character. Speaking of Canada as compared with New Zealand he said : " They had something better to do for women than to give them the suffrage. And what was it they did for them ? In his country, and especially in the Province from which he came—and perhaps they would not be surprised as to the French Province of Quebec—what they did for women was to marry them. Now, in the course of his admirable address Dr. Schaffer gave some very good advice to the young graduates who were entering on the battle of life. Might he be permitted to join his advice to Dr. Schaffer's—to give them the views of one who unfortunately was no longer young and, as he hoped, was not altogether old ? His advice would be to them to do as they did in his country, not wait until they were rich and earned princely incomes in order to marry, but do as they did in Canada, marry young."

July 30.—The Presidents of the various Annual Conferences of the Methodist Church in Canada for the year are stated as follows :

Conference.	Name.	Address.
Toronto	Rev. James Allen, M.A.	Sault Ste. Marie.
London	Rev. A. L. Russell, B.D.	Highgate.
Hamilton	Rev. T. Albert Moore	Hamilton.
Bay of Quinte.	Rev. A. H. Reynar, LL.D.	Cobourg.
Montreal.	Rev. Manly Benson, D.D.	Arnprior.
Nova Scotia	Rev. Arthur Hockin	Amherst.
New Brunswick and Prince Edward Island	Rev. William Harrison	Dorchester.
Manitoba and Territories.	Rev. Edmund E. Scott	Vancouver.

July 30.—The Council of the Dominion Alliance meets in Toronto and President John R. Dougall, of Montreal, criticizes the Manitoba Prohibitionists for being disunited, for having lost an opportunity to score at least a moral victory, and for having failed to help Ontario sentiment by obtaining a substantial vote for Prohibition.

Aug. 7.—At Manitoba College, in Winnipeg, an interesting discussion takes place on the duty of the Church in public affairs. The Rev. Mr. Jacobs introduces the subject and declared it a religious duty to help in the purifying of politics. The Rev. Dr. Kilpatrick supported this view and declared that you could not separate the Church from the general life of the community. The Rev. Dr. Bryce thought that the interests of the Church and the politicians should not be too closely bound up and warmly defended the latter from "the slanders of the press." The Rev. Dr. Wilson deprecated any entry of the Church into politics. The Hon. Colin H. Campbell thought the true method was for the clergy to create and maintain a public conscience and not "to give *ex-cathedra* declarations on the tariff or inspired utterances on Imperial Federation." Mr. J. S.

Ewart, K.C., and the Rev. C. W. Gordon both seemed to think that the pulpit could very well deal with all questions affecting political purity or public morality.

Aug. 20.—The Provincial Synod of the Church of England, in Rupert's L nd, passes the following Resolutions :

1. The Synod heartily thanks the S. P. C. K., the S. P. G. and the Council of Colonial Bishoprics for their generous grants to the See of Keewatin which have made the consecration of a Bishop possible this year.

2. That a cordial vote of thanks be presented to the S. P. C. K. for the vote of a thousand pounds to the See of Mackenzie River, thus adding to the generous help accorded by them to the Church in this Province.

3. That the warmest thanks of the Synod be tendered to the Society for the Propagation of the Gospel for the decision arrived at last spring to suspend reductions in its block grant of £8,000 from the Bi-centenary Fund, for new missions in these Dioceses.

Sept. 25.—The Ontario Conference of Charities and Correction meets in Hamilton. The Rev. James Lediard of Owen Sound gives a most gloomy picture of the lack of protection afforded to children in country districts and declares that while the rural child badly needs protection it is not accorded, as in the cities, and urges the Children's Aid Society to take up the matter. " Vice and iniquity and cruelty do obtain in the rural districts. Population is small and scarce, widely separated. There is a lack of protection in these rural districts because it is not supposed that these iniquities abound or exist at all. This lack of protection grows, first of all, out of the fact that the people themselves and the authorities themselves, being in the country, do nothing."

Oct. 2.—A Prohibition Convention is held in Winnipeg with the Rev. Dr. Stuart in the chair and with addresses from the Rev. Dr. DuVal, Rev. J. B. Silcox, Rev. C. W. Gordon and others. Resolutions are passed denouncing both political parties in the matter of enacting and enforcing Prohibitory liquor laws ; declaring the intention of supporting only candidates in favour of Prohibition at the next Provincial elections, expressing pleasure at the starting of a Dominion Alliance newspaper, and urging the provision of funds for an effective Prohibition campaign.

Oct. 11. Miss Evangeline Booth, Chief Commissioner of the Salvation Army in Canada, publishes a long and eloquent greeting to her father, the General, in which amongst other things she says : " We realize that by your combined and untiring efforts for the solution of our social enigma, in the reform of the most degraded classes, you come to us the greatest philanthropist of modern times. The nineteenth century is rich in theories for the amelioration of the masses, but what others have dreamt of, written of, and speculated about, you have accomplished."

Oct. 15.—General Booth visits St. John and is given an enthusiastic reception by the Sunday School Convention then in session, and on the following day arrives at Halifax and addresses a great gathering with the Lieutenant-Governor in the chair and with the Provincial Premier, Mayor of the City, and many others on the platform.

Oct. 26.—General Booth visits London and holds several large meetings. To the *Free Press* he speaks as follows : " I think," he said, " the people are beginning to see that the Salvation Army is no longer an experiment. We have shown that the work we set out to do can be done, especially in regard to social affairs—dealing with the poor, and the drunkards, and the vicious classes. There are yet many who are very skeptical about the permanence of the reformation of drunkards, and fallen women, and criminals, but that is only on

26

account of an ignorance of what we have done. We have thousands of examples to show them if they will only take the trouble to look."

Oct. 27.—It is announced that Charles Ora Card, the pioneer Mormon of Southern Alberta and founder of Cardston in that region, is released from his position as President of the Alberta State of Zion and has been ordained a Patriarch. His place is taken by Henry S. Allen.

Oct. 30.—General Booth, of the Salvation Army, is welcomed in Toronto by a great gathering at the City Hall, where Mayor Howland declares that "the General did not represent the royalty, the statesmanship or the military power of the Empire, but he represented something without which Kings, statesmen and generals would be inefficient and ineffectual to maintain the Empire's place among the nations. The General was not of any established church or any recognized creed or order, but he was the latest representative of those constantly incoming waves of Christian enthusiasm, without which churches, established or disestablished, would have no life or power." Tho General reciprocates by expressing the hope that he will have the pleasure of meeting the Mayor in the Hallelujah City. On the following day a mass-meeting at Massey Hall in Toronto, presided over by Premier Ross, listens to an address from General Booth and an appeal for aid in his work.

Dec. 4.—One of the campaign circulars issued by the anti-Prohibitionists sums up the conditions under the proposed Act as follows :

1. A brewer may still brew and a distiller may still distill.

2. Liquor may be imported into Ontario from outside the Province and mail orders may be executed from outside the Province by travellers from outside.

3. Liquor may be kept for consumption in private houses which may be searched for its alleged improper use.

4. Husbands may be compelled to testify against their wives and children against their parents.

5. Medical men may carry around two quarts at a time for the use of their patients.

6. There is no prohibition of the manufacture, importation or sale of liquor.

7. It would harass and impede trade ; destroy a yearly Provincial revenue of $700,000 ; increase the trade of Quebec at the expense of Ontario ; discriminate in favour of the wealthy classes ; result in the consumption of more spirits and less beer ; cause secret drinking, illicit traffic and increased home consumption.

Dec. 27.—In the Montreal *Witness* there appears a symposium of interviews with representative clergy, dealing with the question of Church Union as raised by the Methodist General Conference in Winnipeg. The Rev. Professor Scrimger, of the Presbyterian College, declared himself in favour of the union of Presbyterians, Methodists and Congregationalists, in a corporate body which would leave doctrinal differences aside and properly protect individuality of thought and independence of judgment. Variety in Protestantism was a source of strength and individualism better than ecclesiasticism. The Rev. Dr. James Barclay thought the question had not yet reached a practical basis, and deprecated as impossible the Anglican idea of an Episcopate with Presbyterian and Methodist Bishops. The Rev. Dr. W. I. Shaw, of the Methodist College, believed that "the spirit is growing, not merely of unity but union." The Rev. Frank Pedley placed the Christian Church in two divisions—that of the Priest and that of the People. In the latter would be found the Presbyterian, Methodist, Congregationalist and Baptist denominations. Bishop Carmichael stood by the Lambeth propositions and supported a sort of federation of free churches with a common hierarchy consecrated from each division and the preservation of distinctive articles of faith, or practice, outside of the general system of government.

XVI.—EDUCATIONAL AFFAIRS IN CANADA

According to official figures published during 1902, for the year ending June 30th, or December 31st, 1901, there were in all the
General Educational Conditions Provinces of Canada 18,148 Public Schools, and 973 High, Normal and Model Schools; with 941,833 pupils in the former and 144,316 in the latter; and with an average attendance in the Public Schools of 560,063, or 59·47 per cent. of the registered number.* The total number of teachers in the Public Schools was 23,433 and in the others 4,957; while the Government grants were $3,174,327, the revenues from other sources $7,848,082, and the total expenditure $10,034,441. There were 17 Universities in the Dominion, 20 Colleges, 19 Classical Colleges—partly schools and partly colleges in the Province of Quebec—8 Ladies' Colleges and 36 miscellaneous institutions of higher education which it would be a little difficult to classify. The endowment of the Universities and Colleges, as summarized from not entirely complete data in the official Year Book for 1901, was $10,540,551; while the property owned by them was estimated at $10,789,808.

Some interesting personal and general occurrences in educational affairs marked Canadian history during 1902—apart from the Provincial colouring which, in the main, must always characterize their condition and development. Principal Grant opened the year at Queen's University, on January 6th, with one of the most able and eloquent of his many speeches on public matters. Education to him was much more than a thing of Provinces and boundaries. "A nation is saved by ideas; inspiring and formative ideas; and in these Canada is barren, even as compared with the United States." Speaking at Moulton Ladies' College, Toronto, on January 11th, Prof. J. W. Robertson, Dominion Commissioner of Agriculture, strongly deprecated the modern book-learning of the child as obtained in Canadian schools. "The present arrangement of a school with its children in even ranks, its lack of physical motion, its silence and its attempt to make character by hearing instead of doing, was entirely and utterly opposed to the proper method and tended to destroy the power of thought and initiative."

In a contribution to the Toronto *Mail* of February 22nd, Principal J. O. Miller of Ridley College, St. Catharines, dealt with the lack of religious instruction in Canadian public schools. He declared that there was at the present time general indifference in this connection amongst the Protestant denominations of the English-speaking Provinces. The causes of this condition were various. Handing over the education of children to the State had loosened or alien-

---

* Note—The figures for Ontario are those of 1900.

ated the feeling of responsibility on the part of parents in all matters of secular teaching. From this had naturally come indifference or incapacity in the teaching at home of religious subjects. The abatement of religious faith in the community as a whole was a part of the process. And, while the people had become apathetic regarding the matter, their ministers had become adverse. The reasons in this latter connection were (1) that religious education was claimed to be properly the function of the parent and a part of home-training, which in practice it had ceased to be; (2) that the different religious bodies could not unite upon any common ground or scheme of lessons, even though the foundations of their belief were being questioned in many and increasing directions; (3) that it was impossible to trust to a miscellaneous body of men and women the teaching of personal and spiritual doctrines involving the possible inculcation of dogma. The Principal concluded by declaring that all these difficulties could be met and by urging the preparation of a scheme of lessons by the denominations, with the learning by heart from the Bible of its finest passages, in weekly studies, by the pupils.

At Ottawa, on April 24th, His Excellency the Earl of Minto attended a banquet of University representatives and graduates. In his address the Governor-General referred first of all to the games and sports of his own College days and the memories of friends connected with them, and then gave the English ideal of University work in the following words: "We all know that it is to the mental and educational training of our Universities that we look for the higher erudition of our people and perhaps even more for that tone of culture, that old-world knowledge, that refinement which goes to form a polished man of the world." Continuing, he expressed the hope that " the traditions of scholastic study and the chivalry that permeated the barbarism of the Middle Ages " would long be a factor in his own life and opinions. As for the rest : " It is difficult to crystallize, so to speak, public opinion in the Dominion. Canada is so vast, local interests at huge distances apart are of such pressing moment that they would appear to cast a mist over the future outlook. Nevertheless I trust that it will be the outspoken expression of a mature public opinion, irrespective of political bias, that will lead you, and for that we must look in the development of the high moral and intellectual standard which depends so largely upon University life." Principal Peterson of McGill, President Loudon of Toronto, Provost Street Macklem of Trinity, and other speakers followed.

Speaking at Toronto, on May 28th, in his Presidential address to the Royal Society of Canada, Dr. Loudon, of Toronto University, dealt at length with University ideals, systems and research—not only in Canada but in Germany, England, and the United States. " Organized research in Canadian Universities, as a definite system, can scarcely be said to exist as yet, although within the last decade certain beginnings have been made which indicate a movement in that direction. Canada, like the United States, has derived its University ideals from Great Britain. Some of the original Faculties of our Universities are a transplantation, so to speak, of groups of scholars from Britain, who brought with them intact the traditions in which they themselves had been nurtured." But he believed the demand for research was developing and that in time Canada would adopt in this respect something of the policy of the great German institutions of higher learning. Resulting from one of the important educational incidents of the year—the removal of Dr. George R. Parkin to take charge of the Rhodes' Scholarships—was the valedictory of the Principal of Upper Canada College on October 23rd. It was an eloquently-worded address, written from Oxford, and concluded with the following description of his ideal in teaching the boys of an institution which he had tried to make like a great English school :

Nothing stamps a school as really great save the power of turning out men of high and noble character. So long as truth in thought and word and deed is the rule of life within these College walls and on its playgrounds ; so long as honour is the hall mark stamped on the countenance and conduct of every boy who goes out from us ; so long as boys are not ashamed to guard their lips and guard their lives on Christian principle ; so long we need feel no anxiety about the future of Upper Canada College. While our old School remains a trusted place of training for Christian gentlemen, its walls and work will endure ; should it ever become other than this it will deservedly fall. And so the boys of a great School like this, as they inherit noble traditions from the past, have laid upon them a great responsibility for the present and the future.

The two specific questions of rural education and manual training were largely dealt with during the year as a result of the continued benefactions of Sir W. C. Macdonald, of Montreal, and the work done in their practical application by Prof. J. W. Robertson. It was announced early in the year that the plan as proposed, and to be developed, was to promote the consolidation of five, six, or more rural schools into one central graded school with a school garden and a manual training room as part of the equipment. With this object in view Sir William Macdonald offered financial assistance to one locality in each of the Provinces of Ontario, Quebec, New Brunswick, Nova Scotia and Prince Edward Island, so as to give a practical picture of the work and induce people generally to combine in educational improvement under the control of the regularly constituted Provincial authorities. In Ontario it was proposed to also offer the Guelph Agricultural College the gift of a building, including equipment, for the accommodation of teachers while taking a short course in Nature Study for these rural schools. A residence building would also be offered, fully equipped, and fitted to accommodate not less than one hundred female students, for instruction and training in domestic economy and household science. A travelling instructor would be appointed as part of the rural school scheme for each Province and arrangements be made for the transportation of scholars to the central or graded school when necessary. On January 27th, Prof. Robertson spoke in St.

John, with the Lieutenant-Governor, Senator Ellis and others on the platform, and summarized conditions as to manual training in the form of nature studies and school gardens:

The idea was not to make farmers or horticulturists, but capable men and women. The only fault of the present system was its specialization in favour of the professions, whereas it should be general and for the people. Another effect of the gardens would be to beautify the present ugly aspect of country school-houses, generally a disgrace to our civilization. They would also give information and serve to train the pupils to observe, investigate, conclude, and finally do for themselves. The department of household economy was spoken of in its branches of sewing, cooking and housekeeping, and its value as an educational factor elaborated. Manual training schools had been established all over Canada, and in no instance had one failed. There were five each in Nova Scotia and Ontario, at the expense of the Provinces, and these were to be increased during the coming year by five and seven respectively. The Government aimed to establish in New Brunswick this year gardens in connection with ten country schools and to provide a trained teacher for preliminary and regular instruction. In Ontario 150 teachers were being trained for that work.

At Quebec, on May 30th, a largely attended meeting of the Protestant Committee of Public Instruction, with the Rev. Dr. W. I. Shaw in the chair, considered the plan of centralizing and consolidating the small schools in poor districts in the light of Sir William Macdonald's offer to assist in making the experiment. A Resolution was passed thanking the latter and offering to cordially co-operate in every possible way. On August 26th Prof. Robertson announced that the group of consolidated rural schools in Prince Edward Island would be in the Pownal District, in Nova Scotia they would be at Middleton, in New Brunswick at Kingston, King's County, and in the County of Brome, Quebec. To the Toronto *Globe* of December 16th, he summed up concisely the advantages claimed for the system of rural school consolidation and transportation of scholars:

1. It results in the attendance of a larger number of the children in the locality, particularly of those under the age of eight years and of those over fifteen years.
2. It brings about a more regular attendance of pupils of all grades of advancement.
3. It ensures the engagement and retention of some teachers of higher qualifications and longer experience in rural schools.
4. It creates conditions for a proper classification of pupils and for such a grading of the schools as may permit the pupils to be placed where they can work to the best advantage for their own improvement.
5. It permits the time-table to be so arranged that teachers can give each class and every pupil in the class more direct help and supervision.
6. It provides beneficial influences to fairly large classes of pupils of about equal advancement (a) by more companionship; (b) by friendly rivalries to excel; (c) by children learning from each other; (d) by co-operating under careful discipline; and (e) by class enthusiasms.
7. It makes it convenient for boys and girls in rural districts to obtain a high school education without leaving home.
8. It leads to the erection of better school buildings, and more satisfactory equipment in all the requisities of a good school.
9. It makes it practicable for rural schools to enrich their courses for all pupils by nature study, manual training and household science, as well as by better music, and, for advanced pupils, by instruction in agriculture, horticulture and allied subjects.

10. It stimulates public interest in the schools and brings to the pupils of a township an institution in which all can have an equal interest and a worthy pride.

11. It may lead to an improvement of the public roads in the country parts.

12. It would facilitate the rural free delivery of the mail.

The death of Dr. George Monro Grant, C.M.G., after twenty-five years of leadership in Canadian educational work and public life, as Principal of Queen's University, Kingston, removed a vital factor in the progress of the Domin- **Death of Principal Grant** ion. Perhaps the most sympathetic and accurate tribute of the many offered to his memory was that of the Toronto *Globe* on May 12th. "All Canada will mourn the death of George M. Grant. He was a national figure, and where he stood erect the other day there is a great gap of grey sky and bare horizon." Through thirty full and fruitful years his personality had stood out as an ideal expression of "strenuous, resolute, sagacious and sympathetic Canadian nationalism." Through it all, however, though a politician of great ability and a statesman who moulded public and national affairs, he lived and wrought as an educationalist.

The loss to Queen's is great beyond comparison. The University was inseparable from the personality of the Principal. Grant was Queen's and Queen's was Grant. In building up the fortunes of Queen's he best exhibited his extraordinary resource and untiring energy; and that love for truth, and bold and free spirit of inquiry and speculation for which Queen's is distinguished, are of the very essence of the life and character of Grant. The child of his love and of his faith, Queen's was his life's care and his last concern, and it will become his associates who are left behind to perpetuate its spirit, guard its traditions, and continue its work as the enduring monument to his teachings and labours.

A few days later, on May 17th, *The Globe* returned to the task of analyzing Principal Grant's character and influence. "His part in our public life was more subtle than that of the publicist of the usual type and the harder to appraise. Perhaps the key can be found in his attitude in the class-room. In the stricter sense of the word he was a great teacher for he had the gift of educating men. No man was less of a propagandist. He had the rare and delicate gift of abstention from desire to see reproduced in his students his own specific ideas. He developed the men he had to deal with, and each left his hands, not a replica of the Principal moulded by his personality, but a man whose latent faculties had been aroused and developed, and who was deliberately encouraged to form his own views for himself." A personal tribute of a kind somewhat different from these editorial expressions of opinion, was the able sermon preached, in memoriam, at St. Andrew's Church, Toronto, on May 18th, by the Rev. J. A. Macdonald. In it he reviewed the many-sided character and labours of the man and defined what he believed to be the important message of his strenuous life. Unity and liberty were declared to be the organizing principles of his educational work. "It is true he opposed the large scheme of University confederation but that was partly because of conditions at Kingston and partly because he feared the uniformity of type which, he thought, the confederation scheme might produce. During his whole Principalship he laboured to bring Queen's University into close relations with the educational system of Ontario while he safe-guarded the independence of its teaching and life. When the time came and the Queen's type had been definitely and deeply fixed and Queen's University had become the University of Eastern Ontario, doing work of such quality and magnitude as made its position and claims unique, he made that last great venture, making the University wholly and absolutely undenominational— by statute as well as in fact a Provincial institution." Tributes from the pulpits of the country were very numerous. In St. John, on May 12th, the Rev. Dr. Morrison described him as a prophet in the highest sense of the modern use of that word. "His well-trained mind grasped with wonderful comprehension the truths of the Kingdom of God." He was a manly man. "Intellectually strong, emotionally tender and devoutly pious." He was a distinguished patriot. He was "remarkable for plain living and high thinking." At Winnipeg the Rev. Dr. Bryce referred to his wide sympathies, social qualities, pride in the Church, powers as a debater and ability as a business man, and then continued: "Dr. Grant was a great educator. He had a most penetrative mind, and quickly saw through educational shams and fads. He introduced the Scotch university system into Queen's, and in this rather departed from the Canadian model, which is based on the English university system. I have never been able to see the advantage of this change. He, however, made Queen's University well-known and popular, and greatly widened the sphere of its influence. He was also a great public teacher."

In Halifax, the Rev. Principal Pollok, dealt with Dr. Grant's early work in the resuscitation of Dalhousie College, his labours for the Confederation of Canada, his appreciation of the great West at a time when the public knew nothing of it, his early advocacy of Church unity, his patriotic aspirations for the future of Canada. In *The Westminster* of May 17th Prof. William Clark, of Trinity University, paid high tribute to his administration of Queen's. "I will venture to say there is not, on this continent or elsewhere, an institution of the same size which contains a larger number of professors and lecturers of distinguished ability and fitness for their work. Here is one of the tests of greatness—the knowledge of men and the selection of them for their work." Principal Caven expressed a similar opinion. "Queen's University is Dr. Grant's monument. His name must ever represent the immense strides forward made by Queen's in the last 20 years." He went on to say that Dr. Grant most earnestly believed that "any conception of education which failed to bring it into connection with the moral and the spiritual was essentially defective."

THE VERY REV. GEORGE MONRO GRANT, C.M.G., D.D., LL.D., F.R.S.C.
Principal of Queen's University.   Died May 10th, 1902.

GEORGE ROBERT PARKIN, C.M.G., M.A., LL.D., F.R.S.C.
Principal of Upper Canada College, Toronto.   Appointed in 1902 to supervise the Rhodes' Scholarships.

In the same paper the Hon. G. W. Ross, Premier of Ontario, described the late Principal as a man of open vision, great courage and great tenacity of purpose. "Such as Grant are epoch-making men." Dr. George R. Parkin thought him one of the largest and most forceful personalities produced by Canada. "He was a student of the past, a leader in the present, a prophet of the future." In his judgment Grant knew Canada better than any other man of his time. "He had touched Canadian life at every angle and felt its pulse under all conditions." At the funeral of Principal Grant on May 13th, there was a distinguished gathering of publicists and educationalists, including Sir Sandford Fleming, Sir James Grant of Ottawa, Archbishop Gauthier of Kingston, the Rev. Dr. J. Edgar Hill, Rev. Dr. T. G. Williams, and Rev. Dr. Barclay of Montreal, the Rev. Dr. Herridge of Ottawa, Senator Melvin Jones, Mr. Justice Maclennan, Rev. Dr. Milligan, Dr. G. R. Parkin and many others from Toronto, and other places. In his funeral sermon Dr. Milligan referred to the Principal's personal magnetism and qualities; his services to the Church, the country and the Empire. "His death is an irreparable loss to Queen's, all of whose sons will, while life lasts, cherish the memory of Principal Grant. The true monument of all his labours, devotion and sacrifice is this University." In the speech delivered by the Hon. G. W. Ross at the laying of the corner stone of the Grant Memorial Hall at Kingston, on November 6th, a very clear-cut view of Principal Grant as an Educationist was given and should be quoted here :

Principal Grant's views of the kind of education best suited for the Canadian people were quite pronounced. He was not a specialist as that term is generally understood. His rule was first generalize, then, when you have discovered your aptitudes, specialize. He always, so far as I knew (and I think I knew his opinions well), believed that education is breadth, not narrowness ; that the majority of men have to adjust themselves to a variety of conditions in life and so their education should anticipate these conditions. I do not mean to say that Principal Grant did not consider specialization an important part of the University work, but he thought the first duty of the University was to provide a comprehensive course of instruction for the many, placing specialization more in the field of post-graduate work than in the regular course of study. Even in the matter of elective studies I always felt the Principal held somewhat conservative views. A University, in his judgment, represented a certain standard of culture which he claimed could not be divorced from the study of the classical languages. Oxford and Cambridge, though in some respects slow in adapting themselves to modern conditions, represented his ideal of a great University better than Harvard or Cornell, and in this view I believe he is amply sustained by the record in literary circles of those two ideals of scholarship.

An educational event of the year of more than local import was the appointment of George R. Parkin, C.M.G., L.L.D., D.C.L., Principal of Upper Canada College, to the work of organizing **Dr. Parkin and the Rhodes' Scholarships** and managing the special Oxford Scholarships under the terms of Mr. Cecil Rhodes' remarkable bequest. By the latter's will, dated July 1st, 1899, with codicils dated Jan. 18th, 1902, and made public on April 5th of the latter year, Mr. Rhodes appointed as his Executors the

Earl of Rosebery, Earl Grey, Lord Milner, Mr. Alfred Beit, Dr. L. S. Jameson, Mr. L. L. Mitchell and Mr. B. F. Hawksley. Its terms, so far as educational matters were concerned, left (1) for improvements, etc., at Oriel College, Oxford, £100,000; (2) provision for the establishment of 60 Scholarships at Oxford of the yearly value of £300 each, for three years, to be used for instilling into the minds of students the advantage to the Colonies and the United Kingdom of the retention of the unity of the Empire; (3) provision for the endowment of 120 American Scholarships at Oxford of the yearly value of £300 each, for three years, with a view to promoting attachment amongst the rising generations in the United States for the land from which their ancestors came; (4) provision for 15 German Scholarships at the same University worth £250 each, for three years, and subject to nominations by the German Emperor.

This large sum was left, in its Foreign application, because the donor believed that "a good understanding between England, Germany and the United States of America will secure the peace of the world; and educational relations form the strongest tie." There were many and varied criticisms of this document. The curious error, or evidence of ignorance, shown in the limitation of Canada to six Scholarships, was the subject of comment in Great Britain as well as in the Dominion. Under the terms as outlined South Africa was given 24 Scholarships, Australia 21, Newfoundland, Bermuda and Jamaica 3 each and the Provinces of Ontario and Quebec, 3 each. In the Toronto *Telegram* of April 7th appeared a number of interviews upon the nature and possible result of the bequests. President Loudon declared that neither Oxford nor Cambridge had any particular attraction for Canadians—they had no research and were not sufficiently practical or modern. Chancellor Burwash welcomed the gift and said that since 1894 Toronto students had been continuously taking post-graduate courses in both the English Universities. Provost Street Macklem thought the policy of Cecil Rhodes in this connection was calculated to use the two vital factors of increased knowledge and personal intercourse in promoting loyalty or creating friendship. Chancellor Wallace thought the result would be an increased Canadian attendance at English Universities, a broadening of view amongst Canadians generally, a strengthening of Imperial relationship and general good through a linking of scholastic and athletic superiority. Mr. Goldwin Smith's opinion, as expressed in the Philadelphia *Press*, and re-published in the Toronto *Globe* of April 19th, was characteristic:

There can be no doubt that Mr. Cecil Rhodes was the prime author of the conspiracy against the lives of the two South African republics. Were I now engaged in administering the affairs of Oxford University I might find myself somewhat in a moral dilemma. Mr. Rhodes' paramount design seems plainly to be political. His educational policy is subsidiary to his policy of painting the world red, of which he presents himself as the hero in his directions for his unspeakable tomb. He aims at drawing Great Britain and the United States into a league for the purpose of imposing peace, as it is phrased, upon the world ; which as the world does not want to have anything imposed upon it by any league, is not unlikely in the end to lead to an Armageddon.

To the *Telegram* of April 8th, Principal Grant expressed the belief that results would not be as great as were expected, that many of Mr. Rhodes' ideas, as indicated in his will, were "impracticable and characteristic of the man," and that Imperialism in its truest sense would not in his opinion be permanently benefited by these legacies. Dr. Parkin approved warmly of the plan and praised its possibilities while expressing the belief that any mistake made in the reference to Canada would be rectified through the discretionary powers of the Trustees. In this latter connection the Universities of the Maritime Provinces—notably Dalhousie and New Brunswick—hastened to memorialize the Trustees with a view to the extension of the Scholarship privileges to those parts of the Dominion.

On August 12th it was announced that Dr. George R. Parkin was to organize the scheme of these Scholarships and to visit the various countries interested in order to effect a suitable working plan of operation. The comments upon this appointment were very generally favourable—especially in the British countries concerned. The London *Times* of the following day declared that the Trustees had been "singularly fortunate in securing the services of a man peculiarly fitted for the task." His one-time experience at Oxford, his Imperial sympathies, his educational work at Upper Canada College, his knowledge of the Empire, all combined, it was said, to fit him for the position. On August 21st Dr. Parkin arrived in Toronto and at once informed the press interviewers that the Trustees had agreed to give three Scholarships to each Canadian Province. He expressed the opinion to the *Mail and Empire* that the work should be largely post-graduate in its nature ; that the best of Canada's young men should be selected ; that from his own experience the course would have a stimulating and broadening influence ; that it would draw both men and countries together. He intimated that it would take at least two years to settle the conditions and details and that he would at once resign his position at Upper Canada College.

Dr. Parkin was in St. John on Aug. 27th, when he pointed out that Canada would have seven Scholarships each year and twenty-one students at Oxford permanently. The share of the Dominion in the bequest would be $31,500 a year. He visited other places, returned to England and issued from Oxford a series of questions to heads of Colleges in all the countries concerned and, on Nov. 30th, arrived again at New York. On Dec. 19th he was at Sackville, N.B., conferring with the heads of the chief educational institutions and interests in the Maritime Provinces ; on Dec. 22nd he held a similar conference at Montreal for the Province of Quebec ; on Dec. 27th he was at Toronto with a similar mission ; and two days later was in conference at Washington with American leaders in educational affairs. Meanwhile, the authorities of McGill University, Montreal, announced on Dec. 10th their intention to recognize his work in this connection by bestowment of the Hon. degree of LL.D., and on Oct. 23rd some notable words written by Dr. Parkin had been read in a public ceremony at Upper Canada College, Toronto. They dealt with education in general and the Oxford matter in particular:

I write these lines from Oxford. It is a place which nearly thirty years ago gave to me some of the deepest inspirations of life—some of the most powerful impulses to effort that youth can receive. Around me on every side I see magnificent buildings devoted to purposes of intellectual culture. The magnanimous and patriotic thought of men who long ago here dedicated their wealth to the higher life of the English people is seen to be a living power for good to-day, as it has been in centuries past. From these homes of learning has gone forth a steady stream of student-thinkers, writers, statesmen, men of affairs, who have enriched the traditions of our nation, made it famous throughout the world, added the grace of culture to the material good achieved in the fields of mechanical industry. Without such centres of thought and learning no nation can reach its highest possibilities. In the case of the individual, wealth which does not translate itself into personal superiority in those who inherit it, has missed its highest result. In the nation the greatest material prosperity fails to attain its noblest end if it does not minister to the higher intellectual and spiritual life of the people. I crave for all the great centres of our Canadian life more of what I see around me here.

The chief educational institution in the Province of Quebec and one of the leading institutions of learning upon the continent, McGill University, closed its Session of work in 1902 with a very successful record for the year which ended August 31st. The annual Report, signed by Lord Strathcona as Chancellor and by Dr. William Peterson, C.M.G., as Principal, was presented in December to His Excellency the Governor-General, Visitor of the University. According to this statement satisfactory progress had been made in every department and "a really high standard of achievement" reached. "Apart from efficient and successful teaching in all branches of the curriculum it is not too much to say that the researches of some of our most distinguished Professors, whom it would be invidious to mention by name, have made the University even more widely known than it was before." Reference was made to the need of new endowments in the Faculty of Arts; gratification was expressed at the success of the Royal Victoria College for Women during the year and in which the number of resident pupils was stated to be increasing steadily; attention was called to the small proportion of male graduates of the University who went into the Provincial schools as teachers; approval was given to the suggestion made by Professor Adams, of London, as to the establishment of a Chair of Education but fears were expressed that the profession was not sufficiently attractive and remunerative to warrant it at present.

The departments of Civil, Mechanical and Electrical Engineering were reported to be over-crowded and either restriction in numbers, or increased building accommodation, necessary. Reference

was made to the regrettable retirement of Dr. Robert Craik, Dean
of the Faculty of Medicine; to the rank of Professor Emeritus
granted Dr. G. P. Birdwood in the same Faculty; to the removal
by death of Dr. Wyatt G. Johnston, only a month after his
appointment to the Strathcona Chair of Hygiene; and to the
accession of Dr. T. G. Roddick, M.P., to the Deanship of the Faculty.
The thanks of the University were accorded, in the Report, to Sir
W. C. Macdonald for a donation of $20,000 in the preceding March
to enable the Faculty of Arts to acquire certain books, etc., essential
to its work; and approval was expressed of the efforts being made
by the undergraduates for the establishment of a Gymnasium.   It
was stated that Sir William Macdonald had continued his previous
year's Travelling Scholarships and reference was made to the
second year affiliation of Vancouver College.   The agreement
made, as to local examinations in Music, with the Associated Board
of the Royal Academy of Music and the Royal College of Music of
London, was stated to have been renewed, the high standard of
the examinations was referred to and success hoped for from the
coming visit to Canada of Sir Alexander Mackenzie, the head of
the first-named institution.

During the educational year, 1901-2, McGill conferred 176
degrees, including 10 in Law, 82 in Medicine, 41 in Arts, 35 in
Applied Science and 8 in Veterinary Science.   Examinations for
the Certificate of Associate in Arts were held in June, 1902, at 33
different centres and for matriculation into the different Faculties
of the University at 45 centres.   The successful candidates in the
first case numbered 133 and in the second 55—with 130 more in
the preliminary parts only.   The students in attendance during the
sessions were 47 in the Faculty of Law; 455 in that of Medicine;
290 in that of Arts—of whom 129 were women and 161 men; 250
in that of Applied Sciences; and 16 in the Faculty of Veterinary
Science.   Deducting 17 who were registered in different Faculties
the total was, therefore, 1,041 students; while McGill Normal
School contained 168 teachers in training.   New endowments, or
donations, during the year included that of Sir W. C. Macdonald,
already mentioned, together with the gift of a lot of land for
building purposes and $5,000 for miscellaneous objects; $42,500
from Lord Strathcona for the maintenance of the Royal Victoria
College; a continuance by Mrs. Peter Redpath of her late husband's
annual subscription to the Museum and Library of $1,500 and an
addition of $500 to her own yearly gift of $5,000 for the same
purposes; the sum of $9,534 from the subscribers to the Alexander
Mackenzie Memorial Fund for the foundation of Fellowships in
Political Science; and prizes, etc., from various gentlemen or firms
including $125 from Mr. George Hague.

In addition to the changes mentioned by the annual Report
there were several important appointments during the educational
year.   Dr. Robert Craik became a member of the Board of
Governors; R. F. Ruttan, B.A., M.D., succeeded Dr. Girdwood as

Professor of Chemistry; Hermann Walter, M.A., Ph.D., was appointed Professor of Modern Languages; Alfred Stansfield, D.SC., became Professor of Metallurgy; H. T. Barnes, D.Sc., was appointed Assistant Professor of Physics, L. Herdt, E.E., Assistant Professor in Electrical Engineering, and J. G. G. Kerry, Assistant Professor of Surveying. Messrs. W. W. Chipman, B.A., M.D., W. R. Fraser, B.A., Ph.D., G. W. MacDougall and J. W. A. Hickson, M.A., Ph.D., were appointed Lecturers in different departments; while Mr. J. A. Nicholson, M.A., became Registrar of the University. The students of McGill came, during the year, from all parts of Canada and a few from Great Britain and the United States. In the Faculty of Medicine, for instance, there were 140 students from Ontario, 142 from Quebec, 49 from New Brunswick, 20 from Prince Edward Island, 28 from Nova Scotia and 18 from British Columbia. The United States contributed 42, Ireland 1, the West Indies 7, and Newfoundland 6.

Under the corporate and historic name of the Royal Institution for the Advancement of Learning, McGill University showed a balance sheet, on June 30th, 1902, of donations amounting to $2,265,964 and of endowments totaling $3,009,994. Upon the other side of the account were immovable property, such as buildings, etc., valued at $1,297,023; movable property such as collections, apparatus, books and equipment, valued at $816,715; and investments in mortgages, bonds, etc., of $3,485,098. The income for the year was $336,193, of which $68,389 came from fees, $154,132 from investments, and $84,486 from donations and subscriptions. The expenditures were $395,286, of which $171,960 was for salaries and wages, $27,062 for apparatus and equipment and $16,991 for repairs, etc. On capital account $424,441 was received and disbursed during the fiscal year.

On April 30th, the annual Convocation was held and was marked by seven, out of the thirteen Honours awarded, falling to the female graduates. Only one gold medal in the Arts course was given and this went to Miss A. W. Nolan of the Royal Victoria College. The degree of D.Sc. (in course) was granted to Professor Frank Dawson Adams, Ph.D., and to Mr. William Bell Dawson, M.A. A large number of other degrees were conferred and then, with Sir William Macdonald presiding, Dr. Alexander Johnson, Dean of the Faculty of Arts, presented his annual Report. He went at length into the desirability and possibility of creating a McGill College in completion of the work and aim of a University. At present there was only the latter and therefore the educational ideal, the British system of higher education, was only half realized. He suggested the recently formed Christian Association amongst the students as a basis for the social and religious life connected with a College, proper, and referred to 1902 as the Jubilee year of the University under its amended charter and the centennial year under that of the Royal Institution.

Dean Johnson concluded his speech as follows: "In spite of the wonderful progress of the University, half of its ideal is still left for the future to develop. What better time to make a beginning of this half than the present jubilee year, this centennial year? What nobler monument in recognition of the great services of the Board of Governors can the friends of the University raise than a Christian Association building, this new College, or beginning of a new College, of the University?" Professor Henry T. Bovey then submitted a Report as Dean of the Faculty of Applied Science and Professor F. P. Walton, one as Dean of the Faculty of Law. Principal Peterson followed in an address during which he expressed appreciation of Mr. Cecil Rhodes' bequests and described Oxford as a great school of manners as well as of learning and one which turned out four-square men fitted to meet the duties, as well as the business of life. He mentioned the fact of having recently represented McGill at the Universities of Glasgow, Yale, Johns Hopkins and Columbia and continued in the following terms:

There is a growing element of practicality in Universities ; but this does not mean that they should teach money-making. They should enrich the individual life, and the advantage of associating professional pursuits with them is that these pursuits may be uplifted by them. So the profession of law has helped itself by coming unreservedly within the University. So it is equally true of medicine that the University is over, above and around the Faculty. In years to come it will be seen how much can be accomplished by the independence and co-ordination of the Faculties all working together for the good of the University.

As McGill is the heart of English education in the Province of Quebec, so the University of Laval is the centre of French educational life and interests. Some 19 Classical Colleges **Laval University and Other Quebec Colleges** in that Province, comprising a mixed system of higher and elementary learning, conferring certain degrees and including both men and boys amongst their students, are affiliated with Laval. During the year 1900-01 they had 2,170 pupils in the Commercial courses and 3,745 in the Classical courses, with an average attendance of 5,462 and a percentage of attendance to registration of 92·23. Their lay Professors numbered 35 and their Religious Professors (Roman Catholic) totalled 514 in number. Laval University itself is largely under the control and financial management of the Quebec Seminary and its Arts course is chiefly given in the affiliated Colleges. The students at Quebec numbered 358 in 1900-01, and those at the Montreal branch were 719 in number. The latter institution controlled the Montreal Polytechnic School, at which 35 pupils were enrolled during the year, with six graduates receiving the diploma of Civil Engineer. The assets of the Polytechnic School were stated in the Report of the Quebec Department of Public Instruction for 1902 as being $35,990, its liabilities as $16,000 and its receipts $17,431, including a Government grant of $10,000.

In 1902 His Eminence, Miecislas, Cardinal Ledochowski, head of the Congregation of the Propaganda at Rome, was Cardinal Protector of the University. The Apostolic Chancellor was Mgr. Bégin, Archbishop of Quebec, and the Vice-Chancellor was Mgr.

Bruchési, Archbishop of Montreal. The Rev. Dr. Mathieu was Rector at Quebec and the Rev. Canon Archambault, Rector at Montreal. The graduates in 1901-2 as Doctors in Theology numbered 4 and the Licentiates in Theology 1; the Doctors of Law numbered 2, including H. R. H. the Duke of Cornwall and York, the Bachelors at Law were 12, and the Licentiates 10; the Doctors in Medicine numbered 56 and the Bachelors in Medicine 24; the Masters in Arts numbered 7 and the Bachelors in Arts 15. There were also 5 Civil Engineers, 1 Bachelor in Applied Science, 2 Doctors and 4 Bachelors of Veterinary Medicine, 7 Bachelors of Letters and 4 Bachelors in Science who graduated during the year. In the Petit Seminaire at Quebec there were in the same Session 538 students, of whom 265 were in residence.

On June 24th Laval University celebrated at Quebec its Jubilee, or 50th anniversary as a chartered educational institution. Everything that could make such an event impressive or mark it with surroundings of ecclesiastical splendour and public interest was done. The procession was two miles in length and addresses at the University were delivered by the leading men of the Province in varied spheres of public, educational and religious life. During the speech of the Rector, Rev. O. E. Mathieu, D.D., C.M.G., he used these striking words : " Our mission is not so much managing capital as stirring ideas ; not so much lighting up factory fires as shedding afar the home light of religion and high thought. For, as has been said, nothing great or lasting was ever founded upon materialism." On November 4th, following, the Law students of Laval University in Montreal held their annual banquet, with Sir Wilfrid Laurier and Hon. J. Israel Tarte amongst their guests. The Premier's speech was reminiscent in tone and non-political; that of Mr. Tarte was aggressive and dealt with various current topics. The Law Faculty of the Quebec branch of the University held its annual banquet a little later, on November 28th, and amongst the speakers were His Honour Sir Louis Jetté, Mgr. J. C. K. Laflamme, Dean of the Faculty of Arts, Mr. Justice F. Langelier, Hon. M. E. Bernier, Dominion Minister of Inland Revenue, Sir C. A. P. Pelletier, Hon. J. Israel Tarte, Hon. Horace Archambault, Hon. A. Robitaille, Hon. E. J. Flynn, Hon. L. P. Pelletier, Hon. T. Chapais, Hon. Charles Fitzpatrick, Dominion Minister of Justice, and the Hon. H. G. Carroll, Solicitor-General.

The University of Bishop's College, Lennoxville, represents the convictions and educational ambitions of the Church of England in the Province of Quebec. Its Convocation was held on June 19th and was marked by the presentation of the Hon. degree of D.C.L. to Mr. George W. Parmelee and that of D.D. to the Very Rev. L. Evans, D.C.L., Dean of Montreal. The Chancellor, Dr. John Hamilton, M.A., presided, and various prizes were presented and reports received ; while the degree of M.A. was conferred, in course, upon four graduates and that of B.A. upon one. Principal, the Rev. Dr. J. P. Whitney, in his annual Report, stated that the total number of students had been 39, and asked for increased provision in some of their departments of work. It would be an advantage if the suspended Law Faculty could be restored, but this would involve an endowed Professorship or Lectureship. Philosophy should be recognized and the Chair of Mathematics should be separated from its dependence upon the Professor of Theology. English and English Literature should also receive more attention. He hoped much from the efforts of the Alumni Society in raising an additional endowment in Natural Science, and referred with satisfaction to the appointment of the Rev. Harold Hamilton as resident Lecturer. The Rev. Dr. F. J. B. Allnatt, Dean of the Faculty of Divinity, reported 24 of the students in residence as candidates for Holy Orders and referred to the recent appointment of the Rev. E. A. Dunn of Cambridge as Professor of Pastoral Theology. Mr. H. J. H. Petry, Head Master of Bishop's College School, reported 91 boys in attendance at the beginning of the educational year. Four had gone up to McGill for matriculation and 28 new ones had joined during the year now past.

Of the minor institutions of higher learning in the Province there are five of importance—all theological in character. They include the Montreal Presbyterian College, with 53 students in the session of 1902; the Diocesan Theological College (Anglican) with 29 students; the Wesleyan Theological College with 16 students; the Montreal Congregational College with 15 students; and the Wesleyan College, Stanstead, with 141 students. The first four are affiliated with McGill University.* The incidents of the year in the Presbyterian College were the Convocation of April 2nd, and the death in December of its distinguished Principal the Rev. Dr. D. H. MacVicar. At the Convocation the Hon. degree of D.D. was conferred upon the Rev. Professor Kerswill, M.A., B.D., of Lincoln University, Pennsylvania, and the Rev. P. C. MacLeod of Attwell, Ont. Four graduates were given the degree of B.D. and diplomas presented to eight others. A large list of prize winners were announced by Principal MacVicar, who presided and referred, in his address, to the falling off in the United States, in Great Britain, and now in Canada, of candidates for the Ministry. He urged the attention of Christian parents to this requirement and need of the Church and to the present tendency of teaching children social, political and commercial aspirations rather than those of a religious life. The College now had over 300 Alumni serving the Church in various fields. He concluded by saying that another Scholarship had been recently endowed through a bequest from the late Mrs. M. J. Allsopp of Farnham. Dr. MacVicar died suddenly on December 15th. He had built up the institution and presided over it during nearly 35 years and his death was regarded as not only a great loss to education but to the cause and interests of the Church in which he was such a well-known leader.

---

* Note—These figures are given in the Annual Report for 1901-2 of McGill University.

During the year the resignation of the Rev. Dr. J. T. L. Maggs Principal of the Wesleyan Theological College, took place, and went into force on August 1st. He was succeeded by the Rev. Dr. William I. Shaw, Chairman of the Protestant Committee of Public Instruction in the Province. On April 22nd the annual Convocation of the Congregational College of Canada was held in Montreal with Principal, the Rev. Dr. E. Munson Hill, presiding. The annual Report referred to the founding of a new Professorship and asked aid in raising the $25,000 still required in that connection. Medals, prizes and bursaries were awarded and the degree of B.D. conferred upon the Rev. H. G. Rice, B.A. That of Hon. D.D. had been offered to the Rev. Hugh Pedley, B.A., but refused as "sometimes proving a stumbling block to the Pastor in his work." At the opening exercises of the College on October 16th, following, the Hon. degree of D.D. was conferred upon the Rev. Alfred Rowland, B.A., LL.B., of London, England.

The University of Toronto was prominently before the public during 1902. Its new Alumni Associations in different parts of the Province, its financial condition, and its relations **Toronto University in 1902** with the Government, all helped to this end. On January 24th the Guelph Alumni Association held a banquet which was notable for the presence of the University Chancellor, Sir W. R. Meredith, and the Principal of University College, Dr. Maurice Hutton. The former in his speech declared that it was the work of the Alumni in the past year which had largely met the financial difficulties of the institution and pro-cured necessary aid from the Government. He spoke strongly as to the advantage of College federation and hoped yet to see Trinity and McMaster within the circle of consolidation. As to money they only needed from the Government a paltry $30,000 or $40,000 a year. "What he now asked was that the members of the Association would continue to press upon public attention the needs of the University; would continue to educate the people as to the duty of the State toward it; and, if this were thoroughly done, such a case could be made to the Government as to lead it to provide all that was reasonably required. The position of the University was yet critical; but for an unexpected payment received on account of some land there would have been a very considerable deficit on this year's operations. There was absolute need that the Government should add to the sum which was granted last Session." Principal Hutton urged the need of residence buildings at University College—especially for the women—and traced the changes of recent years in the management and character of Universities.

A deputation from the University waited upon the Government on February 12th to urge the granting of $50,000 toward the construction of a proposed medical building—the Faculty of Medicine undertaking to obtain the remaining $75,000 required. Dr. R. A. Reeve, Dean of this Faculty, presented the case and was supported by Dr. John Hoskin, K.C., Chairman of the University Board of

Trustees, and others. The Premier and Minister of Education promised every possible consideration. At the March meeting of the University Senate arrangements were made to separate the Board of Studies for Medicine, Dentistry and Pharmacy into three distinct departments. Convocation was held on June 13th, with the Chancellor in the chair, and the first proceeding was the unveiling of a portrait by Mr. J. W. L. Forster of the Hon. William Mulock, K.C., M.P., for many years Vice-Chancellor of the institution. Speeches in this connection were delivered by Principal Caven of Knox, and Mr. Justice Moss, the present Vice-Chancellor. The Hon. degree of LL.D. was then conferred upon the Hon. J. D. Armour, Chief Justice of Ontario; Dr. Ira Remson, President of Johns Hopkins University; Dr. W. H. Drummond, F.R.S.C., of Montreal; James Pliny Whitney, K.C., D.C.L., M.P.P., Conservative Leader in Ontario; James J. Foy, K.C., M.P.P., Dr. R. A. Reeve, Dean of the Medical Faculty, Professor R. Ramsay Wright, M.D., Professor John Galbraith, Dean of the Faculty of Science, and Principal Maurice Hutton, M.A., of University College. Mr. F. H. Torrington was given the Hon. degree of Mus. Dr. and Messrs. R. Davidson and R. G. Murison, the degree of Ph.D. Many lesser degrees, in course, were conferred as well as medals, prizes and scholarships.

In the speeches various hopes were expressed that the University would receive a greater measure of Government aid. Chief Justice Armour regretted that the Government had not shown more appreciation of the institution in this respect and thought that " in the interest of the public, much more than in the interest of the University itself, they ought to give such aid as would put it beyond want for any learning which might be thought fit to be given within its walls." Mr. Whitney expressed the hope that the public and the politicians would unite in making the path of the great Provincial University smoother and easier than it was to-day. At the banquet of the Alumni Association in the evening President Loudon presided with many prominent guests around him. In replying to one of the toasts Mr. J. P. Whitney expressed the belief that enough attention had not been given to the University during the past twenty years either by its graduates, the public, or the Government. In the discussion of many matters its interests, requirements and possibilities, had been neglected. He urged attention to its special claims upon the Province and asked each graduate to become a centre of influence in making the people understand their duty to the institution. Mr. Goldwin Smith followed and, after claiming to be the father of the University federation idea in Canada, referred to the question of whether the object of a University should be culture, or instruction in practical subjects. " The two," he thought, " were not mutually exclusive ; high instruction in practical subjects brought culture with it. The proper duty of a University was to teach high subjects of all kinds—not handicrafts or trades." Other speakers were Sir W. R. Meredith, President Remson, Dr. R. A. Reeve, and Mr. J. A. Paterson, K.C. At the opening of the Wycliffe Convocation Hall, on October 7th, Sir W. R. Meredith criticised the Government for not giving the University more aid and asked the Minister of Education, who was present, if it was seemly for a great Provincial institution of learning to held its Convocation in a Gymnasium! He then proceeded as follows:

There is strange apathy to the needs of this Provincial University. It may be treated as axiomatic that the highest educational body in this rich Province of Ontario should be properly equipped; but the increasing expenses of modern education have gone beyond our resources for want of proper support from the Province. The real weakness is not with the people, but with those who will not trust the people. When I have tried to excuse the parsimonious treatment we receive from the Legislature, I find that even the rural districts favour proper support for their University. I think that a Legislature which would so endow this University as to enable it to meet the requirements of to-day would have the endorsement of the people of Ontario. The true policy should be to provide what is necessary for the efficient working of the University and that is the proper policy for the Government; and any Government that takes that course will be sustained by the people of Ontario.

The teaching staff of the University, according to the Annual Report of the President for the year ending June 30th, 1902, consisted of 70 Professors, Lecturers, Demonstrators, Assistants, etc., in Arts, 56 in Medicine and 20 in Applied Science. The total number of students was 1,646, of whom 882 were in Arts, 474 in Medicine and 290 in Applied Science. Of the candidates examined and numbering, altogether, 1,885 there were 912 in Arts, 465 in Medicine, 13 in Law, 264 in Applied Science and Engineering, 6 in Pedagogy, 10 in Agriculture, 114 in Dentistry, 51 in Pharmacy and 50 in Music. The degrees conferred during the academic year numbered 350, as follows: Honorary, 15; Ph.D., 2; M.A., 24; B.A., 130; M.D., 1; M.B., 55; LL.B., 6; D.D.S, 30; B.E., 1; B.A.Sc., 15; B.S.A., 7; B.Paed., 2; Mus.Bac., 2; Phm.B., 51. The details of student attendance may be summarized briefly:

ARTS ....University College..Regular (B.A. Course)..	432
" " ..Occasional " ..	128
" " ..Graduate " ..	14
" " ..Ph.D. Course..........	4
University......... "	11
Victoria College....Regular (B.A. Course)..	224
" " ....Occasional " ..	47
" " ....Graduate " ..	19
" " ....Ph.D. Course..........	3
MEDICINE........................Regular...............	407
Occasional............	67
APPLIED SCIENCE...................Regular...............	288
Occasional............	2

Several changes in the staff occurred during the University year. Dr. T. L. Walker, of the University of Calcutta, was appointed to the Chair of Mineralogy and Petrography; Dr. J. C. Fields became Lecturer in Mathematics, Dr. B. Arthur Bensley, Lecturer on Zoology, Dr. W. H. Piersol, Lecturer on Histology and Elementary Biology and Mr. J. H. Faull, Lecturer on Botany.

Various promotions or transfers were also made in different departments of work. A new course leading to the degree of B.A. was instituted in the Department of Biological and Physical Science so as to enable graduates to enter the Faculty of Medicine with third year standing and thus to obtain their degrees of B.A. and M.B. in six years. A curriculum was also arranged for local examinations in Music and arrangements were initiated for instructions in Household Science and Forestry. In another connection President Loudon wrote as follows: " A constant and growing demand exists for young men for business posts who have enjoyed the advantages of a University education and a number of graduates, who have entered upon positions of this nature, have met with remarkable success. In view of a feeling existing widely in business circles that a shorter course leading to a diploma instead of the usual degree in Arts would be of advantage to young men contemplating a business career, and especially in view of the representation made to this effect by the Toronto Board of Trade, the Senate instituted in June, 1901, a two years' course in Commercial Science leading to a diploma in the subject. This course came into operation at the beginning of the Session 1901-02."

Special University lectures were given during the year by Dr. J. C. Glashan of Ottawa and M. Hugues Le Roux of Paris and by Dr. W. H. Drummond, Prof. A. P. Coleman, Prof. Halliday Douglas, Provost Street Macklem, F. C. Wade, K.C., and Prof. McGregor Young. The Library was reported to contain 72,337 volumes and 22,500 pamphlets. The new volumes added in 1901-02 were 4,201 and amongst the special donations were $10,000 from Professor and Mrs. Goldwin Smith for a "King Alfred Memorial Fund"—of which the proceeds were to go towards the purchase of historical publications—and a valuable bequest of books, coins and medals from the late Rev. Dr. Scadding. Buildings were reported in course of erection for medical and scientific purposes and Victoria College had constructed a residence for women students. A new Physics Building, a Convocation Hall and a residence building for University students of both sexes were described by the President as very greatly needed. In financial matters the revenue, in 1901-02, of the Faculty of Arts (University and University College) was $149,-089 and the expenditure $158,650; in the Faculty of Medicine the revenue was $37,094 and the expenditure the same; in that of Applied Science and Engineering the revenue and expenditure each amounted to $37,539. In the departments maintained by the Government and including Chemistry, Physics, Mineralogy, and Geology the expenses were $30,436.

The annual banquet of the University Faculty of Medicine was held on December 3rd and was notable for speeches by the Hon. George E. Foster, Mr. Byron E. Walker and Professor Barker of Chicago. The last-named was a former graduate of Toronto University and stated that in his University of Chicago most of the Fellowships were given to Canadians—because they deserved them—and that most of these men were Toronto graduates.   Mr. Walker expressed the belief that the University should be maintained apart from Government grants and by a direct tax upon the people of a fraction of a mill.   This plan had been adopted in Michigan, Minnesota and other American States.   On December 10th it was announced that the Ontario Government had decided to approve of Toronto University establishing and granting a degree of Bachelor in Household Science.   English, mathematics, and history were to be obligatory in this course, with three other subjects selected from Latin, Greek, French, German and experimental science.   In the first year's examination the principles of cooking and house-keeping were to be amongst the subjects while the candidate must have had a six months' course of physical training.   The second year would include various subjects of learned instruction and the construction, care and conduct of a house.   There was also to be another course in physical training. The third year was to include English, history, economics, political science, biology and practical chemistry.   For three years' successful work along these lines the student might receive a Diploma in Household Science.   The fourth year course was to include English, ethics, economics, and sanitary science, with continued special work in the University laboratories.   Success in this would give the Bachelor's degree and, in the opinion of the Minister of Education, add both dignity and culture to the future household or modern home.

To Queen's University the year 1902 was an eventful period. It opened with the apparent recovery of Principal Grant from his

Queen's University, Kingston

prolonged illness and the delivery, on January 6th, of a careful, rounded and effective address covering the position and prospects of Canada and referring, at some length, to his own 25 years' connection with the institution in which he spoke and of his motives in originally accepting the post of Principal.   " I believed that the highest University ideal was not government by a denomination, but self-government, and that on Boards of Governors only public and educational interests should be represented.   But clearly, Ontario needed more than one University, were it only to save the one from the blight which Napoleon's centralized University of France (with the suppression of the old Universities) brought upon higher education in that country; and Queen's, from its location, traditions and freedom from denominational control seemed peculiarly fitted to be the second, and of all the most value to the Province, from its distinctiveness of type."   Of late years he had felt that even a nominal connection with the Presbyterian Church through its General Assembly should be severed and, accordingly, after careful consideration by the latter body and the University Council the principle of separation had been unanimously accepted and the way was now clear for Legislative action and the establishment of Queen's as " the public and undenominational

University of Eastern Ontario, in particular, and Canada in general."

Convocation was held on April 30th and the day was marked by the absence of the Principal through illness; by Sir Sandford Fleming, Chancellor of the University, laying the foundation stone of the partially-completed Engineering building; by the Ontario Minister of Education laying the corner-stone of a new Physics and Geology building; by the bestowal of the Hon. degree of LL.D. upon Mr. N. W. Hoyles, K.C., and Mr. John Seath of Toronto, and that of D.D. upon the Rev. Dr. Thomas Hart of Manitoba College, Winnipeg, and the Rev. Prof. William Clark of Trinity University, Toronto; and by the Hon. Mr. Harcourt's promise to aid in the organization of a Department of Forestry. The latter in his speech paid a high tribute to Principal Grant as a man of letters and a man of action, referred to the success of the Schools of Agriculture and Mining which had been established in connection with the University, and declared that none of the expenditures of the Province had been more wisely made, in the opinion of the Government, than those relating to Queen's. A little later, on May 18th, it was announced that the Trustees had appointed Mr. P. G. C. Campbell, B.A., to be Professor of Romance Languages in place of Prof. J. McGillivray, Ph.D., who assumed the Professorship of German.

The death of the distinguished Principal occurred on May 10th. Of this event something is said elsewhere, but in its special connection with the University a few more lines may be written. All the tributes paid to Dr. Grant dealt more or less with the essential union of the man and his work. Mr. John Charlton, M.P., in the Ottawa *Journal*, pointed out that when the late Principal assumed charge the financial interests of the University were at a low ebb. He speedily raised an endowment of $150,000. In 1899 he added another endowment of $250,000 to this sum, and thereafter other sums were obtained by his untiring exertions. "This great institution of learning owes its existence, humanly speaking, to the efforts of its honoured Principal." When he took control, it was elsewhere pointed out, there were less than 100 students; now there were about 700. In Ottawa, on May 11th, the Rev. S. G. Bland declared that as a result of his work Queen's was now second to none, "in the spirituality of its aims, the intellectual enthusiasm it awakened amongst the students, and the freedom, disinterestedness and loyalty of its search for truth." In the Halifax *Herald* of May 12th the Rev. Dr. Robert Murray paid a further tribute to this element in the life-work of Principal Grant. Speaking of his going to Kingston and what followed, he said:

The University felt at once the stirrings of a new life. A total revolution —call it evolution of you like—was effected. Men of wealth came to the rescue, but the givings of the rank and file were of still more value. A steady stream of liberality from Kingston, and from the country at large, came in response to the eloquent pleadings and the bright and eager canvassing of the new Principal. He was most fortunate in the men with whom he surrounded himself in all the Faculties. Buildings were erected, Faculties were multiplied, students came in by scores and hundreds from all parts of the Dominion. For example, a School of Mining was established in connection with the University, and though the McGill School of Mining and the School at Toronto are equipped with all that money can secure, the School at Kingston has easily kept pace with each of them in efficiency and popularity. Queen's has now a group of stately buildings to accommodate her work—five of them. When Dr. Grant became Principal there was but one poor little old building, and it was sufficient for the needs of the hour.

At the Presbyterian General Assembly meeting in Winnipeg during June, Mr. G. M. Macdonnell, K.C., presented a Report from Queen's University, and stated that it was now the intention of the institution to become technically and legally independent as it long had been in practice. In other words, it was to be divided in functions and control and, while the Arts Faculty was to be entirely separated from the Church, that of Theology was to be brought into still closer relation with the General Assembly. These changes were later approved by the Assembly under a motion presented by Principal Caven and the Rev. Dr. Robert Campbell, and a Committee was appointed to confer with the Trustees on the matter generally. Following Principal Grant's death some discussion took place as to his successor, and the names of Rev. J. A. Macdonald of *The Westminster*, Rev. Dr. Herridge of Ottawa and the Rev. Dr. Barclay of Montreal were freely mentioned. On September 17th it was announced that the last-named had been unanimously nominated by the Trustees. The salary, it was stated, would be largely increased over the $3,000 which Dr. Grant had received. Dr. Barclay, however, hesitated to accept, and after receiving various expressions of regret from his own church and various city interests, finally declined the position.

On November 21st it was announced that the Rev. Dr. Daniel Minor Gordon, Professor of Theology in the Halifax Presbyterian College and formerly Pastor of St. Andrew's Church, Ottawa, and of Knox Church, Winnipeg, had been offered the Principalship. He was definitely appointed on December 5th following. Approval was very general in the matter. The Winnipeg *Tribune* of November 27th described him as having an unusual number of personal friends, as being a high type of the Canadian scholar and Christian gentleman, as being a manly man and well suited to guide young and earnest men. The Kingston *Whig* of November 22nd declared him to be a man after the late Principal's own heart. " He has had a varied occupation and experience, and they have, no doubt, widened his view and given him the peculiar qualification which the Principalship of a great University requires. Travel, contact with men, pastoral and administrative duty, academic and professional service, have had their effects on this man of high ideals, strong character and progressive spirit, and he will enter upon his new field of labour with the ardour, deliberation and devotion which give assurance of success." The Halifax *Herald* of two days later, thought that Dr. Gordon's whole career had marked him out by native ability, special training, polished manner and knowledge of public affairs to fill just such a post.

Meanwhile, the new Convocation Hall of Queen's, which had been a cherished object of the late Principal's and for which $34,000 had been collected by the students and graduates largely in his honour, had been got well under way. It was now decided to call it the Grant Memorial Hall and, on November 6th, the corner-stone was laid by Sir Sandford Fleming, and a deep, admiring tribute paid by him to the late Principal as a man of many gifts, a man of strong intellect, a scholar, a teacher, a preacher and a theologian, a man of affairs and of singular resourcefulness. The Rev. Dr. Ross of Montreal followed, and then the Premier of Ontario delivered an address which was a broad, harmonious presentation of Dr. Grant's place in the political, national, Imperial and educational life of Canada. It may be added that toward the close of the year Mr. J. C. Gwillun, B.Sc., was appointed Acting-Professor of Mining Engineering and Mr. Reginald Brock, M.A., Acting-Professor of Geology and Petrography.

McMaster University, the intellectual centre of Baptist denominational work in Canada, held its Commencement exercises in Toronto on May 6th and 7th. The event of the first day was the baccalaureate sermon preached by the Rev. Dr. Anderson and the unveiling of a portrait of the Rev. Professor David Morse Welton, M.A., D.D., Ph.D., in the Castle Memorial Hall. On the following day the Walmer Road Baptist Church was the scene of the annual conferment of degrees. Chancellor, the Rev. Dr. O. C. S. Wallace, presided, and the Hon. degree of D.D. was given the Rev. W. W. Weeks of Toronto and that of LL.D. to Professor Alexander Charles McKay of McMaster and the Hon. George W. Ross, Premier of Ontario. The degree of M.A. was granted to three graduates, that of B.A. to 31 graduates, that of B.Th. to three and that of B.D. to two graduates. Prizes and scholarships were then awarded and the Chancellor announced that the Rev. George Cross, M.A., B.Th., Ph.D., had been appointed to succeed the Rev. Dr. Newman as Professor of History. Addresses followed from the Rev. Dr. Weeks, Professor McKay and the Hon. Dr. Ross.

The Premier's speech was one of marked eloquence. He took an outlook upon national conditions and described the requisites for greatness in that respect as three in number—a resolute spirit in meeting difficulties; a responsive statesmanship in the community; a consolidation of national power. The first quality had marked the Greeks and Romans and Swiss and Scotch and English at different and famous periods of their existence as a people. "Let us infuse into all the purposes of our life, whether academic, educational, religious or political, that same confidence, that spirit of self-reliance." The need of the second was shown in the history of Charles I. and James II. and in the loss of the American Colonies. "Society was an organism and the institutions of to-day would not fit the second or third generation which comes after us." Responsive statemanship was going to revolutionize the Imperial system and bring a population of 20,000,000 to Canada in the next 30 years. As to the consolidation of national power everything was in our favour. "I rejoice that there are in Canada so many formative influences—Public Schools so well endowed, Universities with such unselfish aims, freedom in Church and State. If, with these conditions we fail, on us should rest the blame."

At the Baptist Convention in Montreal, on October 16th, Mr. D. E. Thomson, K.C., of Toronto, spoke at length of the great success which had come to their educational work. At McMaster, he said, the attainment of a broad, general culture was the aim, while specialization, when desired, was given in post-graduate work. "On all hands it was admitted that the work done was of the highest character." The enrolment in the B.A. course, was particularly satisfactory and the financial difficulties of the past had been removed. Chancellor Wallace presented on the same day the annual Report of the University and affiliated institutions. It showed an enrolment of 192 students in the University proper, of whom 135 were in Arts and 47 in Theology and presented a marked advance on the previous year. It showed, through Principal A. L. McCrimmon, an enrolment at the Woodstock College of 132 students as compared with 125 in 1900-1 and at Moulton Ladies' College, through Mrs. J. E. Wells, the Principal, a total enrolment of 206 students. These students were of various religious denominations including, at Woodstock, 91 Baptists, 20 Presbyterians, 8 Episcopalians and 12 Methodists and, at the Ladies' College, 72 Baptists and the rest scattering. The Chancellor summarized the condition of the University as follows:

These extracts show that there were gathered in our schools last year more than 500 students; that these young people were for the most part studious and earnest; that many of them were blessed spiritually; that the schools were used for the conversion of a considerable number of our sons and daughters; that the quality of the work done by our several Faculties is unsurpassed by schools of similar rank; and that the Principals of our schools, as they take a close view of the work under their hands, are filled with courage and hopefulness.

Trinity University, Toronto, entered, in 1902, upon a prosperous year and one which was marked by an important event in its history. At the annual reunion of the Alumni, which **Trinity University and its Jubilee** took place on January 7th, the Rev. Dr. Street Macklem, Provost of the University, expressed encouraging views as to the possibility of federation upon satisfactory terms with Toronto University, referred with pride to the acceptance of the Chancellorship of Trinity by Mr. Christopher Robinson, K.C., M.A., and spoke of the coming Jubilee of their foundation. On January 15th one of the most distinguished gatherings in the history of the institution met in Convocation Hall to witness the installation of the new Chancellor. Amongst those present were the Bishop of Toronto, President Loudon, Mayor Howland, C.M.G., Principal Hutton, Dr. G. R. Parkin, G.M.G., the Hon. G. W.

Ross, W. R. Brock, M.P., J. J. Foy, K.C., M.P.P., and amongst the speakers were Sir W. R. Meredith, Chancellor of Toronto University, the Hon. R. Harcourt, Minister of Education, Mr. J. P. Whitney, K.C., M.P.P., Chancellor Burwash of Victoria, Chancellor Wallace of McMaster, Rev. Canon Welch, Mr. Gilbert Parker, M.P., Mr. E. B. Osler, M.P., Lieut.-Colonel H. M. Pellatt, Dr. J. A. Worrell, K.C., Rev. Provost Street Macklem and the Rev. Professor Clark. After receiving the Hon. Degree of D.C.L. the new Chancellor spoke at some length, referred to the great interest he had always felt in the University and to its prolonged good work in the past. He then dealt with present and future issues as follows :

Whether we go on as we have been doing or whether we should enter into closer relations with our Provincial University is a matter for the future. That I cannot tell. One thing is quite certain. Trinity must always remember the object for which she was brought into existence, the combination of religious instruction, according to the doctrines of the Church of England, with secular learning and, next to that, should adhere to the residential system, both in connection with the teaching and for other reasons. These two primary objects must always be safeguarded and her ability to carry out these purposes must never be interfered with or prejudiced. Subject to these two requirements, I believe, speaking now as a general subject entirely, that confederation is desirable. I say so for these reasons : I believe that no one, if higher education was now for the first time to be provided in this Province, would advocate our present system. I believe, in the next place, that it is the result not so much of the differences which now prevail as of old controversies which have long since been settled and of reasons which I trust and believe have entirely passed away.

On January 24th, following this event, it was announced that the Rev. Professor Clark had been appointed Deputy Chancellor by the new head of the University, and that Mr. Frederick Nicholls had been elected to the Corporation in place of the late C. J. Campbell. From the 22nd to the 25th of June the Jubilee celebrations were held. On the first date mentioned, Sunday, sermons on religious education, with special reference to Trinity, were preached throughout the Anglican churches of Ontario. On the following day the students gave a representation of Aristophanes' comedy, "The Frogs," and a University luncheon was given, with addresses by the Provost, the Rev. Dr. C. W. E. Body, Canon Welch, Dr. Goldwin mith, Canon Whitney of Lennoxville, and others. June 4th was marked by a public reception and a reunion of graduates and, on the succeeding day, a thanksgiving service was held at St. James' Cathedral and a Jubilee Convocation at the University. In the latter connection a number of Honorary degrees were conferred. That of D.C.L. was granted to the following prominent Canadians : Sir Oliver Mowat, G.C.M.G., Lieutenant-Governor of Ontario ; Sir John Boyd, K.C.M.G., Chancellor of Ontario ; Mr. Justice P. Æ. Irving, of British Columbia ; Judge Senkler of the County of Perth ; Mr. J. P. Whitney, K.C., M.P.P. and Mr. Edward Douglas Armour, K.C.

Upon the following gentlemen the degree of Hon. D.C.L. was conferred "in recognition of distinguished service to the cause of education ": The Hon. Richard Harcourt, M.A., Minister of Education in Ontario; Dr. William Osler, of Baltimore; the Rev. Dr. J. P. Whitney of Bishop's College, Lennoxville; the Rev. J. O. Miller, M.A., Principal of Ridley College, St. Catharines; and Mr. James Bain, Jr., Chief Librarian, Toronto. It was also granted to the following six elected representatives of the six Dioceses of the Church of England in the Province of Ontario: The Ven. Thomas Llywd, Algoma; Ven. G. C. Mackenzie, Huron; Very Rev. Stuart Houston, M.A., Niagara; Ven. C. L. Worrell, M.A., Ontario; Ven. J. J. Bogert, M.A., Ottawa; Ven. T. W. Allen, M.A., Toronto. The degree of Hon. Doctor of Music was conferred upon Mr. J. Humphrey Anger, and that of Hon. M.A. upon the Rev. F. W. Kennedy, Missionary in Japan. An incident of the celebration was the publication of a handsome and valuable souvenir number of the *Trinity University Review* on June 25th.

The annual general meeting of the Corporation was held on October 24th, with the Chancellor in the chair, and amongst others present the Bishops of Toronto and Ontario and Mr. Justice Burbidge. The report for the academic year, ending September 30th, showed that it had opened with 115 students in Arts and Divinity taking full courses, and with 25 special students. The total number of students during the year in Arts, Divinity, Medicine, Law, Music and Dentistry was about 300. The degrees conferred included B.A., 23; M.A., 26; M.D., 44; D.C.L., 3; B.C.L., 5; B.M., 4; B.D., 2; D.D.S., 9; or a total of 116. The statement of the Board of Endowment showed subscriptions of $166,000 during the year and was presented by Lieut.-Colonel Pellatt. It was announced that prizes of different kinds had been given by Dr. G. S. Cæsar, Dr. C. V. Snelgrove and Mr. E. B. Osler, and that Mr. William McKenzie (himself a Presbyterian) had offered ten entrance Bursaries of $100 each with a view to bringing the "exceptional advantages" of the Trinity Arts course before the young men of Canada.

The University of Ottawa—conducted by the Oblate Fathers of Mary Immaculate—held its closing exercises on June 18th with **Ottawa University and other Ontario Colleges** Archbishop Duhamel, Apostolic Chancellor, presiding. The Hon. degree of LL.D. was conferred upon the Hon. Edward P. Morris, K.C., of St. John's, Newfoundland, and various other degrees, in course, together with gold and silver medals and prizes. The degree of Licentiate of Theology was given to one graduate, that of LL.B. to another, that of Licentiate of Philosophy to five graduates, that of Bachelor of Philosophy to six graduates, that of M.A. to one, and of B.A. to five graduates. From September 1st to date there were in attendance 24 Theolgical students, 52 Scholastic students and 395 students in the Arts, Collegiate, or Commercial courses. The Very Rev. J. E. Emery delivered an eloquent Rectorial address describing what he believed to be the scope and ultimate end of education. It was not simply the making of a living, the obtaining of food and raiment, or the harmonious development and perfecting of the physical, intellectual and moral faculties. It was the inculcation of true religious life:

And, note well, this is true, not only of what is termed religious education, but of education in the full sense of the word, for there is only one kind of education and religion is of its very essence. "A system of education," says Cardinal Manning, "not based on Christianity, is an imposture. It is not education, it cannot educate the people. Call it instruction, if you will, but, in the name of Christianity, and also of truth, let it not be called education." You might as well call the Tower of Babel the way to heaven. All this may be a hard saying to the worldly-minded but it is the truth. Behold then the ultimate end God has in view in the education of His children, the angels included ; Christ in the education of all mankind ; the Church in the education of all nations ; and the University of Ottawa in the education of all those whom Providence has confided to her care—namely the youth of the ecclesiastical Province of Ottawa by right, of the civil Province of Ontario without racial distinction, by privilege, and of all of those who are attracted from every point of the compass by the light of her guiding star. Behold, the ultimate end to which our maxim bids us to look,—human nature, brought to its highest perfection, raised to the most exalted plane possible, and invested with the plentitude of the Divinity.

Victoria University, Toronto, under the guidance of the Methodist General Conference and in affiliation with the University of Toronto, had in attendance during the Session of 1901-2, 271 students in Arts and 140 students in Theology. Deducting those enrolled in two Faculties, the total number of students was 316. Closely associated and affiliated with this institution was Albert College, Belleville, with the Rev. W. P. Dyer as Principal, and 302 students in attendance; the Ontario Ladies' College, Whitby, with the Rev. Dr. J. J. Hare as Principal, and 141 students in attendance; and Alma Ladies' College, St. Thomas, with the Rev. Dr. R. I. Warner as Principal, and 138 students in attendance. The Columbia College, New Westminster, B.C., was also in affiliation. The annual Convocation in Divinity was held on April 29th, when Chancellor Burwash presided, and conferred the degree of D.D. upon the Rev. Henry Youngman of Queensland, Australia, the Rev. Joseph R. Gundy of Strathroy, and the Rev. Robert I. Warner, M.A., of St. Thomas. That of B.D. was granted to 7 graduates, Certificates were awarded to 24 graduates in the Arts Conference, or ordinary Conference course, and a large number of prizes and medals were conferred. The Chancellor in his address drew attention to the fact that nearly sixty per cent. of the Divinity graduates had also taken the full course in Arts. "In this respect we are continually moving forward," he said. "We may soon, as some of our sister Colleges have talked of doing, make the standard for those entering our Ministry include a graduation in Arts as well as the complete course in Divinity. A large number who are now taking the full University course are fired with an ambition to have the best and most perfect preparation possible for their future work." Wycliffe College, an Anglican institution of higher learning in Toronto, held its annual Convocation on May 1st with Mr. N. W. Hoyles, K.C., LL.D., in the chair and surrounded by the Bishop of Calgary and Saskatchewan, Mr. Justice Moss, Principal Sheraton and Principal Caven of Knox. Lengthy results of various examinations were announced and the names of graduates given. Mr. F. C. Jarvis reported that $15,800 had been collected towards the new Convocation Hall in course of erection, and that $1,500 more was required to complete the Library. The corner-stone of this building was laid on June 24th following by Mr. S. H. Blake, K.C. Principal Sheraton, in the course of his address, described the chief aim of the founders of Wycliffe as being "the education of candidates for the sacred Ministry upon the broad and solid basis of the principles of the Reformation." They affirmed their right and liberty as Christian men and Anglican Churchmen to combine in making the doctrines of the Reformation the fundamental and governing principle of life and work and instruction. They contended for "the freedom of voluntary action, within legitimate limits, which has ever been one of the distinguishing characteristics of the Church of England."

Another object of the founders of the College he defined as follows: "Accordingly, one great aim of the founders of Wycliffe College was to bring Theological education into close touch with the educational system of the Province, and with the Provincial University, and to train its students not in a cloistered seclusion, but in the broad fellowship of students of all Churches and professions and to utilize for them every advantage of such fellowship that they might go forth as men among men, with breadth of sympathy as well as strength of conviction, and ready and willing to work with and for their fellow-Christians of different Churches." Dr. Sheraton then referred to the benefactions during the past year of Messrs. S. H. Blake, A. H. Campbell, J. Herbert Mason, T. R. Merritt, R. Millichamp, John Flett, Fred. Nicholls, and others, who had enabled them to put up the new buildings now under way, and which would afford ample room for work and growth during the next twenty-five years. Mr. Blake followed with a high tribute to the learning and ability of the Principal, and to the importance and value of their close association and affiliation with Toronto University. The latter was not perfect but "of all the Universities that we have there is none that can compare with it in its staff, in its varied departments, in the largeness of the men who are there." He then gave an interesting account of the origin and underlying principles of Wycliffe College:

At the period of Wycliffe's foundation there was much disturbance in the Church of England in the Motherland. It was seen that there was an attempt to introduce here the same system that was introduced there, and although it was stated that these matters were small and of little importance, these men of wisdom saw that every change trended only in one direction—towards Rome—and that it was not only a Rome-ward movement, but by the members who were leaving the Church of England and going into the Church of Rome that it was a movement that ended there, and they said: "Let us see, God helping us, if we cannot prevent the introduction into this newer land of that which is sapping the Church of England," and they formed this Theological School. It was essentially Protestant; he was glad to meet those who were not ashamed of that word which had been baptized by the death of so many of the very best that this world has ever seen. It was a good name, a great name, for them to live up to.

A further incident in connection with Wycliffe's progress during the year was the opening of its new Convocation Hall on October 7th. The President of its Corporation, Dr. N. W. Hughes, K.C., presided and with him were the Bishops of Toronto and Ontario, the Provincial Minister of Education, the Chancellor of Toronto University, Mr. Justice Moss, the Hon. S. H. Blake, K.C., the Provost of Trinity, the Chancellor of McMaster and Principal Sheraton. Bishop Mills, in his speech, referred to the bad reading of many clerymen and suggested the advisability of a Professor of Elocution in all Theological Schools. The Hon. Mr. Harcourt paid tribute to Principal Sheraton's work and congratulated the country on the hundred or more men of culture who had been sent out from the halls of this institution since it started. Sir William Meredith followed and declared the great necessity of the day to be education of the highest and most scientific character. Ministers of the Church, in particular, should be equipped to meet and repel attacks and they needed, nowadays, culture and learning as well as piety. Other speeches were made and Mr. Stapleton Caldecott reported that total subscriptions of $19,000 had come in for the new Hall and that more were coming.

Knox College, the old-time seat of Presbyterian learning in Toronto, held its annual closing exercises on April 2nd. In his address Principal Caven referred to the need of better accommodation for their Library of 15,000 volumes and to the endowment of a Scholarship of $2,500 by Mr. W. Mortimer Clark, K.C., in memory of his son. The degree of D.D. was then conferred upon the Rev. W. D. Armstrong of Ottawa and the Rev. Alexander Stewart of Clinton and that of B.D. upon four graduates. Diplomas were given to ten other graduates, a number of scholarships were awarded and an address delivered by the Rev. Alfred Gandier, B.D. There were, during the year, 69 students in attendance, of whom 10 graduated and, according to statements submitted to the General Assembly of the Presbyterian Church in June, the endowment fund of Knox College was $355,000. Upon this latter occasion the annual Report of the College was presented by the Rev. Dr. Thompson of Sarnia, who stated that Mr. David Morrice of Montreal had founded a Scholarship of $1,000 during the past year in addition to that of Mr. Mortimer Clark. A Resolution was passed congratulating the institution upon its intention of founding a Library building to be called Caven Hall in honour of its distinguished Principal. For this latter purpose, it was announced at a meeting of the Alumni on Dec. 9th, that $2,200 had been subscribed out of a total of $5,000 which that Association intended to raise. An incident during the year which was deeply regretted was the death on June 16th of Professor A. Haliday Douglas, M.A. His chair of Apologetics and Homiletics was offered, in November following, to the Rev. John Kelman, M.A., of Edinburgh, but was not accepted by him.

Of the higher institutions of learning in the Maritime Provinces Dalhousie University occupied the most prominent position during 1902. At its closing Convocation on April 29th, the Rev. Principal Forrest reviewed the progress of the academic year ; reported 343 students on the roll and 73 as about to receive their degrees; urged strongly the necessity of a better equipment and declared it a disgrace to the Province that Nova Scotia had no School of Mines. " Has Dalhousie no friend," he asked, " who will erect a monument for himself and prove a benefactor to his country by giving us $25,000 for a suitable building ?" He concluded with a vigorous appeal for University consolidation and the establishment of one strong Provincial University. The degrees were then conferred including B.A., 26 ; B.Sc., 4 ; LL.B., 12 ; M.D., 21 ; M.A., 6 ; B.L., 1 ; M.L., 1. The Hon. Degree of LL.D., was conferred upon Mr. Martin J. Griffin, Parliamentary Librarian at Ottawa and the Rev. Robert Murray of Halifax. On May 29th it was announced that the University would take steps to raise an endowment fund of $200,000 for the purpose of establishing a School of Mines. A few weeks later, on July 3rd, a public meeting, called by the Governors of the institution, was held in Halifax in order to launch an appeal for the sum required.

Mr. John F. Stairs presided and pointed out in his speech that unless Dalhousie kept up with the times and advanced she must fall behind and her students drift away. The young men of the Province were now going to Montreal and Toronto and Kingston for their technical training and many never came back. The $200,000 asked for was imperatively required and Halifax first, and then the Maritime Provinces generally, should share in its contribution. Principal Forrest traced the history and progress of the University and appealed to local patriotism and pride for support ; Mr. H. S. Poole dealt with the great need existing in Nova Scotia for technically-trained men in its coal and gold mines ; Mr. Benjamin Russell, M.P., stated that Dalhousie was very properly trying to meet and aid the great development in mining of the last few years and pointed out that 20 men now in the institution wanted to take a Mining course and, if unable to do so, would probably go elsewhere. Other speeches endorsing the proposal were made by Mr. G. S. Campbell, President of the Board of Trade, the Rev. Dr. D. M. Gordon and the Rev. W. J. Armitage. The Chairman closed the meeting by announcing that the Board of Governors had taken the initiative in the matter by appointing J. E. Woodman, Ph.D., M.A., of Harvard, to be Professor of Geology and Mineralogy ; and a little later it was stated that Mr. H. C. Boynton, B.A., M.Sc., also of Harvard, would be Professor of Metallurgy and Mining. Lecturers were also appointed on Mining, Assaying, etc. ; the course in Chemistry, Physics, and Mathematics was arranged out of the existing staff; and special arrangements were made for courses in Surveying and Civil Engineering.

On Sept. 16th it was stated that great success had been met with in the collection of funds. Halifax had promised $35,000 and at least $10,000 more was expected from that City; while successful public meetings had been held in New Glasgow, Sydney and other places. Several applications from intending students had been received and it was expected that the School would open with about 20 students. At the Convocation of Dalhousie College on Sept. 17th President Forrest was in the chair and, during his address, described the gratifying way in which the public had met their appeal for aid in connection with the School of Mines' project and also in reference to the McDonald Memorial Library, for which the students and graduates had endeavoured to raise $25.000 and for which they already had $18,500. The other speakers included Mr. J. F. Stairs, Senator Mackeen and Professor S. M. Dixon. The last-named dealt at length with the general subject of technical education and concluded with a statement of existing local conditions :

The Governors of Dalhousie having decided that this year a new move should be made to forward technical education, the branch relating to the mining engineer demanded their attention first. It is evident to all in Nova Scotia that the professional man capable of properly developing the mineral resources of the Province and of giving sound advice to the investor is urgently needed ; and just as in Europe the industrial school is in general specially adapted to the industries of the district in which it is situated, so here at Dalhousie a beginning is to be made in that branch of technical education which appeals most generally to the people of the Province. It is clear that the establishment of a School of Mines at Dalhousie, besides aiding in the development of the natural resources of the country, will materially advance scientific and technical education along the lines pointed out, and will benefit the College indirectly—in the ways already mentioned and directly by the additional work that is made possible in chemistry, physics, mineralogy and geology. But this is merely an initial step in a very much larger scheme of technical education which must soon be adopted if Nova Scotians are to develop their own country and not wait for outside help.

King's College, the old-time seat of learning at Windsor, N.S., held its annual gathering and celebration from June 17th to June 19th. The first two days were marked by a careful discussion of the question of amalgamation with Dalhousie, and the Alumni voted against it, while the Governors decided by 17 to 6 in favour of the proposal. On the 19th Convocation was held, with Vice-Chancellor the Rev. Dr. C. E. Willets in the chair, the Lieutenant-Governor of the Province on his left and the Lord Bishop of Nova Scotia on his right. It had been intended to confer the Honorary degree of D.C.L. upon Mr. J. Y. Payzant, but he declined the compliment, and six degrees of M.A. were given prior to various announcements as to matriculation, prizes, etc. The Lieutenant-Governor then spoke at length. He referred to the mixed feelings with which he was present, the regret it was to him, as an old-time Churchman, to see the days upon which King's had fallen and to feel that the Church of England had not kept pace with the other Churches. " It would be ungracious to say that King's College had

28

not done its work. It had done a grand work, but he could not help thinking that for a long time King's had failed to keep in touch with the laity of the Church. The people, therefore, had kept aloof, and to-day there were 100,000 Church people in the Maritime Provinces standing idly by and seeing King's wiped out."

His Honour proceeded to say that he hoped the University would be able to retain its identity and that, even if the proposed arrangement with Dalhousie were carried out, it would be retained as a Divinity School. He concluded by urging an appeal to the people of the Church generally to all join in aiding King's to retain its historic position. Bishop Courtney followed and said there was nothing peculiar about the present crisis. " King's had always been in crises." This present proposal was no less than 78 years old. It should not now be considered from a narrow denominational point of view, however, but with the hope of establishing a great Maritime University—strong, efficient and able to do its proper work. The year which still lay before King's might be used to advantage, but a very large sum of money would be needed to properly maintain it in complete independence. Did they believe it could be obtained? The total number of students in Arts, in attendance during 1902, was 19, in Science 4 and in Theology 13.

The Commencement exercises of the University of New Brunswick were held at Fredericton on May 29th, with Dr. James R. Inch, Provincial Superintendent of Education, in the chair. Degrees were conferred upon 18 members of the graduating class, the Douglas gold medal was given to Chester B. Martin and the Governor-General's gold medal to P. B. Perkins. The degrees and medals were presented by Messrs. J. D. Phinney, K.C., J. Douglas Hazen, K.C., M.P.P., Professor Brydone-Jack and the ˙Rev. Canon Roberts. The degree of M.A., in absentia, was conferred on W. L. Estabrook; that of Ph.D. upon Prof. Cecil C. Jones of Acadia University; and the Hon. degree of LL.D. upon Eldon Mullin, the Rev. W. O. Raymond and Robert Chalmers. The Very Rev. W. R. Harris, formerly Roman Catholic Dean of St. Catharines, addressed the graduating class, as did Professor John Davidson, the latter at considerable length. It was announced during the day that Mr. W. H. Clawson, B.A., of St. John, had been appointed to the vacancy caused by Prof. Stockley's retirement; that Professor Davidson had been granted a year's leave of absence; that the University had decided to build a new Gymnasium; and that Chancellor Harrison, Mr. Justice Barker and Dr. H. S. Bridges had been appointed a Committee to confer with Dalhousie regarding University federation.

Wolfville is the educational centre of the Maritime Baptists, and the annual gathering and exercises of Acadia University and its affiliated institutions are always well attended. On June 1st the Rev. William A. Newcombe of Thomaston, Maine, preached the baccalaureate sermon at the Wolfville Baptist Church, upon " Elements in a Christian Education "; in the evening of the same day the Rev. H. F. Waring of St. John preached at the College upon

" The Religion of a Christian "; on June 3rd the Acadia Seminary held the closing exercises of its most successful year, with a record of 182 students enrolled, 82 in residence and 19 graduating. The affiliated Horton Academy, it may be added, had an attendance during the year of 78 students. The Convocation proceedings took place on June 4th, with President, the Rev. Dr. Trotter, in the chair. The degree of B.A. was bestowed upon 24 young men and women. The Hon. degree of D.D. was conferred on the Rev. W. A. Newcombe of Maine and Prof. J. Alfred Faulkner of Drew Theological Seminary, while that of Doctor of Literature was given Professor H. C. Creed of Fredericton. All were one-time graduates of Acadia. President Trotter's address was an eloquent presentation of the obligations which the graduates of such an institution were under to society. The debt, he declared, should be paid by the use of a trained intellect in objects of social amelioration, by giving currency to noble thoughts and ideals, by giving to the world the blessings of a moral enthusiasm. The annual Report of the Board of Governors was presented to the Baptist Synod of the Maritime Provinces on August 27th and stated amongst other things that the movement commenced 5 years before for the raising of $75,000 was now nearing its end. " Of the $60,750 conditional amount necessary to secure in full Mr. Rockfeller's pledge of $15,000, your Board has raised $50,987." An urgent appeal for the balance was made. The Arts students in attendance during 1902 numbered 129.

The annual gathering of the Halifax Presbyterian College was held on April 30th, with the Rev. Principal Pollok presiding. The Report of the Rev. Professor Falconer showed the smallest number of students in attendance for some years—21 in number, with six graduating. And yet, he pointed out, there had never been such a period of expansion and industrial growth in either the Maritime Provinces or the Dominion. " These conditions, to say nothing of the regions beyond, are sufficiently impressive to dispel utterly the languor of those who dreamed that the Ministry would recruit itself without any effort on the part of the Church to put the claims of the sacred office before its young men. The Senate would respectfully urge upon the attention of the Assembly and Synod the necessity of taking some action in this matter. On the other hand, our future is encouraging. We have good hope that the outward flow has reached its lowest ebb, and there are signs of a returning tide, which we hope will be fuller than ever." Prizes were presented at the close of this statement, six graduates received their degrees, and the Rev. A. H. Denoon, B.A., was awarded (on examination) the degree of B.D. It was announced that the Summer School for Sunday School teachers and Christian workers, recently inaugurated by the Senate, had proved eminently successful. On December 5th, the Rev. Dr. D. M. Gordon, Professor of Systematic Theology, was appointed Principal of Queen's University, Kingston, and the Rev. James Croskery, M.A., B.D., was nominated to succeed him.

At Antigonish, on June 11th, the Commencement exercises of St. Francis Xavier's College took place. The town was crowded with visitors and amongst them were 400 members of the C.M.B.A. of Cape Breton. The Very Rev. Dr. Macdonald, V.G., presided and a great many prizes were distributed and some degrees granted. Three young women received the B.A. degree and seven young men, while that of B.SC. was conferred upon one graduate. The address delivered by the Rev. Dr. Thompson, President of the University, referred to the history of their institution, the benefactions and splendid work of Bishop Cameron and the great progress which the College was making. The words of the speaker concerning Bishop Cameron's aid to the institution were most impressive: "But there is one name the omission of which in this connection would not be tolerated by this or any other assemblage in Eastern Nova Scotia, a name which crowns all, the name of one whose memory will be green in the history of this country when the sapling oak which put forth its bud but yesterday will have crumbled into dust. It was unnecessary to tell them that he referred to Mgr. Cameron, that most venerable and beloved of Bishops, a man whose exceptionally great intellect, broad-mindedness, prudence and energy had been more instrumental than any other agency in putting this College into the very forefront of the institutions of higher education in Canada." There were during the year 118 students in Arts attending together with 6 in Science and 8 in Law.

It may be added here that the University of Mount Allison College, Sackville, N.B., under the Presidency of Dr. David Allison, had a successful year. Representative of Methodist interests in the Maritime Provinces it had 465 students in the University and the affiliated Mount Allison Ladies' College and Mount Allison Academy. The degrees conferred in 1902 included 2 of M.A., in course, and 14 of B.A. St. Anne's College, at Church Point, N.S., an Acadian institution, had during 1902 students in attendance in the Arts course numbering 33.

During many years the question of uniting some, or all, of the chief seats of higher learning in New Brunswick, Prince Edward Island and Nova Scotia has been the subject of
Proposed Federation of Maritime Colleges desultory discussion or organized effort—notably in 1823, in 1829, in 1880 and in 1901. On December 12th of the latter year a meeting of the Board of Governors of King's College, Windsor, was held and, after careful and exhaustive consideration, a Committee was appointed to confer with representatives of the other Universities and Colleges in the three Provinces. It was composed of the Bishops of Nova Scotia and Fredericton ; the Hon. E. J. Hodgson, Chancellor of King's College, and its President, the Rev. Dr. Willets ; the Very Rev. Dean Partridge of Fredericton ; the Rev. W. J. Armitage and Messrs. John Y. Payzant, A. de B. Tremaine, R. J. Wilson and C. E. A. Symonds of Halifax ; Mr. J. Roy Campbell, Jr., and the

Rev. C. D. Schofield of St. John; the Hon. Judge Warburton of Charlottetown; and Mr. C. S. Wilcox, ex-M.P.P., of Windsor, N.S. A Resolution was passed declaring the time "ripe for promoting the federation of the higher educational institutions of the Maritime Provinces" and expressing the belief that united work in one large University was better than divided efforts in scattered Colleges.

On January 2nd, 1902, a meeting of the Board of Governors of Dalhousie University was held at Halifax and consideration given to the action taken by King's. A Resolution was passed approving the principle of united educational work and the general idea of a federation of Maritime Colleges. The following Committee was appointed to confer with the body recently selected by the sister University and to meet any other representatives who might be chosen by other institutions: Messrs. John F. Stairs and Thomas Ritchie, Principal Forrest, Rev. Dr. John McMillan, Mr. Justice Graham, Dr. A. H. Mackay, Superintendent of Education, the Mayor of Halifax, Rev. Robert Murray, the Premier of Nova Scotia, Senator Mackeen, Rev. F. H. W. Archibald, Major H. B. Stairs and Messrs. Charles Archibald and H. McInnes. The action thus taken precipitated considerable discussion of the question. It was pointed out in different quarters that there were now in the three Maritime Provinces no less than eight Colleges having university powers for the conferring of degrees, in the following order of seniority: King's (1787), New Brunswick (1800), Dalhousie (1820), Acadia (1838), Mount Allison (1858), St. Francis Xavier (1866), St. Joseph's (1870), St. Anne's (1882).

Two of these were not under the control of any religious denomination—the Universities of New Brunswick and Dalhousie. The last two on the list were Acadian institutions. Besides these there was the Presbyterian Theological College at Halifax, with power to confer degrees in Divinity; the Catholic Seminary, for the purpose of educating young men for the priesthood of France; St. Dunstan's College at Charlottetown, affiliated to Laval University at Quebec, and without the power of conferring degrees; the Prince of Wales College at Charlottetown. The degree-conferring institutions had about forty salaried Professors teaching the ordinary subjects of the Arts course, or as many as the whole Professorial staff of Edinburgh University. All this work, it was claimed, was being duplicated; men were teaching the same things in different Colleges who ought to be specializing in a central institution; the work of the Professors was often of a character which great Universities give to assistants and inferior officials. At McGill University the salaries in all departments totalled about $100,000; in the Maritime Provinces it was stated that $70,000 a year was being spent mainly upon an Arts course.

The two Committees mentioned above met on February 25th at Halifax and appointed sub-committees to draft a suitable Act of Union and to communicate with other institutions. In this latter connection the replies only promised consideration of the matter.

On April 29th Principal Forrest referred at length to the question at Dalhousie's Convocation. He was profoundly thankful that at last the prospects of Union were hopeful and that the day might not be so very far distant when great denominations would see the folly of spending their funds in maintaining a number of small and necessarily ineffective institutions. " Of course our chief weakness in Nova Scotia is in our divisions. It is perfectly possible for us in the Maritime Provinces to have a University equal to anything on the continent. We have the students. Our people are a healthy and intelligent race, the equal of any people on the face of the globe. We have wealth enough to equip an up-to-date University. Our Government is willing to contribute liberally to its support. The only thing in the way is our disunion. If we could unite to-day we need not have the slightest fear of competition with any University in the world. But we are divided."

Meanwhile, opposition in some places and indifference in others had been very clearly shown. The Board of Mount Allison University declined to confer with the other Committees on the subject ; the Governors of Acadia University remitted the question to the Baptist Convention without appointing a Committee ; the University of New Brunswick appointed a Committee but held out no hope of a satisfactory scheme being propounded for its acceptance. In the Charlottetown *Examiner* of June 7th there appeared an elaborate letter attacking the scheme of union from an ultra-King's College standpoint. The writer pointed to the fact that Roman Catholics, Methodists, Presbyterians and Baptists all supported flourishing Universities in the Maritime Provinces and claimed that the extinction of King's College would be not only the betrayal of a solemn and historic trust but a smashing blow to the *prestige* of the Church of England. He declared that no genuine attempt had been made to save King's despite its splendid work in the past ; that the present scheme was being engineered mainly in the interests of the City of Halifax ; that the movement was not sufficiently open nor had the Church people of the Provinces been given sufficient time and notice ; that in any case the best work was done by small colleges ; and that the religious and residential features of King's should be carefully conserved rather than obliterated.

On June 3rd the Report of the joint Committee of the two Universities had been made public and, after recapitulating the events of the past six months, it recommended Union upon terms elaborately presented in an accompanying draft Act and based upon the removal of King's College to Halifax, the equally apportioned government of the new institution between representatives of the existing Colleges, and the utilization of present endowments along the lines originally intended by the donors—as far as possible. The Alumni Association of King's College and University met at Windsor on June 18th and considered this subject at length. The Report of the Executive presented a review of the position of the

College and declared that the principles upon which and for which it was founded were (1) to further the cause of higher education in the land; (2) to maintain the doctrine and discipline of the Church of England; (3) to secure to students the educative and humanizing influences of College residence; and (4) to provide suitable training for candidates for Holy Orders. The question before them was whether these principles could be adhered to and the educational demands of the day be also properly met.

There was a prolonged struggle upon the issue thus raised. The Rev. V. E. Harris presented a Resolution which eventually passed, almost unanimously, as follows: "That it would be a departure from the principles upon which King's College was founded, and which it had always steadfastly maintained, a nd would involve a change of trust and might result in the cancelling of her charter, to become a party to a scheme for the establishment of a University from which all recognition of the Christian religion is eliminated." The Rev. Canon Maynard, the Rev. S. Weston Jones, the Rev. Dr. Bowman, Judge Hannington and Mr. C. S. Wilcox, opposed amalgamation, while Judge Warbu ton, the Rev. W. J. Armitage, Mr. J. Roy Campbell and, finally the Bishop of Nova Scotia, in a strong speech, favoured the principle of union. A Resolution proposed by the Rev. L. J. Donaldson and the Rev. C. W. Vernon, and warmly supported by the Bishop, expressed pleasure at the movement inaugurated by the Board of Governors to "establish a Maritime University by the federation of existing Colleges," but was in the end defeated by 38 to 25 votes.

On the following day the Governors of King's met and decided by seventeen votes to six in favour of the Report submitted by the joint Committee and of the Act which they had prepared. There was one change made—the introduction into the preamble of a clause declaring that the principles of the new University "shall be in harmony with the principles of Christian truth." A Resolution was carried, also, ordering the printing and distribution of the Report and the Act for consideration by various associated interests. This involved the postponement of final settlement in the matter for a year as one of these bodies would not hold its annual meeting until June, 1903. On June 20th, Bishop Courtney in addressing the Diocesan Synod of Nova Scotia, referred at length to this subject and to the position of King's College. The time had come in his opinion for a change which should adapt the "old order" and the old College—now in the 100th year of its chartered life— to new conditions and to participation in the proposed "University of the Maritime Provinces of Canada." Deliberately and carefully the Synod should consider and deal with the question.

From the first, I have not concealed my own opinion that it would be wise if a centre could be devised for the Maritime Provinces, in which all the Colleges could be embraced, which should set a standard of education for them, conduct the examination of all the students, and in the name of which the various degrees would be conferred. Now and again efforts have been made looking towards the amalgamation of King's College, Windsor, and Dalhousie

College, Halifax, but though this project had the advocacy of Bishop Binney, and was adopted by this Synod and recommended by it to the College authorities, they did not adopt it, and the College has struggled on, with a noisy denunciation of the proposed change, but with little practical support in the way of money subscribed for its better equipment or relief from its financial stringency.

A prolonged debate followed in the Synod and, on June 24th, a Resolution, moved by Rev. Dr. Bullock, approving of Federation, received 62 votes against 40. As, however, both laity and clergy had to give a majority under the Synod constitution, and as the vote of the clergy was 24 in favour and 34 against, the Resolution was necessarily declared lost. During the first days of July the subject was considered in the Diocesan Synod of Fredericton. Bishop Kingdon, in his opening address, favoured the amalgamation of the two Colleges as being of importance and value to King's. Dean Partridge submitted the Report of the joint Committee and moved a Resolution stating that the proposed union " would be in the best interests of higher education in the Maritime Provinces and that the teaching to candidates for Holy Orders in the Maritime Dioceses would thereby be rendered more thorough and effective." There were, he declared, only three courses open to them—(1) to close the College and permit the endowment funds to accumulate ; (2) to continue and eventually to be forced to close its doors ; (3) to amalgamate with Dalhousie, retaining under the terms of union all existing funds and applying them to the maintenance of a Divinity School to be called by the old name. The Resolution was supported by the Rev. C. D. Schofield and vigorously opposed by Mr. Justice Hannington, who contended that the trouble in King's College was largely caused by mismanagement and urged a change in the Faculty rather than consolidation with another institution. The debate was then adjourned and no definite action was taken by the Synod.

Late in July the papers contained a lengthy letter from the Rev. Dr. Trotter, Principal of Acadia University—notably the Charlottetown *Guardian* of July 23rd—dealing with the question of consolidation and explaining why his particular institution had referred the matter to the Baptist Convention. The conditions with respect to Acadia were very different from those affecting King's. Their finances were healthy owing to recent bequests—especially one of $100,000, together with a fund of $75,000 which had also been raised. Moreover, their interests were in New Brunswick as much as in Nova Scotia and, unless the University of New Brunswick went into the union, its friends in that Province in the denomination could hardly be expected to support the proposal. He then summarized the position and objects of Acadia as follows :

It has no state connection but depends for its support upon the voluntary principle. While embracing in its curriculum all the studies of the secular College, which may be handled with the utmost freedom, it provides that the work shall be done under distinctly Christian auspices. It is not denominational in the sense of inculcating denominational tenets, but only it the sense of being controlled by a Christian denomination. Its founders and supporters proceed upon the fundamental assumptions common to all evangelical Christians and believe that the broadest and highest education will take cognizance of these. In such a College the Christian element is not a permitted and incidental but a characteristic and vital element. The student is regarded as being moral and spiritual as well as intellectual—one whose spiritual attitudes and relationships constitute the determinative factor in his life for time and eternity.

When the Baptist Conference of the Maritime Provinces met at Yarmouth on August 26th, they listened to addresses from a visiting delegation composed of the Rev. W. J. Armitage and Mr. A. de B. Tremaine of Halifax, and, after the Rev. Dr. Trotter had replied, a unanimous decision was expressed against the appointment of any Committee to confer upon the question of Union. Meanwhile, the discussion continued in the press and elsewhere. Mr. R. R. McLeod wrote at length to the Halifax *Herald* of July 31st upon the historic environment of the question ; the King's College *Record* in April advocated one strong Arts course for the three Provinces in a single University, together with various independent Divinity Schools ; the *Educational Review*, in July, supported the idea of one properly equipped University conferring degrees in arts, philosophy, science and engineering, instead of several Colleges doing, or attempting to do, the same work ; and the St. John's *Globe* of July 5th defended, to some extent, the management of King's and criticized the policy of the Church of England as the original cause of the trouble. " If the conditions of King's are deplorable, the reason largely is because the Church of England in these Provinces has not taken a firm and honest stand upon the question of Education. When non-sectarian education became the battle-cry of a political party, members of the Church ran with the hare while they held with the hounds. Professing with one breath to be delighted to see education emancipated from clerical control, they declared on the other that there should be religious teaching in education." On August 27th a special meeting of the Associated Alumni of King's College was held at Windsor and a series of Resolutions unanimously passed, which may be summarized as follows :

1. Endorsement of the recently formed organization called the Society of Friends of King's College and of its proposals to raise funds by annual subscription, or by permanent endowment, for the maintenance of the institution.

2. Disapproval of the scheme of amalgamation with Dalhousie and proposals for a re-organization of the Faculty and the appointment of a new President on the ground that scholarship was not now needed so much as business ability and popular qualities.

3. Approval of the appointment of Rev. S. Weston Jones to travel through the Provinces and obtain popular support for the Association ; to encourage the help of Church organizations of all kinds ; and to promote public contributions for adding to the staff, extending the curriculum, and otherwise improving the condition of the University.

4. Protest against any legislation being obtained or attempted for carrying out the proposed amalgamation with Dalhousie.

A mass-meeting was held in the evening, addressed by Mr. Justice Hannington and the Rev. J. R. de Wolfe Cowie. On December 11th the semi-annual meeting of the Governors of King's was held, with Bishop Courtney in the chair. Petitions were received from the " Friends of King's College," asking that action should be taken in June, 1903, as to Faculty re-organization; stating that the Rev. Mr. Weston Jones had collected $2,400 for the institution, and that the membership of the Alumni had increased to 170; and declaring the general feeling to be in favour of maintaining King's as a Church institution. No action was taken by the Board. Mr. Justice Hannington was announced to have been elected a Governor and the Ven. Archdeacon Kaulbach to have resigned his seat.

The Council of the University of Manitoba—representing chiefly the affiliated St. John's College, Wesley College, Manitoba College and the College of St. Boniface—met in prolonged

Western Institutions of Higher Learning session on March 6th, 1902, with Archbishop Machray, Chancellor of the institution, in the chair. Examiners for the year in arts, mathematics, natural science, mental and moral science, English, French, German, history, Hebrew, law and medicine were appointed and the Report of the Board of Studies adopted—after some discussion upon a clause stating that "we see no reason for departing from our custom in refusing to hold examinations above the matriculation in the Province of Manitoba outside of Winnipeg." This referred to a request from Brandon College and an amendment permitting first year students in that place to write on their examinations in Brandon was proposed and defeated.

Various financial statements were presented and the Committee on Domestic Science recommended the grant of suitable accommodation for three years, free of cost, to the Local Council of Women, if they desired to carry out the scheme of teaching this subject which had been propounded by Mrs. Massey Treble of Toronto. On May 15th the Council received a petition from the Evangelical Lutheran Synod praying that the Icelandic language and literature be added to the present curriculum. On May 16th, the presentation of degrees, medals and scholarships took place at the Legislative Buildings. The Rev. Father Drummond, of St. Boniface, presided and Lieutenant-Governor Sir D. H. McMillan and others were present. The Chairman in his address paid high tribute to the late Dean O'Meara and the Rev. Dr. Robertson. He stated that there had been a steady increase in the number of University students during the past year, that no less than 203 candidates had been examined in Arts and Law and 113 in Medicine, that 298 applications had been received for the examination on May 28th, and that this total of 614 students was a most gratifying evidence of prosperity. But there was more than this:

The progress in mere numbers has been more than equalled by the advancement in the curriculum. In proportion as the professional staffs of the various Colleges have developed so also has developed the conviction that time is a necessary factor in academic thoroughness. Hence the addition of one year to the University course, an addition which was carried into practice for the first time this year with very satisfactory results. During the past year the entire curriculum has been overhauled and re-examined under every aspect possible to a Committee composed of men of old and new world experience; most various in their training and personal views yet all agreeing to merge their personal preference in the common good.

The degree of B.A. was then conferred upon 2 graduates from St. Boniface, 8 from St. John's, 24 from Manitoba, 16 from Wesley and 5 from Brandon. Three graduates were granted the degree of M.A. and 5 that of LL.B. An address was given by Dr. D. J. Goggin of Regina upon the purpose and work of a University. "It conserves the accumulated knowledge of the ages, it offers instruction to all who come with trained minds, it offers opportunities for research so that the sum of knowledge may be increased and applied." Its formative influence on public life he also considered at some length. Convocation followed, on June 6th, when the medical degrees were cenferred. The Council of the University held its annual meeting on October 9th with the Rev. Dr. Patrick in the chair. The names of the elected or appointed representatives of the various bodies composing the institution were announced for the succeeding year. Apart from the Government and Convocation there were the four Colleges already mentioned, the College of Physicians and Surgeons and the Manitoba Medical College.

The results of the September examinations were announced and a Resolution was passed appointing a Committee to take measures with a view to securing recognition in the distribution of the Rhodes' Scholarships. The financial Report for the year ending June 30th was also presented and showed receipts from the Provincial Government of $6,000, from the Land Board $4,000, from the Isbester Trustees, for Scholarships, $7,102, and from fees $4,044. The total receipts were $21,169. The disbursements amounted to $21,848 including Scholarships, salaries and interest. The Isbester Trust showed a balance of $14,701 in the bank and the total sales of University lands to August 31st had been 10,020 acres for $60,142. At a Council meeting on December 11th it was announced that the local College of Pharmacy was to be affiliated with the University, and the petition from Brandon College asking for local Examinations, together with Principal Patrick's reply and refusal as head of a special Committee, were presented and discussed.

St. John's College had 56 students in attendance during the Session of 1901-2 and a very successful year's work. At the meeting of the Synod of Rupert's Land on August 20th, the Archbishop's address devoted some space to this valued Church institution. Several requirements were pointed out including more care by the Bishops in sending young men of suitable education and character to take the College course ; increased efficiency through additions to its staff and equipment; and aid in the removal of the Debt. The S. P. G. of England had voted £1,000 to the endowment fund on condition that £4,000 be raised from other sources by December 31st, 1906, and His Grace warmly urged the importance of aggressive action in this respect. At the General Synod meeting in Montreal on September 3rd the Archbishop again referred to this subject and to the lack of any general aid to denominational Colleges by the Church of England in Canada. "I may be allowed to illustrate by St. John's College, the College I have endeavoured to build up in Winnipeg. The Colleges of Presbyterian and Wesleyan Churches in Winnipeg are yearly and largely assisted by their respective bodies, and there is from this not only immediate help through the share of general collections of the denomination, but Colleges being brought prominently before their Churches receive many special gifts. St. John's College has no such assistance. I trust the Synod will not fail to deal practically with this matter. I may say that a measure of outside help is for my own College of vital necessity, not only for its efficiency, but almost for its existence. Any disaster to it would inflict the gravest injury on the Church." During the year the Rev. Mr. Murray, a distinguished graduate of Dublin, was appointed Lecturer on Mental and Moral Philosophy; the Rev. E. E. Phair, B.A., Lecturer on Pastoral Theology; and Mr. R. J. Sprott, B.A., Lecturer in French and German. Commemoration Day occurred on November 4th when prizes were given and addresses delivered by Bishop Grisdale of Qu'Appelle, Dean Matheson and the Rev. J. G. Anderson, B.D.

Manitoba College, Winnipeg, was reported by Principal Patrick, at the General Assembly in June, 1902, to have 145 students enrolled in Arts and 45 in Theology. Alike in the number of its students and in the number of distinctions won it was stated to be first of the four Arts Colleges which composed the University of Manitoba. The Principal favoured the teaching in Arts for some time to come, declared that one reason for Presbyterian success in the West was the scholarship and preaching power of their ministers and urged that this standard be fully maintained. He also asked for power to grant the degree of D.D. and sanction for the raising of a $50,000 fund to endow a Chair of Old Testament Literature in honour of the late Principal King. The Professors in the College, it may be added, numbered 23 at this time, the Lecturers 15, the graduating students 46 and the endowed fund amounted to $94,915. Principal Patrick's wishes, as expressed to the Assembly, were granted and at Convocation on September 16th he was enabled for the first time to confer the Hon. degree of D.D.—the first recipient being the Rev. J. A. Carmichael, the new head of the Presbyterian Missions in the West. On this occasion, also, he was able to describe the past Session as having had the largest enrolment in the history of the College and as being marked by the introduction of a system of practical training which he declared to be unique among Theological Colleges. Reference was made by the Principal to the proposed Dr. King Memorial and to the need of another Professor upon their staff. Various Scholarships, degrees and prizes were then awarded—amongst them being the degree of B.D. upon the Rev. H. Hamilton, B.A., and the Rev. C. McPherson, M.A. An eloquent address by Chancellor Burwash of Toronto closed the proceedings.

Brandon College, the Baptist institution of the West, in its annual Report for the year ending June 25th, 1902, showed total receipts of $11,630, of which $3,673 was in fees; and disbursements of $12,627.   There was a mortgage loan current of $25,000 on building account, in which connection the total expenditures had been $34,057.   Unpaid subscriptions, it was stated, would cover half this indebtedness.   The number of students enrolled was stated by Principal, the Rev. Dr. A. P. McDiarmid, as being 146, or an increase af 33⅓ per cent. over the preceding year.   They were of all denominations, including four Roman Catholics, and were made up of 108 young men and 38 young women.   Attention was drawn to the continued refusal of the University of Manitoba to permit Brandon students writing their examinations locally, and it was pointed out that the Brandon Council, Board of Trade and School Board had united in an unsolicited memorial protesting against the decision.   Regret was expressed, in view of the varied and great benefits accruing from College residence for students, that they had as yet no accommodation for the young women who were in attendance.   The formal Memorial regarding the relations of Brandon College to the University, which had been forwarded by the various public bodies of Brandon as above indicated, was presented in Winnipeg to the Council of the University on December 11th. It declared the decision of the Winnipeg institution to be unjust and apparently based upon nothing better than custom.   Brandon was stated to be a growing educational centre and the students to have suffered material and needless expense and inconvenience in having to go to Winnipeg for examination.   Protest was made against the University Council being composed entirely of local members and therefore not guaranteeing protection to outside interests, against the examining Committee as composed almost entirely of Winnipeg men ; against the whole policy of the University in this connection as being inimical to the interests of higher education in the Province and a hindrance to the establishment of Colleges by private benefaction.

    The Report of the Special Committee in reply was signed by Principal Patrick, as Convener, and described the general position of the University.   It had a "liberal, comprehensive and flexible constitution," created by the Provincial Legislature, and upon its Council was a full representation of all affiliated interests.   If Brandon, or any other outside College, had an Arts course meeting the requirements of the University, it could at any time take its place in the privileges and control of that institution.   As to the main grievance regarding examinations, the Committee described the custom to which they adhered as being one based on high expediency and present necessity.   "This is undoubtedly the case so far as some of the most important examinations of the University are concerned.   The advanced examinations in science require practical work by the student, and this work can only be done in the class-room or in the laboratory.   The corresponding examination in modern languages is partly oral and must therefore be conducted by the same examiners throughout, if equal justice is to be done to all candidates. The first duty of the Council is to see that the examinations of the University are uniform and thorough, and for this there is no guarantee so effectual as the holding of them at one common centre." The conclusion was that, on all grounds of local expediency, of experience elsewhere in Canada, and of economy and efficiency in Manitoba, there should be only one University and it should be strengthened by outside affiliations instead of weakened by dispersion of its forces or work.

Vancouver College, in the City of Vancouver, had been working in affiliation with McGill University, Montreal, in so far as the matriculation and first year work were concerned, until the beginning of 1902. On February 12th, however, it was announced that the College had been admitted to second year privileges and that this would mean the right of a student to study locally for two years and to complete his course at McGill in another two years. At the annual Convocation ceremonies, on October 17th, Mr. J. C. Shaw, M.A., Principal of the College, dealt at length with its position, and congratulated the institution and the Province upon the privileges granted by McGill. They were having difficulties, however. The new Session was opening with more classes than rooms, there was no Assembly room, the gymnasium was unworthy the name, the grounds were worthless for athletic purposes. Better accommodation was essential in view of the progress they were making.

"In the space of three years, I may state, our enrolment shows a gain of 115, or of over 58 per cent., and as against the year 1900-01, of 93, or over 12 per cent.—the numbers for the three years reaching 197, 219 and 312, respectively. And to go back farther would better the showing. The prospects of the present year, based on a comparison of our enrolment of to-day with that of October 17th, 1901, justify the estimate of a gain of 40, or about 13 per cent. for 1902-03 over the phenomenally large numbers of last year—a prospective attainment, in fact, of better than the 350 mark. It is worth while noting in this connection that of the 312 students in attendance last year, no fewer than 56, in round numbers, or 18 per cent. of the whole, were from outside districts." Addresses of a congratulatory character followed from Mr. Alex. Robinson, Superintendent of Education, Mayor Neelands, the Rev. L. Norman Tucker and Capt. R. G. Tatlow, M.P.P. The Columbian Methodist College of New Westminster, B.C., held its first Convocation on December 21st, 1902, with a record of 80 students for the year. The Principal, Rev. W. J. Sipprell, B.D., presided, and had around him the leading Methodists of the Province. A large list of pass examinations was reported and the Hon. degree of D.D. was conferred upon the Rev. Elliot S. Rowe of Victoria, the Rev. E. Robson of Vancouver and the Rev. J. F. Ockley of Collingwood, Ont.

In his annual Report, issued during the year, Mr. Alexander Robinson, Superintendent of Education for British Columbia, made the following reference to a matter in connection with Higher

Education which had been discussed from time to time in the press and educational circles of the Province:

> The question of the establishment of a Provincial University has lately engaged the attention of several newspaper editors throughout the Province. Taking into consideration, however, the small number of University students that will for many years be available from British Columbia, the low rates offered by the Canadian Pacific Railway to young men desirous of prosecuting their studies in the East, and the incomparable advantages to be derived from associating with students from other Provinces, especially in large centres of population such as Toronto and Montreal, it would appear that the agitation for the establishment of such a University is premature. At any rate, when the University of British Columbia is established, the Government must endow it so liberally and equip it so thoroughly that its degrees will be treated with respect by other institutions of learning.

According to the annual Report of the Provincial Minister of Education for 1902, containing the statistics for 1901, there were 5,663 Public Schools in Ontario with a registered **Popular Education in Ontario** attendance of 414,619, an average attendance of 235,084 and an expenditure thereon of $4,328,682. There was an increase over 1900 of 8 in the number of schools, and of $100,150 in the expenditure; but a decrease in the registered pupils of 5,478 and in the average attendance of 2,222. The expenditure included $433,801 upon sites and buildings and $2,874,473 upon teachers' salaries. The teachers numbered 8,676, of whom 2,375 were men and 6,301 women—a decrease of 164 in the number of men during the year and an increase of 174 in the women. The average annual salary of the men was $421 and of the women $306; showing an increase of $17 in the former and of $8 in the latter sum.

Of these teachers 4,427 had attended a Normal School—an increase of 292 over 1900. There were 372 Roman Catholic Separate Schools in the Province with 43,987 pupils, an average attendance of 26,926, instruction by 818 teachers, receipts of $436,721 and expenditures of $391,628. The increase in the number of these schools during the year was 17, in the registered pupils 1,590, and in the average attendance 1,051. The number of Protestant Separate Schools was 7, the pupils 450 in number and the average attendance 249; the Kindergartens numbered 118, the teachers 251, the pupils 11,405 and the average attendance 4,704; the night schools numbered 12, the teachers 22, the pupils 800 and the average attendance 194. The average attendance in proportion to the registered pupils at the Public Schools of the Province was 57 per cent. Of the total population of the Province—in which there were 574,490 persons between the ages of 5 and 21—the percentage enrolled in the schools was 22 as against a similar United States percentage of 20.

The number of High Schools and Collegiate Institutes—teaching all the subjects necessary for matriculation into the University—was 131; the teachers numbered 579; the pupils 22,523 or an increase of 800 over the preceding year; the total expenditure thereon was $728,132, of which $535,521 was devoted to teachers' salaries; the total receipts were $784,626, including $99,864 from fees and $109,200 from Legislative grants. The percentage of average to total attendance was 59 and the cost per pupil $32.33. In connection with this branch of the educational system the Hon. Mr. Harcourt drew attention in his Report to the changing character of High School studies. In 1867 only 1,283 pupils, or 23 per cent. of the whole number, studied book-keeping; in 1901 this subject was taken up by 10,051 pupils, or 45 per cent. of the total attendance. The study of Latin had in the same time changed from 5,171 pupils, or 90 per cent., to 18,710 pupils or 83 per cent.; that of French from 38 to 57 per cent.; that of German from nothing to 14 per cent.; that of Greek from 15 to 3 per cent. The parentage of the pupils attending High Schools was stated to be 6,747 agricultural, 5,984 commercial, 5,862 mechanical, 2,144 professional and 1,786 without occupation. The Minister then proceeded as follows:

When High Schools were first established in the Province their primary object was to prepare pupils for the learned professions, and especially for the University. Although their original purpose has not been ignored, the course of study has been enlarged so as to meet the aims of pupils who intend to follow the ordinary pursuits of life. It is in the High Schools that most students who desire to become Public School teachers receive their non-professional training. This is a valuable function of these institutions and one that has done much to commend them to the general public. Many young men also who intend to follow mechanical pursuits, or prepare themselves for mercantile life or for agriculture, take advantage of the High Schools. The superior culture which is thus received proves a valuable investment. In 1872 the number of High School pupils entering mercantile life was 486. In 1901 the number had increased to 1,300. In 1872, 300 pupils left the High Schools for agricultural pursuits, and the number in 1901 had reached 833.

Turning to miscellaneous matters it may be said that 197,605 pupils in all the schools were receiving instruction during 1901 in Temperance and Hygiene; that the average salary of the male teacher in the cities was $915 and in the counties $359, and of the female teacher $470 and $262 respectively; that there were 55 County Model Schools with 1,189 teachers in training, of whom 1,145 had passed the final examination; that the Normal College had 14 teachers and 113 students and the Normal School 14 teachers and 613 students; that there were 78 Teachers' Institutes in the Province with 8,372 members and total receipts of $13,898. A feature of the year's development was the growth of the Continuation classes commenced some years ago, to enable pupils in places where there were no High Schools to take up studies identical with those in the lower forms of the latter and growing naturally out of their Public School work. The idea was adopted from the United States and soon became popular. In 1902 there were 540 of these classes receiving Legislative aid with 4,933 enrolled pupils and 554 teachers.

In the course of his Report the Minister of Education referred in most appreciative terms to Sir W. C. Macdonald's promised help

LAURENTIAN FRUIT FARM, FRUITLAND, NIAGARA PENINSULA, ONTARIO.

in centralizing rural schools and quoted various cases of successful operation in the United States. He also mentioned the growing popularity of the Travelling Library idea in country districts; the desirability of improvements in rural mail delivery; the advantages of Nature Study in the schools; the development of the manual training scheme; and the desirability of meeting the moral needs of the pupil in an age when intellectual power has supplanted physical force in a sometimes undue measure:

It should never be forgotten that the most important requisite of moral training is a teacher of high moral character; and to secure better teachers, higher qualifications must be exacted. Children naturally look to the teacher for guidance, and if they find him actuated by a spirit of truthfulness, industry and courtesy, the disposition to imitate will soon show itself. As is so often said, the scholars need models rather than critics. The teacher, to have the best moral influence must also be successful in the discharge of his duties. If he is master of his profession, the children are readily trained to habits of punctuality and regularity; and in the present age when so much work is done by machinery, the value of both punctuality and regularity can scarcely be over-estimated. The silence which a good teacher cultivates, forms habits of incalculable value in carrying out those complex arrangements to be found in modern industrial enterprises. The pupil who is properly trained, readily understands the duties he owes to himself and the value of correct habits, constant self-culture, and habits of thrift which should become part of his character.

The annual Meeting of the Ontario Educational Association is of permanent importance because of the extensive ground covered in its discussions. The 1902 gathering was opened **The Ontario** at Toronto on April 1st with Mr John Henderson, **Educational** **Association** M.A., of St. Catharines, in the chair. In his address he referred to the expansion of educational interests in the Province, and dealt at some length with alleged defects such as the very irregular attendance of the school population, the "wretchedly underpaid" condition of the teachers, the country districts without school libraries, etc. He urged reform in these respects and especially in the enforcement of the compulsory regulations as to school attendance. He deprecated the admission of non-matriculants to the Provincial University, opposed strongly the publication of examination results in connection with any special school or centre and declared, in conclusion, that if the commercial spirit of the age were allowed too free a hand in the schools and colleges of Canada it might mean the future elimination of all that is best in knowledge and human thought from the purview of its educational systems. The Hon. Mr. Harcourt, Minister of Education, followed in an elaborate speech of welcome to the City and review of educational conditions in the Province.

He advocated the early establishment of a fourth Normal School, the broadening of the course of instruction at Normal and County Model Schools and the extension of the term in each. He pointed in a general sense to the universal educational unrest now existing as a result of the multiplication of new and peculiar problems; referred to the recent gift by Sir W. C. Macdonald of

29

$125,000 for aiding the study of Domestic Science, etc., and to the gift by the late W. E. H. Massey of $40,000 to the Guelph Agricultural College; urged the extension of the Travelling Library system and the encouragement of Libraries for rural school sections; dealt with technical education and Canada's need for highly trained mechanics, surveyers, engineers, chemists, assayists, and metallurgists; and expressed the hope that a Chair of Forestry would soon be established at the University, and that the Association would aid the movement for consolidating rural schools.

On April 3rd Mr. John Seath, M.A., Inspector of High Schools for Ontario, was elected President for the ensuing year, Mr. R. W. Doan, Secretary, and Mr. W. J. Hendry, Treasurer, and on the following day the Association adjourned after a number of papers had been read and discussed in its different Sections. These included historical contributions by the Rev. Dr. Symonds, Chancellor Burwash, Mr. Barlow Cumberland, B.A., and Mr. J. H. Coyne, B.A., and educational articles by Messrs. John Seath, M.A., J. Squair, B.A., E. W. Hagarty, A. W. Burt, J. P. Hoag, B.A., W. J. Galbraith, B.A., G. A. Smith, F. C. Colbeck, B.A., J. F. Thompson, B.A., I. J. Birchard, Ph.D., W. M. Govenlock, B.A., W. E. Rand, B.A., W. N. Bell, B.A., C. O. Sliter, M.A., M. W. Matchett, S. Morley Wickett, Ph.D., S. B. Sinclair, B.A., Ph.D., W. F. Moore, E. W. Bruce, C. E. Kelly, M.A., F. F. Macpherson, M.A., William Houston, M.A., S. Alfred Jones, Dr. John Noble, D. D. Moshier, B.A., J. G. Elliott, S. Silcox, B.A., W. H. Elliott, B.A., F. Tracy, Principal J. O. Miller, Professor J. G. Hume, W. Johnston, LL.D., J. C. Rogers, B.A., and many others. Some interesting papers on miscellaneous subjects were read by Professor W. Lash Miller, Professor Hutton, Messrs. H. Charlesworth, Eugene Masson, W. H. P. Anderson, A. C. Neff, and Dr. F. J. A. Davidson. The Association passed a Resolution appointing a Committee to examine into the operation and work of the Educational Council, with instructions to report at the next annual meeting; and one favouring the appointment by the Ontario Government of a Commission to examine into the Library question.

In his paper on the Status of the Educational Council Mr W. F. Moore pointed to the changes in function and composition which had come about since its origination in 1846 at the suggestion of Dr. Egerton Ryerson. Composed in 1901 of Professors Burwash, Baker, McCallum, Clark and Farmer, President Loudon, Principal Hutton, Principal Fessenden, Rev. Dr. Teefy, Inspector Tytler, Dr. Knight and G. H. Armstrong, M.A., it was, he claimed, too representative of University interests alone. He urged reform in this respect, with elective members from the Universities, the Collegiate Institutes, the Public Schools, etc., and with duties comprising complete control of text books, full charge of Departmental examinations, control of the College and school curriculum, with executive powers as well as consultative and advisory rights. Mr.

John Squair, B.A., delivered a lengthy address during the proceedings. He declared that industrial training was superceding scholarly subjects in the schools to an undue extent, and urged the commencement of foreign language study at an earlier age, as one of the means of meeting the situation. The chief obstacle to this was the severity of the entrance examination to High Schools. "It is the most important factor in the adjustment of the various parts of our school system, and as things stand at present it has done a great deal to hinder the development of language studies; and not only of language studies but of all higher scholarship as well. For those who are going to the High School and University the time spent in the Public School is too long. If scholarship is to flourish then the entrance examination must either be abolished or made easier." Mr. Squair then passed to a consideration of general conditions in Ontario:

Our schools are not improving very fast, and no increase in the severity of examinations will make them improve. We must have resource to other remedies. The effective remedies are two—an increase in the distinction, stability, and emoluments of the teaching profession, and an increase in the intellectual and artistic culture of the teachers. The first of these involves changes in statutes and regulations regarding Legislative grants, grouping of school sections, retiring allowances and the like, and the second involves a radical change in our ideas regarding the training of teachers. The assumption made by so many in our country that all that is needed by those who have passed the non-professional examinations to make them good teachers is instruction in pedagogics, is absolutely erroneous. They do doubtless need pedagogics, but what they need vastly more is a deeper and wider knowledge of the subjects they are to teach, and, in addition, the knowledge of cognate subjects to give them that grip of themselves and their work which makes efficient teachers. For instance, if one is to teach geography, he should know something about geology ; if he is to teach history he should know something about ethnology ; if he is to teach English he should know something of Latin, and so on. It is for this widening and enriching of the knowledge of prospective teachers that our Normal Schools should mainly exist, for it is what is most needed with us.

His proposals may be summarized as being better teachers, fewer subjects and less rigid examinations and regulations, while his view of the situation as a whole was given in these words: "The low standard of scholarship in our country is produced, not only by imperfect machinery in our schools but, more particularly, by a lack of desire for it in the body of the public." An address by Mr. John Seath, M.A., travelled over a wide field of thought and furnished much important advice to teachers in secondary schools. Like Mr. Squair and others he drew attention to the growth of industrial and commercial subjects and expressed keen regret at the coming disappearance of Greek. "It is a question of maintaining the highest form of literary culture in the Province." He protested against the publication of examination results in the papers as "exploiting the very feature of our system which should be kept in the background." The most serious defect in High School teaching was, in his opinion, the poverty of results. "A large percentage of the results are still raw and the workmanship is unfinished." For this he blamed the matriculation or leaving examinations. The standard was altogether too low and had "crowded the ranks of the Public School teachers with badly equipped members and our Universities with badly equipped matriculants." In other directions he was very critical. Arithmetic work was inaccurate in many schools; derivation and root hunting were not sufficiently taught in connection with grammar; low, indistinct speaking and abrupt, badly-formed sentences were prominent faults everywhere amongst Canadian pupils; the cultivated use of the English language was lamentably deficient amongst teachers; reading aloud was little taught and the neglect in the proper pronunciation of words was a glaring and far too general defect.

Mr. E. W. Hagarty, in his paper, contended that the High School curriculum was greatly over-loaded and that this was caused, amongst other things, by lack of a common educational standpoint and by past regulations being framed too much with a view to the requirements of the Honour course in each department. He advocated a curtailment of the work attempted and the increase of the pass limit to 50 per cent. in suitable papers. Mr. J. P. Hoag, in dealing with the study of English grammar, declared that in many Public Schools the subject of composition was neglected owing to the pressure of other work and that the pupils came up to the High School entrance examinations " without the ability to compose, orally or in writing, with any degree of ease or rapidity." There were a great number of other papers dealing with miscellaneous and interesting subjects such as Latin and Greek instruction, History teaching, book-keeping, commercial courses, arithmetic, nature study, examinations, kindergarten work, rural schools, educational theories and facts, poetry in education, the Bible in Public Schools, education of the deaf, the remuneration of teachers, etc. But they were more of a specific character than of the general application which made those first referred to of public importance.

The Educational system of Quebec Province is differently constituted from that of any other part of the Dominion, owing mainly to the religious and racial complexion of its population. Its Council of Public Instruction consists of two divisions—the Roman Catholic Committee and the Protestant Committee, with the Hon. P. Boucher de la Bruère, Superintendent, as Chairman of the former and as member, *ex officio*, of the latter. When the Report of this official was presented on January 10th, 1902, for the year ending June 30th, 1901, to the Provincial Secretary, the members of the Roman Catholic Committee included the Archbishops of Ottawa, Quebec and Montreal, the Bishops of St. Hyacinthe, Pembroke, Nicolet, Charlottetown, Rimouski, Chicoutimi, Valleyfield, Sherbrooke and Three Rivers, Senator L. F. R. Masson, Mr. Justice F. Langelier, Mr. Justice J. E. Robidoux, the Hon. Messrs. H. Archambault, Lomer Gouin, Thomas Chapais and Gédéon Ouimet, and Messrs. E. Crepéau, K.C., H. R. Gray, M. T. Stenson and Alphonse Pelletier. The Prot-

Public Instruction in Quebec

estant Committee comprised its Chairman, the Rev. Dr. W. I.
Shaw and Bishop Hunter Dunn, of Quebec; Principal Peterson, of
McGill University; the Hon. Sydney Fisher, M.P.; Dr. C. L.
Cotton, the Rev. A. T. Love, and Messrs. George L. Masten, A. W.
Kneeland, Samuel Finley, Herbert B. Ames, G. G. Walker and W.
S. MacLaren, M.P. The Associate Members included the Rev. E. I.
Rexford, Dr. S. P. Robins, Dr. James Dunbar, K.C., the Hon. H.
T. Duffy, M.P.P., and Messrs. W. S. Shurtleff and H. J. Silver.
M. Paul de Cazes was the French Secretary of the Department of
Public Instruction and Mr. George W. Parmelee, English Secretary.

In his annual statement M. Boucher de la Bruère referred with
satisfaction to the course of lectures given at the Mont Ste.
Marie Convent to female lay teachers who had not a Normal School
training. They had attended to the number of 530, and been
greatly aided by the presence and advice of Archbishop Bruchèsi.
School attendance he described as satisfactory, although difficult to
control during winter in the country districts. The construction of
school-houses was greatly improving but not the condition of school
furniture. He urged that the Government should aid in establishing libraries in the schools, and drew attention to the insufficiency
of salaries paid the school inspectors. " We have actually 43 school
Inspectors, 9 of whom are Protestant and 34 Roman Catholic.
With the exception of four whose salaries, for special reasons, are
very small—not exceeding on an average $250 each—they receive an
annual stipend ranging from $650 to $1,000. Their travelling expenses over the wide areas to be traversed run from $225 to $350, and
these expenses are deducted from their salaries ! " The teaching of
drawing in the schools was described as being merely nominal and
without useful result. He regretted this and hoped that more
attention would be paid to the subject. Special importance was
attached in his Report to the desirability of establishing technical
schools in the Province and to an extension of manual training.
" If the Government of the Province has deemed it necessary to
spread among our farming class the teaching which they needed
for the cultivation of the land with method and success, it is urgent
to display the same energy in the industrial field in order that the
child quitting the primary school may not be left to himself but
that he may, if he so wishes, learn a trade under the best possible
conditions by receiving from the State, through the foundation
of technical schools, the assistance which he can legitimately claim."
The following tabulated statement is compiled from the voluminous statistics published by the Provincial Superintendent of Public
Instruction :

ELEMETARY SCHOOLS, 1900-01.	Roman Catholic.	Protest-ant.
Elementary Schools under control of Commissioners and Trustees	4,322	876
Elementary Schools independent of control	47	....
Total number of Pupils in Elementary Schools	174,613	26,511
Average attendance	119,884	18,903

	Roman Catholic.	Protestant.
Percentage of Average attendance...............	68·66	71·31
Number of male lay teachers....................	52	22
Number of female lay teachers..................	4,434	1,084
Number of male teachers in Orders..............	111	1
Number of Nuns teaching.......................	392	....
Average salary of male lay teachers with diplomas..	$281	$1,149
Average salary of female lay teachers with diplomas.	113	201

MODEL SCHOOLS AND ACADEMIES, 1900-01.

	Roman Catholic.	Protestant.
Model Schools under control of Commissioners or Trustees...................................	369	46
Independent Model Schools......................	142	....
Total number of Pupils.........................	77,889	3,350
Average attendance at Model Schools.............	63,355	2,517
Total number of Academies......................	139	29
Total Pupils at Academies......................	26,972	5,546
Average attendance............................	23,093	4,503
Percentage of average attendance at both Model Schools and Academies......................	82·45	78·91
Number of male lay teachers....................	223	79
Number of female lay teachers..................	507	242
Number of male religious teachers...............	778	....
Number of female religious teachers.............	264	....
Average salary of male lay teachers with diplomas..	$510	$802
Average salary of female lay teachers with diplomas.	125	299

Summarized, these and other statistics show 5,245 Elementary Schools in the Province with 185 male teachers, 5,911 female teachers, 201,124 pupils and an average attendance of 138,787; 557 Model Schools with 655 male teachers, 1,809 female teachers, 81,239 pupils and an average attendance of 65,872; 168 Academies with 428 male teachers, 1,213 female teachers, 32,518 pupils and an average attendance of 27,596. There were also in the year 1900-1, 5 Normal Schools with 58 teachers and 353 pupils; 4 schools for the deaf, dumb and blind with 105 teachers and 528 pupils; and 7 schools of Art and Design with 49 teachers and 1,410 pupils. There was a total number of teachers in all kinds of institutions of 6,643 of whom 6,267 were females; and a total of religious teachers in all branches of Provincial education numbering 4,283. In the year under review the total expenditure upon Education was $3,453,754 of which $1,335,045 was the annual tax upon the people, $131,566 was a special tax, $222,132 was in monthly fees, $1,311,061 was in fees from subsidized educational institutions and $453,950 was in direct Government payments.

During the years 1901 and 1902 there was much discussion in the Province as to the condition of Protestant education. Dr. S. P. Robins, Principal of the McGill Normal School, in his annual Report published in the latter year, stated that in the rural Protestant schools the average attendance was barely 16 pupils per school; that they were now threatened with a decrease in the number of teachers under training; and that the steady abandonment of the profession by men was a subject of grave anxiety. It may be said here, in this latter connection, that M. Boucher de La Bruère's annual statement showed that the male lay and religious teachers in 1867-8 numbered 919 and in 1900-1 had increased to 2,326 ; while the growth in female teachers had been from 3,617 to 9,044 in number.

During the latter part of 1901 and the beginning of 1902 the Montreal *Star* had a special correspondent making inquiries into this subject of Protestant education in the Province and amongst the difficulties described were the isolation of school life, the inefficiency often caused by insufficient remuneration, the imperfect system of school inspection, the cost or multiplicity of text books and the lack of popular control over School Boards. On January 11th an interview with Mr. W. A. Weir, K.C., M.P.P. appeared in *The Star.* With every appreciation of the voluntary services rendered by many gentlemen under the existing system he declared that the time had come for elective School Commissioners in Montreal and Quebec. "An active public opinion on school questions and an easy channel for the expression and adoption of the wishes of the public," were now needed. He also thought that the Protestant Committee of Public Instruction was greatly weakened by the absence of country representation from its membership.

On April 23rd Mr. John Adams, M.A., afterwards Professor of Education in the University of London, commenced a two months' investigation into the Protestant educational system of Quebec, under the auspices of the McGill University, and visited many schools of all kinds in all parts of the Province. The result was the publication of a Report in which he recommended (1) a more rational classification of the schools ; (2) more money to give effect to the regulations of the Committee, obtained by the more populous school districts helping the poorer ones ; (3) compulsory education with exemption only granted to those who had passed an examination in reading, writing and arithmetic ; (4) consolidation of small rural schools and of the weaker Model Schools ; (5) appointment of a Chief Inspector of secondary schools with considerable power in effecting minor reforms ; (6) a two years' course of training for teachers and the establishment of a Chair of Education at McGill. In connection with the teachers' position he said : " I should think that teachers are worse paid in the Province of Quebec than in any other part of the world." Speaking at the meeting of the Provincial Association of Protestant Teachers of the Province, which met at Montreal on October 9th, Mayor Cochrane, M.P.P., of that City, made the following reference to this subject :

We are losing to-day in the Province the best element of our teachers, and the reason is low salaries. They are working for nothing compared with Ontario and every small town and village in the United States. I have made inquiries from Trustees of schools in the State of New York, and I have been informed that lady teachers, ordinary teachers and not principals, receive $700 and $800 a year, and some get as much as $1,400. During the last Session of the Quebec Legislature I asked what some female teachers got in this Province, and I was told $80 per annum. How can teachers be retained on such a salary when they can take up other employment at $30, $40, and $50 a month?

In municipalities that cannot afford to pay their teachers from $400 to $500 a year, the Government should supply the money to make up the difference, and have efficient teachers.

At this gathering the Rev. Dr. W. I. Shaw took up the general subject of Quebec Protestant education. He referred to the recent rule by which teachers of all grades were compelled to take a training course at the Normal School; condemned the critics who complained of frequent changes of text books, and pointed out that such changes were contrary to law and that ready redress lay in the hands of voters at the School Board elections; claimed that on the Protestant Committee all educational interests were fairly represented — including 12 members directly connected with elementary education, and others occupied in farming, commerce, medicine, law, politics, etc.; pointed out that in Ontario the Legislative grant in the past year was $782,000, and in Quebec $405,000, and that while Toronto paid for its schools $675,000, Montreal, though a third larger, only paid $347,000; and declared the wonder to be not that they had many inferior schools but that so much had been done with such limited means. As to the teaching he made the following statement: "Salaries are still disgracefully small, but so they are elsewhere. In the United States the average salary in Public Schools is $260; in the Protestant Schools of Quebec it is $240. Of thirty-eight American States reported, the average salary of male teachers is larger only in eight, but the lowest average of female teachers, that of North Carolina, $21.43 per month, is larger than the average of all our female teachers." The Rev. Dr. Barclay and the Rev. Dr. MacVicar followed and strongly deprecated the present utilitarian spirit as a serious danger. The former declared that existing conditions were encouraging a mere smattering of knowledge on many subjects and only a superficial covering of a great area in any one subject. He thought the present salaries paid to teachers a scandal and disgrace.

The depression visible in educational matters in Nova Scotia in 1901 passed away to some extent during the succeeding year;

Popular Education in Nova Scotia and for the twelve months ending July 31st, 1902, the number of pupils in the Schools was 99,059 as compared with 98,410 in the previous period. Of this former total 50,247 were boys and 48,812 girls, while the number of teachers was 2,492—exactly the same as in 1901. The number of Normal School trained teachers, however, had increased from 947 to 1,044. The growth in this latter connection is shown by the fact that in 1893 there were only 408 trained teachers in the schools. During the year under review Mechanic Science Schools increased from three to eight and Domestic Science Schools from two to five; their equipment from $2,800 in value to $6,036; their total expenditure from $7,791 to $10,806. The annual vote of the ratepayers for school purposes also increased from $470,108 in the school year 1901 to

$538,850 in 1902. There was a small increase in the salaries of male teachers and a corresponding decrease in those of female teachers. The total expenditures from the Provincial Treasury rose, slightly, from $254,778 to $257,615. Further details may be seen in the following tabulated statement:

Particulars.	Year ending July 31, 1901.	Year ending July 31, 1902.
School Sections in Province	1,848	1,850
Sections without Schools	145	155
Schools in operation	2,387	2,394
Number of Male Teachers	540	485
Number of Female Teachers	1,952	2,007
New Teachers	466	416
Pupils in Common Schools	91,114	91,919
Pupils in High Schools	7,296	7,140
Value of Property in Sections	$82,026,153	$88,949,231
Value of School Property in Sections	1,632,460	1,777,512
Number of Volumes in School Libraries	14,780	15,085
Total Provincial Aid to Schools	$254,778	$257,615
Total Municipal Assistance	119,876	117,376
Total Section Assessment	470,108	538,850
Total of all voted educational expenditures	844,762	913,841
Average attendance of Pupils	53,643	55,437

The expenditure per pupil in average attendance at the schools of Nova Scotia, according to the annual Report of Dr. A. H. McKay, F.R.S.C., Superintendent of Education, was in this year $15.79 as compared with $17.40 in Ontario and with sums running in the United States from $47.81 in Nevada down to $17.53 in the State of Maine and to very much lesser sums in many of the Southern States. In his Report Dr. McKay mentioned previous efforts to induce a consolidation of rural school sections, deprecated the inertia, in this respect, of the ratepayers and hoped for success from Sir W. C. Macdonald's experiment at Middleton. He warmly approved the Nature Study idea, which was also being tried under the auspices of Sir W. C. Macdonald's money and Prof. J. W. Robertson's energetic work. Upon the matter of teachers and their position he spoke very plainly. After mentioning the popular idea that teaching was only a means of starting in life, the general knowledge as to the lowness of remuneration in the profession and the gradual elimination of men as members of it, Dr. McKay proceeded as follows:

Female teachers can afford to keep school open at a much less cost, it appears. The Trustee who is always haunted by the cry "keep down the taxes," is therefore extremely liable to fall into the error of accepting the lowest figure; and even when he knows better he is often forced by an ignorant democracy to accept its standard of value. This democracy understands the difference between twenty dollars and twenty-five, for by dint of ever-engrossing discrimination its vision is very acute; but it has not the dimmest glimpse of the difference between a teacher worth to the community twenty dollars and one worth a thousand. It is possible that the faith of the masses in the infallibility of the standard of license is partly responsible for this. A good third-class teacher is ready to take a school for a year at $200, but another of the same class will take it for $100. "It is the same article; and, of course, the cheap one is a great bargain," they argue.   This brings us face to face with the greatest defect of all in our system.   We admit teachers into the profession who have simply been able to pass the primitive test of a brief and simple written exam-ination.   There is no practical test of ability to teach or to manage a school. The examiners do not even see the candidate whose very face, or posture, or manners, or accent should rule him out of a teaching profession.

He urged greater care by Trustees in selecting from candidates and more willingness to pay larger salaries.   " Our system is perfect enough to supply in a few years teachers as good, if not better than can be produced in any country, provided it can be arranged to have a reasonable, living wage.   But when teachers are offered less than $20 a month, and unlettered boys can earn from $30 to $40 a month driving a team, or from $50 to $75 a month digging coal, what kind of teachers can we expect to take charge of the schools, and what hopes can we have of improving education in rural districts where there is not at least one man who can lead the people to reasonable effort."   Dr. McKay went on to urge the Legis-lature to intervene in preventing some of the wealthy towns from succeeding in their effort to escape from their share of the Municipal School Fund—as Dartmouth, Windsor and Truro had already done. He urged a small grant to rural teachers for looking after the school libraries.   He approved strongly of the recent affiliation of the School of Agriculture—with its 91 students—to the Provincial Normal School, and urged consolidation also with the School of Horticulture.   At the Normal School the enrolment of teachers was 182, exclusive of 26 who attended the course for bi-lingual teaching in the Acadian schools.

On February 7th Mr. Benjamin Russell, M.P., had a letter in the Halifax *Herald*, severely criticising modern methods of education in the Maritime Provinces.   The weakness of the system lay in its helping to overcrowd the professions.   If a young man wished to become a Civil, or a Mining, or Electrical Engineer he had to go elsewhere for his training.   He declared that there were too many opportunities now for the would-be minister, or lawyer, or doctor. Let others have a chance, and let the Provincial Government help to found a suitable Technical School.   In the Legislature, on March 23rd, a debate took place on teachers' salaries, and Mr. D. D. McKenzie quoted lengthy tables of figures to show how steadily they were falling.   In Grade " A," for instance, male teachers in 1894 received $802 and in 1901 $763 ; in Grade " B " they received $438 and $384, respectively.   Similarly, female teachers received in Grade " A " $653 in 1894 and $433 in 1901 ; and in Grade " B " $319 and $294, respectively.

Two days' later Mr. J. H. Sinclair presented to the Legislature the report of the Committee on Education.   Without reflecting in any way upon the Superintendent, who had inherited a certain system, they reported the opinion that " the schools of this Prov-ince as at present conducted are too much absorbed in book work and in verbal studies which seek to train the memory only, but which fail to give adequate discipline, or to fit the pupil for skilled labour or practical life." They urged more manual and practical instruction in elementary schools and the establishment, as soon as possible, of advanced technical and industrial schools. For these latter, however, there were not at present enough students available with the proper preliminary training. A Commission composed of the best fitted men in the Province was suggested with the duty given it to thoroughly investigate the existing system. In his speech Mr. Sinclair urged this recommendation upon the Government's attention. Good work was being done now but perhaps a still higher grade of achievement might be reached in future. The Hon. Mr. Longley said, in reply, that the Government had not the slightest objection to such an investigation, but he thought it might be very difficult to find enough men thoroughly familar with Common School education, as distinct from University and higher education, to form the Commission. The Government had, he pointed out, done a good deal already to encourage manual training in the Normal School and elsewhere.

Acadian education was given some attention during the year and on April 18, a Commission was appointed by the Government to investigate " the best methods of teaching English in the schools situate in the French districts of the Province " and of improving educational conditions generally therein. It consisted of the Rev. P. Dagnaud, Mr. W. E. Maclellan of Halifax (Chairman), Prof. A. G. Macdonald, Rev. W. M. LeBlanc, Hon. A. H. Comeau, Rev. A. E. Mombourquette, Mr. M. J. Doucet, M.P.P. and Dr. A. H. McKay. They reported the unanimous conclusion that the French-Canadian element in the population was at a very serious disadvantage in respect to education; and that this was due partly to their position in the midst of a different race and partly to misconceptions amongst incompetent teachers. The Committee recommended that English should be freely and fully taught concurrently with a general education in French; that bi-lingual teachers only should be employed; that a special series of French reading-books should be prepared and Inspectors be obliged to report separately upon these schools. The conclusions upon which these recommendations were based were as follows:

Your Commissioners find that the fundamental error in dealing with the French Schools, which must be held responsible for many of their short-comings, has been the assumption that they must be taught exclusively in English. They find that with startling uniformity and persistency attempts have been made and are being made to educate children from French-speaking homes and with none but French-speaking playmates, by means of the English language alone, sometimes from the lips of teachers who speak nothing but English. They find from the testimony of experts that even were such teachers masters of the most approved modern methods of teaching a foreign language but meagre results could be anticipated from their best efforts under such conditions. They find that with the inexperienced, ill-taught and often otherwise incompetent teachers ordinarily available for employment in such schools the efforts, however conscientious, made to teach the children to speak English are, as might be anticipated, largely a failure. They find also that while futile attempts to teach them English are thus being put forth, the general education of French-speaking pupils is being more or less seriously or sometimes even totally neglected.

As in Nova Scotia, the vital question of the neighbouring Province during the year, was that of teachers. In his annual Report, dated February 15th, 1902, Dr. J. R. Inch, Superintendent of Education in New Brunswick, pointed to a decrease of 15 in the number of teachers; estimated the new candidates seeking admission at the Normal School as averaging 240 or 250 each year; and stated that this number would be sufficient to provide for the withdrawal of about one-eighth of the teachers ordinarily employed in the schools. "But under existing conditions a much larger proportion than $12\frac{1}{2}$ per cent. of trained teachers of the higher classes seek and obtain other employments. There are now many more avenues of activity, than formerly, opening up before educated and energetic young people of both sexes, and these new fields of usefulness give promise of much better financial rewards and their cultivation is attended with less nervous strain and self-denial than are usually associated with the charge of a country school." Dr. Inch then pointed out in plain language what followed from this condition of affairs and indicated a possible means of meeting the difficulty:

> The inevitable results are the withdrawal annually from the teaching profession of hundreds of our best qualified teachers and the consequent closing of the schools or, what is scarcely a less evil, placing them in charge of teachers of imperfect education and utterly incompetent for the proper discharge of the functions of a teacher. The time has come when some remedy must be found for this growing evil; otherwise, every effort which has been made to raise the standard of efficiency in the schools by supplying them with a better educated and better trained class of teachers will be rendered abortive. A young man or woman who has spent years in acquiring the necessary education, who has undergone professional training and successfully passed the prescribed examinations, has a right to claim a reasonably remunerative salary from some source. If the public revenues are too limited to admit of increased Provincial grants and if no further assistance can be expected by the augmentation of the County Fund, then I respectfully submit that by legal enactment, the school districts, in proportion to their taxable valuation, should be required to contribute an amount which, when added to the Provincial grant, will make up salaries sufficient to command the services of properly educated and well-qualified teachers.

He had given in a preceding Report a list of 20 school districts with a taxable valuation running from $409,350 to $55,000, and in which the highest sum contributed towards the teacher's salary was $185 and the lowest $85. This he considered unfair to the poor districts as well as to the system as a whole. Everyone should contribute proportionately to the cause of education. In addition to increased taxation of districts in a rate of not less than 50 cents on every $100 of the taxable valuation, he urged the consolidation of rural schools and districts, wherever possible. For the school year 1900-1 Dr. Inch stated that the number of schools in the first term was 1,812 and in the second term 1,741; the number of teachers, respectively, 1,893 and 1,841; the number of pupils 57,629 and 60,420, respectively. The Provincial grant for schools in 1901 was $163,224, the district assessments, approximately, $346,623 and the County Fund grants to Trustees $90,492—a total of $600,339

Popular Education in New Brunswick

For 1900-1 there had been a decrease of 60 in the attendance at the Normal School, but for the current year of 1901-2 the enrolment was 270, or about the average for recent years. Dr. Inch pointed out in his Report that many of these teachers, though trained especially by the Province, dropped away from their profession after a short time, and he thought there should be some specific requirement of three years' service in connection with the course. The following statistics were given, in addition to those mentioned above, for the year 1900-1 :

	First Term.	Second Term.
Proportion of population at School	1 in 5·57	1 in 5·31
Decrease on corresponding term last year	1 in 247·08	1 in 313·7
Number of Pupils under 5 years of age	225	187
Decrease	34	125
Number between 5 and 15	55·111	56·485
Decrease	1,005	522
Number over 15 years	2,293	3,748
Decrease	257	377
Number of Boys	28,435	30,870
Decrease	1,024	680
Number of Girls	29,194	29,550
Decrease	272	344
Average Attendance	37,160	37,717
Decrease	1,092	(Inc.) 188
Number of Male Teachers in Common Schools	375	351
Decrease	10	19
Number of Female Teachers	1,494	1,460
Increase	12	....
Number of Trained Teachers	1,851	1,781
Increase	3	(Dec.) 28
Number of Grammar School Teachers	24	23
Decrease	....	2

The average salary of a male teacher in the Common Schools for the term ended June 30th, 1901, was $520.10 in the 1st class, $276.48 in the 2nd class, and $221.41 in the 3rd class. The average for female teachers was, respectively, $312.69, $226.78, and $179.34. The average salary in the Superior Schools was $576.07. Mr. Eldon Mullin, Principal of the Normal School at Fredericton, referred in his annual Report to the fact that leave of absence had been granted to him for a year from the 1st of February, 1902, to enable him to aid the South African authorities in remodeling their Normal School system, and stated that during the 18 years of his term of office in New Brunswick more than 5,000 teachers had passed through his hands. Dr. William Crocket was appointed to the position.

The annual Report of the Chief Superintendent of Education in Prince Edward Island was made public in March, 1902, with the **Popular Education in Prince Edward Island** statistics of the preceding year. It gave the school districts of the Province as 474 in number and the schools as numbering the same—an increase of three over the preceding year. The teachers numbered 589 in 1901 and 586 in 1900 and, of the former, 299 were males, or a decrease of 15, and 290 females, or an increase of 18.

The pupils enrolled in 1901 were 20,779 and in 1900 they were 21,289. Of the former number 11,319 were boys and 9,460 girls. The average attendance in 1901 was 12,330 as against 13,167 in 1900 and the proportion of population at school in 1901 was one in five or 20 per cent. The expenditure by the Government was $128,288 in 1901 as compared with $129,112 in the previous year and the former total included $113,835 as the statutory allowance to teachers, $920 as a bonus to teachers, and $5,469 as a grant to the Prince of Wales College and Normal School. There were supplementary payments by Trustees of $8,935 to teachers, and other sums running the total expenditure up to $164,935 or $7.93 for each pupil enrolled. Dr. Alexander Anderson in his Report reviewed the conditions indicated by these figures. He had found during the year that the schools were in a fair state of efficiency and the primary teachers better than he had expected.* But he was shocked at the state of the school-houses. "The class-rooms are never ventilated but by opening the windows; they are generally cheerless, cold and uninteresting; frequently their walls and ceilings are begrimed with the smoke of many years; their floors are broken or worn into holes in many places and the furniture is as unsuited as possible to meet the necessities of the present day." Irregular attendance was another evil to which he drew attention—caused either by the scholar being kept at home to work or by simple disinclination to attend. The frequent change of teachers was also a regrettable feature and was caused by the same difficulty which was facing other Provinces. The salaries paid to teachers in 1901, according to grades and sexes, were as follows:

GRADE.	NUMBER OF TEACHERS.	HIGHEST SALARY. Male.	Female.	LOWEST SALARY. Male.	Female.
1st Class	156	$770	$350	$300	$230
2nd Class	315	392	280	225	180
3rd Class	118	200	252	180	130

Such salaries were sadly insufficient and the only remedy was, he declared, in a generous supplementary contribution by the School Trustees towards an increased scale of remuneration. There should also be a higher assessment bye-law in the school districts. Dr. Anderson described the question as having become of vital importance. The very existence of education in the Province depended upon what they did now in this connection. "Salaries are so small that the best students who leave the Prince of Wales College, either do not take situations as teachers or if they do only remain for one, or it may be two years." Then the most of them left the Province. He declared it to be the people who must now act. The Government had done their full duty in this respect and all they could do. Apart from this subject he suggested certain reforms. In the first place men and women alike should teach for three years before being engaged in their native districts; in the second place

---

*Note—Dr. Anderson became Chief Superintendent in 1901 after many years experience as head of the Prince of Wales College.

every effort should be made to consolidate sections and rural schools ; in the third place no woman should receive a license to teach under 18 years of age. The first and last suggestions he considered very important. Most of the recent graduates from Prince of Wales College, who took up teaching, had been girls of sixteen, or thereabouts, with but few of the matured qualities needed for instructing others. Upon the first point he spoke strongly :

There has been no more fruitful source of trouble in school districts than the habit of appointing as teachers young people who have been born and brought up in the district, and who, only a short time ago, were pupils in the schools of which they are now in charge. Manifestly they must be possessed of considerable force of character and of activity and attainments above what is general among our teachers, to command the respect, to ensure the discipline, to direct the instruction, and influence the conduct of their former school-mates. But their frequent failure is undoubted proof of the folly of such a selection. The school does not exist for the purpose of assisting certain individuals in a district to make their first start in life. The school is instituted in the interest of the children and must be conducted so as to benefit them in the highest degree possible.

The Educational system in Manitoba is in the hands of a Department of the Government with the Ministers as members and

Public Instruction in Manitoba with an Advisory Board composed, at the beginning of 1902, of Archbishop Machray (Chairman) representing the University Council ; Messrs. J. D. Hunt, B.A., and Daniel McIntyre, M.A., elected by the the Teachers of the Province ; the Rev. Professor Hart, Rev. A. A. Cherrier, Rev. Canon Matheson, B.D., Prof. R. R. Cochrane, B.A., and Messrs. J. R. Jones, M.D., and John Graham, B.A., appointed by the Department of Education, or, in other words, the Government. On February 22nd, 1902, the Report for the school year ending December 31st previously was presented to the Legislature by the Hon. Mr. Campbell. In this the Inspectors of the Provincial school divisions reported at some length as to local conditions. In Winnipeg, the enrolment of pupils at the Public Schools was 8,246, of whom 4,093 were boys and 4,119 girls. According to Mr. D. McIntyre, the Superintendent for the City, " the general tone of the schools and the spirit in which the work is done is, for the most part, excellent and the quality of instruction good." At the Provincial Normal School the attendance during its four sessions ran from 40 to 47. Principal W. A. McIntyre, in his annual statement, said that " as the work of the School continues, the wisdom of compelling all teachers to take the third-class course and teach a year before the second-class course, is perceived."

In his Division Inspector S. E. Laing found a great lack of school libraries—only 45 per cent. possessing even a semblance of one ; too many small schools ; and very insufficient attention paid to oral reading. Inspector E. E. Best reported a marked absence of sympathetic feeling in his community toward the work of the schools, and he deprecated the local habits of speech. " I regret to say that few schools appear to put forth any special effort to counteract the general tendency towards recklessness in the oral

use of our language." He found also that irregular attendance
was greatly marring the efficiency of the schools, coupled with
insufficient equipment provided by the Trustees.

Inspector A. S. Rose of Brandon reported a most successful
year, the teachers as being well abreast of the times, and a decided
upward tendency in salaries. Amongst the pupils reading was
well taught in the primary forms but apt to be neglected afterwards, and irregular attendance was complained of. Inspector A. L.
Young described the school buildings in his Division as not up to the
standard, attendance also as irregular, and a tendency noticeable
amongst teachers to give undue prominence to certain subjects.

Inspector Roger Goulet had supervision of the French-Canadian
schools of the Province, and he declared a serious need to exist for
qualified bi-lingual teachers. The salary question was the great
drawback. Inspector A. W. Hooper reported "lamentably irregular" attendance, great difficulty in obtaining qualified teachers,
and no opportnity of dealing with the Gallicians—of which
people there were 12,000 in his Division—because of the lack
of teachers understanding both languages. Inspector H. S.
MacLean asked for a compulsory school law as the only means of
ensuring satisfactory attendance. Mr. H. H. Ewart reported for a
Division containing mainly Mennonite schools, and in which the
attendance was very satisfactory and the teachers devoted to their
work. The pupils, however, in accordance with a custom of their
people, would not attend after 12 to 14 years of age. The
statistics of the schools of Manitoba as a whole, may be seen in the
following tabulated statement for the year, ending December 31st
1901:

```
School Population of the Province .................  63,881
Pupils Registered at Schools .....................  51,888
Average Attendance ..............................  27,550
Number of Male Teachers .........................     618
Number of Female Teachers .......................   1,051
Standing and number of Teachers.
    A—Collegiate ............................  46
    B—1st Class .............................  267
    C—2nd Class .............................  725
    D—3rd Class .............................  541
    E—Interim Certificates ..................  90
                                            ——— 1,669
Teachers at Normal School .......................      20
Students at Normal School .......................     260
Legislative Grant to Schools ....................  $113,451
Municipal Taxes for Schools .....................  653,359
Teachers' Salaries ... ..........................  582,325
Total Receipts for Educational purposes .........  1,310,805
Total Expenditures ..............................  1,272,616
Average Teachers' Salaries (urban) ..............  576.41
Average Teachers' Salaries (rural) ..............  435.15
Number of Schools opened with Religious Exercises ..  248
Number of Schools closed with Prayer ............  283
Number of Schools in which the Bible is used ....  169
Schools giving Temperance Instruction ...........  879
Schools teaching Ten Commandments ...............  254
Schools giving Moral Instruction ................  925
```

At the opening ceremonies of the Normal School in Winnipeg, on August 20th, Principal McIntyre spoke at some length and described the great progress made in the Province along educational lines during his 15 years' experience in his present position. "To-day there are practically no teachers who have not had some professional preparation, and about 60 per cent. have had a special training of seven months or over." The average age of their teachers was about 25 years and, more important still to his mind, a higher ideal of duty and responsibility was apparent. "This higher ideal may be termed the ideal of character, and stands over in particular against two imperfect ideals—the ideal of utility and the ideal of scholarship. In a commercial age, an age of intense competition, and in a country where the amassing, rather than the enjoyment and generous disposal of wealth, seems to be the chiefest consideration, it is natural that there should be a great demand for such teaching in the schools as will fit the pupils for the battle of life. Yet everyone will agree that it is vastly more important to learn how to live than to learn how to make a living, and that the hoarding idea is altogether too low for a progressive and enlightened people." He strongly deprecated the idea of turning farmers and mechanics ready-made from the schools, and believed that Manitoba was developing the very much higher conception outlined above :

Now the ideal which our teachers have been reaching, as contrasted with the scholastic ideal and the ideal of utility, might be termed the idea of character. It recognized that the whole boy goes to school, and aims at his physical, intellectual, and moral development. It considers that the products of education should include the acquisition of knowledge, the development of power, the formation of pure tastes and right habits, the cultivation of proper feelings and disposition, and the formation of a strong self-controlled will, which, linked to a sound conscience, is the foundation of a character. It is because so many of our teachers are placing before them the three C's—conscience, conduct, character—as the great aims in education, that we hope for the future of our Province. All true education looks toward the eternities. The great eternities are faith, hope and love, which are the elements of strong, lovable and enduring character.

What has become imbedded in history as the Manitoba School Question was raised from time to time during the year, so far as one distinguished ecclesiastic could succeed in doing

Educational Issues in Manitoba so. On April 13th Archbishop Langevin of Winnipeg issued a Pastoral Letter which was read throughout the Archdiocese of St. Boniface. It declared that of all the questions debated in this young country none was more vital than that of providing and maintaining elementary schools for the Christian education of Catholic youth. If, as his Church believed, religion is an essential part of education, then parents could not conscientiously accept a system where secular instruction was wholly divorced from religious instruction; or one in which a religious training common to all denominations and Churches was prescribed; or one in direct opposition to the tenets of the Catholic Church. "We mean to say that not only Protestant or

30

anti-Catholic Schools are prohibited but even those called non-sectarian schools—such as are at present the Public Schools of Manitoba." It was the duty of Catholic parents to send their children to Catholic schools. "We thank God," added His Grace, "that the greater number of the Catholics in the Diocese have understood and faithfully fulfilled their duty in this matter. Nevertheless, we must not fail to mention a most regrettable action on the part of some negligent or poorly enlightened parents wanting in generosity who, without reason or leave, have sent their children to non-Catholic schools and this when there were Catholic schools at their very doors."

The Archbishop then went on to assert that the School question was not settled although they had been compelled by circumstances to work under a law which disputed and divided the Church's control over her schools wherever a portion of the Government grant was accepted. "The restoration of school rights violated in 1890 is what we claim now"—the right to use Catholic books of history, geography and reading; the complete liberty of religious teaching, exercises and the use of symbols. The Pastoral concluded by instructing parish priests and missionaries that children attending non-Catholic schools were not to be admitted to the first Communion without the Archbishop's permission. Speaking at Ottawa, on October 2nd, His Grace referred again to this subject and stated that in Winnipeg the Catholics supported their own schools and, in addition, had to pay $10,000 a year in taxes to support the Public Schools.

During the succeeding two months Archbishop Langevin spent much time in visiting various parts of Quebec with, it was said, the object of arousing public interest in the North-West and also in its School question. To the press, on November 27th, he declared with vigour that this matter was far from being settled. "It will be settled only when right is done—right such as was promised to the Catholics of the Province in 1870 by the Imperial authorities. The fact that we enjoy a certain degree of toleration, instead of a legal recognition of our rights, is not sufficient; but then we appreciate the increasing good will of the best thinking men in the land." He referred to their financial situation in the West, to the double taxes borne by the Catholic ratepayers of Winnipeg, to the closing of one of their five schools as a consequence and wondered how long the Protestants of Canada would stand it if the minority in Quebec were so treated. Through *Le Journal* of Montreal the Archbishop addressed two appeals to his "French-Canadian compatriots of the Province of Quebec." On December 2nd he made a fervent demand that they insist upon the Dominion Government doing justice to the minority in Manitoba and described, as follows, his reasons for opposing the present conditions in his Province:

1. By the existing school laws we are not able to speak of religion nor even to explain the commandments of God from the Catholic point of view during school hours.

2. By the existing school law we are not able to recite Catholic prayers during class hours.

3. Under the existing school law we are not allowed to supply ourselves with Catholic school-books.

4. Under the existing school law we are not allowed to place a crucifix or other sign of religion in the school.

5. Under the existing school law, as interpreted by the Winnipeg School Commission, our Sisters are not even allowed to wear their costume in the school.

6. Under the existing law each school-master and mistress is called upon to take an oath to safeguard the interests of the neutral school. If this oath has been modified at our demand by the local Government it still remains unjust.

The *Canadian Gleaner* of Huntingdon, in the Eastern Townships of Quebec, took up the Archbishop's reference to the Quebec minority on December 4th. It declared that in those one-time Protestant Townships the schools had originally been neutral and attended by Protestants and Catholics alike ; that they were broken up by the Catholic demand for Separate Schools ; that thousands of English-speaking children were now growing up in ignorance because their parents, while able to support one school, could not support two. The inevitable result had been inefficient and ill-attended institutions. The editorial proceeded to describe " one school for all and perfect religious equality " as the motto of Manitoba and to state that clergymen of all denominations had the right to attend the schools of that Province at fixed hours and give religious instruction. " Would to Heaven we had such schools in our Townships ! If we had, we would not have the sad spectacle, now oft presented to us, of loyal subjects leaving for the United States because unable to get their children educated in this nominally British Province of Quebec."

Another question of importance, though not of such a controversial character, was the problem of education for the Gallician settlers in the Province. On January 2nd the Premier and his Government received a deputation at Winnipeg, composed of Principal Sparling, the Rev. Dr. Bryce, Principal Patrick, the Rev. Professor Hart, Archdeacon Fortin, the Rev. C. W. Gordon, Mayor Arbuthnot, and Messrs. William Whyte, J. A. M. Aikins, K.C., R. J. Whitla and E. L. Drewry, which strongly presented the necessity for establishing Public Schools amongst these people. Archdeacon Fortin stated that " the bulk of the 15,000 Gallicians in the Province had no facility for education of any kind. They were a very intelligent and ambitious people, anxious to get on, although afraid to incur expenses they might not be able to meet. The Government stood *in loco parentis* to them and should do something to establish schools. The most important thing was that English should be taught." Other speakers followed and then the Hon. Mr. Roblin replied, in part, as follows : " The question they had laid before him was not one which had escaped the attention of his Government ; indeed they had given it more attention, perhaps, than any one question that had come before them. They had viewed it from all standpoints, and had come to the conclusion that, apart altogether from the education of the Gallicians, the educational system of the Province demanded re-adjustment. It was because of this that a year ago he had promised that a Bill imposing compulsory education should be introduced at the next Session. That this had not been done was because they found, on examining the cost, that the finances of the Province simply could not stand the extra burden." The Premier's conclusion was a hope that the Federal Governnment would give the Province its rights in connection with the School Lands' question and thus enable the Government to again take up this matter of compulsory education.

Three days later the Archbishop of St. Boniface addressed the Catholic Club of Winnipeg upon the needs and nature of the Gallicians. Education was, he declared, their primary requirement, but there were difficulties in the way. "Schools must be established for them according to the law, and the English language should be taught in those schools. The school law of the country had also consecrated the bi-lingual system, and these people as a matter of right might have their children taught their own language, together with the English, and as a matter of fact they desired it strongly. But, if all agreed that English must be taught, all did not admit the desirability of teaching their national language. Now the Gallicians believed they must keep their language, particularly, because they believed it was the best means to keep their faith." The Catholic Church was already maintaining a school in Winnipeg for these people with 125 children in daily attendance, but, His Grace remarked, no aid had been suggested for this institution by the gentlemen who recently waited upon the Government. Another hundred would come to the school if room were available, and the reason for this was that their language, as well as English, was taught and their faith conserved.

He seemed to think that this phenomenal interest in the Gallicians, as apart from Mennonites and Doukhobors and others, was because the great majority of them were Catholics. He did not like this interference and observed that the Roman Catholic Church was not trying to establish schools for educating Presbyterian children or Methodists! People should not so lightly try to dispose of 4,000 Catholic children. "If they wanted to start a new School Question now was the time. With their increase in numbers during the past ten years, and with the better knowledge they had of their strength, the Catholics were never so well fitted to fight their own battles. People apparently thought the Catholics were sleeping, but this was a mistake; they might not be saying much lately but they were always at work, and even when they slept they were thinking." Archbishop Langevin concluded with a description of the missionary work his Church had done amongst the Gallicians, and was followed briefly by the Rev. Father Drummond and others.

On August 12th, following, the Hon. Mr. Campbell, Attorney-

General of the Province, stated that the Government were going to take up the matter of education amongst the Foreign-born classes in the country as soon as possible. Although they had received some $25,000 a year less from the Federal Government than was expected in the School Lands matter yet they would endeavour to obtain a suitable Superintendent for this work and take it up in some organized form. The position was stated by the Winnipeg *Teleg. am* of the following day in these words : " The difficulties, as far as the Government are concerned, have been twofold. The Foreigners would not avail themselves of the provisions of the law, form school districts, elect Trustees and raise by taxation what was necessary to supplement the Government grants. They appeared to be anxious for education, but they did not seem ready for the system of the Province. If they could not qualify under the law for grants, the only thing the Government could do would be to make an exception in their case and manage everything for them until such time as they were able to do their share. But here the second difficulty came in, for the funds available for education were so limited that in justice to the Province as a whole the necessary amount of money could not be set apart for this exceptional treatment of one class of the people."

During the years 1901 and 1902 the question of Education was one of the most important with which the Government of the Territories had to deal. The vast extent of country, the scattered people, the agricultural and ranching characteristics of the population, the constant and increasing influx of new settlers, the limitation of available funds, all combined to make it a complicated and difficult problem. At the beginning of the former year a re-organization of the system was carried out under the terms of recent legislation. The old-time Council of Public Instruction was superceded, and the control of all matters pertaining to schools and education passed into the hands of a Department of Education presided over by Mr. F. W. G. Haultain, Premier, and now Commissioner of Education, with Mr. J. A. Calder as Deputy Commissioner, and Mr. D. J. Goggin, M.A., D.C.L., as Superintendent. During 1901 the number of school districts was 713, or an increase of 83 over the preceding year; the number of districts having schools in operation was 564, or an increase of 72; the number of departments in operation was 682, or an increase of 94; the number of pupils enrolled was 23,837, or an increase of 3,494; the average attendance of pupils was 11,968, or an increase of 2,538; the average percentage of pupils attending was 50 per cent., or an increase of 3·65 per cent.*

The financial difficulties of the situation were illustrated in the year ending December 31st, 1901, by the fact that the school grants earned by school districts amounted to $185,721, or an

*Education
in the
North-West
Territories*

---

* NOTE—Report of the Department of Education, Regina, for 1901.

increase over 1900 of $22,707; while the total grants paid were $162,215, or a decrease of $6,106. The school debentures authorized during the year amounted to $109,210, and those registered to $90,360. The amount expended on school buildings and grounds was $95,300; the payments for teachers' salaries were $274,040; and the amount expended for school purposes was $179,468. Of the school districts, at the above date, there were 371 in Assiniboia, including 6 Separate Schools; 260 in Athabasca, including 7 Separate Schools; 82 in Saskatchewan, including 3 Separate Schools. There were, therefore, 16 Separate Schools in the Territories at that time—a point of importance in view of the expected assumption of Provincial powers in the near future and the already commenced discussion as to the control and financial place of the Roman Catholic Separate Schools under new conditions.

Of the 23,837 pupils in the Territorial schools, 12,310 were boys and 11,527 girls; 10,060 were in towns and villages and 13,777 in rural schools; in each rural department there was an average enrolment of 27 pupils, and in each urban department of 58 pupils. The salaries of the 762 teachers, employed during the year, varied in accordance with their certificates, with their position in rural, town or village schools, and upon the school being open the whole year or only part of a year. The average salary paid to all teachers employed was $45.00 per month. The following table affords a summary:

CLASS OF CERTIFICATE.	SCHOOLS OPEN THE WHOLE YEAR.				IN ALL SCHOOLS.			
	No.	Salaries per month.			No.	Highest.	Lowest.	Average.
		Highest.	Lowest.	Average.				
		$ c.	$ c.	$ c.		$ c.	$ c.	$ c.
First, male	88	108 33	40 00	59 80	119	108 33	40 00	56 25
,, female	34	66 66	40 00	47 62	52	66 66	40 00	46 04
Second, male	97	65 00	40 00	45 83	213	65 00	35 00	44 53
,, female	129	60 00	30 00	43 12	268	60 00	30 00	42 44
Third, male	1	40 00	....	....	14	45 00	40 00	41 10
,, female	10	66 66	33 33	39 79	42	66 66	30 00	38 45
Permit, male	6	50 00	26 00	41 52	25	50 00	26 00	41 95
,, female	2	50 00	33 33	41 66	28	50 00	30 00	39 70
Kindergarten	1	41 66	....	....	1	41 66	....	....

There were 143 log school-houses in use, 355 frame ones and a small number made of brick, stone, etc. School libraries were reported in 105 of the institutions with a total of 4,229 books. The total receipts of the school districts for 1901 were $620,562—including taxes collected amounting to $243,146, Government grants of $163,843, proceeds of debentures $88,835, and $77,550 borrowed by notes. The assets of these districts were stated at $917,766, of which $559,991 was the estimated value of lands and out-buildings. There were 227 interim certificates granted during the year to teachers who had either completed a course of training at the Regina Normal School or who presented approved professional certificates from the other Provinces or elsewhere. Professional certificates numbering 100 were given to teachers who had taken Normal School training and taught successfully for at least a year on their interim receipts. Provisional certificates were given to 144 candidates. The Normal School during the year had 116 students in attendance. In presenting the above and other statistics to the Department Mr. J. A. Calder stated, in his Report of April 1st, 1902, that progress in a general connection had been more than usually satisfactory.

In every part of the country the keenest interest has been shown in the establishment and maintenance of Public Schools. As may be seen from the statistical tables accompanying this Report, the material advancement that has taken place is most gratifying. The reports received from our Inspectors also indicate that the schools which have been in operation have succeeded in attaining a comparatively high standard of efficiency. That there is a constantly growing healthy sentiment in favour of the best results that our educational system can be made to secure is everywhere manifest. The people have been liberal in their financial support; new and better school buildings are being erected ; greater attention is being given to the equipment of schools, and the care and arrangement of school grounds ; school libraries are being provided ; and Trustees continue to demand the very best teachers that can be secured.

In the matter of teachers there had been the same trouble as elsewhere and it was expected that the demand in 1902 would far exceed the supply. Mr. Calder approved strongly of the recent legislation by which the formation of small school libraries was made compulsory ; urged the consolidation of rural schools and referred to the arrangements made by the Government in cases when transportation was required. Dr. Goggin submitted an elaborate Report detailing in some measure, and summarizing in other respects the reports of the Inspectors. He drew attention to the London *Journal of Education* as warmly approving the Department's programme of studies—describing it as showing "a progressive spirit nowhere excelled." The educational documents of the Territories had also, he said, been highly commended in Great Britain while the Commissioner of Education in the United States had referred to their system as " giving evidence of advanced ideas with reference to the conditions for effective schools." Dr. Goggin concluded as follows: " While we have reason to congratulate ourselves on our progress we still have difficulties to overcome. If we could secure higher scholarship in our teachers and give them longer training ; if we could give sufficient training to those teachers who come to us each year from other Provinces, so as to familiarize them with our conditions, aims, and courses of study ; if we could induce small schools to unite and provide for the conveyance of the children to the central schools and so increase the length of their school year and improve the attendance and the character of the teaching; we should have solved some of our pressing problems and increased the efficiency of our system."

There were, of course, other opinions expressed in this connection. On February 27th, 1902, the Calgary *Herald* reviewed the educational situation in the Territories; declared that it might be all right in theory but it was " fizzling out in practice; " described it as crushing out individuality and referred to the lack of opportunity amongst teachers to exchange ideas; regretted the lack of funds which was making it difficult to procure efficient teachers or to maintain sufficient training opportunities for them; demanded more discipline in the schools and vigorously deprecated the modern fear of applying corporal punishment to pupils; declared the whole system to be in need of a revolution in favour of "the concrete, the practically useful." The following extract gives further detail in this connection:

Children are crammed with abstract theories and few of them acquire a decent knowledge of the practical work by which they expect to earn their daily bread.   If anyone doubts this all that he has to do is to pick out a lad from any of the Territorial High Schools and set him at office work and see how much he can do.   He will probably argue with you about the manner in which to conduct your business but that will be the utmost extent of his usefulness.

In a great many instances the teachers are little better than children themselves.   They stuff themselves full of book knowledge, which they have neither the training nor the perception to apply, attend Normal School at Regina where they listen to lectures upon abstract subjects and are taught that it is nothing short of criminal to take the strap to a boy ; no matter how gross the cause of his offending.

Thus the majority of them become mere pedants stuffed with just enough learning to make them dangerous and entirely deficient in a knowledge of its application.   They walk and work along the rigid lines laid down by their preceptors.   Many of the male teachers—the majority of them we believe—do not enter the teaching profession permanently.   The finished teacher in this country is one of the last persons who should be intrusted with children.   It is not his (or her) fault.   The system is to blame.

On Sept. 24th it was announced that Dr. Goggin had resigned the positions of Superintendent of Education and Principal of the Regina Normal School, which he had held since 1894, in order to remove to Toronto.   Various tributes were paid to his work and that of the Moosomin *Spectator* (Oct. 16th) may be quoted here: " He deserves credit for what he has done in the cause of education in the West.   When he came to Regina the educational sytem of the Territories was in its infancy.   He had an almost free hand to develop the system according to his own ideal and was given valuable assistance in so doing.   Now the educational system of the Territories compares favourably with that of any other part of Canada and has complimentary notices from educationists both in Britain and the United States.   The Regina Normal School has been popular with teachers ever since its organization.   From the first session the attendance has been large, too large for the equipment and staff to handle with satisfaction."

The Canadian Arch Erected in London in Honour of the Coronation.

The Educational system of British Columbia is divided into High, Graded, and Common Schools.   The total enrolment in these for the year ending June 30th, 1901, was 23,615, or an increase of 2,084 over the preceding school year. Of this number 12,069 were boys and 11,546 girls—an increase respectively, of 993 and 1,091.   According to the annual Report of Mr. Alexander Robinson, B.A., Superintendent of Education for the Province, which appeared in 1902 for the period above mentioned, the enrolment of students at the High Schools was 584, an increase of 31 over the previous year; at the Graded Schools it was 15,460 or an increase of 1,647; and at the Common Schools it was 7,571 or an increase of 406. The average daily attendance at all schools was 15,334 or an increase of 1,667; the actual average attendance was 15,098 or an increase of 1,659.   The expenditure by the Government was $312,187 upon Education proper with $38,345 additional spent upon buildings, repairs, etc.   The municipalities of Nanaimo, New Westminster, Vancouver and Victoria also expended $182,160 between them, making a total for the Province of $532,692 as against $389,367 in the year 1899-1900.

Popular Education in British Columbia

The average monthly salary of teachers in city districts was $59.26 and in rural districts $52.66.   There were 318 schools in operation during 1901, or an increase of 20.   Of these there were 5 High Schools with 15 teachers; 55 Graded Schools with 270 teachers; and 258 Common Schools with 258 teachers and monitors—a total of 543 teachers, or an increase of 49 over the previous year.   Mr. Robinson, in the further course of his Report, stated that the Manual Training Schools established by Sir W. C. Macdonald had proved a great success, urged an extension of their centralization policy through the medium of graded schools, and asked for the erection of a new building for the Normal School.

MISCELLANEOUS EDUCATIONAL INCIDENTS

Jan. 1.—The Public Libraries in Ontario are stated to number 415 with 155,361 members, 6,062 newspapers and periodicals, 1,066,117 volumes and 2,668,364 issued during the year. The receipts for the year were $225,796 and the assets of the various institutions $1,080,601. Of the number mentioned 132 were free and 283 not so. During 1901, 27 Libraries did not report to the Department of Education and 35 new Libraries were incorporated in 1902, so that the total number at the end of that year was 477.

Jan. 1.—The Report of the Ontario Department of Education gives the following table relating to teachers' salaries in certain years since Confederation :

YEAR.	Highest Salary paid.	Average salary, male teacher, Province.	Average salary, female teacher, Province.	Average salary, male teacher, Counties.	Average salary, female teacher, Counties.	Average salary, male teacher, Cities.	Average salary, female teacher, Cities.	Average salary, male teacher, Towns.	Average salary, female teacher, Towns.
1867	$1,350	$346	$226	$261	$189	$532	$243	$464	$240
1872	1,000	360	228	305	213	628	245	507	216
1877	1,100	398	264	379	˙251	735	307	583	269
1882	1,100	415	269	˙385	248	742	331	576	273
1887	1,450	425	292	398	271	832	382	619	289
1892	1,500	421	297	383	269	894	402	648	298
1897	1,500	391	294	347	254	892	425	621	306
1900	1,500	404	298	349	255	892	455	624	309
1901	1,550	421	306	359	262	915	470	649	315

May   1.—The Public School Board of Toronto receives the resignation of Mr. James L. Hughes, its Senior Inspector of Schools. It is not accepted and later on is withdrawn. The incident evokes many public references to Mr. Hughes' efficiency and popularity.

May 19.—Mr. James L. Hughes in a local address urges certain educational reforms, as follows : " Much smaller School Boards ; in Toronto one Board to manage education, and with it the Public Library ; the schools open for the use of the people at night, and to become, by lecture courses, etc., centres of social and intellectual advancement for the whole community ; two courses of education throughout the country with University degrees equally honourable—one based on mechanics, the other on culture ; in the city, for boys and girls alike, more planting and growing, more manual training and more play."

July 17.—The Public School Board of Toronto appoints Mr. Hughes Chief Inspector of its Schools, with increased powers subject to future and exact definition. The vote is 12 to 7 in favour of the appointment.

Oct. 17.—The Manual Training Department of the Halifax Public Schools is formally opened, with addresses by the Lieutenant-Governor, Mr. H. L. Chipman and Mr. T. B. Kidner of Truro. Mr. Chipman, in speaking as Chairman of the local Board of School Commissioners, says that Halifax was the first city in Canada to introduce Manual Training into its Public Schools, and then continues : " Is it, therefore, not in the trend of an up-to-date educational system that we should endeavour to give the boys that education which will afford them the means of livelihood in after years ? Is this not in keeping with the industrial progress of the age in which we are now living ? Has it not been the means of the industrial growth of the neighbouring Republic, and to-day, when we have in our own country indications of a similar development, is it not time that we should put forth our strongest efforts to educate the youth of to-day in that direction ? Does not such education mean the keeping of young men and women at home ; does it not mean the growth and success of our country ?

Oct. 22.—Professor J. W. Robertson of Ottawa addresses a large audience in Vancouver upon Manual Training and the rural school system, which it was now proposed to develop in the different Provinces.

Oct. 29.—Professor J. W. Robertson addresses a gathering in Winnipeg upon the aims and principles of the Macdonald Manual Training Schools, and also deals at length with the desirability of graded or consolidated schools in rural districts. The Hon. C. H. Campbell presides and, with Principal Patrick and the Rev. Dr. Bryce, endorses the suggestions of the speaker.

Dec. 10.—A Report dealing with the educational system in Toronto and prepared by Mr. John Seath, B A., LL.D., Inspector of High Schools for Ontario, is made public. In it he describes the condition of the local Collegiate Institutes to be serious, and five additional teachers, five or six new class-rooms and a considerable additional expenditure as necessary in order to meet the increasing attendance. He urges a re-organization of the various independent School Boards into one coherent system and asks the Public Library to take up its work as part of the educational system. He presses for a union of the High and Public School Boards as a preliminary to general re-organization.

Dec. 10.—It is announced that the successor of the late Dr. J. A. McCabe as Principal of the Ottawa Normal School will be Mr. J. F. White, Senior Separate School Inspector of Ontario, and that Mr. J. F. Power of the Simcoe High School will replace Mr. White.

Dec. 19.—The McGill University authorities are advised that the Carnegie Institute of Washington, D.C., has granted the sum of $25,000 to Dr. Frank D. Adams, Professor of Geology at McGill, to enable him to continue certain important scientific experiments.

Dec. 22.—It is announced that Dr. Parkin's successor as Principal of Upper Canada College, Toronto, has been appointed in the person of Mr. H. W. Auden, M.A., of Fettes College, Edinburgh. It is stated that the appointment is made upon the recommendation of Mr. E. B. Osler, M.P., who had recently visited several Schools in England in connection with the matter. Principal Auden was born in 1867, is a graduate of Cambridge, and is said to be a man of wide culture and marked organizing ability.

XVII.—MUNICIPAL INTERESTS

An organization was formed in August, 1901, under the auspices and initiative of Mayor O. A. Howland of Toronto, for the purpose **The Union of Canadian Municipalities** of uniting the municipalities of Canada along lines of common action and for purposes of mutual protection against Legislative or corporate encroachment. Mayor Howland was elected President and Mr. W. D. Lighthall, Mayor of Westmount, became the first Secretary of the Association. On May 14th, 1902, the Executive Committee issued a Report describing the work done during the past few months. They had (1) combined with the Cities of Toronto and Hamilton in resisting a measure at Ottawa intended to enable the Toronto and Hamilton Railway Company to force a connection with Street Railways operating in those cities, without municipal consent; (2) they had received the thanks of Port Arthur for opposing certain concessions asked by corporations from the Ontario Government; (3) they had aided in obtaining from the Legislature of Quebec modifications imposing the consent of municipalities in connection with the Provincial Light, Heat and Power Company, the Beauharnois Light, Heat and Power Company and the Shawinigan Power Company.

At Ottawa, deputations attended from time to time and with more or less success, in connection with the Union, and in opposition to clauses in Mr. W. F. Maclean's Telephone and Telegraph measure and in the similar legislation proposed by the Government; to the Bell Telephone Company's application for power to increase its capital stock from five to ten millions; to the Joint Stock Companies' Bill and to the Canadian Northern Telegraph and Telephone Bill. In connection, especially, with this proposed telephone legislation, 80 petitions were presented by the Union and pressure was brought to bear from many combined municipal interests. The legislation was finally held over. The Terminal Railway matter in Montreal, by which a Company had obtained through Dominion charter what amounted to the power of establishing a street railway in that city without Provincial or Municipal consent, was vigorously and successfully opposed and won a Resolution of appreciation from the Montreal City Council. The Union had received a similar vote of thanks from Winnipeg for its representations against an effort made on behalf of the Canadian Pacific Railway to compel that City to contribute one-half toward the cost of a local Subway. Successful aid was also given to the City of Hamilton in an effort to have the G.T.R. Company ordered to reconstruct its bridge at Burlington. Meanwhile under date of Feb. 17th, a petition was sent to the members of the

Dominion Parliament and to the Quebec and Ontario Legislatures urging, on behalf of 70 cities, towns and other municipalities, the following propositions:

1. That municipalities should have full and exclusive control of their streets, and no legislation should be passed infringing on such control unless the same be subject to the consent of the municipality concerned.

2. The Union has no desire to injure corporations or impair any fair and proper powers, but it prays that the desire of the vast number of citizens whose municipal rights it is called upon to protect, be duly held in view by your Honourable House in connection with the numerous private bills affecting municipalities which are to come before you during the present Session.

3. It also prays that retroactive legislation in the same spirit be duly brought in and passed, by a general statute submitting to municipal consent and control all future works and constructions to be made by corporations in, upon, and under, the streets and highways of municipalities; admitting only of passage across one municipality to another, subject to compensation by arbitration.

This document was signed by Mayor Howland of Toronto, Mayor Lighthall of Westmount, Mayor Hamilton of Halifax, Ald. McRae of St. John, Mayor Arbuthnot of Winnipeg, Mayor Morris of Ottawa, and Mayor Read of Owen Sound. The first annual meeting of the Union of Canadian Municipalities opened at Montreal on Sept. 15th with the President in the chair. In connection with the address of welcome from acting-Mayor Lamarche of Montreal, Mayor Howland replied in both English and French. The Secretary reported a membership of 90 municipalities extending over every Province of the Dominion. Amongst the 85 delegates in attendance at the Convention were Mayor John Arbuthnot of Winnipeg, Mayor Fred. Cook of Ottawa, Mayor Aaron Reid of Owen Sound, Mayor James Warburton of Charlottetown, Mayor J. O. Camirand of Sherbrooke, Mayor Hayes of Richmond, P.Q., Mayor G. W. Sulman of Chatham, Ont., Mayor T. H. G. Denne of Peterborough, Mayor Adam Beck, M.P.P., of London, Mayor J. Morgan Shaw of Kingston, Mayor S. Chant of St. Thomas, Mayor W. H. Keary of New Westminster, Ald. W. P. Hubbard of Toronto, Ald. W. R. Stroud of Ottawa, Ald. J. F. Whear, M.P.P., of Charlottetown, and Ald. H. B. Ames of Montreal. After the formal addresses had been disposed of Ald. Lapointe of Montreal read a paper urging more and better Civic embellishment; more practical and systematic effort in beautifying the towns and cities of Canada; more care by citizens of the appearance of their houses and gardens and of their streets by the public bodies concerned. Discussion ensued at some length upon the following Resolution embodying approval of a plan suggested and strongly favoured by Mayor Howland:

That this Union, having considered the question submitted to it by the last annual meeting looking to joint action on the part of the municipalities throughout Canada for their financial relief, is strongly of the opinion that much good will come from drawing the attention of municipal bodies and financiers to the advantage of municipalities combining (with the assistance of suitable legislation) to borrow on united credit, for the purpose of borrowing favourably; and the Executive is hereby instructed and empowered to prepare a suitable scheme for presentation to the various Provincial Legislatures, with a view to the provision of Provincial machinery for examining debentures and certifying the same; and looking ultimately, if found practicable, to a Dominion guarantee of the whole.

The President briefly explained his proposals as follows : " The object is to enable the municipalities of Canada (which are the whole of Canada, distributed into sections) to borrow the large sums which they do borrow annually, and to maintain the immense debt which they do maintain, on some terms which more nearly approach those of the Dominion of Canada. The debts of the municipalities of Canada, in the aggregate, amount to about one hundred million dollars, an amount of debt which, if it took a consolidated and recognized shape upon the market in some kind of permanent and non-fluctuating form, derived from one central authority and not depending upon the recognition given in Foreign countries to an individual village, or individual township, or individual city in Canada, would be a very permanent and a very important public security and public fund, and would necessarily hold a higher rank than the majority of the municipal securities that are now placed upon the market enjoy." No action was taken upon the matter, further than to leave it in the hands of the Executive to obtain fuller information for future consideration.

The officers were elected as follows, on Sept. 17th, after which the Convention adjourned: President, Oliver A. Howland, C.M.G., K.C., Mayor of Toronto; Secretary-Treasurer, W. D. Lighthall, M.A., F.R.S.L., Mayor of Westmount; Vice-Presidents for Ontario—Mayor Cook of Ottawa, Mayor Denne of Peterborough, Mayor Hawke of Galt, and Mayor Read of Owen Sound ; Vice-Presidents for Quebec —Mayor James Cochrane, M.P.P., of Montreal, Mayor Alexander Montbriant of Ste. Cunegonde and Mayor Camirand of Sherbrooke ; Vice-President for Nova Scotia—Mayor A. B. Crosby of Halifax : Vice-President for New Brunswick—Ald. A. W. McRae of St. John ; Vice-Presidents for Manitoba—Mayor Arbuthnot of Winnipeg and Mayor Kelly of Brandon ; Vice-Presidents for British Columbia— Mayor Hayward of Victoria and Mayor Keary of New Westminster ; Vice-President for Prince Edward Island—Mayor Warburton of Charlottetown. The following is a synopsis of the various Resolutions passed :

1. In favour of a modification of the Quebec Municipal Code so as to authorize local Councils to expend sums not exceeding $1,500 in the construction of macadamized roads, subject to Government approval but without having recourse to popular vote upon a bye-law.

2. Authorizing the establishment by the Executive of a Bureau of Information having special reference to the subject of public ownership of public utilities.

3. Favouring the enactment of a law of compulsory arbitration in the case of all Companies operating public franchises who may have difficulties with their employees.

4. Authorizing the Executive to join with and assist the Dominion Government, under promised permission, in drafting the proposed measure concerning Telephones so that Canadian municipalities, large and small, "may obtain and retain their rightful control of their streets" ; that they may have

full facilities, if desired, to control local franchises ; and that the Government
may be enabled to assume control of long distance connections and an effective
control of rates and class of instruments and service.

5. Affirming the necessity for complete and authoritative recognition of
the rights of municipalities to manage, within reasonable limits, their own
affairs and voicing the determination "to unitedly resist all encroachments by
Parliament, or any Legislature, upon local rights."

6. Urging Legislative and legal action to remedy the evil and loss of life
occasioned by level railway crossings.

7. Authorizing the Executive to assist municipalities, by legislation, in
obtaining power to acquire for municipal purposes water-powers, parks and
other properties at any distance beyond the existing limits of any one
municipality.

8. Petitioning the Legislatures of the various Provinces "to entirely
abolish bonuses to manufacturers by municipalities."

9. Expressing the opinion that all expenses of Provincial registration and
election should be borne by the respective Provinces.

There was much more than local public interest felt in the
election for Mayor of Montreal, which took place on February 1st,
1902. Mr. Raymond Prefontaine, K.C., M.P., had completed his second term of two years and it was known
would be an exceedingly strong candidate if he should
desire to run again. On January 4th, just after leaving for England on a three weeks' trip, a letter was made public
addressed to the municipal ratepayers. In it Mayor Prefontaine
expressed his appreciation of the recent request of a representative
delegation of citizens, which had asked him to again be a candidate,
and stated that he had considered the request most favourably
because (1) he desired to hasten as much as possible the execution
of certain municipal projects and works already under way;
(2) because he wished to settle the question of annexing all the
municipalities on the Island of Montreal and creating a "Greater
Montreal"; (3) because it would take another two years to complete certain works in the Harbour which would make Montreal
the national port of Canada, and which he believed himself in a
position to greatly further. For these and other reasons he would
like to serve the City for a third term. "Nevertheless, gentlemen,
I must assure you that I make this declaration subject to the
decision which may be arrived at by my friends, in whose hands I
have placed myself unreservedly with regard to a new term, and
who, I am convinced, will adopt the necessary measures in order to
place you in a position to freely and frankly express your opinion
in connection with my candidature."

It was thought in many quarters that the Mayor could not be
beaten except by another French-Canadian, despite the fact that
an unwritten law prevailed by which his successor should have
been an English-Canadian and, therefore, a number of his opponents nominated Dr. E. P. Lachapelle, who for many years had been
head of the Provincial Board of Health. Meanwhile, Mr. R. Wilson-
Smith, a prominent broker and financier who had been Mayor in
1896-8, was being urged by many citizens and prominent ratepayers
to again be a candidate. On January 18th two meetings were held

in connection with the matter. Dr. Lachapelle's friends met, with Mr. M. Hutchinson, M.P.P., in the chair, and appointed various officers and committees for the contest. At the Windsor Hotel, a large and representative gathering was presided over by Mr. James Crathern and requisitions presented to Mr. Wilson-Smith, signed by 9,000 citizens. The meeting was addressed by Mr. George Hague, Dr. L. H. Davidson, Lieut.-Col. F. W. Hibbard, Mr. J. C. Holden and other leading business men. In his reply Mr. Wilson-Smith pointed out that he had not taken any personal steps in this connection ; that he had declined to be a candidate unless the election was by acclamation ; and that he had allowed the matter to go as far as it had done simply because he understood that only his candidature at this juncture would preserve the right of an English-Canadian to hold the succession to the Mayoralty.

As for a platform, his policy was (1) retrenchment and economy; (2) the erection of a suitable Contagious Diseases Hospital for the City; (3) reform in the character and control of the Fire Department; (4) improvement in the disgraceful condition of the streets ; (5) abolition of some, at least, of the $38,000,000 of exemption from City taxes ; improvements in the Harbour and transportation facilities of the City. He concluded with a strong appeal to all honest citizens to work for municipal interests. Pressure was applied to persuade a change of determination as to election by acclamation, but Mr. Wilson-Smith again pointed out that he had no personal ambition to be Mayor and was only anxious now to promote unanimity amongst the racial elements of Montreal's population. The formal nominations took place two days later, and it had, meanwhile, been announced that Mr. Wilson-Smith had consented to stand even if the field was not clear. Mr. Prefontaine's name also stood, together with those of Dr. Lachapelle and Mr. James Cochrane, M.P.P. The latter's was somewhat of a surprise, and he stated to the *Herald* of the same date that: "I am coming out as a protest against the candidature of Mr. R. Wilson-Smith. They claim he is a representative of the English-speaking electors of Montreal. I say he is not." He went on to say that he could speak French and Mr. Wilson-Smith could not and that, therefore, he would be elected.

The former gentleman was supported in the ensuing contest by the *Star*, the *Gazette* and *Le Journal*, and opposed by the *Herald*. Mayor Prefontaine's name was ultimately withdrawn after some controversy upon technical points and much doubt amongst his friends as to the desirability of doing so. Dr. Lachapelle also withdrew in deference to the claim for an English-speaking turn at the office, and the issue, therefore, was fought out between Mr. Cochrane and Mr. Wilson-Smith. Various meetings were held and, after a vigorous contest in which it was soon seen that the former candidate was going to get a considerable French vote and the latter a large English vote, it was found, on February 1st, that Mr. Cochrane was Mayor by a majority of 964. The *Witness* declared that the one little fact of Mr. Cochrane speaking French had decided the issue.

Mayor Cochrane's inaugural address was delivered on February 10th. His Worship commenced by presenting his election as another proof of the fair-mindedness of the French population of Montreal; referred to "the judicious legislation and wise administration" which was bringing the City out of a slough of despond in which it had wallowed for years ; spoke of the absolute necessity of reforming and thoroughly equipping the Fire Department; declared the condition of the Civic Contagious Diseases Hospital as a disgrace to the City and a menace to public safety ; deprecated the incomplete condition of the Harbour works and the slipping away of trade from their Port, and promised vigorous action in the premises; congratulated the City upon its financial condition, suggested certain improvements in the Water Works' system, declared the number of Policemen to be entirely inadequate to the City's needs, and deprecated the insufficient grants made for sidewalks and streets. Amongst the more notable Aldermen elected to this Council, it may be added, were Messrs. Joseph Lamarche, L. A. Lapointe, H. Laporte, D. Gallery, M.P., H. B. Ames, C. B. Carter, K.C., H. A. Akers and P. G. Martineau. Mr. Joseph Brunet, M.P., was defeated.

The Toronto municipal election of 1902 was notable for the interjection into the contest of a wide and rather vague matter of public policy in opposition to a personally popular candidate and a general sentiment in favour of a second term. The candidates nominated on Dec. 30th, 1901, were Mayor Oliver A. Howland, C.M.G., K.C., Mr. W. F. Maclean, M.P., of the *World* newspaper and Mr. C. C. Woodley—who expected to capture a few hundred votes for Socialism. Mr. Maclean propounded a lengthy platform. His first principle was the general one of making life more endurable to the great mass of the public by increasing common comforts and conveniences. His second and chief plank was the public ownership of great public franchises and, where that was not possible, the public regulation and control of such franchises. " In so far as this municipal contest is concerned, what I mean by the great conveniences of life and business is the supply of water, light, power and street transportation and I believe that public ownership can do these things better than private corporations." Taking his policy in detail and as propounded in this speech it meant (1) ownership of the Gas plant and gas at 60 cents a thousand instead of 90 cents ; (2) purchase of the Street Railway system and inauguration of a two cent fare instead of a four or five cent fare ; (3) municipal control of the Telephone service and rates of $15 a year instead of $25 or $40. Incidently, he advocated an increased representation of Toronto in the Provincial Legislature, declared his opposition to Prohibition, denounced the corporations as a great corrupting influence and promised to secure the Garrison Common for Park purposes and to improve conditions on the Island.

31

Mayor Howland replied briefly. He deprecated the policy just described as simply out of the question. Mr. Maclean "was going to revolutionize everything. He was going to do everything which never had been done and leave undone all things which had been done." As to his own record the Mayor pointed to his efforts in resisting the encroachment of corporations like the Bell Telephone Company; to his Gas Company agreement under which the City would receive its gas at a reduction of 10 cents a thousand; to his inauguration of the Union of Canadian Municipalities; and to his constant supervision of every Civic interest, assisted by an efficient Board of Control. "They had required information from the heads of departments every time as to the propriety of every act, every item, every proposal. They had checked many evils, stopped many schemes, advanced various plans; some things were enlarged upon, some things were cut down, but by acting as a regulating, controlling and revising body they had advanced a considerable step towards that state of concentrated, responsible government and efficient working of the City's business, which had been his aim and was still his aim." As to municipal ownership, he had publicly favoured the theory before Mr. Maclean had even whispered his approval and was prepared to support it wherever its practicability and advisability were proved—but only in such cases. He concluded by deprecating certain personal misrepresentations in the press of the City during the past year.

In the contest which followed Mr. Howland vigorously denounced his opponent as personally unworthy of public confidence and with equal vigour denounced a large portion of the local press. An Address was issued to the citizens pointing to his careful and just administration of their interests; his defence of the City against corporations such as the Telephone Company and Street Railway; his bringing into effect the co-operation of other municipalities and consequent leadership of Toronto in Provincial affairs; his various efforts along minor lines to advance the common welfare. He made few promises. On Jan. 4th Mr. Maclean had one of the largest meetings ever held in Toronto during a municipal contest and delivered a long and able speech describing his large policy of municipal ownership, representing his opponent as not a friend of the workingman and criticizing him for lack of energy and enterprise. An incident of the campaign was the interjection of Mr. Goldwin Smith's views. In the *Telegram* of Jan. 15th, he declared that after exhausting all experiments in shifting areas and arrangements—even the proposal previously presented by Mr. Howland of a Board of Control elected by the whole City—they would come back to the fact that management of a great city is a special business requiring "a permanent, paid and expert administration."

The result of the elections on January 6th, was the return of Mayor Howland by a majority of 4,607. He polled 13,424 votes, Mr. Maclean 8,816, and Mr. Woodley 635. On January 13th the inaugural meeting of the new Council took place and the Mayor delivered a brief address in which he declared that the past year had laid the foundations for present work; that the agreement with the Gas Company should be ratified by the Legislature; that various projects presented from time to time and dealing with the improvement of the Harbour, the bettering of the Cattle market conditions, the extension of the Street Railway to the north-east and the improvement of the Lake front, should be carefully considered. As to municipal ownership, plans now before the Council would require the expenditure of $3,000,000 and further great responsibilities should not be hastily incurred. " The time has not come for taking over the franchises now controlled by private interests nor will it come until we have proved that we have money enough to carry on the necessary work which the municipality must undertake." Concentration on necessary projects was in his opinion better than the dissipation of energy over a large number of ambitious or perilous schemes.

The Mayoralty contest in Ottawa is generally of public interest, as the municipal head of the capital may have important functions to perform during a year. There was no election, however, in 1902 as Mr. Fred. Cook, the well-known journalist, correspondent of the London *Times* and local Alderman, was elected by acclamation. In London there was a vigorous contest between Mr. Adam Beck, who later in the year was elected as a Conservative to the Ontario Legislature, and Mr. Edward Parnell, a well-known business man and an Alderman for nine years previously. Mr. Beck's personal popularity won the day by 1,820 majority. In Hamilton Major John S. Hendrie—who later on was also elected as a Conservative to the Legislature—was returned a second time, over Mr. William Barrett, by a majority of 3,393. This City is noteworthy as sometimes making little concealment of the political issue in its municipal contests and on this occasion *The Spectator* of January 7th boasted that 16 Tory Aldermen out of 21, together with a Tory Mayor, had resulted from the fight. Some of the principal elections elsewhere in Ontario, on January 6th, were as follows:

Other Municipal Elections in Ontario

City or Town.	Mayor.	City or Town.	Mayor.
Barrie	W. A. Boys	Galt	Dr. Hawke
Belleville	R. J. Graham	Goderich	M. G. Cameron, K.C.
Berlin	J. R. Eden	Gravenhurst	Dr. J. A. C. Grant
Bowmanville	J. B. Mitchell	Guelph	J. Kennedy
Brantford	D. B. Wood	Harriston	J. M. McKay
Brockville	W. H. Harrison	Ingersoll	Walter Mills
Carlton Place	W. A. Nichols	Kincardine	W. J. Henry
Chatham	G. W. Sulman	Kingston	J. Morgan Shaw
Clinton	Thomas Jackson	Lindsay	George Ingle
Cobourg	E. C. S. Huycke	Listowell	John Watson
Collingwood	W. A. Hogg	Midland	J. D. Hamill
Cornwall	W. J. Deruchie	Milton	S. Dice
Forest	W. H. Bartram	Napanee	G. F. Ruttan

City or Town.	Mayor.	City or Town.	Mayor.
Orillia	J. B. Tudhope	Sarnia	Dr. William Logie
Oshawa	T. L. Fowke	Seaforth	J. H. Broadfoot
Owen Sound	Aaron Read	Strathroy	G. A. Stewart
Palmerston	T. G. Burns	Stratford	J. Stamp
Parry Sound	G. G. Gladman	Thorald	Leslie McMann
Pembroke	Peter White, Jr.	Trenton	J. Funnell
Perth	J. M. Balderson	Walkerton	C. W. Cryderman
Peterborough	T. H. G. Denne	Walkerville	E. G. Swift
Port Arthur	I. L. Matthews	Waterloo	David Bean
Port Hope	Henry White	Welland	C. H. Reilly
Prescott	James Glasgow	Whitby	A. M. Ross
St. Catharines	J. B. McIntyre	Wingham	R. Vanstone
St. Thomas	S. Chant	Woodstock	Dr. Mearns

On April 16th Mr. James T. Hamilton, Mayor of Halifax during the past three years, published an Address in which he referred to his years of service in the interests of the City, to the **Municipal Affairs in the Maritime Provinces** arduous duties of the period in which he had held the Civic chair, and to the state of his health, which now compelled retirement. The *Chronicle* of the following day referred to Mr. Hamilton's admitted " purity of motive and unswerving courage " and to his honest and effective services to the City. " We congratulate Mayor Hamilton on the entirely honourable termination of his long and faithful term of public service in the interests of Halifax, and on the peculiarly manly, kindly and good form of his retirement." The candidates for the position were Messrs. C. S. Lane, W. J. Butler and A. B. Crosby. Mr. Butler afterwards retired, and on the day preceding the election—during which a proposed ship-building bonus of $100,000 was being voted upon—Mayor Hamilton published an open letter to the citizens, urging them very strongly to support the measure. The result of the contest on April 30th was the election of Mr. A. B. Crosby by 16 majority and the carrying of the Bonus by-law almost unanimously. On the same day and at a final meeting of the old Council, Alderman R. T. MacIlreith, who had been Deputy-Mayor for the greater part of the preceding year, owing to Mr. Hamilton's ill-health, read a lengthy address on Municipal affairs.

He denounced the existing Assessment Act as bearing heavily upon the manufacturers; deprecated the consequent necessity of class legislation for their relief; declared the present appropriation of $25,000 to keep 100 miles of streets in repair and condition as utterly inadequate; claimed the charter under which the City worked to be unsatisfactory in the extreme and asked for its revision; urged the beautifying of the City by creation of lawn spaces, the judicious planting of trees, shrubs and vines, and some regulation of the advertising nuisance. Mayor Crosby addressed the new Council on May 14th with extreme brevity and the following quotation may be given as embodying his opinions: " Taxation is the all-important topic with the citizens, and to keep the present rate, or perhaps reduce it, I invite your earnest consideration and assistance.   It seems poor encouragement for our citizens that the taxes should go on increasing from year to year without being able to point to any material advantages or accommodation.   If we could boast of good streets, good sidewalks, good and sufficient sewerage and plenty of water all over our City, our citizens perhaps would not have so much reason to complain."

Meanwhile, on February 4th, the cities and towns of Nova Scotia had elected their Mayors.   The most exciting contest was, perhaps, that in Truro, where Mayor George W. Stewart was elected for a fifth term over Mr. J. H. Kent by a majority of 80.   Other elections of note were D. D. McKenzie, M.P.P., as Mayor in North Sydney, Walter Crowe in Sydney, D. M. Burchill in Glace Bay, John McCormack in Sydney Mines, Dr. Augustus Robinson in Annapolis, W. P. Cunningham in Antigonish, E. D. Davison in Bridgewater, E. C. Whitman in Canso, Fred Scarfe in Dartmouth, O. Sproul in Digby, W. Yould in Kentville, A. R. Morash in Lunenburg, A. C. MacDonald in Pictou, R. Keith in Stellarton, W. Conway in Springhill, S. G. Robertson in Westville, George Thomson in Wolfville, and G. W. Johnson in Yarmouth.

On August 15th Dr. Walter W. White was elected Mayor of St. John, N.B., by a majority of 1,914 over Ald. E. B. Colwell.   The inaugural meeting of the new Council took place on May 6th, when the retiring Mayor, J. W. Daniel, who had held the positon for two years, spoke at some length.   He referred to the bad condition of the streets and recommended vitrified brick as a roadway pavement; mentioned the improvements effected in the water supply of the City; dealt with the trade and business of the Port and the increasing local export; urged preparation for the coming volume of business which he foresaw and stated that it would cost $2,000,000 to put the Harbour into a fit condition to receive this increased trade; and referred to the satisfactory condition of Civic finances.   Mayor White followed with his inaugural address.   He described the debt of the City on December 31st, 1901, as being $3,736,784 and the assets $5,000,197, or a credit balance of $1,263,413.   Of the debt $1,523,859 was at 6 per cent. and $2,013,132 at 4 per cent.   He urged increased wharf and warehouse accommodation and quoted the Hon. Mr. Tarte as saying in the Commons that St. John " was undoubtedly the future winter port of Canada."   An improvement in the ferry service between the eastern and western sides of the Harbour, the paving of the streets with asphalt, reform of the Assessment Act, and election of the Aldermen for a term of two years were suggested as matters deserving care and attention.

XVIII.—LABOUR QUESTIONS AND CONDITIONS

Two developments appeared, in a marked degree, through the discussions and legislation of the year in connection with the **Labour Legislation and Labour Interests** alleged, or real, interests of workingmen and the not less vital interest of capital and industry in the welfare of the community. One was the pronounced influence of American organizations and delegates in Canada; the other was an increasing attention paid by political bodies to the representations of organized labour. In the Dominion Parliament, during its Session of 1902, an amendment to the Post Office Act provided for increased pay to the messengers, letter-carriers and other employees of the Department. Mr. Mulock's presentation of his measure for compulsory arbitration in railway disputes, as a preliminary to its formal introduction in 1903, was an important indication of policy along supposedly Labour lines. The following extract from the speech of the Postmaster-General in the House of Commons on April 29th indicates his position in the matter:

The object of this Bill is to prevent lockouts and strikes upon railways, by providing a more satisfactory way than those violent measures afford for the settlement of such disputes and of differences that may from time to time arise between railway companies and their employees. The proposition is, in fact, one for compulsory arbitration between railway companies and employees in regard to the various subjects of controversy that from time to time arise between those parties. The measure is confined entirely to the railway world; it does not deal with any industries other than railway industries, and therefore it is not a precedent for the treatment of disputes between other classes. Whilst strikes and lockouts upon railways affect the Companies and their employees, there is a third interest to be considered, the public interest, perhaps the greatest of all; and that paramount interest appears to give jurisdiction on this occasion for the House to adopt what is apparently an extreme means in order to ward off the evil consequences flowing from railway strikes and lockouts.

By this measure strikes and lockouts were to be made illegal upon railways of all kinds, whether operated by steam, electricity or other motive power, and all disputes were to be referred to a Dominion Board of Arbitration, or to one of seven Provincial Boards of Arbitration, to deal with. Of the five members of the Dominion Board the railways were to appoint two and the employees two, while on the Provincial Boards each interest would have one representative. The Government appointed one in each case. The award was to be current for the year and not subject to appeal. After discussion the measure was allowed to stand over until the next Session. It may be added here that Sir Edmund Barton, Premier of Australia, in an interview at New York on August 29th, described the system in vogue in the Commonwealth as being somewhat along this line. " By the terms of our Arbitration Law great strikes are made practically impossible.   Arbitration is compulsory, and when disputes arise between employers and employed both parties are required to submit the issue to a Board of Arbitration, which is under Government control.   A Judge of the Supreme Court is the head of the Board, and two Assessors are named to act with him, one appointed by each side."

In Ontario the Act relating to the Temiscamingue Railway contained special clauses protecting labourers employed thereon, as did the Act dealing with aid to miscellaneous railways.   Amendments of importance were made to the Mechanics' Lien Act and the Ontario Factories Act.   In Manitoba the Master and Servants' Act was amended and in British Columbia a greater part of the year's legislation was affected by Labour considerations.   The rights and liabilities of Trades Unions were defined by the Public Wages' Act and the security of wages due to workmen on subsidized works was provided for.   A Workmen's Compensation Act was passed and three measures, afterwards vetoed at Ottawa, restricted in different ways the employment of Chinese and Japanese.   On March 17th a large deputation from the Trades and Labour Congress of Canada waited upon the Premier and the Hon. Mr. Mulock, Postmaster-General and Minister of Labour, and presented, with descriptive speeches, a series of Resolutions passed by the meeting of the Congress at Brantford in the previous September.   Each Province of the Dominion was represented, and Mr. Ralph Smith, M.P., in presenting the delegation, declared it to be the largest and most representative ever introduced to a Premier of Canada.

The Government was asked (1) to impose a $500 capitation tax on all Chinese entering Canada; (2) to increase the scale of wages paid to letter-carriers in the Postal Service; (3) to grant an eight-hour day to all employees on Government railways; (4) to establish or aid in establishing Technical Training Schools; (5) to reform the Alien Labour Act by giving the Minister of Labour power to investigate and deport without judicial proceedings; (6) to amend the Conciliation Act so as to prevent the abandonment of labour union membership being a condition of settlement in disputes and enabling the Minister of Labour to intervene in strikes without a request from either side.   Sir Wilfrid Laurier, in reply, said that no Chinese legislation would be introduced until the public had been given an opportunity of studying the Report of the recent Royal Commission; that he believed the eight-hour day was becoming more and more general in private concerns and he would place their view before the Minister of Railways and Canals; that the Government had given strict orders to their agents abroad to induce only settlers to come to Canada who would occupy its vacant lands; that technical schools pertained to Education, and that subject was constitutionally under Provincial control; that deportation of alien workmen without trial would be a departure from the oldest and best principle of British law.   The Minister of Labour promised a measure at the present Session of Parliament which would be designed to meet the wishes of the letter-carriers. Representations were also made by the delegation in favour of Gevernment owner-ship of public utilities.

The work done by the Department of Labour at Ottawa during the fiscal year ending June 30th, 1902, was considerable, and in the annual Report submitted by Mr. W. L. Mackenzie King, Deputy Minister of Labour, under date of September 2nd, it was stated to include: (1) the preparation and publication of the *Labour Gazette;* (2) the settlement of industrial disputes under the Conciliation Act of 1900; (3) the carrying out of the Parliamentary Resolution of March, 1900, which proposed to secure the payment of fair wages and the performance of work under proper con-ditions to those employed on public labour; (4) the management of the Departmental Library and the conducting of a varied corre-spondence. An immense number of reports from local correspond-ents all over the Dominion had been received dealing with the condition of the labour market, of local industries and of particular trades. Special attention was devoted to the collation and study of legal decisions affecting Labour, to the rates of wages and hours of work throughout Canada, and to the cost of living. During the fiscal year the intervention of the Department was asked and given successfully in eleven strikes involving the em-ployment of some 2,130 men. These figures, it was claimed, did not indicate in any clear way the interests affected by such settle-ments or the greater troubles possibly averted.

The most important of these incidents was the strike of 1,200 longshoremen at Halifax on April 2nd, 1902, by which the Harbour was practically closed up. During March the Longshoremen's Union submitted to the Steamship Companies a demand for various changes in the scale of wages and general relations. The request for intervention was made by the Union, and on April 10th Mr. Mackenzie King was in Halifax. Negotiations were entered upon and a settlement effected within forty-eight hours. The agreement provided, amongst other matters, that in future no strike or lock-out should occur without thirty days' notice in writing. It was ratified by a mass meeting of 1,000 men and signed by all the interested parties. The matter of providing fair wages for public contract work was managed through the various Departments of the Government sending in particulars of proposed tenders and an immediate investigation by a Fair Wage officer being made as to the local conditions of work and wages. A schedule was then prepared by the Labour Department, based upon this information, and was inserted in the contract before its final acceptance by the tenderer and the Government. There were a very large number of such contracts arranged and accepted during the year.

Early in 1902 the 2nd Report of the Ontario Bureau of Labour was presented by its Secretary, Mr. Robert J. Glockling, to the Commissioner of Public Works. It dealt with the record of the 12 months ending December 31st, 1901; reviewed the past Labour legislation of the Province at length; gave a synopsis of recent Ontario legal decisions affecting labour interests; supplied a list of 57 Labour organizations in Ontario which were subordinate to United States Unions or Orders; and published various tables relating to wages and hours of labour. A good deal was said about the work of free employment offices. Mr. Glockling stated that there were twenty of them in Toronto and a proportionate number throughout the other centres of the Province, and seemed to think that, upon the whole, they were detrimental to the interests of the working men. A mass of comparative facts and figures given in this Report were of an American character and illustrated, no doubt, the close relationship which is supposed to exist between the problems affecting the workingmen of the two countries.

The 18th annual meeting of the Trades and Labour Congress of Canada was held at Berlin, Ontario, from Sept. 15th to Sept.

The Trades and Labour Congress of Canada 19th, 1902. The attendance of 150 delegates was the largest on record, and credentials were received from 102 Labour organizations. Mr. Ralph Smith, M.P., of Nanaimo, B.C., was in the chair as President of the Congress, for his fourth year, although he had found some slight difficulty in being elected a delegate. His local Union refused to send him, and he had accepted the telegraphed representation of a Vancouver body. Mr. J. H. Watson, the well-known Labour official of Vancouver, told the *Province* of Sept. 7th that the cause of the trouble in Nanaimo was Mr. Smith's opposition to the control of Canadian Unions by American organizations. The first business of the Congress was its President's address. After congratulating the gathering upon the number present and the Congress upon the energetic work of its Secretary, Mr. P. M. Draper, he pointed out the fact that they constituted what was the foundation of a future National Labour Federation of Canada, and dwelt upon the usefulness and purposes of Trades Unions. "They seek to mitigate the struggle of life and yet to maintain its progress. They try to make people more happy, but they are anxious to still keep them free."

He then referred to the legislation at Ottawa during the preceding Session and, in connection with the Minister of Railways' compulsory arbitration proposals, asked why the Railway employees had protested against this policy. "When we remember that all the Unions of the country, including the Trades and Labour Congress of Canada, have in their platforms provisions in favour of such a measure, it seems to me very important that a full explanation should be made to the Government by the railway men as to their reasons for such objection; the intention of the Government being entirely a desire to know just what opinions the Labour Unions hold on this question." Reference was made to the Oriental immigration issue in British Columbia where, Mr. Ralph Smith declared, "the people were unjustly treated," and especially in view of their efforts by petition and Provincial statute to better existing conditions. The recent Taft Vale Railway decision in England where the Imperial Privy Council had declared that Trades Unions could be subject to legal action from employers for damages in strikes, etc., he described as placing their funds in a most dangerous condition, and as tending to make the Law Courts, in Canada also, a battleground for contending economic forces. A measure had already passed the British Columbia Legislature safeguarding their interests in this connection, and similar legislation would, he said, be passed at Ottawa during the next Session. He urged the appointment of a special Labour organizer; demanded loyalty on the part of every one to the Canadian Congress as against any other institution; and protested against allegations in certain quarters that their organization was of a political character.

Following this address, which was formally approved by the Congress, came the exclusion of 10 Knights of Labour Assemblies and some Central Labour Unions from representation; a refusal to recognize any national (Canadian) Unions where international ones in the same craft existed; the decision to extend the fraternal privileges of the Congress only to delegates from the American Federation of Labour and the Trades' Congress of Great Britain. The various Provincial Executives reported upon sundry matters. That of Prince Edward Island protested vigorously against any foreign body such as the American Federation of Labour chartering Canadian Councils, and in this regard it was upheld by the Report of the General Executive. That of Ontario described the formation of more than 80 Labour organizations since the last meeting of the Congress. That of Quebec approved the Hon. Mr. Mulock's Arbitration proposals for railways, while the British Columbia Executive presented a protest from the freight-handlers of Vancouver against Mr. John A. Flett, of Hamilton, Vice-President of the Congress, having organized local Unions in Canada under the American Federation of Labour. That of Manitoba described a desertion of the United Brotherhood of Railway Employees by the Trainmen—conductors, engineers, and firemen—in a recent strike, as traitorous in the extreme. The following Resolution was then passed by the Congress:

That as the Congress has placed itself squarely in accord with the principles of international trades unionism, and as such action will entail the loss of certain revenues from former affiliated bodies, owing to the change in the constitution, it is the opinion of this Congress that, being the national organization of labour in the Dominion, all Federal Labour Unions and central labour councils in Canada should be under the jurisdiction and control of the Congress; and the incoming Executive is hereby instructed to make such arrangements with the American Federation of Labour, looking to the consummation of this object; as in the opinion of this Congress the existence of dual Federal Labour Unions holding charters from the Congress and the American Federation of Labour is not conducive to the solidity and effectiveness of the Labour movement in Canada.

The Committee appointed to deal with the Reports from the various Executives followed with suggestions urging agitation for the appointment of a Factory Inspector in Nova Scotia and the passage of a Factory Act in New Brunswick. Following this came a discussion raised by the President, who withdrew temporarily from the chair, as to certain charges made against him by the Trades and Labour Council of Phœnix, B.C. Summed up they were to the effect that he was "a henchman of a capitalistic party" and had accepted a pass from the C.P.R. In reply Mr. Smith declared himself independent in his views, denied that he had stumped Ontario for the Liberals, stated that the meetings he had addressed were attended at the invitation of local Presidents of Unions, and explained that he took his pass from the C.P.R. under instructions from the Miners' Union of which he was Secretary. The matter was referred, amid cheers, to a Committee which afterwards reported the charges to be "absolutely ridiculous, most unjustifiable, and palpably untrue."

A Resolution was passed on Sept. 18th, after various discussions and by a vote of 78 to 12, disapproving Mr. Mulock's proposed compulsory arbitration legislation in connection with railways, and urging every Labour organization in the Dominion to aid in this protest, and in defeating the measure. "If enacted it would rob the railway employees of their constitutional rights, destroy their organizations and place them absolutely in the hands of the railway Companies." Later on in the proceedings, and in order to preserve an appearance of consistency, the clause in the platform of the Congress which declared in favour of Compulsory Arbitration was changed to read "Voluntary Arbitration." Mr. Ralph Smith refused to be a candidate for re-election as President, and was presented with an Address expressive of good will and confidence. The election of officers on September 18th resulted in the choice of Mr. John A. Flett of Hamilton as President, Mr. J. B. Mack of Montreal as Vice-President, and Mr. P. M. Draper of Ottawa as Secretary. Vice-Presidents of the various Provincial Executives were chosen as follows: J. B. McNiven for British Columbia; A. W. Puttee, M.P., for Manitoba; Samuel Moore for Ontario; A. Gariepy for Quebec; D. A. Wilson for Nova Scotia; P. C. Sharkey for New Brunswick; J. W. Sutherland for Prince Edward Island. A very large number of Resolutions were passed during the Session of the Congress, in addition to those already mentioned, and they may be summarized as follows:

Condemnation of Sunday excursions and approval of a Saturday half-holiday.

Favouring the enactment by the House of Commons of legislation meeting the recent Taft Vale decision in Exgland, or any tendency by the Judiciary in Canada to follow such precedent.

Favouring Dominion legislation (1) incorporating provisions in the Railway Act to compel all railway ccompanies to use air brakes and other safety appliances; (2) increasing the wages on the Intercolonial Railway, and meeting the demand of Post Office employees for increased pay; (3) amending the Fishery laws in British Columbia so as to avert conflict with the Indian modes of obtaining food supplies; (4) paying employees in the Government Printing Bureau for Departmental holidays.

Asking for a more rigid enforcement of the Ontario Factory Act and the appointment of more Inspectors; urging certain amendments to the Quebec Factory Act; and opposing any repeal of the Act in Manitoba.

Condemning any proposal to increase the tariff as being in the interest of the holders of lands and forests and mines, from whose extortion labour was now suffering, and asking instead for the transfer of taxes to those values "which now enable non-production to impoverish industry."

Favouring the removal of taxes from improvements and affirming the right of every Municipality to determine its own system of taxation.

Protesting against magistrates being allowed the right to call out the Militia during strikes, asking that the power be removed to the hands of the Minister of Militia, and urging organized Labour men to abstain from joining military bodies except when the country is invaded.

Deprecating the alleged discharge of certain foremen on Government works for belonging to International Unions; expressing sympathy with the Canadian Northern Railway strikers in Manitoba, with the coal miners in the United States, as well as with several current bodies of strikers in Toronto, Berlin and Montreal.

Endorsing all labels of international and national Unions; favouring the appointment of plumbing inspectors; urging the weekly payment of wages to all Government employees, either Federal or Provincial.

Opposing any system of assisted immigration; the property qualification for Mayor or Alderman; and the present house-leasing system in Quebec.

On September 18th, the day before the Congress adjourned, a new and rival organization was formed at Berlin, Ont.—partly as a consequence of the exclusion of the Knights of Labour and other independent organizations numbering some 10,000 men from the Congress, and partly because of the attitude of the American Federation of Labour in maintaining a superior rather than a parallel jurisdiction in its relations with the Dominion organizations. The new body called itself the National Trades and Labour Congress of Canada, declared itself purely Canadian in character and policy and elected Mr. Omer Brunet, of Quebec City, as President, together with various other officers. Meanwhile, Mr. Ralph Smith, M.P., of Victoria, B.C., had been interviewed on his way home by the Winnipeg *Telegram* of September 23rd. He took occasion to deprecate the influence of American labour officers in the affairs of Canadian Unions. "The Labour cause," he added, "suffers from lack of unity by giving ear to the unreasonable demands of agitators."

There were a number of Labour disputes and troubles in Canada during the year, though they did not compare in scope or importance with those of Great Britain and the United States. In the former country they were also comparatively limited, and the figures for the preceding period of 1901, as given in the British *Labour Gazette*, may be considered an indication. In that year there were 624 strikes or disputes, with 175,165 work-people involved altogether and 107,418 directly concerned. The chief cause was a demand for increased wages and the total financial

Labour Problems and Organizations

disturbance was less than in any recent year. In the United States, according to figures compiled by Mr. Carroll D. Wright, the statistician, there were 22,793 strikes between 1881 and 1900, with 6,105,694 employees thrown out of employment, $257,863,478 loss in wages, $122,731,121 loss to employers, and an average of 50·77 per cent. successful, 13·04 per cent. partly successful, and 36·19 per cent. failures. The Report of the Iowa, U.S., Bureau of Labour Statistics for 1901 stated, in this connection, that in the 94 national and international Trades Unions of the Republic there were in that year 1,550,747 members; that 531,085 of these were working on the 8 hour-a-day basis; that the strikes under their auspices in 1899 and 1900 had numbered 1,427, involved 247,260 persons, and cost the organizations $1,293,181. Of these strikes 1,071 were said to have been successful.

In Canada during 1902 there were 123 new trade disputes, or strikes, referred to the Department of Labour, involving 12,143 work-people and a total loss of 163,125 working days. Of these cases 54 were caused by a demand for higher wages, seven were protests against reduction in wages, seven asked for a decrease in hours of work and 14 were demands for increase in wages and a decrease in hours. Eight were directed against the employment of particular persons; five were against objectionable conditions of service; five were for the recognition of Unions; nine were sympathetic in character; and the balance were for miscellaneous causes. The great bulk of these difficulties (73 in number) were adjusted by negotiation between the parties concerned, 11 were settled by the Department, 12 by replacement of the men, and 20 by a return of the men to work upon the employers' terms. According to trades, 28 of the strikes were amongst builders, 31 amongst metal workers, 10 in wood-working, 10 in food and tobacco preparation, nine in clothing, four in transport and the rest scattering. By Provinces, Ontario headed the list with 65 disputes or strikes as against 53 in 1901; Nova Scotia followed with 12 and five respectively; Prince Edward Island had none in 1901 and two in the succeeding year; New Brunswick increased its number from three in 1901 to seven in 1902; Manitoba rose from three to eight; the Territories from nothing to one; British Columbia and Quebec alone showed reductions—the former from 10 to 8 and the latter from 29 to 20. In Toronto there were 24 strikes reported, in Hamilton 12, in Montreal 9, in Quebec, Halifax and Winnipeg, six each.

This statement, compared with that of 1901, was very favourable. Although the number of strikes, etc., increased from 104 in 1901 to 123 in 1902, the number of work-people involved decreased by 15,880 and the loss in working days by 521,127. The chief strikes of the year were those of the Halifax longshoremen, the Toronto Street Railway men, the C. N. R. employees in Manitoba, and the Fernie miners. The first has been already referred to and the second is specially dealt with elsewhere. That of the Canadian Northern Railway commenced on June 30th and included some 200 men. It was supposed to be partly in sympathy with the machinists who had gone out on May 16th and in both cases the immediate cause was the Company's refusal to recognize certain schedules of rules and regulations as governing their service. At the request of the Strikers' Committee Mr. Mackenzie King, of the Labour Department, later on visited Winnipeg but was assured by the Company that they had no need to enter into negotiations and that any embarrassment caused to them by the strike had been temporary and was now past. Nothing, therefore, was done and the Company maintained their attitude of indifference despite various disturbances which occurred during the next two months. They arranged schedules which satisfied the Brotherhood containing their firemen, conductors and telegraphists and, after a while, most of the freight clerks returned to their work. The Provincial Government intervened at the end of July, under request from the strikers, but were told that no recognition of the latter could be given. After this the strike seems to have died away without any direct settlement.

The troubles at Fernie, B. C., commenced on June 26th and effected 200 miners directly and, after a time, the whole Province indirectly, through tying up the local coal output. It was said to have been caused by a new arrangement made by the management of the Crow's Nest Company mines which added half an hour to the shift and was unsatisfactory to the men. This strike seriously affected some of the smelters of the Province through lack of coke and lasted until August 4th when some mutual concessions were made and the men resumed work. An important incident in connection with Labour questions and through which a probably serious strike was averted occurred in the reference of a difference, as to rate of wages, between the Canadian Pacific Railway and the Brotherhood of Railway Trackmen, to a Board of Arbitration composed of Mr. F. P. Gutelins representing the C. P. R. ; Mr. J. F. Wilson for the Brotherhood ; and Sir John Boyd, Chancellor of Ontario, selected by both of the parties. The first meeting was held at Montreal on May 5th and the award was issued two days later settling the rate of pay for all the maintenance-of-way men on the Railway.

Some discussion took place during the year as to the action of certain Labour bodies in placing themselves in opposition to the Militia. The movement was not, apparently, a very general or effective one but, so far as it went, was obviously an outcome of similar feelings and actions in the United States under very different conditions. Underlying any sentiment which existed in the matter was the feeling that the Militia might at any time have to act against organized Labour in the event of any particular strike leading to violence. Amongst the Resolutions of the Trades and Labour Congress of Canada at its September meeting was one protesting against the calling out of the Militia during strikes and urging members of organized Labour bodies to abstain from joining militiary organizations except in the event of an invasion of the country. What was claimed to be the logical outcome of such a movement, if it should be successful, was described by the Vancouver *World* of Nov. 10th in the following rather interesting words :

Amid all the uncertainties and perplexities of the industrial situation one thing is absolutely certain—that the mass of the public will insist that property and person shall be adequately protected. Any Government, however despotic, which protects person and property is better than any Government, however free it may be called, which does not. If organized Labour withdraws from the Militia because it is summoned to protect persons and property in time of a strike, the Militia will be recruited from portions of the country which are not in sympathy with organized Labour. If it cannot be recruited by volunteers, men of property who value peace and order will raise the necessary amount of money to secure a paid force for the purpose. It such protection cannot be furnished by a Militia, it will be furnished by a standing army.

The question of Labour as a class interest and its general position in the community was dealt with by the Committee on Sociological Questions of the Methodist Church in Canada. In their Report submitted to the General Conference of the Church, on Sept. 17th, an elaborate statement of conditions and opinions was made which may be briefly summarized as follows : (1) The Church is greatly concerned in the various modern methods of obtaining wealth and the uses to which it is put ; (2) all legitimate efforts should be made to secure to workingmen a living wage, to reduce the hours of labour where practicable, and to secure proper sanitary conditions for the workman ; (3) the weekly day of rest and worship should be safe-guarded and the Saturday half-holiday preserved ; (4) the right of the manufacturer to specialize labour in producing his wares, and to combine with other manufacturers for the purpose of reducing the price of distribution, should be recognized as well as the liberty of the labourer to organize for the protection of what he believes to be his rights ; (5) there should be a law for the compulsory arbitration of labour disputes and the assumption by Government of the control of public utilities ; (6) purity of the ballot should be imperatively pressed as important to all classes and a reform effected in the present extreme partizanship in politics.

On July 31st, 1902, there were 430 Labour bodies in Ontario, while 151 were reported at other dates from Quebec and 138 from the Maritime Provinces. The number of new Labour organizations in Canada during 1902, which reported to the Department of Labour, was 190. Of these, 30 were in the building trades, 25 in the metal, engineering and ship-building trades, 9 in the wood-working and furnishing trades, 8 in the printing trades, 15 in the clothing trades, 16 in the food and tobacco industries, 3 in the leather trades, 16 in transportation interests, and 68 were of a miscellaneous character covering every line of labour—miners, fishermen, actors, bartenders, barbers, bootblacks, musicians, firemen, civic employees, and even agricultural labourers. By Provinces, 112 were in Ontario, 27 in

British Columbia, 17 in Quebec, 10 in Nova Scotia, 9 in New Brunswick, 9 in the Yukon, 1 in Prince Edward Island, 1 in Manitoba, and 3 in the Territories. In addition to the Trades and Labour Congress the most important strictly Labour gathering of the year was that held at Kamloops, B.C., on April 14th, to which reference is made elsewhere,* as it was called primarily with a political purpose. Under the terms of the circular issued in this connection to the Trades and Labour organizations of British Columbia, the objects to be served were defined as the uniting and harmonizing of all Labour organizations and Reform bodies in the Province for purposes of common political action in future campaigns and the adoption of a platform and policy which should guide organized Labour in its future course. The result was the formation of a Provincial Progressive Party with a long and varied programme.

The most prominent and probably most important Labour difficulty of the year was the strike of the Street Railway employees in Toronto. The trouble developed in an **The Toronto Street Railway Strike** acute form about the middle of June. Prior to this, however, matters were sufficiently threatening. On May 31st a mass-meeting of the employees of the Company — who belonged largely to the Toronto Railway Employees' Union which, in turn, was affiliated with the International Street Railway Men's Union, with headquarters at Detroit, Mich.—was held to the number of 900 or more, and demands adopted for presentation to the Company which included (1) recognition of the Union; (2) re-instatement of James McDonald, a dismissed employee; (3) working days approximating to nine hours ; (4) special allowances for Sunday, and arrangements for cleaning the cars; (5) leave of absence for employees whenever the Union should require their services. President William Mackenzie of the Street Railway Company replied, on June 13th, to these demands by a statement to the Press in which he announced the refusal to meet a Committee of the Union for their discussion, but expressed his willingness to receive any deputation from the employees, as such, to consider their representations, and to increase wages if circumstances seemed to warrant doing so. He then reviewed the situation in another respect as follows :

The Toronto Railway Company is virtually asked to recognize, and in a sense, put itself under the control of a Labour Union whose headquarters and managing officers are in the United States. I have never yet known a case where a street railway or any other company, employing labour in the United States, has allowed itself to be dictated to by Canadians. Any one can see that foreign control of such Canadian institutions as ours might lead to very grave consequences, and is manifestly unfair, not only to us, but to all Canadians whatsoever. If this foreign intervention with Canadian concerns is to be tolerated, then, so far as I can see, there is nothing to prevent a few American labour leaders from tying up every Canadian street railway, steam railway, and factory whenever it suits them to do so.

---

*Note—See pages 84-5-6.

The Manager of the Company had, meanwhile, written refusing to receive the Committee, and a little later the Chairman of the Executive of the International Union arrived in the city, and remained a very energetic figure through the ensuing troubles. On June 16th a Committee of the Board of Trade, composed of Messrs. A. E. Ames, President, Paul Jarvis, Secretary, J. D. Allan and W. J. Gage, had another meeting of the men called. It was attended by a thousand members of the Union, and was addressed by Mr. Ames and other members of the delegation, as was another and rather slightly attended meeting in the evening called by the Company. The strike was held off until Sunday, June 22nd. Meanwhile, Mayor Howland had done what he could to avert a crisis, and on the 20th, accompanied by Mr. Glockling, Secretary of the Ontario Bureau of Labour, had spent several hours with Mr. E. H. Keating, Manager of the Company, in an effort to effect a compromise. On the evening of the 21st, a crowded and stormy mass-meeting of the men was held and addressed by Mr. Ames and by Mr. Daniel Dilworth, Chairman of the International Executive of Street Railway Employees, who was now a prominent person amongst the men. The feeling, however, was in favour of striking, and next morning the cars were not running. The terms offered by the Company were practically as follows :

1. Wages to be increased : first year, from 15c. to 17c.; second year, from 16 2/3c. to 18c.; third, fourth and fifth years, from 17c. to 19c.; after fifth to tenth year, from 18c. to 20c.; after tenth year, from 18c. to 21c.

2. On Sunday work an increase in wages to be made so as to make the wages earned on that day equal to those earned on other days of the week.

3. The Company undertakes to have the cars cleaned for the motormen and conductors in the morning, but the men shall report ahead of time, as at present, without additional pay, and keep the inside and platforms of their cars clean, as formerly, while on duty.

4. The Company undertakes to prevent, as far as possible, any injustice for men having to suffer by reason of being suspended without just cause, and that all shall have the right to appeal, without prejudice to their positions, to the General Manager at any time.

On Sunday the men did not turn out to work and the Company undertook to run some of their lines of cars, with the result of a riot, in which several people were hurt and cars damaged. The Police Commission, composed of the Mayor, Judge McDougall and Mr. R. E. Kingsford, at once asked for the troops to be called out, on the ground that the Police were insufficient to maintain order, and, on Monday morning, some 700 cavalry and 700 infantry were camped at the Armouries or posted at the barns of the Company. No further attempt was made to run the cars, however, and continuous conferences were held between the Board of Trade Committee, Mr. Keating and a Committee of the men headed by Mr. J. H. Pickles. On the morning of June 23rd the following settlement was arrived at and signed by Mr. E. H. Keating for the Company, Messrs. A. E. Ames, J. W. Flavelle, J. D. Allan and Paul

32

Jarvis for the Board of Trade, and by Mr. Pickles for the Men's Committee :

1. The wage scale which has been published to stand until the first of July. In the meantime the employees may hold a meeting, to be called under the auspices of the Board of Trade Committee, and if a majority of the regular and relief men vote by ballot to substitute the scale of 18 cents per hour for the first year of service and 20 cents thereafter, the Company will substitute it for the present scale.

2. The Company will not interfere with the freedom of the railway employees to organize under any form of constitution, but the Company decline to give recognition to the Union or to receive a Grievance Committee from the Union ; but any employee who may be suspended or dismissed, or who may have any other grievance, shall have the right of an appeal in person to the General Manager, and to bring with him such of his fellow-employees or other witnesses who may have any knowledge of the facts and circumstances of the case.

3. The Company agree that the cars shall be cleaned for the motormen and conductors in the morning, but that the motormen and conductors will report fifteen minutes ahead of the time as at present, without additional pay, and will keep the inside and platform of their cars clean as formerly while on duty ; that on Sunday the increase shall be such as to make the day equal to a working day in the week.

The press gave much credit to the Board of Trade Committee for the settlement, and Mr. Dilworth, the International Delegate, declared to the *World* of June 24th that without their intervention the result would not have been possible at such an early stage in the strike. The trouble lasted three days, involved directly 963 men, and was said to have cost them in wages $6,000 and the Company, in receipts, $15,000. The loss to rolling stock was estimated at $10,000, the cost to the city of securing troops at $12,000, the difference to the Company in the new scale at $112,000, and the addition to salary of old employees at $100,000. The local press had practically made no comment upon the calling out of the troops, though it was, perhaps, the most important incident of the strike so far as the public were concerned. There had been no further violence in connection with the strike, although there developed a strong undercurrent of feeling amongst various Union men in the city against Mayor Howland for having been instrumental in calling the Militia into action. Outside press opinion was very congratulatory upon this point, however, and Toronto's determination to maintain law and order was the text of many comments in the Dominion and the United States.

In welcoming the International Convention of Iron-Moulders to Toronto, on July 7th, Mayor Howland made an explanation of his position in the matter and argued that the Militia had not been called out to force the men in any way but simply to preserve order. " The Street Railway Company, in his judgment, wanted to prove that the city couldn't protect their cars, so as to be able to meet the city's complaint that they were not providing a service. If they had attempted to run cars and had not been protected, they would have sat down, folded their arms, closed their barns, and starved out the other side. But when the Railway Company saw the Militia called out, they knew that their game was up." He then added a remark implying that the leading member of the Board of Trade Committee was interested personally in the Street Railway Company, and this, together with an afterwards repudiated inter- view of the following day in the *World* brought about a personal interchange of letters with Mr. Ames. During the ensuing Mayor- alty election, in which Mr. Howland was defeated by a small major- ity, this calling out of the troops was made an issue amongst a section of the Union men of the city. On December 17th the Mayor defended his position in words which deserve to be recorded here as of permanent interest :

When the peace of the City was threatened by a disorderly youthful class, which despite our educational system was growing up here, as well as in other cities, he had reached the conclusion that it was a time for prompt action. Had this class gained control, had the Police been unable to cope with them, it would have served as an example which would have made the work of the Police difficult for years to come. He was convinced that the Union men were with him when he determined to call out such a force as would show the lawless element that the laws of the land and of society must be observed. They must have no American system of breeding mobs until bloodshed ensued. In Toronto's case the finest disciplined force at the country's command had been called out. There had been no bloodshed. Not a sword had been unsheathed, not a bullet had been fired. No trouble of any kind had ensued. It had been a perfectly peaceful moral demonstration. It had not only stopped the possi- bility of trouble and bloodshed, but had educated the mob element into the knowledge that there was a power behind the Government. If they had not learned it at school they had learned it then. His Worship claimed that in the course he had pursued he had represented all classes, and no class so much as those who had to labour for their daily bread. The strike might have lasted three months, with all the attendant disturbances and upheaval of business, instead of three days.

A somewhat important movement in connection with Labour conditions was initiated in Toronto on October 14th, when a meeting of leading manufacturers and employers was **Protection of** held for the formation of an organization intended to **Employers** protect their interests and to provide a medium for settling strikes and other difficulties marking current industrial development. Mr. James P. Murray, who had started the movement in this connection, occupied the chair and, in his address, objected to Canadian trades unions as being for the most part branches of alien institutions, with aliens for leaders and drawing their political strength from " machine " manipulation of votes; denied the right of any body of men to interfere with an individual in selling his labour for any price he might choose; and described the objects of the new Association as being not the waging of war on Labour Unions but the providing of an organized body of manufacturers to treat with organized Labour. Mr. Murray was elected President, Mr. W. H. Carrick 1st Vice-President, Mr. A. F. Rutter 2nd Vice-President, Mr. Frank Polson Treasurer and Mr. H. G. Hunt Secretary. Each member of the Employers' Asso- ciation was pledged to protect any other member against any unjust demand of Labour organizations and to endeavour, at the same time, to adjust all disputes amicably.   The objects of the Association were defined as follows:

1. To protect its members in their rights to manage their respective businesses, in such lawful manner as they may deem proper.

2. The adoption of a uniform, legitimate system whereby members may ascertain who is, and who is not, worthy of their employment.

3. The investigation and adjustment, by the proper officers or committees of the Association, of any question arising between members and their employees, when such question shall be submitted to the Association for adjustment.

4. To endeavour to make it possible for any person to obtain employment without being obliged to join a Labour organization, and to encourage all such persons in their efforts to resist the compulsory methods of organized Labour.

5. To protect its members in such manner as may be deemed expedient against Legislative, municipal and other political encroachments.

XIX.—LITERATURE AND JOURNALISM

The progress of the year in Canada, so far as literary achievement is concerned, was quiet and not marked by any striking features except, perhaps, the popularity of the Rev.

Literary Progress and Affairs C. W. Gordon's (Ralph Connor) "Man from Glengarry," which first came out in the preceding year, and the appearance of a remarkable poem upon the Coronation by Mr. Bliss Carman—now of New York. The personal element, which enters so largely into all literary work and reputation, found expression in an effort, early in 1902, to erect a memorial at Ottawa to the late Nicholas Flood Davin, K.C., M.P., the scholarly author of "The Irishman in Canada" and many monographs upon public topics, the charming occasional poet, and the always eloquent man of affairs. The project was taken up with earnestness by Mr. Henry J. Morgan, of Ottawa, who issued a circular appeal on Jan. 13th, with considerable success. On April 22nd following, a large gathering took place at Ottawa, with Mr. Charles Magee, President of the Bank of Ottawa, in the chair, and a list of prominent subscribers to the fund was presented by Mr. Morgan. An influential Committee was appointed with Mr. Magee as President, Mr. C. Berkeley Powell, M.P.P., as Treasurer, and Mr. Morgan as Hon. Secretary. A substantial amount was ultimately received.

Early in the year, Mr. Gilbert Parker, M.P., the best known Canadian author abroad, paid a visit to the Dominion and was welcomed in various ways. At Toronto, on Jan. 9th, the Canadian Club tendered him a banquet, with President S. Casey Wood in the chair. The latter paid a personal tribute to the guest of the evening, and then proceeded as follows: "But we, members of the Canadian Club—deeply interested in the growth and development of our country as a whole—wish particularly to acknowledge the great and important fact that he, an English-speaking Canadian, has helped us to understand and appreciate the lives and characters, aims and ideals, of our fellow-Canadians of French origin or extraction; that he has brought us in touch so delightfully with the hearts and minds of that chivalrous, ardent, and ingenuous people; that he has done and is doing so much to establish that mutual understanding and sympathy, that toleration of race and creed, upon which Canadians, both French and English-speaking, are building a united Canadian nation." In his address, Mr. Gilbert Parker dealt with Imperialism and the coming unity of the British realms at some length, deprecated Mr. Rudyard Kipling's criticism of the sportsmen of England, and described in vigorous words the progressive spirit of Canada. The

Hon. George E. Foster and Dr. S. Morley Wickett also spoke. On the following day Mr. Parker visited Kingston as the guest of Principal Grant, and on Jan. 14th was banqueted at Belleville with Sir Mackenzie Bowell in the chair. A very warm welcome was given him in this, his native town, by some 200 guests, and the speeches of Mr. W. B. Northrup, M.P., Mayor Graham, Mr. M. B. Morrison, M.P.P., and others, were naturally eulogistic. His reply was devoted largely to patriotic thoughts and words.

During the year Dr. W. H. Drummond, the author of "The Habitant" and other French-Canadian dialect poems, visited Toronto, read from his works at a gathering in Massey Hall on April 24th, presided over by Mr. J. S. Willison, and was given the Hon. degree of LL.D. by Toronto University. The *Globe* of April 30th referred to the warm reception he had been given in Toronto and to the popular interest felt in his literary work. "Dr. Drummond in some sense stands as the interpreter between the two races. Thoroughly Anglo-Saxon as he is, he yet has become sympathetically conversant with the kindly ingenuous, humorous, volatile side of the *habitant*, and in his broken English has given English - speaking Canadians vital glimpses of it." Another author honoured in 1902 was the veteran antiquarian, ornithologist, and historian of Quebec, Sir James M. Le Moine, D.C.L., F.R.S.C. On Aug. 9th, at his residence, Spencer Grange, near Quebec, he was presented with a portrait in oils and an Address, in the presence of Their Excellencies the Earl and Countess of Minto, His Honour Sir Louis Jetté and Lady Jetté, the Hon. Charles Fitzpatrick, and many of the leading citizens of Quebec. In the course of the Address, read by Mr. J. U. Gregory, Sir James was asked to accept the portrait "as a slight testimonial of our obligation to you for your unwearied labours in making our Province and City known of men the world over. Forty-five years of unremitting toil in the broad domain of Science and Literature; the gathering of rich stores of material for volumes that are a source of joy and pride to every loyal Canadian, whether of French or English extraction."

The works of the year in Canada may be divided into sections and recorded here without comment. They naturally fall into the ranks of romance, poetry, history and politics, biography and works of reference. Besides these there were some valuable pamphlets and monographs published from time to time. The following tabular statement speaks for itself:

Novels and Romances.

Glengarry School Days.   Rev. C. W. Gordon (Ralph Connor).
Why Not, Sweetheart?   Mrs. Julia W. Henshaw.
Where the Sugar Maple Grows.   Adelaide M. Teskey.
Donalblane of Darien.   J. Macdonald Oxley.
A Maid of Many Moods.   Mrs. Virna Sheard.
Tilda Jane.   Marshall Saunders.

With Rogers on the Frontier. J. Macdonald Oxley.
Heralds of Empire. Agnes C. Laut.
The Kindred of the Wild. Charles G. D. Roberts.
Barbara Ladd. Charles G. D. Roberts.
Donovan Pasha and some People of Egypt. Sir Gilbert Parker, D.C.L., M.P.
Thoroughbreds. W. A. Fraser.
Those Delightful Americans. Mrs. Everard Cotes.
Beautiful Joe's Paradise. Marshall Saunders.

Poetry.

Poems. Charles G. D. Roberts.
Tecumseh : A Drama ; and Canadian Poems. Charles Mair.
In Many Keys. J. W. Bengough.
A Coronation Ode. Bliss Carman.
Government Clerks. Charles Gordon Rogers.
Flower Legends and Other Poems. Alma Frances McCallum.
From the Book of Myths. Bliss Carman

History and Politics.

Documentary History of Education in Upper Canada, 1791-1876. Volumes
VIII. and IX. J. George Hodgins, M.A., LL.D.
The Montreal Highland Cadets. Capt. Ernest J. Chambers.
Progress of Canada in the Nineteenth Century. (Edin.) J. Castell Hopkins, F.S.S.
Richardson's War of 1812. (Edited.) A. C. Casselman.
From Quebec to Pretoria, with the Royal Canadian Regiment. W. Hart McHarg.
Histoire de la Paroisse de St. Liguori. Abbé A. C. Dugas.
Speeches by French-Canadians in France. (Edited.) Georges Belleri e.
The French-Canadians. Byron Nicholson.
The Story of the Trapper. Agnes C. Laut.
My Dogs in the Northland. Egerton R. Young.
History of the Queen's Own Rifles of Canada. Capt. Ernest J. Chambers.
The Romance of Canadian History. (Edited.) Pelham Edgar, Ph.D.
Frontenac and his Friends. Ernest Myraud.
Louis Jolliet. Ernest Gagnon.
Documentary History of the Niagara Frontier Campaign of 1813. Part 1.
(Edited.) Lieut.-Col. E. Cruikshank.
Public Men and Public Life in Canada, Hon. James Young, ex -M P
Exploration of the Great Lakes. (Edited) J. H. Coyne, M.A.
Commonwealth or Empire? Goldwin Smith, D.C.L., LL.D.
History of Manitoba and the North-West Territories. D. M. Duncan, M.A.
The Chignecto Isthmus and its First Settlers. Howard Trueman.
The Siege of Quebec and the Battle of the Plains of Abraham. In six volumes.
A. G. Doughty, Hon. T. Chapais, M.L.C., George W. Parmelee, E. T. D.
Chambers.

Biography.

Brief Biographies. Rev. J. O. Millar, LL.D.
Lord Strathcona : The Story of his Life. Beckles Willson.
Charles Heavysege : A Monograph. Lawrence J. Burpee.
E. W. Dadson : The Man and his Message. Prof. J. H. Farmer.
Sir Wilfrid Laurier, Premier of Canada. Henri Moreau.
Henri de Bernières, First Curé of Quebec. Abbé Auguste Gosselin.

Works of Reference.

The Statistical Year Book. George Johnson, Hon.F.S.S.
Morang's Annual Register of Canadian Affairs. J. Castell Hopkins, F.S.S.
The Magistrate's Manual. S. R. Clarke.
The Canadian Mining Review. B. T. A. Bell.
Decisions of the Speakers of the Legislative Assembly of Quebec, 1867-1901.
L. G. Desjardins.
Historical and Parliamentary Guide for Quebec. Joseph Desjardins.

Monographs and Pamphlets.

The French-Canadians in the British Empire.   Henri Bourassa, M.P.
In the Court of History.   Goldwin Smith, D.C.L.
Boundaries of New Brunswick.   W. F. Ganong, LL.D.
The Alaska-Canada Boundary Dispute.   Thomas Hodgins, M.A., K.C.
The First Legislators of Upper Canada.   C. C. James, M.A.
City Government in Canada.   S. Morley Wickett, Ph.D.
City Government in Canada.   W. D. Lighthall, M.A.

Miscellaneous.

From the Great Lakes to the Wide West.   Bernard McEvoy.
Literature in the Nineteenth Century.   Prof. A. B. de Mille, M.A.
Public School Arithmetic for Grammar Grades.   J. A. McLellan, M.A., Ph.D.
Municipal Code of the Province of Quebec.   Robert Stanley Weir, D.C.L.
The Criminal Code and Criminal Evidence.   W. J. Tremeear.
Review of Historical Publications relating to Canada.   Prof. G. M. Wrong, M.A
    and H. H. Langton, B.A.
The Destiny of To-day.   Rev. John Maclean, M.A., Ph.D.
Light for Daily Living.   Rev. John Maclean, M.A., Ph.D.
Christendom Anno Domini 1901.   W. D. Grant, Ph.D.
God's Nation : Her Ancestry and Mission.   Rev. J. M. Simpson.

The question of Copyright as it affects Canadian and other interests is too wide and complicated for any detailed consideration here.   All that can be done is to refer to such action **The Copyright Question in Canada.** as was taken during the year upon any special element which came under discussion—the Canadian or British publisher, the Canadian or British author, the Canadian printer, or the constitutional issue.   On January 2nd the Hon. David Mills, K.C., Minister of Justice, received at Toronto a deputation from the Wholesale Booksellers' Section of the Board of Trade and from the Papermakers and Master Printers and Bookbinders, asking him to remedy the present copyright conditions in favour of protection to the Canadian printer and publisher.   The Minister declared, in his speech, that the authors in England had too much influence with the Imperial Government that they largely controlled the Canadian market *via* the United States ; that Mr. Chamberlain had asked him to prepare a case upon the constitutional point of control over copyright for the Privy Council, but that he had declined.   " The preferable way, I contended, would be to allow us to legislate upon those lines which we think are in the interests of the authors, publishers and people of this country, and then if the authors in England think that we do not possess the power of such legislation let them go before the Judicial Committee and test the validity of the law."

Mr. Mills then dwelt at length upon the constitutional issue and the question of English publishers selling rights in Canada to Americans.   Mr. W. P. Gundy followed with the request of the deputation, as expressed in recent Resolutions, that the Government should make it obligatory that a book " shall be printed and bound in this country in order to secure Canadian copyright, and continue to be so printed and bound in order to retain such copyright." Power was also asked to print English works after 30 days' notice to the author and with due payment of royalties. Mr. John Ross Robertson supported this view and also asked for legislation protecting special cables, articles and letters in newspapers. Considerable discussion followed in the press and elsewhere. Mr. William Tyrrell wrote to the *Globe* of March 22nd condemning the present Copyright law and opposing the proposals of the publishers as above outlined. "By appeals to false sentiment they are now trying to burden British authors and Canadian book-buyers with the extra expense of setting up and reprinting in Canada, and, if the authors refuse to do this, why then our publishers ask for permission to do as a highwayman would; and then, having got valuables for nothing, they virtuously propose to return to the luckless victim so much as they may think he deserves." Mr. W. P. Gundy replied two days later. Meanwhile, Mr. George N. Morang, a Toronto publisher, had addressed on February 19th a long letter to the Board of Trade protesting against the views of the other publishers and approving existing conditions. On April 12th, following, he addressed a similar communication to the Canadian Society of Authors.

The Wholesale Booksellers' and Stationers' Committee of the Toronto Board of Trade reported on March 24th, as to a Memorial for presentation to the Dominion Government, along lines which urged continuous printing and binding in Canada; the right of any citizen of any country granting copyright to British subjects to obtain copyright in Canada; the right of Canadian publishers to receive a license to print any book if not copyrighted in Canada within 30 days of its original publication in country of origin— subject to a reasonable author's royalty; the right to copyright in newspaper cables, articles, etc. On April 2nd a delegation of these Toronto interests and of the Ottawa Board of Trade waited upon the Ministers of Justice and Agriculture at Ottawa and asked for protection to the Canadian printer and protection against the American publisher who might try to obtain control of the Canadian market. Mr. J. F. Ellis, in presenting the deputation, said that they represented the views of various Boards of Trade, and these were afterwards stated to include Kingston, Hamilton, Montreal, Halifax, Edmonton, Vancouver, Winnipeg, Windsor and St. Catharines. In the *Globe* of April 5th Mr. Wm. Tyrrell made a vigorous plea against these contentions and, as he put it, on behalf of the authors and book-buyers. As to the Canadian publisher he now occupied the same position as his colleague in England. "If a Canadian publisher first publishes a book in Canada, he at once possesses absolute and unqualified protection, not only in Canada but throughout the whole British Empire, and in all countries which are parties to the Berne Convention. He can also, by complying with the American law requiring manufacture, obtain the same protection for his work in the United States." Three days later the Secretary of the Canadian Society of Authors made public the following statement as being the views of that body :

1. We endorse any action which the Canadian Government may take towards securing increased Legislative privileges in this, as in all questions where doubt as to the extent of Canada's prerogative exists.

2. While affirming this position we would deprecate any retrogressive legislation which would impair the privileges Canada at present enjoys as a part of the British Empire.

3. We would as strongly register our protest against action being taken that would involve our withdrawal from the Berne Convention. This agreement we regard as an enlightened measure which recognizes the principle of reciprocal international concessions and accords to the author the right to control the products of his own brain.

4. Any licensing clause upon the lines proposed by the Board of Trade would necessitate our withdrawal from the Berne Convention.

5. Canada would then be isolated in the civilized world, a system of retaliation would be substituted for a system of international reciprocity, and Canadian authorship would be seriously hampered in its growth. The Federal Executive by maintaining existing conditions, can, on the other hand, encourage the development of a Canadian national literature.

These views were endorsed by the British Society of Authors which, in its organ, *The Author*, during May declared them to be similar to opinions previously outlined by their own Committee. The *Globe* of April 8th expressed the following editorial view in this connection : "The proposals of the Toronto Board of Trade avowedly involve the isolation of literary Canada from the rest of the civilized world, the establishment of a system whereby Canadian printers may at pleasure print the works of English and Foreign authors without their consent, even if this involves retaliation in England, in the United States and in every other country which now or in the future may afford a market for the works of Canadian authors."

Four days later, in the same paper, Mr. W. J. Gage opposed this view and stated that the Canadian Government had, a few years before, given notice of their desire to withdraw from the Berne Convention but that the Imperial Government had taken no action in the matter. Mr. Tyrrell, on April 26th, also attacked a part of the position taken by the Author's Society as well as the existing Fisher Copyright Act—as it was popularly called. To this letter Mr. G. N. Morang replied in the *Globe* of May 24th. Mr. Tyrrell returned to the charge on June 7th and declared (1) that the existing law was opposed to the principle of Imperial copyright and followed the evil manufacturing conditions of the United States ; (2) that it restricted Canadian book-buyers to editions produced from American stereotype plates ; (3) that it removed the beneficial competition of "Colonial editions" and discriminated against British publishers and authors ; (4) that it enabled a Canadian publisher to control a whole series by copyrighting one volume and a book by copyrighting one story or poem. At the meeting of the Boards of Trade Conference in Toronto, June 4th and 6th, a Resolution was passed in favour of "the right of Canada to make its own laws on on the subject of copyright"

The Royal Society of Canada, which held its annual meeting at
Toronto University from May 26th to May 29th, is the principal
organization in the Dominion along lines of literary,
Royal Society historic, or scientific research. With it are affiliated
and Canadian most of the learned Societies of Canada. Amongst
Authors those who attended the Toronto meeting from different
parts of Canada were Sir Sandford Fleming, Mr. George U. Hay of
St. John, Mr. W. Wilfrid Campbell of Ottawa, Prof. H. T. Bovey, Prof.
R. F. Ruttan, Prof. Alex. Johnson and Prof. D. P. Penhallow of
McGill University, Prof. James Fowler and Prof. W. L. Goodwin of
Queen's University, the Rev. F. G. Scott of Quebec, Henry S. Poole,
the Hon. J. W. Longley and Dr. A. H. McKay of Halifax, Sir James
Grant and Dr. William Saunders of Ottawa, the Rev. Dr. Bryce of
Winnipeg, Abbé P. B. Casgrain and Dr. N. E. Dionne of Quebec,
and Dr. A. D. DeCelles of Ottawa. From Toronto there were
present various numbers, including Dr. G. R. Parkin, C.M.G., Prof.
William Clark, Prof. A. B. Macallum, Mr. R. F. Stupart and the
Rev. Dr. W. H. Withrow. Sir John Bourinot, the Secretary and a
founder of the Society, was ill and unable to be present. President
Loudon of Toronto University was in the chair as President of the
Society. On the first day reports were read from many affiliated
organizations and Dr. Loudon delivered an elaborate opening
address upon " The Universities in relation to Research."
The annual Report dealt with the death of Principal Grant, in
whom the Society lost a member so remarkable for energy, versa-
tility, knowledge, patriotism and educational force ; referred also
to the loss of Abbé Cuoq, Mgr. Tanguay and Dr. Harvey of Newfoundland ; approved of various efforts for preserving and protecting places of scenic and historic interest in the country ; expressed
gratification at the abandonment of the American effort to erect a
Memorial to General Montgomery at Quebec ; urged more definite
and concerted action along ethnological lines in Canada ; and
described the work in surveying tides and currents done by Dr. W.
Bell Dawson. Meetings were held of the Sections devoted to
Mathematics and Chemistry, English and French Literature, Geology and Biology. On May 29th a Canadian Poets' evening was
participated in by Messrs. W. Wilfrid Campbell and Duncan Camp-
bell Scott of Ottawa, the Rev. F. G. Scott of Quebec and Mr. George
Murray of Montreal. Sir James Grant, of Ottawa, was elected
President for the ensuing year ; Lieut.-Col. George T. Denison, of
Toronto, Vice-President ; Sir John Bourinot, Hon. Secretary ; and
Dr. James Fletcher, of Ottawa, Hon. Treasurer. The new members
elected were Dr. J. C. Glashan of Ottawa, Dr. H. T. Barnes of
McGill University, Rev. Chancellor Burwash of Toronto and Mr.
W. D. Lighthall of Montreal.
The Canadian Society of Authors met at Toronto on February
15th and elected Dr. Goldwin Smith, Hon. President ; Hon. G. W.
Ross, LL.D., President ; the Rev. Dr. Bryce of Winnipeg, Dr. W. H.
Drummond of Montreal, Dr. L. H. Fréchette, C.M.G., of Montreal,

Hon. J. W. Longley, K.C., D.C.L., of Halifax, and Duncan C. Scott of Ottawa as Vice-Presidents ; Prof. Pelham Edgar, Ph.D., of Toronto, Secretary ; and John A. Cooper, B.A., Treasurer. The Executive Committee was composed of Byron E. Walker, James Bain, Jr., D.C.L., J. S. Willison, F.R.S.C., J. Castell Hopkins, F.S.S., J. Macdonald Oxley, Mayor O. A. Howland, C.M.G., and Professors J. Mavor, Davidson and A. H. F. Lefroy.

There were a number of interesting incidents in connection with journalistic affairs during the year. The first was an able address delivered at Kingston on February 5th by Principal Grant of Queen's University, upon the defects and possibilities of journalism in Canada. This occupation was, he pointed out, a most vital one. The journalist, according to the measure of his power, formed those currents of opinion which take shape in public policies, in the tone of our thinking and conversation, and in the whole of modern life and its institutions. "Admittedly the ideal is seldom before the mind of the journalist," while, he declared, ordinary publishers simply regard the newspaper as property to be managed on business principles. He accepted a recent expression by Mr. J. S. Willison, stating that the function of the newspaper is " to inform and not rule," but he added to this the dictum that it should also "guide the people." A paper should (1) give space, not as a courtesy but as a right, to different opinions, so long as these are expressed with reasonable brevity, and (2) it should employ upon its staff, as far as its means allow, men competent to ascertain public opinion and to report it, not in the slang of the street, but in good English. " This duty it owes to our noble English speech and to clearness of thought. Uneducated reporters make use of vulgarisms to hide their ignorance ; they are unable to write well because of limited vocabulary and indistinct conceptions." Canadian journalism had, in his opinion, failed to educate the people, and this was the cause of " our undignified treatment of large questions." A sounder training of the people and less self-laudation, coupled with a higher sense of responsibility, were, he thought, the special requirements of Canadian journalism.

Early in the year, February 19th, a meeting of the Directors of *The Colonist* newspaper in Victoria, B.C., resulted in Mr. James Dunsmuir, Premier of the Province and a large shareholder, obtaining control. A new Board was appointed with Mr. Dunsmuir at its head and Mr. A. G. Sargison as Managing-Director. Mr. C. H. Lugrin resigned his position as Editor. In Toronto, on March 29th, the *Mail and Empire* celebrated its 30th year of publication with a special issue and a Dinner to its staff on the following day, with Mr. W. J. Douglas in the chair. In London, about the same time, Mr. John Cameron, Editor of the *Advertiser*, a veteran journalist and one-time Editor of the Toronto *Globe*, resigned, to accept the Postmastership of London, amidst many congratulatory comments from the press throughout Canada. On October 11th the Brant-

Canadian Journalism in 1902

ford *Expositor* celebrated its fiftieth anniversary and the twelfth year of its control by Mr. T. H. Preston, m.p.p.

Two important incidents occurred in Quebec journalism. The first was the announcement on April 11th that Mr. Henri Bourassa, m.p., together with Messrs. J. A. Chicoyne, m.p.p., T. E. Normand, ex-m.p., and others had acquired possession of *Le Pionnier*, of Montreal, and that its policy was to be independent and anti-Imperialist. In October, upon his retirement from the Government, Mr. J. Israel Tarte, m.p., assumed control of *La Patrie*, and turned that paper from a Liberal organ into an occasional critic of the Government—especially along tariff lines. Towards the close of the year he was said to have been approached by Senator Dandurand and other Liberals of prominence with a view to buying his interest in the paper, but to have refused to sell. To the press of Dec. 31st he declared that "the day for a purely political organ is past. As a financial investment, it is not any longer feasible. In these days of liberty of thought and action, for no salary would I go into any newspaper office to simply express the opinions of any one political party. There are always certain matters in which I will remain free to express an opinion." Meanwhile, on October 18th, the Quebec *Mercury* stated that it had been purchased by Mr. Tarte and would immediately be enlarged in equipment and staff with Dr. George Stewart remaining, however, in editorial charge.

A number of minor changes had, meantime, occurred throughout the country. On Jan. 4th the Calgary *Albertan* changed hands and became the property of Mr. William McC. Davidson. On April 1st the St. Thomas *Daily Times* came into the control of Mr. L. H. Dingman, of Stratford. In Nelson, B.C., the *Daily News* made a first appearance on April 22nd under control of Mr. F. J. Deane, and in place of the *Nelson Miner*. The *Westminster* issued its first number as an undenominational monthly in June, with the Rev. J. A. Macdonald as Editor-in-Chief, and the Rev. Dr. S. P. Rose, the Rev. Hugh Pedley, m.a., Prof. J. H. Farmer and Prof. H. J. Cody, as Associates and representatives of other denominations, on its staff. On July 21st Mr. J. P. Earngey, of Toronto, assumed editorial charge of the Rossland *Miner*, and on Oct. 25th *The Yukoner* made its first appearance at Dawson with a strongly British platform. The *Eastern Chronicle* of New Glasgow, N.S., changed hands on Nov. 1st with Mr. James A. Fraser as the new Editor. During the same month the *Banner-News* of Chatham, Ont., became the *Daily News*, and the Labour organ of British Columbia, *The Independent*, was acquired by Mr. T. R. E. McInnes. The Woodstock *Times* ceased publication on Nov. 30th and was merged in the *Daily Express* of that place. On Dec. 31st the Rev. Dr. A. C. Courtice published in the *Christian Guardian* his farewell article upon handing over its editorial charge to the Rev. G. J. Bond, b.a. But the chief journalistic event of 1902 was the retirement of Mr. J. S. Willison from the editorship of the

Toronto *Globe,* which was made public on Nov. 28th and created much interest. Interviewed as to the cause of his resignation, after twelve years' service as Editor of the Liberal organ, Mr. Willison made the following statement to *The World:*

My resolution to leave *The Globe* is due to a determination to enter independent journalism. My relations with *The Globe* during the term of my editorship have been agreeable and harmonious, and, so far as I know, I leave the paper on the best of terms with the Board and the staff. In entering the field of independent journalism, I will be associated with Mr. J. W. Flavelle. He will supply the capital, and all the capital, for the new venture. No money will come from any other source. It is the distinct and clearly-expressed understanding that the paper to be acquired or established shall not be the organ of any political party or of any organized interest, and shall be absolutely independent of all business and corporate enterprises. The only objects in view are free and frank discussion of public questions, in no spirit of hostility to any party and without regard to the effects upon any party; to debate public questions only upon public grounds ; to further in a sane, rational and practical way all movements which seem to make for the public betterment ; and, above all things, not to employ the paper for the promotion of the private interests of any individual or group of individuals.

The comments upon this event were numerous in the press, and personally very complimentary to Mr. Willison. A little later it became known that Mr. Flavelle had acquired the *Evening News* of Toronto, and that this would be the paper which Mr. Willison was to control. On Dec. 6th the latter was presented by the Directors and staff of *The Globe* with an Address and a silver table service. It may be added that the Directors of the paper at this juncture were Messrs. Robert Jaffray (President), W. Barclay McMurrich, K.C., A. F. Rutter, Hugh Blain, N. W. Rowell, K.C., and W. G. Jaffray. On Dec. 30th it became known that the Rev. J. A. Macdonald of the *Westminster* had taken Mr: Willison's place, and that Mr. John Lewis, who had been acting temporarily, would join the *World* staff. It had been stated a short time before that Mr. A. H. U. Colquhoun, B.A., was to be associated with the new management of the *News,* and that the present Editor, Mr. Richmond Smith, was to retire.

On February 27th and the following day the Canadian Press Association held its 44th annual meeting at Ottawa with Mr. A. G. F. Macdonald, President, in the chair. The annual

The Canadian Press Association Report dealt at length with the Paper Combine inquiry and settlement of 1901-2 and the final reduction of duty on news print from 20 to 15 per cent. The President, in his address, described the year as the best in the history of the Association, referred loyally to the Royal visit of 1901, spoke of the Combine investigation and dealt with the visit of the Association to the Maritime Provinces. Addresses were delivered by Mr. E. B. Biggar on Imperial postage ; by Mr. Albert R. Carman, B.A., on London and Paris journals ; by Mr. W. Ireland on Half-Tones and News Print ; by Mr. John A. Cooper on Literature and its handicaps ; by Mr. E. L. Newcombe, K.C., on the Copyright question ; and by Sir Sandford Fleming on cheaper

Telegraph rates.   In this latter connection it was claimed (1) that Canada is the only country in the British Empire where the Telegraph service is not owned by the State; (2) that Canada and the United States are the only civilized nations which do not control their Telegraph services; (3) that the cost of messages in those two countries is practically double the rates charged in all other civilized countries.

Resolutions were passed urging the Government to reduce the duty on paper from 15 to 10 per cent., to remove certain restrictions upon the recent reduction of duty on news print, and to pay the Association's expenses *re* the Combine inquiry; instructing the Executive to arrange a Press excursion to Great Britain in 1903; favouring a lower postage on newspapers, periodicals and books within the Empire; approving the aid given to Mr. Marconi by the Government; and re-affirming belief in Government ownership of cables and land telegraphs.   Mr. D. McGillicuddy of Goderich was elected President, Mr. H. J. Pettypiece, M.P.P., 1st Vice-President, Mr. John A. Cooper, 2nd Vice-President, Mr. J. T. Clark, Secretary-Treasurer, with Mr. M. O. Hammond as Assistant Secretary.   The members of the Executive Committee elected were Messrs. A. H. U. Colquhoun, B.A., J. W. Eedy and Archibald McNee.   The annual banquet was held on February 27th with the Prime Minister, Mr. R. L. Borden, M.P., the Hon. Mr. Paterson, Minister of Customs, Senator Templeman and Mayor Cook amongst the speakers.

An extraordinary incident occurred in British Columbia during the year which attracted the attention and criticism of nearly every newspaper in Canada.   To comprehend it clearly the
The McAdams' Case and the Press   fact should be borne in mind that British Columbia is a Province having a large mining population—partly alien in nationality and accustomed to the elective American Judiciary—with pronounced democratic ideas and Western views not always in harmony with the dignified traditions of Eastern law or British Courts.   In the cities, of course, the conditions do not differ greatly from those in other parts of Canada.   On May 17th, 1902, the Sandon *Paystreak*, a small paper brimful of contempt for dignitaries, monarchy and British ideas generally, contained the following in reference to some case before the Courts: " We pride ourselves on our British fair play, but we maintain a string of Judges who are corrupt, lazy, debauched and prejudiced, and we permit them to conduct the business of the country in a manner that is simply outrageous.   Justice has become foreign to British Columbia Courts.   Unless our Judiciary is quickly revised and corrected we may expect to see the Vigilance Committee spring into existence and find mining litigation settled by the oratory of the six-shooter.   The two-handed gun man is a lesser danger than a corrupt Judiciary."

The Editor, Mr. William McAdams, was called to appear before the Supreme Court and to answer the charge of contempt of Court. He paid no attention to the Order to appear on July 2nd, except to make a further general attack upon the Judiciary in his paper. On July 18th he was, however, present, and the case was heard by Chief Justice Hunter and Justices Drake and Walkem. He admitted that the charge of corruption should not have been made, but would not express any regret, and the Court sentenced him to nine months' imprisonment and to furnish four securities of $1,000 each or receive another year's confinement as the alternative. On August 1st Mr. McAdams was released by order of the Court after writing a full apology for his " inexcusable and insulting language," and receiving the following charge from the Chief Justice:

William McAdams, you have been found guilty of what was one of the greatest contempt of Court cases ever recorded. I have searched the record of such cases, and I have found none which approaches this. In such cases as this the Court must exercise its jurisdiction ; and the only reason the Court will take a lenient course is because the Press has not been checked in such matters as it might have been. Your ignorance of the decencies of one man's behaviour to another man seems to be remarkable. I have perused these few issues of your paper which I have here, and I must say that a more disreputable and atrocious paper I have never seen.

Meanwhile, the comments of the Canadian press as a whole had been very severe—not upon the Editor but upon the Judges for inflicting too heavy a sentence. The country papers of the Province, with the exception of the Kaslo *Kootenaian*, the Rossland *Miner* and one or two more, took this view, and the Eastern papers were almost unanimous in considering the judgment an abuse of power. The more important city papers of British Columbia took a different view. The Vancouver *World* of July 16th described McAdams as " an irresponsible scribbler with anarchistic leanings "; the *News-Advertiser* of the same place declared on August 3rd that such an example had become necessary in the interests of law and authority; and the Vancouver *Province* denounced the Eastern papers as· misinformed and ignorant of local conditions in this connection.

The subject of Canadian news from Great Britain—its origin and character—came in for unusual public consideration during the year. No more succinct description of the general situation could be given than in the following extract from a March number of the *Saturday Review*. After referring to Canadian dependence upon American Press agencies, it proceeded as follows: "The agents of one such agency—numbering perhaps some ten thousand—will send their news to their headquarters in London. From London the daily budget is sent to New York, and thence to such Canadian newspapers as are entitled to the services of the Company. The staff employed in London to collect and forward British news is composed, of course, of Americans; the items they select are naturally those most likely to tickle the palate of a people whose prominent characteristic is certainly not modesty ; and of foreigners whose feelings are not always friendly to the country in which they

The Cable
News Service
of Canada

(the correspondents) dwell." The attention of the public was drawn to the possible danger arising from this condition of affairs by various Canadian papers.

The Victoria *Times* of July 23rd asked for an all-British news service in order to conserve British unity; the Stratford *Beacon* of the same date dealt with the "loaded" American despatches to Canadian papers; the Victoria *Colonist*, on the same day, spoke of the "insidious work" to which the Canadian public had to submit in the view thus presented of British institutions and interests; the Toronto *World* on June 17th and August 20th drew attention to the subject; the Brockville *Times* of September 6th renewed its frequent prayer for the establishment of a Canadian service; the New Westminster *Columbian*, the Toronto *News,* the Vancouver *World* and the Montreal *Witness* took similar ground. The condition of affairs in this respect seemed to particularly attract the attention of visitors during the year. On September 6th Sir James Fairfax, of the Sydney *Morning Herald,* expressed the hope and belief to the *Globe* that a cable service would shortly be established between Britain, Canada and Australia, in which " the news would not have to filter through American channels." Sir Edmund Barton spoke vigorously in various parts of Canada upon this point. At the Toronto banquet, on September 3rd, he declared that Canadians should " buck up " and not remain content to accept news prepared solely for American consumption.

The affairs of your country are not of such interest to the citizens of the United States as they are to you, and it would not be wonderful if the news supplied to you, and relating to the other self-governing portions of the Empire, was rather scanty, as I find it is. It will be necessary for you, if you wish to do business with the Empire, to ascertain fully its conditions, its transactions, its history, its reverses and prosperity. You will not know these unless the dissemination and reception of them are in the hands of those interested in knowing them, and they are not the citizens of the United States, but they are the citizens of Canada.

At Victoria, on September 20th, the Australian Premier repeated these opinions; stated that Canadian cable news from Britain was much less full and true than was that which came thousands of miles further to his own country. He had found some of it very difficult to understand and asked how Imperial sentiment could be preserved with such public and continuous teaching along antagonistic lines. The subject was also considered by the Montreal Board of Trade and a Committee was appointed which went into the matter and found that Canadian newspapers claimed the field to be too small and the demand insufficient to warrant them in undertaking the additional expense of a Canadian press agency in England with special cables. But, if Australia would come into a joint service with lower rates over the Pacific Cable, something might, the Committee thought, be done.

33

Throughout Canada, during 1902, there was considerable controversy as to the propriety of inviting or accepting Mr. Andrew
Carnegie's donations for the erection of Public
The Carnegie Libraries. In Halifax, it was a matter of actual
Library Gifts litigation and in Guelph it was specially discussed.
The issue turned in most cases upon Mr. Carnegie's
one-time bitter denunciation of British institutions and his expressed contempt for Canada as a part of the Empire—mixed
at times with a stirring up of Labour feeling over memories
of Homestead. According to statistics made public in May, 1902,
he had up to that date given, or promised, $52,270,173 to Libraries
in the United States; $564,250 to Libraries in Great Britain; and
$826,000 to Libraries in Canada. The latter list was as follows:

Ontario.

Berlin	$ 15,000
Chatham	15,000
Collingwood	12,000
Cornwall	7,000
Goderich	10,000
Guelph	20,000
Lindsay	10,000
London	10,000
Ottawa	100,000
Palmerston	6,000
Pembroke	10,000
Sarnia	15,000
Sault Ste. Marie	10,000
Smith's Falls	10,000
St. Catharines	20,000
St. Thomas	15,000
Stratford	12,000
Windsor	20,000

Quebec.

Montreal	$150,000
Sherbrooke	15,000

Nova Scotia.

Halifax	75,000
Sydney	15,000
Yarmouth	4,000

New Brunswick.

St. John	50,000

Manitoba.

Winnipeg	100,000

British Columbia.

Victoria	50,000
Vancouver	50,000

XX.—CANADIAN OBITUARY FOR 1902

Adams, M.A., D.C.L., Rev. Thomas—ex-Principal of Bishop's College, Lennox-ville, P.Q. December 26th.

Allen, ex-M.P.P. for York, N.B., William K. April 16th.

Baker, Thomas Bray—President of the Western Elevator Company, Winnipeg. December 7th.

Banting, Lieut.-Col. Richard T.—County Clerk of Simcoe, Ontario. April 1st.

Barss, John W.—Philanthropist of Wolfville, N.S. May 22nd.

Booth, M.P.P., Hon. John Paton—Speaker of the British Columbia Legislature. February 25th.

Boulton, Lieut.-Col. D'Arcy Edward—ex-Mayor of Cobourg. January 1st.

Bourbonnais, B.A., M.P.P. Avila Gonzalve. April 4th.

Bourgeois, Hon. Jean Baptiste—Judge of the Superior Court of Quebec. October 11th.

Bourinot, K.C.M.G., D.C.L., LL.D., D.Litt.,Sir John George—Clerk of the House of Commons, Ottawa; President and afterwards Hon. Secretary of the Royal Society of Canada. October 13th.

Browne, Thomas A.—Postmaster of London. February 20th.

Brine, B.A., Rev. Robert Frederick. February 19th.

Brymner, LL.D., F.R.S.C., Douglas—Dominion Archivist, 1872-1902. June 18th.

Bucke, M.D., Richard Maurice—Superintendent of the Asylum for the Insane, London, Ont. February 21st.

Cassils, John—Merchant of Montreal. May 21st.

Christie, M.D., M.P. of Argenteuil, P.Q., Thomas. August 5th.

Clarkson, B.A., Charles—Ontario Educationalist and Author. March 17th.

Clemow, Hon. Franeis—Senator of Canada. May 28th.

Colin, Abbé Frederic Louis de Gonzague—Superior of the Order of Sulpicians, Montreal. November 27th.

Connolly, V.G., Very Rev. Thomas—Rector of St. John the Baptist Church, St. John, N.B. October 15th.

Crandall, Joseph—Postmaster of Moncton, N.B., 1846-1897. March 29th.

Dawson, C.E., ex-M.P.P., ex-M.P., Simon James. November 20th.

Déchène, M.P.P., The Hon. Francois Gilbert Miville—Minister of Agriculture in Quebec. May 10th.

Dobell, M.P., Hon. Richard Reid—Member of the Dominion Government without Portfolio. January 11th.

Douglas, M.A., Andrew Halliday—Professor of Apologetics, Knox College, Toronto. June 16th.

Douglas, K.C., LL.B., William—Crown Attorney of Kent, Ont. March 28th.

Duff, Lieut.-Col. John—Police Magistrate of Kingston. October 10th.

Ewing, Andrew Stewart—Merchant of Montreal. January 8th.

Fish, Rev. Charles. February 15th.

Fleming, ex-M.P., James—Inspector of Legal Office for Ontario. October 5th.

Fletcher, C.M.G., Lieut.-Col. John. June 7th.

Forde, George—Past County Master of Orange Order in Russell, and formerly Alderman of Ottawa. August 7th.

Gamble, K.C., Clarke—Solicitor for the City of Toronto, 1840-1863. November 23rd.

Gibbs, ex-M.P. for North Ontario, William Henry. November 5th.

Grandin, D.D., Right Rev. Vital Justin—R. C. Bishop of St. Albert, N.W.T. June 3rd.

Grant, Peter—Collector of Customs at New Westminster, B.C. April 2nd.

Gwynne, Hon. John Wellington—Justice of the Supreme Court of Canada. January 6th.

Haines, J.P., George—Formerly Mayor and then Police Magistrate of Bowmanville, Ontario. November 15th.

Hamilton, James T.—Mayor of Halifax. May 23rd.

Hannaford, C.E., Edward P.—ex-Chief Engineer of Grand Trunk Railway. August 18th.

Harding, M.D., of St. John, N.B., William Stenning. December 12th.

Harper, D.D., Rev. Ephraim B. February 5th.

Harrison, John—ex-President of Owen Sound Board of Trade. February 7th.

Hanson, Niels—Mormon Bishop at Cardston, N.W.T. December 11th.

Hart, Frank J.—Merchant and Alderman of Montreal. March 27th.

Hogan, Henry—Proprietor of St. Lawrence Hall, Montreal. October 9th.

Holliday, Thomas—Pioneer Brewer and settler in Guelph, Ont. October 14th.

Horton, J.P., ex-M.P., Horace—Mayor of Goderich, 1872-4. February 18th.

Howland, Henry Stark—Merchant of Toronto and President of the Imperial Bank of Canada. January 28th.

Jarvis, Stephen Maule, Toronto. March 17th.

Johnston, M.D., Wyatt Galt—Professor of Hygiene, McGill University, Montreal. June 19th.

Jones, Stephen James—County Judge of Brant, 1853-1897. November 16th.

Kranz, J.P., ex-M.P. for South Waterloo, Hugo. June 1st.

Laing, M.A., D.D., Rev. John. February 29th.

Lee, Walter Sutherland—Managing-Director of the Canada Permanent Corporation, Toronto. January 4th.

Leeming, Thomas—Merchant of Montreal. March 31st.

Lister, Hon. James Frederick—Justice of the Ontario Court of Appeal. February 9th.

MacCabe, M.A., LL.D., John Alexander—Principal of Ottawa Normal School. November 30th.

Macdonald, Ernest Albert—Mayor of Toronto in 1900. December 18th.

Macdonald, Rev. George W.—First President Reformed Baptist Church of New Brunswick. December 31st.

Mackay, William— Pioneer Lumberman of Montreal and Ottawa. December 1st.

MacVicar, D.D., LL.D., Rev. Donald Harvey—Principal of Montreal Presbyterian College, 1868-1902. December 15th.

Matthews, Jehu—Author, journalist and pioneer Imperialist. January 16th.

Maxwell, M.P. for Vancouver, George Ritchie. November 18th.

McAlister Rev. James. July 21st.

McCrae, John—Merchant and Pioneer of Guelph, Ont. March 17th.

McIntosh, ex-M.P.P., Manitoba, John D. January 15th.

McIsaac, ex-M.P.P., Angus—County Court Judge of Antigonish, N.S. June 12th.

McLeod, M.P., Angus. November 19th.

Mitchell, J.P., James—Clerk of the County Court of Haldimand. November 14th.

Morin, ex-M.P.P., Lieut.-Col. James E.—Registrar of Welland. October 7th.

Moylan, James George—Journalist and formerly Inspector of Dominion Penitentiaries. January 18th.

Muir, M.D., L.R.C.P. (Edin.) William Scott. March 10th.

O'Donohue, K.C., ex-M.P., Hon. John—Senator of Canada. December 7th.

Ogilvie, ex-M.P.P., Alexander Walker—ex-Senator of Canada. March 31st.

Osler, Rev. Henry Bath—Canon of St. Alban's Cathedral, Toronto. March 8th.

Peebles, Lieut.-Col. Adam John Laing—Police Magistrate of Winnipeg, 1879-1901. February 10th.

Primrose, Hon. Clarence—Senator of Canada. December 22nd.

Prowse, ex-M.P.P., Hon. Samuel—Senator of Canada and formerly member of Prince Edward Island Government. January 14th.

Randolph, Hon. Archibald Fitz—Formerly Member of New Brunswick Legislative Council. May 14th.
Reesor, Hon. Daniel—Senator of Canada. April 27th.
Reynolds, William Kilby—Journalist and Author. December 2nd.
Robertson, D.D., Rev. James—Superintendent of Presbyterian Missions in Western Canada ; Moderator of the Presbyterian Church in 1895. January 24th.
Robertson, M.P.P., Hon. Thomas—Speaker of the Nova Scotia House of Assembly. April 19th.
Ross, Mrs. George W. (Catharine Boston, wife of the Premier of Ontario). March 12th.
Rowe, Amos—Collector of Customs at Calgary, N.W.T. January 28th.
Royal, ex-M.P.P., ex-M.P., Hon. Joseph—Formerly Minister of Public Works in Manitoba and Lieutenant-Governor of the North-West Territories. August 23rd.
Ryan, Rev. Francis—Rector of St. Michael's Cathedral, Toronto. March 8th.
Ryan, John—Contractor of Toronto. March 21st.
Scarth, James L.—General Manager North British and Canadian Investment Company, Toronto. November 14th.
Scarth, ex-M.P., William Bain—Deputy Minister of Agriculture at Ottawa. May 15th.
Selwyn, C.M.G., LL.D., F.R.S., F.G.S., F.R.S.C., Arthur Richard Cecil—Director of Geological Survey of Canada, 1869-1895. October 18th.
Seymour, Rev. James Cook—Methodist Minister and Author. September 1st.
Short, Richard Allan—Journalist and editorial writer on the Montreal *Witness*. May 17th
Smallfield, Albert—Editor of the Renfrew *Mercury*. November 16th.
Smith, John Wesley—Merchant and Philanthropist. November 27th.
Smith, D.D., LL.D., Rev. Thomas Watson—Author of " History of Methodism in Eastern British America." March 8th.
Spence, David—Secretary of Ontario Immigration Department. June 14th.
Tanguay, LL.D., F.R.S.C., Mgr. Cyprien—Author and Historian. April 28th.
Teague, John—British Columbia Pioneer, and twice Mayor of Victoria. October 25th.
Tillson, Edwin D.—First Mayor of Tilsonburg. January 31st.
Wardell, M.P.P., Thomas Atkins. April 5th.
Waters, D.D., Rev. Henry Harcourt. February 7th.
Wells, K.C., ex-M.P.P., ex-M.P., Hon. Rupert Mearse—Speaker of House of Assembly, Ontario, 1873-1880. May 11th.
Yeigh, J.P., Edmund Lossing. March 17th.

INDEX TO NAMES.

518

34

INDEX OF AFFAIRS.

35

The London Guarantee and
Accident Company

(Limited)

HEAD OFFICE FOR CANADA

CANADA LIFE BUILDING, TORONTO.

D. W. ALEXANDER, - Manager for Canada.

THE MOST APPROVED BONDS and POLICIES and LOWEST RATES *re*

Guarantee, Accident, Employers'
Liability, Elevator or . . . . } **Insurance**
Workmen's Collective. . . . .

ALL FORMS OF FIDELITY BONDS ISSUED

— SUCH AS —

Government, Court (Administration, Appeal, Liquidators, Etc.)
Bank, Municipal, Agency, Treasurer, Society Officer, Etc.

THE ONTARIO BANK

Capital Paid-up - - - - -	$1,500,000.00
Rest - - - - - - -	425,000.00

HEAD OFFICE - TORONTO.

DIRECTORS:

G. R. R. COCKBURN, ESQ., *President.*   DONALD MACKAY, ESQ., *Vice-President.*

Hon. J. C. Aikins.   R. D. Perry, Esq.   A. S. Irving, Esq.

Hon. R. Harcourt.   R. Grass, Esq.

CHARLES McGILL - General Manager.

BRANCHES:

Alliston	Cornwall	Mount Forest	Sudbury
Aurora	Fort William	Newmarket.	Tweed
Bowmanville	Kingston	Ottawa	Trenton
Buckingham, Q.	Lindsay	Peterboro'	Waterford
Collingwood	Montreal	Port Arthur	

Toronto—Scott and Wellington Streets.
Queen and Portland Streets.
Yonge and Richmond Streets.
Yonge and Carlton Streets.

AGENTS:

London, Eng.—Parr's Bank, Limited.

France and Europe—Credit Lyonnais.

New York—Fourth National Bank and the Agents of the Bank of Montreal.

Boston—Eliot National Bank.

THE TRADERS BANK
OF CANADA

Incorporated by Act of Parliament, 1885.

Head Office, TORONTO

Capital paid-up	$1,500,000
Rest	350,000

H. S. STRATHY, General Manager.   J. A. M. ALLEY, Inspector

Board of Directors

C. D. WARREN, ESQ., President.   HON. J. R. STRATTON, Vice-President

John Drynan, Esq.   C. Kloepfer, Esq., Guelph.   W. J. Sheppard, Esq.,
Waubaushene.   C. S. Wilcox, Esq., Hamilton.

Branches

Arthur	Guelph	Owen Sound	Sault Ste. Marie
Aylmer	Hamilton	Port Hope	Sarnia
Beeton	Ingersoll	Prescott	Schomberg
Burlington	Lakefield	Ridgetown	Stratford
Drayton	Leamington	Rodney	Sturgeon Falls
Dutton	Newcastle	Strathroy	Tilsonburg
Elmira	North Bay	St. Mary's	Windsor
Glencoe	Orillia	Sudbury	Woodstock
Grand Valley			

Bankers—Great Britain—The National Bank of Scotland.   New York—The
American Exchange National Bank.   Montreal—The Quebec Bank.